HANDBOOK ON MIGRATION AND THE FAMILY

ELGAR HANDBOOKS IN MIGRATION

The Elgar Handbooks in Migration series provides a definitive overview of recent research in all matters relating to the study of Migration, forming an extensive guide to the subject. This series covers research areas including internal migration, the global impact of human trafficking and forced labour, and international migration policy, and constitutes an essential new resource in the field. Each volume is edited by an editor recognized as an international leader within the field and consists of original contributions by leading authors. These *Handbooks* are developed using an international approach and contribute to both the expansion of current debates within the field, and the development of future research agendas.

Titles in the series include:

Handbook of Culture and Migration
Edited by Jeffrey H. Cohen and Ibrahim Sirkeci

Handbook on the Governance and Politics of Migration
Edited by Emma Carmel, Katharina Lenner and Regine Paul

Handbook of Citizenship and Migration
Edited by Marco Giugni and Maria Grasso

Handbook of Migration and Global Justice
Edited by Leanne Weber and Claudia Tazreiter

Research Handbook on International Migration and Digital Technology
Edited by Marie McAuliffe

Handbook on Migration and Welfare
Edited by Markus M. L. Crepaz

Handbook of Return Migration
Edited by Russell King and Katie Kuschminder

Research Handbook on Irregular Migration
Edited by Ilse van Liempt, Joris Schapendonk and Amalia Campos-Delgado

Handbook on Migration and the Family
Edited by Johanna L. Waters and Brenda S.A. Yeoh

Handbook on Migration and the Family

Edited by

Johanna L. Waters

Professor of Human Geography, Department of Geography, University College London, UK

Brenda S.A. Yeoh

Professor of Social Sciences, Department of Geography, National University of Singapore, Singapore

ELGAR HANDBOOKS IN MIGRATION

Cheltenham, UK • Northampton, MA, USA

© Johanna L. Waters and Brenda S.A. Yeoh 2023

Cover image: Ginny Rose Stewart on Unsplash

All rights reserved. No part of this publication may be reproduced, stored in a retrieval system or transmitted in any form or by any means, electronic, mechanical or photocopying, recording, or otherwise without the prior permission of the publisher.

Published by
Edward Elgar Publishing Limited
The Lypiatts
15 Lansdown Road
Cheltenham
Glos GL50 2JA
UK

Edward Elgar Publishing, Inc.
William Pratt House
9 Dewey Court
Northampton
Massachusetts 01060
USA

A catalogue record for this book
is available from the British Library

Library of Congress Control Number: 2023930036

This book is available electronically in the Elgaronline
Geography, Planning and Tourism subject collection
http://dx.doi.org/10.4337/9781789908732

Printed on elemental chlorine free (ECF)
recycled paper containing 30% Post-Consumer Waste

ISBN 978 1 78990 872 5 (cased)
ISBN 978 1 78990 873 2 (eBook)

Printed and bound in the USA

Contents

List of contributors   vii

1   Introduction to the *Handbook on Migration and the Family*   1
      Johanna L. Waters and Brenda S.A. Yeoh

PART I   GENDER RELATIONS AND GENDER SUBJECTIVITIES

2   Nanny families and the making of gender (in)equality   16
      Rosie Cox, Terese Anving and Sara Eldén

3   Transnational marriage migration: agency, structures and intimate gendered governmentality   33
      Neil Amber Judge and Margaret Walton-Roberts

4   Nation, gender and location: understanding transnational families in the face of violence   51
      Biftu Yousuf and Jennifer Hyndman

5   Vietnamese masculinities in transition: negotiating manhood in the context of female labour migration   68
      Lan Anh Hoang

6   The transnationalisation of intimacy: family relations and changes in an age of global mobility and digital media   84
      Earvin Charles Cabalquinto and Yang Hu

PART II   AGE AND INTERGENERATIONAL RELATIONSHIPS

7   Mobility and intergenerational transfers of capital: narrating expatriate and globally mobile children's perspectives   102
      Sin Yee Koh and I Lin Sin

8   Young people, intergenerationality and the familial reproduction of transnational migrations and im/mobilities   118
      Caitríona Ní Laoire

9   Split households and migration in the Global South: gender and intergenerational perspectives   135
      C. Cindy Fan

10   Negotiating long-distance caring relations: migrants in the UK and their families in Poland   154
      Weronika Kloc-Nowak and Louise Ryan

11	Analysing youth migrations through the lens of generation Rhondeni Kikon and Roy Huijsmans	170
12	Unaccompanied child migrants and family relationships Katie Willis, Sue Clayton and Anna Gupta	184

PART III   POWER, SOCIAL INEQUALITIES AND SOCIAL MOBILITY

13	Families in educational migration: strategies, investments and emotions Johanna L. Waters and Zhe Wang	200
14	Privileged migration and the family: family matters in corporate expatriation Sophie Cranston and George Tan	217
15	Not as safe as houses: experiences of domestic violence among international migrant women Cathy McIlwaine	232
16	Academic mobility and the family Yanbo Hao and Maggi W.H. Leung	249
17	The heterosexual family ideal and its limitations for bi-national same-sex family formations Claire Fletcher	265

PART IV   SPATIALITIES AND TEMPORALITIES

18	Migrant family separation, reunification and recalibration Denise L. Spitzer and Sara Torres	286
19	'Maybe in the future I'll have two homes': temporalities of migration and family life among Vietnamese people in London Annabelle Wilkins	301
20	Offshoring social reproduction: low-wage labour circulation and the separation of work and family life Thomas Saetre Jakobsen, Sam Scott and Johan Fredrik Rye	315
21	Growing over time: left-behind children in the past three decades Theodora Lam	333
22	Transnational families and mobility regimes Franchesca Morais and Brenda S.A. Yeoh	349

Index   365

Contributors

Terese Anving, Department of Gender Studies, Lund University, Sweden.

Earvin Charles Cabalquinto, School of Communication and Creative Arts, Deakin University, Australia.

Sue Clayton, Department of Media, Communications and Cultural Studies, Goldsmiths, University of London, UK.

Rosie Cox, Department of Geography, Birkbeck, University of London, UK.

Sophie Cranston, Department of Geography, Loughborough University, UK.

Sara Eldén, Department of Sociology, Lund University, Sweden.

C. Cindy Fan, Department of Geography, University of California, Los Angeles (UCLA), USA.

Claire Fletcher, Department of Geography, University College London, UK.

Anna Gupta, Department of Social Work, Royal Holloway, University of London, UK.

Yanbo Hao, Department of Human Geography, Planning and International Development Studies, University of Amsterdam, Netherlands.

Lan Anh Hoang, School of Social and Political Sciences, University of Melbourne, Australia.

Yang Hu, Department of Sociology, Lancaster University, UK.

Roy Huijsmans, International Institute of Social Studies, Erasmus University Rotterdam, Netherlands.

Jennifer Hyndman, Graduate Program in Geography, York University, Canada.

Thomas Saetre Jakobsen, Senior Advisor, Department for Working Environment and Regulations, The Norwegian Labor Inspection Authority, Trondheim, Norway.

Neil Amber Judge, Department of Geography, Wilfrid Laurier University, Canada.

Rhondeni Kikon, the ant (the action northeast trust), Udangshri Dera, Bodoland Territorial Region, Assam, India.

Weronika Kloc-Nowak, Centre of Migration Research, University of Warsaw, Poland.

Sin Yee Koh, Institute of Asian Studies, Universiti Brunei Darussalam, Brunei.

Theodora Lam, Asia Research Institute, National University of Singapore.

Maggi W.H. Leung, Department of Human Geography, Planning and International Development Studies, University of Amsterdam, Netherlands.

Cathy McIlwaine, Department of Geography, King's College London, UK.

Franchesca Morais, Asia Research Institute, National University of Singapore.

Caitríona Ní Laoire, School of Applied Social Studies, University College Cork, Ireland.

Louise Ryan, London Metropolitan University, UK.

Johan Fredrik Rye, Department of Sociology and Political Science, Norwegian University of Science and Technology (NTNU), Norway.

Sam Scott, Geography, School of Natural and Social Sciences, University of Gloucestershire, UK.

I Lin Sin, Independent Scholar, Glasgow, UK.

Denise L. Spitzer, School of Public Health, University of Alberta, Canada.

George Tan, Northern Institute, Charles Darwin University, Australia.

Sara Torres, School of Social Work, Laurentian University, Canada.

Margaret Walton-Roberts, Department of Geography, Wilfrid Laurier University, Canada.

Zhe Wang, Department of Education, University of Oxford, UK.

Johanna L. Waters, Department of Geography, University College London, UK.

Annabelle Wilkins, Kingston University and Queen Mary University of London, UK.

Katie Willis, Department of Geography, Royal Holloway, University of London, UK.

Brenda S.A. Yeoh, Department of Geography, National University of Singapore.

Biftu Yousuf, Graduate Program in Geography, York University, Canada.

1. Introduction to the *Handbook on Migration and the Family*

Johanna L. Waters and Brenda S.A. Yeoh

Migration is inextricably tied to complex and varied familial relationships, some of which are supportive and nurturing, others violent and oppressive. Ideologically, the family functions as a 'deep-rooted social institution' (Yeoh et al., 2018, p. 413) that articulates with the state and capital to create the conditions of modern life (Ong, 1999). States often promote circumscribed definitions of family (nuclear, heterosexual), and immigration regimes reflect dominant and idealised values (Teo and Piper, 2009), facilitating the mobilities of 'typical' families that fit the norm while denying entry to other (atypical) households that are deemed illegitimate. The slippage between state regulation of what constitutes the accepted family and family life on the one hand, and the messier lived realities from grounded perspectives on the other hand, reflects some of the most significant ongoing tensions and negotiations within the social order.

Understanding migration dynamics also requires attending to the social institution of the family at both a societal and a personal level. The family domain is integral to how certain inequalities are bolstered and maintained; and inextricable from the way power is frequently exercised by one group over others. Women and children are, habitually, disadvantaged within the family sphere through migration: gendered relations privilege male employment over female careers, and children have little or no voice when it comes to their mobilities. In the example of marriage migration, women who cross borders as foreign brides often have diminished power over decision-making and are completely dependent upon their male sponsors for their legal status in host countries (Yeoh et al., 2013). Within the domestic sphere, migration can heighten unequal responsibilities, placing far more burden on women to maintain social reproduction in an unfamiliar and uncertain environment. Conversely, migration can also lead to masculinities being challenged and upended, women's heightened sense of freedom, and children having a say, as several chapters in this *Handbook* attest. Thus, there is not one narrative of how families experience migration or, indeed, what a migrant family is, but multiple ones.

We begin this Introduction by reflecting on how research on migration and the family has changed over the past half-century, from an almost exclusive focus on men, male careers and the masculine experience. Where families were included in this narrative, they were part of a nuclear unit, wherein immigration involved a main (male) applicant and so-called dependents. We then consider the work of feminist scholars who, through their critique of 'gender-blind' discussions of migration, highlighted the role of the family as an important site wherein relational and gendered power dynamics were played out. We relate this work to scholarship on transnationalism which has, *inter alia* and as a consequence of feminist interventions, more recently provided a complex and nuanced exploration of familial relations. Within transnationalism, migration involves the spatial separation of family members, and emergent and diverse forms of 'householding' are evoked, as long-distance transnational social formations emerge (Yeoh et al., 2018). As Parreñas (2005) has written: 'Migration engenders changes in a family … Contemporary transnational households have a different temporal and spatial experience from ... families of the past' (p. 317). It is this evolution, of both thematic ideas and migrant experiences, that we seek to tease out in the first half of this Introduction.

This broad temporal sketch of key ideas relating to the cross-currents in migration and family research leads to a more grounded overview of the *Handbook* chapters. These chapters are organised into four interrelated themes: gender relations and subjectivities; age and intergenerational relationships; power, social inequalities and social mobility; and spatialities and temporalities.

THE UNENCUMBERED MALE MIGRANT AND 'ECONOMIC MAN'

Historically, migration studies paid scant attention to the family and its role in migratory movements. In some instances, families were completely ignored: migrants were conceived of as lone and unencumbered travellers, usually male, and always interpreted through an economic lens. Employment or career mobility was seen as a key driver behind much migration in multiple contexts, including Western Europe (Kofman, 2004) and Asia (Yeoh and Huang, 2011). Discussions were dominated by human capital approaches, which treat migration as an individual investment (Cooke and Bailey, 1996). Later, primarily male migrants were accompanied by their 'trailing spouses' (Harvey, 1998). This term represented a subtle shift to recognise that many migrants had partners and families, but still they were viewed as largely unimportant appendages or, worse, as obstacles to successful professional migration (Yeoh and Willis, 2005).

Over time, thinking became extended to recognise the role families could play in (economic forms of) migration. Mincer (1978) was one of the first scholars to include the family in discussions of migration and human capital, articulating 'profit maximising' and the 'net' benefits brought through the migration of dual earner households to the (nuclear) family (Cooke and Bailey, 1996). This dominance of human capital perspectives and an overriding concern with *Homo economicus* blinded scholarship, for a time, to the messy, complex and all-too-human aspects of family migration (Ley, 2003), where financial considerations are only one of many driving forces behind, and outcomes of, migration (or, indeed, they may be inconsequential at any given time). In particular, feminist scholars argued for the importance of examining the gender-differentiated power geometries at work in both the labour market and the workplace, as well as within the family sphere, in shaping who moves, who stays, who gains and who sacrifices (Yeoh and Willis, 2005; Kofman and Raghuram, 2006). This vein of work disrupted assumptions that household decisions regarding migration were guided by 'principles of consensus and altruism'; instead, these decisions may 'equally be informed by hierarchies of power along gender and generational lines' (Mahler and Pessar, 2006, p. 33).

Nation-states also actively help to create and maintain this human capital view of migration, within which family narratives have been drowned out. Several countries in the Global North, during the 1980s onwards, made changes to their immigration criteria and introduced business immigration programmes, in an unabashed attempt to attract skilled and wealthy migrants from overseas (particularly from the so-called 'Asian Tigers'). Ley (2010) describes this 'new immigration paradigm' as a shift away from humanitarian and family reunion routes of immigration to Canada, during the 1980s, towards 'economic migrants' and selection processes seeking 'well educated and adaptive skilled workers, for assessments confirm that skilled migrants speedily make net economic contributions to their host' societies (p. 8).

Canada, Australia, New Zealand, Singapore and the United States have all explicitly selected migrants on their ability to make a valuable (narrowly defined in economic terms) contribution to society, and other immediate family members were able to join them as dependents on that basis. As far as states were concerned, however, the family was an incidental by-product of this immigration, rather than a goal, even though so-called dependent immigrants, over the past 30 years, have had a profound impact upon many major cities around the world, transforming their social and cultural geographies in myriad ways.

FEMINIST APPROACHES, TRANSNATIONALISM AND THE FAMILY

A paradigm shift within academic research on international forms of migration occurred with the widespread adoption of a framework of transnationalism, from the mid-1990s onwards. Transnationalism has famously been defined by Basch et al. (1994, p. 7) as:

> the process by which immigrants forge and sustain multi-stranded social relations that link together their societies of origin and settlement. We call these processes transnationalism to emphasise that many immigrants today build social fields that cross geographic, cultural and political borders. Immigrants who develop and maintain multiple relationships – familial, economic, social, organizational, religious, and political – that span borders we call 'transmigrants'. An essential element of transnationalism is the multiplicity of involvements that transmigrants sustain in both home and host societies.

However, while early work on transnational migration tended to shift the focus away from the purely economic towards migration's multiple dimensions, there was 'nothing inherently transgressive or emancipatory' about transnationalism (Pratt and Yeoh, 2003, p. 159). It took feminist scholars to emphasise the significance of complex power relations within (transnational) households. Feminist scholarship encouraged relational approaches to understanding transnationalism and highlighted the salience of gender politics within the family sphere; Pessar and Mahler (2003) critiqued early work on transnationalism as being 'inattentive' to 'gendered geographies of power' which, significantly, involved the family as a key unit or social institution within which gender was embedded. Gendered, socialised norms structure migrants' lives, produce marked inequalities, and restrict the kinds of activities they are able to undertake (and the lives they are able to live) (Pessar and Mahler, 2003).

However, Pessar and Mahler (2003) also stressed that while gendered politics are enacted in and through the family or household, these politics are often supported and upheld by the state (despite the implication that transnationalism somehow bypasses or undermines state power); something that we touched upon above. As Ong (1999) has likewise argued, the (Chinese) family is an ideological construction promoted by the state for its own ends, ultimately seeking to uphold and maintain patriarchal structures. Thus, the linkages between the family and the state must be always held in mind when discussing transnational family formations.

While feminist scholarship was instrumental in recognising and highlighting the importance of the family and family relations within international migration, through its focus on gender and relationality, particularly interesting for this *Handbook* is the way in which it challenged transnational approaches to be more attentive to familial relations and inequalities. Feminist inspired work on migration and transnationalism (particularly dating from the early 2000s), rendered visible the centrality of family relations within contemporary migration (e.g. Hardill, 2004), in the way that it indicates the 'multi-stranded' and spatially extended social relations (comprised, primarily, of familial relations) that contemporary immigrants often maintain, spanning several nation states (Basch et al., 1994). Here we discuss how a transnational perspective, guided by feminist approaches, has enriched our understanding of the family within migration in a number of ways.

First, it has emphasised the importance of families in all types and forms of migration: documented and undocumented, economic and humanitarian, educational and lifestyle-related (Levitt et al., 2003; Pratt and Yeoh, 2003). Family members often directly support and facilitate migration, whether through financial or material resources, social capital or proffering knowledge of immigration processes. Family can also precipitate the migration of individuals: migration can be a means, for some, to escape the suffocating pressures placed upon them by wider familial relations and expectations (particularly for young women around marriage and childbearing) (Ryan et al., 2009; Walton-Roberts, 2004).

Second, feminist scholars have demonstrated the differential impact of transnational migration on family members, notably parents, children, spouses, siblings and grandparents (Ryan et al., 2009). Adult women within transnational families, for example, have often been forced to suspend or forgo their careers as a consequence of migration (Waters, 2002); migrant children can provide significant caring in the form of 'sibling support' (Baldassar and Brandhorst, 2021). Men can struggle with their identities following challenges, wrought by migration, to their masculinity (Waters, 2010; Walsh, 2011). And transnational grandparenting has significantly increased, changing the age demographics of contemporary migrants in unforeseen ways (Ho and Chiu, 2020; Nedelcu and Wyss, 2020). These different roles and experiences play out within the context of the transnational family, challenging the view that families are inscrutable, and invariably unified in their pursuit of migration goals.

Third, by attending to linkages between home and host country, transnationalism emphasises the often crucial role played by non-mobile family members in the migration process. For example, grandparents caring for children as parents migrate overseas for work (Hoang and Yeoh, 2012), and left-behind children providing direct support for siblings in the absence of parental oversight (Parreñas, 2005), are both central to sustaining transnational families and yet they are, themselves, not migrants. Female migrants such as healthcare and domestic workers, in particular, have notably relied on extended family back home to provide care for their own children in their absence (Bryceson, 2019).

Fourth, transnationalism has challenged the spatial imaginaries attached to family life, promoting the idea that life can be lived within transnational social spaces that transcend ideas of here and there, home and away, and the physical co-locatedness of domesticity. Digital media are having a profound effect on how transnational families are experienced (Madianou, 2016; Wilding et al., 2020), and this has only been heightened with the mobility restrictions imposed around the world as a consequence of the COVID-19 pandemic. Madianou (2016, p. 183) develops the concept of 'ambient co-presence', to describe 'peripheral yet intense' awareness of 'distant others' made possible by the developments in social and digital media in the context of transnational families.

And finally, the very categories that migration scholars have used to discuss migration have been dismantled through transnationalism. Binary categories such as immigrant and emigrant, host society and home society, find roots in methodological nationalism, where the nation-state (and its overriding concern with assimilation, initially, and later integration) has dominated the framing of migration. As mentioned above, these categories have taken their lead from human capital approaches to understanding migration. Whilst such terminology is still prevalent within policy and grey literature on international migration, academic discussions are consequently much more nuanced and 'decentred' in the ways in which they label and demarcate migration and migrants. Whilst the nation-state often continues to be highly important in shaping family life and livelihoods, the thickening of transnational flows in the form of money, material goods, ideas, knowledge, care and emotion across borders has meant that the frame of reference for families is not always the nation-state, as seen in the day-to-day lives of transnational families, who take as much interest in the quotidian mundanity of family members living overseas as they do in those living in close proximity (Madianou, 2016). As will be seen below, many of the chapters in this *Handbook* owe some significant debt to the ways in which transnational perspectives pushed boundaries and challenged thinking on contemporary migration and family from the mid-1990s onwards.

THE HANDBOOK

The *Handbook on Migration and the Family* offers a timely and important contribution to debates concerning contemporary forms of mobility and complex familial ties in the face of changes in how space is configured and experienced, internationally. It argues that the family is not incidental but central to understanding migration. The book prioritises migration that involves the crossing of international borders and boundaries (as opposed to internal or within-state migration). Indeed, borders of one sort or another are a central trope running throughout all the chapters (Silvey, 2005).

The *Handbook* takes a largely qualitative and social science approach to research on migration and the family, aiming to capture a range of views and perspectives across multiple disciplines, including diverse constructions of what constitutes 'family' (for example, nuclear, extended, heteronormative, same-sex) and different types of family structure (traditional, patriarchal, matriarchal, those headed by grandparents or other family members, children as carers, and so on) as well as the role that family members may play in migration itself (some, for example, may be themselves 'immobile'). The chapters provide readers with a critical and insightful review of cutting-edge scholarship on how migration and families have been conceptualised together, providing an overview of key themes in this area. Taken as a whole, the *Handbook* attempts to capture the diversity of family types, arrangements and strategies on display in a global setting.

The *Handbook* is organised into four parts, reflecting key and dominant themes: 'Part I: Gender Relations and Subjectivities', 'Part II: Age and Intergenerational Relationships', 'Part III: Power, Social Inequalities and Social Mobility' and 'Part IV: Spatialities and Temporalities'. It comprises 22 chapters in total, including this Introduction. However, as will become clear, several chapters would fit within multiple parts. The parts are designed as a guide and not as an exhaustive categorisation of the chapters contained within. Contributions are primarily theoretical/conceptual, all addressing, in different ways, the relationship between family and (international/transnational) migration in contemporary times, and the implications of this. The parts are devised to reflect the most recent debates and agendas within social science research on migration and the family. In what follows, we provide a brief overview of each part of the *Handbook* and the main contribution of each chapter contained within.

OVERVIEW OF THE PARTS AND CHAPTERS

Part I: Gender Relations and Subjectivities

Gender has emerged as a key variable in analyses of migrant families over the past two decades, in recognition of the sometimes extreme inequalities in experiences and outcomes that men, women and non-binary individuals face. Research has explored, for example, the fact that women may relinquish their career through migration or find themselves relatively trapped in the home, whilst their male spouses continue to work (experiencing 'business as usual'). Women often find themselves in a subservient position compared to their male counterparts when it comes to their migration status, and yet can also be seen to negotiate and rework this position through, for example, the sending and controlling of remittances (Yeoh et al., 2013). Same-sex couples have faced long-standing discrimination when it comes to immigration laws and policies (Fletcher, Chapter 17, this *Handbook*). We have also, in this part of the *Handbook*, sought to highlight the diversity and socially constructed nature of gendered subjectivities and gender relations (Butler, 2002).

Early work on gender within migration studies invariably prioritised the female experience of international migration within the confines of the heteronormative family. This is understandable and necessary, of course, when we consider the relative neglect of women's experiences and voices within research hitherto. Several chapters in this *Handbook* consider women's experiences of migration.

The domestic space is increasingly a space for transnational familial relations that are also highly gendered. Rosie Cox, Terese Anving and Sara Eldén (Chapter 2) explore the growing phenomenon of privatised childcare in relation to migration and the family. As is increasingly well documented, care work and domestic forms of labour are heavily dominated by (female) migrant workers. This migration has the inadvertent effect of connecting local families employing migrant workers with globalised networks of care. The chapter recognises the state policies that underpin domestic and care work, and seeks to highlight these regimes of care, migration, welfare and work, comparing the cases of the United Kingdom (UK) and Sweden. Although showing interesting differences in many ways, in both countries the employment of domestic workers and au pairs has bolstered extant gender inequalities and assumptions about women and domestic work. Also exploring domestic space, but this time in relation to marriage, Neil Amber Judge and Margaret Walton-Roberts (Chapter 3) attend to the roles and experiences of women in transnational marriage migration. Marriage migration, they argue, can offer women opportunities to exercise agency by engaging in transnational marriages that have the potential to provide them with relative autonomy and social status. Nevertheless, structural factors, including immigration policy, constrain this ability for agency. They note the increasing implementation of 'stronger policies and stricter rules' for the entry of marriage migrants, reflecting states' attempts to craft a 'national imaginary'. The authors draw on the case of marriage and family migration between north India and Canada to illustrate these points, highlighting that 'immigration policy can interact with forms of already existing patriarchy to reproduce social stratification and hierarchy that is damaging to women's security'.

A different perspective on gender relations and migration in the context of the family is provided by Biftu Yousuf and Jennifer Hyndman (Chapter 4). Their chapter discusses human rights advocacy among former refugees from Sri Lanka and Ethiopia living in Canada. They reveal the disagreements that occur within communities, which can arise around the ways in which national identity both 'back home', and within the diaspora, can and should be expressed. Yousuf and Hyndman argue that transnational practices of kinship care, and expressions of pain and suffering, are highly gendered; and whilst both women and men participate in gendered transnational cultural practices, women's roles in reproducing the nation socially, culturally and symbolically were particularly distinct in the research that they encountered.

Male subjectivities and the relations between genders are often neglected within gendered perspectives on family and migration. Chapter 5, by Lan Anh Hoang, examines the experiences of men in Vietnam whose wives and partners had emigrated as labour migrants. The chapter recognises the fluidity and plurality of notions of femininity and masculinity and how, most importantly, they can be seen as relational constructs. How do 'stay-behind' men respond to the migration of their female spouses? Men, in this context, have to juggle competing pressures of the norms associated with masculine subjectivities, and their daily realities encompassing significant uncertainty and unpredictability. They are seen to carve out 'new standards of masculinity' which are not, Hoang points out, necessarily more egalitarian in nature.

Finally for Part I, the chapter by Yang Hu and Earvin Charles Cabalquinto (Chapter 6) takes a broader look at transnational intimacy within the context of the family in the face of mass use of digital communications media and highlights important gendered dynamics. The authors develop the concept of the 'transnationalisation of intimacy' to explore critically the 'performance, embodiment and experience of intimacy' within a fast-moving and increasingly digitised society. The transnationalisation of familial intimacy is characterised by both family change and continuity, signalling both changes to how familial relations are characterised and enacted whilst also, frequently, reinstating established gender norms, relations and ways of 'doing family'. Taken together, the chapters in this part of the *Handbook* offer a rich tapestry of different perspectives on gender ideologies, relations and practices within contemporary migration formations.

Part II: Age and Intergenerational Relationships

Migrant families invariably encompass individuals of varied ages and life-stages, with differing roles, pressures and expectations attendant to this. And yet, age has for many years been neglected by researchers studying migration (White et al., 2011). This is partly a reflection of the methodological nationalism inherent in studies prioritising immigration policy: states have an 'ideal age' for recruiting potential immigrants, and consequently economically productive migrants have, historically, been the most prolifically researched.[1] Likewise, children are often excluded from the discussion because they are not deemed economically productive; they are also a dependent of another family member and therefore not independently significant; and ethically, it is often difficult to research children apart from their parents/carers (Dobson, 2009). Separately, but of course relatedly, intergenerational relations raise some different issues and concerns revolving, largely, around conflicts and divergencies in ideas and identities between grandparents, parents and children (Parreñas, 2001). Intergenerationality can also be embodied within a single migrant; a female migrant, for example, can simultaneously be a grandmother, a mother and a child (with different responsibilities to different generations of their family emerging concomitantly). Consequently, a complex tightrope of expectations and responsibilities must be walked (Yeoh et al., 2013). This part of the *Handbook* explicitly addresses, from different perspectives, the significance of age and intergenerational relationships within migrant families.

Part II begins with Chapter 7, by Sin Yee Koh and I Lin Sin, on capital accumulation and intergenerational transfers among transnational families, focusing on children's perspectives. Three themes are highlighted from their critical review of the academic literature: the values and meanings attached to global mobility and the significance of intergenerational social reproduction; the deconstruction of children's presumed privilege and homogeneity in capital transmission from parents to children; and the need to amplify the 'voices and choices of children in familial capital/mobility projects'. Importantly, the chapter also considers, from a methodological perspective, how researchers might better take account, going forward, of children's perspectives in family migration projects.

The next chapter by Caitríona Ní Laoire (Chapter 8) focuses on intergenerationality and the role it plays in contemporary migration. It explores the complex situation of multigenerational transnational Irish families, and the chapter develops a conceptualisation of the transgenerational reproduction of migration and (im)mobilities, taking account of familial migration histories and legacies. These histories and legacies shape young people's own migration trajectories. Likewise, C. Cindy Fan, in Chapter 9, takes an intergenerational perspective on the phenomenon of long-term split households, and intersects this discussion with consideration of the importance of gender, drawing useful links with chapters in Part I of the *Handbook*. The chapter turns the spotlight squarely onto split households, providing a comprehensive and insightful review of the academic literature in this area, ultimately demonstrating beyond doubt that split households matter significantly and should be subject to further academic enquiry.

Weronika Kloc-Nowak and Louise Ryan in Chapter 10 provide a fascinating look at the 'sandwich generation' of migrant families originally from Poland living in the UK: with caring obligations for their children, but also receiving and providing care at a distance from/ to ageing parents and other family back in Poland. One of the factors they touch on is Brexit (the UK's exit from the European Union) and the ongoing (in)ability of Polish parents to rely on occasional childcare from grandparents, due to the mobility restrictions that have arisen as a consequence. The chapter explores how migrants negotiate current care arrangements and foresee future intergenerational care needs, navigating shifting political and social circumstances.

The final two chapters in Part II focus on younger migrants: children and youth. Rhondeni Kikon and Roy Huijsmans (Chapter 11) reflect upon the general absence of significant scholarship exploring the concept of generation and youth migration, reviewing literature from across several countries. Their ideas are illustrated through a case study of youth migration from an Assam tea plantation (in Northeast India), linking family, a 'generationed political economy' with a plantation labour regime, and the predisposition for youth migration. By contrast, Katie Willis, Sue Clayton and Anna Gupta's chapter (Chapter 12) explores the particular phenomenon of unaccompanied child migrants, where the family has been left behind. The chapter explores children's relationships with distant family members and, in addition, how children can be seen to create new families. They explore how notions of the family and family life become mobilised in both national and international law and protocol to facilitate and/or police migration. Finally, the experiences of other family members, such as parents in the country of origin, are discussed in the context of unaccompanied child migration.

Part III: Power, Social Inequalities and Social Mobility

As suggested in the opening to this Introduction, families are the nexus of particular power configurations, which inevitably result in the exacerbation of social inequalities, both within the family itself and within wider society (Walton-Roberts, 2004). Families are also units of social mobility: spaces within which practices promoting social mobility are focused and sustained (Ong, 1999; Waters, 2006; Finch and Kim, 2012). The migration of one or more family member (as a worker or student, for example) often has the objective of securing social mobility for all family members (Coe and Shani, 2015; Robertson and Runganaikaloo, 2014). The chapters in Part III provide insight into these different relations, but notably focus on how the exercise of power intersects with social inequalities and social reproduction. The first chapter, by Johanna L. Waters and Zhe Wang (Chapter 13), acknowledges the importance of educational migration as a familial strategy to promote social mobility amongst contemporary migrants. Whilst the strategy may be seen to be often successful, a focus on different family members renders a more complex picture, where the 'messy reality of emotions' (Yeoh et al., 2018, p. 423) comes into play. Sometimes, these strategies fail. Always, they result in different outcomes and experiences for different family members, as their focus on emotions and educational migration exposes.

The exercise of power is amply demonstrated through the experiences of so-called 'elite migrants', embodied in the idea of the corporate expatriate worker. Sophie Cranston and George Tan, in Chapter 14, explore the notion that the expatriate is frequently discussed without due attention given to the significance of family within this elite form of migration. They explore literature that foregrounds the motivations and experiences of family members and call for a refocusing on the temporal as well as spatial and relational aspects of expatriate migration. They draw on two case examples (of British and Australian migrants in Singapore) to exemplify these entanglements through time and space.

Cathy McIlwaine, in Chapter 15, focuses specifically on gendered power relations and how gender norms and associated practices are enacted both locally and transnationally 'across multiple spheres from the state to labour markets'. Notably, however, these relations are crucially centred on the family and the space of the household. They also vary according to the power of the woman within the migrant family: whether their migration was independent or dependent, whether they moved as workers or for marriage, or whether they were victims or survivors of trafficking and smuggling. Other factors also come into play: the domestic space can be a space of refuge from wider social hostility, or one of violence or abuse. This chapter considers and discusses the complexity of gendered power dynamics within the context of families and migration, including highlighting the structural and institutional inequalities within immigration processes. It draws, in places, on empirical work with international migrant women in London.

Yanbo Hao and Maggi W.H. Leung (Chapter 16) review the literature on academic mobility, arguing that the family has rarely been placed at the centre of these debates. Their critical overview of the academic literature in this area provides a very useful corrective to this as they endeavour to unpack the family from the perspectives of gender and intersectionality, arguing that academic mobility remains an uneven mobility field. They also highlight some ongoing areas where research has been limited or non-existent and some directions for future research.

In Chapter 17, Claire Fletcher moves the discussion away from heteronormative and nuclear family formations to discuss the unequal socio-legal rights granted to lesbian, gay, bisexual, transgender, queer and intersex (LGBTQI) migrants. There are, she notes, significant 'discrepancies in legal provision for LGBTQI people' when it comes to migration, where 'legal rights that have been granted have been provided only to same-sex unions that replicate the heteronormative ideal'. Using the example of bi-national same-sex partnerships and migration policy in the UK, the chapter explores how immigration rules limit which families are seen as legitimate, and 'deserving', and therefore granted entry and citizenship rights. Power is exercised by the state to uphold particular, circumscribed notions of family.

Part IV: Spatialities and Temporalities

Migration is an inherently spatial issue: not only is it seen to unfold over and through space (and distance), but family migration also actively creates (diverse) spaces. Families are often multi-sited and yet still operating together, 'in sync'. More recently, however, scholars have been attentive to the combined spatialities, materialities and temporalities as a key feature of transnational families (Acedera and Yeoh, 2019; Pascucci, 2016; Xu, 2021). Transnational lives are lived through daily domestic rhythms, whilst they must at the same time contend with the complex temporalities of the state and state institutions (Waters and Leung, 2020). In a pragmatic sense, for example, the state may prescribe whether a stay is temporary or permanent, and this situation can and often does change and mutate over time (Baas and Yeoh, 2019). On a different register, time can affect a migrant family's experience of transnationalism, as Waters's (2011) longitudinal study of women migrants in Vancouver has shown. The chapters in Part IV take different but complementary views on temporality and its role in understanding families in migration.

In Chapter 18, Denise L. Spitzer and Sara Torres tackle head on the implications of spatial and prolonged (and indeterminant) temporal separation of families through migration, resulting from the out-migration of labour migrants. The United Nations Convention on the Rights of the Child, and the International Convention on the Protection of the Rights of All Migrant Workers and Members of their Families, enshrine in law the right to family reunification. And yet, as the authors demonstrate, nation-states situated in the Global North continue to act as gatekeepers through their migration policies that determine the shape and composition of migrant families and the timing of their resettlement, resulting in the stratification of family migrant households. They explore the complexity underpinning the reunification of family members under migration regimes, which is underpinned by particular conceptions of the family. Furthermore, whilst reunification is often, at first, an emotionally uplifting experience for the family in question, the actual process of resettlement can involve the recalibration of gendered familial roles in a way that can be painful for the individuals concerned. They argue that the process of family reunification, and the recalibration of family life that this invariably entails, needs to be related to 'the dynamics of the host society' which serve either to support or undermine families' attempts to adjust to life in their new country and home.

Annabelle Wilkins's chapter (Chapter 19) looks explicitly at the issue of temporality within migration and families research, and how this is often overshadowed by an emphasis on spatial approaches. She argues that extant scholarship on the 'temporalities of home' can advance such discussions. The chapter begins by providing a critical overview of the literature on time, migration and the family, highlighting research on the temporal effects of immigration regimes and the micro-temporalities of transnational family life. The chapter then engages with research on Vietnamese migrants and refugees in East London, informed by work on care temporalities, time and the life course, and temporalities of home and the city. Wilkins argues that a lens of 'home' and temporality can enhance understandings of transnational family practices and how these intersect with different timescales of migration.

Seasonality, within migration, is one way in which temporality and spatiality clearly intersect. Thomas Saetre Jakobsen, Sam Scott and Johan Fredrik Rye, in Chapter 20, consider low-wage labour mobility as circulators rather than settlers, where transnational householding arrangements become commonplace. In other words, household social reproduction and wage work become spatially separated. The chapter asks: what lessons can be learned from the particular case of Norwegian and UK horticulture, where seasonal migrant labour usage is normalised? What impact does this seasonality have on the separation of roles within the (sometimes split) household? The authors argue that the seasonal separation of migrants and their households (in other words, a spatial and temporal division of work and family life) is pivotal to the realisation of surplus value in this sector. The 'offshoring of social reproduction' and its spatialities and temporalities is an area that requires more research.

How do we assemble a picture of 'left-behind' children (and childhoods) over time? Theodora Lam, in her chapter (Chapter 21), reviews the literature on this migration phenomenon over the past decade, of children coping with the inherent ruptures of living prolonged periods without one or both parents under the same roof, and/or under the care of surrogate parents. The chapter provides a valuable take on the evolution of research in this important area, before turning to consider, specifically, the voices of left-behind children in Indonesia and the Philippines, drawing on an empirical study of child health and migrant parents in Southeast Asia. This highlights the importance of time (as well as spatial separation and distance) in how children's lives may have changed over the period of separation from family members.

Transnational families encounter mobility regimes not only in space but also in time as Francesca Morais and Brenda S.A. Yeoh explore in their chapter (Chapter 22) on how nation-states govern contemporary mobility. The term 'mobility regimes' attempts to capture the 'complex modes of differentiation within governing structures of mobility' and the impacts of this upon transnational family members living across nation-state boundaries. Temporality is highlighted as an important lens for understanding how the different life stages of migrants, in relation to other family members, are implicated within mobility regimes. As the COVID-19 pandemic has shown, transnational families encounter various mobility regimes with the closure of national borders, travel restrictions and lockdowns.

CONCLUSION

In conclusion, we offer some suggestions on using the *Handbook* before thinking through future directions that work on migration and the family might take in a world that has been, to a certain extent, reconfigured by the COVID-19 pandemic. As we indicate above, the chapters have been grouped in a way according to their dominant themes. However, as also noted, many chapters would sit easily within or across multiple parts. The parts should not be taken as definitive, therefore, but rather as a mere suggestion for how the chapters might be read. Although interdisciplinary in nature, the chapters are not exhaustive in the disciplinary perspectives they represent. There is a dominance of human geographical and sociological standpoints within these pages, but other disciplines and subdisciplines are undoubtedly represented. The chapters are primarily designed as critical reviews of and engagements with lasting debates within their specific areas, but in many cases some original empirical material is drawn upon to make a particular illustrative point.

In terms of future directions of travel, the chapters indicate where gaps in knowledge undoubtedly remain. We still know little about how LGBTQI families experience migration, and disabled migrants are significantly and woefully underrepresented within contemporary research. Temporality is still largely neglected (in comparison to spatial perspectives) in studies of migration and the family (Xu, 2021), although several chapters in this *Handbook* have gone some way towards addressing this. COVID-19 has highlighted the fragility of mobility and the enduring power of nation-states to shut their borders and separate families for an extend period of time. It is likely that states will continue to exercise their power in this area, and into the future and post-pandemic times. The pandemic has highlighted what is possible and has normalised (to a certain extent) and heightened oppressive mobility regimes. This global crisis – and more particularly the human response to the crisis – has made it all the more important to attend to the complex entanglements of migration and family so as to grasp the multiple ramifications for the fates and fortunes of migrants and their families across the world.

NOTE

1. Many states' immigration point systems reward applicants up a defined 'productive age' and significantly penalise older migrants (for example, after the age of 35, under the Canadian Points System, the number of points you accrue for your age is reduced each year to zero once an applicant reaches 47 years old. Children under the age of 18 are not usually permitted to apply to immigrate independently, only as 'dependent immigrants').

REFERENCES

Acedera, K.A., and Yeoh, B.S. (2019). 'Making time': Long-distance marriages and the temporalities of the transnational family. *Current Sociology*, 67(2), 250–272.

Baas, M., and Yeoh, B.S. (2019). Introduction: Migration studies and critical temporalities. *Current Sociology*, 67(2), 161–168.

Baldassar, L., and Brandhorst, R. (2021). Sibling support in transnational families: The impact of migration and mobility on sibling relationships of support over time and distance. In *Brothers and Sisters* (pp. 239–256). Palgrave Macmillan.

Basch, L., Schiller, N.G., and Blanc, C.S. (1994). *Nations Unbound: Transnational Projects, Postcolonial Predicaments, and Deterritorialized Nation-States*. Routledge.

Bryceson, D.F. (2019). Transnational families negotiating migration and care life cycles across nation-state borders. *Journal of Ethnic and Migration Studies*, 45(16), 3042–3064.

Butler, J. (2002). *Gender Trouble*. Routledge.

Coe, C., and Shani, S. (2015). Cultural capital and transnational parenting: The case of Ghanaian migrants in the United States. *Harvard Educational Review*, 85(4), 562–586.

Cooke, T.J., and Bailey, A.J. (1996). Family migration and the employment of married women and men. *Economic Geography*, 72(1), 38–48.

Dobson, M.E. (2009). Unpacking children in migration research. *Children's Geographies*, 7(3), 355–360.

Finch, J., and Kim, S.K. (2012). Kirŏgi families in the US: Transnational migration and education. *Journal of Ethnic and Migration Studies*, 38(3), 485–506.

Hardill, I. (2004). Transnational living and moving experiences: intensified mobility and dual-career households. *Population, Space and Place*, 10(5), 375–389.
Harvey, M. (1998). Dual-career couples during international relocation: The trailing spouse. *International Journal of Human Resource Management*, 9(2), 309–331.
Ho, E.L.E., and Chiu, T.Y. (2020). Transnational ageing and 'care technologies': Chinese grandparenting migrants in Singapore and Sydney. *Population, Space and Place*, 26(7), e2365.
Hoang, L.A., and Yeoh, B.S. (2012). Sustaining families across transnational spaces: Vietnamese migrant parents and their left-behind children. *Asian Studies Review*, 36(3), 307–325.
Kofman, E. (2004). Family-related migration: A critical review of European Studies. *Journal of Ethnic and Migration Studies*, 30(2), 243–262.
Kofman, E., and Raghuram, P. (2006) Women and global labour migrations: Incorporating skilled workers. *Antipode*, 38(2), 282–303.
Levitt, P., DeWind, J., and Vertovec, S. (2003). International perspectives on transnational migration: An introduction. *International Migration Review*, 37(3), 565–575.
Ley, D. (2003). Seeking homo economicus: The Canadian state and the strange story of the business immigration program. *Annals of the Association of American Geographers*, 93(2), 426–441.
Ley, D. (2010). *Millionaire Migrants: Trans-Pacific Life Lines*. John Wiley & Sons.
Madianou, M. (2016). Ambient co-presence: Transnational family practices in polymedia environments. *Global Networks*, 16(2), 183–201.
Mahler, S.J., and P.R. Pessar (2006). Gender matters: Ethnographers bring gender from the periphery toward the core of migration studies. *International Migration Review*, 40, 27–63.
Mincer, J. (1978). Family migration decisions. *Journal of Political Economy*, 86(5), 749–773.
Nedelcu, M., and Wyss, M. (2020). Transnational grandparenting: An introduction. *Global Networks*, 20(2), 292–307.
Ong, A. (1999). *Flexible Citizenship: The Cultural Logics of Transnationality*. Duke University Press.
Parreñas, R.S. (2001). Mothering from a distance: Emotions, gender, and intergenerational relations in Filipino transnational families. *Feminist Studies*, 27(2), 361–390.
Parreñas, R. (2005). Long distance intimacy: Class, gender and intergenerational relations between mothers and children in Filipino transnational families. *Global Networks*, 5(4), 317–336.
Pascucci, E. (2016). Transnational disruptions: Materialities and temporalities of transnational citizenship among Somali refugees in Cairo. *Global Networks*, 16(3), 326–343.
Pessar, P.R., and Mahler, S.J. (2003). Transnational migration: Bringing gender in. *International Migration Review*, 37(3), 812–846.
Pratt, G., and Yeoh, B. (2003). Transnational (counter) topographies. *Gender, Place and Culture: A Journal of Feminist Geography*, 10(2), 159–166.
Robertson, S., and Runganaikaloo, A. (2014). Lives in limbo: Migration experiences in Australia's education–migration nexus. *Ethnicities*, 14(2), 208–226.
Ryan, L., Sales, R., Tilki, M., and Siara, B. (2009). Family strategies and transnational migration: Recent Polish migrants in London. *Journal of Ethnic and Migration Studies*, 35(1), 61–77.
Silvey, R. (2005). Borders, embodiment, and mobility: Feminist migration studies in geography. In *A Companion to Feminist Geography* (pp. 138–149), edited by Lise Nelson and Joni Seager. Blackwell Publishing.
Teo, Y., and Piper, N. (2009). Foreigners in our homes: Linking migration and family policies in Singapore. *Population, Space and Place*, 15(2), 147–159.
Walsh, K. (2011). Migrant masculinities and domestic space: British home-making practices in Dubai. *Transactions of the Institute of British Geographers*, 36(4), 516–529.
Walton-Roberts, M. (2004). Transnational migration theory in population geography: Gendered practices in networks linking Canada and India. *Population, Space and Place*, 10(5), 361–373.
Waters, J.L. (2002). Flexible families? 'Astronaut' households and the experiences of lone mothers in Vancouver, British Columbia. *Social and Cultural Geography*, 3(2), 117–134.
Waters, J.L. (2006). Geographies of cultural capital: Education, international migration and family strategies between Hong Kong and Canada. *Transactions of the Institute of British Geographers*, 31(2), 179–192.
Waters, J.L. (2010). Becoming a father, missing a wife: Chinese transnational families and the male experience of lone parenting in Canada. *Population, Space and Place*, 16(1), 63–74.

Waters, J.L. (2011). Time and transnationalism: A longitudinal study of immigration, endurance and settlement in Canada. *Journal of Ethnic and Migration Studies*, 37(7), 1119–1135.

Waters, J.L., and Leung, M.W. (2020). Rhythms, flows, and structures of cross-boundary schooling: State power and educational mobilities between Shenzhen and Hong Kong. *Population, Space and Place*, 26(3), e2298.

White, A., Ní Laoire, C., Tyrrell, N., and Carpena-Méndez, F. (2011). Children's roles in transnational migration. *Journal of Ethnic and Migration Studies*, 37(8), 1159–1170. DOI: 10.1080/1369183X.2011.590635.

Wilding, R., Baldassar, L., Gamage, S., Worrell, S., and Mohamud, S. (2020). Digital media and the affective economies of transnational families. *International Journal of Cultural Studies*, 23(5), 639–655.

Xu, C.L. (2021). Time, class and privilege in career imagination: Exploring study-to-work transition of Chinese international students in UK universities through a Bourdieusian lens. *Time and Society*, 30(1), 5–29.

Yeoh, B.S.A., Chee, H.C., Vu, T.K.D., and Cheng, Y.E. (2013). Between two families: The social meaning of remittances for Vietnamese marriage migrants in Singapore. *Global Networks*, 13(4), 441–458.

Yeoh, B.S.A., and Huang, S. (2011). Introduction: Fluidity and friction in talent migration. *Journal of Ethnic and Migration Studies*, 37(5), 681–690.

Yeoh, B.S.A., Huang, S., and Lam, T. (2018). Transnational family dynamics in Asia. In *Handbook of Migration and Globalisation* (pp. 413–430), edited by A. Triandafyllidou. Edward Elgar Publishing.

Yeoh, B.S.A. and Willis, K. (2005). Singaporeans in China: transnational women elites and the negotiation of gendered identities. *Geoforum*, 36(2), 211–222.

PART I

GENDER RELATIONS AND GENDER SUBJECTIVITIES

2. Nanny families and the making of gender (in)equality
Rosie Cox, Terese Anving and Sara Eldén

INTRODUCTION

Families are more than intimate relationships amongst kin. They are intertwined in networks of complex ties between people and across borders, they are part of global flows of labour, and they are always dependent upon national welfare policies. There are over 50 million domestic and homecare workers worldwide who carry out housework and care for children, the elderly and vulnerable adults within private homes. These workers are in a fundamental sense enabling family life, and as a consequence they are part of the 'doing' of family (Morgan, 1996, 2011). The majority are women, and domestic work has become a migrant niche in many countries. The International Labour Organization (ILO) estimates that there are at least 53 million domestic workers worldwide and the number could be as high as 100 million, 83 per cent of whom are women. As the ILO explains, even at its lowest estimate 'if all domestic workers worked in one country, this country would be the tenth largest employer worldwide' (ILO, 2011).

Domestic workers have long been migrants. Traditionally, women would move from rural areas to cities or from poorer to richer regions to take on these roles, but in the late 20th century international migration for domestic work became common. Domestic and care workers are predominantly from Asia, North Africa, South and Central America, and move primarily between countries in the Global South and from South to North. There are some distinct patterns of movement between countries which reflect immigration regulations, historical colonial relationships, income inequalities and language commonalities. These include movements of workers between Latin American countries, from Mexico and the Caribbean to the United States of America (USA), and from Latin America to Spain. Moroccan and Tunisian women move to France; Burmese to Thailand; Filipinos, Indonesians and Sri Lankans to the Middle East, Hong Kong, Singapore and Malaysia; and recently women from Eastern Europe and the former Soviet States have become important sources of care provision in private homes in Central and Western Europe.

The international movement of domestic and care workers is encouraged by policy in both sending and receiving countries. Some policies explicitly target this domain, facilitating either the immigration or emigration of domestic workers. For example, the Philippines has labour export policies which have encouraged over 150 000 people a year to migrate to become domestic and care workers overseas (POEA, 2012; see also Guevarra, 2014). Receiving countries often establish visa regimes for domestic workers which commonly specify that the worker must live in the employer's home (see, for example, the Live-in Caregiver Program in Canada, the au pair scheme in the USA, Norway and Denmark). Government policy can also encourage (or discourage) the employment of domestic and care workers through policy regimes which do not explicitly address this domain; most obvious perhaps are policies which shape gender equality, opportunities to balance family life and paid work outside the home (parental leave, subsidised childcare, and so on). There are broad work, care, migration and welfare regimes which shape both cultural attitudes towards how care work should be done, and the practical possibilities for accomplishing it (Treas and Lui, 2013).

In this chapter we argue that the ways in which families are 'done' (Morgan, 1996, 2011) – that is, the everyday practices that families engage in – are intimately intertwined with opportunities arising in different welfare state regimes. The 'doing of family' is related to and dependent upon politics and policies: not only those explicitly directed at families, but also other areas such as migration and employment regulations (see also Chapters 14 and 17 in this *Handbook*). In the United Kingdom (UK), in common with a number of high-income English-speaking countries, the market and the family are expected to provide care and make possible dual-earner family life. We show how au pairing, which is framed as a 'family-like' relationship, has boomed within this context. In the case of the Nordic countries, political initiatives all aiming to introduce neoliberal agendas of 'freedom of choice' have, in combination with growing income gaps and increased labour migration, created new possibilities for 'doing family' for a growing group of well-off middle-class parents. Through the employment of nannies and au pairs, new ways of doing the – much sought after – gender-equal family have arisen, a doing that in itself reproduces new inequalities, we argue.

This chapter draws on two research projects which explore the ways that care workers were engaged in 'doing family'. The UK study 'Au Pairing After the Au Pair Scheme'[1] (Cox and Busch, 2018) explored the conditions of au pairs since the deregulation of au pairing in 2008. It involved analysis of 1000 advertisements for au pairs on the website Gumtree, interviews with 40 au pairs and 15 people who were currently hosting or had recently hosted au pairs and interviews with key informants engaged in the sector including the British Au Pairs Agencies Association (BAPAA), workers' and migrants' rights groups, and the Home Office.

The study 'Care for Children in an Era of Private Market Services: A Study of Nannies, Children and Parents'[2] had the overarching aim of analysing the practice of doing care and family in Swedish families who hire nannies and au pairs.[3] Nannies/au pairs (n = 26), parents (n = 29) and children (n = 19) were interviewed separately. The nannies and au pairs related their experiences from working in 59 families, the parents had experience of hiring 83 nannies and au pairs (all women) over the years, and the children (aged between 5 and 14 years old) told of experiences of being taken care of by around 80 nannies and au pairs.

The chapter begins by conceptualising the policy and cultural influences which shape family life in different countries. Building on the idea of welfare regimes, we show that the interactions between these and care, migration and employment regimes are significant in different national responses to needs for care. We then explore the case of au pairing in the UK, a deregulated form of live-in childcare provided by migrant workers, before moving on to examine the employment of nannies and au pairs in Sweden and the recent challenges of the 'woman-friendly' Nordic states.

CONCEPTUALISING REGIMES OF CARE AND FAMILY

International differences in the employment of domestic workers to carry out housework and childcare depend on intersections of gender inequality and socioeconomic inequality at national level (Treas and Lui, 2013). Hardly surprisingly, countries which have pronounced gender inequalities and polarised incomes have high rates of domestic worker employment (Milkman et al., 1998; Higman, 2015). However, the organisation of domestic tasks, the types of jobs that are created for domestic workers, and whether migrants are specifically recruited into them, depend on wider social, cultural and economic practices. The 'willingness to outsource assumes a "servant culture" that accepts others to clean up' (Treas and Lui, 2013, p. 141; Pfau-Effinger, 2010), something which has not always sat comfortably with some nations' egalitarian imaginings of themselves.

Building on Esping-Andersen's (1999) influential typology of welfare regimes, Fiona Williams and Anna Gavanas (2008) argue that migration into care and domestic work can be understood as part of the dovetailing of childcare regimes (state policy responses to changes in family and work) with migration regimes (state policy responses to changes in work, population movement and change). National childcare regimes are differentiated by three policy-related factors: the extent and nature of public and market childcare provision, especially for children of under school age; policies facilitating parents' involvement in paid employment such as maternity/paternity or parental leave; and cash benefits for childcare; as well as care cultures, which are the dominant national and local cultural discourses on what constitutes appropriate childcare. Migration regimes are characterised by the rules for entrance into a country, settlement and naturalisation rights, as well as employment, social and civil rights. There are also internal norms and practices which govern relationships between majority and minority groups, all of which are shaped by histories of migration and emigration which themselves emerge from colonialism and old trade routes, and share political, economic or religious alliances. Employment regimes can be added to regimes of care and migration. These provide the institutional context that shapes the experiences of both migrant women care workers and their employers, and the patterns of migrant care work found in different countries (Williams, 2014).

Cross-national studies of gender relations, housework and paid domestic work identify broad groups of countries with particular cultural and policy approaches to the organisation and execution of care work. Williams (2014, p. 17) describes a situation of 'converging variations' across Europe, where there has been a generalised pattern of growth in the employment of migrant domestic workers (also true beyond Europe), but variations in the roles of the state, market and family in the provision of care. In the countries of the Global North, we can identify commonalities amongst: (1) English-speaking nations (particularly the USA and UK) which have high rates of socioeconomic inequality, a laissez-faire approach to employment, declining welfare provision, and an expectation that individual families will use the market to solve their needs for care labour (Treas and Lui, 2013); (2) Southern European nations with less-developed state provision of care and welfare and relatively low rates of paid work for married women, and where marked growth in the employment of migrant domestic workers is replacing a formerly strong reliance on family carers (Williams, 2014); (3) Eastern European countries with their legacies of state socialism have high rates of female paid employment outside the home, relatively high rates of male involvement in domestic work, long-standing provision of collective childcare and low (but now growing) incidence of employment of care workers in private homes; and (4) Nordic countries with strong welfare provision, cultural expectations of gender equality, state provision of childcare and, at least until recently, a cultural reflex against the employment of domestic workers.

We look in more detail at the first and last of these two groups (expanding the Anglophone 'North' to include Australia and New Zealand) to highlight the different approaches to 'doing family' that emerge within these different care regimes, and to examine how gender divisions of labour within households have been affected in different countries by the increasing employment of domestic and care workers. Through this discussion we also question the extent to which the assumption of 'Nordic exceptionalism' in discussions of gender relations and discussions of domestic work still stands.

The Market Will Provide: Privatised Childcare in the Anglophone 'North'

There are substantial and important differences in the cultural and policy environments that frame family life in Canada, the USA, the UK, Ireland, Australia and New Zealand. However, the increasing adoption of neoliberal approaches to care and welfare in all of these countries in recent decades has created some similarities in the ways that migrant domestic workers have been looked to as a solution to the problems of balancing paid work and family life. The combination of relatively long working hours, patchy support for families in terms of parental leave or subsidised childcare, and cultural preferences for 'mother-like' care in private homes (Gregson and Lowe, 1994), creates a demand for the kind of flexible, individual childcare that au pairs and nannies can provide. Migration regimes have responded by creating lightly regulated routes for migrant care workers. In particular, au pair schemes have developed in the USA, UK, Ireland and Australia which provide low-waged (or unwaged) 'helpers' to families in need of childcare, or sometimes eldercare.

In the English-speaking high-income countries, it is useful to consider the operation of care regimes and migration regimes in the light of attitudes and policies towards paid work and the market. In the post-war years these countries have moved, at different paces, from a male breadwinner model, based on men earning a 'family wage' (at least for skilled working-class and middle-class men) towards a 'universal worker' model, which manifests for many families with young children as a 'one and a half breadwinner' pattern, with men in full-time paid work and women working part-time outside the home and taking the brunt of responsibility for domestic and care work at home. These countries also have relatively long working hours and short holidays; people in the most economically unequal countries – a category that includes the UK, USA, Australia and New Zealand – work the equivalent of two to three months more per year than those in more economically equal states (Wilkinson and Pickett, 2010).

Families have been supported through market-focused mechanisms such as government subsidies for private housing (see Cox, 2021), tax breaks or direct payments for care needs (Williams, 2014) rather than, for example, free, universally available childcare. This approach reinforces both the role of the market as the primary provider (albeit one which would not function without quite substantial government intervention), and the family (in particular, mothers) as the unit responsible for organising care. These policies thus have material affects and reinforce ideologies about the responsibilities of families and individuals.

Migration regimes which facilitate the employment of domestic workers could also be considered as market-focused responses, allowing those families who can afford to employ a care worker the opportunity to ameliorate the problems of work–life balance. The USA has a long history of employment of Black American women in white households, and this has been added to more recently by the employment of large numbers of women from Asia (particularly the Philippines), Latin America and the Caribbean to carry out childcare and housework as nannies and housekeepers (see, amongst others, Brown, 2011; Glenn, 1992; Hondagneu-Sotelo, 2001; Macdonald 2010; Parreñas, 2000). Canada, similarly, has relied on migrant care workers to provide both childcare and eldercare in private homes and developed the Live-in Caregiver Program to facilitate this. The programme restricts the employment rights of live-in care workers, for example the right to change employers, thus ensuring a supply of highly flexible workers to Canadian families (England and Stiell, 1997; Pratt, 1999, 2004; Stiell and England, 1997). The UK, Australia (Berg, 2015; Berg and Meagher, 2018) and Ireland (Smith, 2015), and to a lesser extent the USA (Geserick, 2015, 2016), have used au pair schemes to provide flexible, live-in carers within a structure that emphasises the primacy of family as the site of care. Au pairs are not considered to be workers, but are meant to be involved in a cultural exchange scheme and treated like a member of their host's family.

Women-Friendly Welfare States in Change: The Re-emergence of Domestic Workers in the Nordic Countries

Gender equality is often regarded as a core value in the Nordic countries,[4] and the countries are often portrayed as women-friendly welfare states (Hernes, 1987; Borchorst and Siim, 2008; Isaksen, 2010). This self-image is closely connected to the overall understanding of the Nordic welfare states as belonging to a social democratic welfare regime characterised by a social security system for all citizens, as well as a focus on individual autonomy and social mobility (Esping Andersen, 1999). The Scandinavian countries, although differing in certain respects, can all be defined as having a 'universal caregiver model' (Fraser, 1994). Care is both collectivised and a private responsibility, and the availability of affordable public daycare is a cornerstone in this childcare regime. Together with generous parental leave schemes,[5] accessible childcare is an important piece of the puzzle in making it possible for men and women to both work outside of the home and share the caring work; the ideal being that of a family where adult partners have 'dual earner/dual carer' responsibilities (Lundqvist, 2011, p. 72). As a result, a comparatively large proportion of women in the Nordic countries are part of the paid labour force. In Sweden, for example, the number of women in the labour force grew from 38 per cent in 1960 to 83 per cent in 1980, and has since stayed at approximately this level (Lundqvist, 2017). According to Esping Andersen (2009). this can be regarded as a revolution in the lives of women.

However, the revolution can be argued to be incomplete, as neither the dual earner part, and even less so the dual carer part, has been realised in practice. In the Nordic countries, while the majority of small children are enrolled in public daycare, women still do most of the care work at home, they more often stay home with their children during infant years despite initiatives such as 'daddy quotas', and also often work in part-time jobs. While women have increased their participation in the labour force, and well-educated women often work full-time, men have not reduced their working hours and increased their participation in care work at home to the same extent (see, e.g., Borchorst and Siim, 2008; Mósesdóttir and Ellingsaeter, 2019; Statistics Sweden, 2020).

Researchers have argued that the gap between gender equality as a discourse, and the inability to realise sharing care and housework responsibilities between men and women in the everyday lives in families, is a main reason behind the increasing demand for affordable, flexible domestic workers in the Nordic countries (Bikova, 2017; Isaksen and Näre, 2019). This is where the childcare regimes become intertwined with employment and migration regimes: the possibilities for young women to migrate for domestic work has been enabled by changes in migration and labour regulations (e.g. Calleman, 2010; Stenum, 2010; Frödin and

Kjellberg, 2018), and is meeting demands of families struggling to solve the conflicts between work and family responsibilities. The gender equality argument has been at the forefront in debates and political initiatives promoting the establishment of a domestic work market in all Nordic countries. In Denmark, as well as in Norway, the hiring of especially Filipino au pairs has become more common during the last decade, while the au pair programme in Denmark has been described as a way to make possible work–family balance in double-income families (Liversage et al., 2013; Bikova, 2017). In the spirit of freedom of choice, in Finland a 'cash-for-care' system has been introduced to complement public daycare, making it possible for parents to choose whether they prefer to have their children in daycare, receive funding in order to stay at home with them, or to employ a private carer such as a nanny or au pair. For double-income middle-class families, the reason for employing someone is often to make it possible for men and women to engage in paid work, and to allow for greater flexibility in everyday life (Näre, 2016; Näre and Wide, 2019). Also, in Sweden, as we will discuss shortly, when a tax deduction on domestic work was introduced in 2007, resulting in a boom in the market for domestic services, the solving of work–family dilemmas and gender equality arguments were frequently used by its advocates.

The Nordic countries and the Anglophone West illustrate the 'converging differences' which shape the growth in the employment of domestic workers and au pairs internationally. There is convergence in employment regimes towards a 'universal breadwinner' model, established in the Nordic countries in the 1960s and adopted in the decades since at different rates in the English-speaking countries. There are marked differences in care regimes, manifest in the very different state provision of childcare and cultural attitudes towards how and where children should be cared for, but also convergence around the increasing use of market-based solutions organised by individual families. There is also convergence in the migration regimes and the migration policies which have been developed, such as au pair schemes, to facilitate the flow of low-waged, flexible migrant labour into childcare and domestic work in private homes.

AU PAIRS AND 'FAMILY-LIKE' CARE IN THE UK

The UK has one of the most popular au pair schemes in the world, and while numbers are imprecise, it is thought that over 50 000 au pairs were hosted by UK families before the 2016 Brexit vote, and the number may have been as high as 90 000. The rules and details of au pairing vary by country with some national au pair schemes being highly regulated, such as the USA, while others – the UK being the prime example – are not regulated at all (Cox, 2015). All schemes have in common the idea of a young person living with a host family, carrying out household tasks and being treated 'as an equal' (the translation of 'au pair').

Broadly speaking, in the UK, au pairs are imagined to be young people, normally from another EU country, who will do 25–30 hours of childcare and housework in exchange for room and board, pocket money, and being treated as a member of the family. Until 2008 au pairing in the UK was regulated by the Home Office through the Au Pair Visa. The visa set out what an au pair could and could not do, and the guidance provided was applicable to all au pairs, even those from EU and European Economic Area (EEA) countries who did not need a visa (Búriková, 2016). In 2008, the Au Pair Visa was ended and the government ceased to regulate au pairing (Cox, 2012; Cox and Busch, 2018). Currently, the UK government provides a very limited amount of guidance about how to identify an au pair (see https://www.gov.uk/au-pairs-employment-law/au-pairs), but this information is vague and would allow people living and working in vastly different conditions to still be called au pairs. The only categorical statements this guidance provides are that au pairs are not entitled to the National Minimum Wage (NMW) or paid holidays, and that they are not normally classified as workers or employees. Au pairs are constructed as providing 'help' rather than labour for the families they live with. By defining au pairs as 'not workers' the government has removed any protections that may be available to them, and created a sector where exploitation is rife and also largely unseen.

Our research found that demand for au pairs came almost exclusively from families with children who were negotiating the demands of paid work and childcare. Analysis of 1000 advertisements for au pairs on Gumtree.com was carried out to gain an overview of the working hours, tasks and remuneration that characterised au pair posts (Cox and Busch, 2018). Our study found that the average working week being advertised was 38.7 hours long (including babysitting), and that there was great variety in the number of hours an au pair was expected to work. A minority of ads were looking for an au pair for 25 hours a week or fewer (the number of hours specified by the old Au Pair Visa), and 10 percent of all advertisers wanted an au pair to work 50 hours a week or more, with the longest working week specified being 80 hours. In return for this work the average pocket money offered was £108 per week (although only half of the ads revealed the amount on offer). Fourteen per cent offered below the recommended £85 per week. Three ads posted next to each other illustrate this variety in pay and conditions amongst UK au pairs: the first offered £100 per week plus own bedroom and bathroom for 45 hours work looking after four children, one of whom was under 3 and one of whom was under 1; the next offered £100 per week plus own bedroom for 50 hours work looking after one child under 3; and the third offered £110 per week (no information given about bedroom or bathroom) for 25 hours work looking after three children, none of whom was under three years old. The lowest pay offered in the Gumtree ads was no pocket money, just room and board for 30 hours work looking after a child under three years old, cooking and cleaning. The highest pay offered was c. £360 per week to care for two school-age children after school during term time and full time during the holidays, as well as cooking and cleaning. This variety of demands, as well as the long average working hours seen in the whole sample of ads, suggests that the notion of 'au pairing' is used to cover a multitude of roles, and the conceit of 'family membership' can conceal work that is significant in terms of its volume and its place in family life (Cox and Busch, 2018).

Alongside long working hours for parents, the UK also has limited state provision of childcare, and high childcare costs. Collective forms of care, such as nurseries, do not offer the hours many working parents need; and even if these are available, they can actually prove more expensive than hosting an au pair. For families with the space to host an au pair, this can be an affordable and workable solution to the childcare crisis. In 2017, the government's Money Advice Service advised that a registered childminder (someone who provides care for a small number of children in the childminder's home) for a child under 2 years old would cost £212.86 per week (£275.83 in London) and a nursery for one child under 2 would be £222.36 per week (£277.84 in London). Qualified nannies are prohibitively expensive for all but the best-off families, costing up to £650 per week plus tax, national insurance and room and board; that is, £33,800 per year (see https://www.moneyadviceservice.org.uk/en/articles/childcare-costs) (median household disposable income in 2015/16 was £26,300 according to

ONS, 2017). When more than one child needs care, these costs can multiply, and nannies are unlikely to offer the flexibility of an au pair.

All of the hosts we interviewed had decided to host an au pair so that the parent (in the case of lone-parent families) or both parents (in the case of two-parent households) could engage in paid work outside the home. The decision had been made in the context of the perception among those interviewed that they had four main alternatives: public or private nursery for younger children or after-school clubs for older ones; childminder; nanny; or au pair. Parents interviewed worked in a range of industries, and it was notable that many worked non-standard and/or long hours that were difficult to reconcile with school hours or with standard nursery or childminder provision. This might be because one parent's job required that they travel abroad frequently, leaving the other parent needing additional childcare support for short but intense bursts. For others, working shifts meant that they were sometimes required to do night shifts, and sometimes their hours conflicted with the school run. Others again had to be at work early in the morning and/or returned late in the evening, meaning that they needed someone else to deliver children to school or nursery, pick them up in the afternoon, and feed and bathe them in the evening.

They key problem that hosts were trying to solve was the difficulties they encountered holding down jobs that required long and/or unpredictable hours that clashed with their children's timetables. For most of those we interviewed it was neither financially feasible nor desirable for one parent to be the breadwinner and the other a stay-at-home parent. But neither was it possible for both parents (or one parent in the case of single-parent families) to work without having extensive and flexible childcare in place. Parents we interviewed had usually explored a number of options before deciding to host an au pair, and had concluded that live-in childcare by someone who could care for children around parents' work hours, be charged with a range of other household tasks, and be paid pocket money rather than a wage, was the most viable solution to the problem of how to reconcile paid work with family and domestic responsibilities.

For individual host families, hosting an au pair had to fit within the context of family finances, need for flexibility from the childcare provider, and concepts of what constitutes good parenting and, by extension, an adequate form of childcare. These were the lived reality of the regimes outlined above. For example, one host, Eleanor, discussed how hosting an au pair fitted with her finances and affordable collective childcare:

> I'm one of those mums who hasn't been able to work for a good eight years because of child care expense ... none of the salaries I was offered cover the cost of child care and train [fare] and I really think that childcare's very, very expensive and very overrated as well, meaning formal nurseries and stuff.

Eleanor explained that it was only when she and her family moved into a larger house that she had been able to think about returning to work. She said:

> The moment when we moved into a bigger house when we could actually bring an au pair in, we did. I lived in a flat before ... I still haven't got a full-time job. I'm working part time, but it pays off, really. It's cheaper and cost is not just the only thing but it's actually also the flexibility.

Similarly, Lucy, another host, explained that she had tried a number of different arrangements and had settled on an au pair because of the cost and flexibility:

> For a year I had a girl that would come to my house and it was very expensive. At one point, I think I was paying £1000 a month. Unsustainable, you're just getting more and more in debt. [not] getting out of it. Then after that we had a nursery was slightly less than that. Maybe £800 ... an expensive nursery, then we go slightly cheaper. As he got older he got cheaper and we had a very lovely Montessori nursery just before he went off to school. At that point that Montessori nursery finished at four and we had childcare like a girl that would come and pick him up. If I had to work late it was tricky but it was okay, we managed.

These experiences illustrate the way that demands for flexible working combined with very limited subsidised or flexible collective childcare create demand for individual solutions. When these practical aspects are added to hosts' attitudes towards care, and what constitutes good parenting, au pairs became even more desirable. As outlined above, ideas about parenting have been constructed within cultural, social and political contexts, and what is seen as good for a child in one local, national or historical situation might be abhorrent in another. In the UK, it has been widely held that home-based care by a parent or trusted individual was better for a child's development than care in an institution such as a nursery (Gregson and Lowe, 1994). In the UK, parents have often not regarded nursery care as a standard and acceptable solution to combining work and family commitments, nor have they in many cases been able to rely on family networks. Instead, hosts discussed a preference for paid 'mother-substitutes' for babies (and a number had employed qualified nannies before au pairs) and/or a combination of this care with nursery, pre-school then school hours as children grew older.

Host Stacey expressed this in a way which took for granted women's responsibilities for childcare, a preference for 'mother-like' care, and an acknowledgement that many women want to work outside the home. She said:

> It depends on the parent, doesn't it? If you're the kind of woman that needs to go out to work to be fulfilled, and that makes you a better mother when you are at home, then I think it's a very good scheme, because it helps you do that. But I think genuinely speaking for the children, there's nobody better than having their parents there.

Laura had tried a range of childcare options, but expressed her preference for an au pair in terms of consistency and warmth, as well as fitting with work patterns and a local childcare culture which endorsed the use of au pairs:

> [My son] was at a Montessori and because the Montessori finished at 4:00, not at 6:00 – which is what most nurseries finish at – but we really liked the Montessori – we needed somebody to be there from 4:00. We started – initially he was going back to all different people's houses and I was sort of going, picking him up late at night. He was only three or four years old and it just felt really wrong to be dragging him home at sort of six or seven o'clock at night. So we decided to – we just liked the idea of him coming home to his own house even though he might then have his friends back or whatever but he's coming back to an environment he knows. So – and I liked the idea of sort of having the house warm and lit in the evenings for him and when I come home. I just wanted that consistency really. So that was the reason and then lots of our friends have got au-pairs so we just carried on really.

For all our host interviewees, taking on an au pair was a way of balancing the demands of work, particularly demands for flexibility, with finding a form of childcare that was acceptable. In turn, the supply of highly flexible, unregulated au pair labour influenced demand, which then contributed to reaffirming particular local childcare cultures which favour in-home and 'mother-like' care (Williams and Gavanas 2008). The availability of au pairs (something that is challenged by Brexit) has enabled families in the UK to use private and market solutions to provide childcare which is culturally acceptable and flexible enough to support long working hours. Without this, UK families and government might be forced to recognise that childcare should be regarded as a 'central public responsibility and that it is wrong to force families to try to solve the problem of childcare on their own' (Tronto, 2002, p. 48).

AU PAIRS AND NANNIES 'DOING FAMILY' IN SWEDEN

In Sweden, the expansion of the welfare state, which started off in the 1930s, had the aim of fighting poverty and decreasing fertility rates through reforms aiming for greater social equality. The initial solutions to resolve the work–family dilemma emerging when middle-class women started to enter the labour market to a greater extent was to hire a maid or nanny (Öberg, 1999; Platzer, 2006). From the 1960s and onwards, gender equality became an explicit aim in trying to make men and women equally share both paid labour outside of the home and unpaid care work at home. Public and affordable daycare for all became an important question for the women's movement in striving for gender equality (Schmitz, 2007), and in the 1980s and 1990s the public daycare system expanded widely. Today, almost all Swedish children between the ages of one to five attend daycare, at a cost of approximately €135 per month (Swedish National Agency for Education, 2017). This, by and large, made privately employed domestic workers redundant.

However, as noted earlier, gender equality ideals were still not easily realised in practice, and women continued to take on the main bulk of care and housework at home. In response to this, and as part of a general incentive to privatise public services, the idea of introducing a tax deduction on domestic services was brought to the political arena. While initially met with great scepticism – with arguments that introducing such a tax deduction would be a return back to a 'clear and visible class society with masters and maids in people's homes' (Kvist, 2013, p. 215) – the so-called RUT[6] tax deduction was eventually introduced in Sweden in 2007. The reform meant that purchasers of domestic services such as those by cleaners, nannies and au pairs could deduct half of the cost of the service from their taxes.

In debates, and in the government bill initiating the tax deduction, gender equality was a central argument: the aim of the reform was to make it possible for families to outsource parts of the care work at home to somebody else, and thereby making it possible for women to work more outside of the home. Other arguments were also made by the proponents, most notably the possibility of creating jobs for people at the margins of the labour market, and newly arrived migrants and people with few formal qualifications were singled out as prospective employees (Kvist and Peterson, 2010).

Since the introduction of the RUT tax deduction, the market for domestic services in Sweden has grown considerably. In 2017, the total amount deducted was €460 million, compared to €25 million in the year of 2009 (Swedish NAO, 2020). While most of the deduction is made for cleaning services, the nanny market – which hardly existed before the introduction of RUT – has expanded from year to year (Dagens Industri, 2017). The au pair market is more invisible, primarily because most au pairs come from within the EU and are not visible in any statistics due to the European agreement on free movement of labour. However, our qualitative data (Eldén and Anving, 2019) indicates – as do other studies (Platzer, 2006; Calleman, 2010) – that the market has grown considerably during the recent decades, a development paralleled in other Nordic countries (Stenum, 2010; Liversage et al., 2013; Bikova, 2017; Näre and Wide, 2019).

The tax deduction alone cannot explain the growing prevalence and acceptance of employing domestic workers: increasing economic inequality in Sweden during the last two decades (Statistics Sweden, 2018), as well as changes in labour migration laws making it easier for both EU and non-EU citizens to enter the country for work (Calleman, 2010; Frödin and Kjellberg, 2018), are key elements in understanding the current condition. But without doubt, the tax deduction speeded up a more general political process aiming to privatise public welfare, driven by arguments of freedom of choice, and also gender equality. As a result, although public daycare is still the main provider of childcare in Swedish families, a growing number of families choose to hire nannies and au pairs to complement daycare institutions. This indicates a shift in people's attitudes: buying care and housework services – including childcare – has increasingly become an acceptable way of 'doing family' in Sweden (Eldén and Anving, 2016; Carbin et al., 2017).

Given the constantly repeated argument for private domestic services as being a solution for gender equality, has this been the case? And if so, for whom? According to statistics, most tax deductions are claimed by households of higher economic standing (Swedish NAO, 2020), and quantitative studies show that the hiring of domestic workers has indeed meant a reduced pay gap between men and women employed in middle- and high-income jobs (Boye et al., 2014). This is visible also in our study: the employer parents were all dual-earner couples, and most of them – both women and men – were earning high wages in demanding careers that required long working hours. In the interviews, gender equality was argued to be a main reason for employing a nanny or an au pair. The parents talked about how this had made it possible for women to take on a career on (almost) the same terms as men. Without a nanny or an au pair, Leif, father of two children and with the experience of hiring six nannies and au pairs, says: 'it becomes like, the mother stays at home, or works part time or something, actually, really gives up her whole career. And we haven't done that … If you have an au pair you don't need to choose. No one has to take a step back.'

As Leif admits, there are still strong expectations put on mothers to take on the responsibility of primary caregiver, to stay at home when children are small and, when entering paid labour again, to work part-time, all of which considerably affects mothers' careers. Through employing a nanny or an au pair, this can be avoided and equality between the sexes can be achieved, in the sense that no one has to step back from work.

Outsourcing parts of the care and housework is understood as a 'buying of time' by the interviewed parents. Emma, for example, mother of three, explains that through employing different nannies and cleaners over the years she has been able to buy herself time to spend on her career; but also that this has been a buying of time on behalf of her husband: in other words, the domestic workers have taken over his share of care and housework in the family. While acknowledging that their relationship is not actually gender-equal in the original meaning of the word (with dual carer as well as dual earner responsibilities), and while – like most mothers in our study – she still is the one responsible for managing the domestic workers, she says that by buying help, she buys herself a sense of being in a gender-equal relationship. Furthermore Emma, as several other women and men interviewed, attest to this arrangement also having positive consequences for the couple's relationship: conflicts about care and housework are significantly reduced since someone else is taking care of the bulk of this work, as are arguments about whose career is most important.

Another, and related, motive for hiring nannies and au pairs is that it significantly helps in solving what in Sweden is popularly referred to as 'the jigsaw puzzle of life', meaning the work of piecing together all parts of modern family life: paid work, housework, children's activities, family time, and so on. The parents describe the time before they employed nannies and au pairs as very stressful and impossible to manage, despite having their children in daycare. In fact, all of the parents interviewed used the service of nannies and au pairs as a complement to publicly funded daycare, for example, by having the care worker picking up the child early in the afternoon so the parents could stay at work. This enabled 'good parenting' in the eyes of the parents, since being in daycare for too long is considered problematic (Lorentzi, 2011). To 'come home, maybe crash out on the sofa and take it easy', 'with one grown-up you know well and who only focuses on you', as one of the parents says, becomes the ideal solution. Through employing somebody to do parts of the care and housework, parents argue that their 'jigsaw puzzle' is solved and that stress has been reduced, for the parents as well as for the children. This further gives the parents a possibility to avoid feeling shattered between different demands; rather, they can be 'present in the moment' when being together with their children. In the words of Julia, mother of four:

> I can really feel the difference. It is amazing actually. I think I've become calmer and my husband is calmer ... it is for the children's too, it's more harmony. When we put them to bed at night, that's a good example ... It takes a long time to put them to bed and we want to give every child some attention ... Before, after dinner, then you had to do just everything, you know, chaos in the kitchen, you had to do the dishes, put everything away, and prepare everything for the next day, and then put them to bed, and [you] were exhausted, so these were not nice evenings.

By not having to do all the mundane everyday care and household tasks, the parents can give their children full attention in the time they spend together. This, they argue, leads to quality time for the whole family, also making the adults feel like better parents, not as stressed as they otherwise would be.

The parents' solution to the 'jigsaw puzzle' of family life entails assumptions about care as being possible to divide: not between men and women in the family as the dual carer ideal assumed, but rather, a division made for the purpose of delegation to a non-parental party. The nanny or the au pair is expected to do some parts of care, which are often portrayed as easy and menial – usually related to mundane, recurring tasks, such as serving an afternoon snack, or preparing dinner – while the parents keep the parts that are seen as significant, such as tucking in at night or reading a story (Roberts, 1997). Through this, the parents' view of themselves as good and attentive parents can be kept, despite them spending less time with their children.

However, the narratives emerging in the study, in the interviews with nannies, au pairs and children, attest to this idea of the possibility of dividing care being flawed (Eldén and Anving, 2019). Doings of care – and especially everyday mundane activities – entail emotional doings (Mason, 1996), often invisible even to those engaged in them (DeVault, 1991), but crucial for a care situation to be experienced as 'good'. Nannies and au pairs tell about 'simple' routines turning out to be enmeshed with complex and emotionally demanding activities, requiring skills of being closely attuned to and able to interpret the needs, moods, individuality and relationships of the particular child, and also the parents; to think through, organise, and orchestrate the relationship between themselves and the parents and, in addition, the relationships between the children and the parents (Mason, 1996: 27). These sentient activities of care, experienced as necessary by the nannies and au pairs, and also expected by the care receiver, as our interviews with children show, are missing from the ideals and understandings of nanny and au pair work as 'easy' and dividable, as reproduced by parents and in cultural discourse.

The recurrence of privately organised care for children in Sweden, in the form of nannies and au pairs, is making possible gender-equal solutions of work–family dilemmas, while simultaneously reproducing new inequalities. It transforms gender equality from being a political concern aimed at all families, making it into a privilege for some: families who can afford to hire nannies and au pairs and other domestic workers. It further transforms the content of gender equality in itself: by replacing 'dual carer' with 'outsourced care', the understanding of care activities as such change, marking them as 'simple' activities easily delegated to women. Through this, gender equality for one woman, as well as the non-engagement of men in care work at home, becomes possible, and dependent on the continued invisibility of another woman's work: the nanny and the au pair.

CONCLUSION

This chapter has explored the employment of migrant care workers within private families through the lens of welfare, care, employment and migration regimes. This lens highlights the importance of policy and cultural practices working together to shape the precise contours of family life in different states. Across the world there may be convergence between countries in the increasing employment of domestic workers, but there are still differences in cultural attitudes towards how care work should be done, and the practical possibilities for accomplishing it (Treas and Lui, 2013).

By contrasting practices in the UK and Sweden, we have illustrated the ways that policies are developed and play out within particular contexts. In the UK, the au pair scheme has been a popular solution to the competing demands of childcare and long hours at work. In Sweden, the state-supported emergence of a nanny and au pair market has presented new opportunities for well-off families to do 'gender equality' and 'good parenting'. While still diverging in important respects, both cases represent a solution that relies on the notion that care is being provided within the private family and which does not challenge existing gender norms or ideals of family life, even while it relies on the migration of tens of thousands of young women. These solutions for work–family conflict and attempts to achieve gender equality arise from the concerns of middle-class women, and the results often reproduce and are dependent upon social inequalities other than gender. Most obviously, there are the differences, often predicated on racism and unequal citizenship, that divide employing families from the low-paid workers they rely on (Gullikstad et al., 2016) but there are also inequalities between citizen families that are exacerbated by the access of the most privileged families to the labour of domestic workers. Following the argument of Esping Andersen (2009): as long as gender equality is mainly a middle-class affair, it often produces greater social inequalities between well-educated and well-paid parents on the one hand, and low-paid parents on the other (Isaksen, 2010). Families who are able to afford flexible, private childcare can realise the benefits of demanding paid work outside the home as well as less conflict within it.

The employment of nannies and au pairs represents a childcare regime that builds upon a well-known and, by feminist scholars, widely criticised view of care as something women 'just know' and do 'naturally' (Graham, 1983; Waerness, 1984); a view that has long been the grounds for the devaluation of care work in general, and women's care work in particular. Care becomes an activity that can easily be divided up and delegated, preferably to young women, often migrants, who work for low pay and under very weak working regulations (Tronto, 2002; Anving and Eldén, 2016; Cox and Busch, 2018). This increases the invisibility of the actual complex and emotionally demanding activity that these young women do in caring for children. As argued elsewhere (Eldén and Anving, 2019), the nanny or the au pair becomes a sort of invisible glue that keeps the jigsaw puzzle of life from falling apart, while her part in this 'doing family' largely stays invisible – and precarious.

NOTES

1. This research was carried out with Nicky Busch and funded by ESRC grant ES/J007528/1.
2. Funded by the Swedish Foundation for Humanities and Social Sciences: RJ P13-0603:1.
3. In Sweden, the term 'nanny' (*barnflicka*) refers to a live-out, privately employed child care worker, without formal education, usually working in a family a couple of afternoons per week but sometimes more. 'Au pair' refers to migrated, live-in workers who are officially on cultural exchange, under conditions similar to the European Agreement on Au Pair Placement (1969). Both categories of workers engage in everyday care for children in families, both are predominantly occupied by young and often migrated women, and both are poorly paid and weakly regulated (Eldén & Anving, 2019).
4. By the Nordic countries we refer to Sweden, Finland, Norway and Denmark.
5. In Sweden, parents are entitled to 16 months of state-financed parental leave, to be divided between the couple, although three months are reserved for the individual parent, usually referred to as the 'daddy quota'.
6. RUT is an acronym for 'Rengörning, Underhåll, Tvätt' ('Cleaning, Maintenance, Laundry').

REFERENCES

Anving, T. and Eldén, S. (2016) 'Precarious care labor: Contradictory work regulations and practices for au pairs in Sweden'. *Nordic Journal of Working Life Studies* 6 (4), 29–48.
Berg, L. (2015) Hiding in plain sight: Au pairs in Australia. In Cox, R. (ed.) *Au Pairs' Lives in Global Context: Sisters or Servants?* Basingstoke: Palgrave Macmillan, pp. 187–202.
Berg, L. and Meagher, G. (2018) 'Cultural exchange or cheap housekeeper? Findings of a national survey of au pairs in Australia'. Migrant Worker Justice Initiative, November. DOI:/10.13140/RG.2.2.17089.81769.
Bikova, M. (2017) *The egalitarian heart: Glocal care chains in the Filipino au pair migration to Norway.* Bergen: University of Bergen.
Borchorst, A. and Siim, B. (2008) 'Woman-friendly policies and state feminism'. *Feminist Theory* 9. 207–224.
Boye, K., Halldén, K. and Magnusson, C. (2014) 'Könslönegapets utveckling: Betydelsen av yrkets kvalifikationsnivå och familjeansvar' (The gender pay gap. The significance of qualification level and family responsibility). In Evertsson, M. and Magnusson, C. (eds) *Ojämlikhetens dimensioner: Uppväxtvillkor, arbete och hälsa i Sverige (Dimensions of inequalities: Childrearing, work and health in Sweden).* Stockholm: Liber, pp. 185–211.
Brown, T.M. (2011) *Raising Brooklyn: Nannies, Childcare and Caribbeans Creating Community.* New York University Press.
Búriková, Z.S. (2016) 'EU enlargement and au pairing in the United Kingdom'. *Nordic Journal of Migration Research* 6 (4), 207–214.
Calleman, C. (2010) 'Cultural exchange or cheap domestic labour? Constructions of "au pair" in four Nordic countries'. In Isaksen, L.W. (ed.) *Global care work: Gender and migration in Nordic societies.* Lund: Nordic Academic Press, pp. 69–96.

Carbin, M., Overud, J. and Kvist, E. (2017) *Feminism som lönearbete: Om den svenska arbetslinjen och kvinnors frigörelse (Feminism and paid work: Swedish working politics and women's emancipation)*. Stockholm: Leopard förlag.

Cox, R. (2012) 'Gendered work and migration regimes'. In Sollund, R. (ed.) *Transnational migration, gender and rights.* Advances in Ecopolitics, Volume 10. Bingley: Emerald, pp. 33–52.

Cox, R. (2015) 'Conclusion'. In Cox, R. (ed.) *Au pairs' lives in global context: Sisters or servants?* Basingstoke: Palgrave Macmillan.

Cox, R. (2021) *Home improvement: In Aotearoa New Zealand and the UK*. London: Routledge.

Cox, R. and Busch, N. (2018) *As an equal? Au pairing in the twenty-first century*. London: Zed Books.

Dagens Industri (2017) 'Barnpassare tar nya vägar' (New directions for nannies). https://weekend.di.se/nyheter/barnpassare-tar-nya-vagar.

DeVault, M.L. (1991) *Feeding the family: The social organization of caring as gendered work*. Chicago, IL: University of Chicago Press.

Eldén, S. and Anving, T. (2016) 'New ways of doing the "good" and gender equal family: Parents employing nannies and au pairs in Sweden'. *Sociological Research Online* 21 (4), 2.

Eldén, S. and Anving, T. (2019) *Nanny families. Practices of care by nannies, au pairs, parents and children in Sweden*. Bristol: Bristol University Press.

England, K. and Stiell, B. (1997) '"They think you're as stupid as your English is": Constructing foreign domestic workers in Toronto'. *Environment and Planning A* 29, 195–215.

Esping-Andersen, G. (1999) *Social foundations of postindustrial economies*. New York: Oxford University Press.

Esping-Andersen, G. (2009). *Incomplete revolution: Adapting welfare states to women's new roles*. Oxford: Blackwell Publishers.

Fraser, N. (1994) After the family wage: Gender equity and the welfare state. *Political Theory* 22 (4), 591–618.

Frödin, O. and Kjellberg, A. (2018) Labor migration from third countries to Swedish low-wage jobs. *Nordic Journal of Working Life Studies* 8 (1), 65–85.

Geserick, C. (2015) '"She doesn't think it will work out": Why au pairs in the USA leave their host family early'. In Cox, R. (ed.) *Au pairs' lives in global context: Sisters or servants?* Basingstoke: Palgrave Macmillan, pp. 219–234.

Geserick, C. (2016) 'America is the dream of so many things'. *Nordic Journal of Migration Research* 6 (4), 243–251.

Glenn, E.N. (1992) 'From servitude to service work: Historical continuities in the racial division of reproductive labour'. *Signs* 18 (1), 1–43.

Graham, H. (1983) 'Caring: A labour of love'. In Finch, J. and Groves, D. (eds) *A labour of love: Women, work and caring*. London: Routledge & Kegan Paul, pp. 13–30.

Gregson, N. and Lowe, M. (1994) *Servicing the middle classes: Class, gender and waged domestic labour in contemporary Britain*. London: Routledge.

Guevarra, A.R. (2014) 'Supermaids: The racial branding of global Filipino care labour'. In Anderson, B. and Shutes, I. (eds) *Migration and care labour: Theory, policy and politics*. Basingstoke: Palgrave Macmillan, pp. 130–150.

Gullikstad, B., Kristensen, G.K. and Ringrose, P. (eds) (2016) *Paid migrant domestic labour in a changing Europe: Questions of gender, equality and citizenship*. Basingstoke: Palgrave Macmillan.

Hernes, H. (1987) *Welfare state and woman power: Essays in state feminism*. London: Norwegian University Press.

Higman, B.W. (2015) 'An historical perspective: Colonial continuities in the global geography of domestic service'. In Haskins, V.K. and Lowrie, C. (eds) *Colonization and domestic service: Historical and contemporary perspectives*. London and New York: Routledge, pp. 19–37.

Hondagneu-Sotelo, P. (2001) *Doméstica: Immigrant workers cleaning and caring in the shadows of affluence*. Berkeley, CA: University of California Press.

International Labour Organization (ILO) (2011) *Domestic Work Policy Brief Number 4: Global and regional estimates on domestic work*. Geneva: ILO.

Isaksen, L.W. (2010) 'Introduction: Global care work in Nordic societies'. In Isaksen, L.W. (ed.) *Global care work: Gender and migration in Nordic societies*. Lund: Nordic Academic Press, pp. 9–19.

Isaksen, L.W. and Näre, L. (2019) 'Local loops and micro-mobilities of care: Rethinking care in egalitarian contexts'. *Journal of European Social Policy* 29 (5), 593–599.
Kvist, E. (2013) 'A booming market of precarious work: Selling domestic services in women-friendly Sweden'. In Gunnarsson, Å. (ed.) *Tracing the women-friendly welfare state: Gender politics of everyday life in Sweden*. Stockholm: Makadam, pp. 214–233.
Kvist, E. and Peterson, E. (2010) 'What has gender equality got to do with it? An analysis of policy debates surrounding domestic services in the welfare states of Spain and Sweden'. *NORA* 18 (3), 185–120.
Liversage, A., Bille, R. and Jakobsen, V. (2013) *Den Danske au-pair ordning: En kvalitativ og kvantitativ undersøgels* (*The Danish au pair order: A qualitative and Quantitative analysis*), 13:02. København: SFI – Det Nationale Forskningscenter for Velfærd (SFI – The Danish National Center for Social Research).
Lorentzi, U. (2011) *Alla andra hämtar tidigt: En undersökning av öppettider och tider för lämning och hämtning på förskolor* (*Everybody else picks up early: A report on opening hours and times for leaving and picking up at daycare*). Stockholm: Kommunal.
Lundqvist, Å. (2011) *Family policy paradoxes: Gender equality and labour market regulation in Sweden, 1930–2010*. Bristol: Policy Press.
Lundqvist, Å. (2017) *Transforming gender and family relations: How active labour market policies shaped the dual earner model*. Cheltenham, UK and Northampton, MA, USA: Edward Elgar Publishing.
Macdonald, L.C. (2010) *Shadow Mothers: Nannies, Au Pairs, and the Micropolitics of Mothering*. Berkeley, CA: University of California Press.
Mason, J. (1996) 'Gender, care and sensibility in family and kin relationships'. In Holland, J. and Atkins, L. (eds) *Sex, sensibility and the gendered body*. London: Macmillan, pp. 15–36.
Milkman, R., Reese, E. and Roth, B. (1998) 'The macrosociology of paid domestic labor'. *Work and Occupations* 25 (4), 483–510.
Morgan, D.H.J. (1996) *Family connections: An introduction to family studies*. Cambridge: Polity Press.
Morgan, D.H.J. (2011) *Rethinking family practices*. Basingstoke: Palgrave Macmillan.
Mósesdóttir, L. and Ellingsaeter, A.L. (2019). Ideational struggles over women's part-time work in Norway: Destabilizing the gender contract. *Economic and Industrial Democracy* 40 (4), 1018–1038.
Näre, L. (2016) 'Neoliberal citizenship and domestic service in Finland: A return to a servant society?' In Gullikstad, B., Kristensen, G. and Ringrose, P. (eds) *Paid migrant domestic labour in a changing Europe: Citizenship, gender and diversity*. London: Palgrave Macmillan, pp. 31–53.
Näre, L. and Wide, E. (2019) 'Local loops of care in the Helsinki region: A time-economy perspective'. *Journal of European Social Policy* 29 (5), 600–613.
Öberg, L. (1999) 'Ett socialdemokratiskt dilemma: Från hembiträdesfråga till pigdebatt' (A Social Democratic dilemma: From a question of maids to a maid debate). In Florin, C. et al. (eds) *Kvinnor mot kvinnor: Om systerskapets svårigheter* (*Women against women: About the difficulties of sisterhood*). Stockholm: Norstedts Förlag, pp. 159–199.
Office for National Statistics (ONS) (2017) 'Household disposable income and inequality in the UK: financial year ending 2016'. https://www.ons.gov.uk/peoplepopulationandcommunity/personalandhousehol dfinances/incomeandwealth/bulletins/householddisposableincomeandinequality/financialyearending2016 (accessed 11 December 2017).
Parreñas, R.S. (2000) 'Migrant Filipina domestic workers and the international division of reproductive labor'. *Gender and Society* 14 (4), 560–580.
Pfau-Effinger, B. (2010) 'Cultural and institutional contexts'. In Treas, J. and Drobnič, S. (eds) *Dividing the domestic: Men, women and household work in cross-national perspective*. Stamford, CA: Stamford University Press, pp. 125–146.
Philippines Overseas Employment Administration (POEA) (2012) *2008–2012 Overseas Employment Statistics*. www.poea.gov.ph/stats/2012_stats.pdf.
Platzer, E. (2006) 'From public responsibility and back again: The new domestic services in Sweden'. *Gender and History* 18 (2), 211–221.
Pratt, G. (1999) 'From Registered Nurse to Registered Nanny: Discursive geographies of Filipina domestic workers in Vancouver, B.C.' *Economic Geography* 75, 215–236. www.jstor.org/stable/144575 (accessed 20 December 2017).

Pratt, G. (2004) *Working feminism*. Philadelphia, PA: Temple University Press.
Roberts, D.E. (1997) 'Spiritual and menial housework'. *Yale Journal of Law and Feminism* 9 (1), 51–80.
Schmitz, E. (2007) *Systerskap som politisk handling: Kvinnors organisering i Sverige 1968 till 1982 (Sisterhood as political action: Women's organisation in Sweden between 1968 and 1982)*. Lund: Lund University.
Smith, A. (2015) 'Part of the family? Experiences of au pairs in Ireland'. In Cox R. (ed.) *Au pairs' lives in global context. Migration, Diasporas and Citizenship Series*. London: Palgrave Macmillan, pp. 170–184.
Statistics Sweden (2020) *På tal om kvinnor och män. Lathund om jämställdhet 2020 (About women and men: Statistics about gender equality 2020)*. Stockholm: Statistiska centralbyrån.
Stenum, H. (2010) 'Au-pair migration and new inequalities. The transnational production of corruption'. In Isaksen, L.W. (ed.) *Global care work: Gender and migration in Nordic societies*. Lund: Nordic Academic Press, pp. 23–48.
Stiell, B. and England, K. (1997) 'Domestic distinctions: Constructing difference among paid domestic workers in Toronto'. *Gender, Place and Culture* 4 (3), 339–359.
Swedish NAO (2020) *Rutavdraget: konsekvenser av reformen (The RUT tax deduction: Consequences of the reform)*. Stockholm: Riksrevisionen.
Swedish National Agency for Education (2017) 'Barn och personal i förskolan 2017' (Children and staff in daycare institutions 2017). https://www.skolverket.se/getFile?file=3949.
Treas, J. and Lui, J. (2013) 'Studying housework across nations'. *Journal of Family Theory and Review* 5, 135–149. DOI:10.1111/jftr.12006.
Tronto, J.C. (2002) 'The "nanny" question in feminism'. *Hypatia* 17 (2), 34–51.
Waerness, K. (1984) 'The rationality of caring'. *Economic and Industrial Democracy* 5, 185–211.
Wilkinson, R. and Pickett, K. (2010) *The spirit level: Why equality is better for everyone*. London: Penguin Books.
Williams, F. (2014) 'Making connections across the transnational political economy of care'. In Anderson, B. and Shutes, I. (eds) *Migration and care labour: Theory, policy and politics*. Basingstoke: Palgrave, pp. 11–30.
Williams, F. and Gavanas, A. (2008) 'The intersection of childcare regimes and migration regimes: A three-country study'. In Lutz, H. (ed.) *Migration and domestic work: A European perspective on a global theme*. Aldershot: Ashgate, pp. 13–28.

3. Transnational marriage migration: agency, structures and intimate gendered governmentality

Neil Amber Judge and Margaret Walton-Roberts

INTRODUCTION

Family migration is the largest channel of migration to Organisation for Economic Co-operation and Development (OECD) countries, and includes international adoptions, family reunification (where kin ties predate initial applicants' migration), accompanying family (where family members accompany the principal immigrant), and family formation (where a resident national or foreigner marries a foreigner and sponsors them for admission) (OECD, 2019). Family migration accounted for almost 40 per cent of new permanent migrants to OECD nations in 2017 (OECD, 2019). Within this, family formation (marriage migration), ranged from 48 per cent of all family migration to France, to 28 per cent in Germany, and 9 per cent in the United States (OECD, 2017). Moreover, 10 per cent or more of all marriages in the OECD were 'mixed marriages' (between a citizen and foreign spouse), ranging from about 15 per cent of all marriages in France, to less than 5 per cent in Japan (OECD, 2017). Marriage migration, or family formation, is closely linked to the processes of globalisation (Brettell, 2017). Increasing international migration, and developments in travel and communications technologies, have led to more people engaging in transnational relationships and seeking spouses or partners from other countries (Sirriyeh, 2015). While the majority of migrants are able to live with their spouse in the host country (in all OECD countries, the share of migrants whose spouse is absent remains below 20 per cent), processing delays for family reunification are common, with only 54 per cent of married migrants arriving within 12 months of their spouse (OECD, 2019).

Despite the numerical significance of family migration, analysis of how family migration policies inform settlement and integration patterns, especially their gendered consequences, are not well understood (OECD, 2019). The relationship between labour and family migration in Europe has been assessed in gendered terms, in that once labour migration slowed or stopped, as it did in the mid-1970s, family reunification, and an associated rise in female migration, emerged as a growing migration route (Zlotnik, 1995). Some of the major family migration flows are towards a few OECD countries that are permanent settlement sites, such as the United States, Canada and Australia, accounting for about two-thirds of the total flow of family migration (OECD, 2017). However, a rising trend of family migration can be observed in countries such as France, Australia, Denmark and Finland between the years 2008 to 2015, and in Canada it has been largely consistent (OECD, 2017). In cases where a decline in family migration has been noted, it tends to follow overall migration trends, such as Southern European countries where the decline in family migration numbers followed the overall decline in migration, primarily as a result of the 2008 global financial and economic crisis. In the United Kingdom (UK) similar observations could be made as family migration fell between 2010 and 2013, but it rebounded in 2014–2015. In countries such as Sweden, the Netherlands, Austria and Germany the fall in the share of family migration can be attributed to the rise in other migration channels, but the absolute numbers of family migrants have been stable or increased slightly (OECD, 2017).

While a significant share of permanent migration to OECD nations is classed as by family migrants, the growth of this channel has been accompanied by increased surveillance and more intimate controls and verification processes, that have the effect of multiplying border enforcement in ways that have disproportionately gendered consequences (Bhuyan et al., 2018; see Chapters 2 and 9, this *Handbook*). Moreover, several developed Western countries are increasingly moving toward greater skills and economic selectivity in their immigration policies (Root et al., 2019; Bragg and Wong, 2016), which again have gendered consequences (Boucher, 2016). Such policy directions intersect with issues of citizenship, sovereignty, security and the idea of the nation-state exercising border control (Moret et al., 2019; D'Aoust, 2013). These policies control the process of family formation and reunification, but also govern social reproduction practices and intimate relations, and are informed by, among other things, anxieties surrounding demographic and cultural change, and the national welfare state (Bonizzoni, 2018).

In the next section we review literature on marriage migration through the lens of migrant agency, and structural factors of policy and state control. In doing this we aim to address Bélanger and Flynn's (2018, p. 198) call that 'a deeper integration of transnational perspectives to examine both agency and structural constraints would facilitate an appreciation of the "gendered geographies of power" (cf. Mahler and Pessar, 2001) underlying the current global era of marriage migration'. We then consider marriage migration as an example of gendered governmentality where border control becomes intimately focused on relations of love and intimacy. We then contextualise the wider consideration of agency, structure and gendered governmentality, using the case of Punjabi migration from India to Canada. We explore how Canadian spousal and family sponsorship immigration policies have intimately shaped community formation, while also attempting to manage and control marriage migration through discourses of defending national border integrity against possible 'inauthentic' marriages.

POSITIONING THE MARRIAGE MIGRANT: AGENCY

We can usefully understand the position of women in transnational marriage migration by focusing on it as a practice that resides between the complex confluences of agency, autonomy and choice, as well as a process that is structured by multiple cultural, spatial, economic, social and politico-legislative constraints framed by transnational marriage contexts. Scholars have highlighted how gendered shifts occur in response to changing migration corridors, drivers and desires linked to international migration policy constraints, often with initial male-dominated labour migration followed later by female-dominated family migration (Zlotnik, 1995; Abel, 2018). For Bélanger and Flynn (2018), examining women's agency from the perspective of political economy alone renders them as passive agents in international migration, but they reveal how migrants' decision to enter transnational marriages can be viewed as a strategy that women consciously choose over other options in order to reach their goals (see also Brennan 2003). Studies show that migrant women negotiate their gender roles in both the sending and receiving societies. They may choose to enter into an international marriage in order to improve their socio-economic status back home and attain more autonomy in decision-making (Yeung and Mu, 2019; Huang et al., 2008). Bélanger and Flynn's (2018) study of marriage migration from Vietnam to East Asia confirms that international migration can be a significant element in transforming the role and position of women in sending communities. Emigrant women make a considerable economic contribution to their family back home, which certainly has an impact on their status and enhances a preference for women and/or daughters in the family and community. Emigrant women may also achieve greater power in marital transactions to express and negotiate their desires, having more freedom to choose who to marry, either locally or in another country. Migrant women's agency is evident as they enter into various transnational relationships and find new ways of shaping their identity and sense of self in the opportunity structures offered in their transnational worlds. For example, Faier (2007) found that Filipino women from poorer families married rural Japanese men in order to define their status and success through being able to work and stay in Japan and send money home to their families in the Philippines, thereby using their rural marriage in Japan to build up their transnational status and agency at home in the Philippines. Certain other motivations for marrying abroad could be the prevalence of gender-based inequalities and lack of opportunities in their own society, or a chance to remarry in a new and more accepting context if remarriage is perceived negatively in their own society (Belanger and Flynn, 2018). In this way transnational marriage migration offers diverse options that must be seen as relative to the different socio-spatial contexts women are able to access (see Chapters 2, 5 and 13, this *Handbook*).

Patriarchal and gender subordination can constrain or impose limits on the exercise of agency. Cultural and social practices, including marriage norms that position women in a subordinate role, can be sustained or reshaped through transnational marriage migration (Walton-Roberts, 2004b; Mooney, 2006). While motivated to pursue the opportunities for upward mobility that international migration provides, migrant women are often made vulnerable by economic, cultural and legal constraints imposed upon them and their agency, resulting in women continuously negotiating between the constraints and various opportunities that they face (Yeung and Mu, 2019; Fair, 2010; Constable, 2009; Walton-Roberts, 2004a). Constable (2009) notes certain developments of the global capitalist economy that lead to the 'commodification of intimacy', where intimacy and intimate relations are understood as market transactions, to be sold and consumed like a commodity and framed by market constraints. Marriage migration is transformed through such commodification, with transnational marriage brokers providing services for international marriage partners and mail-order brides (Constable, 2009). This results in decisions about transnational marriage being determined through culturally mediated economic transactions, all of which can constrain the potential brides' autonomy (Walton-Roberts, 2004b). Countering this, we can see how women's agency can be enhanced through legislative protections. We see this in the work of Charsley (2005), who found that women married to husbands from their parent's place of origin in Pakistan did not necessarily experience subordination to their spouse; rather, their UK citizenship status placed them in a relatively empowered position with regard to their migrant husbands. They were able to exploit relative structural differences (citizenship status) to their advantage.

Transnational marriage migration does then provide women with certain amount of agency, but family aspirations, the desire to migrate and cultural norms may incrementally situate women in a subordinate position (Mooney, 2006; see Chapter 13, this *Handbook*). For example, the desire for endogamy, to seek marriage partners from within one's cultural and religious community, is widely practiced among some migrant communities (Beck-Gernsheim, 2007; Judge and Bal, 2006; Charsley, 2005). The reasons are varied, but religious factors are significant, and assimilationist pressures may actually encourage immigrant groups to preserve their religious identity through transnational marriage (Lucassen and Laarman 2009). The practice and desire can endure into the second generation, as Lievens (1999) demonstrates in the case of marriage migration from Turkey and Morocco to Belgium. Lievens (1999) details how second-generation women migrants may prefer to marry a partner of lower status from the homeland rather than a higher-status partner in Belgium, since it may allow them greater autonomy and agency in the relationship, while still obliging their parent's wishes. Extended family and community pressures in one's country of origin may also result in demands for marriage opportunities (Walton-Roberts, 2004b). Beck-Gernsheim (2007) highlights the development gap between low- and high-income nations as a significant motivational factor to pursue cross-border marriages. International migration in such contexts provides the opportunity for upward socio-economic mobility potentially for the whole family, and transnational marriages as a result become highly sought after as a popular migration route to wealthier countries (Beck-Gernsheim, 2007; Charsley, 2005). This provides transnational marriages with important motility and social capital, thus introducing the potential for enhanced agency to be exercised for some women as they negotiate these transactions. However, these opportunities must also interact with state policy norms and structures, and Beck-Gernsheim (2007) notes that increasing structural restrictions on migration in most Western countries means that marriage migration is one of the few remaining pathways available for less-skilled migration to the West.

POLICY AND STATE CONTROL: STRUCTURES

Women's agency can be constrained by the way immigration policies are structured, especially concerning spousal and family sponsorship rules in destination countries (Bhuyan et al., 2018). Immigration policies in many developed Western countries are moving towards preferring high-skilled economic immigrants, and family migration, although significant, is increasingly facing more restrictions, surveillance and forms of control that have disproportionately gendered consequences (Root et al., 2019; Bhuyan et al., 2018; Bragg and Wong, 2016). Family formation migration remains a durable and desirable form of transnational migration, but it has also increasingly become a concern for states and incurs increased criminalisation for those who violate immigration rules. Stricter eligibility rules and conditions, such as income thresholds, age and language requirements, have also been imposed (Moret et al., 2019; Bhuyan et al., 2018; Gabriel, 2017; Satzewich, 2015; Tyldum, 2013). Restrictive policies with regard to family and spousal sponsorship have a particularly targeted influence, since there are few remaining pathways that allow family migration for migrants who do not fit privileged categories of skilled or investor immigrants (Moret et al., 2019). Concerns and anxieties over marriage migration intersect with issues of national security, risk management, citizenship and the idea of the nation-state. They are seen as challenging the boundaries of nation-states and the ideal versions of family and marriages. These ideal versions of family and marriage are based on Western ideas of affection, gender equality and individual autonomy (Moret et al., 2019; D'Aoust, 2018, 2013). D'Aoust (2013) uses the term 'technologies of love' in the governmentality of marriage migration, defined as the various processes involved in 'love', how an emotion such as 'love' is understood and constitutes the self and others. 'Technologies of love' is limited in relation not only to its meaning and role to the self, but also to how it is learned and recognised by others, especially within bureaucratic processes of recognition and control in immigration. For D'Aoust (2018), such ideas have become central to the biopolitical governmentality of marriage migration.

States actively create categories during policy formation and implementation to differentiate between those who belong to the imagined national community and those who do not. Certain customs and practices of immigrant communities may be linked to negative versions of family and marriage; such classifications help justify the implementation of restrictive immigration policies (Moret et al., 2019; D'Aoust, 2018). Nation-states see the trend among migrants to seek partners from their home countries as an indication of integration failures, despite this being an overly simplistic view with little analytical support (Charsley et al., 2017). Block (2021) highlights how strong legislation on marriage migration in Germany are justified by some policy-makers in the name of gender rights, along with ideas of 'proper' and 'improper' marriages that select those deemed to belong to the liberal national community. For Sirriyeh (2015), the state exercises control over the family unit and governments introduce measures informed by exclusionary discourses around citizenship and national belonging in order to control and govern particular kinds of international family formation. Contrary to the argument that sponsored immigrants may risk becoming a welfare burden, the reality is that settlement stresses can be ameliorated by the presence of family members, and family presence can be associated with higher immigrant earnings over time (OECD, 2019). The benefits of family migration remain undervalued, and the costs of separation are not properly highlighted in various economic calculations (Bragg and Wong, 2016). Neoliberal austerity policies may also adversely affect immigrant women through increased social, economic and household responsibilities, which negatively affect their labour force participation (Root et al., 2019). Neoliberalism promotes gender-divided workplaces, leading to hyper-masculinisation, prioritising economic class migration, more self-sufficient and flexible (usually male) workers and professionals. These lead to further downgrading of the contributions made by the women in their role as workers and family members (Arat-Koç, 2012).

Scholars have examined the increasing control and management of marriage migration, in countries including the UK, Denmark, Finland, Germany, South Korea and Canada, through income and language requirements. Measures such as income requirements give less family unification rights to poorer migrants, suggesting that class is used as a form of policy exclusion (Moret et al., 2019). High income and language requirements in Finland and Germany sometimes become the basis for denying visas. A couple's income can become a marker of belonging to the nation-state and their love for each other, which can determine their approval for a residence permit (Block, 2021; Pellander, 2021). Marriage migrants in South Korea may be refused a visa unless they pass a certain level of Korean language competency. Further, the Korean Nationality Act requires marriage migrants to prove their basic economic abilities; the condition also provides immigration officers with considerable discretionary powers to judge the diverse economic circumstances that marriage migrants usually face (Lee-An, 2020). In the case of the UK, several restrictions were introduced under family migration rules in 2012, including significant increases in the minimum income required for sponsoring partners or family members (D'Aoust, 2018; Sirriyeh, 2015). Canada's introduction of a two-year probation period, or Conditional Permanent Residence status, before a sponsored partner could apply for permanent residency, represent similar forms of intimate control (Bhuyan et al., 2018; Gabriel, 2017). Denmark's minimum age and 'combined attachment' rule dictates that a couple's combined attachment to Denmark must to be greater than their attachment to any other country, and they must each be a minimum of 24 years of age (D'Aoust, 2013; Fair, 2010).

These measures may cause couples and families to remain separated, and lead to unnecessary hardship (Bhuyan et al., 2018; D'Aoust, 2018; Sirriyeh, 2015). Women may find themselves particularly disadvantaged by marriage migration rules, since immigration policies structure processes of subordination: for example, immigrant men are more likely to have the occupational experience coded as skilled, whereas immigrant women's social reproduction work is not considered 'skilled' for purposes of immigration (Boucher, 2016). This, rhetorically and materially, embeds a condition of dependency for women immigrants in most immigration policy contexts. For example, Tyldum (2013) examines how some migrant women from Thailand married to Norwegian citizens find themselves dependent on their husbands, as migrant spouses are required to stay married for three years to secure independent residency in Norway. Female migrant spouses become severely disadvantaged as a result of their limited economic independence, and lack of language skills and understanding of the legal system and their rights. Such situations can lead to women being unfavourably dependent on their husbands or in some cases exploited.

Marriage practices among migrant communities may also have various implications for women who marry someone in a foreign country, including a person from their parents' country of origin. Marriage migration has traditionally been based on women's position as sponsored spouses, which can place women in a subservient position to the typically male sponsor. Women may face various forms of violence as a result of the intersection of these structural aspects of patriarchy and migration governance (Bhuyan et al., 2018; Gabriel, 2017; Bal, 2015; Walton-Roberts, 2004a). Transnational marriages always involve vulnerabilities and risks for women and their families, since spatial and social distance may increase opportunities for concealing questionable biographies of a potential spouse, the existence of premarital relationships, and other undesirable behaviours or traits that may damage the reputation of the family and the relationship's future. These structures of family, community, honour and reputation, when interlinked with restrictive immigration policies, can have intimately gendered consequences and result in forms of economic abuse (Walton-Roberts, 2008; Anitha, 2019).

Structural power is particularly acute around interpretations of marriage processes that might position women as trafficked or as victims in transnational migration (Constable, 2009; Faier, 2007). Tyldum (2013) understands trafficking as 'systematic exploitation of vulnerabilities' inherent in migration. Vulnerabilities are not created by the traffickers or exploiters, but are already present due to poverty, gender discrimination and lack of opportunity. Immigration policies and regulations can underpin and even enhance or exploit these vulnerabilities (Jayasuriya-Illesinghe, 2018). For example, in the case of cross-border marriage migration between Mainland China and Hong Kong, institutional, legal and economic barriers intensify the vulnerability of women due to the long-term separation experienced because of prolonged immigration processes, and social protection limits imposed on housing and economic assistance (Chiu, 2017). Such vulnerabilities are inherent in migration pathways from poorer countries to richer countries, and can also be exploited in labour market as well as marriage migration processes (Tyldum, 2013). The intersection of structures of migration management in the realm of family formation and social reproduction mark important forms of gendered governmentality that reflect ideas of the global and the intimate.

MARRIAGE MIGRATION POLICY: NEW FORMS OF INTIMATE GENDERED GOVERNMENTALITY

Processes of globalisation are increasingly being understood from the scale of the 'body', where bodily experiences of individuals reveal an intimate perspective towards understanding the experiences of violence, fear and (in)security that are produced through various processes occurring at global and local scales that are understood to be interconnected and intertwined phenomena (Pain and Staeheli, 2014; Mountz and Hyndman, 2006; Pratt and Rosner, 2006). State bordering practices are now done precisely at the scale of the body, resulting in biopolitical governance and governmentality of border controls where regulation is displaced from physical borders to that of border crossers: to people and populations (Hyndman, 2012; Paasi, 2012). Scholars highlight the growing focus on intimate issues such as love, sex, relations, family and conjugal matters in shaping transnational migration and the creation of transnational spaces.

Legislation and restrictions on marriage migration in several Western European countries are justified in the name of resisting the victimisation of women, along with portraying spousal migration as invariably leading to large number of forced marriages (Block, 2021; Leutloff-Grandits, 2021). Many migrant receiving countries also justify mechanisms of governing and controlling marriage migration through concern about fraudulent marriages or 'marriages of convenience' (D'Aoust, 2013). The former Canadian Immigration Minister Jason Kenney identified fraudulent marriages as 'Marriages in which both spouses collude to fake true love so that one can bring the other to Canada' (D'Aoust, 2013). Increasingly, governments employ these discourses to characterise those who violate immigration rules or take advantage of the spousal sponsorship rule to migrate as a threat to the integrity of the immigration system as a whole, and one that poses a burden on the welfare system of the country (Innes and Steele, 2015; Satzewich, 2015). According to Innes and Steele (2015), the spousal visa is a tool explicitly used by the state to limit what it considers 'undesirable' immigration. The requirements and regulations of spousal law often comply with Western cultural understandings of family life, and it can result in harm if the family life does not comply to the desired definitions of the state (Innes and Steele, 2015). D'Aoust (2018) notes the increased legislation around 'sham' marriages in the UK, and suggests that it has more to do with reducing immigration from former colonies in Asia and Africa.

Since the introduction of the Canada's Immigration and Refugee Protection Act in 2002, many new amendments and regulations have been introduced to spousal sponsorship rules, including the introduction of Conditional Permanent Residence (CPR) in 2012. This new regulation stipulated requirements for couples in common law relationships to live together for two years after a spouse arrives in Canada, and if that relationship breaks down within that time frame the permanent resident status of the sponsored spouse may be revoked; but if it happens after two years then the sponsored spouse can retain their status, but they are barred from sponsoring a new spouse for three to five years from their date of arrival in Canada (Satzewich, 2015). Sponsorship regimes have been said to be discriminatory towards immigrant women who are sponsored by their husbands, and have been criticised for creating several disadvantages for the sponsored spouse (the majority being women), since they place undue power in the hands of the sponsoring applicant (Bhuyan et al., 2018; Gabriel, 2017; Satzewich, 2015). It is not clear how the CPR governance measure deters marriage fraud, but it does disproportionately affect some racialised minorities, since the top three countries for sponsored spouses from 2012 to 2014 were from India, China and the Philippines (Gabriel, 2017). Research has also revealed that even protecting women from CPR enforcement if they faced domestic violence generated situations where the shadow state regulates racialised immigrant women (Bhuyan and Bragg, 2019). The CPR was removed in 2017 after much opposition from various Canadian women's and civil society groups, arguing that new conditions introduced in permanent residence would further exacerbate the problems faced by women immigrants (Bhuyan et al., 2018; Gabriel, 2017). The Government of Canada also recognised that fake marriages do exist, but the majority of relationships are genuine and spousal sponsorship applications are made in good faith (Citizenship and Immigration Canada, 2017).

Detecting cases of marriages of convenience is a significant responsibility for overseas immigration visa offices, as they review applications for their eligibility and admissibility for temporary or permanent residence in Canada. Eligibility conditions include reviewing applicants to determine if they have sufficient funds to sponsor a spouse, and checking to see whether the applicant has a 'genuine' relationship with the sponsored spouse. Admissibility includes reviewing applicants for their security risk, criminality, or other kinds of burdens including health and finances, for which they could be barred from entering or removed if within Canada. Visa officers are trained to recognise genuine relationships in accordance with the culture they are operating in, which means that arranged marriage and other culturally and geographically specific marriage norms are normally deemed authentic (Bhuyan et al., 2018; Satzewich, 2015). Indeed, immigration procedures involve various agents of the state who investigate and scrutinise the everyday development of love and the family life of spousal visa applicants in order to rule out fraudulent marriages (Satzewich, 2015). In the evaluation of visa applications, couples are encouraged to submit physical evidence supporting their story; these include documents such as photographs, letters, emails, chat history, telephone bills, bank statements, wills, school certificates, and anything which supports their case (Satzewich, 2015). D'Aoust (2013) refers to the materialisation of and quantification of love as taking different forms, from the careful choice of 'convincing photographs' to the submission of documents and receipts that act as material testimony of the couple's genuine relationship. This materiality of love thus needs to be learned and recognised not only by the couples involved, but also by the various actors and administrative technologies involved in the evaluation process. How love is recognised and experienced might vary significantly for persons experiencing it and for those observing or evaluating it (D'Aoust, 2013).

INTERNATIONAL MARRIAGE MIGRATION IN CONTEXT: NORTH INDIA–CANADA MIGRATION

We now turn to examine these issues more closely using the case of north Indian migration to Canada. Marriage migration from Punjab in north India has contributed towards Punjabi-Canadian community formation in Canada. Family and spousal migration rules of Canadian immigration policy have framed the course of migration from the region, and recent policy changes reflect various Canadian state anxieties regarding the nature of immigration and family formation.

The history of migration from Punjab to Canada dates back to the 19th century. Early Punjabi Sikh settlers arrived in Canada in the late 19th century and set the foundation for subsequent migrations (Walton-Roberts, 2017, 2003; Taylor, 2013). Early Punjabi immigrants to Canada were diverse in terms of their religious background, but the majority were Sikhs belonging to the rural landowning *Jat* caste (Nayar, 2004). They were largely males who had come to find work in Canada, and many of them were single, or had left their wives and children in India (Bal, 2015). Family reunification was largely discouraged and restricted by the Canadian state to prevent South Asian immigrants from forming permanent communities; for example, between 1904 and 1920 only nine women from India were allowed to land in Canada (Jagpal, 1994). These policies largely remained unchanged till the 1960s (Bal, 2015). In the period after the Second World War Canada needed immigrant labour, and by 1967 Canada had liberalised its immigration policies to be skills/human capital-based, rather than race/nationality-based, which permitted family reunification (Kelley and Trebilcock, 2010; Walton-Roberts, 2017; Bal, 2015). Once new family and spousal sponsorship regulations were in place, Indian immigrant women mostly arrived in Canada as dependants – as mothers, wives or daughters – and this process continued into the 1990s and 2000s (Bal, 2015; Judge and Bal, 2006). This family reunification and formation migration built upon and strengthened transnational connections between Punjabi-Canadian communities in Canada and their relatives in India (Walton-Roberts, 2004b). This resulted in important socio-cultural connections that are central to understanding the 'gendered geographies of power' operating across this transnational space (Mahler and Pessar, 2001), and how they informed marriage arrangements and norms.

In India's patriarchal system the status of women could be said to be subordinate, with a woman expected to join the household of her husband after marriage (Chakravarti, 1993). The institution of marriage in India is largely characterised by the social norm of arranged marriages, or at least arranged introductions, and matrimonial advertisements in popular local and national newspapers are widely used in this process. Research has demonstrated how these advertisements employ gendered language that reproduces and stabilises the social norms related to traditional gender role expectations (Ramasubramanian and Jain, 2009). Although gender roles and the status of women are changing in contemporary Indian society, matrimonial advertisements tend to present men as breadwinners and professionals with jobs outside the home, and women as being of the household (Ramasubramanian and Jain, 2009). Divorce is viewed negatively and is highly stigmatising for women; it is often avoided for the sake of respect in the community, which can place women into positions of vulnerability (Bal, 2015; Walton-Roberts, 2008).

In Punjab, transnational marriage unions are highly sought after since they offer social and spatial mobility through migration. Family migration strategies have revealed that women being used as the means for entire families to migrate overseas (Bal, 2015; Judge and Bal, 2006). The marriage union is enforced both by the family a woman marries into, and by her own parents in Punjab, because the woman's marriage becomes the key to her whole family's potential mobility. Many families give priority to seeking marriage unions with a permanent resident status-holder in countries such as Canada, the United States and the UK. It has been reported that instant match-making takes place in Punjab often at the expense of the woman's interests, as families compete for their daughter to marry returning migrants or non-resident

Indians (Bal, 2015; Walton-Roberts, 2008). The spatial and social distances entailed by these transnational matches can erode full knowledge about the potential groom's background and family. After migration, the relative isolation of a woman in a foreign country can become problematic, as she is away from the safety of her own family, and access to relevant supports and services may be difficult due to social, cultural, legal and financial issues (Bal, 2015; Walton-Roberts, 2008; Judge and Bal, 2006). Layered onto these structures of gender subordination are the structural restrictions imposed by Canadian policy.

Canadian immigration policies impose structural constraints through financial, legislative and processing demands, and these have gendered consequences when imposed upon already existing cultural norms of gendered subordination. Canadian family migration and spousal sponsorship policy has introduced greater restrictions, more stringent eligibility requirements for sponsoring spouses, along with expanding deportability measures, and has imposed longer waiting periods for spousal applications, especially from certain countries (Bhuyan et al., 2018). This includes introducing measures such as the Conditional Permanent Resident (CPR) status from 2012 to 2017, which required newly sponsored spouses to remain in a marital relationship for a minimum of two years. Despite the repeal of CPR in 2017, various measures to check marriage fraud continue to affect racialised immigrants, and these disproportionately impact upon women (Bhuyan et al., 2018). The neoliberal restructuring of immigration policy in Canada is promoting immigrants who are self-reliant, skilled and capable of integrating easily with less state support (Root et al., 2019; Bragg and Wong, 2016). These policy developments challenge family reunification, which ironically serves as an important support in the long-term successful settlement and integration of new immigrants to Canada (Bragg and Wong, 2016; OECD, 2019). Some of these policy restrictions have oscillated depending on the government in power: for example, the annual cap on parent and grandparent sponsorship was limited to 5000 by the Harper Conservative government, but increased to 10 000 by the Trudeau Liberal government (Root et al., 2019; Bragg and Wong, 2016). However, the enduring negative discourse on family immigration devalues the contributions made by the family, and the role of parents and grandparents in immigrant families, especially in terms of childcare provision (Bragg and Wong, 2016). Family migration is increasingly negatively compared to economic immigration, but the value of family migration in terms of securing social reproduction is never fully acknowledged or evaluated in these economist arguments (Martin, 2019; Root et al., 2019; Gabriel, 2017).

Global economic competitiveness necessitates countries to move towards neoliberal structuring of policies that prefers highly educated, skilled and wealthy immigrants who are seen as contributing to the economy of the country. Although family class remains highly significant in the current immigration policy of Canada, its share of total immigrants admitted has reduced since the 1990s, when it represented about 42 percent of total immigrant flows, down to about a quarter of all immigrant entries by 2012 (Satzewich, 2015). There are particular gender consequences of this rebalancing of immigration streams since, as Bhuyan et al. (2018) note, men are overrepresented in all the temporary and permanent immigration streams, and male immigrants accounted for 70 per cent of the Canadian Experience Class and 76 per cent of those who applied through Provincial Nominee Programs (points-based immigration streams based on skills). Although women represent a growing number of economic immigrants to Canada, the majority of female immigrants continue to enter as spouses/partners or dependents. In 2019, females accounted for 58 per cent of those admitted to Canada as spouses, partners and children (IRCC, 2020). Dominant neoliberal policy stipulates that immigrant families should

Table 3.1   Change in family immigration rules 2012–2019

Rule	Details
2012 Five-year ban for sponsored spouses Conditional Permanent Residence (CPR) (repealed in 2017)	Immigrants who are sponsored spouses must wait for five years to be able to sponsor a subsequent partner themselves (in the event of death or divorce from the partner who sponsored them). Two-year probationary period before applying for permanent residence, couples are required to live together for that time.
2013 Temporary Resident Biometrics Project Penalty for misrepresentation	Requires all foreign nationals seeking temporary resident visas in Canada to submit electronic biometric data. Expands the collection and sharing of biometric data in the form of fingerprints, digital photo for background check and identity verification. Individuals held for immigration misrepresentation will be inadmissible for the period of five years, and also face a five-year ban from applying for permanent residence (increased from the previous two-year ban).
2014 Super-visa for parents and grandparents Sponsorship undertaking for parents and grandparents Parent and Grandparent Sponsorship Program	Parents and grandparents can visit Canada for up to two years and will be granted a ten-year valid visitor visa. They will be responsible for their own financial support and medical insurance during the time of their visit. Increased sponsorship undertaking for sponsoring parents and grandparents to 20 years (for all provinces except for Quebec) in 2014 from the previous ten-year commitment. The cap on the number of new applications accepted was set at 5000 in 2014 and 2015.
2015 Excluding proxy relationships	'Excluded relationships' for all forms of marriage that are made by telephone, fax, internet or similar means for all temporary and permanent immigration programmes.

Sources: Data for table from five-year ban for sponsored spouses, Conditional Permanent Residence (CPR), Temporary Resident Biometrics Project, Penalty for misrepresentation, and excluding proxy relationships, from Bhuyan et al. (2018) and Corrigan (2014).

financially provide for sponsored family members, and they should not be dependent on welfare and settlement services. Various austerity measures affect services considered vital for the settlement and integration of family class immigrants (Root et al., 2019; Bragg and Wong, 2016). Table 3.1 details the various policy changes made between 2012 and 2019 that manage family immigration policy and impose penalties in cases where misrepresentation or fraud are deemed to have occurred.

Fraudulent marriages are a concern for immigration authorities, as there have been cases of manufacture, sale and reproduction of fake documents, and the staging of entire wedding ceremonies in Punjab. These are carried out by certain business ventures skilled in organising sham weddings and receptions designed to convince Canadian visa officers of the authenticity of the marriage (Keung, 2008). There may be mutual agreement in undertaking such strategies between the families of the spouses, but often the women's position and their role in the decision-making process within their family may be subordinate. State categorisation of cross-border marriages as either 'sham' or 'genuine', along with imposed ideals of romantic love, undermines the bargaining power of women (Andrikopoulos, 2021). While these arrangements are used to circumvent immigration rules, they may also lead to violence for the women involved if abuse, abandonment and isolation follow, since the sponsored spouse may be aware of the fabrication involved in their application, and their immigrant status may be in jeopardy if they report their concerns (Bal, 2015; Bhamra, 2006).

The migration of Punjabi women to Canada has been central to the formation of the Punjabi-Canadian community (Bal, 2015; Judge and Bal, 2006). With the formation of a community there also emerged challenges for the status of women. It is because of their important position in the representation and imagination of the community that women's behaviour is often the subject of control and confinement in both the public and the private sphere (Virdi, 2013; Walton-Roberts, 2008). The Punjabi diaspora has marked its position in Canada through socio-cultural, and political-economic activities (Judge and Bal, 2006). A woman migrating from India to join her husband and his family is entering a context that has predetermined her positionality as a dependent, arguably placing her in an inferior position in the matrix of the citizen-worker that determines the discursive and material consequence of Canadian immigration policy (Boucher, 2016). The expectations of the 'trailing spouse', the 'dependent applicant', are constructed through both the structures of immigration policy and the cultural understandings and expectations of the daughter-in-law's role in the diasporic household. She will be expected to work (unpaid and paid), contribute to the family income, bear children, and maintain and reproduce the cultural traditions and norms of the community in those children. The process of adjustment, learning a new language, entering the labour market, and satisfying domestic responsibilities in a new country, can pose immense challenges for immigrant women (Bhamra, 2006; Judge and Bal, 2006).

Women's economic participation in the post-migration context may provide limited autonomy, but family roles remain in place for the 'double shift' the majority of women have to satisfy. Women's participation in the economy does provide them some bargaining space in the patriarchal family, and some assertion in the community, but the tensions created between freedom from economic integration, and resistance towards confinement and conforming to traditional roles, can create considerable disruption within families (Judge and Bal, 2006). This includes situations where the woman might replace her husband as the main breadwinner due to economic restructuring (Gill and Matthews, 1995) and systemic deskilling and non-recognition of credentials in Canada (Walton-Roberts, 2004a; Bal, 2015). Women's vulnerability in Canada may also arise from their tenuous legal status, which immigration policies can add to since they are structured to grant control of the immigration process to the resident spouse in Canada.

These social, legal and economic structures exercise a considerable effect on immigrant women as they participate in the economy and manage the household. In times of difficulty or abuse in the household, various avenues for formal and informal support and assistance may be limited, or deemed inappropriate, especially if divorce is viewed negatively by extended family and the wider community (Walton-Roberts, 2004b; Bal, 2015). However, immigrant women have exercised their rights by acting decisively to report abuse and have sought support from various formal services (Bal, 2015; Walton-Roberts, 2008; Judge and Bal, 2006). Immigrant service providers also play an important role for immigrant women who may be unable to secure a range of necessary services (Bhagat et al., 2002). Austerity measures have negatively affected the ability of immigrant and gender-based service providers to offer essential supports which many immigrant women depend upon, presenting another form of intersectional disadvantage that immigrant women face in their settlement processes (Walton-Roberts, 2008, 2004a).

The discussion on the position of women in transnational migration networks may situate them as helpless victims of various kinds of intersectional violence, but many women have asserted their independence to be equal consumers of the benefits of international migration and globalisation. It is also important to consider that Indian society, and especially Punjabi society, has changed over time, with more and more women securing education and participating in the rapidly liberalising Indian economy (Judge, 2015, 2012). Gender differences in Punjab have been changing as well. The gender gap is narrowing in education enrollments at all levels, and there has also been an improvement in the sex ratio, with the increase in number of females born in proportion to males between the 2001 to 2011 censuses (Srinivasan, 2018).

More women are migrating as skilled workers or as students to countries such as Canada. Canadian immigration policies have opened pathways for international students to both study and work in Canada. India has replaced China as the number one source country for international students to Canada, and students from Punjab make up a considerable share of these (Keung et al., 2019). Although many women continue to migrate as dependents through spousal sponsorships, there has been an increasing trend for women to migrate independently as a result of their better educational and workplace performance (Chabba, 2020; Todd, 2017; Vasdev, 2011). Certain professional courses and occupations, such as nursing, present significant opportunities for women in the international job market (Walton-Roberts et al., 2017). Such transnational opportunities may lead to gendered shifts in international migration from this region, and contribute towards changing women's status and rights. These changes may suggest increasing agency and autonomy, but the role of family in the decision-making process still plays an important role in women's spatial mobility (Walton-Roberts, 2015). Marriage migration has also shifted with the changes in the immigration policies of countries such as Canada. For example, matrimonial advertisements in local newspapers in Punjab indicate how marriage partners are sought based on their English language test scores. Sometimes the man's family may offer to pay for a women's education abroad if she secures entry to Canada through a study visa. This type of 'two-step' migration poses various risks in such cases, since the sponsoring partner initially offers informal support for the migration process, and enforcement of any breaches of contract will be challenging, thus posing problems for these female migrants (Chabba, 2020; Todd, 2017; Vasdev, 2011).

CONCLUSION

Family formation and reunification migration is significant in terms of the inflows of migrants to OECD nations, but it is subject to specific forms of migration management and control that intrude on intimate relations. Marriage migration embodies the complex processes and outcomes in a globalised world with new opportunities for people to migrate to ever more distant parts of the world, and create relationships that traverse transnational boundaries. Communities are increasingly connected through diasporas and personal networks, and opportunities for economic and social mobility are connected to family formation and reunification immigration pathways. Marriage migration offers women opportunities to exercise their agency by engaging in transnational marriages that might offer them relative agency, autonomy and status, if they can generate resources that enhance their status in their home communities, or when women can marry men from their parents' homeland, and then enjoy relatively more secure status (in terms of citizenship) then their husbands. Women's ability to enact agency in marriage migration is, however, constrained by structural factors, including immigration policy (see, for another example, Chapter 17, this *Handbook*). We reviewed this complex confluence of migrant agency, and structural factors of policy and state control in transnational marriage migration, with an appreciation of Bélanger and Flynn's (2018, p. 198) call for 'a deeper integration of transnational perspectives'.

Insecurities regarding marriage migration and the resulting family formation have been a growing concern for the states as they struggle to exercise their sovereignty and to control who can be considered part of the nation. We observe the increasing implementation of stronger policies and stricter rules for the entry of marriage migrants as one way in which the state can impose the boundaries of the national imaginary. State concern regarding family reunification and formation processes has been posited as reflective of anxieties linked to ideas of who belongs in the idealised national community in terms of race, gender, religion, and so on. Structures of patriarchy and marriage practices intersect with immigration policies, and these politico-cultural formations can be place-specific, in both cultural formulation and policy intersection. Conceptualising these structural impositions on marriage migration practices illustrates the point that women's intimate experiences of love and marriage can be understood as inextricably linked to structural global processes of state policy and control (Mountz and Hyndman, 2006). Immigration governance of marriage migration needs to be carefully examined in terms of its potential reinforcement of structural and intimate processes of gendered disadvantage.

We illustrated these matters in more detail using the case of marriage and family migration between north India and Canada. Women face subordinate positions in Indian patriarchal structures, and in transnational migration processes women's bodies can become objectified in marriage migration strategies that have become commodified in the search for the economic benefits attached to international migration. The resultant policy responses to the intense desire for marriage migration reveals government understandings of 'culture as a problem', but this obscures how immigration policy can interact with forms of already existing patriarchy to reproduce social stratification and hierarchy that is damaging to women's security.

Changing socio-economic conditions, selective immigration policies and enhanced education for women suggest the potential for improved female autonomy and agency within their families and across wider society. Nonetheless, there are gendered constraints that can be reinforced through immigration policies that discursively and materially position women in subservient positions in terms of the rights and resources they are accorded (see Chapter 2, this *Handbook*). The India–Canada case reveals how women have historically engaged in migration to Canada mainly through the family and spousal sponsorship rules. We assessed the nexus of cultural marriage traditions, economic accumulation and modern educational habitus through marriage migration, and identified how women are now migrating independently to work or study in Canada, which may suggest that changes in migration gender dynamics from Punjab are under way. The case from north India shows how patriarchy and family strategies towards socio-economic mobility are embraced, and can be embedded in and reproduced through transnational opportunities. Nonetheless, gender roles in immigration decision-making need to be carefully explored, and their interaction with and response to immigration governance processes assessed more fully.

REFERENCES

Abel, G.J. (2018). Estimates of global bilateral migration flows by gender between 1960 and 20151. *International Migration Review*, 52(3), 809–852.
Andrikopoulos, A. (2021). Love, money and papers in the affective circuits of cross-border marriages: Beyond the 'sham'/'genuine' dichotomy. *Journal of Ethnic and Migration Studies*, 47(2), 343–360. https://doi.org/10.1080/1369183X.2019.1625129.
Anitha, S. (2019). Understanding economic abuse through an intersectional lens: Financial abuse, control, and exploitation of women's productive and reproductive labor. *Violence against Women*, 25(15), 1854–1877.
Arat-Koç, S. (2012). Invisibilized, individualized, and culturalized: Paradoxical invisibility and hyper-visibility of gender in policy making and policy discourse in Neoliberal Canada. *Canadian Woman Studies*, 29(3), 6–18.
Bal, G. (2015). Migration of Sikh women to Canada: A social construction of gender. In P.S. Judge (ed.), *Indian Diaspora: Between Modernity and Tradition*. New Delhi: Rawat Publication.
Beck-Gernsheim, E. (2007). Transnational lives, transnational marriages: A review of the evidence from migrant communities in Europe. *Global Networks*, 7(3), 271–288. https://doi.org/10.1111/j.1471-0374.2007.00169.x.
Bélanger, D., and Flynn, A. (2018). Gender and migration: Evidence from transnational marriage migration. In Nancy E. Riley and Jan Brunson (eds), *International Handbook on Gender and Demographic Processes* (pp. 183–201). Dordrecht: Springer.
Bhagat, R., Johnson, J., Grewal, S., Pandher, P., Quong, E., and Triolet, K. (2002). Mobilizing the community to address the prenatal health needs of immigrant Punjabi women. *Public Health Nursing*, 19(3), 209–214.
Bhamra, S.A. (2006, 15 December). Bartered brides. *The Tribune*.
Bhuyan, R., and Bragg, B. (2019). Epistemologies of bordering: Domestic violence advocacy with marriage migrants in the shadow of deportation. *Migration Studies*, 9(2), 159–178. https://doi.org/10.1093/migration/mnz025.
Bhuyan, R., Korteweg, A.C., and Baqi, K. (2018). Regulating spousal migration through Canada's multiple border strategy: The gendered and racialized effects of structurally embedded borders. *Law and Policy*, 40(4), 346–370.
Block, L. (2021). '(Im-)proper' members with '(im-)proper' families? Framing spousal migration policies in Germany. *Journal of Ethnic and Migration Studies*, 47(2), 379–396. https://doi.org/10.1080/1369183X.2019.1625132.
Bonizzoni, P. (2018). Policing the intimate borders of the nation: A review of recent trends in family-related forms of immigration control. In *Gendering Nationalism* (pp. 223–239). Cham: Palgrave Macmillan.
Boucher, A. (2016). *Gender, Migration and the Global Race for Talent*. Manchester: Manchester University Press.
Bragg, B., and Wong, L.L. (2016). 'Cancelled dreams': Family reunification and shifting Canadian immigration policy. *Journal of Immigrant and Refugee Studies*, 14(1), 46–65.
Brennan, D. (2003). Selling sex for visas: Sex tourism as a stepping-stone to international migration. In A. R. Hochschild and B. Ehrenreich (eds), *Global Woman: Nannies, Maids, and Sex Workers in the New Economy* (pp. 154–168). New York: Metropolitan Books.
Brettell, C. (2017). Marriage and migration. *Annual Review of Anthropology*, 46, 81–97. http://dx.doi.org/10.1146/annurev-anthro-102116-041237.
Chabba, Seerat (2020, 5 May). 'IELTS marriages' – India's 'ideal bride' is proficient in English. *DW*. https://www.dw.com/en/ielts-marriages-indias-ideal-bride-is-proficient-in-english/a-53341947.
Chakravarti, U. (1993). Conceptualising brahmanical patriarchy in early India: Gender, caste, class and state. *Economic and Political Weekly*, 579–585.
Charsley, K. (2005). Vulnerable brides and transnational Ghar Damads: Gender, risk and 'adjustment' among Pakistani marriage migrants to Britain. *Indian Journal of Gender Studies*, 12(3), 381–406. https://doi.org/10.1177/097152150501200210.
Charsley, K., Bolognani, M., and Spencer, S. (2017). Marriage migration and integration: Interrogating assumptions in academic and policy debates. *Ethnicities*, 17(4), 469–490.

Chiu, T.Y. (2017). Marriage migration as a multifaceted system: The intersectionality of intimate partner violence in cross-border marriages. *Violence against Women*, 23(11), 1293–1313.

Citizenship and Immigration Canada (2017). Notice – Government of Canada eliminates conditional permanent residence. https://www.canada.ca/en/immigration-refugees-citizenship/news/notices/elminating-conditional-pr.html.

Constable, N. (2009). The commodification of intimacy: Marriage, sex, and reproductive labor. *Annual Review of Anthropology*, 38(1), 49–64. https://doi.org/10.1146/annurev.anthro.37.081407.085133.

Corrigan, E.C. (2014, 10 January). Dramatic changes to sponsorship of parents and grandparents for Canadian citizenship. *The Rabble*. https://rabble.ca/news/2014/01/dramatic-changes-to-sponsorship-parents-and-grandparents-canadian-citizenship.

D'Aoust, A. (2013). In the name of love: Marriage migration, governmentality, and technologies of love. *International Political Sociology*, 7(3), 258–274. https://doi.org/10.1111/ips.12022.

D'Aoust, A.M. (2018). A moral economy of suspicion: Love and marriage migration management practices in the United Kingdom. *Environment and Planning D: Society and Space*, 36(1), 40–59. https://doi.org/10.1177/0263775817716674.

Faier, L. (2007). Filipina migrants in rural Japan and their professions of love. *American Ethnologist*, 34(1), 148–162. https://doi.org/10.1525/ae.2007.34.1.148.

Fair, L.S. (2010). 'Why can't I get married?' Denmark and the 'twenty-four year law'. *Social and Cultural Geography*, 11(2), 139–153. https://doi.org/10.1080/14649360903514392.

Gabriel, C. (2017). Framing families: Neo-liberalism and the family class within Canadian Immigration Policy. *Atlantis: Critical Studies in Gender, Culture and Social Justice*, 38(1), 179–194.

Gill, D.S., and Matthews, B. (1995). Changes in the breadwinner role: Punjabi families in transition. *Journal of Comparative Family Studies*, 26(2), 255–263.

Huang, S., Yeoh, B.S.A., and Lam, T. (2008). Asian transnational families in transition: The liminality of simultaneity. *International Migration*, 46, 3–13. https://doi.org/10.1111/j.1468-2435.2008.00469.x.

Hyndman, J. (2012). The geopolitics of migration and mobility. *Geopolitics*, 17(2), 243–255. https://doi.org/10.1080/14650045.2011.569321.

Immigration, Refugees and Citizenship Canada (IRCC) (2020). *Annual Report to Parliament on Immigration, Immigration, Refugees and Citizenship Canada*. https://www.canada.ca/en/immigration-refugees-citizenship/corporate/publications-manuals/annual-report-parliament-immigration-2020.html#gender.

Innes, A.J., and Steele, B.J. (2015). Spousal visa law and structural violence: Fear, anxiety and terror of the everyday. *Critical Studies on Terrorism*, 8(3), 401–415. https://doi.org/10.1080/17539153.2015.1081755.

Jagpal, S.S. (1994). *Becoming Canadians: Pioneer Sikhs in Their Own Words*. Vancouver: Harbour Publishing.

Jayasuriya-Illesinghe, V. (2018). Immigration policies and immigrant women's vulnerability to intimate partner violence in Canada. *Journal of International Migration and Integration*, 19(2), 339–348.

Judge, P. (2012). Love as rebellion and shame. *Economic and Political Weekly*, 44, 44–50.

Judge, P. (2015). Punjab at the Crossroads. *Economic and Political Weekly*, 42(1), 17–19.

Judge, P., and Bal, G. (2006). Diaspora, gender and nation: Exploring Punjabi diaspora literature.In K.A. Sharma, A. Pal and T. Chakrabarti (eds), *Critiquing Nationalism, Transnationalism and Indian Diaspora*. (pp. 156–171). New Delhi Creative Books.

Kelley, N., and M. Trebilcock (2010). *The Making of the Mosaic: A History of the Canadian Immigration Policy*. Toronto: University of Toronto Press.

Keung, N. (2008, 23 May). 'Rent-a-guest' schemes tipped off Immigration. *Toronto Star*. http://www.thestar.com/news/gta/2008/05/23/rentaguest_schemes_tipped_off_immigration.html.

Keung, N., Teotonio, I., and Lafleche, G. (2019, 27 September). Dreams of better life can come at a cost. *The Standard*, p. A1.

Lee-An, Jiyoung (2020). 'Fake' or 'real' marriage? Gender, age, 'race' and class in the construction of un/desirability of marriage migrants in South Korea. *Studies in Social Justice*, 2020(14), 125–145.

Leutloff-Grandits, C. (2021). When men migrate for marriage: Negotiating partnerships and gender roles in cross-border marriages between rural Kosovo and the EU. *Journal of Ethnic and Migration Studies*, 47(2), 397–412. https://doi.org/10.1080/1369183X.2019.1625133.

Lievens, J. (1999). Family-forming migration from Turkey and Morocco to Belgium: The demand for marriage partners from the countries of origin. *International Migration Review*, 33(3), 717–744.
Lucassen, L., and Laarman, C. (2009). Immigration, intermarriage and the changing face of Europe in the post war period. *History of the Family*, 14(1), 52–68.
Mahler, S.J., and Pessar, P.R. (2001). Gendered geographies of power: Analyzing gender across transnational spaces. *Identities*, 7(4), 441–459.
Martin, Beth (2019). Immigrants are family members too. In H. Bauder (ed.), *Putting Family First: Migration and Integration in Canada* (pp. 23–44). Vancouver, BC: UBC Press.
Mooney, N. (2006). Aspiration, reunification and gender transformation in Jat Sikh marriages from India to Canada. *Global Networks*, 6(4), 389–403. https://doi.org/10.1111/j.1471-0374.2006.00151.x.
Moret, J., Andrikopoulos, A., and Dahinden, J. (2019). Contesting categories: Cross-border marriages from the perspectives of the state, spouses and researchers. *Journal of Ethnic and Migration Studies*, 47(2), 325–342. https://doi.org/10.1080/1369183x.2019.1625124.
Mountz, A., and Hyndman, J. (2006). Feminist approaches to the global intimate. *Women's Studies Quarterly*, 34(1–2), 446–463. Retrieved 9 April 2020, from www.jstor.org/stable/40004773.
Nayar, K. (2004). *The Sikh Diaspora in Vancouver: Three Generations Amid Tradition, Modernity, and Multiculturalism*. Toronto, Buffalo and London: University of Toronto Press. Retrieved 10 May 2021, from http://www.jstor.org/stable/10.3138/9781442682368.
OECD (2017). *International Migration Outlook 2017*. OECD Publishing. Paris, https://doi.org/10.1787/migr_outlook-2017-en.
OECD (2019). *International Migration Outlook 2019*. OECD Publishing. Paris, https://doi.org/10.1787/c3e35eec-en.
Paasi, A. (2012). Border studies reanimated: Going beyond the territorial/relational divide. *Environment and Planning A*, 44(10), 2303–2309. https://doi.org/10.1068/a45282.
Pain, R., and Staeheli, L. (2014). Introduction: Intimacy-geopolitics and violence. *Area*, 46(4), 344–347. https://doi.org/10.1111/area.12138.
Pellander, S. (2021). Buy me love: Entanglements of citizenship, income and emotions in regulating marriage migration. *Journal of Ethnic and Migration Studies*, 47(2), 464–479. https://doi.org/10.1080/1369183X.2019.1625141.
Pratt, G., and Rosner, V. (2006). Introduction: The global and the intimate. *Women's Studies Quarterly*, 34(1/2), 13–24. Retrieved 10 May 2020, from www.jstor.org/stable/40004728.
Ramasubramanian, S., and Jain, P. (2009). Gender stereotypes and normative heterosexuality in matrimonial ads from globalizing India. *Asian Journal of Communication*, 19(3), 253–269. https://doi.org/10.1080/01292980903072831.
Root, J., Shields, J., and Gates-Gasse, E. (2019). Neoliberalism and the framing of contemporary Canadian immigration policy. In H. Bauder (ed.), *Putting Family First: Migration and Integration in Canada* (pp. 45–66). Vancouver, BC: UBC Press.
Satzewich, V. (2015). *Points of Entry: How Canada's Immigration Officers Decide Who Gets In*. Vancouver: UBC Press.
Sirriyeh, A. (2015). 'All you need is love and £18,600': Class and the new UK family migration rules. *Critical Social Policy*, 35(2), 228–247. https://doi.org/10.1177/0261018314563039.
Srinivasan, S. (2018). Transnationally relocated? Sex selection among Punjabis in Canada. *Canadian Journal of Development Studies / Revue canadienne d'études du développement*, 39(3), 408–425. https://doi.org/10.1080/02255189.2018.1450737.
Taylor, S. (2013). Searching for ontological security: Changing meanings of home amongst a Punjabi diaspora. *Contributions to Indian Sociology*, 47(3), 395–422. https://doi.org/10.1177/0069966713496301.
Todd, Douglas (2017, 3 July). International students in fake marriage schemes to Canada. *Vancouver Sun*. https://vancouversun.com/news/local-news/international-students-in-b-c-caught-in-fake-marriage-schemes.
Tyldum, G. (2013). Dependence and human trafficking in the context of transnational marriage. *International Migration*, 51(4), 103–115. https://doi.org/10.1111/imig.12060.
Vasdev, K. (2011, 11 October). Australia is new address of sham marriages. *The Tribune*.
Virdi, P.K. (2013). Barriers to Canadian justice: Immigrant Sikh women and izzat. *South Asian Diaspora*, 5(1), 107–122.

Walton-Roberts, M. (2003). Transnational geographies: Indian immigration to Canada. *Canadian Geographer*, 47(3), 235–250. https://doi.org/10.1111/1541-0064.00020.

Walton-Roberts, M. (2004a). Rescaling citizenship: Gendering Canadian immigration policy. *Political Geography*, 23(3), 265–281. https://doi.org/10.1016/j.polgeo.2003.12.016.

Walton-Roberts, M. (2004b). Transnational migration theory in population geography: Gendered practices in networks linking Canada and India. *Population, Space and Place*, 10(5), 361–373. https://doi.org/10.1002/psp.343.

Walton-Roberts, M. (2008). Weak ties, immigrant women and neoliberal states: Moving beyond the public/private binary. *Geoforum*, 39(1), 499–510. https://doi.org/10.1016/j.geoforum.2007.10.006.

Walton-Roberts, M. (2015). Femininity, mobility and family fears: Indian international student migration and transnational parental control. *Journal of Cultural Geography: Immigrant Identity and Place*, 32(1), 68–82. https://doi.org/10.1080/08873631.2014.1000561.

Walton-Roberts, M. (2017). Immigration policy change and the transnational shaping of place. *Rethinking International Skilled Migration*, (January), 227–248. https://doi.org/10.4324/9781315688312.

Walton-Roberts, M., Runnels, V., Rajan, S.I., Sood, A., Nair, S., Thomas, P., et al. (2017). Causes, consequences, and policy responses to the migration of health workers: Key findings from India. *Human Resources for Health*, 15(1), 28–28. https://doi.org/10.1186/s12960-017-0199-y.

Yeung, W.J.J., and Mu, Z. (2019). Migration and marriage in Asian contexts. *Journal of Ethnic and Migration Studies*, 46(14), 2863–2879. https://doi.org/10.1080/1369183X.2019.1585005.

Zlotnik, H. (1995). The south-to-north migration of women. *International Migration Review*, 29(1), 229–254. https://doi.org/10.1177/019791839502900110.

4. Nation, gender and location: understanding transnational families in the face of violence

Biftu Yousuf and Jennifer Hyndman

INTRODUCTION

Transnational subjects are individuals who belong to multiple societies and maintain relationships across borders. Transnational families, likewise, reside in more than one location and country (Lam et al., 2002). This distributed geography of the family is not necessarily of its own making. Research shows that transnational notions of family include people who are forced to make decisions to leave their country of origin and make a new home elsewhere. Transnational scholarship about people migrating for jobs and to escape acute poverty abound, but much less has been said about the transnational families that scatter or disperse – two definitions of diaspora – due to violence and conflict. Despite a longstanding and burgeoning transnational literature, few studies examine the distinctive relationships forged by families who face persecution or violence, and feel that they must leave their countries of origin. This chapter aims to fill this gap, and illustrates how: (1) people who flee a violent home country still experience an ethnonational kinship connection to those left behind, even if they are not immediate family members; and (2) the well-being of transnational family members in one country depends on the status of its most at-risk members 'back home'. We employ two original studies conducted by each of us to show how transnational families navigate national, generational and gender identities amid violence that generates displacement.

Transnational families are geographically distributed across neighbourhoods, cities and countries. The term 'diaspora' originally referred to the scattering of people, often in reference to the Atlantic slave trade or Jewish persecution and flight. Hyndman et al. (2020) utilized the term 'diaspora geopolitics' to examine transnational politics that traverse geographies of violence and displacement as expressed by members of the Tamil diaspora in Canada (p. 1). They canvass Tamils who came to Canada from Sri Lanka as adult immigrants (often initially as asylum seekers – the 'first generation'), children who immigrated to Canada (the so-called '1.5 generation'), and children born to at least one Tamil parent in Canada (the 'second generation'). Their focus on familial and generational views on the politics of violent and competing nationalisms 'back home', and life-altering displacement across borders, raises specific questions about how families connected transnationally to sites of political conflict might be distinct from those created through other dynamics, such as highly skilled economic migration (Kofman, 2000; Kofman and Raghuram, 2006; Walton-Roberts, 2020) or temporary labour migration (Kearney and Nagengast, 1989; Mahler, 1995).

Although there is considerable research on political transnationalism, with formative roots in the works of Schiller et al. (1992, 1995; see also Basch et al., 2005), a relatively small number of scholars have traced the transnational families formed through forced migration, especially diasporas generated through violent conflict and war (Al-Ali et al., 2001; Al-Sharmani, 2010; Hopkins, 2010; Horst, 2007). Likewise, there are many important studies of transnational families and related labour migration – both elite and not – between East and Southeast Asia and North America (Lam and Yeoh, 2018; Pratt, 2004; Parreñas, 2001; Waters, 2002; see, for example Chapters 10 and 14, this *Handbook*). The transnational ties among families separated by war, violence and human rights atrocities in these same regions have received less attention, with important exceptions (Amarasingam, 2015; Pratt, 2012; Smith, 2015). We aim to elaborate upon and contribute to this work by analysing our two cases of diasporas in Canada, produced out of ongoing political conflicts and violence connected to competing nationalisms in Sri Lanka and Ethiopia.

This chapter traces transnational family formation in Canada constituted by and through war and human rights atrocities that incite fear, threat and displacement from South Asia and the Horn of Africa. In the case of Tamils living in the Greater Toronto Area (GTA), Canada, original research shows that they experience insecurity and a desire for protection for their ethnonational kin in Sri Lanka when they are under siege, as they were during the 2009 military conflict, even if their immediate family members are in Canada. In the second case, of Oromos forced to flee Ethiopia to Canada, peace and security in their new home are not possible until the pain and suffering of Oromos in Ethiopia are addressed. In other words, the well-being of Oromos in Canada is also closely related to how their families and ethnonational kin are doing in the Horn of Africa. This study also demonstrates transnational aspects of the emotional lives of families.

Below we provide a brief analysis of transnational families in the context of war, violence and related displacement, acknowledging that a single chapter cannot capture the entire body of research about this field, which has emerged over more than two decades. First, our review identifies several kinds of transnational families, but focuses on political transnationalism connected to targeted violence, what has been called 'refugee transnationalism' (Hyndman, 2010; Nolin, 2006). Second, we include a brief review of select scholarship that analyses gender relations and subjectivities within the dynamics of transnational family relations. Third, our two sets of original empirical findings are analysed within the specific context of transnational families uprooted by violent conflict. Lastly, these findings are interpreted against the backdrop of existing theories and analyses of transnational families.

WHY FAMILIES BECOME TRANSNATIONAL

Transnational families are generally understood as those whose members are geographically separated but maintain regular social and familial connections. Well-known and important literature on transnational families has focused on 'elite' economic migrants and the economic rationales for transnationalism, examining how families are organized around economic immigration (Waters, 2002, 2010), highly skilled migration (Kofman, 2000; Kofman and Raghuram, 2006; Walton-Roberts, 2020), and temporary labour migration (Graham et al., 2012; Kearney and Nagengast, 1989; Lam and Yeoh, 2018; Lam et al., 2002; Mahler, 1995). We contend that these analyses are foundational, but underplay relations of violence that produce, shape and sustain some families transnationally. A cursory analysis of scholarship about transnationalism illustrates that economic drivers of migration, separation, and often struggle, are salient. Political transnationalism and the power relations and communications that traverse borders through familial and ethnonational networks are less common in comparison (see Chapter 12, this *Handbook*).

Scholars in the field of migration studies have investigated political transnationalism to analyse the specific networks and activities that involve politics across territorial borders (Bauböck, 2003; Hyndman and Walton-Roberts, 2000; Sheffer, 1994). Refugee transnationalism is a variant of political transnationalism, in that it is normally not a planned migration strategy or path but one highly structured by the threat of violence or persecution (Hyndman, 2010). 'Refugee transnationalism' is an oxymoron of sorts, in that 'refugee' is part of international, state-centric discourse: a refugee is someone who has crossed an international border in search of protection, whereas transnationalism is about forging human relations, fields and networks despite such borders. Nonetheless, refugee transnationalism is characterized by diasporas whose members develop bonds and relationships in exile, and organize activities to maintain connections with the home countries they have physically left behind.

Diasporas made up of refugees (among others) are forcibly separated from their family members out of necessity and for protection, while families organized around economic migration rationales are more likely to decide on emigrating and thereby separating from members of their family. As Waters (2002) finds in her study, some families discuss and plan transnational arrangements prior to emigration, citing improvement of economic security and acquiring an additional passport as a kind of political protection as driving factors. In a prescient fashion, Waters (2003) appears to know, from the families she speaks with, that new opportunities stem from their immigration to Canada following arrangements conceived as calculated and strategic. Likewise, studies have observed that the dispersal of families through labour migration (Bryceson, 2019; Lam and Yeoh, 2018; Lam et al., 2002; Yeoh et al., 2005) are often calculated strategies implemented for the purpose of securing economic well-being.

If leaving improves chances for stability and survival, those faced with the threat of violence may also decide to move in order to find more reliable political status and security elsewhere. As Waters (2010) argues, to dichotomize transnationalism as something that migrants do or do not enact oversimplifies their globalized familial arrangements. Notwithstanding the different circumstances and rationales underpinning transnational family formations, a desire to hold together during separation is a constitutive factor in the migration of family members. A unique characteristic of families in situations of violent conflict is the strong kinship ties that are maintained transnationally with countries of origin and sites of displacement. Empirical studies about political/refugee transnationalism provide seminal insights into the transnational kinship relations that emerge from violence and displacement.

TRANSNATIONAL KINSHIPS: THE DYNAMICS OF VIOLENCE AND DISPLACEMENT

Members of diasporas who are forcibly separated from their families and support networks remain invested in family ties and relations across transnational spaces. Distinct from transnational families organized around economic rationales, personal obligations and cultural imperatives motivate and inform the practices of transnational families structured by forced migration. Grace's (2019) study illustrates how former refugees negotiate and maintain extended familial relations across spaces of resettlement, war and encampment. Drawing upon data from a multi-sited ethnography of the Somali Zigula refugee community in the United States (US) and their kin in Tanzania and Kenya, Levitt (1998) uses the concept of 'social remittances' to explain how families are connected transnationally through traditions and rituals (p. 927). Likewise, Grabska's (2010) research on the expensive transnational marriages of Sudanese men resettled to the US and other Global North countries, to Sudanese refugee women in Kenyan refugee camps, exposes marriage to be a survival strategy or at least a livelihood one, for families stuck in refugee camps or impoverished post-war regions of South Sudan. Despite war and vast geographical distances across borders, kinship norms are maintained and ties are reproduced through transnational marriages. Grabska's (2010) study provokes thinking about transnational families in a new way, namely as it concerns the intentional transnational formation of a household after years of displacement.

Grace (2019) and Grabska (2010) elucidate transnational kinship relations by emphasizing how social relations and cultural diffusion galvanize diasporas to re-imagine family life. Lim's (2009) research with Southern Sudanese refugees resettled in San Diego also draws attention to the ways in which cultural value systems shape transnational family practices, but her study emphasizes the affective dimensions of these familial relations. Like Grace (2019) and Grabska (2010), Lim's (2009) research emphasizes the close ties that exist between diaspora and family members who remain behind. The metaphors of loss and death are used by several of Lim's (2009) participants to express what it would mean to forgo contact with family 'back home'. Her work is indicative of the strong familial bonds that diasporas forge and maintain across distance. Lim's (2009) research also finds that transnational families extend 'beyond bloodlines to include in-laws, relatives of relatives, and neighbors' (p. 1032). The scaling up of family from household to extended family to community engenders questions about other variations of transnational kinship in the context of violence and displacement, including 'ethnonational kin', which we employ here.

While these examples of refugee transnationalism illustrate how transnational kinship networks provide important social and cultural supports, the political aspects of these relationships are underplayed. As Al-Ali et al. (2001) note, the transnational connections between refugees and the places they call home can be political in ways that are distinct from labour migrants (see Chapter 12, this *Handbook*). Establishing connections between violence, displacement and family within a framework of transnational political practices can yield new insights into transnational kinship formations and dynamics. An analysis of gender relations and gender subjectivities is one such way to analyse the politics of transnational kinship, albeit at a finer scale.

GENDERED DYNAMICS OF TRANSNATIONAL FAMILY RELATIONS

The literature adduces some salient examples of how gender analyses have featured in the scholarship on transnational families (see Part I, this *Handbook*). Transnational processes and practices shape gender relations across various sites and family formations. Many early studies focused primarily on the analytical concept of care, which allows the perspectives of migrant women as departed mothers to be foregrounded (Ducu, 2018). Hondagneu-Sotelo and Avila (1997) coined the term 'transnational motherhood', which was one of the first concepts to shed light on the relationship dynamics between migrant mothers and children left behind. The notion of transnational motherhood pertains to migrant mothers who relocate to higher-income countries in search of a better life for their families. In so doing, transnational mothers continue to care for their children by maintaining emotional and economic connections transnationally. Hondagneu-Sotelo and Avila's (1997) key contribution continues to permeate the research field on transnational mothering, most notably as it concerns the sacrifices made and the pain felt by transnational mothers (Parreñas, 2001). Although this scholarship thoughtfully examines the effects of migration on gender roles and how they are reconstituted, the relational, shared and gendered nature of suffering among family actors is underexamined (Horton, 2009). Specifically, the experiences of women as migrants, and the person or people left behind (Kobayashi and Preston, 2007; Waters, 2002; Pratt, 2012), has garnered considerable attention in studies that have stressed the gendered nature of transnationalism. The views and experiences of migrant men are underrepresented except in a few studies (Lam and Yeoh, 2018; Waters, 2010).

At the site of families influenced by refugee transnationalism, scholarship that addresses forced migration and displacement establishes crucial interconnections between gender and violence, and how they circulate transnationally. Al-Sharmani's (2010) work provides a good entry point into how gender features in refugee transnationalism as it relates to survival, coping and aspirations for a better life. This research finds that women are the economic and emotional sustainers of transnational families, a finding that echoes concerns around the highly gendered nature of transnational emotional labour often carried out by women (Grace, 2019). For example, Al-Sharmani's (2010) study describes how one young teenage woman in the family was plucked from a refugee camp in Kenya and sponsored by extended family members to go and live in Cairo, where she was assigned highly gendered care duties for an ageing family member. Her own aspirations to attend university and to have a career were truncated, at least in the short term, and displaced by the designs of more senior family members who funded her flight to Cairo along with her food and accommodation. While the decision to bring this young, unmarried woman to Cairo was for her protection and well-being, her own volition and autonomy was undermined nonetheless. Family members may be geographically distant across borders, but each may assert different goals, revealing competing 'family' interests among members and across space.

By placing gender relations at the centre of transnational analysis, researchers have ascertained more nuanced understandings of gendered practices across a variety of transnational family formations. These studies exemplify the flexible and fluid nature of gender subjectivities in transnational family formations, and how relations and power differentials play out among family members. The different forms of family relations and exchanges on a transnational scale illustrate the emotional and physical labour required to facilitate and maintain connections through separation. Diasporas undertake sacrifices to sustain transnational kinships across borders – including countries of origin and other sites of refugee displacement – in ways that are distinct from families shaped by economic rationales of migration. For instance, refugees are less likely to have economic capital because of their unplanned migration.

Transnational families organized around competing nationalisms may have distinct journeys and experiences of their new homes, findings that we foreground below in illustrating the lives of Tamil and Oromo families in Canada. Our conceptualization of transnational families connects households – with a focus on gender and generation – and ethnonational identities to violent conflicts and sites of displacement. Transnational families are generally analysed at the scale of the household. Marston (2000) argues that the household scale is routinely overlooked in human geography, and that the masculinist conventional scales of city, region, state and global scales prevail. Building on an argument made by feminist geographers for decades (Domosh and Seager, 2001), the household is normally considered a domestic, private space and is valued less than the public domain. The domestic private sphere is a gendered site of social reproduction. Our chapter aims to expand research on transnational families by reclaiming the household scale – though not necessarily the nuclear family – as relevant to transnational studies.

A TALE OF TWO DIASPORAS

Transnational families produced by war or human rights atrocities that generate displacement are, we contend, distinct from those whose distributed geography may be predicated on different relations of power and decisions to move, whether social, economic or political. In the context of armed conflict, war crimes, persecution and other forms of violence such as famine, the range of decisions people can make is truncated. To leave one's country, home and life's assets is often an act of last resort. The concept of diaspora stems from the Greek term *diaspeirein* (to scatter about, disperse), and has developed as a frame for understanding movements under conditions not of one's own making (Abraham, 2015; Fuglerud, 1999). In our case studies, we aim to illustrate how diasporas maintain transnational connections with family and what we call 'ethnonational kin': people who may share many of the insecurities of those who leave, but are themselves unable to depart.

In the discussions that follow, each of the authors develops an analysis based on her original research that aims to extend knowledge about diaspora-generated transnational families. Hyndman's research about Tamil displacement generated by violent, competing nationalisms, and humanitarian responses to it, was initially based in Sri Lanka, but after the end of military conflict in Sri Lanka in 2009, more political space to conduct research and interview various actors in the diaspora opened up.

The Tamil Diaspora

Since the anti-Tamil pogroms of 1983, an estimated 1 million Tamils have left Sri Lanka (Collyer, 2012). Dozens of countries have become new homes for these transnational families, from Norway and the United Kingdom to Australia and India. Canada hosts the single largest Tamil diaspora from Sri Lanka, with upwards of 300 000 members (Amarasingam, 2015). While many Canadians of Tamil heritage still have extended family members in Sri Lanka, almost all in the original study we cite remain connected to the Tamil nation irrespective of whether they have family members abroad (Hyndman et al., 2020). As a minority ethnic group persecuted and dispossessed, transnational family connections became more vivid in the wake of deadly violence in 2009 when an estimated 40 000 Tamil civilians were killed in military conflict. Militarized violence between competing nationalisms has characterized Sri Lanka for decades, with the Sinhalese majority largely controlling the government and military, at the expense of Tamils and, more recently, Muslims. The guerilla Liberation Tigers of Tamils Eelam (LTTE), a militant separatist group, has fought for a Tamil homeland and self-rule until the death of the LTTE leader in 2009. Some would argue that the LTTE lives on in the Tamil diaspora (Amarasingam, 2015).

From late 2008 to May 2009, the Sri Lankan armed forces faced off against the LTTE in Mullivaikkal, a small spit of land near the coast of northeastern Sri Lanka, with tens of thousands of Tamils civilians caught in the crossfire, also known as 'the cage' (Weiss, 2012).

Meanwhile, in Canada, specifically the GTA, a large number of resident Tamils with familial and ethnonational connections to Tamils in Sri Lanka took to the streets. A peaceful 'human chain' kilometres long was organized, and a call on the Canadian government to condemn violence against civilians was issued. In April 2009, some 30 000 people protested against the violence on Parliament Hill in Ottawa, despite evidence of acute violence in Sri Lanka against Tamil civilians in the northern part of the country. Our point here is that diasporas maintain solidaristic connections with others in their persecuted ethnonational kin group across space. As Thiranagama (2011) contends, some Tamils who wanted to leave could not afford to, and instead form a kind of 'shadow diaspora', highlighting the importance of class position in being able to leave.

For Van Hear (2005), 'refugee diasporas' are groups of people targeted with violence and forced to flee protracted conflicts and widespread human rights abuses. Recently, Van Hear et al. (2018) developed the idea of *refugia*, a kind of diaspora citizenship and belonging that grants one residency rights in a particular – often Global North – country, but citizenship is practiced within a diaspora governance structure. Van Hear's research history in Sri Lanka and with Tamil diaspora families and communities in London and Toronto influences his proposal.

The study we wish to draw from was conducted by a research team of three, led by Hyndman, with Drs Amarnath Amarasingam and Gayathri Naganathan. The study included two qualitative methods: four focus groups, convened in 2012, and 52 semi-structured interviews, held in 2013. The interviews were conducted with both first- and second-generation Tamil Canadians in the GTA, extending to parts of southwestern Ontario. The interviews were all coded using NVivo, a qualitative research software program, with parent codes that included, for example 'Tamil nationalism in Canada' and 'LTTE – opinion of' (Hyndman et al., 2020).

The research found that: (1) Tamil-identified people in Canada were strongly connected to the plight of family members and ethnonational kin 'back home' during the acute violence of the final months of the war; and (2) the geopolitics of conflict between the military and the LTTE in Sri Lanka were alive and well in Canada, and constituted grounds for disagreement within diaspora families living there. While united by their concern for Tamil people as a minority facing violence and discrimination in Sri Lanka from which their own families had fled, they were often divided in their support for the LTTE in the diaspora and within their transplanted transnational family formation.

One second-generation man born in Canada was asked whether his take on the LTTE had changed over time:

> My feelings on the LTTE generally haven't changed. I was not a Tiger supporter. My dad generally felt that, you know, the things they did weren't good. And he didn't like the fact that they would extort money back. He felt, like a lot of other people, that they [the Tigers] were the only people who dared fight back. And so for that they, he wouldn't put it this way, but this is the way I read it. That they could be excused for some of the things that they did. I definitely did not feel that way. I have a lot more problems with that idea. (Interview 216)

Both men felt a connection to the Tamil nation in Sri Lanka, in a sense, but the expression of this allegiance was distinct for father and son.

A woman born in Canada of Tamil background narrated tensions in her family and the disagreement about the LTTE between her parents:

So, in our house it's controversial, because my dad is very pro LTTE, while my mom is very, she thinks that like regardless, whichever side it is, they killed people on both sides. So, it's still, it's wrong regardless of whether who does it, but obviously the Sinhalese government has done worse injustice than the LTTE. So it always like, I was always critical of that. Yes, I would say yes I support an organisation that supports the cause of the Tamils, but obviously you have to be critical of what they did in their past too. (Interview 231)

Again, views differ about the politics and legitimacy of the LTTE, but the identification with anti-Tamil violence by the government was seen as far worse. Ongoing connections to Tamils in Sri Lanka are clear; they are what we call here ethnonational kin, if not direct family members. For the Tamil diaspora, transnational ties among ethnonational kin remain strong, and yet fraught because of the distance between members. Building on this, the Oromo case will elucidate how ethnonational kinship networks traverse borders to influence the emotional lives of diasporas and the gendered nature of these dynamics.

The Oromo Diaspora

Despite the long history of violence against Oromo people in Ethiopia, their plight has gained more widespread recognition by the international community since 2004 (Advocates for Human Rights, 2009). International human rights organizations have published multiple reports that detail the rampant patterns of oppression in Ethiopia and the Ethiopian government's violent policies and practices (HRW, 2014). Amnesty International released a report which exposed the contemporary Ethiopian regime's ceaseless campaign to quash real or imagined dissent. The measures taken by Ethiopia's state government include systematic, widespread and arbitrary arrests of Oromo citizens; the prolonged detention of citizens who have not been charged; enforced disappearance; and torture, brutality and murder (Amnesty, 2014; HRW, 2016). Some argue that these human rights atrocities occurred simply because Oromo people attempted to assert their natural and legal rights (Amnesty, 2014; Dugassa, 2017; HRW, 2016). In essence, Ethiopia's state government has targeted, criminalized and killed Oromo people for exercising these rights, causing many Oromos to become displaced and dispossessed.

Oromo people have been subjugated to ongoing systematic violence perpetrated by successive Ethiopian dictators and rulers who give little space for the political voices of the country's largest ethnonational group. Widespread human rights abuses arising from competing nationalisms have forced Oromos into exile (Gudina, 2007; Jalata, 2010, 2011). Although Oromo people have been fleeing Ethiopia for decades, landing in neighbouring countries and making homes in other parts of the world, the actual number of Oromo refugees resettled to Canada is unknown because census statistics group them as Ethiopian. One source suggests that by 1981, at least half of the more than 2.5 million refugees who fled Ethiopia were Oromo (*Cultural Survival Quarterly Magazine*, 1981), and as conflict has continued in Ethiopia over the years, Oromos have continued to seek refuge. As we demonstrate below, historical and ongoing circumstances provide context for understanding how social and political determinants of well-being construct pain and suffering among transnational families. Before turning to findings that illustrate these interconnections, we first provide an outline of the research methods used for this case.

The primary method for this research by Yousuf was semi-structured in-depth interviews. The second method involved participant observation at select ethnocultural events. Data collection took place over a period of six months spanning 2016 and 2017. The interview participants included Oromo women and men who came to Canada as refugees, or who were sponsored by formerly resettled refugees, or who were second-generation children of refugee parents. A total of seven women and seven men between the ages of 20 and 65 were interviewed. Yousuf attended four participant observation events, whereby roughly 250 people participated in total. Coding, analysis and interpretation were performed using NVivo.

Yousuf's reading of the data reveals that: (1) members of the Oromo diaspora in Canada experience their emotional lives transnationally; and (2) their well-being in Canada is contingent on the well-being of family members and ethnonational kin who remain in Ethiopia. By incorporating analyses from both men and women, we will illustrate a better understanding of the gendered nature of transnational family dynamics.

Emotional Lives of Transnational Kinship

Transnational families generated through relations of violence often make difficult decisions to separate geographically from their home country and loved ones, due to danger and insecurity. In the case of ongoing violence in one's country of origin, diaspora members also struggle to feel at peace in their new homes in far-flung countries. Al-Sharmani (2010) argues that transnational families offer 'an essential support system for refugees and their families to cope with both the on-going armed conflict in the homeland and with displacement and its multiple marginalizing effects' (p. 500). Yousuf (2018) shows – in a similar vein – how pain and suffering continue to affect the transplanted Oromo families, despite living in the relative safety of three Canadian cities: Calgary, Ottawa and Vancouver.

The emotional lives of Oromos in Canada are transnational, as evidenced by how participants identified and reflected on their understandings of what constitutes a meaningful life:

> I'm very much connected to my roots back home, really. This is the thing ... I can't really say I'm having a good life because for me to go back home, work with my people, and at least share their sufferings there, and bring something of a change, it would have been a good life for me before I really die, before my life, I get much older than this. I would never say that I'm having a good life just eating or having a good sleep, having a good car, having a good house is not a good life for me. I can't define that really as a life. My life would be more aesthetic, more of mental, more of mental satisfaction, more of reality, more of fact where people can live peacefully and where they have got their rights. Particularly I'm talking of people of the Oromo because our focus is about the Oromo people. (Bilchina, Interview 13)

Bilchina explained how a 'good life' revolves around being able to do good for those who are suffering in his place of origin, which is a viewpoint held by most participants. Bilchina also expressed an important distinction between the emotional and economic aspects of transnationalism. Living in Canada has afforded some Oromos opportunities to secure economic well-being. They have had access to education, employment, healthcare and assets such as owning vehicles and homes. Notwithstanding the structural and systemic barriers that can limit upward mobility for all resettled refugees, participants for the most part acknowledged that they were materially satisfied. Laafaa (Interview 4) said, 'like I'm well off here. I have a big house, a car, and family and work'. Similarly, Ogeessa (Interview 5) commented, 'I have a decent home, that's even good enough for me. I drive a car that is safe. And decent enough in terms of mechanical efficiency.' The history of conflict and violence that has generated

Oromo displacement would have made comparable economic prosperity unattainable had they remained in Ethiopia. However, as the quotes adduce, participants also recognized that their well-being is intimately tied to those Oromos left behind, and entailed much more than simply being able to attain a good life through economic advancement for oneself and within one locale.

When participants expressed what well-being meant to them and how they could achieve it, they tended to articulate their responses vis-à-vis the historical and ongoing political conflicts and violence in Ethiopia. As two interview participants passionately shared:

> I come from an extended family. My sisters, brothers, uncles, and cousins, they are all over there. Some are toiling in prison, some are ... and I have to pitch in money over there every month, every time from my salaries I have to send them some money back home to support those. Because they are no more with their parents, most of, them are jailed in jail, some are killed. And you know, we live in a very extended family, in a clan-ish type society. So, I, you can't just segregate yourself, put yourself aside and say, 'yeah, I'm now living a good life.' That a good life will never ... it will never be whole. (Bilchina, Interview 13)

Bilchina highlighted two vital points in the excerpt above: first, families are extended, not just nuclear; and second, the conditions for family members 'back home' can be difficult and violent. As another participant shared:

> Oromo never had a good life. Sorry to say this, Oromo ... like I'm well off here. I have a big house, a car, and family and work. But at the back of my mind, I've never been happy. The reason is, it's obvious and I'm for, we have to call it anyway probably, but when your people die, killed, tortured, disappeared, and you can't do anything about it, it's ... I don't see happiness. I don't see happiness. But yes, we can forget sometimes ourselves. We have a better life here, but I don't think so until our people are free, have a democracy in that country, and live without fear, without imprisonment, without torture, you know? My heart, you know when I see a mom cry for her son or her daughter, shot or killed, then I become helpless and I can't be happy. I think for the last nine months I am kind of in depression myself because I watch too much graphic images ... but this is connected for all of us, and we still live. You know, our soul is back home. Physically we're here, our soul is back home. So, happiness? I don't know happiness. Is not only about having money and having a good job. Happiness is when you're happy fully. But one part of us is not happy. (Laafaa, Interview 4)

These excerpts exemplify how visions of well-being among Oromos in the diasporas are grounded in transnational connections to their place of origin. Their reflections demonstrate patterns of collectivism characterized by close-knit relationships within their ethnonational group. Given their collectivist orientation and longing for cohesion and community (Gow, 2013), ethnonational identity is found to be an important thread that interconnects Oromos in addition to familial ties. It is thus unsurprising that transnational bonds and social ties among families and ethnonational kin separated by violence remain strong, and at the forefront of Oromo people's lives as they live in diasporic communities.

Bilchina and Laafaa's excerpts also illustrate how the long history of violence against Oromos continues to negatively impact upon their well-being in the present. Both expressed how the pain and suffering endured by Oromos in Ethiopia has deprived them of feeling whole and happy. A common sentiment among participants was that in order to achieve a good life and be well in the diaspora, their family and ethnonational kin 'back home' had to be free from repressive and oppressive social forces. As Dursaa (Interview 11) shared:

Well-being for me is basically the [Oromo] people having their freedom. Being able to live their lives how other Ethiopians are living their life, and actually having the freedom to keep their land, and also to not be oppressed, you know, to keep them silent. They need to be able to have the freedom to speak their mind, and basically, we shouldn't be, not just silenced, we shouldn't be jailed, we shouldn't be murdered. And just a continuation, basically of our people, and repopulating, and continuing that through generations.

These sentiments permeated the narratives collected from participants despite them having resettled in Canada, a country that has provided safety, security and access to healthcare. Additionally, many participants struggled with the reality that the rights and protections afforded to them through resettlement remained inaccessible to those they left behind.

Those who partook in the participant observation events engaged in certain actions that corroborate the interviewees' viewpoints. At an Oromo wedding in Calgary, Yousuf's participant observation turned into an unplanned, full-fledged participant protest. Through discussions with wedding guests, she learned that a fundraising event for the Ethiopian government of the day was under way in one of the two rooms at the wedding venue. Knowledge of this event ignited a fierce protest that was endorsed by the bride and groom, who forfeited their wedding ceremony to stand in solidarity with the Oromo struggle for liberation. By this time, other people from the local and adjacent Oromo diaspora who were not planning on attending the wedding had travelled to the site to join the escalating protest.

Hundreds of Oromos spent hours collectively chanting: 'PLEASE PLEASE, STOP STOP, KILLING KILLING, OROMO PEOPLE', 'THIEVES THIEVES', 'LIARS LIARS.' Participants expressed anger as they recounted the horrors that Oromos have been made to experience, pain and sadness as tears streamed down their cheeks, and frustration as they yelled at the police in an effort to get them to understand their discontent. At the time, Oromo people in Ethiopia and across the world routinely staged peaceful protests and demonstrations to raise awareness of the plight of Oromos (Amnesty, 2016; HRW, 2015; Jeffrey, 2016). These actions, and how interview participants envisioned their well-being, indicate that the emotional lives of Oromo families are transnational and extend beyond households to include ethnonational kin. In short, the well-being of Oromos in the diaspora is emotionally framed by the impacts of violence that circulates transnationally, but especially in Ethiopia. These accounts illustrate the transnational dimensions of well-being, as illustrated through affect and emotion, but the Oromo case also provides some evidence to support the gendered nature of these experiences.

Gendered Practices of Well-being Among Transnational Kin

Research participants engaged actively in organizing spaces to address the transnational trauma of Oromos. Civic awareness and engagement are two such examples, and were widespread practices among the participants. A few of the goals that influence this type of involvement include a shared desire to stay connected transnationally, to congregate around mutual interests, and to work for and toward the collective well-being of Oromos. For participants, this included political awareness and participation, keeping up to date on Oromo politics and news, holding regular meetings to discuss the current atrocities that plague Oromo people in Ethiopia, as well as staging protests and demonstrations. Their diasporic practices, including weddings, are highly gendered in various ways. Although all participants expressed that they had a certain burden of responsibility to raise awareness and to be engaged, men tended to lead *teessoos*, which directly translates to mean 'meeting'; while women organized *afooshaas*, or community meetings.

A *teessoo* can have many purposes and aims, as there are many reasons for people to come together (for example, political gatherings or fundraising events). However, findings suggest that Oromo people tend to congregate when there is a death in the community, either locally or abroad. In the words of one participant: 'if there's a death people pool together and help with you know being there physically, or offering resources, or money, or moral support' (Gammadu, Interview 1). Similarly, Laafaa (Interview 4) stated:

> For example, on many occasions in [my local community], we collect money for people who died or the refugees in Kenya, Somalia, and Sudan and somewhere else. And the victims back home, there's a little bit of politics. But they, we have to be. That even gives you the well-being of the community by helping people across the ocean, you know? So, you feel good about it, like when we collect. We come together and discuss and that, that's well-being.

Laafaa explained that the local diaspora fundraises money to support the families of people who have died 'across the ocean' in other places where many Oromos have been displaced by violence.

Another example of acknowledging death relates to getting news that someone had died 'back home'. According to Barsiisaa (Interview 9) 'in terms of when the times of death and bad news come from back home or somebody dies here, yes, we come together and share, yes'. The participants acknowledged that they congregate to grieve deaths that happen locally, in other parts of the diaspora (for example, common hubs for Oromo refugees such as refugee camps), as well as back in Ethiopia. These findings show how transnational families transcend geography and connect across borders, linking those in Canada to households much closer to sites of conflict, violence and displacement.

Like *teessoos* (meetings), *afooshaas* (or community gatherings) include men as well as women; men hold *afooshaas* too. In the study, however, women talked about *afooshaas* extensively in terms of the various women's groups that they have formed and participated in. *Afooshaas* are similar to *teessoos* in that they provide Oromo people in the diaspora with community spaces to connect with other Oromos and engage in important events such as celebrating a birth or sharing grief over death. *Afooshaas* differ from *teessoos* because they tend to have gendered, ancestral, religious and geographical orientations, whereas *teessoos* tend to be broader. A few passages quoted below help to unpack some of these nuances:

> Yeah, we have a woman's group separately, and also, we have men and women, all the community together. We support each other, yes. (Jiraatuu, Interview 6)
> In our country, they call it 'afooshaa.' 'Afooshaa' is a group of people that, in our country they do it, and men and woman it doesn't matter. From any kind, it could be Christian, it could be Muslim, it could be anybody. They come together, like neighbours and all in the area. They come together and then they do it 'afooshaa.' (Jeynittii, Interview 12)

Both *teessoos* and *afooshaas* can be seen as sites of ethnonational kinship care that have served as lifelines for diasporic social support networks to thrive. The transnational networks of which they are comprised are protective factors of emotional well-being that can buffer against pain and suffering.

Gendered Productions of Pain and Suffering

The wedding event turned to protest, as described above, is emblematic of the gendered productions of pain and suffering among participants. Beginning with the accounts leading up to the main protest, there was a noticeable difference between how women and men mobilized. Inside the wedding venue, one woman took it upon herself to interrupt the fundraising event by voicing her anger at the attendees. Another woman arrived at a table visibly upset and insisted that wedding guests go and express their concerns to those attending the fundraising event. Shortly after this encounter, a man addressed all people in the hall and said, 'All of us let's get up and take a stance, let's join the protesters outside.'

When the bride and groom signalled – by crossing their forearms into an 'x', a widely used symbol expressing Oromo solidarity during contemporary protests – that the guests should go outside to protest, everyone left the wedding venue. While men mobilized the groups of people to come outside from the community hall, women were at the front line and the most vocal. Like the bride and groom, Oromo women stood tall with raised arms, crossed at the wrist above their heads. The gesture symbolizes the arrest of Oromo people by Ethiopian authorities. This is a famous protest gesture for Oromo people all over the globe, and it was banned by the Ethiopian government (see Duggan, 2016, for a list of banned activities proposed under Ethiopia's state of emergency). Women would also lie down in a non-violent fashion while crying out in pain for loved ones stolen by violence. The positioning of women's bodies on the ground was a striking observation of how they made themselves vulnerable and non-threatening.

Most of the men at the event were dressed in mainstream Western clothing, although they wore Oromo flags as necklace tags, or colours that were emblematic of specific political allegiances. Conversely, most women were dressed in traditional Oromo outfits, reflecting their ethnonational heritage (Hordofa, 2020). Women stood as the bearers of culture, in addition to the reproducers of the Oromo nation (Anthias and Yuval-Davis, 1989; Yuval-Davis, 1993). These findings illustrate that political and social transnational ties are always in play; diaspora members do not forget about their families and ethnonational kin back home when they attend a wedding in Calgary, Canada. Conflicts and the history of violence in Ethiopia encompass immense human suffering that has had lasting effects on displaced and dispossessed Oromo people across borders.

CONCLUSION

The literature on transnational families is replete with examples of families formed through economic transnationalism across class lines, with some attention to managing risk in the context of political uncertainty; while transnational families produced by war, violence and human rights atrocities are less represented. The two studies presented highlight the ways in which transnational families generated from the violence of competing nationalisms and related displacement actively participate in the politics of 'back home' in the diaspora. Their transnational connections to family members and ethnonational kin who may be threatened by violence abroad shape their daily worlds in Canada in highly gendered ways that vary across generation. The notion of ethnonational kin extends one's understanding of transnational family in the context of violent, competing nationalisms, where members of a persecuted or minority ethnonational group make the decision to leave their homes and country of origin.

This chapter has underscored how transnational families, specifically those among former refugees from Sri Lanka and Ethiopia who live in Canada, participate in politics and human rights advocacy in Canada that relates to conditions for Tamil and Oromo people back in these countries. The Tamil study shed insights into the nuances, analyses and disagreement about the ways in which Tamil nationalism should or was expressed, especially in relation to the widespread killing of civilians in Sri Lanka during 2009. Research with Oromos living in the diaspora revealed similar connections to politics. The ongoing persecution of Oromos in Ethiopia, stoked by the violence of competing nationalisms, deeply affects Oromos in the diaspora. Oromos in Canada maintain deep emotional connections to those left behind, which in turn galvanizes them to mobilize against the violence and human rights atrocities that gave rise to their displacement. The Oromo study illustrates how transnational practices of kinship care, and expressions of pain and suffering, are highly gendered. While both women and men participate in transnational cultural practices organized around gender roles and subjectivities, women undertook distinct roles in reproducing the nation socially, culturally and symbolically.

While the desire to hold together during separation may be common among the distinct transnational family dynamics, the strong bonds between diasporas and ethnonational kin complexify one's understanding of what constitutes transnational kinship. Displacement and diaspora formation due to violence and human rights atrocities spawn different kinds of transnational relationships, both with ethnonational kin and with family members left behind. Transnational family members may be divided politically, but can share the same concerns as their ethnonational kin. Likewise, diasporas are physically distant from their family and ethnonational kin, but are not separate from their insecurities. These notions of family, which extend beyond the household to include ethnonational kin who remain connected to sites of violent political conflict, illustrate a variant form of transnational kinship.

REFERENCES

Abraham, I. (2015). How India became territorial: Foreign policy, diaspora, geopolitics. *International Affairs*, *91*(4), 915–916.
Advocates for Human Rights (2009). *Human rights in Ethiopia: Through the eyes of the Oromo diaspora*. Retrieved from https://www.theadvocatesforhumanrights.org/uploads/oromo_report_2009_color.pdfAl-.
Al-Ali, N., Black, R., and Koser, K. (2001). The limits to 'transnationalism': Bosnian and Eritrean refugees in Europe as emerging transnational communities. *Ethnic and Racial Studies*, *24*(4), 578–600.
Al-Sharmani, M. (2010). Transnational family networks in the Somali diaspora in Egypt: Women's roles and differentiated experiences. *Gender, Place and Culture: A Journal of Feminist Geography*, *17*(4), 499–518.
Amarasingam, A. (2015). *Pain, pride, and politics: Social movement activism and the Sri Lankan Tamil diaspora in Canada*. Athens: University of Georgia Press.
Amnesty International (2014). *'Because I am Oromo': Sweeping repression in the Oromia region of Ethiopia*. Retrieved from https://www.amnesty.org/en/documents/afr25/006/2014/en/.
Amnesty International (2016). *Ethiopia: Dozens killed as police use excessive force against peaceful protesters*. Retrieved from https://www.amnesty.org/en/latest/news/2016/08/ethiopia-dozens-killed-as-police-use-excessive-force-against-peaceful-protesters/.
Anthias, F., and Yuval-Davis, N. (1989). *Woman-nation-state*. New York: Palgrave Macmillan.

Basch, L., Schiller, N.-G., and Blanc, C.S. (2005). *Nations unbound: Transnational projects, postcolonial predicaments, and deterritorialized nation-states*. London: Routledge.
Bauböck, R. (2003). Towards a political theory of migrant transnationalism. *International Migration Review*, *37*(3), 700–723.
Bryceson, D.F. (2019). Transnational families negotiating migration and care life cycles across nation-state borders. *Journal of Ethnic and Migration Studies*, *45*(16), 3042–3064.
Collyer, M. (2012). Deportation and the micropolitics of exclusion: The rise of removals from the UK to Sri Lanka. *Geopolitics*, *17*(2), 276–292.
Cultural Survival Quarterly Magazine (1981). Oromo continue to flee violence. Retrieved from https://www.culturalsurvival.org/publications/cultural-survival-quarterly/oromo-continue-flee-violence.
Domosh, M., and Seager, J. (2001). *Putting women in place: Feminist geographers make sense of the world*. New York: Guilford Press.
Ducu, V. (2018). Afterword: Gender practices in transnational families. In Ducu, V., Nedelcu, M., and Telegdi-Csetri, A. (eds), *Childhood and parenting in transnational settings* (Vol. 15, pp. 191–204). Cham: Springer.
Dugassa, B.F. (2017). Collective violence and public health: The experience of the Oromo people in Ethiopia. *Sociology*, *7*, 102–127. doi: 10.4236/sm.2017.73008.
Duggan, B. (2016, 18 October). Ethiopia's list of banned activities. *Cable News Network*. Retrieved from http://www.cnn.com/2016/10/18/africa/ethiopia-banned-activities/index.html.
Fuglerud, O. (1999). *Life on the outside: The Tamil diaspora and long-distance nationalism*. London: Pluto Press.
Gow, G. (2013). *The Oromo in exile*. Melbourne: Melbourne University Publishing.
Grabska, K. (2010). Lost boys, invisible girls: Stories of Sudanese marriages across borders. *Gender, Place and Culture*, *17*(4), 479–497.
Grace, B.L. (2019). Family from afar? Transnationalism and refugee extended families after resettlement. *Journal of Refugee Studies*, *32*(1), 125–143.
Graham, E., Jordan, L.P., Yeoh, B.S., Lam, T., Asis, M., and Su-Kamdi (2012). Transnational families and the family nexus: Perspectives of Indonesian and Filipino children left behind by migrant parent(s). *Environment and Planning A*, *44*(4), 793–815.
Gudina, M. (2007). Ethnicity, democratisation and decentralization in Ethiopia: The case of Oromia. *Eastern Africa Social Science Research Review*, *23*(1), 81–106.
Hondagneu-Sotelo, P., and Avila, E. (1997). 'I'm here, but I'm there': The meanings of Latina transnational motherhood. *Gender and Society*, *11*(5), 548–571.
Hopkins, G. (2010). A changing sense of Somaliness: Somali women in London and Toronto. *Gender, Place and Culture: A Journal of Feminist Geography*, *17*(4), 519–538.
Hordofa, E. (2020, 19 October). How clothes reflect growing Oromo ethnic pride in Ethiopia. *British Broadcasting Corporation*. Retrieved from https://www.bbc.com/news/world-africa-54513438.
Horst, C. (2007). *Transnational nomads: How Somalis cope with refugee life in the Dadaab camps of Kenya*. New York: Berghahn Books.
Horton, S. (2009). A mother's heart is weighed down with stones: A phenomenological approach to the experience of transnational motherhood. *Culture, Medicine, and Psychiatry*, *33*(1), 21.
Human Rights Watch (HRW) (2014). *'They know everything we do': Telecom and internet surveillance in Ethiopia*. Retrieved from https://www.hrw.org/report/2014/03/25/they-know-everything-we-do/telecom-and-internet-surveillance-ethiopia.
Human Rights Watch (HRW) (2015). *Ethiopia: Lethal force against protesters*. Retrieved from https://www.hrw.org/news/2015/12/18/ethiopia-lethal-force-against-protesters.
Human Rights Watch (HRW) (2016). *'Such a brutal crackdown': Killings and arrests in response to Ethiopia's Oromo protests*. Retrieved from https://www.hrw.org/report/2016/06/15/such-brutal-crackdown/killings-and-arrests-response-ethiopias-oromo-protests.
Hyndman, J. (2010). Introduction: The feminist politics of refugee migration. *Gender, Place and Culture: A Journal of Feminist Geography 17*(4), 453–459.
Hyndman, J., Amarasingam, A., and Naganathan, G. (2020). Diaspora geopolitics in Toronto: Tamil nationalism and the aftermath of war in Sri Lanka. *Geopolitics*, 1–20. doi: https://doi.org/10.1080/14650045.2020.1819248.

Hyndman, J., and Walton-Roberts, M. (2000). Interrogating borders: A transnational approach to refugee research in Vancouver. *Canadian Geographer/Le Géographe Canadien*, 44(3), 244–258.

Jalata, A. (2010). *Contending nationalisms of Oromia an Ethiopia: Struggling for statehood, sovereignty, and multinational democracy*. Binghamton: Global Publishing at Binghamton University.

Jalata, A. (2011). The Oromo in Exile: Creating knowledge and promoting social justice. *Societies Without Borders*, 6(1), 33–72.

Jeffrey, J. (2016, 24 November). Why is the Ethiopian diaspora so influential? *British Broadcasting Corporation*. Retrieved from https://www.bbc.com/news/world-africa-38076389.

Kearney, M., and Nagengast, C. (1989). *Anthropological perspectives on transnational communities in rural California*. Working paper no. 3. Davis, CA. California Institute for Rural Studies, Working Group on Farm Labor and Rural Poverty.

Kobayashi, A., and Preston, V. (2007). Transnationalism through the life course: Hong Kong immigrants in Canada. *Asia Pacific Viewpoint*, 48(2), 151–167.

Kofman, E. (2000). The invisibility of skilled female migrants and gender relations in studies of skilled migration in Europe. *International Journal of Population Geography*, 6(1), 45–59.

Kofman, E., and Raghuram, P. (2006). Gender and global labour migrations: Incorporating skilled workers. *Antipode*, 38(2), 282–303.

Lam, T., and Yeoh, B.S. (2018). Migrant mothers, left-behind fathers: The negotiation of gender subjectivities in Indonesia and the Philippines. *Gender, Place and Culture*, 25(1), 104–117.

Lam, T., Yeoh, B.S., and Law, L. (2002). Sustaining families transnationally: Chinese-Malaysians in Singapore. *Asian and Pacific Migration Journal*, 11(1), 117–143.

Levitt, P. (1998). Social remittances: Migration driven local-level forms of cultural diffusion. *International Migration Review*, 32(4), 926–948.

Lim, S.L. (2009). 'Loss of connections is death' Transnational family ties among Sudanese refugee families resettling in the United States. *Journal of Cross-Cultural Psychology*, 40(6), 1028–1040.

Mahler, S.J. (1995). *American dreaming: Immigrant life on the margins*. Princeton: Princeton University Press.

Marston, S.A. (2000). The social construction of scale. *Progress in Human Geography*, 24(2), 219–242.

Nolin, C. (2006). *Transnational ruptures: Gender and forced migration*. Aldershot: Ashgate.

Parreñas, R.S. (2001). Mothering from a distance: Emotions, gender, and intergenerational relations in Filipino transnational families. *Feminist Studies*, 27(2), 361–390.

Pratt, G. (2004). *Working feminism*. Philadelphia: Temple University Press.

Pratt, G. (2012). *Families apart: Migrant mothers and the conflicts of labor and love*. Minneapolis: University of Minnesota Press.

Schiller, N.-G., Basch, L., and Blanc, C.S. (1995). From immigrant to transmigrant: Theorizing transnational migration. *Anthropological Quarterly*, 68(1), 48–63.

Schiller, N.-G., Basch, L., and Blanc-Szanton, C. (1992). Transnationalism: A new analytic framework for understanding migration. *Annals of the New York Academy of Sciences*, 645(1), 1–24.

Sheffer, G. (1994). Ethno-national diasporas and security. *Survival*, 36(1), 60–79.

Smith, E.P. (2015). *To build a home: The material cultures, gender relations and the cultivation of meaning by Karen refugees from Burma*. Doctoral dissertation, York University, Toronto. Retrieved from http://hdl.handle.net/10315/30741.

Thiranagama, S. (2011). *In my mother's house: Civil war in Sri Lanka*. Philadelphia: Pennsylvania Press.

Van Hear, N. (2005). Refugee diasporas or refugees in diaspora. In M. Ember, C.R. Ember, and I. Skoggard (eds), *Encyclopedia of Diasporas* (pp. 580–591). Boston: Springer.

Van Hear, N., Barbelet, V., Bennett, C., and Lutz, H.A. (2018). Imagining refugia: Thinking outside the current refugee regime. *Migration and Society*, 1(1), 175–194.

Walton-Roberts, M. (2020). Intermediaries and transnational regimes of skill: Nursing skills and competencies in the context of international migration. *Journal of Ethnic and Migration Studies*, 1–18. doi: 10.1080/1369183X.2020.1731988.

Waters, J.L. (2002). Flexible families? 'Astronaut' households and the experiences of lone mothers in Vancouver, British Columbia. *Social and Cultural Geography*, 3(2), 117–134.

Waters, J.L. (2003). Flexible citizens? Transnationalism and citizenship amongst economic immigrants in Vancouver. *Canadian Geographer* 47(3), 219–234.

Waters, J.L. (2010). Becoming a father, missing a wife: Chinese transnational families and the male experience of lone parenting in Canada. *Population, Space and Place 16*(1), 63–74.

Weiss, G. (2012). *The cage: The fight for Sri Lanka and the last days of the Tamil tigers*. New York: Bellevue Literary Press.

Yeoh, B.S., Huang, S., and Lam, T. (2005). Transnationalizing the 'Asian' family: Imaginaries, intimacies and strategic intents. *Global Networks: A Journal of Transnational Affairs*, *5*(4), 307–315.

Yousuf, B. (2018). *'The sufferings and persecution of my people back home is the one that really burns and boils in me every single day': Exploring expressions of well-being in the Oromo diaspora*. MA/MSc Thesis, Simon Fraser University, Vancouver, Canada. Retrieved from http://summit.sfu.ca/item/18548.

Yuval-Davis, N. (1993). Gender and nation. *Ethnic and Racial Studies*, *16*(4), 621–632.

5. Vietnamese masculinities in transition: negotiating manhood in the context of female labour migration

Lan Anh Hoang

INTRODUCTION

Universally, work and money are the prerequisites for men's assertion of their masculinity and claims to patriarchal authority within and beyond the family (Brittan 1989; Osella and Osella 2000; Thai 2010). Work is integral to the masculine identity (Connell 1995: 33), while money begets power, enabling men to better orchestrate their parental identities, fathering activities and family arrangements (Marsiglio and Pleck 2005: 261). However, men's access to work and money is no longer guaranteed in the late-capitalist global economy, where capital has reached an unprecedented level of transnational mobility and labour relations have been increasingly flexiblised to ensure that profits are maximised for capital owners (Harvey 2005; Lewis et al. 2015). Workers' insecurity and precarity – the hallmarks of neoliberal globalisation – are crucial government technologies that keep them disciplined, exploitable and disposable. As boys continue to be socialised into the gender role of family provider, men's increasingly precarious place in the labour market undermines their ontological security and threatens to disrupt the gender relations in which they are embedded. While it may be an overstatement to conclude that men are currently experiencing a 'crisis of masculinity' (see Faludi 1999; Edwards 2006; Morgan 2006, for example), as the impacts of neoliberal globalisation on men are deeply classed and raced and vary widely across time and place, it is evident that many men today experience their own masculinity as fragile and vulnerable (see also Bly 2001). Understanding how men navigate the disjuncture between the growing insecurities they experience in their lives and the rigidity of the prevailing masculinity ideals will shed important light on their emergent gendered subjectivities and social practice, and enrich our knowledge of how the patriarchal system within which they are embedded is being reconfigured by migration (see also Chapters 2, 3 and 4, this *Handbook*).

The continued expectation for men to perform their provider's role explains the intimate links between money and masculinity in Vietnamese society, which is experiencing rapid social stratification. In recent decades, nationalistic and communist ideologies have been giving way to an intensifying materialistic fever. Hung Cam Thai (2006, 2014), for example, meticulously documents how low-waged American *Việt Kiều* (overseas Vietnamese) men are willing to endure great sacrifice in order to remit money to Vietnam, in an effort to assert their social worth, status and manhood which have been shattered by their low status in the United States. In her ethnography of Vietnam's sex industry, Kimberly Kay Hoang (2015) provides a compelling account of how Vietnamese men engage in conspicuous consumption as an avenue for contesting the global hierarchy of masculinities, which is predicated on Western dominance and superiority, and affirming the ascendancy of Asian masculinities. Money is equally crucial for rural, working-class men in performing hegemonic masculinity. In their comparative study of both rural and urban men in Northern Vietnam, Horton and Rydstrom (2011: 550) observe that a man's financial status is believed to mirror his level of masculinity. The strong relationship between money and masculinity must be seen in a context where lived realities of femininity and motherhood are becoming increasingly diverse and complex, due to women's greater mobilities and exposure to modern, foreign values. Although marriage and the family remain important, and good mothering continues to be a priority for women of younger generations (Hoang 2020b), the notion of femininity is beginning to incorporate new aspirations for 'modernity, urbanity, beauty, and sexuality' (Werner 2006: 314).

In this chapter, I provide a critical review of how men left behind by migrant women in Vietnam (re)negotiate their masculinities when they can no longer perform the traditionally ascribed role of the family provider. Masculinities, as compellingly argued by Connell (1995), are both multiple and fluid, with internal complexities and even contradictions. As masculinity and femininity are relational terms defined in opposition to each other, changes in women's roles and identities would logically result in changes in men's lives (Kimmel 1987; Brittan 1989). Focusing on Vietnamese stay-behind men in both internal and transnational migrant families, I advance the feminist view of migration as a gendered process, but depart from the migrant woman-centred tradition and shift my analytical gaze to the gendered experiences of immobile men. In so doing, I heed Choi and Peng's (2016: 13) call for bringing men's voices, subjectivities and experiences into the centre of the gender and migration debates. The chapter enriches the scholarship on masculinities, and at the same time addresses the 'mobility bias' in migration and mobility, that is, the tendency to give mobility a conceptual priority over immobility, and privilege nomadic accounts at the expense of sedentary ones (Sheller 2018; Schewel 2020).

THE FEMINISATION OF LABOUR MIGRATION IN POST-REFORM VIETNAM

Labour migration in Vietnam has become increasingly feminised since the launch of the economic reforms (also known as Đổi mới[1]) in the late 1980s. The number of female migrants in inter-provincial flows, which tend to be for work rather than for marriage purposes, rose rapidly in the 1990s to match that of male migrants just before the turn of the century (GSO 2011: 24). By 2009, women had outnumbered men in both intra- and inter-provincial flows. According to the 2015 National Internal Migration Survey, women accounted for 52.4 per cent of all internal migrants (GSO and UNFPA 2016). While rural–urban disparities in income and access to infrastructure, social services and social protection are seen the key drivers of rural out-migration in general (Nguyen and Locke 2014), it is the rapid expansion of the private sector and the increasingly gender-segregated labour market that spur the unprecedented growth in female internal migration. Qualitative research also suggests that, in many contexts, female labour migration is a strategic livelihood decision made by the household, based on the assumption that women are more altruistic and self-sacrificial than men in their financial management and, therefore, tend to save more money and not to engage in city 'vices' (especially sexual infidelity) (Resurreccion and Ha 2007; Agergaard and Thao 2011). Much female labour from rural areas is absorbed by the foreign direct investment sector, which largely comprises manufacturing industries in urban and peri-urban areas in the Red River Delta and the Southeast (Angie 2004; Belanger and Pendakis 2009; GSO and UNFPA 2016: 112). Urban small trade is particularly attractive for married women who come from rural areas in close proximity to metropolitan centres, as it affords them the much-needed flexibility to perform the so-called 'translocal householding', juggling both breadwinning and familial roles while migrating (Resurreccion and Ha 2007; Vu and Agergaard 2012; Nguyen and Locke 2014).

A similar trend of 'feminised migration' can be observed in transnational contract labour migration flows which are regulated by bilateral agreements between the government of Vietnam and those of labour-receiving countries. The rate of female contract workers increased steadily from 30.1 per cent in 2009 (Hoang and Yeoh 2012) to 42 per cent in 2017.[2] As of 2018, 500,000 Vietnamese labour migrants were working overseas,[3] mainly in Taiwan, Japan and the Republic of Korea, which together hosted 90 per cent of contract workers from Vietnam.[4] Women were predominately employed in domestic and care services as well as manufacturing industries. Although the deployment of migrant contract workers experienced significant setbacks in 2020 due to the COVID-19 pandemic, the migration industry remains optimistic about the long-term prospect for Vietnamese labour exports.[5]

In a society where a woman's identity continues to be anchored in marriage and domesticity, and judgements of her social worth and moral standing are centred on her performance in the reproductive sphere (see Hoang 2016, 2020b), it is not surprising that the feminisation of migration has produced a great deal of social anxiety. Unlike migration studies in China, where the young (unmarried) female migrant has captured much scholarly attention (see Fan 2004; May 2010; Ge et al. 2011, for example), Vietnamese scholarship is more interested in the implications of married women's migration for social reproduction and gender relations within the household (Resurreccion and Ha 2007; Hoang and Yeoh 2011; Vu and Agergaard 2012; Hoang 2016). Research indicates incremental change in attitudes to female migration among rural households since the 1990s, from disapproval to grudging acceptance and, in some contexts, even encouragement (Resurreccion and Ha 2007; Agergaard and Thao 2011; Hoang 2011a; Locke et al. 2012; Nguyen 2014).

However, the increasingly relaxed attitude to women's participation in labour migration does not seem to be accompanied by any fundamental shift in gender ideologies. Migrant women continue to be expected to live up to the femininity ideals of caring and dutiful mothers and wives despite their now crucial economic contributions to the household. Although there are clear differences between international and internal migrants, especially in regard to their ability to continue to perform physical care-giving duties while migrating, migrant women are generally found to be keen to preserve the conventional familial arrangements and patriarchal hierarchies of power (Truong 2009; Hoang and Yeoh 2012; Locke et al. 2012a 2012b; Vu and Agergaard 2012). Migrant women's loyalty to patriarchy does not necessarily reflect their internalisation of women's subordination, but as I have discussed extensively elsewhere (see Hoang 2016), tends to be a carefully crafted strategy to ensure their long-term social and economic security, because the financial rewards of their labour migration are generally neither significant enough nor effectively invested in ongoing income-generating activities to guarantee self-sufficiency and independence in old age. Within a rigid patriarchal system, women are compelled to conform to traditional femininity ideals in order to preserve their parental authority and moral standing (Agergaard and Thao 2011: 115). Doing gender 'appropriately' is women's primary avenue for building symbolic capital and legitimating their claims on family support in the future.

The heavy focus on how migrant women negotiate the contradictions and dilemmas emerging from their assumption of the family breadwinner's role and their extended physical absence from home has overshadowed the challenges faced by their stay-behind husbands. Because migration is selective, female labour migration tends to happen in the context of men's limited economic power or poor health, which have already compromised their ability to live up to the hegemonic breadwinner ideal (see Agergaard and Thao 2011; Hoang and Yeoh 2011; Hoang and Yeoh 2015a, for example). The vast majority of Vietnamese female labour migrants come from poor rural households in the North and North Central, which means that their husbands tend not to be formally employed. However, men are more likely than women to earn cash incomes from off-farm work, such as construction, carpentry or small trade, before migration becomes a livelihood strategy for the household (Hoang 2011a; Hoang and Yeoh 2011; Hoang and Yeoh 2015a). Despite the irregular and low-paid nature of their off-farm work, men's incomes are crucial resources for cash-strapped rural households given that farming is no longer sufficient to provide for basic household maintenance needs, not to mention to cover large expenditures such as house construction or major healthcare needs (Hoang 2011a). The woman's assumption of the family breadwinner's role upon her migration therefore implies difficult, if not painful, adjustments on the part of her stay-behind husband.

MEN AND MASCULINITIES IN POST-REFORM VIETNAM

Gender norms in contemporary Vietnamese society exhibit both the East Asian patriarchal values that are rooted in Confucian ideologies of social order, and relatively more liberal elements of Southeast Asian cultures where the bilateral kinship system affords women greater mobility and bargaining power. In the Confucian worldview of social harmony, which has a particularly strong and enduring influence in Northern Vietnam (see Hickey 1964; Bélanger and Li 2009), women are expected to submit to and depend on their husbands in every aspect of their lives (Santillán et al. 2002; Rydstrom 2004). Men's power is consolidated by the continued practice of patrilineality and patrilocality, which provides them with secure access to land and vital support from kinship-based social networks (Hirschman and Nguyen 2002; Bélanger and Li 2009; Hoang 2011a; Horton and Rydstrom 2011). Unlike China where daughters in sonless families are allowed to perform ancestor worship and funeral rites, which legitimises their right to inherit parents' property (see Bélanger and Li 2009), in Vietnam male members of the family have an exclusive responsibility for ancestor worship rituals, which translates directly into economic privileges (especially inheritance rights) for men, greater symbolic value of sons, and ultimate authority of the male patriarch in family decision-making.

However, the privileges conferred on men by the patriarchal and patrilineal structures come with the expectation that they fulfil the duties of the breadwinner and protector of the family. This is expressed through the metaphorical references to men as the 'pillar' (*trụ cột*) of the household or the 'roof' of the house,[6] affirming their status as the most superior and important member of the unit, without whom both the marriage and the household would fall apart (Rydstrøm 2006: 334; Horton and Rydstrom 2011: 556). The primary markers of Vietnamese masculinity centre around men's relationship to the family, which is reaffirmed by a recent survey of 2,567 rural and urban men from four different cities and provinces across the country (ISDS 2020). 'Good manhood', therefore, is fundamentally about the man's fulfilling his family duties, including displaying filial piety to his parents, performing ancestor worship rituals, ensuring the continuation of the lineage through marriage and procreation, providing for the household's sustenance, and building and protecting the honour and reputation of the family by setting himself as a moral example and supervising the social conduct of his wife and children. Given the central place that the family occupies in the Vietnamese construction of masculinity, men's work has not only important symbolic value but also the practical value of enabling men to perform their family provider and protector's role. However, the expectation for men to look after the family's welfare tends to cause them significant stress and even mental health problems (ISDS 2020: 1).

As the 'pillar' of the household, men are believed to have the right to 'discipline' and 'educate' junior members, including their wives and children, as illustrated by the popular proverb, '*Dạy con từ thuở còn thơ, dạy vợ từ thuở bơ vơ mới về*' (Educate/discipline your children from early days of childhood, educate/discipline your wife as soon as she moves into your family home). Here, educating and disciplining involve not only moral and social guidance but also physical punishment, if necessary. The idea of men's use of violence as a masculine practice is introduced to them through childhood disciplining by their fathers and grandfathers (see Rydstrøm 2006, for example), and reinforced by their sense of superiority within the patriarchal system. The high prevalence and normalisation of men's perpetration of gender-based violence in Vietnam has been attributed to the pressure for them to be a strong 'pillar' for the household, and their experiences of corporal punishment during childhood (Hoang et al. 2013; Yount et al. 2016). A recent qualitative study by James-Hawkins et al. (2019) suggests that the 'status conflict' driven by increases in female labour force participation and greater gender equity in the public sphere are important factors contributing to intimate partner violence in post-*Đổi mới* Vietnam. Facing unemployment and poverty, men tend to resort to violence as a measure to reassert their masculine dominance and authority within the family.

Given the essentialised stereotypes about feminine attributes as cool, passive, gentle and easy to control, and masculine attributes as hot (also bad-tempered), active, aggressive and hard to control (see Rydstrom 2004), society is more permissive when men engage in high-risk social activities or supposedly disgraceful behaviour such as drinking, smoking, gambling and extramarital affairs (Horton and Rydstrom 2011). Men's use of violence to resolve conflicts is therefore considered justifiable, because it is their 'nature' to be aggressive and violent, while women are expected to 'endure' because their cool nature enables them to do so (Rydstrøm 2006: 336). When a man seeks sexual relationships outside marriage, the blame tends to be put on his wife, who is believed to have failed to meet her husband's sexual needs, while female sexual infidelity is heavily stigmatised and subject to severe social sanctions including divorce and ostracisation (Horton and Rydstrom 2011; Hoang and Yeoh 2015a).

Although social institutions, especially the family, are male-centred and male-dominated, Vietnamese women have always been active economic actors, keeping the household economy afloat through their earnings from small trade or home-based work (Kabeer and Tran 2000; Leshkowich 2015; Horat 2017). With their crucial economic contributions to the household, women are able to leverage their soft power in household decision-making processes, effectively asserting their preferences in quiet and hidden ways, and avoiding open confrontation which would compromise their reputation and moral standing. Women's voices in household decision-making have been enhanced further by their increased mobility and the nucleation of the household since *Đổi mới*. Research shows that while rural women still move to their husbands' villages upon marriage, the typical three-generation, patrilineally organised household in Northern and Central Vietnam is becoming less common (Rydstrøm 2003; Werner

2004). However, the perception of the domestic sphere as women's space persists. The 2020 survey on men and masculinities shows that men's definition of a good wife still emphasises women's domestic skills, subordination to their husbands, and dedication to the family (ISDS 2020). Specifically, the four most important qualities of a good wife for the surveyed men are: 'domestically skillful' (90 per cent), 'always sacrifice for the family' (88 per cent), 'always listen to and agree with the husband's opinions' (84 per cent), and 'have jobs that allow plenty of time for family' (73 per cent) (ISDS 2020: 163).

In Northern and Central Vietnam, where independent female labour migrants tend to come from, men's ability to measure up to the breadwinner ideal has long been constrained by the shrinking agricultural land and the lack of viable off-farm opportunities. While official statistics indicate that Vietnam has one of the lowest unemployment rates in the world – 2.17 percent as of 2019[7] – the figure is highly inaccurate due to dubious statistical methods.[8] A recent World Bank report found that about 38 million (or 76 per cent) of Vietnam's 50 million jobs are in family farming, household enterprises or uncontracted labour; the jobs that are characterised by low productivity, low profits, meagre earnings and few worker protections (Cunningham and Pimhidzai 2018). Underemployment is widespread in rural areas. According to the government's official statistics, 6.8 per cent of all workers in Vietnam were time-related underemployed as of 2009 (7.7 per cent of rural workers were underemployed), and men were significantly more affected by time-related underemployment (7.3 per cent) than women (6.2 per cent) (MOLISA 2010: 19). Like the official unemployment statistics, underemployment tends to be underestimated. Nguyen and Ezaki (2005: 11), for example, suggest that around 70 per cent of rural residents can be seen as underemployed if full-time employment is to involve 2000 hours of work annually.

The economic constraints men face are compounded by the 'socialisation' (privatisation) of education and healthcare, and inflated cost of living, since Đổi mới. According to the 2012 Vietnam Household Living Standards Survey, the monthly income per capita in the Red River Delta was VND2,337 million (US$100) and the monthly total consumption expenditure per capita in the same region was VND1,889 million (US$82) (GSO 2012). The insignificant margin between income and consumption gives households little wiggle room to account for major expenditures such as house construction, or shocks, not to mention long-term investment in productive activities. This explains how female labour migration has emerged as a new route for poor rural households in the Red River Delta to get out of debt and poverty. Research shows that remittances from migrant women are vital to the sustenance of the household (Vu and Agergaard 2012; Hoang and Yeoh 2015b), significantly improve their standards of living and children's well-being (Resurreccion and Ha 2007; Locke et al. 2015), help the family to pay debt and build up savings for the future (Vu 2013; Locke et al. 2015; Hoang 2020a), and radically transform the physical landscape of the countryside (Vu 2014; Hoang 2020a).

FLEXIBLE MASCULINITIES: MEN RENEGOTIATING THE GENDERED DIVISION OF LABOUR

When I conducted field research for my doctoral project on internal migration in early 2005 in Thái Bình – a Red River Delta province 110 km southeast of Hà Nội – female labour migration was commonly framed by local men as 'the last resort', and many thought that only 'losers' would swap places with their wives, staying behind to do care and domestic work and letting their wives migrate to provide for the household (Hoang 2011a: 1447). A woman's migration was seen as an indication of her husband's poor capacity to fulfil his masculine roles. However, both internal and international female labour migration grew quickly towards the end of the first decade of the 21st century, and by the time I returned to Thái Bình in 2009 to conduct fieldwork for a large-scale mixed-method study on transnational contract labour migration,[9] many rural communities in the province had been given a new nickname, 'Taiwan villages', by the media due to a high number of local women who had migrated to Taiwan for contract work (Hoang and Yeoh 2011). The substantial shifts in both volumes of and social attitudes to female labour migration are also observed by Catherine Locke and colleagues (Locke et al. 2008, 2012a, 2012b, 2014), who highlight the strong influence of the 'happy family' discourse – which is premised upon both husband and wife's productive income generation – on these changes. Within nearly three decades since the introduction of Đổi Mới reforms, female labour migration had become well established in many rural areas of the Red River Delta.

Research indicates distinctively different gender dynamics between translocal and transnational households, which are attributable, in the first place, to the selective nature of migration (that is, translocal and transnational female migrants tend to come from different household and marital situations), the usually significant differences in their respective migration's economic costs and benefits, and the ability of translocal migrants to visit home regularly (and transnational migrants' inability to do so). The extant literature on internal female migration in Vietnam emphasises continuity, rather than change, in gender identity and practice, especially in regard to labour division (Resurreccion and Ha 2007; Vu and Agergaard 2012). The resilience of patriarchy is also observed in China, where scholars note the 'shattering effects' of rural–urban migration on the 'foundation of the peasant patriarchy', particularly the norms of patrilocality and female domesticity (Choi and Peng 2016: 4), but point out that the freedom and autonomy which young women achieve through migration tend to be short-lived, and the generational and gender hierarchies that structure the patriarchal family remain largely intact post-migration (Fan 2003; Ge et al. 2011; Zhang 2013; Jacka 2014; Chuang 2016).

In Vietnam, while evidence shows that stay-behind men and migrant women in both translocal and transnational households are keen to preserve patriarchal values and structures, mainly for the symbolic value deriving from them, their capacity to do so in the latter situation is compromised by the physical distance and restrictive contract labour migration regimes in Asia (Resurreccion and Ha 2007; Locke et al. 2009; Hoang and Yeoh 2011; Vu and Agergaard 2012; Hoang 2016). A typical contract for transnational migrant workers is for three years, and renewable for a limited number of times (see Hoang 2017 for a detailed discussion of transnational labour contract migration in Asia). Migrants are not allowed to bring dependents or to settle down permanently in the host country. Due to resources constraints and mobility restrictions associated with their contract work, migrants tend to visit their families back home only at the end of the contract term, or between contracts. In such a context, rigid patriarchal structures and gender roles within the household become untenable, at least temporarily.

While transnational contract labour migration choices tend to be the result of market demands and the household's rational cost–benefit analysis, the choices that translocal households make with regard to migrant women's destination, livelihoods and work regimes often reflect their desire to sustain patriarchal structures during migration. Research on rural female migrants in Hanoi – the capital city of Vietnam – shows that they tend to come from nearby provinces in the Red River Delta, engage in small trade or waste collection/trade, and live in temporary housing, all of which allow them to easily shuttle between the city and the village, juggling breadwinning and familial duties at the same time (Resurreccion and Ha 2007; Locke et al. 2008; Locke et al. 2012a; Vu and Agergaard 2012; Nguyen 2014; Nguyen and Locke 2014). This so-called 'gendered translocal householding' practice (Nguyen and Locke 2014: 870) has become central to rural–urban migration in the Red River Delta, allowing migrants to diversify and improve their household incomes while minimising potentially disruptive effects of migration on the stability and harmony of the household unit. Although stay-behind husbands willingly take on care and domestic duties during migrant women's absence, both of them consider this arrangement to be ad hoc and distinctively temporary (Resurreccion and Ha 2007; Agergaard and Thao 2011). To assure their husbands of their manhood, migrant women return regularly to do traditionally feminine tasks in agriculture such as rice transplanting or harvesting (Vu and Agergaard 2012) and, more importantly, to fulfil their wifely and motherly duties (Resurreccion and Ha 2007; Locke et al. 2012b; Nguyen 2014). Women's continued efforts to perform gendered work, albeit at a reduced capacity, enable their stay-behind husbands to hold on to their symbolic role as the pillar of the family and stake claims to the remittances which, in their view, would not have been possible without them staying put and taking on domestic tasks (Agergaard and Thao 2011; Nguyen 2014; Vu 2014).

It is in transnational households that we are more likely to see a complete reversal of gender roles than in translocal households. In patriarchal systems, men's dominance over women is essentially based on a rigid division of labour that reserves the public realm and productive work for men, and confines women to the domestic sphere and reproductive work (Mann 2011). However, men's adjustments to female labour migration tend to be less painful if gender boundaries had already been transgressed before migration. My past research on transnational families in Vietnam shows that the stay-behind men who accept the reversed gender roles with ease tend to have been involved in care and domestic work, and benefited from their wives' off-farm incomes, before migration (Hoang and Yeoh 2011). This corroborates Menjívar's (1999) observation of the differences between ladino Guatemalan and Salvadorian men and indigenous Guatemalan men in the United States. She found that the former group felt threatened by their wives' assumption of the main provider's role after migration to the United States, while the latter group, who came from a more gender-egalitarian background, welcomed the change and even encouraged the women to get ahead. Recent research shows relatively high rates of Vietnamese men who have engaged in domestic and care work in the household before they reach 18 (ranging from 61 per cent to 70 per cent, depending on the specific task), and these rates tend to be higher in rural areas (ISDS 2020: 82). This explains the significant differences between Vietnam and other major labour-sending countries in terms of stay-behind men's participation in domestic and care work.

A comparative review of migration studies across Asia underscores the importance of the pre-migration gendered division of labour in how men adapt to their new roles and responsibilities after their wives migrate overseas. Research shows the persistence of the woman carer model in mother migrant families in Sri Lanka and the Philippines where female relatives, especially the maternal grandmother, take on the care and domestic duties vacated by the migrant mother (Gamburd 2000; Parreñas 2005; Save the Children 2006). According to a Save the Children (2006) study of 1200 migrant mother households in Sri Lanka, fathers only made up 25.9 per cent of primary carers. Likewise, children in the Philippines are more likely to be cared for by their female relatives than their fathers when their mothers migrate (Tacoli 1999; Parreñas 2001). However, our past research, which surveyed 287 migrant mother households in Vietnam, showed that the stay-behind father was more likely than other family members to become the primary carer of his children when the mother migrates (70.8 per cent), which reflected relatively greater gender equities in Vietnam (Hoang and Yeoh 2011; Hoang et al. 2015). The differences between Vietnam and other Asian countries in terms of childcare arrangements are consistent with cross-country variations in female labour force participation. According to the World Bank, 73 per cent of Vietnamese women participated in the labour force as of June 2020, while the equivalent figures for the Philippines and Sri Lanka were 46 per cent and 35 per cent, respectively.[10] The more egalitarian gendered division of labour in Vietnam partly explains why, unlike their counterparts in other Asian contexts, Vietnamese men consider fatherhood as integral to their masculine identity, and childcare as an essential part of fatherhood (Locke et al. 2009; Agergaard and Thao 2011; Hoang and Yeoh 2011).

Men's access to off-farm work and cash incomes is equally crucial for how they experience changes within the household following their wives' migration. Research on migrant families in the Philippines show that men are more willing to do a greater share of domestic and care work if their masculinity is already made secure by their own employment status and incomes (Parreñas 2005; McKay 2015). Work and money are important means for men to safeguard their prestige, self-respect and masculine identity against the threat posed by migrant women's increased economic power (Gamburd 2000; Parreñas 2005). In Vietnam, similar links between men's paid work and their participation in domestic and care work can be found in both translocal and transnational female migrant households (Locke et al. 2009; Hoang and Yeoh 2011; Vu 2014; Hoang et al. 2015). Stay-behind husbands tend to continue working during their wives' migration, even if their incomes are often irregular, insignificant and unpredictable, and despite the significant stress of juggling multiple roles at the same time. The symbolic value of work cushions their manhood against the damage their wives' labour migration may cause (Hoang and Yeoh 2011). In rare situations where the stay-behind husband's income even surpasses that of his migrant wife, his economic success works as an invisible yet powerful form of control over the woman's social conduct and sexual life, thereby minimising possible frictions and disruptions in their marriage (Hoang and Yeoh 2015a).

HYPERMASCULINITY: TEMPERING THE DEMASCULINISING EFFECTS OF FEMALE LABOUR MIGRATION

Although labour migration does not always lead to economic success or elevate the status of the household, especially for transnational contract workers whose migration tends to be debt-induced and debt-financed (see Hoang and Yeoh 2015b; Hoang 2017, 2020a), the causal relationship between migration and upward social mobility is readily assumed in Vietnamese society (Carruthers 2002: 439; Hoang 2020c: 157). Besides, there is clear evidence of the positive relationship between women's remittances and their increased bargaining power (Locke et al. 2008; Agergaard and Thao 2011; Hoang 2011b; Vu 2014), which threatens men's place in household decision-making processes. In a context where men are socialised into the idea that they should do only 'grand things' and perform only the work 'worthy' of them (Hoang 2011a: 1447), it is only natural that stay-behind husbands of migrant women feel that their masculinity, authority and social worth are under attack (Locke et al. 2008; Agergaard and Thao 2011). Although most of them accept the reversed gender roles on a temporary basis, they actively seek to assert their authority and temper the demaculinising effects of their wives' migration in various ways.

While many migrant women in my previous research had worked off-farm (mostly as petty traders) and been de facto households providers before migration, the stay-behind husbands who I interviewed were keen to emphasise that they were still the heads and decision-makers of their households (see Hoang and Yeoh 2011: 727). A similar narrative was picked up by Thao Vu in her study of translocal households in the Red River Delta. More than 90 per cent of the husbands she interviewed claimed that their 'pillar of the household' position remained intact, despite the fact that their income from farming was equal to roughly a quarter of their wives' remittances (Vu and Agergaard 2012; Vu 2014). Claiming power while being dependent on their migrant wives for economic provisioning is a delicate balancing act which, if not done in a measured and sensitive manner, may lead to conflict or even marital dissolution. Migration studies in the Red River Delta show that men's common response to their tricky situation is to perform their masculinities more explicitly, through compensatory behaviours in financial management and sexual relationships. For example, they may deliberately misuse remittances (Locke et al. 2008), make large purchases without consulting their migrant wives (Vu 2014), put up with extreme financial hardships rather than requesting remittances from the women (Hoang and Yeoh 2011), and use their wives' hard-earned migration dollars to pay for transactional sex (Hoang and Yeoh 2015a). Although women's subordination to their husbands is still highly valued by Vietnamese men, the 2020 survey by the Institute for Social Development Studies indicates that joint decision-making is becoming more common among Vietnamese married couples: nearly 50 per cent of the surveyed men reported that they made decisions on the family's large spending and investment with their wives (ISDS 2020: 6, 94). The same survey also reveals that 'paternalistic' (tyrannical) and 'caring too much about keeping face' are considered by the surveyed men as the most prominent negative traits of Vietnamese men (ibid.: 109). The contradictions between rigid gender norms and men's increasingly diverse and complex lived experiences are accentuated by female labour migration. Here, men's capability to cope with women's increased mobility and power is severely constrained by their immobility and lack of economic resources. They therefore covertly and silently refuse to acknowledge women's voices in household decision-making in a bid to 'keep face' and resist the ongoing onslaught on their masculinity.

Men's compensatory behaviours are encouraged by their migrant wives' sense of guilt for not being able to perform their motherly and wifely duties and, to some extent, for compromising the men's 'pillar' status by taking over their provider role (Resurreccion and Ha 2007; Locke et al. 2012a; Locke et al. 2014; Vu 2014; Hoang 2016). Tolerating men's vices is framed as a necessary act of sacrifice on the part of their wives, not only because endurance and self-sacrifice are core values of Vietnamese moral womanhood (see Gammeltoft 1999; Werner 2009; Hoang 2016), but also because of the essentialisation of men's primal urges, which are intensified by the lack of their wives' care and intimacy. Sexual infidelity, as has been observed in other Asian contexts, is seen as a manifestation of stay-behind men's sense of inadequacy and a means for them to reassert their masculinity and self-worth (Gamburd 2000; Piper 2008; Acedera and Yeoh 2019). What is reported by migration studies in Vietnam echoes findings from Indonesia and the Philippines, where migrant women not only turn a blind eye to their stay-behind husbands' extramarital sexual adventures, but also deliberately play down their economic success and assure their husbands' role as head of the family to allay the men's anxieties, avoid hurting their feelings and prevent possible cracks in their marriages (Pe-Pua 2003; Lam and Yeoh 2015, 2018; Acedera and Yeoh 2019).

The important role that women play in encouraging hegemonic masculinity performances and upholding patriarchal values is well established in the gender scholarship (Kimmel 2000; Schippers 2007). In the public discourse on the 'happy family' in Vietnam, women are held exclusively responsible for preserving family harmony, raising healthy and well-mannered children, and sustaining the marriage, even if these come at the cost of their own happiness and freedom (Hoang 2020b). This is affirmed by the 2020 survey on men and masculinities, which shows that 89 per cent of the surveyed men consider 'having a happy family' as the most important indicator of women's success in life, while 'having a high income' is rated as the most important indicator of men's success in life (ISDS 2020: 134). The higher stakes that women have in an intact and unblemished family explain why they strive to fulfil motherly and wifely duties throughout their migration process, tolerate their husbands' hypermasculine behaviours, and downplay the men's economic dependence by not closely monitoring their management of remittances or even by allowing them to squander remittances away on gambling and womanising (Vu and Agergaard 2012; Vu 2014; Hoang 2016). Stay-behind husbands, on the other hand, feel that their 'vices' are justifiable, not just because men are unable to control their high libido, but also because those guilty pleasures are the necessary compensation that enables them to cope with their wives' extended absence and the additional responsibilities at home.

CONCLUSION

The case of Vietnamese migrant households shows that men are neither rigid nor tyrannical as is often assumed, but judiciously oscillate between essentialised stereotypes about men and malleable standards of masculinity, tailoring their masculine behaviour as a strategy to deal with the tension between hegemonic masculinity ideals and the growing insecurities they experience in life. By performing these seemingly incoherent and incompatible fragments of the so-called 'mosaic masculinity' (Coles 2008: 238), they soften the demasculinising effects of women's migration, de-emphasise the elements of hegemonic masculinity that they are unable to conform to, and reformulate new standards of masculinity. Findings from Vietnam corroborate Choi's (2016) research on husbands of internal migrant women in China. Subaltern peasant men in her study accept and support their wives' labour migration as long as it is consistent with their material and familial aspirations, while rejecting financial dependence on their wives. The emergence of mosaic masculinity among subaltern men in the face of female labour migration and changing gender roles, therefore, does not necessarily signify a shift toward more egalitarian gender relations. Neoliberal globalisation might have altered the material relations embedded in patriarchy, but not its cultural meanings.

Despite the persistence of patriarchal values in Vietnamese society, research reveals a growing gap between hegemonic constructions of masculinity and men's increasingly diverse lived experiences. By placing men at the centre of my inquiry in this chapter, I have provided important comparative insights into the deep-seated structures of power and inequalities between men and women within the family. The 'gender doings' of stay-behind men in migrant households reflect the important influence of early childhood socialisation, and at the same time highlight the relationality, fluidity and spatio-temporality of gender (see also West and Zimmerman 1987; Hoang 2016). The active role that migrant women play in guaranteeing the dominant position of men underscores the need to incorporate the voices, subjectivities and experiences of both men and women in masculinities research. Femininity and masculinity exist in a relationship that is relational, complementary and hierarchical (Budgeon 2014), which means that migrant women have a vested interest in upholding hegemonic masculinity values if they are to maintain hegemonic femininity ideals. The case of Vietnam cautions against the tendency to attribute any unconventional gendered division of labour, particularly men's participation in care and domestic work, exclusively to female labour migration and the attendant empowerment of women. Because migration is selective, female labour migrants tend to come from households where gender boundaries, particularly in terms of labour division and decision-making, have already been disrupted before they leave home. In other words, the unconventional gender relations and familial structures that we see in migrant households tend to represent continuity rather than change.

NOTES

1. *Đổi mới* ('Renovation') refers to the economic reforms launched in Vietnam in 1986, moving the country from the command economy to the so-called socialist-oriented market economy. The most important reforms included the decollectivization of agricultural production, the permission of private ownership, and a multi-sector economy, and the liberalisation of foreign trade and investment.
2. Source: 'Xuất khẩu lao động đạt số lượng kỷ lục trong năm 2017' (Labour exports set a new record in 2017), http://thoibaotaichinhvietnam.vn/pages/xa-hoi/2018-01-16/xuat-khau-lao-dong-dat-so-luong-ky-luc-trong-nam-2017-52751.aspx, accessed 8 September 2018.
3. Source: 'VN to send 100,000 workers abroad annually', https://english.vietnamnet.vn/fms/society/193095/vn-to-send-100-000-workers-abroad-annually.html, accessed 8 September 2018.
4. Source: 'Xuất khẩu lao động: Một số thị trường đã mở cửa với lao động Việt Nam', https://laodong.vn/xa-hoi/xuat-khau-lao-dong-mot-so-thi-truong-da-mo-cua-voi-lao-dong-viet-nam-826834.ldo, accessed 3 September 2020.
5. Source: 'Xuất khẩu lao động: Một số thị trường đã mở cửa với lao động Việt Nam', https://laodong.vn/xa-hoi/xuat-khau-lao-dong-mot-so-thi-truong-da-mo-cua-voi-lao-dong-viet-nam-826834.ldo, accessed 3 September 2020
6. This is expressed through the proverb, '*Con không cha như nhà không nóc*' ('Children without the father are like a house without its roof').
7. Source: General Statistics Office, https://www.gso.gov.vn/default_en.aspx?tabid=774, accessed 13 October 2020.
8. Source: 'Dubious statistical methods skew Vietnam's unemployment rate', http://english.vietnamnet.vn/fms/business/108082/dubious-statistical-methods-skew-vietnam-s-unemployment-rate.html, accessed 21 June 2015.
9. CHAMPSEA is a mix-method study that surveyed members of more than 4000 migrant and non-migrant households in Indonesia, the Philippines, Thailand and Vietnam in 2008, and interviewed 200 caregivers of children 'left-behind' by migrant parents in the study countries in 2009. See Hoang (2016) for a detailed explanation of CHAMPSEA methodology.
10. Source: 'Labour force participation rate, female (% of female population aged 15+)', World Bank, https://data.worldbank.org/indicator/SL.TLF.CACT.FE.ZS, accessed 30 September 2020.

REFERENCES

Acedera, K.A. and B.S. Yeoh (2019). 'Until death do us part'? Migrant wives, left-behind husbands, and the negotiation of intimacy in transnational marriages. *Journal of Ethnic and Migration Studies* 46(16): 3508–3525.

Agergaard, J. and V.T. Thao (2011). Mobile, flexible, and adaptable: Female migrants in Hanoi's informal sector. *Population, Space and Place* 17(5): 407–420.
Angie, T.N. (2004). What's women's work? Male negotiations and gender reproduction in the Vietnamese garment industry. *Gender Practices in Contemporary Vietnam*: 210–235.
Bélanger, D. and X. Li (2009). Agricultural land, gender and kinship in rural China and Vietnam: A comparison of two villages. *Journal of Agrarian Change* 9(2): 204–230.
Bélanger, D. and K. Pendakis (2009). Daughters, work, and families in globalizing Vietnam. In M. Barbieri and D. Belanger (eds), *Reconfiguring Families in Contemporary Vietnam*. Stanford, CA: Stanford University Press: 265–297.
Bly, R. (2001). *Iron John: Men and Masculinity*. London, Rider.
Brittan, A. (1989). *Masculinity and Power*. Oxford, Basil Blackwell.
Budgeon, S. (2014). The dynamics of gender hegemony: Femininities, masculinities and social change. *Sociology* 48(2): 317–334.
Carruthers, A. (2002). The accumulation of national belonging in transnational fields: ways of being at home in Vietnam. *Identities: Global Studies in Culture and Power* 9(4): 423–444.
Choi, S.Y. (2016). Gendered pragmatism and subaltern masculinity in China: Peasant men's responses to their wives' labor migration. *American Behavioral Scientist* 60(5–6): 565–582.
Choi, S.Y.-P. and Y. Peng (2016). *Masculine Compromise: Migration, Family, and Gender in China*. Oakland, CA: University of California Press.
Chuang, J. (2016). Factory girls after the factory: Female return migrations in rural China. *Gender and Society* 30(3): 467-489.
Coles, T. (2008). Finding space in the field of masculinity: Lived experiences of men's masculinities. *Journal of Sociology* 44(3): 233–248.
Connell, R.W. (1995). *Masculinities*. Berkeley, CA: University of California Press.
Cunningham, W. and O. Pimhidzai (2018). *Vietnam's Future Jobs: Leveraging Mega-Trends for Greater Prosperity Vol. 2*. Washington, DC: World Bank.
Edwards, T. (2006). *Cultures of Masculinity*. London and New York: Routledge.
Faludi, S. (1999). *Stiffed: The Betrayal of the American Man*. New York: W. Morrow & Company.
Fan, C. (2003). Rural–urban migration and gender division of labour in transitional China. *International Journal of Urban and Regional Research* 27(1): 24–47.
Fan, C.C. (2004). Out to the city and back to the village: The experiences and contributions of rural women migrating from Sichuan and Anhui. In Arianne M. Gaetano and Tamara Jacka (eds), *On the Move: Women and Rural-to-Urban Migration in Contemporary China*. New York and Chichester, UK: Columbia University Press: 177–206.
Gamburd, M.R. (2000). *The Kitchen Spoon's Handle: Transnationalism and Sri Lanka's Migrant Housemaids*. Ithaca, NY and London: Cornell University Press.
Gammeltoft, T. (1999). *Women's Bodies, Women's Worries: Health and Family Planning in a Vietnamese Rural Community*. Richmond: Curzon Press.
Ge, J., et al. (2011). Return migration and the reiteration of gender norms in water management politics: Insights from a Chinese village. *Geoforum* 42(2): 133–142.
GSO (2011). *Vietnam Population and Housing Census 2009: Migration and Urbanisation in Vietnam – Patterns, Trends and Differentials*. Hanoi: Vietnam General Statistics Office.
GSO (2012). *Viet Nam Household Living Standards Survey 2012*. Hanoi: General Statistics Office.
GSO and UNFPA (2016). *The 2015 National Internal Migration Survey: Major Findings*. Hanoi: General Statistics Office and United National Population Fund.
Harvey, D. (2005). *A Brief History of Neoliberalism*. Oxford: Oxford University Press.
Hickey, G.C. (1964). *Village in Vietnam*. New Haven, CT and London: Yale University Press.
Hirschman, C. and H.M. Nguyen (2002). Tradition and change in Vietnamese family structure in the Red River Delta. *Journal of Marriage and Family* 64: 1063–1079.
Hoang, K.K. (2015). *Dealing in Desire: Asian Ascendancy, Western Decline, and the Hidden Currencies of Global Sex Work*. Berkeley, CA: University of California Press.
Hoang, L.A. (2011a). Gender identity and agency in migration decision making: Evidence from Vietnam. *Journal of Ethnic and Migration Studies* 37(9): 1441–1457.
Hoang, L.A. (2011b). Gendered networks and migration decision-making in Northern Vietnam. *Social and Cultural Geography* 12(5): 419–434.

Hoang, L.A. (2016). Moral dilemmas of transnational migration: Vietnamese women in Taiwan. *Gender and Society* 30(6): 890–911.
Hoang, L.A. (2017). Governmentality in Asian migration regimes: The case of labour migration from Vietnam to Taiwan. *Population, Space and Place* 23(3): 1–12.
Hoang, L.A. (2020a). Debt and (un) freedoms: The case of transnational labour migration from Vietnam. *Geoforum* 116: 33–41.
Hoang, L.A. (2020b). The Vietnam Women's Union and the contradictions of a socialist gender regime. *Asian Studies Review* 44(2): 297–214.
Hoang, L.A. (2020c). *Vietnamese Migrants in Russia: Mobility in Times of Uncertainty*. Amsterdam: Amsterdam University Press.
Hoang, L.A., et al. (2015). Transnational labour migration, changing care arrangements, and left-behind children's responses in Southeast Asia. *Children's Geographies* 13(3): 263–277.
Hoang, L.A. and B.S.A. Yeoh (2011). Breadwinning wives and 'left-behind' husbands: Men and masculinities in the Vietnamese transnational family. *Gender and Society* 25(6): 717–739.
Hoang, L.A. and B. Yeoh (2012). Sustaining families across transnational spaces: Vietnamese migrant parents and their left-behind children. *Asian Studies Review* 36(3): 307–327.
Hoang, L.A. and B. Yeoh (2015a). 'I'd do it for love or for money': Vietnamese women in Taiwan and the social construction of female migrant sexuality. *Gender, Place and Culture* 22(5): 591–607.
Hoang, L.A. and B.S.A. Yeoh (2015b). Transnational labour migration, debts, and family economics in Vietnam. *Transnational Labour Migration, Remittances and the Changing Family in Asia*. L.A. Hoang and B.S.A. Yeoh. Basingstoke, UK and New York: Palgrave Macmillan: 283–310.
Hoang, T.-A., et al. (2013). 'Because I am a man, I should be gentle to my wife and my children': positive masculinity to stop gender-based violence in a coastal district in Vietnam. *Gender and Development* 21(1): 81–96.
Horat, E. (2017). *Trading in Uncertainty: Entrepreneurship, Morality and Trust in a Vietnamese Textile-Handling Village*. Cham: Palgrave Macmillan.
Horton, P. and H. Rydstrom (2011). Heterosexual masculinity in contemporary Vietnam: Privileges, pleasures, and protests. *Men and Masculinities* 14(5): 542–564.
ISDS (2020). *Men and masculinities in a globalising Viet Nam*. Hanoi: Institute for Social Development Studies.
Jacka, T. (2014). *Rural Women in Urban China: Gender, Migration, and Social Change: Gender, Migration, and Social Change*. New York: Routledge.
James-Hawkins, L., et al. (2019). Norms of masculinity and the cultural narrative of intimate partner violence among men in Vietnam. *Journal of Interpersonal Violence* 34(21–22): 4421–4442.
Kabeer, N. and T.V.A. Tran (2000). *Leaving the Rice Fields but not the Countryside: Gender, Livelihood Diversification and Pro-Poor Growth in Rural Vietnam*. Geneva: United Nations Research Institute for Social Development.
Kimmel, M. (1987). Men's responses to Feminism at the turn of the century. *Gender and Society* 1(5): 261–285.
Kimmel, M.S. (2000). *The Gendered Society*. Oxford: Oxford University Press.
Lam, T. and B.S. Yeoh (2015). Long-distance fathers, left-behind fathers and returnee fathers: Changing fathering practices in Indonesia and the Philippines. In M.C. Inhorn, W. Chavkin and J.-A. Navarro (eds), *Globalized Fatherhoods: Emergent Forms and Possibilities in the New Millenium*. New York: Berghahn: 103–128.
Lam, T. and B.S. Yeoh (2018). Migrant mothers, left-behind fathers: The negotiation of gender subjectivities in Indonesia and the Philippines. *Gender, Place and Culture* 25(1): 104–117.
Leshkowich, A.M. (2015). *Essential Trade: Vietnamese Women in a Changing Marketplace*. Honolulu: University of Hawai'i Press.
Locke, C., et al. (2015). A mother who stays but cannot provide is not as good: Migrant mothers in Hanoi, Vietnam. In M. Unnithan-Kumar and S.K. Khanna (eds), *The Cultural Politics of Reproduction: Migration, Health and Family Making*. New York: Berghahn: 127–151.
Locke, C., et al. (2008). *The Institutional Context Influencing Rural–Urban Migration Choices and Strategies for Young Married Women and Men in Vietnam*. Norwich: Overseas Development Group, School of Development Studies, University of East Anglia.

Locke, C., et al. (2009). What does migration mean for relations with children and spouses left-behind? Reflections from young married men and women on the move in Vietnam. *The IUSSP 2009 Conference*. Marrakech.

Locke, C., et al. (2012a). Struggling to sustain marriages and build families: Mobile husbands/wives and mothers/fathers in Ha Noi and Ho Chi Minh City. *Journal of Vietnamese Studies* 7(4): 63–91.

Locke, C., et al. (2012b). Visiting marriages and remote parenting: Changing strategies of rural-urban migrants to Hanoi, Vietnam. *Journal of Development Studies* 48(1): 10–25.

Locke, C., et al. (2014). Mobile householding and marital dissolution in Vietnam: An inevitable consequence? *Geoforum* 51: 273–283.

Lewis, H., et al. (2015). Hyper-precarious lives: Migrants, work and forced labour in the Global North. *Progress in Human Geography* 39(5): 580–600.

Mann, S.L. (2011). *Gender and Sexuality in Modern Chinese History*. New York: Cambridge University Press.

Marsiglio, W. and J.H. Pleck (2005). Fatherhood and masculinities. In M. Kimmel, J. Hearn and R.W. Connell (eds), *Handbook of Studies on Men and Masculinities*. Thousand Oaks, CA; London; New Delhi: SAGE Publications: 249–269.

May, S. (2010). Bridging divides and breaking homes: Young women's lifecycle labour mobility as a family managerial strategy. *China Quarterly* 204: 899–920.

McKay, S. (2015). 'So they remember me when I'm gone': Remittances, fatherhood and gender relations of Filipino migrant men. *n* L.A. Hoang and B. Yeoh (eds), *Transnational Labour Migration, Remittances and the Changing Family in Asia*. Basingstoke: Palgrave Macmillan: 111–135.

Menjívar, C. (1999). The intersection of work and gender: Central American immigrant women and employment in California. *American Behavioral Scientist* 42(4): 601–627.

MOLISA (2010). *Vietnam Employment Trends 2010*. Hanoi: National Centre for Labour Market Forecast and Information, Bureau of Employment, Ministry of Labour, Invalids and Social Affairs.

Morgan, D. (2006). The crisis in masculinity. In Kathy Davis, Mary Evans and Judith Lorber (eds), *Handbook of Gender and Women's Studies*. London; Thousand Oaks, CA; New Delhi: SAGE Publications: pp. 109–123.

Nguyen, M.T. (2014). Translocal householding: Care and migrant livelihoods in a waste-trading community of Vietnam's Red River Delta. *Development and Change* 45(6): 1385–1408.

Nguyen, M.T. and C. Locke (2014). Rural–urban migration in Vietnam and China: Gendered householding, production of space and the state. *Journal of Peasant Studies* 41(5): 855–876.

Nguyen, T.D. and M. Ezaki (2005). Regional economic integration and its impacts on growth, poverty and income distribution: The case of Vietnam. *Review of Urban and Regional Development Studies* 17(3): 197–215.

Osella, F. and C. Osella (2000). Migration, money and masculinity in Kerala. *JRAI* 6: 117–133.

Parreñas, R.S. (2001). Mothering from a distance: Emotions, gender and inter-generational relations in Filipino transnational families. *Feminist Studies* 27(2): 361–390.

Parreñas, R.S. (2005). *Children of Global Migration: Transnational Families and Gendered Woes*. Stanford, CA: Stanford University Press.

Pe-Pua, R. (2003). Wife, mother, and maid: The triple role of Filipino domestic workers in Spain and Italy. In N. Piper and M. Roces (eds), *Wife or Worker? Asian Women and Migration*. Lanham, MD: Rowman & Littlefield Publishers: 157–180.

Piper, N. (2008). Feminisation of migration and the social dimensions of development: The Asian case. *Third World Quarterly* 29(7): 1287–1303.

Resurreccion, B.P. and T.V.K. Ha (2007). Able to come and go: Reproducing gender in female rural–urban migration in the Red River Delta. *Population, Space and Place* 13: 211–224.

Rydstrøm, H. (2003). *Embodying Morality: Growing up in Rural Northern Vietnam*. Honolulu: University of Hawaii Press.

Rydstrom, H. (2004). Female and male 'characters': Images of identification and self-identification for rural Vietnamese children and adolescents. In L. Drummond and H. Rydstrom (eds), *Gender Practices in Contemporary Vietnam*. Singapore: Singapore University Press: 74–95.

Rydstrøm, H. (2006). Masculinity and punishment: Men's upbringing of boys in rural Vietnam. *Childhood* 13(3): 329–348.

Santillán, D., et al. (2002). Limited equality: Contradictory ideas about gender and the implications for reproductive health in rural Vietnam. *Journal of Health Management* 4(2): 251–267.
Save The Children (2006). *Left Behind, Left Out: The Impact on Children and Families of Mothers Migrating for Work Abroad.* Sri Lanka, Save the Children.
Schewel, K. (2020). Understanding immobility: Moving beyond the mobility bias in migration studies. *International Migration Review* 54(2): 328–355.
Schippers, M. (2007). Recovering the feminine other: Masculinity, femininity, and gender hegemony. *Theory and Society* 36(1): 85–102.
Sheller, M. (2018). Theorising mobility justice. *Tempo Social* 30(2): 17–34.
Tacoli, C. (1999). International migration and the restructuring of gender asymmetries: Continuity and change among Filipino labour migrants in Rome. *International Migration Review* 33(3): 658–682.
Thai, H. (2006). Money and masculinity among low wage Vietnamese immigrants in transnational families. *International Journal of Sociology of the Family* 32(2): 247–271.
Thai, H. (2010). Towards a theory of money and masculinity in the Vietnamese transnational gift economy. Paper presented at the workshop *The Nexus of Migration and Masculinity in the Asian Context*, Asia Research Institute, National University of Singapore, Singapore, 15–16 July.
Thai, H. (2014). *Insufficient Funds: The Culture of Money in Low-Wage Transnational Families.* Stanford, CA, Stanford University Press.
Truong, H.C. (2009). A home divided: Work, body, and emotions in the post-Doi moi family. In M. Barbieri and D. Belanger (eds), *Reconfiguring Families in Contemporary Vietnam*. Stanford, CA: Stanford University Press: 298–328.
Vu, T.T. (2013). Making a living in rural Vietnam from (im) mobile livelihoods: A case of women's migration. *Population, Space and Place* 19(1): 87–102.
Vu, T.T. (2014). When the pillar of the home is shaking: Female labor migration and stay-at-home fathers in Vietnam. In M.C. Inhorn, W. Chavkin and J.-A. Navarro (eds), *Globalized Fatherhood*. New York: Berghahn: 129–151.
Vu, T.T. and J. Agergaard (2012). 'DOING FAMILY' Female migrants and family transition in rural Vietnam. *Asian Population Studies* 8(1): 103–119.
Werner, J. (2004). Managing womanhoods in the family: Gendered subjectivities and the state in the Red River Delta in Vietnam. In L. Drummond and H. Rydstrom (eds), *Gender Practices in Contemporary Vietnam*. Singapore: Singapore University Press: 26–46.
Werner, J. (2006). Between memory and desire: Gender and the remembrance of war in Doi moi Vietnam. *Gender, Place and Culture* 13(3): 303–315.
Werner, J. (2009). *Gender, Household and State in Post-Revolutionary Vietnam*. Oxford and New York: Routledge.
West, C. and D. Zimmerman (1987). Doing gender. *Gender and Society* 1(2): 125–151.
Yount, K.M., et al. (2016). Men's perpetration of intimate partner violence in Vietnam: Gendered social learning and the challenges of masculinity. *Men and Masculinities* 19(1): 64–84.
Zhang, N. (2013). Rural women migrant returnees in contemporary China. *Journal of Peasant Studies* 40(1): 171–188.

6. The transnationalisation of intimacy: family relations and changes in an age of global mobility and digital media

Earvin Charles Cabalquinto and Yang Hu

INTRODUCTION

The contemporary era is characterised by a rapid movement of people, objects, technologies, finances and digital information. Scholars have articulated this phenomenon through a 'new mobilities paradigm' (Sheller and Urry, 2006; Urry, 2007), pinpointing how various forms of corporeal and non-corporeal movements shape individual, familial and social life. In a mobile era, everyday practices have been transformed by social, economic, political and technological changes. Notably, the performance and experience of intimacy in the context of family life, as a form of practice (Jamieson, 1999, 2011; Morgan, 1996), has been reconfigured by expanding markets, national and border policies, as well as the advent of modern transportation and communication technologies. These developments highlight new ways in which personal and social relationships are reworked, adjusted and negotiated through personal choices, mobilities and media consumption. Against this backdrop, rapidly developing trends of global mobilities and digitalisation, which have moved far beyond the original context in which eminent sociologists such as Giddens (1992), Bauman (2003), Beck and Beck-Gernsheim (2002) and Cherlin (2009) theorised intimate family relationships, thus provide a great opportunity for us to rethink the transformation of intimacy in a transnational context.

This chapter offers a roadmap for understanding the performance, embodiment and experience of intimacy in the context of transnational family life. We develop the 'transnationalisation of intimacy' as an important perspective to grasp how familial intimacy – that is, practices enacted to maintain the intimate bonds between family members such as parents and children, intimate partners, spouses and relatives – is reconfigured and transformed at the intersection of global mobilities and digitalisation. This development follows three steps. Firstly, we critically assess existing theorisations of the transformation of intimacy and note their apparent lack of attention to transnationalism. Secondly, we consider how material, symbolic and technological forces engender and undermine intimate family life across borders. Here, the entanglement between a global market, national and border policies, and digitalisation of everyday life, has created transnational arrangements among family members (Bryceson and Vuorela, 2002; Parreñas, 2001). We discuss the role played by an asymmetrical distribution of and access to material and digital resources in enabling, structuring and constraining intimate practices of dispersed family members. Thirdly, we consider how the transnationalisation of intimacy (de) normalises and creates new forms of intimate family relationships and practices. To achieve our objectives, we bring together and review scholarship on intimacy, family life and digital cultures in a transnational context, with a critical focus on the implications of the processes of transnationalisation for understanding family changes.

THE TRANSFORMATION OF INTIMACY REVISITED: THE ROLE OF TRANSNATIONALISM?

Since the 1950s, decades of scholarship on the sociology of families and personal relationships has attempted to theorise how family relations have evolved hand in hand with broader social changes. In a pre-industrial setting, the conception of the family was defined based on composition and function, highlighting the definitive roles – reproductive, economic, and so forth – that each family member must enact (Murdock, 1965). However, the industrial revolution, further development of post-industrial societies, and the participation of women in the workforce, have brought about considerable changes to familial arrangements (see Chapter 2, this *Handbook*).

Scholars such as Beck and Beck-Gernsheim (2002) argue that family relationships have become increasingly 'individualised'. Here, the individualisation of personal relationships refers to 'social processes of separating out, delimiting, focusing on or giving place to [the] individual, allowing some differentiation from rather than being subsumed within social categories and collectives, and enabling room for manoeuvre rather than constraining through anchorage to traditional moorings' (Jamieson and Simpson, 2013, p. 18). A consequence of the trend of individualisation, as argued by sociologists such as Bauman (2003), Beck and Beck-Gernsheim (2002) and Giddens (1992), is the emergence of 'an ideology, philosophy or set of beliefs that celebrate or place particular significance on the individual' (Jamieson and Simpson, 2013, p. 18). From an individualisation perspective, the conception of family is no longer solely determined through its composition or definitive roles of its members, but through practices (Morgan, 1996). Family members perform 'familyhood' by 'doing' family through, for example, dining together, confiding, and providing support and care for each other. More recently, with the global mobility of family members, the meaning of family is understood as a product of obligations, cultural norms and highly mediated practices (Wilding, 2018).

In this chapter, we approach the family as 'practice-based' and we build on a range of scholarly works that highlight the role of intimacy in shaping family life. Intimacy, in this context, is defined by Jamieson (2011, p. 1) as 'the quality of closeness between people and the process of building this quality ... Closeness may also be physical, bodily intimacy, although an intimate relationship need not to be sexual and bodily and sexual contact can occur without intimacy'. Ultimately, we use the term 'familial intimacy' to refer to practices enacted to maintain a sense of closeness and familyhood between family members. Thus, non-familial forms of intimacy, such as casual sexual encounters, are beyond our remit.

The individualisation thesis has evolved in tandem with the development of post-materialism (Inglehart and Norris, 2003). For Giddens (1992), the movement of modern families away from the cornerstone of materialist, functional exchange and interdependence has given rise to what he termed the 'pure relationship', in which intimacy is no longer sustained by normative and material structures, but rather by equal, 'mutual self-disclosure and appreciation of each other's unique qualities' (Jamieson, 1999, p. 477). Similarly, writing of the changing institution of marriage, Cherlin (2009) posits that the foundation of modern marriages has shifted from functional subsistence to companionship between intimate partners, and then to the individualised pursuit of self-growth. In late modernity, intimate (family) relationships are characterised by increasingly liquid and fragile interpersonal bonds (Bauman, 2003).

Over the past few decades, transnational cross-border mobilities have been a major feature and driver of social changes across the globe (Urry, 2007), and intimate family relationships are increasingly forged and maintained in a transnational context (Wilding, 2018). Nevertheless, existing theorisations of the transformation of familial intimacy have yet to fully engage with the rapid and ongoing development of transnationalism. In the words of Beck and Beck-Gernsheim (2014, p. 549), 'family sociology has paid little attention to globalisation and cosmopolitanisation'. Although there is now a rich and diverse body of empirical research on transnational families, there is still insufficient theoretical development in understanding the implications of transnationalisation for changing forms and nature of family relationships and practices.

Our attempt to bring together the literature on migration studies and the sociology of families responds directly to the question raised by Beck and Beck-Gernsheim (2014, p. 558): 'what happens when globalisation hits home?' The cross-fertilisation between the two bodies of literature requires us to interrogate how transnational family relationships stretching across national borders reinforce or problematise the assumptions of post-materialist families, 'individualisation' and 'pure relationships'. Specifically, we ask what role materiality plays in shaping the practice of transnational familial intimacy. We explore how, if at all, 'doing' family in a transnational context unmoors people from the familial collective and normative familial roles in leading to an 'individualisation'. We examine what equal, mutual disclosure – the key notions underpinning Giddens's (1992) 'pure relationships' – mean for transnationally located family members. Finally, we discuss how the transnationalisation of intimacy (un) equally affects the changing ways in which people experience their family relationships.

MOBILITY REGIMES, INFRASTRUCTURES AND THE MAKING OF TRANSNATIONAL INTIMACY

Transnational families are borne out of cross-border migration. The entanglements of changing global markets, national and entrepreneurial policies, border control, and the rapid development of transportation and communication technologies, have shaped people's mobilities (Urry, 2007), helping to forge new family relationships beyond the confine of nation-states (for example, through transnational marriage) and for pre-existing family ties (for example, between parents and children, siblings, and so on) to stretch across borders (Bryceson and Vuorela, 2002). Transnationally located family members often express intimacy via money transfers, circulation of consumer goods (Parreñas, 2005) and digital device use (Madianou and Miller, 2012). Against this backdrop, our conceptualisation of the transnationalisation of intimacy considers the role of regimes, infrastructures and processes that produce, sustain and sometimes hinder transnational familial arrangements. As transnational family members often 'do' intimacy at a distance, void of physical co-presence, it is also key to understand how physical distance and efforts to bridge the distance constitute a key part of their familial arrangements (see Chapter 8, this *Handbook*).

Examining transnational familial intimacy necessitates a critical engagement with the role of various systems that engender, govern and potentially undermine practices of cross-border mobilities. It requires us to go beyond the familial institution and specific nation-states to consider the role of a broader, global system that produces the physical mobility and separation of family members. In this case, we need to situate our discussion in the new mobilities paradigm, highlighting how a range of mobility systems and infrastructures facilitate the stretching of relationships beyond borders (Sheller and Urry, 2006; Urry, 2007). Moreover, the paradigm also argues that interconnected and unevenly distributed mobility systems and infrastructures – transport, communication, and so forth – yield and reinforce hierarchy, division and exclusion (Sheller and Urry, 2006; Urry, 2007). Noting how the new mobilities paradigm maps the intertwined systems across the world and their influences on the conduct of transnational family relationships, we must move away from approaching intimate familial practices from the perspective of methodological nationalism (Wimmer and Schiller, 2009), which privileges the dominant role of national and local contexts, systems and processes in shaping personal and social experiences. Rather, we need to approach intimate family life as produced in a transnational social space (Hannam et al., 2006).

By reflecting on the material and symbolic systems that govern transnational mobilities (Sheller and Urry, 2006), we first build the conceptualisation of the transnationalisation of intimacy on 'regimes' (Glick Schiller and Salazar, 2013). Glick Schiller and Salazar (2013, p. 189) defined a 'regime' as 'the role both of individual states and of changing international regulatory and surveillance administrations that affect individual mobility'. For instance, migration policies (Glick Shiller and Salazar, 2013) and profiling technological and border systems (Shamir, 2005) may discriminate migrants based on class, age, gender and ethnicity, resulting in containment or entrapment in particular spaces and territories (Turner, 2010). The stasis of certain family members vis-à-vis the mobility of others can then produce the transnationalisation of ties and linkages (Bryceson and Vuorela, 2002). In a sense, as noted by Shamir (2005), regimes demonstrate how globalisation consists of various systemic patterns and processes of exclusion. Therefore, examining transnational family arrangements involves and necessitates a critical engagement with a transnational mobility regime, which classifies, segregates and moors people and their family relations through policies or regulatory processes (Turner, 2007) and profiling technologies (Shamir, 2005).

As hegemonic norms about the family permeate mobility regimes, it is crucial to note that not all forms of familial intimacy enjoy a similar level of legitimacy under the same mobility regime. For example, mobility regimes and migration policies in Europe continue to give prominence to and reinforce marriage and the nuclear family as a normative, legitimate form of family (Wray, 2016). Against this backdrop, unmarried cohabitation holds far less currency than marriage when it comes to transnational migration, as family migrants' access to a temporary family visa, permanent residence and citizenship tends to be legitimised on the ground of marriage more than unmarried cohabitation (Probert, 2012). Capitalising on the normative nuclear family model, the United Kingdom's migration regime, for example, insufficiently recognises intergenerational and extended family relations beyond the nuclear family (Tu, 2019). Therefore, as different mobility regimes are closely shaped by their respective cultures and family systems, members of transnational families often experience a normative disjuncture because the legitimacy of distinct dimensions of their family relations come to be challenged and reconstituted as they move across national borders.

Further advancing our understanding of the transnationalisation of intimacy requires an engagement with the infrastructural turn in migration studies (Lindquist and Xiang, 2018; Xiang and Lindquist, 2014). According to Xiang and Lindquist (2014), migrant mobilities are typically produced and undermined by an assemblage of non-human and human actors, which can be categorised into five components: the commercial (for example, intermediary agents), the regulatory (for example, state apparatus and procedures for documentation, licensing and training), the technological (for example, transport and communication), the humanitarian (for example, non-government and overseas organisations) and the social (for example, migrant networks). For instance, in Asian labour migration, infrastructures may refer to passports, migration documents, brokers and agents, work permits and policies, and so forth (Lin et al., 2017). Compared with the concept of mobility regime, the infrastructural perspective covers a broader range of components (for example, commercial institutions, network, and communication technologies) that channel transnational migration, highlighting the holistic assemblage of and interplay between different infrastructural components.

Taken together, the mobility regime and infrastructure perspectives complement each other in helping us to understand how familial intimacy is produced, facilitated, conditioned and curtailed in a transnational context, particularly in terms of people's differential access to transnational migration. While existing literature on migration infrastructure has mostly focused on labour migration, several recent studies have begun unpacking the role of various infrastructures underpinning transnational family relations (Brandhorst, 2020; Hu et al., 2020; Merla et al., 2020; see Chapters 14 and 16, this *Handbook*). Here, the focus revolves around how numerous and interconnected systems, such as institutional contexts (Kilkey and Merla, 2014), gender norms and expectations (Baldassar and Merla, 2014), and technological landscapes (Cabalquinto, 2018a; Baldassar and Merla, 2014; Wilding, 2006), shape transnational familial intimacy.

Take, for example, the well-studied case of labour migration from the Philippines. The out-migration of Filipino workers from their homeland and the production of transnational families are dependent on and shaped by mobility regimes and infrastructures. In host countries such as the United States and Saudi Arabia, the 'denationalisation policies' facilitate the recruitment, selection and employment of cheap labour, often in a gendered and classed manner, birthing the transnationalisation of family life (Parreñas, 2015). In this process, brokers, agents, training centres, employers and various border agencies coalesce to 'infrastructure' the cross-border mobility of Filipino workers (Guevarra, 2010; Rodriguez, 2010). However, through 'renationalisation of policies', labour migrants and their families are often denied access to (full) work rights, citizenship and welfare services in their host country (Parreñas, 2015). These conditions can place migrants in temporary or long-term separation from their family members.

Mobility regimes and infrastructures, along with their stratifying effects in the creation of transnational families, work in a broader context of global capitalism (Robinson, 2004). The political economy of transnational mobilities suggests that material and capital transactions permeate the motivation and consequence for people to 'do' transnational families. For example, Polish cleaners working in German households, and Filipino nannies taking care of American babies, are driven by an aspiration to achieve economic mobility through transnational migration (Beck and Beck-Gernsheim, 2014). As the migrants send remittances back home, the functional, material exchanges in these families extend across national borders. Meanwhile, a new global wave of privately sponsored international education mobility is only made possible through the sustained exchange of economic and other resources between transnationally located family members (Brooks and Waters, 2011; Ma, 2020). Here, it is important to note that global labour and education mobilities, as well as transnational familial intimacy resulting from such mobilities, are as much driven by the uneven distribution of resources across the world as by the post-colonial cultural imaginaries of the world underpinning the construction of 'desirable' destinations (Constable, 2003; Hu, 2017). Therefore, transnational family relations resulting from phenomena such as the 'global care chain' and transnational education mobility are closely embedded in the materiality and symbolic hierarchies fashioned by global capitalism.

DIGITALISATION AND THE MEDIATION OF TRANSNATIONAL INTIMACY

Once transnational family relationships are established through mobility regimes and infrastructures, such relationships are often sustained and mediated through digital communication technologies (Baldassar et al., 2007; Cabalquinto, 2018a; Madianou and Miller, 2012; McKay, 2012). Significantly, the multiple affordances of digital communication technologies and diverse modes of communicative routines mobilise the transnationalisation of familial intimacy.

Technologies shape the nature, quality and dynamics of intimacy between transnationally located family members. A key aspect of the transnationalisation of familial intimacy is the use of smartphones, social media platforms, mobile applications and broadband infrastructures in mediating intimate family lives. Since its mass adoption, mobile phones have been considered an 'intimate object' of everyday life (Fortunati, 2002). They are used to convey intimate expressions, a unique self, and to exchange personalised information (Fortunati, 2002; Lasén, 2004). In transnational families, ubiquitous digital communication technologies help to overcome the challenge of physical separation. Historically, migrants relied on letters and cassette tapes for intimate expressions (Madianou and Miller, 2011). The advent of mobile phones enabled the consumption of prepaid calling cards, serving as a social glue in maintaining a relatively costly connection (Vertovec, 2004). Subsequently, the prevalence of computers led to the utilisation of chat rooms and emailing services (Baldassar et al., 2007; Wilding, 2006). The further advancement of mobile networks, apps and platforms not only provided migrants with new modes of transnational communication, but also reduced the cost of such communication.

Transnational family life is performed, embodied and negotiated through a plethora of rapidly evolving and ubiquitous digital communication technologies. Many studies have highlighted this by coining a range of terms, including 'long-distance intimacy' (Parreñas, 2005), 'virtual intimacy' (Wilding, 2006) and 'ambient intimacy' (Hjorth et al., 2012). Of particular relevance to the transnationalisation of intimacy, different media use, informed by a range of emotions (Boccagni and Baldassar, 2015), may produce different levels of disclosure and intimate affect (Wilding, 2006). Notably, the concept of 'polymedia' proposed by Madianou and Miller (2012) proves useful in examining the intricacies of transnational family lives embedded in a web of communication technologies and affordances. Madianou and Miller (2012) have highlighted the role of personalised communication technologies in enabling both closeness and distance among transnational family members, and how these outcomes for transnational linkages are situated within social and familial structures as well as domains of technological access and competencies.

More recently, several scholars have studied the enactment of transnational intimacy in a polymedia environment, uncovering the possibilities, tensions and negotiations in digital practices for sustaining transnational intimacy. Digital media use often produces co-presence routines (Nedelcu and Wyss, 2016), contributing to producing transnational affective capital or a sense of belonging and ontological security (Leurs, 2014). More specifically, multiple mobile platforms, such as WhatsApp (O'Hara et al., 2014), Facebook (Acedera and Yeoh, 2018; Cabalquinto, 2018a; Mintarsih, 2019) and Skype (Marino, 2019), have been used to produce mundane, random and personalised content and to maintain transnational familial intimacy (Hjorth et al., 2020).

In addition to using diverse platforms, transnational family members also develop a diverse range of personalised and carefully crafted practices to manage their emotional distance and sustain transnational familial intimacy (Alinejad, 2019; Madianou, 2019). For example, migrants select and share carefully a range of customised contents with their family members on social media to protect their autonomy and privacy while remaining connected beyond borders (Alinejad, 2019, 2021). Disconnective practices such as not sharing, hiding or removing information are often deployed (Alinejad, 2019; Acedera and Yeoh, 2018; Cabalquinto, 2018a; Hu et al., 2020). In some cases, despite a lack of access to modern communication technologies, refugees reproduce transnational familial intimacy via 'family imaginary' by collating photographs of dispersed family members and photoshopping and putting them in a collage (Robertson et al., 2016). In moments of navigating physical immobility and forced family separation, smartphones function as 'pocket archives' through which migrants and refugees reconstruct transnational intimate connections via synchronous and asynchronous modes of communication (Leurs, 2017; Smets, 2019). These practices illustrate the diverse ways in which transnational familial intimacy is produced and negotiated in a networked environment.

To understand the implications of digitalisation for transnational familial intimacy, it is therefore important to pay attention to the types of communicating via a range of digital devices and online platforms (Alinejad, 2019, 2021; Madianou, 2019). Specifically, we need to ask whether people have access to communicative technologies, to what technologies they have access, what the nature of the access is, and the contexts in which connections are established, sustained and negotiated. Certainly, technological apparatuses can mediate, enhance or undermine intimate experiences and sociality (Paasonen, 2017). However, differential technological access and competencies are crucial to generating distinct intimate expressions and affective experiences (Alinejad, 2019; Madianou, 2019). Cross-border intimate communication is not only moulded by the mobility, networked connectivity and ubiquity of digital technologies; it is also influenced by gender and locality (Hjorth, 2011, 2015), familial duties and obligations, and individual capacities (Baldassar et al., 2007). As Elliott and Urry (2010, p. 101) argued, digital communication technologies are constitutive of 'mobile intimacy', which 'involves routine, ongoing, mundane and continual communicational orderings of relationships and family'.

STRUCTURAL INEQUALITIES, DIGITAL RUPTURES AND INTERRUPTED TRANSNATIONAL INTIMACY

While thus far we have discussed how mobility regimes, infrastructures and, particularly, communication technologies have enabled people to develop and maintain transnational family relationships, it is equally important to examine how they can constrain and disrupt transnational familial intimacy. As discussed earlier, mobility regimes and infrastructures structure the mobilities and settlement of migrants in their country of destination. Migration legislation and policies on citizenship and social welfare tend to treat migrants as productive subjects and limit their access to essential family rights (Brandhorst, 2020; Merla et al., 2020). For instance, migrants often have limited rights to reunite with their family members in the host countries, and their rights to form a family through pathways such as unmarried cohabitation, marriage and adoption are closely scrutinised and censored by their host countries (Hu, 2016; Papademetriou and Sumption, 2011). Migration policies may also limit the temporary visit or settlement of migrants' left-behind family members (Baldassar et al., 2007; Brandhorst, 2020). While restrictive migration regimes often produce lengthy or even permanent family separation, many transnational family members are found to reclaim family life through sending remittances and care packages to fulfil essential family functions and alleviate the emotional burden of family separation (Parreñas, 2005, 2015).

The reliance on communication technologies to sustain transnational familial intimacy can also be challenging and frustrating. Firstly, due to the uneven financial status of family members (Baldassar, 2008; Madianou and Miller, 2012; Parreñas, 2005), the circulation of remittances and care through mobile device use can place extra financial pressure and demands on migrants. Recent studies have shown how transnational communication can be exploited by left-behind family members, to ask for money and extra gifts from their migrant family members (Cabalquinto, 2020; McKay, 2007; Singh et al., 2012). Secondly, asymmetrical technological landscapes between the home and host countries can produce differential communicative capacities. For example, for some migrants, stable internet access may be limited in their areas of origin (Cabalquinto, 2018b; Madianou and Miller, 2012; Parreñas, 2005; Wilding, 2006). Some left-behind family members may not have access to broadband-equipped digital devices and online platforms (Brandhorst, 2017; Madianou and Miller, 2012). Moreover, a lack of technological competency in using mobile devices and online platforms can considerably constrain one's communicative capacities (Baldassar, 2008; Cabalquinto, 2018b; Madianou and Miller, 2012). Notably, according to the International Telecommunication Union (2019), 3.6 billion people remain offline worldwide, and a majority of them are found in low- and middle-income countries and regions. Yet, resource scarcity and deprivation are likely reasons for people to out-migrate from these countries and regions, thus birthing transnational family relations. As a result, migrants from low- and middle-income countries and their family members staying in the country of origin are particularly likely to experience interrupted familial intimacy.

Even when people have access to up-to-date communication technologies, such technologies have a fixed set of parameters. Certainly, digital media use allows dispersed family members to convene, exchange information and generate a sense of intimacy. However, smartphone or social media use does not constitute a qualitatively equivalent alternative for in-person contact (Hu and Qian, 2021; Madianou and Miller, 2012). Several studies have shown how transnational family members longed for physical expressions of intimacy (Cabalquinto, 2018a; Madianou, 2012; Madianou and Miller, 2012), and such longing is particularly prominent on a much larger scale during the COVID-19 pandemic in the context of lockdowns and border closure (Nehring and Hu, 2021). Crises such as illness and death in transnational families are particularly telling of the limitations of communication technologies (Baldassar et al., 2007). Therefore, digital devices and platforms are often referred to as 'sunny day technologies' (Wilding, 2006). Despite technological advancements, it is still necessary for individuals to travel in order to maintain close family bonds and experience familial intimacy that is bound with socially, culturally and symbolically significant places and events (Urry, 2002).

While communication technologies and digital platforms often operate on a transnational scale, they are also interpenetrated by state regulations and censorship. For example, the state censorship of mainstream platforms such as Google, Facebook, Twitter and WhatsApp in mainland China (King et al., 2014) means that Chinese migrants enjoy a limited repertoire of technological affordances to communicate with their families. Amid the United States–Sino trade war, attempts made by the Trump administration to ban TikTok and WeChat in the United States (Paul, 2020) suggest that the mediation of transnational intimacy between family members is susceptible to not only national policies but also international relations between nation-states.

Although digital technologies facilitate the maintenance of a sense of familyhood, such digitally mediated familial intimacy can also reinforce stringent familial norms and gendered expectations despite physical separation (Cabalquinto, 2018b; Hu, 2016; Madianou and Miller, 2012; Parreñas, 2015). For instance, digital connectivity has created distinct 'transnational mothering' and 'transnational fathering' practices (Parreñas, 2001, 2008). Here, communicative practices are typically influenced by an individual's conformity to gendered familial expectations (Madianou, 2012; Parreñas, 2015). In some cases, overseas migrants conform to familial expectations by acting the role of a filial family member: one who is readily available, supportive and self-sacrificing for the family's needs (Cabalquinto, 2018b).

Digitally mediated transnational familial intimacy can be charged with communicative tensions. For example, overseas mothers may feel ambivalent about their ability to provide care and financial support from afar because their left-behind children do not completely understand their physical absence and virtual presence (Madianou, 2012). Moreover, ambivalent experiences can also be compounded when uneven technological access and literacies impede the ability of overseas migrants and their left-behind family members in meeting familial duties, such as managing tasks via constant communication (Cabalquinto, 2018b). Nevertheless, these outcomes reflect digital connection as both a blessing and a burden in sustaining transnational family ties (Horst, 2006, 2013). By closely examining the ruptures in digital media use, we can unpack how inequalities exist in the transnationalisation of familial intimacy (Goggin and Hjorth, 2009). Indeed, structural and technological forces, at the same time, facilitate, destabilise and disrupt the performance and experience of transnational familial intimacy.

THE TRANSNATIONALISATION OF INTIMACY: A MOSAIC OF CONTINUITY AND CHANGE

As family relationships increasingly stretch across national borders and become heavily structured by mobility regimes and infrastructures, as well as mediated by digital technologies, it is crucial to consider how the transnationalisation of intimacy has reconfigured the familial institution. Early sociologists suggested that traditional family relations were predicated on the materialist foundation of resource exchange and functional interdependence (Murdock, 1965), but the foundation has since been eroded by processes such as societal modernisation and the gender revolution (Cherlin, 2009; Giddens, 1992). However, the question remains as to how, if at all, the transnationalisation of familial intimacy has changed family forms, norms and practices.

Extensive research has shown that migrant mobilities, which are responsible for creating transnational families, are partly driven by motivations for material gains for the family (Parreñas, 2001, 2005; Urry, 2007; Wilding, 2018). For example, it is not uncommon that labour or marriage migration is directly driven by people's aspirations to economic and symbolic mobility on a global stage (Constable, 2003; Xiang and Lindquist, 2014). Transnational family relations are often maintained by the exchange of gifts and remittances between family members (Hondagneu-Sotelo and Avila, 1997; Wilding, 2018). Although the transnationalisation of familial intimacy has substantially changed the temporal and spatial modalities of practices enacted by family members to maintain a sense of closeness and familyhood (Beck and Beck-Gernsheim, 2014), it does not seem to have substantially altered the material exchange and functional interdependence between family members (Bryceson, 2020). As we have shown, materiality also permeates the infrastructuring process responsible for forging transnational familial intimacy (Lin et al., 2017; Lindquist and Xiang, 2018), and for sustaining the mediated means through which family relationships are maintained (Cabalquinto, 2018b; Madianou and Miller, 2012).

The highly gendered pattern of the transnational division of reproductive labour means that the gendered division of domestic and care labour persists to a large extent in transnational families. In the 'global care chain', for example, the international division of productive and reproductive labour serves to reinforce the (gendered) division of labour between family members, thus reinforcing their interdependence (Parreñas, 2015). The difficulty of providing in-person care and parenting from afar means that migrants may be free from the vicissitudes of familial responsibilities such as in-person housework and physical care provision (Bryceson, 2020). But this does not mean that migrants are free from care responsibilities altogether. As Parreñas (2005, 2015) has shown, what migrant mothers miss out on in terms of the provision of physical care is often compensated by their performance of mediated forms of care, such as supervising their children's schoolwork and providing emotional support online. In his study, Kyle (2000) finds that Ecuadorian male migrants in New York and Europe deliberately restrict the information they share about their migrant lives with their left-behind wives and families, as a strategy of gender control to maintain their sense of masculinity. It is clear from extensive research that the transnationalisation of familial intimacy has not substantially altered gender norms and relations in the familial institution (Lim, 2014; Parreñas, 2015).

Nevertheless, there is also some evidence that transnational migration provides a creative solution for people to lift anchor from familial norms imposed at their places of origin (Sassen, 2003). In his research on Chinese–Western intermarriage, Hu (2016) finds that transnational migration enabled some professional Chinese women to evade social pressure imposed by the stigma of 'leftover women', which vilifies their socioeconomic achievements and singlehood. In this case, transnational migration provides the women with a viable way to individualise their choice of whether and when to marry. While forced hypogamy – highly educated professional women being normatively compelled to marry a man of a lower educational and socioeconomic status as a way of maintaining male domination in the family – is not uncommon in patriarchal societies such as China and India (Hu and Qian, 2019; Lin et al., 2020), transnational migration has certainly created a pathway for some people to individualise their spouse selection and marital strategy.

Going beyond a heteronormative framing of family and intimacy, recent research has focused on lesbian, gay, bisexual, transgender and queer (LGBTQ) transnational families. For example, scholars have examined Russian queer diasporas in London and Berlin, showing that in countries where non-heterosexual relationships are criminalised or marginalised, transnational migration helps LGBTQ individuals to evade hegemonic heteronormativity and potential persecution (Mole, 2018; Mole et al., 2014). An emerging body of research on LGBTQ families has shed new light on the families' use of transnational surrogacy as a non-traditional pathway of reproduction and family formation, with particular attention to its ethical and inequality implications (Brainer et al., 2020). Despite a growing body of research on gender in transnational families, sexuality has yet to receive due scholarly attention. As a result, important questions such as how LGBTQ people negotiate sexuality, heteronormativity, and family roles and norms in a transnational context remain unanswered, which should be an important direction for future research.

The transnationalisation of familial intimacy, particularly via the intensified use of digital media, also engenders asymmetries between one's display of familial intimacy online and practice of intimacy offline. The mediated means of maintaining transnational family relations foreground the performative quality of intimacy (Cabalquinto, 2018a, 2018b). As members of transnational families communicate their respective lives across distances by sharing information in a family WhatsApp chat group, on Facebook and via Skype, the representation of their intimate family lives is often self-censored and thus partial (Alinejad, 2019; Cabalquinto, 2018a; Madianou, 2019). In this sense, mediated communication between family members enables strategic and selective rather than equal and full disclosure between family members, as predicted by Giddens (1992). Furthermore, the asymmetries in access to communication technologies and differential digital literacy between family members also mean that equal disclosure is practically difficult (Madianou and Miller, 2012), if not impossible, even if people had a desire to achieve full mutual disclosure.

In the context of communicative asymmetries, studies found that the mediation of transnational familial intimacy often centres on the re-animation and reliving of imagined family rituals, which in turn serves to reify rather than challenge traditional family norms (Cabalquinto, 2018b; Hu, 2016). In their recent study on how Chinese international students in the United Kingdom and their parents in China communicate online during the COVID-19 pandemic, Hu et al. (2020) show that in order to maintain a sense of normalcy, the students and parents are found to strategically express and suppress information and emotions to strike a delicate balance between appearing concerned, calm and authentic in 'doing' transnational family relationships. Indeed, the performance of normative families and normalcy in a transnational context often involves intense emotional mobilisation (Quah, 2018; Vermot, 2015). Therefore, it is pivotal for scholars to account for the emotional contour of the transnationalisation of intimacy.

In sum, the transnationalisation of familial intimacy is characterised by a mosaic pattern of family change and continuity. It has brought about considerable changes to how people practise family relationships, but in many ways, it has not changed the (gendered) norms and materialistic functions underpinning the familial institution. As we have shown, this mosaic pattern of family change in a transnational context features prominently a divergence between intimacy in practice, in terms of substantially reconfigured ways of 'doing' family relations, and intimacy in ideation, in terms of largely fixated family norms which people conjure up and (re)live to maintain a sense of 'familyhood'. Moreover, insofar as transnational family members selectively represent their lives online to reproduce their (imagined) family lives attached to their places of origin, while pursuing individualised life biographies offline, the process of transnationalisation is also likely to create internally paradoxical intimate subjects under the condition of mosaic transnational family change.

CONCLUSION

This chapter contributes to the reconceptualisation of the conduct of family relationships and intimacy in a global and digital era. Over the past few decades, eminent social theorists such as Giddens (1992), Bauman (2003), Cherlin (2009) and Beck and Beck-Gernsheim (2002, 2014) have predicted that in late modernity, intimate family relations would become more fluid, individualised, tumultuous and post-materialist. Although the rise of global mobilities and transnationalism has been a characterising feature of 'late modernity' (Urry, 2007), theorisations of the transformation of familial intimacy have not typically engaged with processes of transnationalisation. Arguably, the present-day state of intimacy between family members cannot be understood without probing its transnational and mediated dimensions. Filling this pertinent gap, we have developed the 'transnationalisation of intimacy' as a conceptual lens to understand the conditions, embodiment, practice and social consequences of transnational family relations.

The transnationalisation of intimacy encourages us to consider the role played by mobility regimes, infrastructures and digital environments in shaping transnational and intimate family relationships. A complex set of political, legal, policy, social, cultural and economic forces coalesce to produce transnational mobilities that are responsible for creating transnational families (cf. Lin et al., 2017; Lindquist and Xiang, 2018). Furthermore, the interpenetration of mobility regimes and infrastructures into the birthing and doing of transnational family relations suggests that materiality plays a central role in the transnationalisation of familial intimacy. In other words, transnational mobilities are often motivated by (anticipated) economic and symbolic mobility, and intimate familial bonds spanning across borders often sustain the transfer and conversion of economic and other forms of resources.

In situating the enactment of transnational intimacy in a networked environment, we have shown how the rapid development of communication technologies brings about communicative benefits, challenges and negotiations for dispersed family members. Certainly, digital connectivity has helped family members to maintain a sense of intimacy across borders. However, uneven social and technological structures can often produce tensions in transnational family lives. In order to manage and nurture family relations, disrupted transnational familial intimacies are often repaired through diverse personalised communicative tactics of boundary making.

We have also highlighted that as family members' capacity to forge and maintain a sense of intimacy relies on very material and not so mobile facilities and infrastructures (Beck and Beck-Gernsheim, 2014), the transnationalisation of intimacy is close embedded in an unequal terrain of globalisation. Thus, while scholars such as Giddens (1992) and Bauman (2003) argued that the transformation of intimacy is borne out of post-materialist conditions in late modernity, we have illustrated the selective nature of and inequalities inherent in such transformations. It is likely that mobility regimes and infrastructures will continue to evolve to accommodate and favour the needs, desires and aspirations of certain privileged bodies, groups and institutions (Glick Schiller and Salazar, 2013). Notably, as we enter an era of 'big data', the intertwining of intimate familial practices and digital technologies has fuelled new forms of commercialisation and a rapid development of platform capitalism on a global scale (Srnicek, 2017). Technology companies and social media platforms are seen to accrue an increasing amount of data on people's intimate lives (van Dijck, 2013). In so doing, they not only benefit from the operations of the migration industry for connective services for remittances, sending care packages and philanthropy (Cabalquinto and Wood-Bradley, 2020; Peile, 2014), but also profit from colonising the intimate domain of people's lives. In this new form of digital colonisation, migrants, along with their families and networks, are subject to new forms of control and exploitation (Peile, 2014).

In conclusion, we have demonstrated the value of the cross-fertilisation between the literature on the sociology of families and that on transnational mobilities and communication. The transnationalisation of intimacy lays bare the intimate fabrics of transnationalism and underlines the importance of understanding globalisation not only as a grand scheme of social change but also as changes taking place through the nuanced vicissitudes of everyday intimate lives. The transnationalisation of intimacy also reflects critically on methodological nationalism, in both explicit and implicit forms, in the theorisation of global family change. It is clear from this chapter that the transformation of familial intimacy cannot possibly be understood without references to incessant mobilities and interconnections across nation-state borders. In a globalising world, people's intimate family lives are interpenetrated by transnationalism no matter whether they are on the move or remain immobile, as the transnationalisation of intimacy takes place here, there, in-between and everywhere.

REFERENCES

Acedera, K.A., and Yeoh, B.S.A. (2018). 'Making time': Long-distance marriages and the temporalities of the transnational family. *Current Sociology*. doi:10.1177/0011392118792927.

Alinejad, D. (2019). Careful co-presence: The transnational mediation of emotional intimacy. *Social Media + Society*, 5(2), 1–11.

Alinejad, D. (2021). Techno-emotional mediations of transnational intimacy: Social media and care relations in long-distance Romanian families. *Media, Culture and Society*, 43(3), 444–459.

Baldassar, L. (2008). Missing kin and longing to be together: Emotions and the construction of co-presence in transnational relationships. *Journal of Intercultural Studies*, 29(3), 247–266.

Baldassar, L., Baldock, C., and Wilding, R. (2007). *Families Caring across Borders: Migration, Ageing and Transnational Caregiving*. Basingstoke: Palgrave Macmillan.

Baldassar, L., and Merla, L. (2014). Introduction: Transnational family caregiving through the lens of circulation. In L. Baldassar and L. Merla (eds), *Transnational Families, Migration and the Circulation of Care: Understanding Mobility and Absence in Family Life* (pp. 3–24). New York: Routledge.

Bauman, Z. (2003). *Liquid Love: On the Frailty of Human Bonds*. Cambridge: Polity.

Beck, U., and Beck-Gernsheim, E. (2002). *Individualization: Institutionalized Individualism and its Social and Political Consequences*. Thousand Oaks, CA: SAGE.

Beck, U., and Beck-Gernsheim, E. (2014). The global chaos of love: Toward a cosmopolitan turn in the sociology of love and families. In M. Richards, J.L. Scott and J. Treas (eds), *The Wiley Blackwell Companion to the Sociology of Families* (pp. 547–559). Oxford: Wiley Blackwell.

Boccagni, P., and Baldassar, L. (2015). Emotions on the move: Mapping the emergent field of emotion and migration. *Emotion, Space and Society*, 16, 73–80.

Brainer, A., Moore, M.R., and Banerjee, P. (2020). Race and ethnicity in the lives of LGBTQ parents and their children: Perspectives from and beyond North America. In A.E. Goldberg and K.R. Allen (eds), *LGBTQ-Parent Families* (pp. 85–103). Cham: Springer.

Brandhorst, R.M. (2017). 'A lo lejos' – Aging in place and transnational care in the case of transnational migration between Cuba and Germany. *Transnational Social Review*, 7(1), 56–72.

Brandhorst, R.M. (2020). A regimes-of-mobility-and-welfare approach: The impact of migration and welfare policies on transnational social support networks of older migrants. *Australian Journal of Family Research*, *3*, 1–19.

Brooks, R., and Waters, J.L. (2011). *Student Mobilities, Migration and the Internationalization of Higher Education*. New York: Palgrave Macmillan.

Bryceson, D.F. (2020). Transnational families negotiating migration and care life cycles across nation-state borders. *Journal of Ethnic and Migration Studies*, *45*(16), 3042–3064.

Bryceson, D.F., and Vuorela, U. (2002). Transnational families in the twenty-first century. In D.F. Bryceson and U. Vuorela (eds), *The Transnational Family: New European Frontiers and Global Networks* (pp. 3–30). Oxford: Berg.

Cabalquinto, E.C. (2018a). Ambivalent intimacies: Entangled pains and gains through Facebook use in transnational family life. In A.S. Dobson, B. Robards and N. Carah (eds), *Digital Intimate Publics and Social Media* (pp. 247–263). Cham: Springer.

Cabalquinto, E.C. (2018b). 'We're not only here but we're there in spirit': Asymmetrical mobile intimacy and the transnational Filipino family. *Mobile Media and Communication*, *6*(2), 1–16.

Cabalquinto, E.C. (2020). Elastic carework: The cost and contradictions of mobile caregiving in a transnational household. *Continuum*, *34*(1), 133–145.

Cabalquinto, E.C., and Wood-Bradley, G. (2020). Migrant platformed subjectivity: Rethinking the mediation of transnational affective economies via digital connectivity services. *International Journal of Cultural Studies*, *23*(5), 787–802.

Cherlin, A.J. (2009). *The Marriage-Go-Round: The State of Marriage and the Family in America Today*. New York: Alfred A. Knopf.

Constable, N. (2003). *Romance on a Global Stage: Pen Pals, Virtual Ethnography, and 'Mail Order' Marriages*. CA: University of California Press.

Elliott, A., and Urry, J. (2010). *Mobile Lives*. Hoboken, NJ: Taylor & Francis.

Fortunati, L. (2002). Italy: Stereotypes, true and false. In J. Katz and M. Aakhus (eds), *Perpetual Contact: Mobile Communications, Private Talk, Public Performance* (pp. 42–62). New York: Cambridge University Press.

Giddens, A. (1992). *The Transformation of Intimacy: Sexuality, Love and Eroticism in Modern Societies*. Cambridge: Polity.

Glick Schiller, N., and Salazar, N. (2013). Regimes of mobility across the globe. *Journal of Ethnic and Migration Studies*, *39*(2), 183–200.

Goggin, G., and Hjorth, L. (2009). The question of mobile media. In G. Goggin and L. Hjorth (eds), *Mobile Technologies: From Telecommunications to Media* (pp. 21–32). New York: Routledge.

Guevarra, A.R. (2010). *Marketing Dreams, Manufacturing Heroes: The Transnational Labor Brokering of Filipino Workers*. New Brunswick, NJ: Rutgers University Press.

Hannam, K., Sheller, M., and Urry, J. (2006). Mobilities, immobilities and moorings. *Mobilities*, *1*(1), 1–22.

Hjorth, L. (2011). It's complicated: A case study of personalisation in an age of social and mobile media. *Communication, Politics and Culture*, *44*(1), 45–59.

Hjorth, L. (2015). Intimate cartographies of the visual: Camera phones, locative media and intimacy in Kakao. In R. Wilken and G. Goggin (eds), *Locative Media* (pp. 23–38). New York: Routledge.

Hjorth, L., Ohashi, K., Sinanan, J., Horst, H., Pink, S., Kato, F., and Zhou, B. (2020). *Digital Media Practices in Households: Kinship through Data*. Amsterdam: Amsterdam University Press.

Hjorth, L., Wilken, R., and Gu, K. (2012). Ambient intimacy: A case study of the iPhone, presence, and location-based social media in Shanghai, China. In L. Hjorth, J. Burgess and I. Richardson (eds), *Studying Mobile Media: Cultural Technologies, Mobile Communication, and the iPhone* (pp. 43–62). New York: Routledge.

Hondagneu-Sotelo, P., and Avila, E. (1997). I'm here, but I'm there: The meanings of Latina transnational motherhood. *Gender and Society*, *11*(5), 548–571.

Horst, H. (2006). The blessings and burdens of communication: Cell phones in Jamaican transnational social fields. *Global Networks*, *6*(2), 143–159.

Horst, H. (2013). The infrastructures of mobile media: Towards a future research agenda. *Mobile Media and Communication*, *1*(1), 147–152.

Hu, Y. (2016). *Chinese–British Intermarriage: Disentangling Gender and Ethnicity*. London: Palgrave Macmillan.
Hu, Y. (2017). Attitudes toward transnational intermarriage in China: Testing three theories of transnationalization. *Demographic Research*, *37*, 1413–1444.
Hu, Y., and Qian, Y. (2019). Educational and age assortative mating in China. *Demographic Research*, *41*, 53–82.
Hu, Y., and Qian, Y. (2021). COVID-19, inter-household contact and mental well-being among older adults in the US and the UK. *Frontiers in Sociology*, *6*, 1–15. doi: 10.3389/fsoc.2021.714626.
Hu, Y., Xu, C-L., and Tu, M. (2020). Family-mediated migration infrastructure: Chinese international students and parents navigating (im)mobilities during the COVID-19 pandemic. *Chinese Sociological Review*. doi: 10.1080/21620555.2020.1838271.
Inglehart, R., and Norris, P. (2003). *Rising Tide: Gender Equality and Cultural Change around the World*. Cambridge: Cambridge University Press.
International Telecommunication Union (2019). New ITU data reveal growing Internet uptake but a widening digital gender divide. https://www.itu.int/en/mediacentre/Pages/2019-PR19.aspx.
Jamieson, L. (1999). Intimacy transformed? A critical look at the 'pure relationship'. *Sociology*, *33*(3), 477–494.
Jamieson, L. (2011). Intimacy as a concept: Explaining social change in the context of globalisation or another form of ethnocentrism? *Sociological Research Online*, *16*(4), 1–28.
Jamieson, L.A., and Simpson, R. (2013). *Living Alone: Globalization, Identity and Belonging*. Basingstoke: Palgrave Macmillan.
Kilkey, M., and Merla, L. (2014). Situating transnational families' care-giving arrangements: The role of institutional contexts. *Global Networks*, *14*(2), 210–229.
King, G., Pan, J., and Roberts, M.E. (2014). Reverse-engineering censorship in China: Randomized experimentation and participant observation. *Science*, *345*(6199). doi: 10.1126/science.1251722.
Kyle, D. (2000). *Transnational Peasants: Migrations, Networks, and Ethnicity in Andean Ecuador*. Baltimore, MD: Johns Hopkins University Press.
Lasén, A. (2004). *Affective Technologies – Emotions and Mobile Phones*. Digital World Research Centre.
Leurs, K. (2014). The politics of transnational affective capital: Digital connectivity among young Somalis stranded in Ethiopia. *Crossings: Journal of Migration and Culture*, *5*(1), 87–104.
Leurs, K. (2017). Communication rights from the margins: Politicising young refugees' smartphone pocket archives. *International Communication Gazette*, *79*(6–7), 674–698.
Lim, S.S. (2014). Women, 'double work' and mobile media: The more things change, the more they stay the same. In G. Goggin and L. Hjorth (eds), *Routledge Companion to Mobile Media* (pp. 356–364). New York: Routledge.
Lin, W., Yeoh, B.S.A., Lindquist, J., and Xiang, B. (2017). Migration infrastructures and the production of migrant mobilities. *Mobilities*, *12*(2), 167–174.
Lin, Z., Desai, S., and Chen, F. (2020). The emergence of educational hypogamy in India. *Demography*, *57*(4), 1215–1240.
Lindquist, J., and Xiang, B. (2018). The infrastructural turn in Asian migration. In G. Liu-Farrer and B.S.A. Yeoh (eds), *Routledge Handbook of Asian Migrations* (pp. 152–161). New York: Routledge.
Ma, Y. (2020). *Ambitious and Anxious: How Chinese College Students Succeed and Struggle in American Higher Education*. New York: Columbia University Press.
Madianou, M. (2012). Migration and the accentuated ambivalence of motherhood: The role of ICTs in Filipino transnational families. *Global Networks*, *12*(3), 277–295.
Madianou, M. (2019). Migration, transnational families, and new communication technologies. In J.J. Retis and R. Tsagaousianou (eds), *The Handbook of Diasporas, Media and Culture* (pp. 577–590). London: John Wiley & Sons.
Madianou, M., and Miller, D. (2011). Crafting love: Letters and cassette tapes in transnational Filipino family communication. *South East Asia Research*, *19*(2), 249–272.
Madianou, M., and Miller, D. (2012). *Migration and New Media: Transnational Families and Polymedia*. Abingdon: Routledge.
Marino, S. (2019). Cook it, eat it, Skype it: Mobile media use in re-staging intimate culinary practices among transnational families. *International Journal of Cultural Studies*, *22*(6), 788–803.

McKay, D. (2007). 'Sending dollars shows feeling' – Emotions and economies in Filipino migration. *Mobilities*, 2(2), 175–194.
McKay, D. (2012). *Global Filipinos Migrants' Lives in the Virtual Village*. Bloomington, IN: Indiana University Press.
Merla, L., Kilkey, M., and Baldassar, L. (2020). Introduction to the special issue 'Transnational Care: Families Confronting Borders'. *Journal of Family Research*, 1–22. doi:10.20377/jfr-420.
Mintarsih, A.R. (2019). Facebook, polymedia, social capital, and a digital family of Indonesian migrant domestic workers: A case study of the voice of Singapore's invisible hands. *Migration, Mobility and Displacement*, 4(1), 65–83.
Mole, R.C.M. (2018). Identity, belonging and solidarity among Russian-speaking queer migrants in Berlin. *Slavic Review*, 77, 77–98.
Mole, R.C.M., Parutis, V., Gerry, C.J., and Burns, F.M. (2014). The impact of migration on the sexual health, behaviours and attitudes of Central and East European gay/bisexual men in London. *Ethnicity and Health*, 19(1), 86–99.
Morgan, D. (1996). *Family Connections: An Introduction to Family Studies*. Cambridge: Polity.
Murdock, G. (1965). *Social Structure*. New York: Free Press.
Nedelcu, M., and Wyss, M. (2016). 'Doing family' through ICT-mediated ordinary co-presence: transnational communication practices of Romanian migrants in Switzerland. *Global Networks*, 16(2), 202–218. doi:10.1111/glob.12110.
Nehring, D., and Hu, Y. (2021). COVID-19, nation-states, and fragile transnationalism. *Sociology*. doi: 10.1177/00380385211033729.
O'Hara, K., Massimi, M., Harper, R., Rubens, S., and Morris, J. (2014). *Everyday dwelling with WhatsApp*. Paper presented at the Proceedings of the 17th ACM Conference on Computer Supported Cooperative Work and Social Computing, Baltimoe, MD.
Paasonen, S. (2017). Infrastructures of intimacy. In R. Andreassen, K. Harrison, M. Petersen, and T. Raun (eds), *Mediated Intimacies: Connectivities, Relationalities and Proximities* (pp. 103–116). Abingdon: Routledge.
Papademetriou, D., and Sumption, M. (2011). *Rethinking Points Systems and Employer-Selected Immigration*. Washington, DC: Migration Policy Institute.
Parreñas, R.S. (2001). Mothering from a distance: Emotions, gender, and intergenerational relations in Filipino transnational families. *Feminist Studies*, 27(2), 361–390.
Parreñas, R.S. (2005). Long distance intimacy: Class, gender and intergenerational relations between mothers and children in Filipino transnational families. *Global Networks*, 5(4), 317–336.
Parreñas, R.S. (2008). Transnational fathering: Gendered conflicts, distant disciplining and emotional gaps. *Journal of Ethnic and Migration Studies*, 34(7), 1057–1072.
Parreñas, R.S. (2015). *Servants of Globalization: Women, Migration and Domestic Work* (2nd edition). Stanford, CA: Stanford University Press.
Paul, K. (2020). Trump's bid to ban TikTok and WeChat: Where are we now? *The Guardian*. https://www.theguardian.com/technology/2020/sep/29/trump-tiktok-wechat-china-us-explainer.
Peile, C. (2014). The migration industry of connectivity services: A critical discourse approach to the Spanish case in a European perspective. *Crossings: Journal of Migration and Culture*, 5(1), 57–71.
Probert, R. (2012). *The Changing Legal Regulation of Cohabitation: From Fornicators to Family, 1600–2010*. Cambridge: Cambridge University Press.
Quah, E.L.S. (2018). Emotional reflexivity and emotion work in transnational divorce biographies. *Emotion, Space and Society*, 29, 48–54.
Robertson, Z.O.E., Wilding, R., and Gifford, S. (2016). Mediating the family imaginary: Young people negotiating absence in transnational refugee families. *Global Networks*, 16(2), 219–236.
Robinson, W.I. (2004). *A Theory of Global Capitalism: Production, Class, and State in a Transnational World*. Baltimore, MD: Johns Hopkins University Press.
Rodriguez, R.M. (2010). *Migrants for Export: How the Philippine State Brokers to the World*. Minneapolis, MN: University of Minnesota Press.
Sassen, S. (2003). Global cities and survival circuits. In B. Ehrenreich and A.R. Hochschild (eds), *Global Woman: Nannies, Maids and Sex Workers in the New economy* (pp. 254–318). London: Granta Books.
Shamir, R. (2005). Without borders? Notes on globalization as a mobility regime. *Sociological Theory*, 23(2), 197–217.

Sheller, M., and Urry, J. (2006). The new mobilities paradigm. *Environment and Planning A*, *38*(2), 207–226.
Singh, S., Robertson, S., and Cabraal, A. (2012). Transnational family money: Remittances, gifts and inheritance. *Journal of Intercultural Studies*, *33*(5), 475–492.
Smets, K. (2019). Media and immobility: The affective and symbolic immobility of forced migrants. *European Journal of Communication*, *34*(6), 650–660.
Srnicek, N. (2017). *Platform Capitalism*. London: John Wiley & Sons.
Tu, M. (2019). The transnational one-child generation: family relationships and overseas aspiration between China and the UK. *Children's Geographies*, *17*(5), 565–577.
Turner, B. (2007). The enclave society: towards a sociology of immobility. *European Journal of Social Theory*, *10*(2), 287–303.
Turner, B. (2010). Enclosures, enclaves, and entrapment. *Sociological Inquiry*, *80*(2), 241–260.
Urry, J. (2002). Mobility and proximity. *Sociology*, *36*(2), 255–274.
Urry, J. (2007). *Mobilities*. Cambridge: Polity.
van Dijck, J. (2013). *The Culture of Connectivity: A Critical History of Social Media*. New York: Oxford University Press.
Vermot, C. (2015). Guilt: A gendered bond within the transnational family. *Emotion, Space and Society*, *16*, 138–146.
Vertovec, S. (2004). Cheap calls: The social glue of migrant transnationalism. *Global Networks*, *4*(2), 219–224.
Wilding, R. (2006). 'Virtual' intimacies? Families communicating across transnational contexts. *Global Networks*, *6*(2), 125–142.
Wilding, R. (2018). *Families, Intimacy and Globalization: Floating Ties*. London: Palgrave Macmillan.
Wimmer, A., and Schiller, N.G. (2009). Methodological nationalism and beyond: Nation-state building, migration and the social sciences. *Socialni Studia*, *6*(1), 11–47.
Wray, H. (2016). *Regulating Marriage Migration into the UK: A Stranger in the Home*. New York: Routledge.
Xiang, B., and Lindquist, J. (2014). Migration Infrastructure. *International Migration Review*, *48*(1), 122–148.

PART II

AGE AND INTERGENERATIONAL RELATIONSHIPS

7. Mobility and intergenerational transfers of capital: narrating expatriate and globally mobile children's perspectives
Sin Yee Koh and I Lin Sin

INTRODUCTION

There is a well-established literature examining the link between transnational mobility and the intergenerational social reproduction and mobility of expatriate and globally mobile families (see Wan et al., 2017 for a review of 'global families'; see Chapter 13, this *Handbook*). Transnational migration is often viewed as part of a familial strategy to accumulate and enhance capital (in economic, cultural, social and symbolic forms) that would ensure sustained or improved material wealth and status for the family and the next generation (Hanisch, 2020; Oso and Suárez-Grimalt, 2017; Waters, 2005). The centrality of the family in transnational mobility research lies in the fact that migrants are not isolated individuals, but part of family systems with interlocking ties, obligations and resources that sustain intergenerational capital pursuits (Coe and Shani, 2015). The literature predominantly approach family-led transnational mobility from the perspectives of parents, without taking equal account of children's views (see Part II, this *Handbook*). Using parents as the starting and focal point gives very little voice to the children who may have conflicting views on what transnational mobility primarily means to them. Furthermore, it does not shed light on the extent to which the children are motivated to pursue mobility-related goals and trajectories aspired for and expected of them. Moreover, this parent-centric approach assumes simplistically that the capital transmission from parents to children is even and straightforward, and that each child will be able to draw from and accumulate the same amount and form of capital with equal success. There is therefore a missed opportunity to examine children's diverse and unexpected mobility outcomes (that is, the extent to which they are able to improve or maintain the social status and privilege of their parents).

While some specific studies on expatriate and globally mobile people have given attention to their childhood mobility experiences, these often involve adults reflecting on and reconstructing their past (Bell-Villada et al., 2011; Eidse and Sichel, 2004b; Fail et al., 2004; Kwon, 2019), rather than children speaking as children. These retrospectives are at best, partial and selective, given the passing of time and the influence of adult-guided reminiscing on the now-adult children's autobiographical memory (Bjørnsen, 2020). By contrast, studies on international school students' mobility and future aspirations have focused on these young people's viewpoints (e.g., Cranston, 2020; Maxwell and Aggleton, 2016; Young, 2017). As Orellana et al. (2001) have argued, children and young people are also active and independent participants of migration, whose lives, relationships and experiences are altered through the migration process. Moreover, 'the *presence* of children is central to the families' decision-making process' (ibid., p. 587). There is therefore a need to place equal emphasis on children's perspectives (Fechter and Korpela, 2016; Hatfield, 2010; Kang, 2013; Sander, 2016; Tse and Waters, 2013). Not only does this give agency and voice to children as (transnational, expatriate or serial) migrants, but it also offers a more comprehensive understanding of familial migration by highlighting the differential perspectives of individual family members.

This chapter first explores the values attached to, and meanings of, migration and global mobility for parents and their children, and the significance of intergenerational social reproduction and mobility to both groups.[1] Second, it deconstructs the children's presumed privilege and homogeneity by highlighting the complexities and specificities of capital transmission from parents to children. Third, it highlights the relatively unheard voices and choices of children in familial capital/mobility projects. The chapter concludes with some methodological suggestions for taking into account children's perspectives of and roles in intergenerational pursuits of capital and transnational im(mobility).

EXPATRIATE AND GLOBALLY MOBILE CHILDREN

Terms and Definitions

Existing literature in migration and cross-cultural education have used various terms to describe and characterize children who move across borders with their families,[2] often on multiple occasions. These terms include 'third culture kids' (TCK) (Useem, 1973; Pollock and Van Reken, 2009), 'global nomads' (McCaig, 2002; Mclachlan, 2007), 'nomadic children' (Eidse and Sichel, 2004a) and 'serial migrants' children' (Désilets, 2015). The common feature amongst these myriad terms is the experience of: (1) moving across borders with the family as a child; and (2) schooling and growing up in a foreign context that is not one's (or either parent's) country of origin. To better capture the experience of growing up in-between cultures, Van Reken proposed another term, 'cross-cultural kids' (CCK), defined as 'a person who is living in – or meaningfully interacting with – two or more cultural environments for a significant period of time during the developmental years of childhood (up to age 18)' (Van Reken, 2011, p. 33). However, this term does not explain in depth the roles, aspirations and trajectories of children who have become involved in their family's capital/mobility projects.

In this chapter, we define expatriate and globally mobile children as children who primarily move overseas with their families, often temporarily, due to their parents' work (see Chapter 14, this *Handbook*). The parents may be self-initiated expatriates or company assignees in a range of industries (for example, oil and gas, education, finance, consulting), aid workers, embassy and diplomatic staff, military staff or missionaries (see McNulty and Selmer, 2017, Parts III–IV). These families have been referred to as 'expatriate families', especially in the human resources and business management literature (Lazarova et al., 2015). As we have highlighted elsewhere, the term 'expatriate' has colonial and racial connotations (Koh and Sin, 2020; also see Kunz, 2020). However, we use it in this instance to capture the notion of choice and the relative ease of global mobility enjoyed by these families. Furthermore, using the term 'expatriate' also enables us to interrogate the commonly assumed privilege that is associated with the term (Kunz, 2016, 2020). As we will later show, focusing on the children's perspectives challenges their presumed privilege and homogeneity as members of the expatriate family.

The term 'expatriate and globally mobile children' used in this chapter does not include first- and further-generation migrant children, who have already been the subject of many studies in the migration literature (e.g. Nyíri, 2014; Waters and Levitt, 2002; Wessendorf, 2016; Zhou, 1997). However, as migrant children can also be globally mobile, we will review a few works on them where relevant to the discussion on expatriate and globally mobile children (for example, migrant children in transnational split household arrangements). There are fundamental differences between the first group (expatriate and globally mobile children) and the second (migrant children) (Dillon and Ali, 2019). Migrant children are likely to have families who have set up roots in the host country and view cross-border mobility as a permanent or long-term move. On the other hand, expatriate and globally mobile children are likely to partake in multiple, shorter-term and occasionally multidirectional cross-border mobility. They are often associated with the term 'TCK', although there are differences between these two groups.

The term 'expatriate and globally mobile children' focuses on the mobility aspect of the children's lives rather than the 'third culture' connotation in the term TCK. TCK suggests that children who experience multiple international relocation during their formative years do not belong to either the culture of their country of citizenship or the culture of their host country (Pollock and Van Reken, 2009). Instead, they occupy a third culture space where they interact with many cultures but do not fully belong in any of them, and struggle to locate a sense of home. On the other hand, the term 'expatriate and globally mobile children' shifts the focus from 'culture' (which may be difficult to define and can be subject to continual change) to 'mobility' (which can be traced and mapped). Examining the mobility of the children allows for a consideration of cultural context and individual resources, characteristics and circumstances not afforded in the term 'TCK' (Dillon and Ali, 2019; Fanning and Burns, 2017). It enables us to circumvent the arbitrary and broad categorization of mobile children of relative privilege into static either/or cultures. We therefore posit that it is much more useful to focus on the mobility (rather than the cultural) dimension of the children's lives, specifically in the context of family expatriation.

Invisibility in the Literature

The relative invisibility of expatriate and globally mobile children in migration research lies in the common treatment of the children as passive dependents in the familial migratory project (cf. Chapter 12, this *Handbook*). More attention has been paid instead to the agency of parents as primary migrants, and their strategies in utilizing economic (for example, financial wealth) and cultural capitals (for example, knowledge, skills, dispositions, qualifications) for household social mobility and reproduction (Selmer and Lam, 2004). Ackers and Stalford's (2004) study of internal family migration within the European Union noted that some parents subjected their children to 'future oriented consent' (p. 111), where migration was made with the justification that their children would reflect positively about the decision in future. Some children had more voice in the decision-making process, having being offered restricted choices between particular options from what Ackers and Stalford described as the 'children's menu' (ibid.). However, the children as a whole lacked control over the eventual family decision. The privileging of parents' voices and choices in the dominant migration literature is problematic, as it dismisses the consideration of children and young people as equal movers.

Following on from Ackers and Stalford's line of argument, but applied to the context of family expatriation, Hutchins (2011) argued that children's roles in familial migratory decision-making are often framed in the literature around the discourse of best interest, seen from their parents' perspectives. This discourse supports a common justification by expatriate and globally mobile parents that transnational mobility is made with their children's education in mind (usually alongside parents' own career-related considerations), and that moving will bring future economic and status benefits to the children (Sander, 2016). However, as we will later show, the expected future benefits may not materialize in the same form and to the same degree as originally envisaged by the parents. Moreover, expatriate and globally mobile children are differentially involved and included in the familial migration decision-making process.

Research on expatriate and globally mobile children's experiences rarely extends beyond their educational experiences in international schools (Adams and Fleer, 2016; Fail et al., 2004; Tanu, 2014, 2018), and their identity, coping and belonging issues as they traverse borders, cultures, languages and friendship groups (Benjamin and Dervin, 2015; Dixon and Hayden, 2008; Kwon, 2019). Little has been done to link their experiences of international schools and frequent relocations with their relationships with their parents (with the exception of a few works, such as Adams, 2014; Lijadi and Van Schalkwyk, 2017; Mclachlan, 2007; Sander, 2016). Moreover, the centring of parents' needs and aspirations has led to a gap in the literature where the children's individual capital accumulation strategies and mobility trajectories are often being overlooked (see Ní Laoire, 2020 for a rare exception). As there are multiple subjectivities within families, there is a need to take into account that children's opinions and experiences are not necessarily representative of or congruent to those of their parents (Hatfield, 2010, p. 244). The individuality of each child and their unique viewpoints and preferences need to be considered in relation to the familial global mobility project.

To address these gaps in the literature, this chapter departs from a parent-centric approach to highlight and incorporate children's perspectives on transnational mobility and intergenerational social reproduction and mobility. In what follows, we examine parents' and children's perspectives respectively, before turning to the challenges and limits of familial capital accumulation and transfer across borders. We then focus on parent–child decision-making with regard to mobility. Throughout these two sections, we highlight the nuances and insights that arise from a focus on children's lived experiences.

CAPITAL ACCUMULATION THROUGH GLOBAL MOBILITY

(Familial) Mobility-Related Capital

The notion of global mobility as capital has been mainly framed in existing literature around Bourdieu's influential and frequently cited concept of cultural capital. It is worth outlining the ways in which the concept has been applied in the family migration context. Bourdieu's original conception of cultural capital (Bourdieu, 1986; Bourdieu and Passeron, 1977) notes that cultural capital in forms such as exclusive knowledge, competences and dispositions were used by elite families in 1960s France to ensure social reproduction, that is, the transmission of power, social distinction and privilege to the children. The schooling system recognizes and rewards the cultural capital embodied by children of the dominant class, leading to their high educational attainment and subsequent occupational and status advantages.

Drawing from Bourdieu's concept of cultural capital, literature in migration research have conceptualized cross-border mobility as a resource consisting of an accumulation of knowledge and experiences of mobility that can be drawn upon to inform decisions to move overseas and to stay put when the situation calls for it (Moret, 2020). This resource, also known as 'motility' or mobility capital when utilized (Kaufman et al., 2004; Leivestad, 2016; Ní Laoire, 2020), is unevenly distributed based on social position(ing) (Basaran and Olsson, 2018; Moret, 2020): individuals who occupy dominant social position(ing)s (for example, along class, gender, ethnicity and nationality lines) and with advantaged access to capital (for example, economic, cultural, social and linguistic) are able to move countries and, at other times, be strategically immobile with more ease than individuals from lower social position(ing)s. Mobility capital can facilitate the accumulation and enhancement of economic (for example, income), cultural (for example, distinctive intercultural experiences; globally recognized and transferable credentials, knowledge, and skills), social (for example, networks of support) and symbolic (for example, prestige and recognition) capital at different times and in different (transnational) places (Moret 2020; Ní Laoire, 2020). In this chapter, we refer interchangeably to these capitals as mobility-related capital (see also Chapter 13, this *Handbook*).

Migration literature have noted the pursuit of transnational education migration by middle-class families (typically the parents' decision) as a strategy for social distinction. Children's education in international schools and boarding schools – or, at the very least, a school in an English-speaking country – is seen as a crucial first step that paves the path towards accumulating future familial mobility-related capital (Kang, 2013, pp. 329–330). In these projects, the family would 'migrate' on paper, with the children physically crossing international borders for schooling while the parents engage in circular/transnational mobilities or split household arrangements (Waters, 2005, 2006; Tse and Waters, 2013). Terms such as 'astronaut families' and *kirogi kajok* (lit. 'wild geese families') (Abelmann et al., 2014; Okazaki and Kim, 2018) have been used to describe the ways these families partake in transnational living for the sake of their children's education and future capital rewards.

Parents' Perspectives

In the context of expatriate and globally mobile families, it has been argued that parents have access to mobility-related capital that can be mobilized across borders and transferred to their accompanying children (Adams and Agbenyega, 2019; Mclachlan, 2007; Weenink, 2008). Mclachlan's (2007) study of expatriate and globally mobile children and their families in a private international school in southern England showed how the parents actively coached their children to manage global mobility. The strategies include making friends with children of similar mobility backgrounds, and observing and learning local norms and behaviour. Similarly, Weenink (2008, p. 1095) found that some globally mobile parents went to the extent of 'arrang[ing] cultural shocks to impart a cosmopolitan cultural openness in their children'.

These examples highlight the importance of a kind of 'international mindedness' (Elwood and Davis, 2009), 'open-mindedness' (Fechter, 2016), or 'cosmopolitan capital' (Igarashi and Saito, 2014; Tanu, 2018; Weenink, 2008) that parents insist on imparting to their children. Having already led globally mobile lives, these parents understood and appreciated the value of capital that can ease one's adaptation to different cultural contexts. The ability to become 'cultural chameleons' (Dillon and Ali, 2019) and relate to people of diverse backgrounds is a form of mobility-related capital that is valued by multinational corporations and transnational organisations. By extension, the recognition of mobility-related capital by employing organisations means that the children will become competitive in the global job market. More importantly, this form of capital is assumed to be obtainable only through global mobility.

As a result of such an assumption (that is, global mobility can translate into capitals with future use and exchange values), newer cohorts of aspiring families have joined the global mobility bandwagon. Kim and Okazaki (2017), for example, highlighted how less affluent middle-class South Korean families arranged early study abroad (*chogi yuhak*) programmes for their children. Instead of moving to traditional destination countries in the West (for example, Australia, the United Kingdom, the United States) which are preferred by elite and more affluent middle-class families, these families moved to more affordable Southeast Asian countries which offer English-medium education and English-language immersion experiences (for example, Singapore, Malaysia, the Philippines). Similarly, Huang and Yeoh (2005) found that 'study mothers' from China (that is, mothers who join their children's education migration as accompanying guardians) believed that their children's acquisition of English language skills and other mobility-related capital in Singapore would bring future positional benefits. Specifically, with the accumulated cultural capital, their children would be able to enjoy greater flexibility in their future global mobilities and be competitive in global and local contexts, including the 'origin' context if they chose to 'return'.

What is clear here is that, regardless of social class and the extent of global mobilities, parents typically hold capital accumulation aspirations for their children. For parents who are already living globally mobile lives and whose children are born into the family's global mobility trajectory, the mobility project continues automatically and organically. By contrast, for parents who have yet to live globally mobile lives, it is the children who are often deliberately positioned as the means and basis to kickstart familial capital accumulation. As we have discussed in this section, this is usually pursued through the children's overseas education.

Children's Perspectives

As key participants and often anchors to their family's capital accumulation, expatriate and globally mobile children have varying levels of agreement with their parents regarding the value and desirability of global mobility. On the one hand, they may fully agree with and embrace the globally mobile lives that their parents have set out for them, carrying the same aspirations into their adult lives and even reproducing them for their own children. On the other hand, they may yearn for a more sedentary lifestyle and disagree with the value that their parents associate with global mobility. Moreover, there may also be groups that sit in between these two extremes; while they may agree with the value of global mobility, their agreement does not discount the emotional and psychological challenges that they face from being globally mobile.

Primary school-age expatriate children in Bangkok who Dixon and Hayden (2008) interviewed through online questionnaires experienced a sense of grief and loss as relocation to another country caused and/or prolonged their separation from extended family members, friends and pets. However, moving brought the opportunity to reinvent the self and accumulate new experiences of schools, people, cultures, food and landscapes. It is this acquisition of mobility-related capital that former expatriate and globally mobile children, now adults, tend to appreciate, as Kwon (2019) argued. Equipped with the right knowledge and resources gained through mobility, the children-turned-adult expatriates in her study were keen to maintain the life of a global nomad, extending a transnationally mobile lifestyle from childhood into adulthood.

The former Irish child return migrants in Ní Laoire's (2020) study expressed a desire to leave Ireland again in their young adulthood to acquire more worldly experience before an eventual return to their home country. Their desire for future mobility was shaped by their pasts and family histories of mobility (p. 5), reflecting how mobility-related capital first introduced by their parents can reproduce intergenerational mobility aspirations. Mobility was seen by the former child migrants as a rite of passage, a necessary move for self-development and becoming adult. They also used their past familial mobility experiences, and the mobility-related capital that they have acquired through those experiences, to distinguish themselves from their peers. Through their selective narrativization of hypermobility, they positioned themselves as 'knowledgeable and experienced mobile subjects' (p. 8). In this way, they mobilized their mobility-related capital to establish their social distinction in the present and future. Such use of capital would appear to be in line with the parents' aspirations discussed in the preceding section.

However, as now adults confronting their own present and future mobilities that are independent from their families', some former child migrants in Ní Laoire's (2020) study developed nuanced attitudes towards moving. While they appreciated the value of global mobility and the accompanying capitals, they also valued 'the right to immobility' (Forsberg, 2019): to stay put and accumulate local place-based capitals. Ironically, their previous global mobility trajectories have resulted in them losing out on locally based capitals (for example, social networks, local knowledge) that could aid in securing occupational and status advantages in the home country. Ní Laoire's (2020) findings highlight the need to examine expatriate and globally mobile children's changing understandings of capital accumulation and their attitudes towards global mobility as they transition from childhood to adulthood.

CHALLENGES AND LIMITS TO THE FAMILIAL GLOBAL MOBILITY PROJECT

Capital: Accumulation, Conversion, Transfers

As we have highlighted earlier, the familial global mobility project is often embarked upon with the expectation that capital accumulation and intergenerational transfers from the parents to children can take place. However, it has to be noted that capital in various forms do not constitute fixed sets of properties and attributes, and have varying exchange values across countries, social settings and situations (Basaran and Olsson, 2018; Jarvis, 2020). In addition, due to various contextual and intersectional factors, there may be limits to capital acquisition, conversion and transfers (Igarashi and Saito, 2014; Hanisch, 2020; Waddling et al., 2019). In other words, global mobility in and of itself does not translate directly and unproblematically to higher forms of capital (Basaran and Olsson, 2018), for the purpose of intergenerational social reproduction and mobility.

In many familial global mobility projects there is a tendency to assume that the capital accumulated in one location can be easily converted into privileged forms of capital in another location. However, the literature suggest that such an assumption may not necessarily be true. This is because certain types of capital (for example, habitual language, location-specific informational knowledge, social networks) are locally embedded and situated in geographical contexts. This means that the capital in question may lose meanings and value once it is disembedded from its context. As Waddling et al. (2019, p. 714) highlight in Bourdieusian terms, it is the inertia of habitus (enduring habits, skills and dispositions shaped by past experiences) as embodied capital that poses challenges for cross-border capital conversion and habitus establishment in new and different sites and spaces.

While expatriate and globally mobile families may be relatively better positioned than other migrant families in regard to the acquisition of mobility capital, the same cannot be said about the success of intergenerational social reproduction and mobility at the transnational level. In their discussion of cosmopolitanism as a form of capital that sits at the intersections of globalization, education and stratification, Igarashi and Saito (2014) highlighted key factors that complicate the accumulation, conversion and transfers of such capital. Firstly, there is variance and heterogeneity within the category of expatriate and globally mobile families (pp. 227–229).[3] This means that families may have unequal access to different forms of mobility-related capital that they can utilize. Secondly, there are also diversities and stratification in parental ownership of capital and their abilities to transfer those capital to their children (pp. 229–231). As we have discussed, parents with pre-existing mobility-related capital may be better positioned to create opportunities for their children to attain similar forms of capital. Additionally, individual parents may have accumulated a mixed bag of emplaced and mobile resources, some of which can be more easily converted into capital in transnational contexts than others.

Finally, the benefits of cosmopolitanism are unevenly distributed, as its value may differ across locations and contexts (Igarashi and Saito, 2014, pp. 231–233). For example, mobility-related capital may lose its value in localized contexts where locally embedded capital carries more weight and recognition (Jarvis, 2020). By contrast, in transnational contexts, those exact capital may be prioritized and valued. We have argued elsewhere that Anthias's (2008) concept of translocational positionality[4] aptly captures the shifting and contradictory value of capital as borders are crossed (Koh and Sin, 2020). The concept calls for attention to differential social position(ings) where individuals are located at different times, places and spaces. This helps to uncover the situated nature of migrant experiences: in this case, the varying degrees of success in mobilizing and transmitting capital.

In contexts where parents are successful in transferring various forms of capital to their children, the children may not profit equally from those capital. Depending on context and circumstances, there may be mismatches or unexpected loss of value between parental accumulated capital and children's inherited capital. Furthermore, there are diversity and heterogeneity within the broad category of 'expatriate and globally mobile children' that need to be taken into account.[5] For example, in terms of the differential propensity for siblings to embrace mobility, '[i]n the same family, some will be more mobile than others' (Murphy-Lejeune, 2003, p. 57) due to differences in personality and desire to live a globally mobile life. We add that personal characteristics such as age, gender (Koh and Sin, 2020) and order in the family can further complicate individual aspirations and experiences of (im)mobility. We did not find any literature which explored in depth the intersectional workings of social positions and social positionings that frame children's roles in familial mobility projects. This is a crucial area which future research should work on to understand not only the possibilities, but also the limitations that global mobility represent.

Competing Values of Capital and Transnational (Im)mobility

Another key factor that challenges and limits the parent-led project of global mobility is the fact that accompanying child(ren) may disagree with the parental ascription of value to certain forms of mobility-related capital. As we have highlighted earlier, children do have agency, perspectives and subjectivities that may differ from those of their parents. They may also develop their own preferences and aspirations that are independent of the family's or their parents'. This is especially so for expatriate and globally mobile children who grow up on the move: they may instead yearn for a more sedentary lifestyle tied to a location, seeking a sense of stability, certainty and belonging that they never really had. More importantly, they may develop alternative understandings of the value of capital.

Sander (2016, p. 89) observed how German-born and raised Chinese expatriate youths in Shanghai straddled shifting cultural and linguistic systems as they faced a tension between parental and school ideals of what constitutes good values, speech and behaviour. The youths performed Western-related cultural capital (for example, critical thinking and questioning) in the international schools they attended, while switching to Chinese-related cultural capital (for example, deference to parents) at home. The parents' choice of international schooling for them, in addition to housing in upscale gated communities, reinforce a local–expatriate divide in Shanghai which limited the children's immersion into cultural capital linked to the host country. There can therefore be contradictions in the valuing of capital within the family.

All the expatriate young people from the Middle East and North Africa region in Wilkins's (2013) study chose to study in the United Arab Emirates, basing their decision on parental preference. It is not certain how much of this decision had to do with a higher valuing of regional cultural capital, but what this suggests is that parent–child relations frame, and at times constrain, possibilities of capital accumulation and future (im)mobilities. The findings also suggest that there is value in place embeddedness (Ní Laoire, 2020), and global mobility projects may not necessarily result in the imperative for hypermobility. The former Irish child return migrants in Ní Laoire's (2020, p. 8) study articulated their need for safe and secure careers in addition to being close to familial, emotional and social ties in Ireland. Immobility (but with financial stability for occasional international travel) or temporary transnational mobility (with a view of returning permanently to Ireland) made pragmatic sense to them as they navigated the tension between the need for security and support embedded in place, and aspirations for further transnational mobility.

In their study of young women (aged 14–18 years) attending elite private schools in England, Maxwell and Aggleton (2016) found that the majority of their respondents who had grown up in expatriate and globally mobile families were ambivalent and circumspect about committing to a mobile lifestyle for themselves and their future children. While the young women did not discount the benefits that they had personally gained from their familial global mobilities (worldliness and a more mature outlook compared to their peers), the authors suggested that they sought an alternative life locally where cultural capital could be equally if not better pursued. This is because they were on the cusp of entering prestigious universities in the local vicinity (for example, Oxbridge, London) which would not entail further global mobility, at least in the near future. Maxwell and Aggleton's (2016) findings reiterate the importance of examining young people's views and responses to familial capital accumulation. It cautions against the easy assumption that hypermobility is the be all and end all for those who have led a mobile life.

Unintended Consequences and Human Cost

The 'success' of transnational mobility – at least at surface value and in terms of physical mobilities – can bring human costs, which have received less attention in the literature. It is not uncommon for expatriate parents to feel guilty (Nukaga, 2013) about relocations as their children constantly experience grief and losses in relationships, activities, and places and objects of familiarity and comfort (Lijadi and Van Schalkwyk, 2017). There is abundant literature on the emotional and psychological negotiations of identity and (un)belonging amongst TCKs (e.g., Eidse and Sichel, 2004b; Gilbert and Gilbert, 2011), but a relative dearth of literature on other aspects of the human cost of global mobility, especially in terms of parent–child relations.

Being on the move entails having to depend on the family for physical, emotional, social and spiritual support, and this has to some extent brought families closer together, but also manifested tension between children and their parents, as Mclachlan's (2007) study shows. Fathers tend to spend less time with their children due to work-related travel, while mothers tend to give up time, and in most cases their careers, to attend to caring responsibilities (Adams, 2014; Mclachlan, 2007; Van Schalkwyk, 2017). Former Norwergian Foreign Service children in Bjørnsen's (2020, p. 131) study felt a sense of emotional estrangement towards their parents and within themselves, as they assumed a silent narrative within the family to embrace the privileged status and exceptional opportunities that came with global mobility, and not display insecurity towards their many relocations.

While the children of Hong Kong astronaut families in Vancouver in Tse and Waters's (2013) study understood the rationale of their parent-led familial migration project, they resented being treated as young children who were incapable of independence. Their parents and extended family members' sporadic visits were perceived as inconveniences that disrupted their lives in Vancouver. As they transitioned into adolescence, they developed alternative imaginaries about their future mobility pathways that differed from what their parents had planned for them. However, like Tu's (2019) participants (Chinese students turned labour migrants in the United Kingdom) who were bounded by notions of filial piety and life-long reciprocity between parent and child, they felt a sense of responsibility to achieve the family's dream of foreign (Western) cultural capital appropriation. For Tu's (2019) participants, this involved studying and eventually working and remaining in the United Kingdom (UK), where the symbolic capital of mobility could be maximized by their parents in China. Symbolic capital was important for their parents, and in some cases justified their continuing financial investments in their adult children (for example, remittances to the UK).

While Tu's (2019) and Tse and Waters's (2013) participants may not fit the label 'expatriate', their narratives capture the shared and competing roles that children, including expatriate and globally mobile ones, play in parental aspirational transfers beyond childhood and national borders. The human cost to the mobility project involves long-term uncertainties, emotional struggles and intergenerational compromises as the now-adults were caught between continuing their parent-led transnational mobility strategies, and their lack of commitment to remaining overseas. These studies highlight the everyday tensions of family and parent–child relations that develop in unexpected ways as the familial mobility project materializes in transnational spaces.

PARENT–CHILD DECISION-MAKING

Extant literature have noted that expatriate and globally mobile children have different degrees of involvement in the familial migration decision-making process, ranging from not being included, to negotiating with their parents, and right through to exerting some choice in their aspirations for geographical and social mobility (Bjørnsen, 2020; Hutchins, 2011; Sander, 2016). It has to be emphasized that the inclusion or exclusion of children in familial decisions on migration and capital accumulation is not a one-off process but occurs at different mobility and life stages, as the following works highlight.

Hutchins (2011, p. 1233) argued that different conceptions of childhood operate in parallel within the family, and particular conceptions may be invoked at different times of migration. The conceptions involve the notions of 'childing' (when adults position themselves as decision-makers to dependent, developing children), 'adulting' (when children assert their independence in relation to adults) and interdependent relations (balancing adult interests with children's interests) (p. 1228). Hutchins found that childhood was mostly constructed based on childing relations among migrant families in her study: the parents placed their self-interests ahead of their children's as the primary motivation for migration to Australia, as much as those interests involve a consideration of the ideal family life (for example, work–life balance, safety for children) that they wished to live. Where children's interests were taken into account, they were mainly constructed in terms of their future adulthood: that is, the better life the parents aspired for the children in future.

Some studies involving migrant families highlight the consequences of childing that arise when aspiring middle-class parents kick-start the familial mobility project without directly consulting their then pre-teen children, or fail to re-evaluate their children's desires later on (Hanisch, 2020; Tse and Waters, 2013). The children may have agreed with the family's strategies for capital accumulation and the roles assigned to them at the onset of the familial global mobility project. However, partaking in the familial project may result in the curtailment of the children's independent mobility options in the future (for example, early childhood migration resulting in lost opportunities to accumulate locally embedded capital at home that can facilitate return migration), in ways seen and as discussed earlier in Ní Laoire's (2020) study.

Hutchins's (2011) different conceptions of childhood are noticeable in studies on expatriate and globally mobile families. For example, former Norwegian Foreign Service children in Bjørnsen's (2020, p. 129) study felt pressured to conform to an adult-centric narrative of a successful expatriate family which was projected onto their childhood. As children, they were culturally constructed as becoming and not being; that is, their future adulthood was given more attention than their personhood (Hutchins, 2011). In turn, the then-children felt compelled to assume and perform characteristics such as having freedom of mobility, having bountiful resources, and becoming internationally competent and economically successful. They learned to put their anxieties and exhaustion aside to live up to expectations of a privileged expatriate childhood.

Expatriate and globally mobile children are commonly positioned by their parents as vulnerable and requiring decisions to be made for them, a position which the children usually passively accept; at least at first. Adams and Agbenyega (2019) used the term 'futurescaping' to describe how mothers in their study (globally mobile families who were residing in Malaysia) imagined futures of a better life beyond national borders for their children, based on their own personal experiences. Having received passive education in the home country, where rote learning and compliance were emphasized, the mothers aspired for their children to escape the system through transnational mobility and international schooling. Transnational mobility was imagined by the mothers not in terms of the social reproduction of educational experiences, but in terms of an intergenerational advancement in the acquisition of valuable mobility-related capital such as active learning skills and a global worldview that would position the children favourably for competitive global employment.

Wilkins's (2013) study of the higher education choices of expatriate young people in Dubai further illustrates the strong influence that parents can have on children's (im)mobility and capital accumulation. A vast majority of his study's participants chose universities in countries (primarily the UK and United Arab Emirates) where their parents and/or immediate family members were or would be located. The reason for their decisions lies in their need for a sense of home: not so much defined in terms of a physical space, but in the strong socio-emotional relationships formed with their parents and families while on the move (Fail et al., 2004; Van Schalkwyk, 2017). These studies remind us of the need to explore the familial mobility project throughout the life course, involving both parents and children equally.

CONCLUSION

This chapter has reviewed some of the key works on intergenerational capital accumulation and transfers among expatriate and globally mobile families. It explored the perceived role of global mobility in enabling familial social reproduction and mobility. We paid particular attention to children's perspectives shared by children themselves and children-turned-adults in order to uncover how these individuals position themselves or are positioned in relation to their parents in familial mobility projects. We made the argument that these perspectives are crucial to understand fully the processes, practices and outcomes of familial global mobility at different times, life stages and locations. Importantly, children's individual characteristics and circumstances, as well as familial relations, dynamics and social position(ing)s of different members, have to be taken into account. A closer look at children's voices and choices offers insights into the dislocations and discomfort that they face, essentially bringing to the fore the complexities and relatively unspoken vulnerabilities and limitations of this purportedly privileged and homogeneous group of migrants.

To gain deeper insights into children's perspectives of and roles in intergenerational transfers of capital and transnational im(mobility), we propose a few research methods. The methods involve longitudinal research (for example, involving the same migrant actor over longer periods of time at different life stages: as a child, adult, parent), multi-sited research (to take into account the transnational social fields where the individual and the family's mobility trajectories come to be embedded), and intergenerational research (for example, involving comparisons of various members of the family, especially parent–child comparisons and involving the grandparents where relevant) (see Ní Laoire, 2020; Oso and Suárez-Grimalt, 2017), that can take into account the multiple and relational subjectivities in the familial mobility project. Child-centred creative arts and participatory methods such as multimedia ethnography (Kang, 2013), storyboarding (Cranston, 2020), drawing (Hutchins, 2011) and photography (Hatfield, 2010) are useful as they position and empower children as knowledgeable about their own lives. They recognize children as independent agents with the ability to articulate and reflect on what matters to them in the migration process.

For children in younger age groups who may not be as articulate in their thoughts and perspectives, creative observational methods can be used. For example, Adams's (2014) combined use of observational videos (at schools and homes) and video interviews (with parents, teachers and children), alongside field notes and photographs, facilitate the triangulation of data in examining younger age children's reciprocal relationships and interactions with others and their environments. The data can then be cross-examined with more traditional research methods such as interviews and questionnaires when the child enters adolescent, young adult and adult life stages. Essentially, using different single and combined research methods that are appropriate to life stages enables more comprehensive and nuanced understanding of the shared and shifting values of transnational (im)mobility and capital to children and their families.

NOTES

1. Due to the lack of literature on children's perspectives, we include studies of adults reflecting on their globally mobile childhood. We take 'children' to mean anyone below the age of 18, but will refer to those between 14 and 17 years as young people where specificity is required.
2. This chapter excludes the discussion of refugee children who may move under very different circumstances than expatriate and globally mobile children.
3. See Waddling et al.'s (2019) point on the diversities and stratifications within the global middle class.
4. Originally used to study migrant identity construction and belonging.
5. See Tanu (2015) on the diversities within the category of TCK.

REFERENCES

Abelmann, N., Newendorp, N., and Lee-Chung, S. (2014). East Asia's astronaut and geese families: Hong Kong and South Korean cosmopolitanisms. *Critical Asian Studies*, 46(2), 259–286. doi: 10.1080/14672715.2014.898454.

Ackers, L., and Stalford, H. (2004). *A community for children? Children, citizenship, and internal migration in the EU*. Ashgate.

Adams, M. (2014). Emotions of expatriate children and families transitioning into Malaysia: A cultural historical perspective. *Asia-Pacific Journal of Education in Early Childhood Education*, 8(2), 129–151.

Adams, M., and Agbenyega, J. (2019). Futurescaping: School choice of internationally mobile global middle class families temporarily residing in Malaysia. *Discourse: Studies in the Cultural Politics of Education*, 40(5), 647–665. doi: 10.1080/01596306.2019.1576266.

Adams, M., and Fleer, M. (2016). Social inclusion and exclusion of a young child: A cultural–historical perspective of an international mid-semester transition into an international school in Malaysia. *Australasian Journal of Early Childhood*, 41(3), 86–94.

Anthias, F. (2008). Thinking through the lens of translocational positionality: An intersectionality frame for understanding identity and belonging. *Translocations: Migration and Social Change*, 4(1), 5–20.

Basaran, T., and Olsson, C. (2018). Becoming international: On symbolic capital, conversion and privilege. *Millennium: Journal of International Studies*, 46(2), 96–118. doi: 10.1177/0305829817739636.

Bell-Villada, G.H., Sichel, N., Eidse, F., and Orr, E.N. (eds) (2011). *Writing out of limbo: International childhoods, global nomads and third culture kids*. Cambridge Scholars Publishing.

Benjamin, S., and Dervin, F. (eds) (2015). *Migration, diversity, and education: Beyond third culture kids*. Palgrave Macmillan.

Bjørnsen, R.H. (2020). The assumption of privilege? Expectations on emotions when growing up in the Norwegian Foreign Service. *Childhood*, 27(1), 120–133. doi: 10.1177/0907568219885377.

Bourdieu, P. (1986). *Distinction: A social critique of the judgement of taste.* Trans. R. Nice. Routledge.
Bourdieu, P., and Passeron, J.-C. 1977. *Reproduction in education, society and culture.* SAGE Publications.
Coe, C., and Shani, S. (2015). Cultural capital and transnational parenting: The case of Ghanaian migrants in the United States. *Harvard Educational Review, 85*(4), 562–683. doi: 10.17763/0017-8055.85.4.562.
Cranston, S. (2020). Figures of the global: Mobility journeys of international school pupils. *Population, Space and Place, 26,* e2305. doi: 10.1002/psp.2305.
Désilets, G. (2015). 'Third Culture Kids' as serial migrants' children: Understanding some of the impacts of a highly mobile transnational upbringing. In S. Benjamin and F. Dervin (eds), *Migration, diversity, and education: Beyond third culture kids* (pp. 143–162). Palgrave Macmillan.
Dillon, A., and Ali, T. (2019). Global nomads, cultural chameleons, strange ones or immigrants? An exploration of third culture kid terminology with reference to the United Arab Emirates. *Journal of Research in International Education, 18*(1), 77–89. doi: 10.1177/1475240919835013.
Dixon, P., and Hayden, M. (2008). 'On the move': Primary age children in transition. *Cambridge Journal of Education, 38*(4), 483–496. doi: 10.1080/03057640802489418.
Eidse, F., and Sichel, N. (2004a). Introduction. In F. Eidse and N. Sichel (eds), *Unrooted childhoods: Memoirs of growing up global* (1st edn, pp. 1–6). Intercultural Press; Nicholas Brealey.
Eidse, F., and Sichel, N. (eds) (2004b). *Unrooted childhoods: Memoirs of growing up global* (1st edn). Intercultural Press; Nicholas Brealey.
Elwood, C., and Davis, M. (2009). *International mindedness: A professional development handbook for international schools.* Optimus Education.
Fail, H., Thompson, J., and Walker, G. (2004). Belonging, identity and third culture kids: Life histories of former international school students. *Journal of Research in International Education, 3*(3), 319–338. doi: 10.1177/1475240904047358.
Fanning, S., and Burns, E. (2017). How an Antipodean perspective of international schooling challenges Third Culture Kid (TCK) conceptualisation. *Journal of Research in International Education, 16*(2), 147–163. doi: 10.1177/1475240917722277.
Fechter, A.-M. (2016). Between privilege and poverty: The affordances of mobility among aid worker children. *Asian and Pacific Migration Journal, 25*(4), 489–506. doi: 10.1177/0117196816674397.
Fechter, A.-M., and Korpela, M. (2016). Interrogating child migrants or 'third culture kids' in Asia: An introduction. *Asian and Pacific Migration Journal, 25*(4), 422–428. doi: 10.1177/0117196816676565.
Forsberg, S. (2019). 'The right to immobility' and the uneven distribution of spatial capital: Negotiating youth transitions in northern Sweden. *Social and Cultural Geography, 20*(3), 323–343. doi: 10.1080/14649365.2017.1358392.
Gilbert, K.R., and Gilbert, R.J. (2011). Echoes of loss: Long-term grief and adaptation among third culture kids. In G.H. Bell-Villada, N. Sichel, F. Eidse and E.N. Orr (eds), *Writing out of limbo: International childhoods, global nomads and third culture kids* (pp. 246–262). Cambridge Scholars Publishing.
Hanisch, S. (2020). Chinese migration to Lesotho as a springboard toward a better future? The ambiguous social class positions of migrants' children. *Africa Today, 66*(3–4), 45. doi: 10.2979/africatoday.66.3_4.03.
Hatfield, M.E. (2010). Children moving 'home'? Everyday experiences of return migration in highly skilled households. *Childhood, 17*(2), 243–257. doi: 10.1177/0907568210365747.
Huang, S., and Yeoh, B.S.A. (2005). Transnational families and their children's education: China's 'study mothers' in Singapore. *Global Networks, 5*(4), 379–400. doi: 10.1111/j.1471-0374.2005.00125.x.
Hutchins, T. (2011). 'They told us in a curry shop': Child–adult relations in the context of family migration decision-making. *Journal of Ethnic and Migration Studies, 37*(8), 1219–1235. doi: 10.1080/1369183X.2011.590926.
Igarashi, H., and Saito, H. (2014). Cosmopolitanism as cultural capital: Exploring the intersection of globalization, education and stratification. *Cultural Sociology, 8*(3), 222–239. doi: 10.1177/1749975514523935.
Jarvis, J.A. (2020). Lost in translation: Obstacles to converting global cultural capital to local occupational success. *Sociological Perspectives, 63*(2), 228–248. doi: 10.1177/0731121419852366.

Kang, Y. (2013). Global citizens in the making: Child-centred multimedia ethnographic research on South Korean student migrants in Singapore. *Ethnography*, *14*(3), 324–345. doi: 10.1177/1466138113491673.

Kaufmann, V., Bergman, M.M., and Joye, D. (2004). Motility: Mobility as capital. *International Journal of Urban and Regional Research*, *28*(4), 745–756. doi: 10.1111/j.0309-1317.2004.00549.x.

Kim, J., and Okazaki, S. (2017). Short-term 'intensive mothering' on a budget: Working mothers of Korean children studying abroad in Southeast Asia. *Asian Women*, *33*(3), 111–139. doi: 10.14431/aw.2017.09.33.3.111.

Koh, S.Y., and Sin, I.L. (2020). Academic and teacher expatriates: Mobilities, positionalities, and subjectivities. *Geography Compass*, *14*(5), e12487. doi: 10.1111/gec3.12487.

Kunz, S. (2016). Privileged mobilities: Locating the expatriate in migration scholarship. *Geography Compass*, *10*(3), 89–101. doi: 10.1111/gec3.12253.

Kunz, S. (2020). Expatriate, migrant? The social life of migration categories and the polyvalent mobility of race. *Journal of Ethnic and Migration Studies*, *46*(11), 2145–2162. doi: 10.1080/1369183X.2019.1584525.

Kwon, J. (2019). Third culture kids: Growing up with mobility and cross-cultural transitions. *Diaspora, Indigenous, and Minority Education*, *13*(2), 113–122. doi: 10.1080/15595692.2018.1490718.

Lazarova, M., McNulty, Y., and Semeniuk, M. (2015). Expatriate family narratives on international mobility: Key characteristics of the successful moveable family. In L. Mäkelä and V. Suutari (eds), *Work and family interface in the international career context* (pp. 29–51). Springer International Publishing.

Leivestad, H.H. (2016). Motility. In N.B. Salazar and K. Jayaram (eds), *Keywords of mobility: Critical engagements* (pp. 133–151). Berghahn Books.

Lijadi, A.A., and Van Schalkwyk, G.J. (2017). Place identity construction of third culture kids: Eliciting voices of children with high mobility lifestyle. *Geoforum*, *81*, 120–128. doi: 10.1016/j.geoforum.2017.02.015.

Maxwell, C., and Aggleton, P. (2016). Creating cosmopolitan subjects: The role of families and private schools in england. *Sociology*, *50*(4), 780–795. doi: 10.1177/0038038515582159.

McCaig, N.M. (2002). Raised in the margin of the mosaic: Global nomads balance worlds within. *International Educator*, Spring, 10–17.

Mclachlan, D.A. (2007). Global nomads in an international school: Families in transition. *Journal of Research in International Education*, *6*(2), 233–249. doi: 10.1177/1475240907078615.

McNulty, Y., and Selmer, J. (eds). (2017). *Research handbook of expatriates*. Edward Elgar Publishing.

Moret, J. (2020). Mobility capital: Somali migrants' trajectories of (im)mobilities and the negotiation of social inequalities across borders. *Geoforum*, *116*, 235–242. doi: 10.1016/j.geoforum.2017.12.002.

Murphy-Lejeune, E. (2003). *Student mobility and narrative in Europe: The new strangers*. Routledge.

Ní Laoire, C. (2020). Transnational mobility desires and discourses: Young people from return-migrant families negotiate intergenerationality, mobility capital, and place embeddedness. *Population, Space and Place*, *26*(6), e2310. doi: 10.1002/psp.2310.

Nukaga, M. (2013). Planning for a successful return home: Transnational habitus and education strategies among Japanese expatriate mothers in Los Angeles. *International Sociology*, *28*(1), 66–83. doi: 10.1177/0268580912452171.

Nyíri, P. (2014). Training for transnationalism: Chinese children in Hungary. *Ethnic and Racial Studies*, *37*(7), 1253–1263. doi: 10.1080/01419870.2014.878029.

Okazaki, S., and Kim, J. (2018). Going the distance: Transnational educational migrant families in Korea. In M.R.T. de Guzman, J. Brown and C.P. Edwards (eds), *Parenting from afar and the reconfiguration of family across distance* (Vol. 1, pp. 321–338). Oxford University Press.

Orellana, M.F., Thorne, B., Chee, A., and Lam, W.S.E. (2001). Transnational childhoods: The participation of children in processes of family migration. *Social Problems*, *48*(4), 572–591.

Oso, L., and Suárez-Grimalt, L. (2017). Migration and intergenerational strategies for social mobility: Theoretical and methodological challenges. *Migraciones. Publicación Del Instituto Universitario de Estudios Sobre Migraciones*, *42*, 19–41. doi: 10.14422/mig.i42.y2017.002.

Pollock, D.C., and Van Reken, R.E. (2009). *Third culture kids: Growing up among worlds*. Nicholas Brealey.

Sander, M. (2016). *Passing through Shanghai: Ethnographic insights into the mobile lives of expatriate youths*. Heidelberg University Publishing.

Selmer, J. and Lam, H. (2004), 'Third-culture kids': Future business expatriates? *Personnel Review*, *33*(4), 430-445. doi: 10.1108/00483480410539506.

Tanu, D. (2014). Becoming 'international': The cultural reproduction of the local elite at an international school in indonesia. *South East Asia Research*, *22*(4), 579–596. doi: 10.5367/sear.2014.0237.

Tanu, D. (2015). Toward an interdisciplinary analysis of the diversity of 'Third Culture Kids'. In S. Benjamin and F. Dervin (eds), *Migration, diversity, and education: Beyond third culture kids* (pp. 13–35). Palgrave Macmillan.

Tanu, D. (2018). *Growing up in transit: The politics of belonging at an international school*. Berghahn Books.

Tse, J.K.H., and Waters, J.L. (2013). Transnational youth transitions: Becoming adults between Vancouver and Hong Kong. *Global Networks*, *13*(4), 535–550. doi: doi.org/10.1111/glob.12014.

Tu, M. (2019). The transnational one-child generation: Family relationships and overseas aspiration between China and the UK. *Children's Geographies*, *17*(5), 565–577. doi: 10.1080/14733285.2017.1393499.

Useem, R. (1973). Third culture factors in educational change. In C.S. Brembeck and W.H. Hill (eds), *Cultural challenges to education: The influence of cultural factors in school learning* (pp. 469–481). Lexington Books.

Van Reken, R.E. (2011). Cross-cultural kids. In G.H. Bell-Villada, N. Sichel, F. Eidse and E.N. Orr (eds), *Writing out of limbo: International childhoods, global nomads and third culture kids* (pp. 25–44). Cambridge Scholars Publishing.

Waddling, J., Bertilsson, E., and Palme, M. (2019). Struggling with capital: A Bourdieusian analysis of educational strategies among internationally mobile middle class families in Sweden. *Discourse: Studies in the Cultural Politics of Education*, *40*(5), 697–716. doi: 10.1080/01596306.2019.1598610.

Wan, M., Singh, R., and Shaffer, M.A. (2017). Global families. In Y. McNulty and J. Selmer (eds), *Research Handbook of Expatriates* (pp. 468–489). Edward Elgar Publishing.

Waters, J.L. (2005). Transnational family strategies and education in the contemporary Chinese diaspora. *Global Networks*, *5*(4), 359–377. doi:10.1111/j.1471-0374.2005.00124.x.

Waters, J.L. (2006). Geographies of cultural capital: Education, international migration and family strategies between Hong Kong and Canada. *Transactions of the Institute of British Geographers*, *31*(2), 179–192. doi: 10.1111/j.1475-5661.2006.00202.x.

Waters, M.C., and Levitt, P. (eds). (2002). *The changing face of home: The transnational lives of the second generation*. Russell Sage Foundation.

Weenink, D. (2008). Cosmopolitanism as a form of capital: Parents preparing their children for a globalizing world. *Sociology*, *42*(6), 1089–1106. doi: 10.1177/0038038508096935.

Wessendorf, S. (2016). *Second-generation transnationalism and roots migration: Cross-border lives*. Routledge.

Wilkins, S. (2013). 'Home' or away? The higher education choices of expatriate children in the United Arab Emirates. *Journal of Research in International Education*, *12*(1), 33–48. doi: 10.1177/1475240913479519.

Young, J.G. (2017). An investigation into how a globalised lifestyle, international capital and an international schooling experience influence the identities and aspirations of young people. *Journal of Research in International Education*, *16*(1), 108–108. doi: 10.1177/1475240916669080.

Zhou, M. (1997). Segmented assimilation: Issues, controversies, and recent research on the new second generation. *International Migration Review*, *31*(4), 975. doi: 10.2307/2547421.

8. Young people, intergenerationality and the familial reproduction of transnational migrations and im/mobilities
Caitríona Ní Laoire

INTRODUCTION

This chapter explores the role of intergenerationality in migration, with a focus on the ways in which migrations and im/mobilities unfold over multiple generations within families (see also other Chapters in Part II of this *Handbook*). The central argument is that migrations and mobilities are experienced and reproduced intergenerationally, in ways that connect past, present and future generations within families. The consequences of past migrations reverberate, often in unpredictable ways, across multiple generations. The chapter seeks to go beyond the here and now or snapshot in time approach to understanding migration and family dynamics and to take a broader temporal perspective on how migration and im/mobilities articulate within families. This perspective can draw our attention to long-term processes of social reproduction and the role of migration and im/mobilities in these processes. The socio-economic, cultural, political and legal implications of transnational migrations can have long-term consequences within families. It is important to examine the role of intergenerational dynamics in these processes: in other words, how relations within families and between generations shape patterns of migration, and vice versa, over time. I explore these processes by focusing on the ways in which mobility capital is transferred, and how narratives of migration and identity circulate and shift, across generations within transnational and migrant families. The chapter focuses in particular on how young people from migrant backgrounds engage with their familial migration histories and legacies.

First, I discuss recent developments in migration studies which highlight the relationality and interdependence of migration flows and the relevance of such perspectives for understanding the role of migration in social reproduction. Next, drawing on family studies literature, I explore the role of family in social reproduction and argue for the value of longitudinal, qualitative and narrative-based approaches in researching intergenerational dynamics in families that experience migration. Building on these bodies of literature, the following section explores the potential for transnationalism, diaspora and mobilities perspectives to shed light on intergenerational dynamics in transnational/migrant families. The final section draws on empirical studies and on research with transnational Irish families to discuss how young people from migrant backgrounds relate to their own migration histories, or legacies, and imagine their own futures. A conclusion summarises the main arguments and identifies some implications for understandings of transgenerational migration legacies and reverberations.

MIGRATION AS RELATIONAL, ENFOLDED AND LINKING LIVES OVER TIME

Recent literature on migration has explored the idea that migrations and mobilities interrelate with, and enfold through, each other. Williams et al. (2011) refer to 'enfolded mobilities', or how individual migrations/mobilities are enfolded with the migrations/mobilities of others. In other words, individual migrations often give rise to, or are integrally interwoven with, other migrations, such as when family members migrate to join others who have already migrated, or a period of study abroad produces opportunities and desires for future long-term migration (Findlay et al. 2017; King and Lulle 2015; Weichbrodt 2017). In particular, some literature suggests that transnational migrations experienced early in life can create circumstances that encourage and facilitate future migrations, and children born into migrant families often themselves go on to migrate as adults (Devlin Trew 2009; Veale and Doná 2014). It is now recognised that transnational migration is characterised by complex patterns of step migrations, chain migrations, onward migrations, returns, re-migrations, seasonality and circularity (Amelina et al. 2016; Paul and Yeoh 2021). The concept of return mobilities can help to shed further light on the complexities of transnational migration flows, referring to the 'range of return spatialities and temporalities' that connect home and host societies, as migrants and their children migrate, move onwards, return and re-migrate in complex patterns of mobility, settlement and family (re)formation (King and Christou 2011: 454). Individual migrations can also be embedded within wider chains or cultures of mobility. The interconnections that foster these enfolded migrations can be economically driven, such as, for example, in the case of global care chains (Oso and Ribas-Mateos 2013). They can also be cultural and historical in nature, such as the long-standing diasporic connections that foster ongoing (re-)migrations to and from diaspora destinations.

Migration almost always occurs in the context of family relations of some kind (even if these are relations of inequality or tension; see Chapter 1, this *Handbook*), which can in turn give rise to further migrations, such as family reunification, familial chain migration, return migration for family reasons, second-generation re-migration or return (Baldassar et al. 2014; Cooke 2008; Jiménez-Alvarez 2017). It is also increasingly recognised that migration is relational in the sense that it involves 'linked lives', whereby individual migrant lives connect with, and are interdependent with, the lives of others, over time (Bailey 2009; Holdsworth 2013; Huijsmans 2017). For example, migrants rely on social, family and wider networks for contacts, opportunities and support, and migrations are structured by (often uneven) family and household relations, and *vice versa* (Findlay et al. 2015; Holdsworth 2013; Kraler et al. 2011; Williams et al. 2011). However, the literature on family and migration tends to focus on relations within migrant or transnational families as they are experienced in the here and now, rather than taking longitudinal and long-term perspectives that could go beyond the individual lifespan. This reflects a broader tendency in migration studies to focus on snapshots in time or on individual life-courses. In this context, some have called for more longitudinal migration research (Findlay et al. 2015; Ryan and D'Angelo 2018). This resonates with recent calls for greater attention to questions of temporality in migration studies, to recognise migration not as a linear journey but as an open-ended process which connects past, present and future (Collins 2018; Griffiths et al. 2013; Cheung Judge et al. 2020). Thus, a long-term perspective could illuminate how migration in one generation of a family can shape migration/staying trajectories in subsequent generations, as well as how members of migrant families engage with their own family migration histories and imagine their futures. In other words, a wider temporal lens opens up questions about how migration and mobility are reproduced through family relations.

In order to understand how mobility is reproduced across multiple generations of migrant families, it is necessary to also examine the role of immobility. Migration can often result in spatial or geographical immobility for migrants, such as in contexts of restrictive immigration regimes or precarity (Brandhorst et al. 2020; Menjívar 2006). Mobility and immobility are both intimately bound up with questions of power; both can be manifestations of marginality or of privilege. However, as many have argued (e.g., Morokvasic 2004), empowerment and enforcement in migration lie on a spectrum rather than being a binary. Thus, mobilities and immobilities are enfolded through the linked lives of the im/mobile, intersecting with the transmission of privilege or marginalisation, and spanning international borders.

FAMILY, INTERGENERATIONAL DYNAMICS AND SOCIAL REPRODUCTION

While a wealth of literature exists that explores intergenerational dynamics in families, much of this is focused on concurrent or contemporaneous relationships between different generations. To explore how intergenerational family dynamics unfold over longer time periods, life-history scholarship provides useful conceptual tools. Biographical or life-history approaches view family as a site of social change and a lens through which to explore the micro-level articulations of macro-level historical and social processes (Bertaux and Thompson 2009). Longitudinal qualitative research with multiple generations of the same families can illuminate wider processes of social change (Edwards 2008; Gray et al. 2016). This type of research can also allow us to explore the role of family in social reproduction, and how narratives and meanings are negotiated and transmitted in families through long-term intergenerationality (between generations) or transgenerationality (across generations).

As illuminated by Thomson and Taylor (2005), a qualitative longitudinal perspective can reveal dynamic intergenerational patterns of continuity and change over time within families and communities. Thus, the ways in which family intersects with, and is embedded in, class, gender and geographical power relations can be unpacked through exploring individual trajectories and family dynamics over time. Family, from this perspective, plays a key role in social reproduction, understood here as the processes through which social structures (class, gender, race, and so on) are maintained over time (Bertaux and Thompson 2009), as it is through family in particular that resources and capital are exchanged between generations, and values and norms are negotiated intergenerationally. There are different ways of conceptualising social reproduction, but Bourdieu's (1986) conceptualisation, oriented around the idea of different types of capital, is particularly helpful when focusing on the family. According to Bourdieu's framework, social reproduction occurs through the intergenerational transmission of economic capital (wealth), social capital (social networks) and cultural capital (cultural competences) (Bourdieu 1986; Edgerton and Roberts 2014). Crucially, these processes of transmission involve tensions, negotiations and ruptures, such that social reproduction is rarely complete or predictable (Guhin et al. 2020). Thus, for example, children and young people can actively resist or re-work values, identities and assumptions that are learned, through socialisation, from parents and grandparents (Hutchby and Moran-Elllis 1998). According to James (2013), socialisation is not something that is 'done to' children, but is something they actively participate in: children are their own biographical agents, but they form their life-paths within the possibilities afforded by their family and social circumstances. These possibilities are comprised of forms of economic, social and cultural capital, and also, as discussed below, mobility capital.

James (2013) highlights that the emotional and relational aspects of social and cultural capital transmission are particularly important. Socialisation is not a set of rational transactions, but is bound up with emotions, identities, values and expectations, the less tangible things that structure and underpin intergenerational relationships and dynamics. Therefore, it is necessary to pay attention to the stories that people tell about their lives, their identities and their families. Narratives can reveal how people feel, how they relate to each other, how they make sense of the possibilities of their social contexts. Narratives are even central to the constitution of family itself, it is argued by some, pointing to the role of family memories in the development of collective narratives that resonate down through generations and connect present to past, though meanings change or are reworked in different contexts (Smart 2011; Thomson et al. 2010). These moments of change and re-working are the outcomes of intergenerational negotiations and tensions, often reflecting wider processes of social change playing out within families.

When family members experience transnational migration, these intergenerational negotiations come into sharp focus. James (2013) points out that while much socialisation involves the absorption of taken-for-granted norms, and thus is largely 'implicit', some socialisation processes are more explicit, such as when children may reject or resist parents' (or familial) cultures/traditions. James (2013) uses the example of ethnic or religious affiliation, but the point can be applied to the wider context of socialisation in migrant families. Much literature attests to conflicts and tensions that exist between parents and children in migrant families, often characterised as cultural differences (Cook and Waite 2016; Foner 2009; Tyyskä 2009). However, the emphasis on cultural conflict has been critiqued for its reification of cultural boundaries, lack of attention to younger generations' subjectivities, and assumptions of progressive linear integration of migrant families with each generation (Mannitz 2005; Olwig 2003). This chapter is not concerned specifically with intergenerational tensions around ethnic identities, but with a broader understanding of intergenerational dynamics in migrant families. It is concerned with aspects that tend to receive less attention, such as transmission of capital, negotiation of family narratives of im/mobility and belonging, and the unfolding of migration and im/mobility trajectories over time.

TRANSGENERATIONAL REVERBERATIONS IN MIGRANT AND TRANSNATIONAL FAMILIES

In seeking to develop a conceptualisation of transgenerational migration dynamics in families, this chapter draws inspiration from theorisations of migration as relational, non-linear and enfolded through processes of social reproduction that involve transmission of capital within families and negotiation of family narratives. However, much existing literature on the lives of migrant second (and subsequent) generations tends to takes a linear and predictive perspective on temporality, which does not adequately recognise the circularity or provisionality of migration, or the incomplete and iterative nature of transmission of capital within families. There is a paucity of research focusing explicitly on micro-level intergenerational reproduction of migration and im/mobility within families which conceptualises migration as relational and non-linear. Studies often focus on questions of assimilation and social mobility and are framed within a 'settlement' or 'integration' perspective on migrant families (Ní Laoire et al. 2011; Olwig 2003; Yeh 2014). This perspective presumes that migration is followed by settlement, and an ideal of upward social mobility, in place, of subsequent generations.

However, despite this lack of attention, there is a wealth of empirical research with migrants and transnational families that, in different ways, does illuminate processes of intergenerational reproduction of migration/mobility within families (e.g., Chamberlain 2006; Tyrrell 2013; Zontini and Reynolds 2018). This type of empirical research tends to be influenced by theories of transnationalism, diaspora or im/mobilities. In other words, research that pays attention to transnational family linkages, or to complex im/mobilities in migration, frequently unearths valuable insights into processes of intergenerational reproduction of migration and im/mobility. Therefore, it is helpful to explore the insights that can be gleaned from the theoretical currents of transnationalism, diaspora studies and the mobility turn, before going on to a closer examination of some specific studies.

Research influenced by the mobility turn in migration studies has opened up the study of migration to the plurality of transnational mobilities, circulations and relations that frame the worlds of migrants and their families (Hannam et al. 2006; King 2012). Veale and Doná (2014), in their edited collection, point to what they call a transgenerational temporal connection in the ongoing cyclical nature of migration, a cycle in which children grow up in migrant families, go on to become migrants, and in turn have children who also grow up in migratory contexts. Veale and Doná's (2014) concept of the transgenerational is valuable for capturing the long-term nature of intergenerational dynamics and the wide temporal arc of the interconnections of individual and collective migrations through family relations, continuities and negotiations that have reverberations far beyond the immediately visible.

Others use the lens of transnationalism to shed light on intergenerational dynamics over time in migrant families. Zontini and Reynolds (2018: 418) propose the concept of transnational family habitus to denote 'a structured set of values, ways of thinking and "being" within the family built up over time through family socialization, practices and cultural traditions that transcend national boundaries'. Similarly, Levitt and Waters (2002) argue that second, and subsequent, generations in migrant families are embedded in transnational social fields that have a powerful effect on their identities, belonging and life trajectories, if viewed over long time periods. In other words, they emphasise the intangible but important ways in which younger generations, gradually over time, learn how to live transnationally from their childhood family contexts.

Scholarship on diaspora, transnational families and return mobilities sheds further light on long-term transgenerational reverberations. The well-established concept of chain migration refers to the phenomenon whereby individual migrations are made possible because of familial or other close contacts in destination societies, which in turn enable other family members to 'follow', in a pattern that can continue over many generations (Johnston et al. 2006). This phenomenon produces transnational social and familial networks that are constantly being renewed through ties of kinship, love, obligation, reciprocity and identity. For example, Chamberlain's (2006) multigenerational oral history with African-Caribbean diasporic families in England reveals the strength of intergenerational family ties in the transmission of familial cultural capital and connecting family members across time, generations and geographical locations. Her work also highlights the important role played by narratives in this process, as a means of giving voice to the ways in which individuals make sense of their family customs in diasporic contexts.

Other research on diasporic family narratives foregrounds the role of gender, recognising the expectations placed upon women to reproduce 'home' cultures and maintain families and homes in the diaspora, and the pressures placed upon women to uphold hegemonic cultural ideals in diasporic communities (Gray 2003; Zontini 2010). For example, De Tona's (2004) research with women in the Italian diaspora draws attention to the role of narrative in the gendered reproduction of Italian identity in the diaspora. Others taking a gender lens have also pointed to the ways in which second and subsequent generations of migrant families construct narratives that reflect their complex relationships with parental or ancestral cultural heritage (Dwyer 2000; Temple 1999). To understand long-term transgenerational family dynamics in contexts of migration, then, it is important to recognise the role of gendered and other power relations that structure families and kin networks, and to engage with the (gendered) narratives that reproduce, resist and transform them.

These transgenerational dynamics in diasporic and transnational families frame the contexts in which members of such families form identities, develop place attachments and imagine their futures. These contexts form part of the landscape of identity and belonging in which young people who grow up in transnational or migrant families form feelings about where home is, or might be, where and to whom they have meaningful connections, and where they can envisage their futures unfolding. Such feelings are often ambiguous and complex (Bloch and Hirsch 2018; Ní Laoire et al. 2011). These complexities are particularly evident in research on second-generation or ancestral return migration, where second or subsequent generations in migrant families migrate, or 'return', as adults, to the countries where their parents or ancestors were born (Christou 2006; Hannafin 2016; King and Christou 2011; Reynolds 2010; Tsuda 2009). The phenomenon of second- or subsequent generation return is linked to social, material and emotional ties that connect disparate members of transnational families. Reynolds (2010) and Zontini (2010), for example, highlight the role of transnational family ties and networks as a source of social capital for young people growing up in migrant families.

This type of transnational social capital can be viewed as one aspect of what could be termed mobility capital, that is, the resources and capital that enable cross-border mobility, including accumulation of past experiences of mobility and control over one's im/mobility (Brooks and Waters 2010; Moret 2020). I argue elsewhere that a transnational migrant background can be a valuable source of mobility capital, in the form of social capital (transnational family ties), cultural capital (migration competence) and symbolic capital (global 'experience') (Ní Laoire 2020). In other words, migration is enabled by the possession of particular mobility-related knowledge and resources (mobility capital) that can be utilised in planning and undertaking migration journeys, and mobility capital is tied up with accumulated migration experience and history. Thus, mobility capital can be transferred between generations in migrant families. This does not mean that mobility itself is always a privilege: mobility can be a result of marginalisation and can be painful. The value of the concept of mobility capital lies in its recognition of the role of power; that is, the degree of control it allows one over their own mobility or immobility.

To summarise, insights into intergenerationality in migrant families from studies influenced by transnationalism, diaspora studies and the mobilities turn highlight the importance of long-term perspectives on temporality, the role of gender, transnational social fields and mobility capital, the complexities of intergenerational relations, and the circulation of narratives of migration, mobility and belonging in families. Taking this approach to the life trajectories of young people growing up in migrant families, then, it becomes clear that the destination society is not necessarily an end-point for all family members, and that second and subsequent generations negotiate their own im/mobility life-paths as autonomous adults. In contrast, research that focuses on 'integration' of immigrant youth tends to view children of migrants in quite narrow terms, identified only in terms of their position in relation to other migrants – that is, their parents – without considering their own diverse social positions, life-worlds and pathways. As Yeh (2014) highlights, it is important to pay attention to children's own mobilities, which often transcend ethnic or familial ties and patterns. Children of migrants develop migration and im/mobility trajectories in their own right and engage in different ways with their family's migration history as they do so.

YOUNG PEOPLE FROM MIGRANT BACKGROUNDS AND THEIR TRANSGENERATIONAL CONNECTIONS: INSIGHTS FROM EMPIRICAL STUDIES

The analysis above raises two key points that are explored further in this section, focusing on young people from migrant backgrounds and how they relate to their own migration histories and their own futures. First, growing up in migrant family contexts (that are structured by power relations) shapes their life-worlds and possibilities in many ways, through their access to mobility capital, closing off some life possibilities while opening up others. Second, these young people carry their memories and legacies of childhood/family migration with them as they transition to adulthood; shaping dispositions towards migration, place and global/local identities, dispositions that are part and parcel of how they negotiate future im/mobilities and migrations. In this section, I draw on a number of empirical studies to illustrate both of these points.

Migrant Background and Mobility Capital

Existing literature sheds some light on the social and material circumstances shaping the childhoods and transitions to adulthood of children and young people who grow up in migrant families, as first, 1.5 or second generations. Qualitative research conducted with young people from migrant backgrounds, as they are transitioning to adulthood and contemplating their future life plans, can shed light on how they make sense of their own social positions and the possibilities of migration or settlement that are open to them. It can reveal the extent and nature of the social, material and emotional connections that tie these young people to their places of residence as well as to other places elsewhere and the degree of mobility capital they can access. For example, in her research with young teenage 1.5-generation migrants from Eastern and Central European countries living in Ireland, Tyrrell (2013) found that despite having lived in Ireland for a number of their most formative years, her participants did not express strong feelings of connection to Ireland. They had undertaken a number of residential relocations within Ireland, and many had strong family connections to their countries of origin. Their life-worlds were more transnational than local/national, and they imagined their futures in an open-ended way, open to prospects of re-migrating transnationally or staying in Ireland, depending on where the best opportunities lay. As Tyrrell (2013) points out, in this sense the transitory aspects of their lives continued, with transnational migration viewed as an ongoing process.

An openness to onward migration among the 1.5 generation was also found by Ramos (2018) in her research with Latin American migrant families in Spain. She found that a lack of opportunity in Spain, related to the economic crisis, propelled many young people (who had moved to Spain as children with their parents) to migrate onwards independently as young adults to the United Kingdom (UK). Their knowledge of how to navigate immigration systems, together with their ties to family contacts in the UK, often intergenerational, comprised crucial mobility capital that enabled them to make their own migration decisions independently of their parents. These studies (Ramos 2018; Tyrrell 2013) show how young people from migrant backgrounds navigate social and structural circumstances in the countries in which they grow up, relating to, for example, economic crisis, precarity or marginalisation, by drawing on their transnational and mobility capital to forge their own pathways.

Both groups discussed above (young Central/Eastern European migrants in Ireland, young Latin Americans in Spain) came of age at a time of economic crisis, in countries where they did not have strong ties, and as members of immigrant populations that experience labour market marginalisation. It is likely that young migrants in such contexts may not have access to valuable local social connections, kinship networks or family property/wealth. Their local place-specific capital may not be deeply rooted in ways that could give them added advantages in the labour market or education system. Relatedly, they may also have ambiguous feelings towards the places in which they have grown up (Andall 2002; Ní Laoire et al. 2011; Reynolds 2010; Tyrrell 2013). However, they do possess strong mobility capital, and may be positively disposed to transnational migration, as a result of their familial transnational connections and familial migrant histories (Ní Laoire 2020; Ramos 2018). In this sense, migrant (family) background can be viewed as playing a role in the complex intersection of structural processes (intersecting with social class, legal status, ethnicity, race, gender) that shape the possibilities open to young people as they transition to adulthood and navigate their life-paths.

Case Study 1: Mobility Capital and Young People in Transnational Multigenerational Irish Families

To illustrate this further, I draw here on my own research with multigenerational Irish transnational families, conducted over a period of approximately 12 years. Continuous flows of emigration, return and re-migration have maintained an Irish diasporic presence in global destination societies – particularly the UK and the United States (US) – and are reflected in the existence of translocal family networks and deep transnational social connections (Hannafin 2016; O'Carroll 2018; Ryan 2004; Walter 2013). I conducted qualitative research with young people who had migrated to Ireland as children with their Irish return-migrant parents during the Celtic Tiger economic boom period (late 1990s to late 2000s). The first phase of the research sought to explore their experiences, as children, of migration to a place considered 'home' by their parent/s (Ní Laoire et al. 2011). The families had moved to the south-west of Ireland, from a wide range of international locations, with Britain and the US being the two most common countries of origin. The initial set of data was gathered through multi-modal qualitative research with 36 children and teenagers in 16 such families over a period of two years in 2007–2009, between one and 12 years since their move to Ireland. Interviews were also conducted with their parents. A follow-up study was conducted between 2014 and 2018, involving return interviews with ten of those young people (seven women and three men), when they were aged between 18 and 31.

For the purposes of this discussion, I focus on four of these families, selecting those families where there were at least three generations of migrants and return migrants. For example, Orla[1] moved to Ireland at the age of eight, from England, with her second-generation Irish parents, during the Celtic Tiger period. Her parents were both born in England, to Irish-born parents (Orla's grandparents) who themselves had migrated to England as part of the large wave of Irish emigration in the mid-20th century. Another family, Ellie's, had some similar characteristics but in this case the transnational extended family was stretched between Ireland and a US city. Ellie had moved to Ireland from the US at a young age with her parents and brothers. Her parents were born in Ireland and had emigrated to the US as young adults during the 1980s wave of Irish emigration, a move that was enabled by the friendship and family contacts they had in the US. Both of these family histories are stories of transnational migrations, returns and re-migrations, within Irish diasporic networks, encouraged and enabled by the social capital of their transnational family connections, or what could be termed strong mobility capital that is transmitted between generations. They are also stories of how prevailing social and economic climates at particular time periods, such as the ebbs and flows of waves of migration from and back to Ireland, play out in people's biographies and reverberate through the generations. Their migrations are not one-off migratory events by individuals, but form part of a web of transgenerational and transnational migrations and settlements that shape the life-worlds of young people like Orla and Ellie.

Both Orla's and Ellie's immediate families had been affected by the post-2008 economic crash in Ireland. Ellie's father lost his job in the construction sector. He then re-migrated to the US, where job opportunities were more plentiful, and a large network of family and friends could support him to find work and accommodation. One of Ellie's brothers also returned to the US, to the city where he had lived as a young child, also to work in the construction sector. Similarly, Orla's father lost his job during the crash and spent a long time looking for work locally in Ireland, eventually taking up a job in a different part of the country which necessitated long-distance weekly commuting. She commented that his difficulties in finding employment in Ireland were related to his lack of 'connections' (valuable social contacts, or social capital) there.

While mobility capital enables members of transnational families to migrate or commute in response to crises such as unemployment, one outcome of ongoing, transgenerational migrations and re-migrations in such families can be a certain lack of local place-specific capital. In a similar way, Van Houte et al. (2015) find that for some migrants, particularly involuntary migrants, transnational migration actually weakens their already limited ties in both source and destination societies, thus further marginalising them. (On the contrary, for other migrants, who have more control over their migration, it is possible to benefit from establishing ties and investments in more than one place; Waters 2006.) Thus, migrant background intersects in complex ways with social class, ways that are not always captured in discussions about linear social mobility in migrant families. For both Orla and Ellie, the possibilities open to them as they transitioned to adulthood were shaped by their access to strong mobility capital, which they were very aware of, along with the fragility of their local place-based ties. For both, this meant that they viewed their life-paths as potentially involving transnational migration or mobility: Orla had moved back to England, while Ellie was planning to travel.

The gendered nature of this phenomenon is also notable, as gendered norms and structures shape the possibilities open to different family members at times of crisis. In both Ellie's and Orla's families, and a number of other families in my research, mothers continued to hold down local jobs during the crisis, even though they were often low-paid, part-time or seasonal, while travel/migration provided possibilities for well-remunerated full-time employment for fathers and young men (usually in construction or related sectors). Employment opportunities for women in the diasporic networks were less lucrative. While most of the young people of the next generation that I interviewed were pursuing higher education, it was clear that some of the young women were particularly keen to establish stable and secure professional careers, viewing higher education as the means to do so. This must be viewed in the context of the gendered nature of migration opportunities in the Irish diaspora. Decisions about staying or leaving are shaped by gendered realities which intersect with migrant background in specific ways. The mobility capital that is transmitted intergenerationally in transnational families is not gender-neutral; thus, the legacy of familial migration histories and capitals can be experienced differently by men and women. These intersectional processes permeate the patterns of transgenerational mobilities, migrations and settlements within transnational families.

Im/mobility Dispositions and Narratives

While migrant background plays a structural and intersectional role in processes of social reproduction (involving social class and gender), the examples discussed above also indicate the role of the less tangible meaning-making processes through which family members make sense of their migration histories, mobility capital and social worlds. Social reproduction is never complete or predictable, as values, identities and expectations are constantly becoming, and as narratives and dispositions surrounding migration/mobility are negotiated by and between different generations. Thus, focusing on narratives about and dispositions towards migration and mobility among young people from migrant backgrounds can shed further light on intergenerational reproduction.

Thomson and Taylor's (2005) research demonstrates the key role of parental values and influence on young people's dispositions towards mobility or immobility, mediated through social class and gender. Some have pointed to the existence of 'cultures' of migration within certain families and communities, such as Kandel and Massey's (2002) research, which demonstrates that particularly pro-migration aspirations exist among young people from families that already have some migratory involvement. Other research shows that young people in transnational families develop transnational ways of being and belonging, as a result of childhoods being permeated by taken-for-granted transnational ties and belongings (Bloch and Hirsch 2018; Levitt and Glick Schiller 2004; Levitt and Waters 2002). For example, in the context of Irish transnational families, Walter (2013) demonstrates the role of memories of childhood visits 'back home' to Ireland in identity constructions among second-generation Irish people in England. Cairns's (2014) research with undergraduate students in Northern Ireland finds that family and personal factors were important in their orientations towards future migration, where strong local family ties could discourage migration or, on the other hand, a 'pro-mobility' habitus may exist in some families. In the context of recent Irish migration, Moriarty et al. (2015) highlight the crucial role played by previous mobility experiences and family migration histories in enabling graduate emigration and producing what they term a 'graduate mobility habitus'. My earlier research found that Irish return migrant parents expressed a desire for their own children to experience some transnational mobility in the future, which the parents tended to construct in terms of valuable life experience. Those same children in return migrant families, when they were older, in turn drew on their family histories of migration as a repository of meaning in relation to their own (actual or imagined) migrations, referring to relatives' past migrations in constructing transnational migration, or mobility, as a viable option for themselves (Ní Laoire 2020).

Research by Yeh (2014) with young British-Chinese people who had grown up in Britain shows how their parents' transnational migration trajectories had shaped their own childhood experiences in many ways, including growing up with a familiarity with the idea of travelling long distances around the world for reasons of work, study and love. However, as the young people transitioned to adulthood, experiencing racialisation and marginalisation in Britain, they forged social worlds that involved virtual mobility and transnational cultural consumption, taking on globalised 'Oriental' youth identities in resistance to the strong 'national' identities associated with their parents (Yeh 2014).

Thus, research shows that young people do not necessarily absorb familial identities or narratives of mobility intact and unchanged. They actively engage with them, being selective, and changing them in the process (Tyrrell et al. 2019). For example, in Kelly's (2017) research with Iranian second-generation youth migrating from Sweden to the UK, the young people's decisions to migrate are shaped in part by their parents' social aspirations, and enabled by diasporic connections. However, the young people construct their own narratives of migration, which are more nuanced and complex than their parents' aspirational narratives, reflecting gendered and generational differences (Kelly 2017). Thus, exploring how different generations narrate their own migration and mobility trajectories and imaginaries can reveal ruptures, shifts and tensions in intergenerational dynamics, reflecting the particular circumstances in which each generation grows up, and how they experience and make sense of them.

Case Study 2: Mobility Narratives of Young People in Multigenerational Transnational Irish Families

Intergenerational dynamics of dis/continuity are evident in the narratives of different generations in my own research. For example, Niamh had moved back to Ireland at the age of four with her parents and siblings. Her own parents were both born in England to Irish-born parents who were part of the mid-20th century wave of Irish migrants who had settled in and around London. Niamh's father, Donal, recalled his childhood growing up in an Irish family in England in the 1970s, participating in Irish diasporic cultural activities, and returning to rural Ireland for long summer holidays every year. He also remembered vividly his own parents' ambiguous desire to return to live in Ireland, which they planned incessantly but did not actually fulfill. His own subsequent decision as a young father to move to live in Ireland, a second-generation 'return', must be viewed in the context of his family's strong connections to Ireland, his memory of his parents' unfulfilled dream to return, along with his disillusionment with the lack of opportunity in England, where his employment situation was insecure and they were experiencing financial difficulties. While the move to Ireland did not resolve all of their troubles, Donal's narrative constructed it as the right decision for the family, and one they would not change.

Niamh herself grew up from the age of four, then, in a family who struggled to an extent to establish themselves in Ireland in terms of employment and social acceptability in their local area (as a 'blow-in' family with English accents living in a rural area). Thus, in her teens she talked nostalgically about England as she struggled to position herself in relation to the binary constructs of Irishness and Englishness shaping her social world. I met Niamh again when she was in her early twenties and still living in Ireland, having spent a year travelling abroad. At this point, for her Ireland was home, and she planned to settle in Ireland, but she had a strong desire to travel, in which a return to live in England was just one option among many, including a variety of possible global destinations. In other words, her identity was bound up with the idea of transnational mobility and cosmopolitanism, an identity she embraced as a form of resistance to a kind of small-town mentality that she associated with people who had never moved, that is, who did not have a migrant background. She also distinguished herself from other migrants, however, constructing her time abroad in terms of travel and life experience rather than migration for work: 'I kind of went over there to work and travel whereas a lot of Irish people go over there to work. I know people who have been over there for 3 years and I saw more of [that country] in 8 months than they did since they've been there' (Niamh).

For Niamh, a migrant-background identity was important, and was possible because of her own family history, echoing back to her grandparents' migrations. But it was also a different type of migrant identity to that of either her parents or her grandparents, being much more open-ended, cosmopolitan and, to an extent, located in the past and in the future rather than the present. The migration stories of all three generations are intimately interlinked, but each also reflects the particular historical and biographical circumstances of their own generation, their intergenerational relationships, and the ways in which they each make sense of, and continue to make sense of, these stories.

These types of intergenerational continuities and ruptures also reflect wider societal discourses surrounding migration, as these shift and change over time. The young people I interviewed tended to construct their own future possibilities in terms of travel and global mobility, as distinct from the 'emigration' of their parents and grandparents, even as they drew on their family histories of migration as valuable cultural capital. (In fact, discursive efforts to replace the term 'emigration' with 'migration' have been a recurring feature of ideological battles over e/migration in Ireland since the late 20th century; MacLaughlin 1994.)

The impact of the legacy of historical narratives of e/migration is particularly poignant in the case of Emer (who had moved back to Ireland as a young child with her second-generation Irish parents). As a young adult, she travelled around the world, and was living abroad when I re-interviewed her. By then, the economic crash had happened in Ireland, and although she was ready to move back to Ireland, there were no job opportunities for her there, and her father had also lost his job, so she could not rely on her parents to support her during a transition back to life in Ireland. As a result of prevailing economic conditions, intersecting with her migrant background, she was unable to return to Ireland, finding herself in effect stuck on the other side of the world.

> I'm really angry that you know in 2007 when I was studying about Irish emigration, I was like ... as if that was another generation, I felt like I was lucky you know reading about people's past experiences, that I would never have to emigrate and I wouldn't you know ... my generation families wouldn't be torn apart and it just makes me really angry. (Emer)

The shock she experienced at finding herself living through an experience (involuntary exile) that she had considered to be consigned to history, and to the history of her own family, is palpable in this quote from Emer. Her shock reflects the unexpectedness of the realisation that the linear discourse of progress is just that, a discourse, and her coming to terms with the way in which her own life trajectory carries echoes of the emigrations of previous generations of her family.

To summarise, the narratives of members of multigenerational migrant families reveal something of how intergenerational reproduction of migration and im/mobility is experienced and lived out by different generations. Young people from migrant backgrounds engage with family memories and stories of migration and settlement, and their own memories of being migrant children, as they navigate the social and economic circumstances and prevailing discourses that shape their social worlds. In doing so, they re-produce and re-make family narratives surrounding migration while producing new narratives.

CONCLUSIONS

There is a lack of attention given to the role of intergenerational dynamics in the unfolding of migration and im/mobility trajectories over time, a gap that is linked to the tendency to view migration through lenses that emphasise snapshots in time, or individual biographies. I argue here that a transgenerational perspective can bring new insights by drawing the gaze to a longer temporal perspective, while also grounding analysis in contextualised understandings of the structural and historical circumstances in which each generation experiences childhood/ youth and forms attachments, hopes and desires. A key element of these sets of contextualised circumstances is the family context, its history, its present and the intergenerational relationships that constitute it. This chapter has drawn on migration and family studies literature, and specifically on transnationalism, diaspora and mobilities perspectives (e.g., Thomson and Taylor 2005; Veale and Doná 2014; Zontini and Reynolds 2018) to propose a framework for understanding transgenerational reproduction of migration and im/mobility. In this way, migration can be reproduced within families and, in some cases, multigenerational migrant families become established through ongoing migrations, returns, re-migrations and mobilities that connect family members across transnational borders and generations (e.g., Chamberlain 2006). The concepts of mobility capital (Moret 2020) and place-based capital are useful in illuminating how such families both benefit from, and are disadvantaged by, the nature of their transnational and locally rooted resources and ties. Thus, intergenerational migration dynamics are intimately bound up with processes of social reproduction, involving social structures such as, for example, social class and gender.

Focusing on the ways in which young people from migrant families make sense of their migrant backgrounds as they develop their own life trajectories and narratives reveals the very dynamic and iterative nature of intergenerational relations. Processes of social reproduction are bound up with power relations and tensions within families; young people form their own im/mobility dispositions in the context of their family histories, their own histories of child migration and settlement, the transnational social worlds of their families and the local worlds in which they live (Levitt and Waters 2002; Yeh 2014; Ní Laoire 2020). As a result, they may seek to deepen their place-based roots and/or to continue the patterns of migration and mobility. Either way, members of multigenerational transnational families are constantly navigating mobility and settlement imperatives in their lives, and in the process reproducing, and reinventing/remaking, migration and mobility. Thus, migration and settlement events can be seen to have effects that reverberate through generations, often manifesting in new migrations, returns and re-migrations, but also in settlement and embedding, as family members navigate their own trajectories against the backdrop of family histories.

NOTE

1. Pseudonyms are used throughout, and some minor details have been changed to protect anonymity.

REFERENCES

Amelina, A., Horvath, K. and Meeus, B. (eds) (2016) *An Anthology of Migration and Social Transformation: European Perspectives*. Cham: Springer.

Andall, J. (2002) Second-generation attitude? African-Italians in Milan. *Journal of Ethnic and Migration Studies*, 28(3), 389–407. DOI: 10.1080/13691830220146518.

Bailey, A. (2009) Population geography: lifecourse matters. *Progress in Human Geography*, 33(3), 407–418.

Baldassar, R., Kilkey, M., Merla, L. and Wilding, R. (2014) Transnational families. In J. Treas, J. Scott and M. Richards (eds), *The Wiley Blackwell Companion to the Sociology of Families* (1st edn). Oxford: John Wiley & Sons, pp. 155–175.

Bertaux, D. and Thompson, P. (eds) (2009) *Pathways to Social Class: A Qualitative Approach to Social Mobility*. London, UK and New Brunswick, NJ, USA: Transaction Publishers.

Bloch, A. and Hirsch, S. (2018) Talking about the past, locating it in the present: the second generation from refugee backgrounds making sense of their parents' narratives, narrative gaps and silences. *Journal of Refugee Studies*, 31(4), 647–663, https://doi.org/10.1093/jrs/fey007.

Bourdieu, P. (1986) The forms of capital. In J. Richardson (ed.), *Handbook of Theory and Research for the Sociology of Education*. Westport, CT: Greenwood, pp. 46–58.

Brandhorst, R. Baldassar, L. and Wilding, R. (2020) Introduction to the special issue. Transnational family care 'on hold'? Intergenerational relationships and obligations in the context of immobility regimes. *Journal of Intergenerational Relationships*, 18(3), 261–280. DOI: 10.1080/15350770.2020.1787035.

Brooks, R. and Waters, J. (2010) Social networks and educational mobility: the experiences of UK students. *Globalisation, Societies and Education*, 8(1), 143–157. DOI: 10.1080/14767720903574132.

Cairns, D. (2014) 'I wouldn't stay here': economic crisis and youth mobility in Ireland. *International Migration*, 52(3). doi: 10.1111/j.1468-2435.2012.00776.x.

Chamberlain, M. (2006) *Family Love in the Diaspora*. New Brunswick, NJ: Transaction Publishers.

Cheung Judge, R., Blazek, M. and Esson, J. (2020) Editorial. Transnational youth mobilities: emotions, inequities, and temporalities. *Population, Space and Place*, 26, e2307. https://doi.org/10.1002/psp.2307.

Christou, A. (2006) *Narratives of Place, Culture and Identity: Second-Generation Greek-Americans Return 'Home'*. Amsterdam: Amsterdam University Press

Collins, F. (2018). Desire as a theory for migration studies: temporality, assemblage and becoming in the narratives of migrants. *Journal of Ethnic and Migration Studies*, 44(6), 964–980. doi: 10.1080/1369183X.2017.1384147.

Cook, J. and Waite, L. (2016) 'I think I'm more free with them': conflict, negotiation and change in intergenerational relations in African families living in Britain. *Journal of Ethnic and Migration Studies*, 42(8), 1388–1402. DOI: 10.1080/1369183X.2015.1073578.

Cooke, T. (2008) Migration in a family way. *Population, Space and Place*, 14(4), 255–265.

De Tona, C. (2004) 'I remember when years ago in Italy': nine Italian women in Dublin tell the diaspora. *Women's Studies International Forum*, 27(4), 315–344.

Devlin Trew, J. (2009) Migration in childhood and its impact on national identity construction among migrants from Northern Ireland. *Irish Studies Review*, 17(3), 297–314. doi: 10.1080/09670880903115512.

Dwyer, C. (2000) Negotiating diasporic identities: young British South Asian Muslim women. *Women's Studies International Forum*, 23(4), 475-486.

Edgerton, J. and Roberts, L. (2014) Cultural capital or habitus? Bourdieu and beyond in the explanation of enduring educational inequality. *Theory and Research in Education*, 12(2), 193–220. doi:10.1177/1477878514530231.

Edwards, R. (ed.) (2008) *Researching Families and Communities: Social and Generational Change.* London: Routledge.

Findlay, A., McCollum, D., Coulter, R. and Gayle, V. (2015) New mobilities across the life course: a framework for analysing demographically linked drivers of migration. *Population, Space and Place*, 21: 390–402. doi: https://doi.org/10.1002/psp.1956.

Findlay, A., Prazeres, L., McCollum, D. and Packwood, H. (2017) 'It was always the plan': international study as 'learning to migrate'. *Area* 49(2): 192–199. doi: 10.1111/area.12315.

Foner, N. (2009) *Across Generations*. New York: New York University Press.

Gray, B. (2003) *Women and the Irish Diaspora*. London: Routledge.

Gray, J., Geraghty, R. and Ralph, D. (2016) *Family Rhythms: The Changing Textures of Family Life in Ireland*. Manchester: Manchester University Press.

Griffiths, M., Rogers, A. and Anderson, B. (2013) Migration, time and temporalities: review and prospect. COMPAS Research Resources Paper, University of Oxford. https://www.compas.ox.ac.uk/2013/migration-time-and-temporalities-review-and-prospect/; accessed on 28/04/2021.

Guhin, J., McCrory Calarco, J. and Miller-Idriss, C. (2020) Whatever happened to socialization? SocArXiv Papers. https://doi.org/10.31235/osf.io/zp2wy, accessed 20 November 2020.

Hannafin, S. (2016) Place and belonging: the experience of return migration for the second generation Irish from Britain. *Irish Geography*, 49(1): 29–46. DOI:10.2014/igj.v49i1.644.

Hannam, K., Sheller, M. and Urry, J. (2006) Mobilities, immobilities and moorings. *Mobilities*, 1(1), 1–22. doi: https://doi.org/10.1080/17450100500489189.

Holdsworth, C. (2013) *Family and Intimate Mobilities*. London: Palgrave Macmillan.

Huijsmans, R. (2017) Children and young people in migration: a relational approach. In C. Ní Laoire, A. White and T. Skelton (eds), *Movement, Mobilities and Journeys. Geographies of Children and Young People 6*. Singapore: Springer Science+Business Media, pp. 45–66.

Hutchby, I. and Moran-Elllis, J. (1998) *Children and Social Competence: Arenas of Action*. London: Psychology Press.

James, A. (2013) *Socialising Children*. London: Palgrave Macmillan.

Jiménez-Alvarez, M. (2017) Autonomous child migration at the southern European border. In C. Ní Laoire, A. White and T. Skelton (eds), *Movement, Mobilities, and Journeys. Geographies of Children and Young People 6*. Singapore: Springer Science+Business Media, pp. 409–432.

Johnston, R., Trlin, A., Henderson, A. and North, N. (2006) Sustaining and creating migration chains among skilled immigrant groups: Chinese, Indians and South Africans in New Zealand. *Journal of Ethnic and Migration Studies*, 32(7), 1227–1250. DOI: 10.1080/13691830600821935.

Kandel, W. and Massey, D. (2002) The culture of Mexican migration: a theoretical and empirical analysis. *Social Forces*, 80(3), 981–1004. https://doi.org/10.1353/sof.2002.0009.

Kelly, M. (2017) Searching for 'success': generation, gender and onward migration in the Iranian diaspora. *Migration Letters*, 14(1), 101–112.

King, R. (2012) Geography and migration studies: retrospect and prospect. *Population, Space and Place*, 18, 134–153.

King, R. and Christou, A. (2011) Of counter-diaspora and reverse transnationalism: return mobilities to and from the ancestral homeland. *Mobilities* 6(4), 451–466. DOI: 10.1080/17450101.2011.603941.

King, R. and Lulle, A. (2015) Rhythmic island: Latvian migrants in Guernsey and their enfolded patterns of space-time mobility. *Population, Space and Place*, 21, 599–611. doi: 10.1002/psp.1915.

Kraler, A., Kofman, E., Kohli, M. and Schmoll, C. (eds) (2011) *Gender, Generations and the Family in International Migration*. Amsterdam: Amsterdam University Press.

Levitt, P. and Glick Schiller, N. (2004) Conceptualizing simultaneity: a transnational social field perspective on society. *International Migration Review*, 38, 1002–1039. https://doi.org/10.1111/j.1747-7379.2004.tb00227.x.

Levitt, P. and Waters, M. (2002) *The Changing Face of Home: The Transnational Lives of the Second Generation*. New York: Russell Sage Foundation.

MacLaughlin, J. (1994) *Ireland: The Emigrant Nursery and the World Economy*. Cork: Cork University Press.

Mannitz, S. (2005) Coming of age as the third generation: children of immigrants in Berlin. In J. Knörr (ed.), *Childhood and Migration: From Experience to Agency*. Bielefeld: Verlag, pp. 23–49.

Menjívar, C. (2006) Liminal legality: Salvadoran and Guatemalan immigrants' lives in the United States. *AJS*, 111(4), 999–1037.

Moret, J. (2020) Mobility capital: Somali migrants' trajectories of (im)mobilities and the negotiation of social inequalities across borders. *Geoforum*, 116, 235–242. https://doi.org/10.1016/j.geoforum.2017.12.002.

Moriarty, E. Wickham, J., Daly, S. and Bobek, A. (2015) Graduate emigration from Ireland: navigating new pathways in familiar places. *Irish Journal of Sociology*, 23(2), 71–92. https://doi.org/10.7227/IJS.23.2.6.

Morokvasic, M. (2004) 'Settled in mobility': engendering post-wall migration in Europe. *Feminist Review*, 77, 7–25. doi: https://doi.org/10.1057/palgrave.fr.9400154.

Ní Laoire, C. (2020) Transnational mobility desires and discourses: young people from return-migrant families negotiate intergenerationality, mobility capital, and place embeddedness. *Population, Space and Place*, 26, e2310. https://doi.org/10.1002/psp.2310.

Ní Laoire, C., Carpena-Méndez, F., Tyrrell, N. and White, A. (2011) *Childhood and Migration in Europe: Portraits of Mobility, Identity and Belonging in Contemporary Ireland*. Farnham: Ashgate.

O'Carroll, Í. (2018) *Irish Transatlantics: 1980–2015*. Cork: Attic Press.

Olwig, K. (2003) Children's places of belonging in immigrant families of Caribbean background. In K. Olwig and E. Gullov (eds), *Children's Places: Cross-Cultural Perspectives*. London: Routledge, pp. 217–235.

Oso, L. and Ribas-Mateos, N. (eds) (2013) *The International Handbook on Gender, Migration and Transnationalism: Global and Development Perspectives*. Cheltenham, UK and Northampton, MA, USA: Edward Elgar Publishing.

Paul, A. and Yeoh, B. (2021) Studying multinational migrations, speaking back to migration theory. *Global Networks*, 21(1), 3–17. doi: 10.1111/glob.12282.

Ramos, C. (2018) Onward migration from Spain to London in times of crisis: the importance of life-course junctures in secondary migrations. *Journal of Ethnic and Migration Studies*, 44(11), 1841–1857. doi: 10.1080/1369183X.2017.1368372.

Reynolds, T. (2010) Transnational family relationships, social networks and return migration among British-Caribbean young people. *Ethnic and Racial Studies*, 33(5), 797–815. DOI: 10.1080/01419870903307931.

Ryan, L. (2004) Family Matters: (e)migration, familial networks and Irish women in Britain. *Sociological Review*, 52(3), 351–370.

Ryan, L. and D'Angelo, A. (2018) Changing times: migrants' social network analysis and the challenges of longitudinal research. *Social Networks*, 53, 148–158.

Smart, C. (2011) Families, secrets and memories. *Sociology*, 45(4), 539–553. doi:10.1177/0038038511406585.

Temple, B. (1999) Diaspora, diaspora space and polish women. *Women's Studies International Forum*, 22(1), 17–24.

Thomson, R., Hadfield, L., Kehily, M. and Sharpe, S. (2010) Family fortunes: an intergenerational perspective on recession. *Twenty-First Century Society*, 5(2), 149–157. DOI: 10.1080/17450141003783389.

Thomson, R. and Taylor, R. (2005) Between cosmopolitanism and the locals: mobility as a resource in the transition to adulthood. *Young*, 13(4), 327–342, doi: 10.1177/1103308805057051.

Tsuda, T. (ed.) (2009) *Diasporic Homecomings: Ethnic Return Migration in Comparative Perspective*. Stanford, CA: Stanford University Press.

Tyrrell, N. (2013) 'Of course I'm not Irish': young people in migrant worker families in Ireland. In C. Crowley and D. Linehan (eds), *Spacing Ireland: Place, Society and Culture in a Post-Boom Era*. Manchester: Manchester University Press, pp. 32–44.

Tyrrell, N., Sime, D., Kelly, C. and McMellon, C. (2019) Belonging in Brexit Britain: Central and Eastern European 1.5 generation young people's experiences. *Population, Space and Place*, 25, e2205. https://doi.org/10.1002/psp.2205.

Tyyskä, V. (2009) Immigrant families in sociology. In L. Lansford, K. Deater-Deckard and M. Bornstein (eds), *Immigrant Families in Contemporary Society*. New York: Guilford Press.

Van Houte, M., Siegel, M. and Davids, T. (2015) Return to Afghanistan: migration as reinforcement of socio-economic stratification. *Population, Space and Place*, 21, 692–703. https://doi.org/10.1080/1369183X.2011.590928.

Veale, A. and Doná, G. (eds) (2014) *Child and Youth Migration: Mobility-in-Migration in an Era of Globalization*. Basingstoke: Palgrave Macmillan.

Walter, B. (2013) Transnational networks across generations: childhood visits to Ireland by the second generation in England. In M. Gilmartin and A. White (eds), *Migrations: Ireland in a Global World*. Manchester: Manchester University Press, pp. 17–35.

Waters, J. (2006) Geographies of cultural capital: education, international migration and family strategies between Hong Kong and Canada. *Transactions of the Institute of British Geographers*, 31, 179–192. https://doi.org/10.1111/j.1475-5661.2006.00202.x.

Weichbrodt, M. (2017) Lessons in transnationality: education-related mobility of young people in Germany and its self-reinforcing effects. In C. Ní Laoire, A. White and T. Skelton (eds), *Movement, Mobilities, and Journeys. Geographies of Children and Young People 6*. Singapore: Springer Science+Business Media, pp. 187–208.

Williams, A., Chaban, N. and Holland, M. (2011) The circular international migration of New Zealanders: enfolded mobilities and relational places. *Mobilities*, 6(1), 125–147. DOI: 10.1080/17450101.2011.532659.

Yeh, D. (2014). New youth mobilities: transnational migration, racialization and global popular culture. In A. Veale and G. Doná (eds), *Child and Youth Migration: Mobility-in-Migration in an Era of Globalization*. Basingstoke: Palgrave Macmillan, pp. 91–115.

Zontini, E. (2010) Enabling and constraining aspects of social capital in migrant families: ethnicity, gender and generation. *Ethnic and Racial Studies*, 33(5), 816–831. DOI: 10.1080/01419870903254661.

Zontini, E. and Reynolds, T. (2018) Mapping the role of 'transnational family habitus' in the lives of young people and children. *Global Networks*, 18(3), 418–436.

9. Split households and migration in the Global South: gender and intergenerational perspectives
C. Cindy Fan

INTRODUCTION

Migrants all over the world have probably been separated from their family members at one time or another. While short-term separation may be inevitable, split households that last beyond the short term are in fact quite common. This chapter draws on selected studies on migration, especially migration for work, that results in split households, in order to highlight this phenomenon as well as its gender and intergenerational impacts.

The works reviewed in this chapter showcase how a focus on households rather than individual migrants helps elucidate intra-household dynamics that are essential for understanding migration, including concepts of householding, household division of labor, household strategies, and translocal and multilocational households. These studies shed light on temporary and circular migration and question whether one-way and permanent migration is inevitable. They also illustrate how gender is central to household arrangements in relation to migration, manifested through gender selectivity of migration, gender division of labor, and how migration impacts or fails to impact deep-rooted patriarchal gender norms. Likewise, these studies highlight the impacts of householding and split households on the next generations, emphasizing remittances, care, left-behind children and migrant children, and new-generation migrants (see also Chapters 4, 7 and 13, this *Handbook*). Together, the scholarly contributions that inform this chapter underscore that a focus on split households is fundamental and essential for contemporary migration research and theories.

Rather than being exhaustive in reviewing the literature on migration, which is astronomically large, this chapter emphasizes studies on internal migration and on the Global South, though not exclusively. Two reasons explain this approach. First, while the literature on migration focuses disproportionately on international migration, internal migration is much more sizable. Second, recent decades have seen fruitful and rigorous research on migration in the Global South, including split households and the gender and intergenerational impacts of migration. The next two sections of the chapter review, respectively, how migration research has approached families and households, and key studies on split households, circular migration and multilocality. They are followed by a section on split households and gender, and another on split households and intergenerational impacts. The chapter closes with a summary of findings from the literature.

FAMILIES AND HOUSEHOLDS IN MIGRATION RESEARCH

Most early research and theories on migration considered individuals, namely the migrants, as the primary unit of analysis (see Chapter 1, this *Handbook*, for a discussion of this). For example, Ravenstein's (1885) "laws of migration," based on data from the United Kingdom (UK) in the 19th century, were concerned with migrants seeking work in the urban areas of rapid commercial and industrial development. While Ravenstein did observe migration of entire families among Irish emigrants, his explanations of migration decision-making focused on individuals. Widely seen as the first published work that analytically explains the "push–pull" framework for understanding migration, Lee (1966) outlined four factors that influence migration decision-making: those associated with the area of origin; those associated with the possible destination; intervening obstacles such as distance; and personal factors such as knowledge of potential destinations. The unit of analysis, similarly, is the migrant or prospective migrant. Another influential theory is that of mobility transition. Zelinsky (1971) linked migration to the stages of urbanization, from the premodern society with limited mobility to transitional societies with high fertility, massive rural–urban migration and rapid rise of cities, to advanced societies characterized by interurban and intra-urban population movements. In short, the theory is more about historical transition than explanations at the individual or household level. Seeking to explain high levels of rural-to-urban migration in Africa and other less-developed countries with high levels of urban unemployment, the Todaro (1976) model described migration as a response to urban–rural differences in expected rather than actual earnings, popularizing the view that migration decisions should be approached over a long time horizon. Still, like most theories that interpret migration as an investment of human capital (e.g., Sjaastad 1962), Todaro's approach emphasized rational decision-making at the individual level rather than the household or family level.

The new economics of labor migration theory postulates that remittances are part of an implicit and cooperative agreement between the migrant and the left-behind, under the assumption that the migrant will eventually return. For example, Stark and Lucas (1988) used Botswana as an illustration and called attention to the relationship between the migrant and the household. It is more recent research, however, especially work using a feminist framework and highlighting power relations and dynamics, that has more fully illustrated the analytical and empirical centrality of the household for understanding migration (Nagel and Boyle 2020). Lawson (1998), for example, foregrounded household divisions of labor and argued for seeing households as neither fixed nor static, but with an expanded conceptualization, including households that incorporate multiple members in diverse places. Focusing on women migrants in Indonesia to export processing zones and to overseas locations, Silvey (2000) found that they were motivated not only by higher wages but also by personal desires and struggles over gender ideology. Wallace (2002) argued that household strategies are especially critical for understanding societies that are subject to rapid change, when households are in situations of risk and uncertainty, when an increasing number of women enter the labor force, and when the informal economic sectors are large; all conditions that are common to many international and internal migrants today. In the same vein, Douglass (2006) proposed the concept of "householding," which emphasizes the household as a unit of analysis, as well as the social processes that sustain and reinvent the household in a changing environment. By extension, "global householding" refers to the forming and sustaining of a household globally, involving multiple locations in the world.

A householding approach highlights social processes in addition to the economic motivation of migration. Specifically, remittances are at the core of traditional explanations for labor migration, by reducing poverty and raising standards of living, diversifying risk, and improving investment in human and physical capital (e.g., Sana and Massey 2005; Taylor 1999). But migration and remittances are also part of the social processes that shape the meanings of the home and household. To the migrants, "home" takes on new meanings as a physical site that offers security but is distanced from daily life (Fan 2009; Fan and Wang 2008; Graham et al. 2012). "Being family" also takes on new meanings in the face of geographic separation and reconfiguration that impact intimate relationships (Bustamante and Aleman 2007; Yeoh 2009). The productive and reproductive relations between migrants and the left-behind are constantly reworked, negotiated and renegotiated, constrained by and challenging traditional gender and generational roles and norms (Asis et al. 2004; Hugo 2002; Xiang 2007). Who is the migrant, and who is/are left behind, are not only economic questions but also fundamentally social questions.

The two terms "family" and "household" are often used interchangeably, though they are not exactly the same. A family consists of individuals who are related to one another by blood or marriage, whereas a household usually refers to family members who are living under the same roof. While both terms include both social and spatial relationships, the term "family" tends to focus more on the social than the spatial. For example, members of the extended family are related to one another but may not live together. The term "household" tends to focus more on the spatial than the social. For example, non-family households may consist of individuals who are living together but not related to one another by blood or marriage. For migration research, neither term is perfect, but they have considerable overlaps. For the purpose of this chapter, the term "household" is preferred. First, when using this term, most researchers are de facto referring to family households rather than non-family households. Second, the term "household" in migration research helps to specify the family members who under normal circumstances are expected to live together. A family member migrating for work may therefore constitute a circumstance that deviates from the normal practice because the household is split temporarily or for a longer period. Third, a household is not only a spatial unit but perhaps more importantly it is usually also a social and budgetary unit where decisions made individually or collectively have direct impacts on other household members. Finally, the household as a unit for research is already common in studies on migration and families, especially those emphasizing strategies and changes, for example, householding (Douglass 2006), household division of labor and household strategies (Lawson 1998), translocal households (Nguyen and Locke 2014), and multilocational households (Schmidt-Kallert 2012).

SPLIT HOUSEHOLDS, CIRCULAR MIGRATION, AND MULTILOCALITY

Early studies on migration have tended to consider migrants' separation from the rest of the household to be temporary, and expect that migrants would avoid splitting the household. Ravenstein (1885: 196), for example, observed that "Whilst emigrants from England or Scotland depart in most instances without 'incumbrances,' it appears to be a common practice for entire families to leave Ireland in search of new homes." And Lee (1966) seemed to suggest that wives do not make migration decisions, but follow their husbands instead.

Indeed, the traditional notion of the family is that it is a spatially intact unit where family members are expected to stay together in one place (Mincer 1978; Stacey 1990; Walsh 2003; Yanagisako, 1979). Accordingly, conventional understanding about migration assumes that when one household member migrates for work, their absence is temporary and any household-splitting is short-lived. The concepts of tied movers and trailing spouses, for example, focus on family members following the migrants rather than splitting the household (e.g., Mincer 1978), and on families forgoing economic benefits in order to stay together (e.g., Odland and Ellis 1988). However, long-term separation of family members due to migration is not uncommon, nor is it a new phenomenon. For example, it has been practiced by goldmine workers in South Africa, 19th century Chinese coolies, Mexican *braceros* in the American Southwest, and post-World War II migrants in guest-work programs (Glenn 1983; Kaufmann 2007; Nelson 1976). Today, many Mexican families are divided by the United States–Mexico border, maintaining a transnational relationship with left-behind children and family members (Dreby 2007). A focus on the split household, along with issues of parenting, family relations, family organization, children's education, and the emotional cost of family separation (Bustamante and Aleman 2007; Fan 2015; Silvey 2006; Waters 2002), informs not only research on migration but also an updated concept of the family. Research on household-splitting, though not voluminous, draws attention to the long-term separation of family members as a practice, though obviously not desirable, pursued by many migrants.

The phenomenon of split households also challenges the assumption that migration is one-way and permanent, and that migrants always wish to and will become permanent residents in the host location. For example, Zelinsky (1971: 225–226) defined migration as "any permanent or semipermanent change of residence," practically excluding non-permanent mobility other than short trips. The prevalence of temporary and circular migration, however, questions the inevitability of one-directional and permanent migration. Temporary migration, in essence, refers to non-permanent migration. It could involve migration of short duration. For example, based on a study of south-central Bangladesh, Call et al. (2017) showed that households are highly responsive to environmental variability by using temporary migration to cope with such shifts. Temporary migration may also refer to migrants who are not expected to access local membership in the host location, including many internal and international labor migrants (e.g., Hugo 2009). In China, due to the household registration (*hukou*) system, rural migrants may not be able to obtain a permanent status in urban destinations, regardless of how long they have worked there (e.g., Liu and Xu 2017). In Vietnam, similarly, the *hộ khẩu* system ties rural and urban citizens to their household registration in a particular location (Nguyen and Locke 2014). While in both countries the household registration instruments no longer prevent mobility, rural–urban migrants are best described as temporary, circular and translocal rather than permanent migrants.

Circular migration is a form of non-permanent mobility and has been a common migration strategy (e.g., Deshingkar and Start 2003; Newland 2009; Skeldon 2010). Hugo (2013), who has written extensively on circular migration, defined it as "repeated migration experiences between an origin and destination involving more than one migration and return." He also linked circular migration to multilocality, by pointing out that circular migration effectively "involves migrants sharing work, family, and other aspects of their lives between two or more locations." Hugo's (1982) work on Indonesia was among the earliest studies documenting and offering the sociocultural and economic explanations of the widespread phenomenon of circular migration, and is relevant to understanding migration in many other countries as well as transnational migration. He observed that when migrants "earn in the high-income, high-cost destination but spend in the low-income, low-cost origin," they can maximize the purchasing power of their earnings from migrant work (Hugo 2013). However, Newland (2009) argued that while circular migration brings about many benefits to migrants, it is not always positive, and that much depends on "the degree of choice that individuals can exercise over their own mobility." Sometimes, institutional barriers to permanent migration are a main reason for circular migration. In China, for example, due to *hukou* restrictions and the continued value of rural land, rural–urban migrants may choose to migrate circularly (Chen and Fan 2016; Hu et al. 2011). The rural places of origin are also where migrants can identify with and can find a sense of security and social support (Fan and Wang 2008). In this connection, Roberts (2007) highlighted the parallel between Chinese circular migrants, who face institutional and other impediments to permanent settlement in urban areas, with Mexican migrants to the United States.

In an editorial of a special issue on internal migration in Asian developing countries, Zhu et al. (2013) argued that the conventional conceptualization of migration as a one-way, permanent move from origin to destination is inadequate. Citing the four articles on India, Cambodia and China in the special issue, the editorial called for more extensive examination of the ways in which migration forges rural–urban linkages, through temporary migration, remittances, family and emotional support, and other means. Drawing on research in an agricultural community in Paraguay, Finnis (2017) highlighted how circular migrants blur the conceptual line between rural and urban. While rural spaces cannot exist economically without urban migrant jobs, the former offer relationships and a sense of security, safety, ownership and control. At the same time, circular migrants are both rural locals identified with rural life and aspirations, as well as cosmopolitan workers with urban skills and experiences.

Split households may also be described as multilocational, multilocal and/or translocal. The circular migration and multilocality phenomena may be extensive and may continue for a long time, rather than being merely a stage in the stepwise progression toward permanent settlement in the host location. Dick and Duchêne-Lacroix (2016) observed that rural–urban multilocality is common in the Global South, especially in Africa where migrants who work and live in the city have strong rural family roots. They noted that in the Global North multilocality tends to involve second homes or children of separated parents instead. Schmidt-Kallert (2012) showed that multilocational households, often involving both a rural and an urban location, are both prevalent and sustained livelihood strategies in Namibia, South Africa and China. He highlighted multilocality as a conscious decision by households who take advantage of opportunities at two or more places, diversify risks, and fulfill important social functions such as caregiving and schooling.

Hall and Dorrit (2018) showed that in South Africa oscillating rural–urban labor migration has continued despite the removal of legal restrictions on permanent urban settlement, resulting in family members who are related by blood and marriage often living apart. They also highlighted the fluidity of household form and relationships, as functions of migrant work, children's schooling, and other changes. In the same vein, Fan et al. (2011) and Fan and Li (2020) have identified different types of household arrangements among rural–urban migrants in China, in response to work opportunities, caregiving needs, and other family changes. The most popular household arrangements include single migrants (an unmarried person migrating alone); sole migrants (a married migrant leaving the spouse and children behind); couple migrants (both spouses migrating, leaving their children behind); and family migrants (both spouses and their children all migrating). Drawing from a comprehensive review of research on rural–urban migration in Vietnam and China, Nguyen and Locke (2014) illustrated how translocal households straddle the city and the country, as household members migrate and return over their life course, simultaneously undertaking care and livelihood activities from different locations.

A focus on split households allows foregrounding those who do not migrate as also part and parcel of migration. In an editorial for a special issue that includes papers on Laos, China, Thailand, Vietnam, and Indonesia, Toyota et al. (2007) observed that the left-behind are often seen as passive recipients of migrant remittances, and instead advocated for bringing them closer to center stage in migration research, and for investigating the "migration–left behind nexus." Similarly, Oakes and Schein (2006) argued that translocality involves not only people but also capital, ideas, and other forms of connectedness, such that those who do not leave are indeed also translocal.

Research on return migration underscores further that permanent migration is not inevitable and that the long-term plan of migrants may very well be return to the place of origin or areas near the place of origin. Chen and Fan (2016) showed that it is a myth that rural–urban migrants in China all prefer urban *hukou* and hence permanent migration to urban areas. Rather, many want to hold on to their rural *hukou* and the option to eventually return to their places of origin. Gibson and Gurmu (2012) found that jobs and services are limited in Ethiopian urban centers and that most rural–urban migrants return to their villages within one year. Studies of return migrants also highlighted how they have changed. Drawing on the experiences of migrants to Hanoi, Anh et al. (2012) argued that even when migrants do return they do so with altered priorities and on different terms. In other words, while migrants may not become urban in the fullest sense, their homeland has become a space of familial origin and emotional identification, not a place where people necessarily seek to reside, work, raise their children, and build their lives. Gibson and Gurmu (2012) noted that one benefit for return migrants to rural areas in Ethiopia may be through enhanced social prestige and mate-acquisition. Focusing on return migration within Thailand and Vietnam, Junge et al. (2015) showed that migrants who return to other places within their home provinces have higher levels of education and greater likelihood to engage in non-farm employment than those who return to their home village. Fan and Chen (2020) also illustrated rural migrants who chose to return to urban areas near their places of origin, but not to their original villages. These findings highlight correlations between return migrants' spatial selection, human capital, and potential for diversifying household income.

The use of split households, multilocality, and translocality as household strategies requires that household members be flexible, collaborative, and creative, including reinventing gender and intergenerational responsibilities and relations. Focusing on rural–urban migrants in China, Fan (2009) showed that migrants and their family members are flexible in terms of work, location, and roles, and they are collaborative and creative in household arrangements and division of labor, as part of household livelihood strategies. Likewise, Kõu et al. (2017) observed for transnational and high-skilled migrants from India to the Netherlands and the UK that they and their extended families are flexible in terms of location and caregiving responsibilities.

SPLIT HOUSEHOLDS AND GENDER

Gender ideology and norms are central to understanding when and if split households are practiced, as well as what constitutes migrants' specific household arrangement. This section focuses on two important aspects of the role of gender in migrant households: gender selectivity of migration, and gender division of labor.

Gender Selectivity of Migration

Drawing on cases from around the world and especially the Global South, and using a critical lens, Chant (1998) highlighted the significance of intra-household dynamics for understanding the gender selectivity of migration. As discussed earlier, the concepts of tied movers and trailing spouses describe family members following the migrants rather than splitting the household. Most tied movers are women, hence the trailing wife phenomenon, which has been explained by differential and expected earnings between men and women; but Cooke (2008) argued that this human capital explanation is not adequate without also addressing the gender roles that assign men as the breadwinner. At the host location, the trailing wife may look for a new job or leave the labor market permanently or temporarily, becoming a homemaker and/or providing caregiving to children. While the increasing prevalence of dual-earner families has given rise to commuter partnership, where one partner lives near work part of the time, as a household arrangement (Van der Klis and Mulder 2008), the wife giving up her job to follow the husband is still the norm rather than the exception, even for high-skilled workers (e.g., Kõu et al. 2017).

When split households are pursued as a household strategy, traditional gender norms may prescribe women and girls' roles as tied to the home and the domestic sphere, so that they are left behind when males in the family take up migrant work. In China, the age-old patriarchal ideology that governs gender roles and divisions of labor within families is aptly summarized by the saying, "the woman's place is inside the family and the man's sphere is outside the family" (Mann, 2000). While this inside–outside dichotomy refers to women being responsible for domestic duties and caregiving, and men being responsible for earning income and activities outside the home, Jacka (2006) noted a shift in the boundary between women's "inside" realm and men's "outside" sphere among rural households. As husbands undertake migrant work, left-behind wives are now responsible for all rural tasks, including not only domestic and caregiving duties but also farming, animal husbandry, and other non-farm work. Fan and Chen (2020) noted that only when children have grown older would these wives consider joining migrant work.

In other parts of the world where patriarchy similarly dictates gender norms, the migration of women and girls may need permission and acceptance by parents and husbands. Paul's (2015) research on Filipino women who work as domestic workers overseas highlighted how women migrants reframe their migration as a duty to the family, rather than an activity that challenges traditional gender norms in a patriarchal society that prescribes men rather than women as the breadwinners. As such, Paul (2015: 282–283) approached migration as a household strategy and as a process and outcome of intricate negotiations between the migrant and her family members. Specifically, she showed that when women migrants face resistance from their father, husband or relatives to their leaving home to pursue migrant work, they adopt strategies that involve a "very particular performance of gender," by emphasizing their "gendered identities as dutiful daughters, caring mothers, and/or supportive spouses" via augmenting income to support the family. Drawing on case studies in Mali, Nigeria, Tanzania, and Vietnam, Tacoli and Mabala (2010) found that it is increasingly common for young women to migrate, in part because they have no land rights and few prospects at home, and that such migration has become more accepted as their remittances contribute to household income.

In societies which subscribe to the notion that women and girls' spheres are in the home, their participation in rural–urban migration to find work may be imbued with negative moral connotations beyond the inside–outside gender division of labor. This is especially the case for single women. For example, Gaetano (2015: 51) noted that in rural China, young women joining migrant work risk being associated with negative stereotypes about morals and money which contradict a deep-rooted gendered construction of virtue that defines womanhood. Similarly, Silvey's (2000) research in Indonesia highlighted young women's concerns that their time doing migrant work might tarnish their reputation as "good, marriageable" girls. On the other hand, men's participation in migrant work does not impede their marriageability. On the contrary, Fan (2018) found that in China men's marriageability is advantaged as a result of the remittances sent back by them or other migrant workers in the same household that improve standard of living such as housing (see also the subsection on "Gender Division of Labor," below).

Despite the sociocultural barriers to women's joining the migrant work labor force, the conventional model of the husband being the primary source of income and the primary migrant worker is quickly outdated. In particular, sex selectivity of the migrant labor market has created gendered migration streams. Large numbers of women from the Philippines, Indonesia, Thailand, and Sri Lanka are employed in Hong Kong, Taiwan, and Singapore, where wage increases over the past decades have resulted in shortages of low-skilled labor in domestic work, restaurants, and low-end services. At the same time, Filipino men dominate the global seafarer labor market (McKay 2015). In fact, the Philippines has maintained a well-oiled and successful recruitment system, and by doing so has enabled a sustained flow of remittances from migrant workers abroad, which account for 10 percent of the country's gross domestic product (Martin 2013). In Gulf Cooperation Council (GCC) countries, foreigners account for large proportions of the population, ranging from 30 percent in Oman and Saudi Arabia, to over 75 percent in Qatar and the United Arab Emirates (UAE), attributable first to primarily male migrant workers from other Middle Eastern countries to build infrastructure such as construction, and more recently to female migrants from India, Pakistan, Indonesia, and the Philippines to work in services (Martin 2013).

Indeed, the feminization of labor migration has been one of the main foci of migration scholarship over the recent decades, highlighting the increase in the number of female migrants and of women-dominated jobs, such as domestic workers, hotel and restaurant servers, nurses, and entertainers. Nevertheless, Kofman and Raghuram (2015) pointed out that men have dominated migration theories, and that these theories do not adequately address how women's forms of circulation are distinct from men's, and how the presence of women and men in migration streams is intimately related. They argued that women are not simply followers or being left behind, but are engaging in production and social reproduction in multivariate contexts.

Gender Division of Labor

In a household where one of the spouses has left for migrant work, what happens to gender division of labor? According to Ye (2019), left-behind women in China, particularly in the countryside, amounted to 61 million. As described earlier, the shifting of the inside–outside boundary has rendered left-behind wives shouldering not only caregiving and domestic work responsibilities, but also farming, non-farm work, and all other rural tasks, thus making it possible for their husband to pursue migrant work (e.g., Fan 2018; Jacka 2006). Many studies, including Fan and Chen (2020), have reported that left-behind wives may pursue migrant work once their children are older, underscoring that caregiving remains their primary responsibility.

When men are the left-behind, the intra-household dynamics may be more contested, especially in patriarchal societies (see Chapter 5, this *Handbook*). Lam and Yeoh's (2018) research in Indonesia and the Philippines, two countries that have had high rates of female labor migration especially for domestic and care work in Asia and the Middle East, found that left-behind husbands "do family" by assuming the domestic and care-providing duties that their wives can no longer do, without "undoing gender." They identified a "package deal" of reconstructed masculinity with one or more of the following four elements: the left-behind husbands emphasizing their taking up new responsibilities; reporting themselves as working or actually engaging in part-time, paid work; taking pride in being "the capable 'mothering' father;" and being, and being seen as, the family's decision-maker. Focusing on family and spousal separation among rural–urban migrants in Vietnam, Locke et al. (2012) highlighted the tension between migration on one hand, and being a good father/mother and a good husband/wife on the other. They observed that gendered ideologies and power relations offer more support to men than to women, and that absent mothers may construct themselves as parenting their children remotely. Also researching in Vietnam, Resurreccion and Khanh (2007) examined female rural–urban migrants in the Red River Delta who work as junk collectors and buyers. They showed that left-behind husbands taking up domestic work is fraught with ambivalence and anxiety, morally compelling women to compensate by accepting the difficult conditions in the city; and that rather than challenging conventional notions of gendered work, women and men are reassured by women's frequent visits, and the expectation that the current arrangement is temporary.

The above studies show that in translocal households where women may not be present to do gendered work such as caregiving and domestic work, they and the males in the family continue to uphold patriarchal gender norms. In other words, migration has not fundamentally challenged gender ideology. Nguyen and Locke (2014) found that in Vietnam and China what male and female migrants do may be challenging conventional familial arrangements, yet they still seek to perform and cast their practices in ideal traditional terms of the patriarchal family. Using stories of love life, fatherhood, and elderly care, Choi and Peng (2016: 152) highlighted the "masculine compromises" that are made by rural men in China, such as relaxing the "men outside, women inside" gender boundary, while insisting on preserving patrilineal and patrilocal practices as two pillars of the Chinese patriarchy. Fan (2018) noted that the remittances that rural–urban migrants in China send back to the home village are often used to build big houses, to increase the marriageability of rural men, thus also reinforcing the transactional nature of marriages in a patriarchal society. Fan and Chen (2020) also found that gender norms remain strong among the new generation of migrants, so that young women too are expected to assume caregiving as their primary responsibility, regardless of their opportunities and desire to pursue wage work.

Despite the above findings that migration has not challenged deep-rooted patriarchy, there is some evidence that intra-family relationships have been shaped by household-splitting. For example, Waters's (2010) research on transnational split households in Vancouver, where the wife is the "astronaut" who returns to the home country to work, showed that the husbands who stay behind in the host location have indeed changed their attitude toward life, including placing higher value on their relationships with their children.

SPLIT HOUSEHOLDS AND INTERGENERATIONAL PERSPECTIVES

As aptly described by Douglass (2013), "Householding is a longitudinal process: it is not solely about the fate of one member or one generation." This section focuses on the next generations, providing an overview of research on migration and care, migration's impacts on children, and new-generation migrants. It appears that much of the published research on these topics is drawn from experiences in Asia and China, hence this section's focus on those regions.

Migration and Care

Expenditures associated with children are among the main usages of migrant remittances, including basic maintenance such as food and clothes, but also more long-term usages such as education, and future marriage and housing expenses. Remittances are therefore a form of care. In an introductory chapter to a volume including cases of the Philippines, Indonesia, Sri Lanka, Bangladesh, China, Vietnam, and Thailand, Hoang and Yeoh (2015: 5) argued that remittances tend to become a primary currency of care in the context of Asian transnational labor migration, and raise questions about the meanings and purpose of the family in an increasingly mobile world. Research on care highlighted the importance not only of remittances, but also of the left-behind and the extended family. Studies on China have shown that the amount of remittances that migrants send back is a function of the extent of caregiving provided by the non-migrants (Fan and Wang, 2008; Fan et al., 2011). Nguyen et al. (2006) highlighted the impact of migration on the health of the left-behind, children who grow up in spatially and even globally extended family networks, and the left-behind males and elderly. In the same vein, Graham et al. (2012) used the "care triangle" to examine interactions between the left-behind children, the non-migrant parents and other caregivers, and the migrant parents in Indonesia and the Philippines, thus giving voice to the left-behind.

Kõu et al.'s (2017) biographic interviews with highly skilled migrants from India to the Netherlands and the UK highlighted life course events and "linked lives" (Findlay et al., 2015) within and beyond the immediate nuclear family. For example, the extended families might be heavily involved with childcare, especially grandmothers, including possibly international travel to host locations and/or the migration of children back to the home country to be cared for by the grandparents. Kõu et al. (2017) observed that the Western literature focuses mainly on the individual or (nuclear) household phenomenon, which does not sufficiently address cultural contexts where the extended family has a strong presence (Kõu and Bailey 2014).

Through the biographical stories of rural women in China, Fan and Chen (2020) highlighted Chinese families that stick together as a safety net, as well as rural women who provided multigenerational caregiving, to both their children and grandchildren. These women's availability and willingness to provide care, both at the place of origin and at the host location, has enabled their husbands and children to pursue migrant work. Like the stories described by Kõu et al. (2017), Fan and Chen's (2020) research underscored that the gender norms associated with caregiving has determined that mothers—across generations—are the designated care-providers.

The Next Generation

Research on migrants' children has been concerned with diverse topics. Studies on immigration to the Global North, for example, tend to focus on issues of adaptation, assimilation, and identity (e.g., Portes et al. 2009; Zhou and Bankston III 2016). Studies of children of migrants in the Global South, on the other hand, seem to pay more attention to impacts of migration on left-behind children, migrant children, and second-generation migrants. These are the foci of the rest of this chapter (see also Chapters 7 and 12, this *Handbook*).

Impacts on children

There is a significant body of research on the impacts of not living with parents on China's left-behind and migrant children, given their sheer extent, but the results tend to be mixed. Focusing on the challenges facing the 100 million children of migrants in China, both left-behind children and migrant children, Chan and Ren (2020) highlighted the prevalence of split families, the plight that rural migrants experience, and a vicious generational cycle of poverty and exclusion related to China's *hukou* system. The book also examined the effects of parental separation on children's delinquency and subjective health. Reviewing both English-language and Chinese-language publications on rural–urban migration in China, Wang and Mesman (2015) concluded that both migrant children and left-behind children show significantly less favorable emotional, social, and academic developmental outcomes than other children, and suggested that economic and acculturation stress and disrupted parent–child relations have undermined child functioning. Analyzing data from a migrant worker survey in six provinces, Liu et al. (2020) concluded that the childhood left-behind experience is adversely associated with correlates of human capital, especially mental health, and may subsequently affect employment in adulthood.

Yet, Xu and Xie's (2015) analysis of data from a 2010 national survey of nearly 2500 children in China found that children's migration has significant positive effects on their objective well-being, but no negative effects on their subjective well-being, and that there is little difference between the left-behind and non-migrant children across multiple life domains. Focusing on quality of education, Wang et al. (2017) compared migrant students in Shanghai and Suzhou who were born in and come from specific source communities in Anhui, and students who are in rural public schools in the same source communities, and showed that the latter outperform the former by more than one standard deviation. The findings highlight the role of teachers in rural public schools who are more qualified than those in urban private migrant schools. Analyzing data covering 141 000 children in ten provinces in China, Zhou et al. (2015) reported that for all nine selected indicators of health, nutrition, and education, left-behind children performed as well as or better than children living with both parents.

While parents who work in cities may access more financial resources, Zhou et al. (2015) argued that all children in rural China are vulnerable and need extra care and resources.

The above mixed results suggest that, in China, migration and split households have impacts on children, but the impacts are neither direct nor straightforward: migrant work improves objective well-being, but absentee parenting may undermine subjective well-being of children, whereas children's educational outcomes are functions of both parenting and schools. While studies on migration's impacts on children in other parts of the world are not as numerous, they too appear to have yielded mixed findings. For example, Bryant (2005) found some evidence in the Philippines, Indonesia, and Thailand that parental migration improves the material conditions of the left-behind children, as reflected in their health and schooling, and that the social costs of parental separation are strongly mitigated by the involvement of the extended family. Lahaie et al. (2009), on the other hand, noted that the impact of parental migration from Mexico to the United States (US) has had negative impacts on left-behind children in terms of academic, behavioral, and emotional problems compared to non-migrant households.

Second-generation and new-generation migrants
Studies on international migration have produced a rather fruitful body of research on second-generation immigrants, usually referring to children born in the destination country to first-generation immigrants who are foreign-born, and the one-and-a-half generation or those who arrived at the destination country before they reached adulthood (e.g., Plaza 2006; Portes et al. 2009; Zhou and Bankston III 2016). Specific to the US, Zhou and Bankston III (2016) distinguished further between an old second generation and a new second generation, referring, respectively, to those with foreign-born parents arriving before and after the 1965 Immigration and Nationality Act. This research area has tended to focus on issues of adaptation, assimilation, and identity of immigrants who stay permanently in the destination country.

Research on internal migration, however, also pays attention to second-generation migrants who are circular rather than permanent migrants. Some studies have hinted at a generational shift in attachment to the rural home and in circular migration. Hall and Dorrit (2018), for example, suggest that in South Africa the strength of rural ties for migrant children depends on where they grew up. The country where a large body of research on "new-generation" migrants has been done is China, where internal migrants are numerous and have remained so for decades, and where a new generation of migrants have fast become the majority among migrant workers and have established themselves as a group quite distinct from "old-generation" migrants (e.g., Chen and Liu 2016; Fan and Chen 2013; Liu et al. 2020; Xiao et al. 2020; Zhao et al. 2018). Most commonly, the term "new-generation migrants" is defined as migrants who were born after 1980, that is, the post-1980 generation (e.g., Liu et al. 2020). However, sometimes the term is interchangeably used with "second-generation migrants," and may also refer specifically to migrants who are children of first-generation migrants (e.g., Liu and Cheng 2008; Zhu and Lin 2014). Finally, the term "new-generation migrants" may also include individuals who began migrant work no earlier than 1990, as opposed to those who began migrant work before 1990 (e.g., Wang 2001). While this definition may include migrants who started migrant work later in life, such as women who joined migrant work after their children are grown, more often than not it is younger people who belong to this group. In other words, the three definitions of new-generation migrants – the post-1980 generation, the second-generation, and post-1990 migrants – have significant overlaps and all tend to involve younger migrants.

Research on new-generation migrants in China have found increased participation of women, hence a more balanced sex ratio, than old-generation migrants (e.g., Wang et al. 2011). This finding reflects changes in migrants' household arrangements, as it is increasingly acceptable for not only single women but married women to join migrant work, even entailing leaving their children behind to be raised by grandparents, or bringing their children along. Studies have indeed found that new-generation migrants are more likely than old-generation migrants to bring their spouse and children to the city, hence an increased prevalence of couple migration and family migration (Fan and Li 2020; Fan et al. 2011; Zhao et al. 2018). New-generation migrants have also received more years of education than old-generation migrants, most having finished junior high school and attended senior high school. Still, the former are not sufficiently skilled for the urban labor market other than the manual, labor-intensive and less desirable jobs, and their wages remain low (Duan and Ma 2011).

Growing up observing migrant work as a way of life for their parents and fellow villagers, the new-generation migrants in China tend to start migrant work at a younger age, typically immediately or shortly after finishing junior high school (Fan and Chen 2013). As a result, they have had little or no farming experience (e.g., Liu and Cheng 2008). The new generation are more likely than the old generation to work in manufacturing and services than construction (Duan and Ma 2011; Zhao et al. 2018). They move longer distances, and are more likely than the old generation to move across provincial borders (Fan and Chen 2013; Zhao et al. 2018). They change jobs frequently in pursuit of better pay, and they work as hard as the old generation, with long working days and weeks (Duan and Ma 2011).

New-generation migrants in China earn about the same as old-generation migrants, but they send home less remittances (Liu and Cheng 2008; Zhao et al. 2018). This difference begs the question whether the new-generation are increasingly assuming an urban lifestyle (Duan and Ma 2011). Compared to the old generation, the new generation tend to pursue migrant work not only for the purpose of earning money, but also for the urban experience and "seeing the world" (Zhao et al. 2018; Zhu and Lin 2014). Their expenses are increasingly accounted for by consumption such as food, clothing, housing, transportation, leisure, and entertainment, although their spending is still much lower than the average urbanite. New-generation migrants also have a stronger desire to integrate into the city, are less tolerant of low pay and poor working conditions, and are more ready to express their frustration, including resorting to protests and even suicide (e.g., Chan and Pun 2010; Chen and Wang 2015).

All the above suggests that new-generation migrants in China are more ready and have stronger aspirations than old-generation migrants to chart out their own future. While new-generation migrants may be more integrated into urban life than old-generation migrants, full integration is still out of reach (Zhao et al. 2018). Zhu and Lin (2014) noted that new-generation migrants are still similar to old-generation migrants in terms of their disadvantaged housing situation, lack of access to various insurance programs and occupational mobility, and self-identification as rural people and with the places of origin. The skill levels and incomes of new-generation migrants remain low; the cost of living in big cities is high; and the *hukou* system still exists. New-generation migrants are more aware of their rights and have wider social networks in the city than old-generation migrants, but they continue to rely heavily on native-place ties, though those ties may have become weaker (Zhao et al. 2018). Compared to old-generation migrants, many of whom plan to return to farming in the rural village, new-generation migrants who do not and cannot settle down in cities may be more likely to "return" to towns and cities near their native place where they can engage in non-farm work (e.g., Fan and Chen 2020).

CONCLUSION

Through reviews of selected studies, focusing on work-related migration and drawing especially from research on the Global South and on internal migration, this chapter has highlighted key findings on split households in particular from gender and intergenerational perspectives.

Unlike early migration theories that focus primarily on migrants as individuals, research using the new economics of labor migration theory and/or a feminist framework elucidates the processes and phenomena of householding, household division of labor, household strategies, and translocal and multilocational households. Likewise, while early research on migration emphasizes households who stay and move together, studies on split households, circular migration, and multilocality draw attention to an updated concept of the family, as well as households that straddle multiple locations. A focus on split households challenges the assumption that migration is one-way and permanent. The prevalence of temporary and circular migration signals that migrants strategize to make the best of both their sending and host worlds, take advantage of the cost of living differences between locations, diversify risks, access social and other support, and fulfill familial social functions by being locationally flexible. The form and arrangement of their households may be quite fluid, as members migrate and return over their life course. By doing so, rural–urban migrants both forge linkages and blur the conceptual line between rural and urban areas. Studies of split households also shed light on those who do not migrate and those who return, their roles in migration decision-making and household arrangements, and migration's impacts on them.

Gender plays a central role in household arrangements in relation to migration. The phenomena of trailing wives and of left-behind women and girls both reflect patriarchal ideology that ties females to the domestic sphere. In addition, left-behind wives in rural areas may have to shoulder all rural tasks, including farming and non-farm work. When women and girls are recruited for migrant work, they face risks of being associated with negative stereotypes, and they reframe their migration as a duty to the family rather than a challenge to gender norms. The feminization of labor migration calls for migration theories to address more seriously women's presence in and experiences of migration. When men are left behind, the intra-household dynamics are even more contested, and both women and men tend to reconstruct their roles in terms of "doing family" without "undoing gender" and without challenging deep-rooted patriarchy.

Householding and split households often involve multiple generations and have significant impacts across generations. Remittances are a form of care, connecting the migrant parents, left-behind children, and non-migrant parents and other caregivers. Often, members of the extended family are critical to caregiving arrangements, such that women may find themselves being the designated multigenerational care-providers. Research on the impacts of migration on left-behind children and migrant children, both especially voluminous in China, has yielded mixed results. In short, parents' migrant work improves children's objective well-being, but separation from parents undermines their subjective well-being. The amount of research on the second generation or new generation of rural–urban migrants in China is also considerable. These younger migrants start migrant work early in life, have no or very little farming experience, are more likely to bring their family members to the host location, and have a stronger desire to integrate into the city than old-generation migrants. Nevertheless, their full integration into urban life is still out of reach, and many may eventually decide to return to towns and cities near their rural places of origin.

REFERENCES

Anh, Nguyen Tuan, Jonathan Rigg, Luong Thi Thu Huong, and Dinh Thi Dieu. 2012. "Becoming and being urban in Hanoi: Rural–urban migration and relations in Viet Nam." *Journal of Peasant Studies* 39(5): 1103–1131.

Asis, M.M.B., Shirlena Huang, and Brenda S.A. Yeh. 2004. "When the light of the home is abroad: Unskilled female migration and the Filipino family." *Singapore Journal of Tropical Geography* 25: 198–215.

Bryant, John. 2005. "Children of international migrants in Indonesia, Thailand and the Philippines: A review of evidence and policies." Innocenti Working Papers No. 2005/05, United Nations.

Bustamante, Juan Jose, and Carlos Aleman. 2007. "Perpetuating split-household families: The case of Mexican sojourners in mid-Michigan and their transnational fatherhood practices." *Migraciones Internacionales* 4(1): 65–86.

Call, Maia A., Clark Gray, Mohammad Yunus, and Michael Emch. 2017. "Disruption, not displacement: Environmental variability and temporary migration in Bangladesh." *Global Environmental Change* 46: 157–165.

Chan, Jenny, and Ngai Pun. 2010. "Suicide as protest for the new generation of Chinese migrant workers: Foxconn, global capital, and the state." *Asia-Pacific Journal* 8(37 No. 2): 1–33.

Chan, Kam Wing, and Yuan Ren (eds). 2020. *Children of Migrants in China*. Abingdon: Routledge.

Chant, Sylvia. 1998. "Households, gender and rural–urban migration: Reflections on linkages and considerations for policy." *Environment and Urbanization* 10(1): 5–22.

Chen, Chuanbo, and C. Cindy Fan. 2016. "China's hukou puzzle: Why don't rural migrants want urban hukou?" *China Review* 16(3): 9–39.

Chen, Shaowei, and Zhilin Liu. 2016. "What determines the settlement intention of rural migrants in China? Economic incentives versus sociocultural conditions." *Habitat International* 58: 42–50.

Chen, Yu, and Jufen Wang. 2015. "Social integration of new-generation migrants in Shanghai China." *Habitat International* 49: 419–425.

Choi, Susanne, and Yuk-Ping Yinni Peng. 2016. *Masculine Compromise: Migration, Family, and Gender in China*. Oakland, CA: University of California Press.

Cooke, Thomas J. 2008. "Migration in a family way." *Population, Space and Place* 14(4): 255–265.

Deshingkar, Priya, and Daniel Start. 2003. "Seasonal migration for livelihoods in India: Coping, accumulation and exclusion." Overseas Development Institute, Working Paper 220.

Dick, Eva, and Cédric Duchêne-Lacroix. 2016. "Multi-local living in the Global South and Global North: Differences, convergences and universality of an underestimated phenomenon." *Trialog: A Journal for Planning and Building in a Global Context* 116/117: 4–9.

Douglass, Michael. 2006. "Global householding in Pacific Asia." *International Development Planning Review* 28(4): 421–445.

Douglass, Michael. 2013. "Global householding and social reproduction in migration research." *Ewha Journal of Social Sciences* 29(2). https://papers.ssrn.com/sol3/papers.cfm?abstract_id=2583197.

Dreby, Joanna. 2007. "Children and power in Mexican transnational families." *Journal of Marriage and Family* 69(4): 1050–1064.

Duan, Chengrong, and Xueyang Ma. 2011. "Dangqian woguo xinshengdai nongmingong de xin zhuangkuang (A study on the new situation of the younger generation of farmer-turned migrant)." *Renkou yu Jingji (Population and Economics)* 4: 16–22 (in Chinese).

Fan, C. Cindy. 2009. "Flexible work, flexible household: Labor migration and rural families in China." Pp. 377–408 in *Research in the Sociology of Work*, edited by Lisa A. Keister. Bingley, UK: Emerald Press.

Fan, C. Cindy. 2015. "Migration, remittances, and social and spatial organization of rural households in China." Pp. 194–226 in *Transnational Labour Migration, Remittances and the Changing Family in Asia*, edited by Lan Anh Hoang and Brenda S.A. Yeoh. Basingstoke: Palgrave Macmillan.

Fan, C. Cindy. 2018. "Migration, gender, and space in China." Pp. 305–319 in *Modernity, Space and Gender*, edited by Alexandra Staub. New York: Routledge.

Fan, C. Cindy, and Chen Chen. 2013. "The new-generation migrant workers in China." Pp. 17–35 in *Transient Urbanism: Migrants and Urbanized Villages in Chinese Cities*, edited by Fulong Wu, Fangzhu Zhang, and Chris Webster. London: Routledge.

Fan, C. Cindy, and Chen Chen. 2020. "Left behind? Migration stories of two women in rural China." *Social Inclusion* 8(2): 47–57.

Fan, C. Cindy, and Tianjiao Li. 2020. "Split households, family migration and urban settlement: Findings from China's 2015 National Floating Population Survey." *Social Inclusion* 8(1): 252–263.

Fan, C. Cindy, Mingjie Sun, and Siqi Zheng. 2011. "Migration and split households: A comparison of sole, couple, and family migrants in Beijing, China." *Environment and Planning A* 43: 2164–2185.

Fan, C. Cindy, and Wenfei Wang Wang. 2008. "The household as security: Strategies of rural–urban migrants in China." Pp. 205–243 in *Migration and Social Protection in China*, edited by Russell Smyth and Ingrid Nielsen. New York: World Scientific.

Findlay, A., D. McCollum, R. Coulter, and V. Gayle. 2015. "New mobilities across the life course: A framework for analysing demographically linked drivers of migration." *Population, Space and Place* 21: 390–402.

Finnis, Elizabeth. 2017. "They go to the city, and sometimes they come back: Conceptualising rural and urban spaces through experiences of circular migration in Paraguay." *Critique of Anthropology* 37(4): 383–400.

Gaetano, Arianne M. 2015. *Out to Work: Migration, Gender, and the Changing Lives of Rural Women in Contemporary China*. Honolulu, HI: University of Hawai'i Press.

Gibson, Mhairi, and Eshetu Gurmu. 2012. "Rural to urban migration is an unforeseen impact of development intervention in Ethiopia." *Plos One* 7(11): 1–8.

Glenn, Evelyn Nakano. 1983. "Split households, small producers, and dual wage earners: An analysis of Chinese-American families strategies." *Journal of Marriage and Family* 45(1): 35–46.

Graham, Elspeth, Lucy P. Jordan, Brenda S.A. Yeoh, Theodora Lam, Maruja Asis, and Su-kamdi. 2012. "Transnational families and the family nexus: Perspectives of Indonesian and Filipino children left behind by migrant parent(s)." *Environment and Planning A* 44: 793–815.

Hall, Katharine, and Posel Dorrit. 2018. "Fragmenting the family? The complexity of household migration strategies in post-apartheid South Africa." WIDER Working Paper 2018(8).

Hoang, Lan Anh, and Brenda S.A. Yeoh. 2015. "Introduction: Migration, remittances and the family." Pp. 1–23 in *Transnational Labour Migration, Remittances and the Changing Family in Asia*, edited by Lan Anh Hoang and Brenda S.A. Yeoh. Basingstoke: Palgrave Macmillan.

Hu, Feng, Zhaoyuan Xu, and Yuyu Chen. 2011. "Circular migration, or permanent stay? Evidence from China's rural–urban migration." *China Economic Review* 22(1): 64–74.

Hugo, Graeme. 1982. "Circular migration in Indonesia." *Population and Development Review* 8(1): 59–83.

Hugo, Graeme. 2002. "Effects of international migration on the family in Indonesia." *Asian and Pacific Migration Journal* 11: 13–46.

Hugo, Graeme. 2009. "Best practice in temporary labour migration for development: A perspective from Asia and the Pacific." *International Migration* 47(5): 23–74.

Hugo, Graeme. 2013. *What We Know About Circular Migration and Enhanced Mobility*. Washington, DC: Migration Policy Institute.

Jacka, Tamara. 2006. *Rural Women in Contemporary China: Gender, Migration, and Social Change*. Armonk, NY: M.E. Sharpe.

Junge, Vera, Javier Revilla Diez, and Ludwig Schätzl. 2015. "Determinants and consequences of internal return migration in Thailand and Vietnam." *World Development* 71: 94–106.

Kaufmann, Florian. 2007. "Emigrant or sojourner? Migration intensity and its determinants." Political Economy Research Institute, Working Paper Series (University of Massachusetts Amherst) 154.

Kofman, Eleonore, and Parvati Raghuram. 2015. *Gendered Migrations and Global Social Reproduction*. Basingstoke: Palgrave Macmillan.

Kõu, Anu, and Ajay Bailey. 2014. "'Movement is a constant feature in my life': Contextualising migration processes of highly skilled Indians." *Geoforum* 52: 113–22.

Kõu, Anu, Clara H. Mulder, and Ajay Bailey. 2017. "'For the sake of the family and future': The linked lives of highly skilled Indian migrants." *Journal of Ethnic and Migration Studies* 43(16): 2788–2805.

Lahaie, Claudia, Jeffrey A. Hayes, Tinka Markham Piper, and Jody Heymann. 2009. "Work and family divided across borders: The impact of parental migration on Mexican children in transnational families." *Community, Work and Family* 12(3): 299–312.

Lam, Theodora, and Brenda S.A. Yeoh. 2018. "Migrant mothers, left-behind fathers: The negotiation of gender subjectivities in Indonesia and the Philippines." *Gender, Place and Culture* 25(1): 104–117.

Lawson, Victoria A. 1998. "Hierarchical households and gendered migration in Latin America: Feminist extensions to migration research." *Progress in Human Geography* 22(1): 39–53.

Lee, Everett. 1966. "A theory of migration." *Demography* 3(1): 47–57.

Liu, Chuanjiang, and Jianlin Cheng. 2008. "Di'erdai nongmingong chengshihua: Xianzhuang fenxi yu jincheng cedu (The urbanization of the second generation migrant workers: An analysis on the current progress)." *Renkou Yanjiu (Population Research)* 32(5): 48–57 (in Chinese).

Liu, Jianbo, Xiaodong Zheng, Marie Parker, and Xiangming Fang. 2020. "Childhood left-behind experience and employment quality of new-generation migrants in China." *Population Research and Policy Review* 39(4): 691–718.

Liu, Ye, and Wei Xu. 2017. "Destination choices of permanent and temporary migrants in China, 1985–2005." *Population, Space and Place* 23(1): e1963.

Locke, Catherine, Nguyen Thi Ngan Hoa, and Nguyen Thi Thanh Tam. 2012. "Visiting marriages and remote parenting: Changing strategies of rural–urban migrants to Hanoi, Vietnam." *Journal of Development Studies* 48(1): 10–25.

Mann, Susan. 2000. "Work and household in Chinese culture: Historial perspectives." Pp. 15–32 in *Re-Drawing Boundaries: Work, Household, and Gender in China*, edited by Barbara Entwisle and Gail Henderson. Berkeley, CA: University of California Press.

Martin, Philip. 2013. "The global challenge of managing migration." *Population Bulletin* 68(2): 1–16.

McKay, Steven. 2015. "'So they remember me when I'm gone': Remittances, fatherhood and gender relations of Filipino migrant men." Pp. 111–135 in *Transnational Labour Migration, Remittances and the Changing Family in Asia*, edited by Lan Anh Hoang and Brenda S.A. Yeoh. Basingstoke: Palgrave Macmillan.

Mincer, Jacob. 1978. "Family migration decisions." *Journal of Political Economy* 86(5): 749–773.

Nagel, Caroline, and Paul Boyle. 2020. "Migration." Pp. 81–88 in *International Encyclopedia of Human Geography*, 2nd edition, vol. 9, edited by Audrey Kobayashi. Amsterdam: Elsevier.

Nelson, Joan M. 1976. "Sojourners versus urbanites: Causes and consequences of temporary versus permanent cityward migration in developing countries." *Economic Development and Cultural Change* 24(4): 721–757.

Newland, Kathleen. 2009. "Circular migration and human development." *Human Development Research Paper (HDRP) Series* Vol. 42.

Nguyen, Liem, Brenda S.A. Yeoh, and Mika Toyota. 2006. "Migration and the well-being of the 'left behind' in Asia." *Asian Population Studies* 2(1): 37–44.

Nguyen, Minh T.N., and Catherine Locke. 2014. "Rural–urban migration in Vietnam and China: Gendered householding, production of space and the state." *Journal of Peasant Studies* 41(5): 855–876.

Oakes, Tim, and Louisa Schein (eds). 2006. *Translocal China: Linkages, Identities, and the Reimagining of Space*. Abingdon: Routledge.

Odland, John, and Mark Ellis. 1988. "Household organization and the interregional variation of out-migration rates." *Demography* 25(4): 567–579.

Paul, Anju Mary. 2015. "Negotiating migration, performing gender." *Social Forces* 94(1): 271–293.

Plaza, Dwaine. 2006. "The construction of a segmented hybrid identity among one-and-a-half-generation and second-generation Indo-Caribbean and African Caribbean Canadians." *Identity* 6(3): 207–229.

Portes, Alejandro, Patricia Fernández-Kelly, and William Haller. 2009. "The adaptation of the immigrant second generation in America: A theoretical overview and recent evidence." *Journal of Ethnic and Migration Studies* 35(7): 1077–1104.

Ravenstein, E.G. 1885. "The laws of migration." *Journal of the Statistical Society of London* 48(2): 167–235.
Resurreccion, Bernadette P., and Ha Thi Van Khanh. 2007. "Able to come and go: Reproducing gender in female rural–urban migration in the Red River Delta." *Population, Space and Place* 13(3): 211–224.
Roberts, Kenneth D. 2007. "The changing profile of Chinese labor migration." Pp. 233–250 in *Transition and Challenge: China's Population at the Beginning of the 21st Century*, edited by Zhongwei Zhao and Fei Guo. Oxford: Oxford University Press.
Sana, Mariano, and Douglas S. Massey. 2005. "Household composition, family migration, and community context: Migrant remittances in four countries." *Social Science Quarterly* 86(2): 509–528.
Schmidt-Kallert, Einhard. 2012. "Non-permanent migration and multilocality in the Global South." *Die Erde* 143(3): 173–76.
Silvey, Rachel M. 2000. "Stigmatized spaces: Gender and mobility under crisis in South Sulawesi, Indonesia." *Gender, Place and Culture* 7(2): 143–161.
Silvey, Rachel M. 2006. "Consuming the transnational family: Indonesian migrant domestic workers to Saudi Arabia." *Global Networks* 6(1): 23–40.
Sjaastad, Larry A. 1962. "The costs and returns of human migration." *Journal of Political Economy* 70(5, Part 2): 80–93.
Skeldon, Ronald. 2010. "Managing migration for development: Is circular migration the answer?" *Whitehead Journal of Diplomacy and International Relations* 11(1): 21–34.
Stacey, Judith. 1990. *Brave New Families: Stories of Domestic Upheaval in Late Twentieth-Century America*. Oakland, CA: Basic Books.
Stark, Oded, and Robert E.B. Lucas. 1988. "Migration, remittances, and the family." *Economic Development and Cultural Change* 36(3): 465–481.
Tacoli, Cecilia, and Richard Mabala. 2010. "Exploring mobility and migration in the context of rural—urban linkages: why gender and generation matter." *Environment and Urbanization* 22(2): 389–395.
Taylor, J. Edward. 1999. "The new economics of labour migration and the role of remittances in the migration process." *International Migration* 37(1): 63–88.
Todaro, Michael P. 1976. *Internal Migration in Developing Countries: A Review of Theory, Evidence, Methodology and Research Priorities*. Geneva: International Labour Office.
Toyota, Mika, Brenda S.A. Yeoh, and Liem Nguyen. 2007. "Bringing the 'left behind' back into view in Asia: A framework for understanding the 'migration–left behind nexus'." *Population, Space and Place* 13(3): 157–161.
Van der Klis, Marjolijn, and Clara H. Mulder. 2008. "Beyond the trailing spouse: The commuter partnership as an alternative to family migration." *Journal of Housing and the Built Environment* 23(1): 1–19.
Wallace, Claire. 2002. "Household strategies: Their conceptual relevance and analytical scope in social research." *Sociology* 36(2): 275–292.
Walsh, Froma (ed.). 2003. *Normal Family Processes: Growing Diversity and Complexity*. New York: Guildford Press.
Wang, Chunguang. 2001. "Xinshengdai nongcun liudong renkou de shehui rentong yu chengxiang ronghe de guanxi (The relationship between social identities and rural–urban integration among the new generation migrant workers)," *Shehuixue Yanjiu (Sociological Studies)* 3: 63–76 (in Chinese).
Wang, Dianli, Baojun Liu, and Suping Lou. 2011. "Xinshengdai nongmingong de chengshi rongru – kuangjia jiangou yu diaoyan fenxi (The integration of new generation of migrant workers into urban society—Framework and analysis)." *Zhongguo Xingzheng Guanli (Chinese Public Administration)* 2: 111–115 (in Chinese).
Wang, Lamei, and Judi Mesman. 2015. "Child development in the face of rural-to-urban migration in China: A meta-analytic review." *Perspectives on Psychological Science* 10(6): 813–831.
Wang, Xiaobing, Renfu Luo, Linxiu Zhang, and Scott Rozelle. 2017. "The education gap of China's migrant children and rural counterparts." *Journal of Development Studies* 53(11): 1865–1881.
Waters, Johanna L. 2002. "Flexible families? 'Astronaut' households and the experiences of lone mothers in Vancouver, British Columbia." *Social and Cultural Geography* 3(2): 117–134.
Waters, Johanna L. 2010. "Becoming a father, missing a wife: Chinese transnational families and the male experience of lone parenting in Canada." *Population, Space and Place* 16: 63–74.
Xiang, Biao. 2007. "How far are the left-behind left behind? A preliminary study in rural China." *Population, Place and Space* 13(3): 179–191.

Xiao, Yang, Siyu Miao, and Chinmoy Sarkar. 2020. "Social ties, spatial migration paradigm, and mental health among two generations of migrants in China." *Population, Space and Place* 27(2): e2389.

Xu, Hongwei, and Yu Xie. 2015. "The causal effects of rural-to-urban migration on children's well-being in China." *European Sociological Review* 31(4): 502–519.

Yanagisako, Sylvia Junko. 1979. "Family and household: The analysis of domestic groups." *Annual Review of Anthropology* 8: 161–205.

Ye, Jingzhong. 2019. "Nongcun liushou renkou yanjiu: Jiben lichang, renshi wuqu yu lilun zhuanxiang (Research on rural left-behind population: Basic perspective, mistakes, and theoretical turn)." *Renkou yanjiu* 43(2): 21–31 (in Chinese).

Yeoh, Brenda S.A. 2009. "Making sense of 'Asian' families in the age of migration." *Asian Population Studies* 5: 1–3.

Zelinsky, Wilbur. 1971. "The hypothesis of the mobility transition." *Geographical Review* 61(2): 219–249.

Zhao, Liqiu, Shouying Liu, and Wei Zhang. 2018. "New trends in internal migration in China: Profiles of the new-generation migrants." *China and World Economy* 26(1): 18–41.

Zhou, Chengchao, Sean Sylvia, Linxiu Zhang, Renfu Luo, Hongmei Yi, Chengfang Liu, et al. 2015. "China's left-behind children: Impact of parental migration on health, nutrition, and educational outcomes." *Health Affairs* 34(11): 1964–1971.

Zhou, Min, and Carl L. Bankston III. 2016. *The Rise of the New Second Generation*. Cambridge: Polity Press.

Zhu, Yu, Martin Bell, Sabine Henry, and Michael White. 2013. "Rural–urban linkages and the impact of internal migration in Asian developing countries: An introduction." *Asian Population Studies* 9(2): 119–123.

Zhu, Yu, and Liyue Lin. 2014. "Continuity and change in the transition from the first to the second generation of migrants in China: Insights from a survey in Fujian." *Habitat International* 42: 147–154.

10. Negotiating long-distance caring relations: migrants in the UK and their families in Poland

Weronika Kloc-Nowak and Louise Ryan

INTRODUCTION

Since the pioneering work of anthropologists such as Glick Schiller et al. (1992), there has been increasing focus on how migrants maintain links between countries of origin and destination. It should be noted that long-distance relationships are not an entirely new phenomenon and migrants in the past maintained communication with family back home through letters, remittances and visits to the country of origin (Fitzgerald, 2008). Nonetheless, innovations in communication and travel have impacted upon the ease, affordability, speed and frequency of maintaining transnational ties (Parreñas, 2014). By these means, geographically separated families and relatives not only maintain a sense of kinship but also continue to care for each other at a distance, exchanging emotional and material support and, if possible and culturally expected, participating in personal care provision (Baldassar and Baldock, 2000; Baldassar et al., 2007).

Poles are not the first major group of European migrants in the United Kingdom (UK) emanating from a strongly family-oriented culture, as they were preceded by others such as the Irish (Ryan, 2004, 2007) and Italians (Zontini, 2006). Yet the massive inflow of Poles to the UK following the 2004 European Union (EU) enlargement contributed to making this migrant group ideal for studying contemporary transnational family practices, in three particular ways. Firstly, immediately after Poland's accession to the EU, Polish migrants to the UK were enjoying freedom of movement, not only for workers but also for their families, allowing family reunification to occur (Ryan et al., 2009). Secondly, relative geographical closeness, enabling people to travel between the two countries by land and sea within 24 hours, was further enhanced by the growing availability of cheap flights and the establishment of airports in new regions (Stenning and Dawley, 2009). Thirdly, maintaining family ties was facilitated by the rapid development of communication technology, including videocalls (Pustułka, 2015; Share et al., 2018).

In this chapter, we critically discuss research and theoretical reflection on the long-term relationships and care culture among the families of Polish post-accession migrants for whom the UK was the primary destination. We begin by identifying how family ties and care issues emerged in the analysis of this wave of migration; initially perceived as temporary. The next two sections discuss Polish migrants' family lives, employing theoretical perspectives of social networks and conceptualisations of care in transnational families, indicating the complex and dynamic ways in which these relationships are negotiated and gendered. The following section, drawing upon our recent research, introduces the issues of Brexit and COVID-19 as challenges to the transnational caring practices of Polish migrant families. Looking beyond the Polish context, we conclude by reflecting on how the previously elaborated theoretical perspectives can be combined and adapted to respond to the recent challenges and future prospects of EU migrants in the UK and their transnational families.

EARLY APPROACHES: THE EMERGENCE OF FAMILY AND CARE ISSUES IN RESEARCH ON POLISH MIGRANTS TO THE UK

Early academic approaches to Polish post-accession migration to the UK focused on the ease of transnational mobility. Scholars expected this wave of migration to be temporary, flexible and 'liquid' (Engbersen et al., 2010), following the earlier post-communist transformation patterns of pendulum or 'incomplete migration' (Okólski, 2001).[1] However, in the early 'intentional unpredictability' (Eade et al., 2007) discourse on Polish migrants there was little discussion of family life or care needs (whether current or future). The issues of intergenerational ties and kin support only emerged from in-depth research on social networks and the families of pioneer migrants (Ryan et al., 2008, 2009; White, 2010).

The context for this development in academic conceptualisation was the immense growth of the Polish migrant population. Poles' migration to the UK dates from the aftermath of World War II, and the size of the diaspora was estimated at 60 000 in the 2001 UK census. However, it was only after the 2004 EU enlargement that the number of Polish-born people in the UK escalated, exceeding pre-enlargement predictions (Pollard et al., 2008). In 2016 the number of people in the UK population who were born in Poland reached a peak size of 911 000. Since then, it has been diminishing, due to increased return or further emigration, in addition to passing away of the oldest World War II diaspora members (for the age structure, see Kaczorowski, 2015, p. 10). Hence, Poland became second to India as the most common non-UK country of birth from 2019 onwards. Regarding citizenship, Polish has remained the most numerous non-British nationality since 2007 (ONS, 2022a). Between 2010 and 2019, women born in Poland had the largest number of children among all foreign-born mothers, contributing to around 3 per cent of all births in England and Wales each year (ONS, 2022b).

Following EU enlargement in 2004, there was a widely held assumption in British political circles that new waves of European migrants would be mainly temporary (for a critical overview, see Ryan and Sales, 2013). For example, an Institute for Public Policy Research (IPPR) report concluded that it was probable that many migrants from new EU member states to the UK would indeed return (Pollard et al., 2008). Moreover, the decision to allow these new EU citizens to enter the British labour market can be seen as part of the 'managed' migration policy to replace third country nationals (Ryan and Sales, 2013, p. 91). The assumed temporariness of these migrants was reflected in the publications of many academic researchers (e.g. Fihel et al., 2006) who argued that EU membership, by opening up legal access to the labour market in Britain, allowed people to come and go freely, facilitating temporary – and often multiple – stays or so-called 'commuter migration' (Morokvaśic, 2004). However, under this freedom of movement, EU migrants, including Poles, gained the freedom not only to go and work in another member state but also to settle and take partners, children and other relatives to live with them in the destination society (Ackers, 2004). As EU citizens, they not only have the opportunity to maintain family relationships through the ease of mobility between the origin and destination countries (Ackers and Stalford, 2004), but they can also engage in family reunion strategies which may shift transnational attachments over time (Ryan, 2011).

Qualitative studies in the years following accession, by researchers such as Ryan et al. (2008)[2] showed that the assumed transient nature of post-accession migration as flexible or even footloose was changing into one whereby migrants gradually extend their stay in the UK. This emerging settlement pattern was further evidenced by signs of family reunification, as individual migrants were increasingly joined by partners (Ryan et al., 2009; White, 2011; White and Ryan, 2008). A study by White (2010), conducted both among migrants in the UK and in migrant-sending regions of Poland, questioned the 'incomplete' migration model derived from the post-communist transformation period (Okólski, 2001), in which the family home and children remained in Poland. White observed that, while leaving children in the care of their grandparents was practiced and socially acceptable when one or both parents undertook temporary migration, a new family migration model emerged as the desired family arrangement: the complete transfer of the nuclear household abroad.

One consequence of the family migration pattern and relatively young demographic profile of Polish post-accession migrants was the growing visibility of Polish children entering British primary schools (Ryan and Sales, 2013). The increasing number of children born and raised in Polish migrant families spawned new research on how childcare and extended kinship relations are negotiated across distances (Barglowski and Pustulka, 2018; Kloc-Nowak, 2018; Lopez Rodriguez, 2010; Moskal, 2011; Pustułka, 2014; White, 2011), including a focus on the use of information and communication technology (ICT) in maintaining intergenerational family ties (Kędra, 2021; Pustułka, 2015; Share et al., 2018). In a study on the parental decision-making of Polish migrants conducted in the UK in 2012 (Kloc-Nowak, 2018), two contrasting strategies regarding grandparents' help with raising children have been identified. One is treating family help as the default: for example, postponing childbearing to the moment when a couple can afford a home with a spare bedroom for a visiting grandmother. The other is insisting on self-reliance: such migrants stated that as they emigrated to gain their independence, they did not want to be dependent on anyone's assistance or for anyone to interfere. However, independent living abroad does not exclude the sense of obligation to visit family in Poland (Pustułka and Ślusarczyk, 2016), or the interconnectedness of the migrants with extended family networks, including relatives who also migrated and resided nearby (Heath et al., 2015). Among young families in the UK, teaching children the Polish language and traditions, and sustaining their ties with grandparents and relatives in Poland, was a way of keeping the return option open (Moskal and Sime, 2015). Ties to family members of various generations, living both in the UK and in Poland, meant that some migrants treated their settlement abroad in an open-ended, flexible way, adjusting to the life-course stage and care needs of their immediate family and wider kin. While some people suffered from conflicting obligations, others shaped their family lives in a flexible way, thanks to their social rights in both countries, and the security offered by their EU migrant status (Kay and Trevena, 2018).

SOCIAL NETWORKS AND THEIR ROLE FOR FAMILIES

While migration scholars often refer to the importance of social networks in explaining patterns of mobility (Haug, 2008), there is a tendency to simplify networks as a rather general and all-encompassing metaphor (for a critique, see Ryan, 2007). Migration researchers have been increasingly urged to go beyond the network metaphor and, instead, to draw upon the well-stocked toolbox of social network analysis (Bilecen et al., 2018). As Wellman (1979) has argued: 'The utility of the network perspective is that it does not take as its starting point putative solidarities – local or kin … Instead, social network analysis is principally concerned with delineating structures of relationships and flows of activities' (p. 1203).

In other words, rather than taking for granted the relationships within ethnic or migrant communities, or the assumed solidarities among kinship groups, social network analysis (SNA) focuses on what is going on within those ties. In this section, we discuss how adopting a social networks lens has offered insights into the relationships and flow of resources between Polish migrants' networks, both locally and transnationally.

The work of Ryan (2011) has been especially important in bringing a social networks lens to the analysis of Polish migration to Britain (see also White and Ryan, 2008). Using a visual tool (sociogram) as well as in-depth interviews, Ryan mapped Polish migrants' social networks in order to analyse the nature of their social relationships and the specific resources that flow between particular ties (Ryan, 2016). A network perspective focuses attention on the nature of relationships between particular ties (parents, siblings, friends, cousins, workmates, neighbours, and so on) as well as the resources flowing between those ties (emotional support, practical aid such as financial help, informational support and advice, as well as hands-on care). Different relationships may exchange different kinds of resources (Ryan, 2011). Kinship ties, for example, may be underpinned by loyalty, trust, mutual support and responsibility (Faist, 2004), while friendship ties may be a source of sociality and, especially for migrants, a means of creating a sense of belonging, familiarity and embedding in a new location (Ryan, 2018).

Moreover, it is necessary to understand networks as fluid and dynamic over time. The relationships that migrants rely upon when they first arrive in a new location are not static and may develop and shift as migrants forge new ties with different people. Furthermore, the addition of the life-course lens (Elder, 1994) allows an understanding of how social networks may evolve and change through different stages of the life cycle (Bidart and Lavenu, 2005; Ryan and D'Angelo, 2018). While young single people may have large networks of friends with whom they socialise frequently, becoming a couple and having children may change the size and density of networks as, for example, parents often turn to kinship ties for help with childcare (Bidart and Lavenu, 2005). Hence, a network lens enables an examination of how social relationships evolve over time, and the different kinds of resources, including care, exchanged through those ties (Ryan and D'Angelo, 2018). In studying migrant networks, therefore, it is important to consider not only how migrants forge new ties in the destination society, but also how long-distance ties in the country of origin are maintained over time. The work of Bojarczuk and Mühlau (2018), for example, offers particular insights into how Polish migrants in Dublin manage caring relationships through a combination of local friendship networks and transnational kinship ties. Their work adds to the developing body of research using a networks lens to analyse how care is mobilised and managed in contexts of migration.

In her pioneering paper on migrant networks, Boyd argued that 'families represent a social group geographically dispersed. They create kinship networks which exist across space and are the conduits for information and assistance which in turn influence migration decisions' (Boyd, 1989, p. 643). Thus, through transnational mobility, kinship groups become extended through space and time as geographically dispersed relatives form part of 'multi-stranded social relations which link together migrants' societies of origin and settlement' (Baldassar and Baldock, 2000, p. 63). As Zontini (2004, p. 1114) argues, a transnational perspective is useful in challenging the assumed linearity of the migration process as a one-way journey and acknowledging the 'fluid relationships between two or more countries'. Moreover, a transnational lens allows us to see how gendered caring practices are stretched across national borders, placing specific expectations on women (Kraler et al., 2011).

However, transnationalism is often used in a vague way, lacking in precision (Vertovec, 2001). The extent and dynamism of transnational relationships need to be researched in more detail (Ryan, 2011). As Dahinden (2005, p. 192) notes, 'the initial euphoria' about transnationalism 'has been replaced by a certain sobriety'. Indeed, the fact that migrants have transnational connections tells us very little about what is actually going on in those relationships. Taking up Dahinden's (2005) call for more differentiated analysis of transnational relations, Ryan (2019) argues that the nature, extent and, perhaps, limits of transnationalism can be studied through an exploration of migrant networks. As argued elsewhere (Ryan and D'Angelo, 2018), a network lens can provide a means of assessing the extent to which transnational relationships may change in form and intensity over time with migrants' needs and circumstances.

Iza and Staszek, a young married couple, arrived in London in 2002 to stay with Staszek's cousin (Ryan et al., 2008). They later had a child and built up extensive family networks in London. In a classic example of chain migration, Staszek, having been helped by a cousin, later facilitated the migration of his brother and his father, who he now employs in his building firm. When their baby was born, the couple relied on the grandmothers for practical, hands-on caring. Iza reported: 'My mum came … firstly my mother-in-law came, when the baby was a month old, my mother-in-law came and she left in August … and I asked my mum if she could come … Mum has been here … for over two years.'

The case of Iza and Staszek clearly suggests a gender division of labour: the father and brother were invited from Poland to work in the new business, while the mothers were invited to come and look after the new baby; we return to gender discussions later. Moreover, this example illustrates the salience of propinquity, especially for hands-on care (Ryan, 2007; Wellman, 1979). It is apparent that providing practical support, such as hands-on care for a grandchild or an elderly relative, cannot be done at a distance and requires physical relocation, at least on a temporary basis (Bojarczuk and Mühlau, 2018; Ryan, 2011). For Iza and Staszek, bringing relatives from Poland to help with childcare was the ideal solution.

Finally, it cannot simply be assumed that migrants' transnational ties are fixed and permanent. Relationships within transnational networks are fluid, and ebb and flow over time (Ryan and D'Angelo, 2018). Depending on the age of the migrant and the number of years in the destination society, dyadic ties to friends back home may fade with passing time as they require more energy to maintain (Eve, 2002). Kinship ties are often reinforced by webs of overlapping connections, for example with siblings and other relatives, as well as expectations and obligations (Faist, 2004). However, that is not to imply that transnational family relationships are always positive and supportive. Over time, relationships can fracture, and migrants may feel burdened by family expectations or disappointed by the lack of support in times of need (Ryan, 2008). Hence, network analysis brings to light the changing dynamics of specific social ties in particular places over time and, as discussed below, allows a more nuanced understanding of how care is negotiated within migrant families.

CONCEPTUALISATION OF CARE IN POLISH MIGRANTS' FAMILIES

In this section we elaborate on the conceptualisations of care and analytical approaches to care applied to Polish migrant families, such as care circulation (Baldassar and Merla, 2014), situated transnationalism (Kilkey and Merla, 2014) and the ethnomorality of care (Radziwinowiczówna et al., 2018). The development of these theoretical frameworks has been preceded by a period of analytical reliance on the global literature on transnational families (Bryceson and Vuorela, 2002) and global care chains (Ehrenreich and Hochschild, 2003; Hochschild, 2000; Parreñas, 2003). Prior to EU accession, due to the established pattern of women migrating alone to work in the domestic sector, Polish scholars focused on the consequences of female migration for families (Slany and Małek, 2005; Urbańska, 2009), often referring to the global literature on women's migration and transnational motherhood (e.g. Hondagneu-Sotelo and Avila, 1997; Parreñas, 2001). Post-EU enlargement, the initial masculinisation of Polish migration resulted in the themes of family roles and practices being combined analytically with studies on male migrants (Bell and Pustułka, 2017; Fiałkowska, 2019; Kilkey, 2014; Kilkey et al., 2014) showing, for example, how economically providing for one's family can be an aspect of caring. Subsequently, as family migration strategies evolved, as described in the previous sections, the focus of academic research shifted to current and envisioned future multigenerational care arrangements, on which this section concentrates.

In Poland, the traditional expectation of family provision of aged care as the default arrangement, coupled with the fast pace of population ageing (Perek-Białas and Slany, 2016), make the issue of care provision for ageing parents a growing challenge, exacerbated by the volume of outward migration in the adult children generation. Researchers analysing caring relations between Polish migrants and their ageing parents left behind (Krzyżowski, 2013; Radziwinowiczówna et al., 2018) often employed the types of care distinguished by Baldassar et al. (2007), based on the original Finch (1989) typology of economic, accommodation, personal, practical, emotional and moral support. Showing that Polish migrants do provide care for their ageing parents despite being spatially separated is important, given that the underdeveloped social care system in Poland relies heavily on family care provision (Perek-Białas and Racław, 2014). In such elderly care regimes, women's migration is particularly problematic, as they are treated as carers by default (Krzyżowski, 2011; Perek-Białas and Slany, 2016).

In contrast to a one-directional understanding of older persons as needy, and their children as caregivers, Baldassar and Merla (2014) proposed the framework of care circulation. In this perspective, care in transnational family networks flows in many directions, not symmetrically exchanged but governed by the expectation of generalised reciprocity and subject to constant negotiation. Care circulation captures the fluctuations of care-giving and -receiving during the phases of the migration process and over the life-course. This perspective is relevant to the relatively young Polish post-accession migrants, who sometimes receive care from their parents in the initial period of migration (Kloc-Nowak, 2018, p. 177; Radziwinowiczówna et al., 2018, pp. 167–168), subsequently rely on grandparental childcare, and often contemplate providing care for ageing parents in the future. In addition, Kilkey and Merla (2014) point out that within transnational families, particular members can be mobile or immobile and this status can change over their life-course depending also on their care needs.

Care in migrant families is shaped by factors operating on different levels (see Chapters 2, 13, 19 and 21, this *Handbook*). Kilkey and Merla (2014) situate the care arrangements in migrants' families in the institutional context of several national and international regimes: migration, welfare, working time and gendered care regimes, transport and communication policies. Thus, in the situated transnationalism perspective, by identifying the parameters of each of these regimes that applied to Poles migrating to the UK after the 2004 EU enlargement, their relatively privileged position as EU citizens is emphasised.[3] Another theoretical perspective, the ethnomorality of care (Kordasiewicz et al., 2018; Radziwinowiczówna et al., 2018),[4] contextualises the migrants, their ageing parents and other kin on the local level: their communities of origin and local care institutions.

The ethnomorality of care addresses the normative beliefs about care, care intentions and practical care arrangements (Radziwinowiczówna et al., 2018). It differs from the circulation of care framework in that it gives more emphasis to the discursive elements (care beliefs and intentions) preceding the practical care arrangements. On the normative level, determined mostly by the Polish familialistic care culture, the ethnomorality of care approach draws attention to the local care regimes in the migrants' places of origin. Beliefs about which arrangements are acceptable or unacceptable are rooted in the locally available care institutions and practices of the population. For example, it is a popular practice to delegate aged care to trusted female neighbours in a region with a long emigration tradition (Grabowska and Engbersen, 2016, p. 110; Radziwinowiczówna et al., 2018, p. 52). When migrants acquire knowledge about care homes in the UK, sometimes by working there as carers, their beliefs may evolve towards the appreciation of the professionalism of residential care (Radziwinowiczówna et al., 2018, pp. 76–77). The care arrangements in Polish post-accession migrants' families are, to a large extent, a result of the life-course stage and the number of generations involved. Migrants' parents living in Poland are often around 60 years old, sometimes struggling with deteriorating health but usually still independent. Some belong to the 'sandwich generation' (Grundy and Henretta, 2006), struggling with obligations to support both adult children and their own parents. When they have to provide personal care for the oldest generation, it hinders their ability to visit or move to help their adult children in the UK.

In the ethnomorality of care framework, Radziwinowiczówna et al. (2018, p. 98) identified five types of support (personal, emotional, material, financial and accommodation), quite close to the typology proposed by Baldassar et al. (2007). Importantly, support belonging to one type, such as financial or material gifts, often becomes an emotional gift, such as, for example, when a Polish grandmother saves a considerable part of her pension to offer to a grandchild living abroad. Conversely, material support from adult children is easier to accept for Polish parents who insist on their self-reliance, if it is offered on a special occasion or as a birthday present rather than simply as necessary provision; such as, for example, new pyjamas. Certain emotional gifts, such as children's drawings or framed photos meant for display, serve the function of co-presence by proxy (Baldassar, 2008). Another aspect of emotional care are the conversations, held by telephone or online platforms. In order not to worry loved ones from afar, information is carefully managed. Such a communication strategy includes parents hiding bad news, so as not to trigger the obligation for their adult children to offer practical help or make them feel guilty for not being physically present.

Radziwinowiczówna et al. (2018, p. 100) proposed a typology of care arrangements based on two dimensions: the intensiveness of care, and the complexity of the arrangement (number of actors involved). Polish migrants settled in the UK, who often cannot travel due to their work and nuclear family obligations, sometimes have to rely on a network of several actors to provide care to their parents. Such a care arrangement would be identified as a loose network if a moderate amount of care (hours, activities) was sufficient, and could become a dense network if the need for more intense care occurred. For example, Martyna, a woman aged 44 living in the UK, could visit her parents (aged 70 and 75, with multiple health issues) only once a year. The rest of the time she resorted to the delegation of care (cf. Kilkey and Merla, 2014) to local trusted persons. In addition, Martyna and her sister, living in another EU country, frequently called and sent material support to the parents, such as specialised wound dressings. Yet, the network-based arrangement proved unstable, due to a conflict between the family and the local carer, when Martyna's mother partly recovered and the hours of paid care were reduced. The migrant was aware that the local care arrangement was insufficient for her parents' needs; she could provide better care for them if they joined her abroad, but her father would not agree to move. Envisaging future care if the mother was left alone, Martyna declared that she would bring her over to a care home in the UK. According to Martyna, UK care homes offered more dignified conditions for their older residents than the institutions in Poland.

Some migrants declared their intention to provide personal care by taking their parents to live with them abroad. For example, Melania and her sister, who both live in the UK, have already decided about their mother's future, as Melania declared in 2016:

> And so we agreed. If she required our care, she would be with me part-time and with my sister part-time. It is quite normal – father has died, there is nobody to help her … the [health] care is good here … Mum doesn't know but it's already settled.

When not all siblings have emigrated, the future personal care provision is usually envisaged in Poland and presented as an obligation for the non-mobile sister or brother, with a financial contribution from the migrant. Interestingly, the non-mobile siblings are referred to as 'local' or 'on the spot', disregarding geographical distance within the country, and with no declared preference for a female carer if only sons remained in Poland. Some migrants and ageing parents explained their intention not to bring their parents to the UK, using a Polish proverb: 'You do not uproot old trees' (Radziwinowiczówna et al., 2018, p. 79). This is an expression of the Polish social norm which respects the attachment of older people to their familiar environment.

While the ethnomorality framework has been developed with the focus on aged care, it can also be applied to analyse childcare provision, as the study documented how Polish grandparents had earlier provided care for their grandchildren, or continued to give care and support to the younger generations (both abroad and in Poland) while also, at the same time, being recipients of care. Looking at the normative level expressed by Iwona, interviewed in an earlier study (Kloc-Nowak, 2018, p. 111), we note how this migrant mother of two justified her decision not to ask her parents for help with childcare because of their old age and lack of strength. At the same time, Iwona sees her sister, a single mother, as entitled to receive childcare from their ageing parents. Iwona does not criticise her sister for relying so heavily on their parents. In the perspective of this migrant mother, the adult children should not expect equal assistance from grandparents but, rather, depend on it according to their individual situation and needs.

BREXIT, COVID AND WHAT NEXT? A VIEW FROM 2021

From the perspective of 2022, in this section we discuss Brexit and the COVID-19 pandemic as new external challenges to transnational family life that can undermine the care arrangements and intentions of the families of Polish migrants in the UK. As discussed earlier, network scholars have long highlighted the salience of propinquity for hands-on care (Wellman, 1984). Migrants' access to proximate support through local networks may take time to develop (Ryan, 2007), underlining the importance of a temporal perspective and the need to take into account how the composition of networks evolves and changes through the life-course (Erel and Ryan, 2019). This section discusses Brexit and the COVID-19 pandemic as new external challenges to transnational family life that can undermine the care arrangements and intentions of the families of Polish migrants in the UK. These new challenges show that situated transnationalism (Kilkey and Merla, 2014) can be a useful framework for focusing on the consequences of changes in the institutional context, the macro level. As noted earlier, some scholars have raised concerns about transnationalism and urged caution in how migrants' apparent cross-national mobility has been taken for granted in the literature (see Dahinden, 2005). Pandemic-related global restrictions on international travel reinforce those concerns. New empirical data gathered during the pandemic, therefore, have significance beyond the Polish context and can help to inform wider debates about the possible limits of transnational practices in the future.

The term 'unsettling events' has been coined by Kilkey and Ryan (2021) to describe transformations at the structural level that have implications for the individual level in ways that can provoke re-evaluations of migration projects. Geopolitical episodes such as, for example, the global financial crisis, Brexit, war or indeed a virus pandemic, can trigger multilayered processes consisting of interlinked material, relational and subjective dimensions. As Kilkey and Ryan (2021) acknowledge, such geopolitical events impact on everyone – including all societal residents – but may be especially unsettling for migrants and provoke questions about continued stay in the destination society, return to the origin country or moving on elsewhere. Moreover, these unsettling events need to be understood within the context of the life-course and linked lives of family members (Elder, 1994). Thus, the ways in which a structural transformation impacts on people may differ according to where they are in their life-course. For example, a young, single migrant may be impacted upon differently to a middle-aged couple with school-age children, or a retired, older person with particular care needs. We draw upon this notion of unsettling events, through a life-course lens, throughout this section of our chapter.

The result of the EU referendum in June 2016 shocked many Britons and EU migrants and, initially, a large emigration flow was predicted (McKiernan, 2017; Shapira, 2018). Yet the long-term reactions to the Brexit process vary between individuals: many feel unclear about the future; others are determined to stay (Jancewicz et al., 2020). Those determined to remain in the UK had to await new regulations and adjust their transnational family practices to the emerging new legal context (Kilkey, 2017). Given the ambivalence of future plans, it was not surprising to also find polarised attitudes among the migrants re-interviewed in mid-2018 by Radziwinowiczówna et al. (2020). In the accounts of their care arrangements and future caring intentions, some spoke of their plans to return to Poland, partly under family pressure, while another planned to take a parent to the UK. There were also references to Brexit as an additional argument to justify not intending to take parents to live with them abroad.

Part of the problem of adjusting family life to Brexit was the period of uncertainty about what the future regulations would be. While the lack of clarity might have encouraged the 'wait and see' approach, it might be more reasonable to act swiftly and take parents to the UK as residents (register with a doctor and obtain a National Insurance number) under EU regulations. Otherwise, transferring a parent, especially in poor health, would become more difficult when freedom of movements rights for EU migrants in the UK ended. Melania, when previously interviewed, had expressed her intention to take her mother to the UK. When she was re-interviewed in 2018, it seemed that Brexit had undermined that plan: 'Even if we wanted [my mum] to come, she will not get free health care. ... Because she would have to be here for at least two years. No, a year, or two years, something like that.'

The COVID-19 pandemic can be understood as another unsettling event because it is a geopolitical episode, at the macro structural level, that has significantly impacted on individuals and families at the micro level. A significant group among the Polish families participating in our projects before the pandemic had talked about precise schedules of travel between the two countries to provide care for infants (see Iza and Staszek's case above) or older children during the summer holidays. With the onset of the coronavirus pandemic and the introduction of travel restrictions, these family visit schedules and the peace of mind based on flight availability eroded immediately. According to grandparents participating in focus group discussions[5] in July 2020, the COVID-19 pandemic meant that all previously planned family visits had to be cancelled, including grandparents' trips to Britain or Ireland, as well as migrants' visits to Poland related to Easter, and scheduled family celebrations such as baptisms or weddings. Even when international travel has been allowed again, some people were not willing to risk becoming infected on the plane or spending the whole visit housebound due to quarantine rules. The travel restrictions imposed at short notice at the beginning of the pandemic, and changing many times in its further stages, show how the old sense that the UK and Poland are geographically close and easily accessible is no longer valid. Established family visiting practices have been disturbed, which is difficult to accept, as evidenced in this focus group discussion in July 2020 with men aged 50+ who have grandchildren in various locations, of whom those of R1 are in the UK:

> R1 I, too, tell my daughter that I do not think we will see each other this year for Christmas. She says, 'How is that possible'? It has already been 18 years that she has been abroad, for 12 or 13 years, every year we have been there – and so how come now – 'it is impossible'. I say 'Possible'.
> R2 We got so used to this good, fast communication...
> R1 Reasonably inexpensive ...
> R2 ... that we cannot imagine the dangers through which all of this could collapse, like with this coronavirus, everything has suddenly changed. We simply cannot predict it.
> R1 Flights used to be fairly cheap, now there is no way to expect them to be cheap. Cheap flying is over ... Well, who will be able to afford it? Retirees? What kind of pensioners?!

Brexit may cause some migrants to return to Poland, which will be beneficial for the left-behind parents. However, the majority of migrants plan to stay put, and their ability to care personally for their ageing parents will be largely negligible, putting particularly at risk those parents with no access to local kinship networks, and especially not to their adult children. COVID-19 has shown how suddenly organising emergency visits has become impossible. The pandemic has abruptly limited transnational visits and will probably affect the way they are organised in the future. While people have learnt to rely even more on ICT-based co-presence (Baldassar et al., 2016), not all care needs can be satisfied virtually. Cultural care norms may still bind family members, making them feel guilty that they cannot visit to help personally.

CONCLUSIONS

In this chapter we have presented an overview of salient academic research on transnational family practices between migrants in the UK and their families in Poland, focusing on the post-2004 EU enlargement period. Freedom of movement, family reunification and ease of travel and communication all contributed to the popularity of step-wise nuclear family migration and, at the same time, enabled multiple generations and wider kinship networks to visit each other, cooperate, and participate in caring for those in need and caring about each other at a distance.

Moreover, moving beyond that existing body of literature, our chapter has looked at recent, unfolding contexts. We suggest that the model of transnational family practices shaped in the years since the EU accession cannot be maintained after Brexit and COVID-19. These 'unsettling events' (Kilkey and Ryan, 2021) have heavily impacted upon the institutional context (migration regime and transport policy) of transnational family care. EU migrants with pre-settled status in the UK may be reluctant to leave Britain for periods of time to care for their family members, as a prolonged absence may endanger their legal path to settlement (Radziwinowiczówna et al., 2020). When facing external limitations to travel, hindering personal caregiving, the migrants who had been socialised under familial care regimes, may feel a stronger conflict between their care beliefs and the actual care arrangements they can offer to parents in Poland. Travel limitations disrupt the grandchildren's visits and grandparents' care schedules. Grandmothers, in particular, can be anticipated to suffer more due to the inability to fulfil their traditional obligation of supporting their adult children through childcare (Leopold and Skopek, 2014). At the normative level, it was earlier claimed that migrants may gradually accept the less familialistic norm of care provision as seen in their country of immigration (Krzyżowski and Mucha, 2014). Yet high mortality rates from COVID-19 among aged care home residents in the UK may hinder the acceptance of institutionalised care and make migrants reconsider personal care provision for their dependent ageing parents at home, even if it means reversing their emigration.

The pandemic, with its limitations on mobility (sometimes even to the perimeter of the neighbourhood), pushes people, including migrants, to establish more local support networks. Looking at Polish migrants' engagement in their local neighbourhood, beyond the lens of the diaspora and family, has shown that the majority contribute voluntarily to their close social environment; for example, by collecting donations or organising actions (Nowosielski and Nowak, 2020). Therefore, as argued throughout this chapter, a network lens is useful in understanding how migrants' reliance upon local and transnational sources of care may change over time (Ryan, 2018).

Even when societies eventually overcome the COVID-19 pandemic, another unsettling event may result in sudden and unanticipated risk, causing an abrupt change to the functioning of societies. Such a situation may occur again in the future due to another pandemic or war, such as Russia's invasion of Ukraine in 2022, significantly impacting on the Polish border, or an environmental or political crisis (such as the risk of Poland leaving the EU). We should continue to study whether and how migrants and their transnational family networks respond to such wider changes. Adjusting or risk-proofing their extended households will be a challenge for families, hitting hardest those who are the most economically vulnerable.

NOTES

1. 'Incomplete migration', according to Okólski (2001), was the phenomenon of prolonged engagement of selected family members in labour mobility, accompanied with the lack of a plan of settlement (or family reunification) abroad, limited integration of the migrant abroad, and social and labour market marginalisation of the migrant in the country of origin. This pattern was characteristic for post-communist countries, whose citizens migrated to Western Europe to work irregularly using short-term tourist visas.
2. In this chapter we draw on bodies of data that we collected with separate teams of colleagues.
3. Poles and other intra-EU migrants acquired certain entitlements upon entry and the full range of social rights after 12 months of residence. EU citizens' family members enjoyed freedom of entry and exit, and there were no criteria for sponsoring the migration of dependent relatives (Ackers, 2004).
4. The ethnomorality of care framework was developed by the team led by Anna Rosińska (earlier published as Kordasiewicz), with Agnieszka Radziwinowiczówna and Weronika Kloc-Nowak, during the realisation of the research project 'Unfinished Migration Transition and Ageing Population in Poland. Asynchronous Population Changes and the Transformation of Formal and Informal Care Institutions (Mig/Ageing)', funded by the National Science Centre, Poland (grant number 2013/08/A/HS4/00602, PI Prof. Marek Okólski). All the quotations in this section, coded with pseudonyms, come from the 'Ethnomorality' dataset of in-depth interviews, conducted in the period 2014–2018, with the inhabitants of two small Polish towns and with migrants from there living in the UK.
5. The focus group discussions with grandparents in Poland were conducted and analysed within the framework of the project 'Grandparenting at a Distance – Beliefs and Practices Regarding Relationship with Grandchildren in Spatially Mobile Polish Families', funded by the National Science Centre, Poland (grant number 2018/30/M/HS6/00279; PI Dr Weronika Kloc-Nowak, foreign partner Prof. Louise Ryan).

REFERENCES

Ackers, L. (2004). Citizenship, migration and the valuation of care in the European Union. *Journal of Ethnic and Migration Studies*, *30*(2), 373–396. https://doi.org/10.1080/1369183042000200759.

Ackers, L., and Stalford, H. (2004). *A Community for Children? Children, Citizenship and Internal Migration in the EU*. Ashgate.

Baldassar, L. (2008). Missing kin and longing to be together: Emotions and the construction of co-presence in transnational relationships. *Journal of Intercultural Studies*, *29*(3), 247–266.

Baldassar, L., and Baldock, C. (2000). Linking migration and family studies: Transnational migrants and the care of ageing parents. In B. Agozino (ed.), *Theoretical and Methodological Issues in Migration Research* (pp. 61–91). Ashgate.

Baldassar, L., Baldock, C., and Wilding, R. (2007). *Families Caring Across Borders: Migration, Ageing and Transnational Caregiving*. Palgrave Macmillan.

Baldassar, L., and Merla, L. (2014). Locating transnational care circulation in migration and family studies. In L. Baldassar and L. Merla (eds), *Transnational Families, Migration and the Circulation of Care: Understanding Mobility and Absence in Family Life* (pp. 25–58). Routledge.

Baldassar, L., Nedelcu, M., Merla, L., and Wilding, R. (2016). ICT-based co-presence in transnational families and communities: Challenging the premise of face-to-face proximity in sustaining relationships. *Global Networks*, *16*(2), 133–144. https://doi.org/10.1111/glob.12108.

Barglowski, K., and Pustulka, P. (2018). Tightening early childcare choices: Gender and social class inequalities among Polish mothers in Germany and the UK. *Comparative Migration Studies*, *6*(1), 1–16. https://doi.org/10.1186/s40878-018-0102-6.

Bell, J., and Pustułka, P. (2017). Multiple masculinities of Polish migrant men. *NORMA*, *12*(2), 127–143. https://doi.org/10.1080/18902138.2017.1341677.

Bidart, C., and Lavenu, D. (2005). Evolutions of personal networks and life events. *Social Networks*, *27*(4), 359–376. https://doi.org/10.1016/j.socnet.2004.11.003.
Bilecen, B., Gamper, M., and Lubbers, M.J. (2018). The missing link: Social network analysis in migration and transnationalism. *Social Networks*, *53*, 1–3. https://doi.org/10.1016/j.socnet.2017.07.001.
Bojarczuk, S., and Mühlau, P. (2018). Mobilising social network support for childcare: The case of Polish migrant mothers in Dublin. *Social Networks*, *53*, 101–110. https://doi.org/10.1016/j.socnet.2017.04.004.
Boyd, M. (1989). Family and personal networks in international migration: Recent developments and new agendas. *International Migration Review*, *23*(3), 638–670.
Bryceson, D., and Vuorela, U. (2002). *The Transnational Family: New European Frontiers and Global Network*. Berg.
Dahinden, J. (2005). Contesting transnationalism? Lessons from the study of Albanian migration networks from former Yugoslavia. *Global Networks*, *5*(2), 191–208. https://doi.org/10.1111/j.1471-0374.2005.00114.x.
Eade, J., Drinkwater, S., and Garapich, M.P. (2007). *Class and Ethnicity: Polish Migrant Workers in London*. Research Report. ESRC End of Award Report RES-000-22-1294 ESRC. CRONEM, University of Surrey. http://www.surrey.ac.uk/cronem/files/POLISH_FINAL_RESEARCH_REPORT_WEB.pdf.
Ehrenreich, B., and Hochschild, A. (eds) (2003). *Global Woman: Nannies, Maids, and Sex Workers in the New Economy*. Owl Books.
Elder Jr, G.H. (1994). Time, human agency, and social change: Perspectives on the life course. *Social Psychology Quarterly*, *57*(1): 4–15.
Engbersen, G., Snel, E., and de Boom, J. (2010). 'A van full of Poles': Liquid migration from Central and Eastern Europe. In R. Black, G. Engbersen, M. Okólski and C. Panţîru (eds), *A Continent Moving West? EU Enlargement and Labour Migration from Central and Eastern Europe* (pp. 115–140). Amsterdam University Press.
Erel, U., and Ryan, L. (2019). Migrant capitals: Proposing a multi-level spatio-temporal analytical framework. *Sociology*, *53*(2), 246–263. https://doi.org/10.1177/0038038518785298.
Eve, M. (2002). Integrating via networks: Foreigners and others. *Ethnic and Racial Studies*, *33*(7), 1231–1248. https://doi.org/10.1080/01419871003624084.
Faist, T. (2004). The border-crossing expansion of social space: Concepts, questions and topics. In T. Faist and E. Ozveren (eds), *Transnational Social Spaces: Agents, Networks and Institutions* (pp. 1–34). Ashgate.
Fiałkowska, K. (2019). Remote fatherhood and visiting husbands: Seasonal migration and men's position within families. *Comparative Migration Studies*, *7*(1). https://doi.org/10.1186/s40878-018-0106-2.
Fihel, A., Kaczmarczyk, P., and Okólski, M. (2006). *Labour mobility in the enlarged European Union*. CMR Working Papers 14(72). http://www.migracje.uw.edu.pl/wp-content/uploads/2016/12/014_72.pdf (accessed 2 March 2021).
Finch, J. (1989). *Family Obligations and Social Change*. Polity Press.
Fitzgerald, P. (2008). Exploring transnational and diasporic families through the Irish emigration database. *Journal of Intercultural Studies*, *29*(3), 267–281. https://doi.org/10.1080/07256860802169204.
Glick Schiller, N., Basch, L., and Blanc-Szanton, C. (1992). Transnationalism: A new analytic framework for understanding migration. *Annals of the New York Academy of Sciences*, *645*(1), 1–24.
Grabowska, I., and Engbersen, G. (2016). Social remittances and the impact of temporary migration on an EU sending country: The case of Poland. *Central and Eastern European Migration Review*, *5*(2), 99–117. doi: 10.17467/ceemr.2016.05.
Grundy, E., and Henretta, J.C. (2006). Between elderly parents and adult children: A new look at the intergenerational care provided by the 'sandwich generation'. *Ageing and Society*, *26*(5), 707–722. https://doi.org/10.1017/S0144686X06004934.
Haug, S. (2008). Migration networks and migration decision-making. *Journal of Ethnic and Migration Studies*, *34*(4), 585–605. https://doi.org/10.1080/13691830801961605.
Heath, S., McGhee, D., and Trevena, P. (2015). Continuity versus innovation: Young Polish migrants and practices of 'doing family' in the context of achieving independence in the UK. *Studia Migracyjne – Przegląd Polonijny*, *3*(157), 139–156.

Hochschild, A.R. (2000). Global care chains and emotional surplus value. In A. Giddens and W. Hutton (eds), *On the Edge: Living with Global Capitalism* (pp. 130–146). Jonathan Cape.

Hondagneu-Sotelo, P., and Avila, E. (1997). 'I'm here, but I'm there': The meanings of Latina transnational motherhood. *Gender and Society*, *11*(5), 548–571.

Jancewicz, B., Kloc-Nowak, W., and Pszczółkowska, D. (2020). Push, pull and Brexit: Polish migrants' perceptions of factors discouraging them from staying in the UK. *Central and Eastern European Migration Review*, *9*(1), 101–123. https://doi.org/10.17467/ceemr.2020.09.

Kaczorowski, P. (2015). *Polacy oraz osoby urodzone w Polsce w wybranych krajach europejskich*. Główny Urząd Statystyczny. http://stat.gov.pl/spisy-powszechne/nsp-2011/nsp-2011-wyniki/polacy-oraz-osoby-urodzone-w-polsce-w-wybranych-krajach-europejskich-na-podstawie-wynikow-spisow-ludnosci-i-mieszkan-rundy-2011,23,1.html (accessed 11 May 2021).

Kay, R., and Trevena, P. (2018). (In)security, family and settlement: Migration decisions amongst Central and East European families in Scotland. *Central and Eastern European Migration Review*, *7*(1), 17–33. https://doi.org/10.17467/ceemr.2017.17.

Kędra, J. (2021). Performing transnational family with the affordances of mobile apps: A case study of Polish mothers living in Finland. *Journal of Ethnic and Migration Studies*, *7*(13), 2877–2896. https://doi.org/10.1080/1369183X.2020.1788383.

Kilkey, M. (2014). Polish male migrants in London: The circulation of fatherly care. In L. Baldassar and L. Merla (eds), *Transnational Families, Migration and the Circulation of Care: Understanding Mobility and Absence in Family Life* (pp. 185–199). Routledge.

Kilkey, M. (2017). Conditioning family life at the intersection of migration and welfare: The implications for 'Brexit families'. *Journal of Social Policy*, *46*(4), 797–814. https://doi.org/10.1017/S004727941700037X.

Kilkey, M., and Merla, L. (2014). Situating transnational families' care-giving arrangements: The role of institutional contexts. *Global Networks*, *14*(2), 210–229. https://doi.org/10.1111/glob.12034.

Kilkey, M., Plomien, A., and Perrons, D. (2014). Migrant men's fathering narratives, practices and projects in national and transnational spaces: Recent Polish male migrants to London. *International Migration*, *52*(1), 178–191.

Kilkey, M., and Ryan, L. (2021). Unsettling events: Understanding migrants' responses to geopolitical transformative episodes through a life-course lens. *International Migration Review*, *55*(1), 227–253. https://doi.org/10.1177/0197918320905507.

Kloc-Nowak, W. (2018). *Childbearing and Parental Decisions of Intra-EU Migrants. A Biographical Analysis of Polish Migrants to the UK and Italy*, Vol. 5. Peter Lang.

Kordasiewicz, A., Radziwinowiczówna, A., and Kloc-Nowak, W. (2018). Ethnomoralities of care in transnational families: Care intentions as a missing link between norms and arrangements. *Journal of Family Studies*, *24*(1), 76–93. https://doi.org/10.1080/13229400.2017.1347516.

Kraler, A., Kofman, E., Kohli, M., and Schmoll, C. (2011). *Gender, Generations and the Family in International Migration*. Amsterdam University Press.

Krzyżowski, Ł. (2011). In the trap of intergenerational solidarity: Family care in Poland's ageing society. *Polish Sociological Review*, *173*(1), 55–78.

Krzyżowski, Ł. (2013). *Polscy migranci i ich starzejący się rodzice: Transnarodowy system opieki międzygeneracyjnej*. Wydawnictwo Naukowe Scholar.

Krzyżowski, Ł., and Mucha, J. (2014). Transnational caregiving in turbulent times: Polish migrants in Iceland and their elderly parents in Poland. *International Sociology*, *29*(1), 22–37. https://doi.org/10.1177/0268580913515287.

Leopold, T., and Skopek, J. (2014). Gender and the division of labor in older couples: How European grandparents share market work and childcare. *Social Forces*, *93*(1), 63–91. https://doi.org/10.1093/sf/sou061.

Lopez Rodriguez, M. (2010). Migration and a quest for 'normalcy': Polish migrant mothers and the capitalization of meritocratic opportunities in the UK. *Social Identities*, *16*(3), 339–358.

McKiernan, J. (2017, 7 September). 'Brexodus' to hit Aberdeen hard as nearly half of EU citizens say they will leave Scotland. *Press and Journal*. https://www.pressandjournal.co.uk/fp/news/politics/1321762/brexodus-could-hit-aberdeen-hard-as-nearly-half-eu-citizens-say-they-will-leave-scotland/.

Morokvasić, M. (2004). 'Settled in mobility': Engendering post-wall migration in Europe. *Feminist Review*, *77*(1), 7–25.

Moskal, M. (2011). Transnationalism and the role of family and children in intra-European labour migration. *European Societies*, *12*(1), 29–50.
Moskal, M., and Sime, D. (2015). Polish migrant children's transcultural lives and transnational language use. *Central and Eastern European Migration Review*, *5(*1), 35–48.
Nowosielski, M., and Nowak, W. (2020). (In)formal social participation of immigrants – are migrants from Poland socially active? *CMR Spotlight*, *21*, 2–6. http://www.migracje.uw.edu.pl/publikacje/cmr-spotlight-nr-21/.
Okólski, M. (2001). Incomplete migration: A new form of mobility in Central and Eastern Europe: The case of Polish and Ukrainian migrants. In C. Wallace and D. Stola (eds), *Patterns of Migration in Central Europe* (pp. 105–128). Palgrave Macmillan.
ONS (2022a). *Population of the UK by Country of Birth and Nationality: Year Ending June 2021*. Office for National Statistics. https://www.ons.gov.uk/peoplepopulationandcommunity/populationandmigration/internationalmigration/bulletins/ukpopulationbycountryofbirthandnationality/yearendingjune2021#population-of-the-uk-by-country-of-birth-and-nationality-data (accessed 3 January 2023).
ONS (2022b). *Parents' Country of Birth, England and Wales, 2021*. https://www.ons.gov.uk/peoplepopulationandcommunity/birthsdeathsandmarriages/livebirths/datasets/parentscountryofbirth (accessed 3 January 2023).
Parreñas, R.S. (2001). *Servants of Globalization: Women, Migration and Domestic Work*. Stanford University Press.
Parreñas, R.S. (2003). The care crisis in the Philippines: Children and transnational families in the new global economy. In B. Ehrenreich and A. Hochschild (eds), *Global Woman: Nannies, Maids, and Sex Workers in the New Economy* (pp. 39–54). Owl Books.
Parreñas, R.S. (2014). The intimate labour of transnational communication. *Families, Relationships and Societies*, *3*(3), 425–442. https://doi.org/10.1332/204674313X13802800868637.
Perek-Białas, J., and Racław, M. (2014). Transformation of elderly care in Poland. In M. León (ed.), *The Transformation of Care in European Societies* (pp. 256–275). Palgrave Macmillan. https://doi.org/10.1057/9781137326515_12.
Perek-Białas, J., and Slany, K. (2016). The elderly care regime and migration regime after the EU accession: The case of Poland. In U. Karl and S. Torres (eds), *Ageing in Contexts of Migration* (pp. 27–38). Routledge.
Pollard, N., Latorre, M., and Sriskandarajah, D. (2008). *Floodgates or Turnstiles? Post-EU Enlargement Flows To (and From) the UK*. Institute for Public Policy and Research. https://www.fiw.ac.at/fileadmin/Documents/floodgates_or_turnstiles.pdf.
Pustułka, P. (2014). Child-centred narratives of Polish migrant mothers: Cross-generational identity constructions abroad. *Studia Migracyjne – Przeglad Polonijny*, *3*(153, 40), 151–170.
Pustułka, P. (2015). Virtual transnationalism: Polish migrant families and new technologies. *Studia Migracyjne – Przegląd Polonijny*, 3(157), 99–122. http://www.kbnm.pan.pl/images/pdf/SM_PP_3_2015/St_Migr_3_15_6_P.Pustulka.pdf.
Pustułka, P., and Ślusarczyk, M. (2016). Cultivation, compensation and indulgence: Transnational short-term returns to Poland across three family generations. *Transnational Social Review*, *6*(1–2), 78–92. https://doi.org/10.1080/21931674.2016.1182312.
Radziwinowiczówna, A., Rosinska, A., and Kloc-Nowak, W. (2018). *Ethnomorality of Care: Migrants and their Aging Parents*. Routledge.
Radziwinowiczówna, A., Kloc-Nowak, W., and Rosińska, A. (2020). Envisaging post-Brexit immobility: Polish migrants' care intentions concerning their elderly parents. *Journal of Family Research*. https://doi.org/10.20377/jfr-352.
Ryan, L. (2004). Family matters: (E)migration, familial networks and Irish women in Britain. *Sociological Review*, *52*(3), 351–370. https://doi.org/10.1111/j.1467-954X.2004.00484.x.
Ryan, L. (2007). Migrant women, social networks and motherhood: The experiences of Irish nurses in Britain. *Sociology*, *41*(2), 295–312. https://doi.org/10.1177/0038038507074975.
Ryan, L. (2008). Navigating the emotional terrain of families 'here' and 'there': Women, migration and the management of emotions. *Journal of Intercultural Studies*, *29*(3), 299–313.

Ryan, L. (2011). Migrants' social networks and weak ties: Accessing resources and constructing relationships post-migration. *Sociological Review*, *59*(4), 707–724. https://doi.org/10.1111/j.1467-954X.2011.02030.x.

Ryan, L. (2016). Looking for weak ties: Using a mixed methods approach to capture elusive connections. *Sociological Review*, *64*(4), 951–969. https://doi.org/10.1111/1467-954X.12395.

Ryan, L. (2018). Differentiated embedding: Polish migrants in London negotiating belonging over time. *Journal of Ethnic and Migration Studies*, *44*(2), 233–251.

Ryan, L. (2019). Narratives of settling in contexts of mobility: A comparative analysis of Irish and Polish highly qualified women migrants in London. *International Migration*, *57*(3), 177–191.

Ryan, L., and D'Angelo, A. (2018). Changing times: Migrants' social network analysis and the challenges of longitudinal research. *Social Networks*, *53*, 148–158. https://doi.org/10.1016/j.socnet.2017.03.003.

Ryan, L., and Sales, R. (2013). Family migration: The role of children and education in family decision-making strategies of Polish migrants in London. *International Migration*, 51(2), 90–103.

Ryan, L., Sales, R., Tilki, M., and Siara, B. (2008). Social networks, social support and social capital: The experiences of recent Polish migrants in London. *Sociology*, *42*(4), 672–690. https://doi.org/10.1177/0038038508091622.

Ryan, L., Sales, R., Tilki, M., and Siara, B. (2009). Family strategies and transnational migration: Recent Polish migrants in London. *Journal of Ethnic and Migration Studies*, *35*(1), 61–77.

Shapira, M. (2018). Brexodus of EU citizens from the UK is picking up speed. *The Conversation*, 22 February. http://theconversation.com/brexodus-of-eu-citizens-from-the-uk-is-picking-up-speed-92089.

Share, M., Williams, C., and Kerrins, L. (2018). Displaying and performing: Polish transnational families in Ireland skyping grandparents in Poland. *New Media and Society*, *20*(8), 3011–3028. https://doi.org/10.1177/1461444817739272.

Slany, K., and Małek, A. (2005). Female emigration from Poland during the period of the systemic transformation (on the basis of the emigration from Poland to the USA and Italy). In K. Slany (ed.), *International Migration: A Multidimensional Analysis* (pp. 115–154). AGH University of Science and Technology Press.

Stenning, A., and Dawley, S. (2009). Poles to Newcastle: Grounding new migrant flows in peripheral regions. *European Urban and Regional Studies*, *16*(3), 273–294. https://doi.org/10.1177/0969776409104693.

Urbańska, S. (2009). Matka migrantka: Perspektywa transnarodowości w badaniu przemian ról rodzicielskich. *Studia Migracyjne – Przegląd Polonijny, 1*(131), 61–84.

Vertovec, S. (2001). Transnational social formations: Towards conceptual cross-fertilization (WPTC-01-16). Paper presented at the workshop 'Transnational Migration: Comparative Perspectives', Princeton University, 30 June to 1 July 2001, https://pure.mpg.de/rest/items/item_3012240/component/file_3012241/content.

Wellman, B. (1979). The community question: The intimate networks of East Yorkers. *American Journal of Sociology*, *84*(5), 1201–1231.

Wellman, B. (1984). *Domestic Work, Paid Work and Networks*, No. 149. Centre for Urban and Community Studies, University of Toronto. https://tspace.library.utoronto.ca/handle/1807/94573.

White, A. (2010). *Polish Families and Migration since EU Accession*. Policy Press.

White, A. (2011). The mobility of Polish families in the West of England: Translocalism and attitudes to return. *Studia Migracyjne – Przegląd Polonijny*, *37*(1), 11–32.

White, A., and Ryan, L. (2008). Polish 'temporary' migration: The formation and significance of social networks. *Europe-Asia Studies*, *60*(9), 1467–1502.

Zontini, E. (2004). Immigrant women in Barcelona: Coping with the consequences of transnational lives. *Journal of Ethnic and Migration Studies*, *30*(6), 1113–1144. https://doi.org/10.1080/1369183042000286278

Zontini, E. (2006). Italian families and social capital: Care provision in a transnational world. *Community, Work and Family*, *9*(3), 325–345.

11. Analysing youth migrations through the lens of generation

Rhondeni Kikon and Roy Huijsmans

INTRODUCTION

The literature on youth migration has grown impressively over the past decade. This is the case in the realm of both the academic and the policy literature (e.g. Ní Laoire et al. 2017; United Nations 2011). As a result, youth are increasingly recognised as a distinct category in migration. This is evident, for example, from the 2019 International Dialogue on Migration[1] which was dedicated to the topic of 'youth and migration'.

Similar to the early days of 'women and migration' research, the focus on youth as migrants is driven by a realisation that youth constitute a good part of the global migration stock. The International Organization for Migration (IOM 2020: 3) reported that 'of the 258 million international migrants, approximately 11 per cent of them were under 24 years of age in 2017', a percentage that would be much higher if accurate figures had been available for short-duration cross-border mobility (Huijsmans 2019a) and internal migration (Grabska et al. 2019). The parallel between the emergence of youth and women on global migration agendas, however, ruptures at the level of theorisation.

From its early days, the literature on women and migration realised a shift in analytical emphasis from women to gender (Chant 1992). This entailed moving beyond recognising women as migrants towards understanding how gender relations matter in diverse ways throughout the social process of migration (see also, discussion in Chapter 1, this *Handbook*). It also includes appreciating how gender relations and gender roles are reinforced, negotiated or possibly reworked throughout the migration process. Such a parallel shift has yet to fully take place in relation to youth (or any other age-based category). As a result, the phenomenon of young people in migration remains largely approached from an age-based perspective; that is, youth are identified as a target population using age-based criteria, which then gives rise to discussion about age-specific needs and concerns. Although such approaches have a function, relatively few studies have taken the next step by teasing out how age as a social relation, and generation as a concept with diverse interpretations, matter for understanding the interplay between being young and mobilities (e.g. Huijsmans 2017; Punch 2015).

Studies that use the lens of generation can take many forms, but in essence it is about moving away from age-based categories as self-evident because of biological realities. While recognising that biology and brain development provide a context to human development, generationed analyses illuminate the social formation of age-based structures and identities (Huijsmans 2016a). In this chapter, after introducing different interpretations of the concept of generation, we apply these insights to the study of youth migration in relation to and beyond the realm of the family. We do so on the basis of research from across the globe, combined with concrete illustrations from a case study conducted with youth on an Assam tea plantation (northeast India). The case study also underscores the importance of adopting a dynamic approach to studying youth migration, while simultaneously showing that youth migration as an ever-unfolding social phenomenon is not without limits.

YOUTH MIGRATION AND DIVERSE INTERPRETATIONS OF GENERATION

Alanen (2009: 160) defines generational relations as 'the relationships between individuals located in different life stages (intergenerational relations) or between individuals sharing the [same] life stage (intragenerational relations)'. Despite her emphasis on individuals, generational relations are by no means limited to micro-level analyses and neither do these exclude the role of institutions. This is well illustrated in the work by Ní Laoire (2000) on analysing youth migration from rural Ireland (see also Chapter 8, this *Handbook*). Drawing on Halfacree and Boyle's biographical approach, Ní Laoire (2000: 229) conceptualises 'migration as part of individual biographies as well as social structures'. In this way she shows how migration at the youth phase of the life-course is tied up with various other transitions taking place during youth. Moreover, she demonstrates that youth's migration decisions are situated within the micro institution of the household and localised gender regimes, but also within larger institutions such as the labour market and the education system that shape the manifestation of youth transitions of Irish rural youth in distinctly spatial ways.

The generationed approach that is implicit in Ní Laoire's work (2000: 235) is developed in more detail by Huijsmans (2016b). He does so by making an analytical distinction between three interpretations of the concept of generation: generation as kinship descent, generation as life-phase, and a Mannheimian understanding of generation. Before discussing each of these approaches, we note that a common feature of these diverse interpretations of the concept of generation is that they call for relational analysis. This means acknowledging that the very idea of youth is a relational construct (that is, it can only exist in relation to other age-based groupings such as children, adults, and so on) and that young people's lives are situated in sets of social relations that shape what it means to be young, while these forces of influence are also negotiated, reworked and resisted by young people themselves. In relation to migration, this means teasing apart how mobility and staying put affects young people's scope for (re)positioning themselves in a particular way in the generational order (as well as how relevant others position them), while also appreciating the role of moving (or staying put) in the social experience of being young (Huijsmans 2019a).

Diverse interpretations of the concept of generation emphasise different dimensions and manifestations of the interplay between being young and mobility. Collectively, these interpretations constitute what other authors have called the 'wider generational order', which refers to 'a complex set of processes through which people become (are constructed as) 'children' [or youth for that matter] while other people become (are constructed as) 'adults'' (Alanen 2001: 20–21, in Punch 2020: 132). Relations of generation, however, do not work in isolation from other social relations (such as gender or class), and are shaped by broader processes of development and change while also affecting them (Huijsmans 2016a).

Interpreting generation as kinship descent directs focus to the scale of the household. It illuminates the intra- and intergenerational dynamics through which migration decisions unfold within the household. This focus connects with the broader shift in migration theory brought about by the new economics of labour migration (e.g. Stark and Bloom 1985) that called for household-based analyses of migration as opposed to viewing migrants as utility-maximising individuals. It also connects with Douglass's (2006: 423) concept of 'householding', described as the ongoing, dynamic social processes of creating and sustaining a household that covers all life-cycle stages and extends beyond the family. For migration studies, it is important to note that the work of householding increasingly takes a translocal or even transnational form, with household members dispersed across space in their efforts to create and sustain their households (Brickell and Yeoh 2014).

The specific contribution that the notion of generation as kinship descent makes can be discerned in situating migration decision-making within the social fabric of parent–child relations, or more explicitly the intergenerational contract (Whitehead et al. 2007). As our case study of the Assam tea plantation illustrates, in contexts where a state system of welfare is lacking or poorly functioning, 'families are the dominant welfare institutions' (Kabeer 2000: 465, in Punch 2015: 264). The idea of the intergenerational contract refers to the social norms underpinning the welfare function of the family: the normative responsibility that parents care for their children when they are young, and the reversal of roles over time. When young people migrate, stay put or return, this may coincide with the interests of their parents. More commonly, though, there is some friction. The idea of generation as kinship descent provides the conceptual language for analysing such contested and negotiated migration decision-making as it unfolds between parents and children as well as between siblings (Whitehead et al. 2007: 15).

Generation as kinship descent requires dynamic analyses. The position of child or parent may be permanent, yet the privileges and responsibilities associated with these roles change as both parents and children progress through the life-course. In addition, households are also in flux for other reasons (Huijsmans 2014). Roles and responsibilities within the household fluctuate in response to outside forces (that is, crises of all kinds) as well as the dynamics of the household development cycle as people leave or join households (Huijsmans 2014). It is further worth noting that roles and responsibilities are also differentiated by gender and birth order. This means that the exact form the interdependencies take between parents and children, and between siblings, and how these impact upon migration, is often less clear than the term 'intergenerational contract' suggests (Huijsmans 2014). Rather, these relations are constantly being worked out, leading Punch to prefer the phrase 'negotiated interdependencies' (Punch 2015: 264).

The idea of generation as life-phase illuminates how migration is related to the construction and performativity of youth. This approach sheds light on the interplay between institutional dynamics which make migration a likely option during certain points in the youth phase of the life-course (Ní Laoire 2000), and young people's desire to migrate or stay put in order to enact a particular generationed identity (Hertrich and Lesclingand 2013; Rodan and Huijsmans 2021). From an institutional perspective, labour markets and the provision of education are typically more developed and diverse in urban settings than in rural areas. For young people from rural areas, this means that migration is often necessary simply in order to continue their studies beyond levels of education provided locally, or to seek forms of work beyond what is available in the countryside (Chea and Huijsmans 2018). In addition, becoming mobile also needs to be recognised as a means of becoming youth (Huijsmans 2019a). This includes being recognised as 'cool' by one's peers (Huijsmans et al. 2021: 83), seen as socially 'up-to-date' (Mills 1997), as well as being recognised by parents and older adults for having an opinion and experience that matters (Soonthorndhada et al. 2005).

Recognising the important role that migration may play in becoming youth also makes it possible to problematise 'non-migration', rather than treating it simply as the unquestioned norm. This insight leads Jónsson (2008: 37) to write about 'involuntary immobility' among young Soninke men in Mali, for whom the inability to migrate 'undermined interpersonal relations and impaired the social becoming of young men'.

A Mannheimian interpretation of generation draws attention to how widespread involvement in migration among youth can become a feature in how people identify with others in their generation and as a generation (Rodan and Huijsmans 2021). This perspective draws on Karl Mannheim's seminal work (Mannheim 1952) on the role of generations in social change. Although different generations may share the same historical time, they experience time as qualitatively different because each new generation necessarily comes in contact with the accumulated heritage of the previous generations in a partial and particular way. Mannheim termed this generation-specific way in which young people come to experience and respond to existing social realities 'fresh contact' (ibid.: 294). This rhythm of generations, Mannheim argued, 'facilitates reevaluation of our inventory and teaches us both to forget that which is no longer useful and to covet that which has yet to be won' (ibid.: 294).

These Mannheimian insights are especially relevant in contexts of migration because the differences in generational identities are often rooted in or reinforced by the generationally differentiated migration experience. A Mannheimian approach helps to explain why young people as a generation may develop attitudes towards migration that are different from those of the previous generation. For example, Somaiah et al. (2020) explain that young Indonesian women increasingly aspire to stay put rather than recreate the burdens of migration they have experienced growing up as children of absent migrant parents. A Mannheimian interpretation of generation can also be recognised in studies employing the concept of '1.5 generation'. This draws attention to how the migration experience of those who have migrated during their formative years (before or during their teenage years) differs from that of their parents. Because of different positions in the generational order, in most cases these children have had little say in the migration decision, and yet have come to engage with the host society in a much more intensive way than their parents (for example, because they attend school in the host society). Thereby, these 1.5 generation migrants may come to experience a particularly strong sense of in-betweenness (Bartley and Spoonley 2008: 67–69). Finally, Mannheimian analytics may also be relevant in relation to second-, third- and further-generation migrants in order to grasp the generation-specific ways that 'the lives of the young might be located within the historical trajectory of a [migrant] society', as Hart (2014: 221) argues on the basis of his research with Palestinian youth who were born and raised in camps in Jordan.

MIGRATION, STAYING PUT, AND THE GENERATIONED POLITICAL ECONOMY OF ASSAM'S TEA PLANTATIONS

In the remainder of the chapter, we apply a generationed analysis to the specific case of migration by young people who have grown up on an Assam (India) tea plantation. We do so by privileging the voices of young migrants (and stayers). However, our concern with the analytics of generation means that we do not simply follow the common approach in childhood and youth studies of countering an adult-centric perspective with a child-centred or youth-centred one. Rather, our contribution is best described as privileging young people's voices by decentring adults (Huijsmans 2016b: 7). Concretely, this means creating the conceptual space for the perspectives of young people, without losing sight of how such perspectives are situated in the broader generational order.

Further, it should be noted that in the Indian context, giving voice to young migrants is more than a matter of methodology. The phenomenon of youth migration has over recent years predominantly been framed as a problem of trafficking; this includes the migration by youth from the Indian northeast to other parts of India (*The Guardian* 2014; UNICEF and Government of Assam 2014). Conflating the widespread phenomenon of youth migration with the specific problem of human trafficking is controversial for conceptual and theoretical reasons. But perhaps most importantly, such framing is problematic because it tends to aggravate rather than reduce the difficulties young people may encounter in their migrations (e.g. Huijsmans and Baker 2012). Another problematic consequence of viewing the phenomenon of youth migration through the lens of human trafficking is that it reduces young migrants to victims of trafficking. Such framing renders young migrants voiceless. Consequently, studies conducted from a human trafficking perspective have little to say about what migration means to young people themselves, what drives their decisions to either stay put or leave, and how this is intertwined with the work of householding and the generationed political economy of the plantation.

An important starting point to the analysis is appreciating that much of the present-day labour force of Assam's tea plantations has its roots elsewhere. Under British colonial rule, the Assam tea plantations recruited labour from what was then called the Chotanagpur region (stretching across parts of the present-day states of Bihar, Chhattisgarh, Jharkhand and Odisha). In order to keep the cost of labour recruitment low, planters induced entire families to move to the Assam plantations based on the promise of salaried work and accommodation (Bhowmik et al. 1996). Family recruitment created an on-site reserve army of labour consisting of children, youth and women who could be mobilised when demand for labour peaked; and in the case of children and adolescents, for just half the amount of the adult wages (Bhowmik et al. 1996: 11).

The generationed political economy described above may have been introduced by the British, yet it can still be recognised in the plantations' present-day labour regime. Bernstein (2000: 253) defines a labour regime as the specific method 'of mobilizing labour and organizing its production'. The one used on the Assam tea plantations revolves around the idea of *badli*.[2] Labour is organised into three categories: permanent workers, temporary workers, and other category (OC) workers. Permanent workers or *badli* have secured regular work and thus income, and also benefit from other entitlements. Most importantly, all permanent workers are provided with family accommodation[3] by the plantation, and upon retirement receive a one-time payment of provident funding (Rosenblum and Sukthankar 2014: 34).

The generationed dynamics of this labour regime become visible when we zoom in on the role of youth. Youth enter the plantation workforce as temporary workers. This status is locally referred to by the derogatory term *faaltu* labour (translating literally as 'useless' labour). As *faaltu* labour, youth have no access to regular work on the plantation during the lean season, making migrating for work to other destinations in India a logical option and, for some, a necessity. In the Assam tea plantations, one can only acquire *badli* status after someone with such status has retired or died. In practice this means that *badli* status is typically transferred within the household from parents to children. Only in exceptional circumstances, when there is no one within the household to take over a vacant *badli* status, is it transferred to someone beyond the household. In such cases, a sum of money is usually paid for acquiring someone's *badli* status.

While *badli* status is tied to an individual, the question of who takes over a vacant *badli* seat is central to the work of householding. Plantation youth are well aware of this, as the following quotation from an informal conversation with Raju[4] shows:

> Now I need to pull in an application. She [Raju's mother] left because of sickness; she couldn't work. Having thought about the seat [*badli* status], someone has to take it (*lena pareka*). He is good at studies [referring to a younger brother]. He has done higher secondary, so my thought is we should not give him [*badli* status]. He says that he will take it, but I am not supporting him that he should. It is like that, for one mother there may be two sons, but we also have our individual lives. (10 August 2019)

A person holding *badli* status earns little,[5] but has access to housing benefits that are of critical importance to the entire household. If the holder of *badli* status gets involved in migration work, which is typically better paid, they risk losing the status and associated benefits. Thus, the *badli* system effectively ties people in place, in terms of labour and residence. Raju's quotation shows that he is cognisant of the individual sacrifices taking over parental *badli* status might entail. Being tied to the plantation delimits one's life-world as a youth as well as the chances of realising life aspirations that go beyond the plantation. Further, his assertion that 'for one mother there may be two sons' indicates that the question of who takes over the *badli* is not only an intergenerational issue: it is an intra-generational question too.

Teasing apart the various ways in which youth's decisions to migrate, return or stay put were concurrently shaped by relations of generations unfolding through the work of householding, constrained by the plantation labour regime and expressive of young people's own aspirations, required an ethnographic approach. For this, the first author lived in a plantation labour quarter for a period of nearly five weeks between July and August 2019. During this period, research was conducted with a group of 18 young people (11 young men, seven young women) who had all been involved in migrant work elsewhere in India, doing things such as domestic work, restaurant work, construction work, working as security guards, and factory work. Additional research was conducted with relevant adults such as parents, labour union representatives and plantation management staff (for a full methodological account, see Kikon 2019).

GOING *BAHAR* FOR THE FIRST TIME

Our data show that most young people first got involved in migration during their second decade of life. The majority (12) did so when they were between 15 and 19 years of age, and another three first migrated at the age of 13. Overall, girls became involved in migration at a younger age than their male peers. Out of the seven young women, six had already migrated at least once by the age of 16, as opposed to five of the 11 young men. This age–gender pattern of youth migration is similar to what has been observed elsewhere in the Southeast Asian region (Huijsmans 2019b).

The age pattern of first-time migration and the motivations young people gave indicate the importance of understanding these initial migrations from a life-phase perspective. Young people start to develop their own outlook on life, and increasingly act on these new life perspectives, as peers become important next to family. These changes do not just happen as a result of human biological development but also stem from the social conditions shaping their lives. For example, in the second decade of life, full-time education is no longer a given for plantation youth and paid employment starts playing a more important a role. Paid work is at times to support the family but also because being a teenager often requires taking part in particular forms of consumption. Further, the generationed political economy of the plantation is such that youth enter the plantation labour force as 'temporary workers'. Since work is not guaranteed for temporary workers and the wages are low, migration becomes a logical option during the second decade of life. Using generation in its interpretation of life-phase, it becomes evident that plantation youth are structurally dispositioned towards becoming mobile, while becoming mobile is also a means of establishing oneself as youth (Huijsmans 2019a).

In the decisions about their first migrations, the family featured in broadly two ways. For some young people migration was a way of dealing with non-harmonious family relations. For example, Suchitra left home at the age of 13. She explained her decision to migrate as follows: 'My father used to quarrel a lot, it was every day, so I got tired and decided to go out.' She left with another youth who had worked away from the plantation before and who put her in contact with a placement agency in New Delhi. It was through this placement agency that she got a job as a live-in domestic worker. Nina also first migrated at the age of 13 (after having completed middle school, standard 8). Her migration started with her going out with friends to a nearby river. As she had stayed out late, she was too afraid to return home, fearing her father's reaction as he was a hot-tempered man. She stayed close to the plantation for a week, staying with a woman who regularly helped youth find work outside the plantation.[6] Her friends then counselled that not returning home for a week had probably made the situation worse with her father, and it was then that she decided to leave for a job as a domestic worker in Punjab with the help of the woman she was staying with. In these instances, young people draw on peers and on their own networks to realise their migration projects without necessarily informing their parents.

In other cases, it was the inability of the family to provide for young people's needs and aspirations that emerged as an important factor triggering their first-time migration. For example, Rajesh first migrated at the age of 13. At that time, his father had already passed away and his mother was the only adult earning an income. As the first-born child (he had two younger siblings), Rajesh felt that he had to go *bahar* (outside) and earn money to support his poverty-stricken household. Years later, his mother still remembered clearly the difference this made, when she remarked, 'it helped me a lot when he went out'.

Poverty was also a main driving factor behind Raju's first migration at the age of 16:

> After matric [class 10th] I should study, I should not leave schooling, but if you have to take admission, you need money. I needed about 3250 rupees (40.95 euros). At that time, working in the tea garden was 94 rupees (1.18 euros) wages per day. So, it was not possible. I knew then, you will eat at home or should give for schooling? So, I thought about it and went to Delhi in 2010.

In many other cases, though, the decision to leave the plantation was the result of a combination of factors. In the case of Rishi, he left home for work in Bangalore at the age of 17. He explained his 'going outside' as follows: 'I got bored sitting at home, I also didn't like the things at home ... there were problems with money, then sickness [of his ageing father and younger brother] ... so I thought as times passes, I also need to move up.'

The illustrations above indicate that the young people interviewed all emphasised their agency in their first migration decision. Indeed, this counters the human trafficking discourse which views young people as objects, rather than agents, in migration. However, recognising young people as agents in migration does not mean ignoring the structural and life-phase specific conditions under which decisions are made (that is, youth's status as temporary workers at the plantation), and the various other constraints shaping their decisions (for example, household poverty). At the same time, the illustrations above also show the increasingly important role of young people's own social networks in realising their migrations. This is not to say that such non-family-related networks are risk-free (Huijsmans 2012). Yet, they help young people to establish themselves as social actors in migration independently from their households, thereby positioning themselves more firmly as youth with their own perspectives and goals.

BACK TO THE PLANTATION: MIGRATION DECISION-MAKING RECONFIGURED

Too often the literature portrays youth migration as a singular event. In practice, it is often a cumulative phenomenon. Young people migrate, often return for shorter or longer periods of time, and may then re-migrate again (Huijsmans 2012). A generationed perspective illuminates how this cumulative and temporal dimension of youth migration matters. Youth, just as any other age-related construct, is a temporal construct. This makes it different from gender, class or ethnicity, which are social categories that one rarely moves out of. Since migration, especially first migration, is an important formative experience for young people (Grabska et al. 2019; Hertrich and Lesclingand 2013: 182; Huijsmans 2018), it then follows that when young people return they are no longer the same as when they left. In addition, a generationed analysis also requires appreciating that the household which young migrants return to has progressed through the household development cycle (Huijsmans 2014). Analytically this implies that young people's migration decisions are not only made afresh for each subsequent migration; rather, they are also made afresh in a reconfigured constellation of relations of generation within the household, and from a reconfigured sense of generation identity of the young person concerned.

Raju's case illustrates some of the dynamics described above. Raju first migrated at the age of 16 and re-migrated twice thereafter. When we met him in 2019 at the age of 25, he had decided to stop migrating and stay on the plantation:

> Physically they [Raju's parents] are weak now, even now if I go, in my thoughts it won't be nice. Yes, you will get more money, but right now my duty is towards my family. Yes, even that time I had duty but it was a time to do something for myself, it's not that it is not there now, it is there now also, but at that time there was more opportunity to do for myself. If I go now, '*mere se jyada burbhak koi nahi hoga*' (there won't be any bigger fool than me) because my duty to look after my family, to look after them is mine now. My mummy and papa's *sampatti* (wealth) is me, *mai chota se itna bara huwa, main hi hun property* (then I was a child, I am grown-up now, I am the property). I went that time, I did whatever I could, and now it is my duty to look after them. I cannot leave them and go. Here I am not able to earn, whatever I earn is less, but since we live together we are happy, whatever, we are eating together, there is more happiness.

Raju's explanation of his decision to stay put is a highly nuanced account. When he first left it was not that he did not feel an obligation to stay, and now that he has decided to stay put for the time being, it is also not that he has no desire to remigrate. The quotation shows that the dramatic change in the outcome of the decision (from leaving to staying) results from a relatively small shift in the overall balancing act he performs between responding to changing family obligations and his evolving aspirations as a young man.

In addition, the first experience of migration may also feature in subsequent migration decisions. If the initial migration was not a positive experience, it may induce staying put. For example, Himanshu returned at the age of 17 after having worked in Delhi and Himachal Pradesh for one year. Seeing that his mother was getting old, he insisted that he now planned to stay on the plantation. However, his decision to stay was also informed by his migration experience: 'Now I won't go outside. It is difficult. I have gone and come back'.[7]

In the case of Himanshu, prior migration experience and his sense of filial duty reinforced each other, leading to his decision to stay put. This is not always the case. For example, Rita had worked in Delhi for a year at the age of 17. Ever since she had returned to the plantation seven years ago, she had wanted to re-migrate, but as the youngest child and daughter of an ageing mother she was not given the opportunity to act on this desire: 'Yes, I wanted to go again but my mother was very sick, and she needed to be given bath and all, which others in the family could not do'. The considerations informing Rita and Himanshu's respective migration decisions hence reflect broader gender patterns. For young women, the obligations that come with their position as daughters were, in general, much more difficult to negotiate than was the case for sons, which could predispose them towards either (re-)migrating or staying (as Rita's case illustrates).

Finally, in contexts in which youth migration is widespread, as is the case for the Assam tea plantations, using the lens of generation illuminates the imprint that migration may make on youth as a generation, even if returning youth decide to stay put. Raju put this perhaps most clearly when he made the following point: 'they don't know biryani, my father has eaten but there are people in the village even now those in the older generation they have not eaten biryani or seen biryani. It is different, their generation and our generation.'

Here, Raju uses the example of having eaten biryani to argue that having stayed and worked away from the plantation has changed plantation youth as a generation. Various others made a similar point in relation to speaking in Hindi. Hindi is not widely spoken on the plantation, and only poorly among the older generation. Having stayed and worked in Hindi-speaking parts of India, various young returnees were keen to point out that their Hindi language skills were much better than was the case among their parents' generation (who often were more comfortable in Orriya and Sadri languages). As Hindi is key to the political construct of the Indian nation-state and is also central to Indian popular culture (Beazley and Chakraborty 2008), facility in the language matters in how plantation youth understand their position as a generation, in relation to the broader imagined community of contemporary India (cf. Huijsmans and Trần 2015).

BECOMING *BADLI*: TEMPORARY RETURN BECOMING PERMANENT

So far we have emphasised the importance of a dynamic analysis when using the lens of generation in relation to young people's migration decisions. Generation in its interpretation as life-phase may be the driving force underpinning a first migration. Yet, for a subsequent migration decision, it may well be that generation in its interpretation of kinship descent has more analytical purchase, because the constellation of factors and relations within which migration decisions are made have shifted. Despite the importance of a dynamic analysis, for at least some of the plantation youth, their status may not stay in flux forever but assumes a degree of fixity in the context of the plantation's generationed political economy.

As explained, obtaining a permanent worker status (*badli*) may not be very attractive for individual youth because the plantation wages are low and it would obstruct realising alternative futures (for example, migrant work). Yet, since *badli* status comes with a number of social provisions (most importantly, housing), it is key that someone in the family holds it. Consequentially, young people – both young men and young women – have no doubts that someone in the household has to take over the *badli* status. If this responsibility comes their way, they claim that there would be no option (*lena padega*) other than to take it.

Rita's case illustrates the above reasoning very well. She is the youngest of four children (two older brothers and a sister). When we met her in 2019 at the age of 25, she had been back on the plantation, working as a temporary worker, for about a year (following two migrations). Rita said that she was preparing to take over her mother's *badli* status in the near future.[8] Becoming *badli* is shaped by her position as the only remaining daughter in the family, and sealed by the fact that her sister-in-law had left the household following divorce. This put Rita in the position of carer for her sick and ageing mother, and for the children of her separated brother who himself had embarked on migration again. In this scenario, the social logic was such that taking over her mother's *badli* came her way because her sister had married and left the household, and the second-born brother was already employed in the customer service point of a kiosk bank.

Less common were scenarios in which the social logic of whom should take over the *badli* status pointed towards a son. One such exception is the case of Himanshu. At the age of 17 he was already certain that he would have to take over his mother's *badli* status in the near future. Here, this prospect was determined by the household composition, but this time shaped by age and ability rather than by gender. His older sister had a disability and his other sibling was a younger seven-year-old sister. In this household there was no other option than for Himanshu, as the only able-bodied young person in the household, to take on the *badli* status.

For young migrants, staying is essentially a temporary condition. It can always be undone by going out again. Yet, taking over a *badli* status renders staying fairly permanent. Rishi was very aware of this reality. As the oldest son (out of three) in a family where both parents held *badli* status, he was anticipating taking over his father's *badli* status in due course, well aware that this would put an end to his sojourns:[9]

> I will have to take [*badli*]. My father has around 10 years to work until he retires. In the meantime, I plan to continue migrating for another 10 years and after that I cannot. But if I have to take the responsibility for *ghar chalana pareka* [have to manage the house] and it won't be possible for me to continue migrating for that long. If I cannot continue migrating for 10 years, it is okay, I will at least continue migrating for 5 years and then I will return for good.

Among sons in households in which there were various potential candidates to take over the *badli* status, we often heard the word *dekhenge* in response to the question of whether they would step forward. *Dekhenge* can best be translated as 'we shall see when the time comes'. This response usually indicated that the question of who would take over the *badli* status was still being negotiated among siblings and between parents and their children. The outcome of such negotiations was difficult to foresee as it depended on the particular state of affairs when the moment arrived.

Additionally, young men's utterance of *dekhenge* also reflected another possible and not uncommon approach to resolving the question of *badli*: marriage. Marriage featured frequently as a motivation for migration. Young men would go out to earn money needed for their marriage, or young people would go out to earn in order to raise funds needed for the marriage of a sibling. Young men would often claim that after marriage they would stop migrating and stay on the plantation. However, in practice, staying was often only temporary. Young wives would move into their husbands' households and take over various care responsibilities – including the *badli* status – thereby allowing their husbands to engage in other forms of livelihood or re-migrate (cf. Huijsmans et al. 2021).

CONCLUSION

Youth have been recognised as an important population in migration in both policy and the academic literature. Yet, to date, relatively few studies have accounted for this generationed characteristic of migration in analytical terms. In this chapter, we have contributed to such an objective by working with diverse interpretations of the concept of generation. The lens of generation demands viewing youth's decisions to migrate, return or stay put in relation to the broader generational order, which includes recognising how these decisions connect with the identity work of being young, young people's changing roles and responsibilities in the everyday work of householding, and the effects it has on the formation of youth as a generation. Similar to gender, the particular way in which the concept of generation is applied brings to light distinct generationed dimensions and effects of youth migration. In other words, there is no definite way of applying the concept of generation. Rather, a generationed approach demands analytical sensitivity to the diverse ways in which generation matters at different moments in the social process of migration.

Adding to this discussion, the case study from the Assam tea plantation highlighted both the importance but also the limits of a dynamic analysis in studying youth migration. Relative to other social categories such as gender, class and ethnicity, age-related categories such as youth are constantly in motion. For young people, youth is necessarily a temporal condition. In addition, the social meaning of youth as a structural location in the generational order is also subject to change over time. We have argued that migration fuels this changing of the meaning of youth. Since youth migration is rarely a singular event, but rather a cumulative process comprised of series of migrations, returns and periods of staying put, it follows that each youth migration needs to be appreciated afresh in relation to a reconfigured constellation of generational relations within the household, and the young person's reconfigured sense of generation identity. At the same time, our case study has also shown that a dynamic and ever-unfolding understanding of youth migration is not always sustainable. For the plantation youth in our study, limits to mobility were brought about by the generationed political economy underpinning the plantation labour regime. While such a labour regime predisposes youth to migrate, the eventual taking over of the *badli* seat would for some youth curtail their mobility beyond the plantation, and by implication, draw to a close a specific way of being youth.

NOTES

1. This is an annual International Organization for Migration-led 'multistakeholder forum for migration policy dialogue and main space for the analysis of overall migration governance at the global level' (IOM 2020: 3).
2. The idea of *badli* is also observed in the Calcutta jute industry, albeit with some slight differences compared to the labour regime of the Assam tea plantations (e.g. De Haan 1999).
3. Such housing typically measures 10.30 ft by 11.00 ft. The accommodation consists of two bedrooms, a small entrance room and a kitchen area.
4. Raju, a 25-year-old son, is the second-born out of five siblings. His older sister has married and left the household, next are two sisters (one single, the other a divorcee), and the last-born is a brother. His mother has *badli* status but is sickly, and his father runs a tea stall next to their house on the plantation.
5. Cash remuneration in tea estates in Assam is only 40–60 per cent of the central government's minimum wage. At the time of research, workers' daily wages on the plantation are 167 rupees (€2.12), and after deductions for benefits such as housing, water and provident fund, they can earn 880 rupees (€11. 04) a week for a six-day work week.
6. From the perspective of plantation youth, this woman is an agent who they approach if they cannot access migrant work through their own networks. However, the anti-trafficking community would look at her as a trafficker, mainly because she facilitates youth migration.
7. Here, Himanshu referred especially to his migrant work experience in a mustard oil factory in Himachal Pradesh, where they had to work long hours and were provided with tiny amounts of food only twice a day.
8. Her father had passed away.
9. Rishi was so certain about this likely course of events because his family preferred that his sister would just do household chores and not get involved in plantation work. In addition, his youngest brother had returned sickly from a previous migration and had never fully recovered.

REFERENCES

Alanen, L. 2009. 'Generational Order.' Pp. 159–174 in *The Palgrave Handbook of Childhood Studies*, edited by J. Qvortrup, W.A. Corsaro and M.-S. Honig. Basingstoke, UK and New York, USA: Palgrave Macmillan.

Bartley, A. and P. Spoonley. 2008. 'Intergenerational Transnationalism: 1.5 Generation Asian migrants in New Zealand.' *International Migration* 46(4): 63–84.

Beazley, H. and K. Chakraborty. 2008. 'Cool Consumption: Rasta, Punk and Bollywood on the Streets of Yogyakarta, Indonesia and Kolkata, India.' Pp. 195–214 in *Youth, Media and Culture in the Asia Pacific Region*, edited by U.M. Rodrigues and B. Smaill. Newcastle: Cambridge Scholars Publishing.

Bernstein, H. 2000. 'Colonialism, Capitalism, Development.' Pp. 241–270 in *Poverty and Development: Into the 21st century*, edited by T. Allen and A. Thomas. Oxford: Open University with Oxford University Press.

Bhowmik, S., V. Xaxa and M.A. Kalam. 1996. *Tea Plantation Labour in India*. New Delhi: Friedrich Ebert Stiftung (India Office).

Brickell, K. and B.S.A. Yeoh. 2014. 'Geographies of Domestic Life: "Householding" in transition in East and Southeast Asia.' *Geoforum* 51: 259–261.

Chant, S. 1992. *Gender and Migration in Developing Countries*. New York, USA and London, UK: Belhaven Press.

Chea, L. and R. Huijsmans. 2018. 'Rural Youth and Urban-based Vocational Training: Gender, Space and Aspiring to "Become Someone".' *Children's Geographies* 16(1): 39–52.

De Haan, A. 1999. 'The Badli System in Industrial Labour Recruitment: Managers' and Workers' Strategies in Calcutta's Jute Industry.' *Contributions to Indian Sociology* 33(1–2): 271–301.

Douglass, M. 2006. 'Global Householding in Pacific Asia.' *International Development Planning Review* 28(4): 421–445.

Grabska, K., M. de Regt and N. Del Franco. 2019. *Adolescent Girls' Migration in the Global South: Transitions into Adulthood*. Cham: Palgrave Macmillan.
The Guardian. 2014. 'The Tea Pickers Sold into Slavery.' 2 March.
Hart, J. 2014. 'Locating Young Refugees Historically: Attending to Age Position in Humanitarianism.' *European Journal of Development Research* 26(2): 219–232.
Hertrich, V. and M. Lesclingand. 2013. 'Adolescent Migration in Rural Africa as a Challenge to Gender and Intergenerational Relationships: Evidence from Mali.' *ANNALS of the American Academy of Political and Social Science* 648(1): 175–188.
Huijsmans, R. 2012. 'Beyond Compartmentalization: A Relational Approach towards Agency and Vulnerability of Young Migrants.' *New Directions for Child and Adolescent Development* 136: 29–45.
Huijsmans, R. 2014. 'Becoming a Young Migrant or Stayer Seen through the Lens of "Householding": Households "In Flux" and the Intersection of Relations of Gender and Seniority.' *Geoforum* 51: 294–304.
Huijsmans, R. 2016a. *Generationing Development: A Relational Approach to Children, Youth and Development*. London: Palgrave Macmillan.
Huijsmans, R. 2016b. 'Generationing Development: An Introduction.' Pp. 1–31 in *Generationing Development: A Relational Approach to Children, Youth and Development*, edited by R. Huijsmans. London: Palgrave Macmillan.
Huijsmans, R. 2017. 'Exploring the "Age Question" in Research on Young Migrants in Southeast Asia.' *Journal of Population and Social Studies* 25(2): 122–134.
Huijsmans, R. 2018. '"Knowledge That Moves": Emotions and Affect in Policy and Research with Young Migrants.' *Children's Geographies* 16(6): 628–641.
Huijsmans, R. 2019a. 'Becoming Mobile and Growing Up: A "Generationed" Perspective on Borderland Mobilities, Youth, and the Household.' *Population, Space and Place* 25(3): 1–10.
Huijsmans, R. 2019b. 'Young Women and Girls' Migration and Education: Understanding the Multiple Relations.' Pp. 31–42 in *Supporting Brighter Futures: Young Women and Girls and Labour Migration in South-East Asia and the Pacific*, edited by IOM. Geneva: International Organization for Migration (IOM).
Huijsmans, R., A. Ambarwati, C. Chazali and M. Vijayabaskar. 2021. 'Farming, Gender and Aspirations across Young People's Life Course: Attempting to Keep Things Open while Becoming a Farmer.' *European Journal of Development Research* 33(1): 71–88.
Huijsmans, R. and S. Baker. 2012. 'Child Trafficking: "Worst Form" of Child Labour, or Worst Approach to Young Migrants?' *Development and Change* 43(4): 919–946.
Huijsmans, R. and T.H.L. Trần. 2015. 'Enacting Nationalism through Youthful Mobilities? Youth, Mobile Phones and Digital Capitalism in a Lao–Vietnamese Borderland.' *Nations and Nationalism* 21(2): 209–229.
IOM. 2020. 'Youth and Migration: Engaging Youth as Key Partners in Migration Governance. Unlocking the Potential of Youth to Respond to New Challenges and Opportunities of Migration.' Geneva: International Organization for Migration (IOM).
Jónsson, G. 2008. 'Migration Aspirations and Immobility in a Malian Soninke Village.' Oxford: International Migration Institute (IMI), James Martin 21st Century School, University of Oxford.
Kikon, R. 2019. 'Leaving, Returning, and Staying: Youth Negotiating Gendered and Generational (Intra- and Inter) Householding within the Plantation Labour Regime in Assam, India.' International Institute of Social Studies, Erasmus University.
Mannheim, K. 1952. 'The Problem of Generations.' Pp. 276–320 in *Essays on the Sociology of Knowledge*, edited by K. Mannheim. London: RKP.
Mills, M.B. 1997. 'Contesting the Margins of Modernity: Women, migration, and consumption in Thailand.' *American Ethnologist* 24(1): 37–61.
Ní Laoire, C. 2000. 'Conceptualising Irish Rural Youth Migration: A Biographical Approach.' *International Journal of Population Geography* 6(3): 229–243.
Ní Laoire, C., A. White and T. Skelton. 2017. *Geographies of Children and Young People Volume 6: Movements, Mobilities, and Journeys*. Singapore: Springer.
Punch, S. 2015. 'Youth Transitions and Migration: Negotiated and Constrained Interdependencies Within and Across Generations.' *Journal of Youth Studies* 18(2): 262–276.

Punch, S. 2020. 'Why Have Generational Orderings been Marginalised in the Social Sciences Including Childhood Studies?' *Children's Geographies* 18(2): 128–140.

Rodan, L. and R. Huijsmans. 2021. '"Our Generation ...": Aspiration, Desire, and Generation as Discourse Among Highly Educated, Portuguese, Post-Austerity Migrants in London.' *European Journal of Development Research* 33(1): 147–164.

Rosenblum, P. and A. Sukthankar. 2014. '"The More Things Change ..." The World Bank, Tata and Enduring Abuses on India's Tea Plantations.' New York: Columbia Law School Human Rights Institute.

Somaiah, B.C., B.S.A. Yeoh, and S.M. Arlini. 2020. '"*Cukup* for Me to be Successful in This Country": "Staying" Among Left-Behind Young Women in Indonesia's Migrant-Sending Villages.' *Global Networks* 20(2): 237–255.

Soonthorndhada, A., S. Kittisuksathit, S. Punpuing, A. Varangrat, A. Malhotra, S.R. Curran and S.B. Martin. 2005. 'Youth at Odds: Thai Youth's Precarious Futures in a Globalized World.' Phuttthamonthon (Nakon Pathom): Institute for Population and Social Research (Mahidol University), International Center for Research on Women (USA), Office of Population Research (Princeton University).

Stark, O.and D.E. Bloom. 1985. 'The New Economics of Labor Migration.' *American Economic Review* 75(2): 173–178.

UNICEF and Government of Assam. 2014. 'Report: Secondary Data Analysis on Trafficking of Women and Children in Assam.' Guwahati: Unicef Field Office Assam, Government of Assam.

United Nations. 2011. 'International Migration in a Globalizing World: The Role of Youth.' New York: Population Division, United Nations.

Whitehead, A., I.M. Hashim, and V. Iversen. 2007. 'Child Migration, Child Agency, and Inter-generational Relations in Africa and South Asia.' Brighton: Development Research Centre on Migration, Globalisation and Poverty, Sussex University.

12. Unaccompanied child migrants and family relationships

Katie Willis, Sue Clayton and Anna Gupta

INTRODUCTION

Family members or carers are commonly seen as vital in the protection, socialisation and support of children. Thus, when children migrate internationally without the presence of such individuals, these young people are seen as particularly vulnerable. This has led to the creation of the official category of 'unaccompanied minor' (UAM) by national governments and international organisations to facilitate the support for these children (UN CRC General Comment Number 6, Point 7, cited in UNICEF Innocenti Research Centre, 2006, p. 46; Eurostat, 2021). The absence of an adult family member is a key part of the UAM definition; it is what makes those individuals 'unaccompanied'. However, this physical absence does not reflect the ongoing importance of family relationships for individual young people, as well as new forms of family that are created and experienced during the migration journey, and through the asylum and welfare system. The construction of being alone may be very different from how the young people feel about themselves, having arrived in a new country (Herz and Lalander, 2017). In this chapter, we explore the constructions and experiences of 'family' in relation to UAMs to highlight the importance of using the lens of the family to understand the lives of UAMs, and their search for safety and stability through their physical and institutional journeys.

Families are inherently dynamic due to births, deaths, marriages, divorce, adoption and other routes by which people join or leave a familial unit. Such dynamism would be experienced by individuals through the life-course regardless of mobility, but migration can add complexity to the forms of family created and the experiences of family life. For unaccompanied children, their international migration is experienced alongside a move towards adulthood, where a transition to the legal status of 'adult' is often associated with a sharp break between a receiving state's legal responsibilities to protect children, and the right of states to police their borders. Uncertainty about what may happen when they turn 18 can have a detrimental impact on young people's well-being, and affect their ability and willingness to develop caring and supportive relationships (Williams, 2019).

The notions and experience of family may change over time during a young person's journey from their natal family to a new country, and through the asylum system and beyond. For example, Eide et al. (2020), in their discussion on transition in Norway, use the notion of 'resettlement' as a form of re-rooting in a new location. This is not just the setting up of a new place of residence, but also the dynamism of existing social connections and the evaluation of new ones.

This chapter explores debates around family and UAMs in Europe. In 2020, 13 600 unaccompanied minors made asylum applications within the European Union (EU) (Eurostat, 2021), and 2291 applied in the UK (Home Office, 2021). This number is a significant reduction from the EU-wide figures of 92 000 in 2015 (Eurostat, 2021), but still represents a significant number of vulnerable young people who have arrived in Europe without an adult family member or other responsible adult.

This chapter first focuses on the construction of 'the family' in law relating to unaccompanied child migrants, and how laws are implemented through particular regulatory processes (see also Chapters 17 and 18, this *Handbook*). We then move to a discussion of the ongoing nature of transnational ties to family members 'left behind'. This stresses the often continuing emotional ties between child migrants and family members, as well as feelings of responsibility and guilt which are taken on by young people who may have been sent away by family members for their own safety, but at great emotional and often financial cost. The following sections consider different and novel forms of family or family-like relationships that may emerge as young people move through the asylum process. Key to these in a European context is the nature of the formal care provision for UAMs. This varies greatly between countries, from a widespread use of foster carers, to UAMs being accommodated in immigration service reception centres. In some contexts, carers and/or young people may see the relationships and environments as 'like family', but there are also significant issues around the provision of emotional care and support for young people within the child welfare systems. Young people may also develop their own social relationships with other young migrants, local people of their own age, members of migrant or religious organisations, and volunteers. These relationships often help young people to feel a sense of stability and belonging, although in many cases this is threatened by the pervading sense of uncertainty about being able to stay once they reach legal adulthood. The chapter concludes with a summary of the perspectives on family that emerge when considering unaccompanied child migrants.

ROLE OF FAMILY IN LAW

The family, as a concept within law, is seen as a 'natural and fundamental group unit of society' entitled to 'protection by society and the state' (Pobjoy, 2017, p. 70). This view of the family is reflected in a number of international treaties. However, what 'family' consists of within law, and what protection the family enjoys, is much less clear. For unaccompanied child migrants, it is separation from adult family members, particularly a parent or parents, that constructs the individual as a vulnerable subject requiring protection (Sirriyeh, 2015).

Within the 1951 Refugee Convention, people (including children) can claim asylum based on imputed identity, such as the political views of family members. Asylum claims can also be based on fears of persecution, not for one's own views, but as an indirect route to target other family members (Pobjoy, 2017, pp. 165–166). While the 1951 Refugee Convention does not include the right to family unity, the family is given specific attention in other international agreements. For example, in the United Nations (UN) Convention on the Rights of the Child (CRC) signed in 1989 and now ratified by all UN member states apart from the United States of America, Article 9 states that:

> States Parties shall ensure that a child shall not be separated from his or her parents against their will, except when competent authorities subject to judicial review determine, in accordance with applicable law and procedures, that such separation is necessary for the best interests of the child. (OHCHR, 2021)

Further, Article 10 states that 'applications by a child or his or her parents to enter or leave a State Party for the purpose of family reunification shall be dealt with by States Parties in a positive, humane and expeditious manner' (OHCHR, 2021).

While these two articles appear to suggest that children have a right to family reunification, in reality this does not usually materialise. In particular, there is an asymmetrical approach to the implementation of family reunification, whereby parents can extend protection to children, but not the other way round (Pobjoy, 2017, p. 50). This means that children may be able to join parents who have crossed international borders for refuge, but parents (or other family members) usually cannot join children.

Family protection for vulnerable children is part of the European Dublin III regulation (Regulation (EU) No. 604/2013) which was adopted on 23 June 2013 and implemented from 1 January 2014. Under Dublin III, unaccompanied children arriving in any EU country and claiming asylum have the right to be united with family members in another EU state. They can then have their asylum claims assessed in that member state while living with their family member. The regulation makes the distinction between 'family', meaning a parent, legal guardian or sibling, and 'relative', which includes adult aunts and uncles, as well as grandparents (British Red Cross, 2019). Despite the adoption of Dublin III by EU member states, its operation has not always been straightforward. This can be clearly exemplified by events in 'the Jungle', an informal refugee settlement in Calais, northern France, which had nearly 10 000 inhabitants in 2016 (Clayton and Willis, 2019, p. 23). An estimated 1900 unaccompanied children were in the camp in mid-2016, but no child from the camp had been able to travel to the UK under the Dublin III regulation until the UK charity Safe Passage started negotiating with the UK Home Office, and other grassroots groups working in Calais challenged the Home Secretary in the UK courts. Even with the principle established in law, reliance on volunteers and charities to locate, monitor and advocate for these children meant that progress was very slow, with only two or three children a week being able to travel (Clayton and Willis, 2019, p. 24). Following the French police clearance of the Jungle camp in October 2016, more than 550 unaccompanied children were expedited by the UK in a more orderly way to join family members in the UK (UNICEF and Save the Children, 2017). It is likely that there were many more who were eligible to travel to the UK under Dublin III, but they were not processed by the Home Office. This reflects both an understandable lack of awareness of this law on the part of the young people, but also, more importantly, a failure to act according to European agreements on the part of the UK authorities. Following the Brexit transition period, the Dublin III regulation no longer applies to the UK (Gower, 2020). As of January 2022, there has been no agreement about family reunification processes for unaccompanied children who are in the EU but have family members in the UK.

The notion of 'best interests' of the child is fundamental to the CRC, and being with family members is usually part of these perceived best interests. However, the opinions of the young persons themselves are often ignored in such decisions, despite the CRC including an explicit requirement to consider young people's agency. Allsopp and Chase (2019) also argue, in an EU context, that notions of 'best interests of the child' are usually based on 'Westernised' concepts of family reunification whereby children will be reunited with a parent or parents in their country of origin. Such assumptions fail to acknowledge the complexities of the migration process, feelings of collective obligation to the family (discussed below), and the potential harms of reunification.

This assumption about family reunification is also expressed through regulations around family tracing, whereby authorities are tasked with seeking to find a young person's family members. In the EU, this is stated in the EU Reception Directive, Article 19(3), which requires member states to try and trace family members of unaccompanied asylum seekers, provided that this is in the best interests of the child. There is also a clear statement that this tracing should not be undertaken if it could lead to harm for the young person or family members (York and Warren, 2019). As with all European directives, interpretation and implementation is decided by individual member states. For instance, in the UK it is the Home Office which has the duty to trace family members as soon as possible after an unaccompanied child has made an asylum claim (Home Office, 2020, p.13). In Sweden, the responsibility is placed on municipalities (Lundburg and Dahlquist, 2012). Issues around family tracing are fraught with difficulty, not least because of the lack of resources available to conduct such research, particularly in countries where there is ongoing conflict and displacement. Young people may be fearful of the ramifications for their asylum claims, or their family's safety if they provide information (York and Warren, 2019).

The importance given to the unit of the family in international law was outlined earlier; at the same time, the family has also been used as a basis for making claims to remain in a country once a young person becomes a legal adult. For example, under Article 8 of the European Convention on Human Rights, there is a right to a private and family life. As will be discussed in more detail later in this chapter, young people who arrive unaccompanied by adult family members may develop new family relationships after arrival in a country of destination where they claim asylum. This may be with existing kin, with foster families or with new partners, perhaps including having children of their own. As young people approaching the age of 18, if they have not been granted leave to remain due to their asylum claim, they may use Article 8 as a reason to stay in the country after they reach legal adulthood. However, this route has not been successful, with judgments including the reasoning that they can maintain their relationship with any children they may have over the phone from another country (Allsopp, 2017). In the UK context, state authorities take the view that some asylum seekers are having children so as to be able to stay in the UK. This example demonstrates the contradictory ways in which 'family' is interpreted and mobilised in migration law: keeping parents and children together is seen as desirable and in the best interests of a child in one context, while in others the creation of a family is interpreted as a strategy to avoid forced removal which would involve the separation of a child from a parent (Griffiths and Morgan, 2017).

TRANSNATIONAL FAMILY LINKS

While UAMs are legally defined based on the absence of adult family members, as with all migrants, it is vital to understand their position within transnational family networks of emotional attachment, material obligation and social identity. While immigration and welfare policies usually deal with lone child migrants in an individualistic manner, the reality for these young people may be very different; their success in their new home is not just about their own achievements, but encompasses the family sphere. Belloni (2016) draws on her work with Eritrean migrants in Ethiopia, Sudan and Italy, as well as family members in Eritrea, to argue that, '[t]he moral, emotional and social ties between migrant and relative in the diaspora are based on implicit rules of ethnic and family membership' (p. 52).

Feelings of love and care for family members left behind are very apparent from numerous studies, with mothers being the particular focus of attention (Allsopp, 2017; Behrendt et al., 2022). However, these emotions are also frequently intertwined with fear about the safety of family members due to the insecurity and violence that the young people may have fled (Hughes, 2019). For example, Thommessen et al. (2015) outline the fears of young migrants in relation to their families in Afghanistan, while Behrendt et al. (2022) discuss the fears of unaccompanied young people in Belgium. Chase and Statham (2014, p. 226) describe the fears of young migrants to the UK, as well as emotions of grief at the death of family members at home or along the journey.

Keeping in touch with family members is often very important for young people's sense of belonging and well-being. Drawing on research with service providers working to support unaccompanied young migrants in Scotland, Hopkins and Hill (2010) stress the crucial role of ongoing family connections and also awareness of events happening in the home country. However, this connection is sometimes tempered by logistical issues around international communication, especially if there has been significant displacement due to violence and insecurity. Phone calls and social media, such as Facebook, are of great importance in maintaining contact (Behrendt et al., 2022).

There may also be some reticence on the part of UAMs to divulge ongoing family connections in the country of origin in case this has a negative impact on an asylum claim (see above). In Lundburg and Dahlquist's research with unaccompanied young migrants in Sweden, they highlight how '[t]heir earlier life, including family life, is restricted to the parts of their life that may allow them to stay in Sweden' (Lundburg and Dahlquist, 2012, p. 73). Young people's narratives about their natal family are shaped by the perceived requirements of the immigration system. This disavowal of ongoing family ties can also add to feelings of guilt among young migrants, contributing to the psychological difficulties they may face in their new home. Based on their research, Lundburg and Dahlquist argue that, '[w]hether or not one has family should not affect the right to apply for asylum or having their asylum grounds tested' (ibid., p. 74).

Forms and levels of connection with family members vary over time. Limited connections early in the migration journey may reflect logistical challenges in accessing technology, such as having no mobile phone, or having no signal or credit. Family displacement may also mean that young migrants do not know where other family members are, or how to contact them. This, combined with worries about the asylum process, may result in significant periods of disconnection from family members. In their longitudinal study in Belgium, Behrendt et al. (2022) highlight how most of the young people in their study did not have contact with families when they first arrived, but that this increased over time as they moved through the asylum system and were logistically able to reconnect with family members.

For many young migrants, there is a feeling of 'collective obligation to family' (Allsopp and Chase, 2019, p. 298) in relation to finances, as family members will have paid for the journey and there is likely to be an expectation (sometimes implicit, rather than expressed overtly) that financial remittances will come from successful migration. There is an assumption that members of the diaspora have greater access to resources than those at home (Belloni, 2016). The inability to provide resources to repay the family back home can lead to feelings of guilt among young migrants as they are not able to meet what are felt to be their socially sanctioned obligations. Such shame and guilt may result in young people choosing not to contact their family members (Belloni, 2020b). This may be the case even for those young people who have been sent away from their natal families against their will (Allsopp, 2017).

Gulwali Passarlay's journey from Afghanistan to the UK demonstrates the emotional resonances of decisions to send children away for their own safety. Following the killing of his father and grandfather, 12-year-old Passarlay was sent away from Afghanistan with his brother Hazrat. The family were concerned that their lives would be threatened due to perceived allegiances, as they were caught between loyalties to the Taliban and North Atlantic Treaty Organization (NATO) forces. Passarlay acknowledges the reasons for his exile: 'My mother sent me away so she didn't have to bury another person whom she loved' (Passarlay with Ghouri, 2015, p. 350). However, this decision came with significant personal loss: 'By sending me away she definitely saved her son, but she also lost him' (p. 354).

Such narratives of exile are very common, as it is usually family elders who make decisions about the movement of young people. Drawing on her work on Eritreans, Belloni (2020a) provides a counterpoint in critiquing the blanket representations of young migrants' lack of agency in decisions to migrate. Her ethnographic work in Italy, Ethiopia, Sudan and Eritrea suggests that sometimes decisions are made individually by young people themselves, albeit within the context of wider family relations. It should be stressed at this point that Belloni's work includes both young people above the age of 18 (so not included in official definitions of unaccompanied minors), as well as those who crossed international borders before the age of 18.

Rather than fleeing immediate physical danger, many Eritreans move in response to 'protracted crisis' in the country, and a future which Belloni describes as a 'wasted life'. All Eritreans are required to complete military service at age 17, but despite this service being of a specified length, in many cases young people are stuck in a form of perpetual servitude, with low pay in remote locations, unable to escape (OHCHR, 2015). Thus young people are confronted with the dilemma of staying at home and having no future, or embarking on a hazardous migration journey. For Belloni, the Eritrean situation demonstrates the intersecting of individual and family aspirations: 'Personal aspirations to access freedom, contribute to family stability and achieve moral recognition are thus intrinsically intertwined with more or less explicit social pressures to achieve a life deemed impossible at home' (Belloni, 2020a, p. 349). As well as this perception of a bleak future among many young Eritreans, for some, restrictions on religious freedom and the persecution of religious minorities (Amnesty International, 2018; OHCHR, 2015) prompt their departure.

In some cases, as outlined in the previous section on law, it is the family links themselves that have created situations of danger for the young people, due to family-based persecution resulting from perceived or actual political activities of family members or family feuds (Allsopp, 2017). In other situations, it is fear of violence from family members which has driven young people to flee (Allsopp, 2017) and claim asylum, such as in cases of female genital mutilation (FGM) (Home Office, 2020; Middleburg and Balta, 2016; Mishori et al., 2020; UNHCR, 2013).

Establishment in a new location does not necessarily mean a breaking of existing emotional and material ties with family members, but rather can lead to a new form of transnationality whereby the young person settles into a new life with opportunities that come from stability and security, while keeping in touch with natal family members, and perhaps sending money. Börjesson and Söderquist Forkby (2020, p. 480) discuss the case of Zabihullah, who arrived in Sweden as an unaccompanied child. Following the processing of his application and granting of a residence permit, he was able to contact his birth family to say that all was well, as he could now pursue an education. This reflected a form of belonging in a new location, as well as ongoing transnational familial belonging. Eide et al. (2020) discuss similar cases in Norway whereby most of the young people in their study kept in touch with families and sent money back, but they also wanted to have a good life in Norway.

Ongoing emotional attachment and obligation also mean that for many young migrants the ideal outcome would be for their family members to join them in their new home country through a process of family reunification (see Thommessen et al., 2015 on Sweden; Kalverboer et al., 2017 on the Netherlands). However, this is very rarely permitted in immigration law (see the earlier discussion of asymmetry in family reunification) (Pobjoy, 2017). In Sweden, family reunification is allowed under the 1951 Refugee Convention if UAMs have been granted a residence permit, with reunification including parents and any siblings who are under 18 (Lundburg and Dahlquist, 2012). However, Swedish immigration laws were made increasingly restrictive in 2015 in the context of the massive increase in refugee numbers in Europe (Lidén, 2019). Similarly, Kauko and Forsberg (2018) outline the impact of the tightening of immigration law in Finland, whereby parental or sibling reunification with children was increasingly restricted, leaving young people to abandon hopes of permanent reunification and instead focus on desiring frequent visits.

Transnational family networks operate not just between the current country of residence and the country of origin, but also through a wider kinship network. Behrendt et al. (2022) outline the role of other kin in Europe in providing practical and emotional support and advice to unaccompanied young people who arrive in Belgium (see also Jani, 2017 on similar forms of cross-border kinship support for unaccompanied children arriving into the United States). The networks of family relationships across international boundaries demonstrate the complexity of diaspora links. As Allsopp and Chase (2019, p. 305) state, '[t]he family itself maybe part of a diaspora that does not map neatly onto traditional geographical mappings of the "nation"'.

FOSTER FAMILIES

The child status of UAMs requires them to be given particular support because of their perceived vulnerability. As discussed in the section on law above, the state needs to provide the care, protection and support expected of family members. The nature of this welfare and care provision varies between countries, and also depends on the age of the child and, in some cases, the stage of the asylum process. A study by the European Union Agency for Fundamental Rights (the Fundamental Rights Agency, FRA) concluded that younger children should be placed with adult relatives or foster families, whereas older, more mature young people could be placed in residential group care that offers more independence, but still with adults responsible for their care (FRA, 2011). In terms of accommodation arrangements, the main forms of provision in the EU are foster care in a private household, a residential home with live-in staff, or semi-independent living with other young people with social services support.

However, at particular times when a large number of unaccompanied young migrants arrive in a particular location within a short period of time, there may be insufficient local authority provision. For example, in France, in cities such as Poitiers and Toulouse, the local authority welfare infrastructure has been insufficient to provide accommodation for the numbers of unaccompanied children arriving from 2015 onwards. This has led to informal systems of host families or even squatting as solutions (Gimeno-Monterde and Gutiérrez-Sánchez, 2019). Similarly, in 2018 the four accommodation centres for unaccompanied young people in Brussels were full and hence unable to house the estimated 1855 unaccompanied 14–17-year-olds in the city (Papadogiannakis, 2020). In Kent, in South-East England, the local authority has also highlighted the challenges that it has faced in meeting the needs of unaccompanied children who it has a statutory duty to look after. From 2021, there has been an increasing number of UAMs arriving by boat across the English Channel, on lorries travelling through the Channel Tunnel, or on ferries (*The Guardian*, 2021). Many of these young people were held initially in detention facilities, including the Kent Intake Unit (KIU), about which a report by the Chief Inspector of Prisons, concluded that unaccompanied minors placed there 'experience very poor treatment and conditions' (HM Inspectorate of Prisons, 2021, p. 3).

In the UK and the Republic of Ireland, children under 16 are usually placed with a foster family. Older children are also fostered if they are seen as particularly vulnerable (Gupta, 2019; Sirriyeh and Ní Raghallaigh, 2018). In the Netherlands, children under 15 are usually fostered (Rip et al., 2020). The notion of 'family' in 'foster family' can be seen as a way of upholding the perceived value of family-like relationships in caring for, supporting, encouraging and guiding young people. However, as Sirriyeh (2013) argues, drawing on her work on fostering in England, different forms of relationship can exist within foster families. She categorises these as lodger, guest and family-like relationships. Viewing the foster child as a lodger suggests that the focus is on the service provision that foster carers are providing for which they receive payment, in this case from a local authority. Guest relationships stress hospitality and respect, but the dynamics suggest that the child is separate from the host family. A 'family-like' relationship suggests something more meaningful and engaging, involving trust and reciprocity. As Wade et al. (2012) discuss in their research on fostering unaccompanied asylum-seeking young people in England, 'In the best of the families that we studied, family structure, relationships, routines and practice were adjusted to incorporate the young person as an active participant, enabling them to help shape family practices in ways that were meaningful to all concerned' (p. 5).

Sirriyeh (2013) draws on the work of Morgan (1996) and Finch (2007) to discuss domestic practices that can be seen as ways of 'doing family'. This may include activities such as communal cooking and meals together, and involving the fostered child in family celebrations. Drammeh (2019) draws on the narratives of young people and foster carers whom she met as a local authority social worker to highlight how dynamics within the home may change over time, reflecting different aspects of Sirriyeh's typology. The development of trust and understanding is not automatic, and is built through small daily interactions which may help a young person to feel secure and 'at home'. For Sirriyeh, foster families in her research 'did not seek to replace bonds with birth families, but rather used family practices to enact new creative kinship' (Sirriyeh, 2013, pp. 12–13).

In the Netherlands, foster families are also seen to provide a better environment for the care of unaccompanied young people than other forms of residential support. This is partly because of the perceived benefits of the emotional support that comes from such a setting, but also because living with a local family helps them to develop language skills and an understanding of Dutch culture, and therefore helps to facilitate integration (Kalverboer et al., 2017). While there is a diversity of experience in fostering situations for young people under 15 in the

Netherlands, Rip et al. (2020) found that most young people in their research preferred to live with foster carers than in asylum centres.

As with fostering and adoption more generally, there are debates around whether culturally similar foster families are more appropriate to provide support to an unaccompanied young person who has experienced significant disruption and trauma. A familiar language, cuisine and/or religious practice may help a child to adapt to their new environment; but evidence is very mixed. In the Netherlands, children under 15 are put in foster care, with a preference for a culturally similar foster family if possible. This can be very positive, especially if there are co-resident children of about the same age (Rip et al., 2020). In Flemish foster families, it is the nature of the relationships that is more important, rather than the similarity of cultural backgrounds. This is also the case in England and Ireland according to Ní Raghallaigh and Sirriyeh (2015), who also warn against essentialising culture. In placing children with foster carers who have the same cultural background, there is a need to be particularly careful about the safety of the birth family if there are links back to the country of origin (Rip et al., 2020). A review of the research on unaccompanied refugee minors and foster care (Van Holen et al., 2020) found it impossible to conclude from the literature a preference for culturally matched or cross-cultural placements, and that the individual needs and wishes of the young person should determine the placement.

The foster family environment can be seen as 'family-like' not just by the unaccompanied young person, but also by other family members. Fostering a child who has fled violence and insecurity, experienced the difficulties of the migration journey, and arrived in an alien environment, can come with challenges that even the most experienced foster parents may find difficult to deal with. Additionally, many carers may be unfamiliar with the asylum system and the threat of forced removal after the age of 18 if the young person is not given leave to remain (Drammeh, 2019). All of this can generate significant emotional work and impact on carers, although there has been less research on these elements of the fostering experience (Sirriyeh and Ní Raghallaigh, 2018).

OTHER FORMS OF SUPPORT AND SIGNIFICANT RELATIONSHIPS

While the foster family notion has a very clear engagement with the idea of familial relationships, albeit ones that may vary greatly in reality, state-provided welfare support for unaccompanied minors may take on other forms. These again may be discursively constructed as 'family-like' or may involve experiences which young people or others may describe in terms of family relationships, although there is significant diversity.

In the UK, foster families are the usual caring environments for UAMs aged 15 and under, but in other parts of Europe, fostering is much rarer. There is, however, some acknowledgement of the different needs of young people, differentiated by age. In Norway, for example, during the asylum process UAMs are looked after in 'care centres' run by child welfare services if under 15, and in immigration authority-run reception centres if aged 15–18 (Eide et al., 2020).

In Sweden, unaccompanied young people are often accommodated in residential care units with live-in staff (Börjesson and Söderquist Forkby, 2020; Söderquist et al., 2016). The shared living space between the adult employees and the young migrants involves shared responsibility for all those cohabiting. The residential care unit staff use the word 'family' to describe the situation, but as Söderquist et al. (2016) outline, the legal and institutional regulations place boundaries on the nature of this family relationship. For example, staff time is controlled, and the flexibility which a parent might have to interact with a child does not exist. In addition, there are clear rules banning the exchange of personal gifts between staff and young people. For the staff, they are seeking to provide care and safety for the young people, but are not seeking to replace existing family relationships; they 'act and think of themselves as substitutes rather than complements to absent parents and significant others' (Söderquist et al. 2016, p. 595). Due to young people's precarious legal position while they navigate the asylum system, residential accommodation may be less like a family home and more like a space of incarceration, as limits are placed on overnight stays elsewhere (Herz and Lalander, 2017).

Guardianship schemes are also part of some formal support for unaccompanied young people, for example in Austria (Raithelhuber, 2021), Belgium (De Graeve, 2015; De Graeve and Bix, 2016, 2017), the Netherlands (Kalverboer et al., 2017), Scotland (Crawley and Kohli, 2013) and Sweden (Börjesson and Söderquist Forkby, 2020). Guardianship involves supporting a young person through the asylum system, playing the role of advocate for that young person. The relationship between guardian and young person is officially defined, and may remain distant and formal, but there are examples of such relationships being described and experienced as more like 'family' relationships, with some young people participating in the family life of the guardian, although they would not be living with them. Drawing on their work in Sweden, Börjesson and Söderquist Forkby (2020, p. 481) describe how Ali, one of the young people involved in their study, said that he was 'like a son' to his guardian, and his guardian's family also described him as 'one of the family'. However, as Thommesen et al. (2015) highlight in their study of guardians in the Swedish system, while some provide guidance and give advice when asked, not all those involved in the study were positive about their role.

Similar debates and experiences around guardians' roles have been revealed in studies by De Graeve and Bex (2016, 2017) in Belgium. All unaccompanied minors are provided with a guardian, but that role formally ends when the young person becomes 18. The guardian plays a number of roles in the young person's life, including being a legal representative, and being responsible for supporting their social well-being and being involved in decisions about their accommodation and education (de Graeve and Bex, 2017). All of these may be seen as replacing what a parent or other adult family member would do, but it is in the sphere of emotional care that there are contrasting viewpoints. Many guardians do not want to be seen as a parent, replacing someone who is not physical present or may even have died. However, in some cases young people may see them in that role (De Graeve and Bex, 2016). Guardians may also consider the importance of keeping a 'professional distance' (De Graeve and Bex, 2017, p. 84) between the guardian and the young person. This may be because of the concerns about safeguarding, but also because of the potential traumatising impact of a close relationship being ripped apart once the young person becomes 18 and may be forced to leave the country if their asylum or other humanitarian claims are not met. In such cases the guardian may feel that it is in the best interests of the child not to set up a situation of family-like relationships which are likely to be fractured in the near future. As in the Swedish case, some guardians consider that the individual child's need for emotional support in a family-like environment is important and they seek to include the young person in their family's activities, although the young person would not be living with them. In De Graeve and Bex's (2016, 2017) research, some of the young people appreciated these invitations, using family terms to describe individuals and seeing themselves as part of the family. In some cases, guardians continued to support a young person after the age of 18. For De Graeve and Bex, the inadequate provision of emotional care reveals a gap in the system:

> The current Belgian care system for unaccompanied minors does not structurally provide the minors with an emotional caregiver, someone who is supposed to have a close and affectionate relationship with the minor (apart from foster parents, yet only a small minority of the unaccompanied minors is placed in foster care). (De Graeve and Bex, 2017, p. 87)

Stability in terms of relationships in a new location can be incredibly important to young people who have experienced significant physical and social disruption during their migration. As part of formal care systems, young people may be moved to different accommodation at short notice. While this may be seen as in the best interests of the child for physical security, it may involve further dislocation from significant relationships, as outlined by Herz and Lalander (2017) in the Swedish context and Behrendt et al. (2022) in Belgium. Kauko and Forsberg (2018) point to similar disruptions in Finland, giving the specific example of a young man separated from his girlfriend and girlfriend's family once he had received his residence permit.

In the UK, the spatial mismatch between the number of unaccompanied young people requiring support and the ability of local authorities to provide the statutory care required has led to a 'transfer protocol', whereby young people are relocated from their point of arrival to elsewhere in the country. As Humphris and Sigona (2019) argue, this is driven by budget restrictions, rather than the 'best interests of the child', particularly in a context where funding for children's services has experienced massive cuts as part of austerity measures. Such relocation can be a vital part of the provision of appropriate shelter, healthcare and education, but there can be significant problems if young people are uprooted from the social relationships and familiarity they may have developed during their journey. This also includes a lack of a continuity of care from individual social workers (Humphris and Sigona, 2019).

Plans for future families are also important in supporting young people in their new home, alongside their aspirations for education and employment. Kauko and Forsberg (2018), in their research in Finland, found that many of the young people they spoke to included setting up their own families in their visions of their future lives. However, for young people who are stuck in a position of significant uncertainty due to temporary residency rights and the threat of removal when they become adults, such dreams of a future family life may be too difficult to contemplate.

Finally, it is important to acknowledge the myriad other relationships which young people develop and from which they gain different forms of support after leaving their original family home. These relationships may provide material, emotional and practical support that may be seen as often coming from family members, and young people may use the language of family to describe the relationships, although it is important not to homogenise the notion of family and how an ideal family should operate. However, some contacts and networks may be fleeting (Wells, 2011), and the nature of these networks are likely to change over time. For example, research in Belgium (Behrendt et al., 2022) revealed that social networks shift from consisting of co-ethnic young people met on the journey and on first arrival, to including other members of diaspora groups with religious organisations being particular important for some nationalities. Over time, local peers become more important as young people become more familiar with the context and feel more established. This develops alongside relationships with formally appointed social workers and guardians, as well as volunteers working in support services. These social relationships help to create a sense of belonging (Drammeh, 2019), which can be devastatingly ruptured if an asylum claim is not accepted and a young person is forcibly removed once they have legally become an adult. This destruction of a settled life and supportive relationships is clearly seen in the interviews with young people who were forcibly removed from the UK to Afghanistan (Allsopp and Chase, 2019, p. 304), and in the experiences of Hamedullah, whose story of forcible removal from the UK to Afghanistan is shown in *Hamedullah: the Road Home* (2013), a film directed by Sue Clayton.

CONCLUSIONS

This chapter has highlighted how the experiences of family and the mobilisation of 'family' as a concept are woven into the international migration of unaccompanied children, using examples of migration to and within Europe. The family situation may be the driver for young people to migrate alone, being sent away by family members for their own safety, or fleeing violence from other family members. A sense of obligation and responsibility towards the natal family may also push individual young people to migrate and continue to shape their emotional and material links to family members during the migration journey. There may be significant logistical challenges in maintaining contact, but the operation of migration and asylum regimes may also restrict contact, often implicitly through the concerns that young people have of mentioning details about their families in case it undermines their asylum claim. The very slim chance of family reunification in the country of destination means that young people are embarking on a journey which will likely result in a future of transnational family practices before they have even reached adulthood.

Experiences of family or family-like relationships may be part of an unaccompanied child's experience of state-supported welfare provision after claiming asylum. The degree to which a sense of emotional well-being, care and safety are experienced will vary significantly depending on the form of support provided, but also the individual relationships involved. A significant challenge for the development and maintenance of these relationships is the threat of forcible removal once a young person reaches 18 if they have not been given residency or leave to remain.

The notion of family is mobilised in a number of ways by state and non-state actors involved in the migration of unaccompanied young people. For the young people themselves, members of the family 'back home' often remain the most important familial relationships. Some seek and find solace from family-type relationships in their new homes, while others may not have this available to them, or they may feel guilty about developing such relationships with foster carers, guardians or friends. There may be similar ambivalence on the part of foster families, guardians and live-in staff in group accommodation facilities.

'The family' is identified as a particularly important social unit in law, requiring protection. However, as this chapter has outlined, what counts as a family, or a family member, can be highly constrained, and its protection is highly context-dependent. For unaccompanied child migrants, laws construct them as vulnerable due to the lack of co-present family members. The state therefore has a duty to step in and provide care and guidance in the absence of family. Despite the value placed on the family, family reunification policies are usually very asymmetrical, with children being able to cross international borders to join parents or other family members, but not the other way round. Similar downplaying of the importance of family and acting in the best interests of the child is also seen in the forcible removal of young people whose asylum claims have not been successful once they reach 18, even if they have family members (including children) from whom they will be separated. Here, the desire for strong national borders outweighs the importance and value placed on a universal notion of the family.

REFERENCES

Allsopp, J. (2017) 'Agent, victim, soldier, son: Intersecting masculinities in the European "refugee crisis"', in J. Freedman, Z. Kivilcim and N. Özgür Baklacıoğlu (eds) *A Gendered Approach to the Syrian Refugee Crisis*, London: Routledge, pp. 155–174.

Allsopp, J. and E. Chase (2019) 'Best interests, durable solutions and belonging: Policy discourses shaping the futures of unaccompanied migrant and refugee minors coming of age in Europe', *Journal of Ethnic and Migration Studies*, 45(2): 293–311.

Amnesty International (2018) *Amnesty International Report 2017/18 – Eritrea*, 22 February. https://www.refworld.org/docid/5a99390ba.html.

Behrendt, M., I. Lietaert and I. Derluyn (2022) 'Continuity and social support: A longitudinal study of unaccompanied refugee minors' care networks', *Journal of Immigrant and Refugee Studies*, 20(3): 398–412.

Belloni, M. (2016) '"My uncle cannot say 'No' if I reach Libya": Unpacking the social dynamics of border-crossing among Eritreans heading to Europe', *Human Geography*, 9(2): 47–56.

Belloni, M. (2020a) 'Family project or individual choice? Exploring agency in young Eritreans' migration', *Journal of Ethnic and Migration Studies*, 46(2): 336–353.

Belloni, M. (2020b) 'When the phone stops ringing: On the meanings and causes of disruptions in communication between Eritrean refugees and their families back home', *Global Networks*, 20(2): 256–273.

Börjesson, U. and Å. Söderquist Forkby (2020) 'The concept of home – Unaccompanied youths voices and experiences', *European Journal of Social Work*, 23(3): 475–485.

British Red Cross (2019) *Guide to Joining Family Under the Dublin Regulation*, London: British Red Cross.

Chase, E. and J. Statham (2014) 'Families left behind: Unaccompanied young people seeking asylum in the UK', in J. Ribbens McCarthy, C-A. Hooper and V. Gillies (eds) *Family Troubles? Exploring Changes and Challenges in the Family Lives of Children and Young People*, Bristol: Policy Press, pp. 223–231.

Clayton, S. and K. Willis (2019) 'Migration regimes and border controls: the crisis in Europe', in S. Clayton, A. Gupta and K. Willis (eds) *Unaccompanied Young Migrants: Identity, Care and Justice*, Bristol: Policy Press, pp. 15–38.

Crawley, H. and R. Kohli (2013) *She Endures with Me. An Evaluation of the Scottish Guardianship Pilot*. Scottish Government.

De Graeve, K. (2015) 'Classed landscapes of care and belonging: Guardianships of unaccompanied minors', *Journal of Refugee Studies*, 30(1): 71–88.

De Graeve, K. and C. Bex (2016) 'Imageries of family and nation: A comparative analysis of transnational adoption and care for unaccompanied minors in Belgium', *Childhood*, 23(4): 492–505.

De Graeve, K. and C. Bex (2017) 'Caringscapes and belonging: an intersectional analysis of care relationships of unaccompanied minors in Belgium', *Children's Geographies*, 15(1): 80–92.

Drammeh, L. (2019) 'Spaces of belonging and social care', in S. Clayton, A. Gupta and K. Willis (eds) *Unaccompanied Young Migrants: Identity, Care and Justice*, Bristol: Policy Press, pp. 159–186.

Eide, K., H. Lidén, B. Haugland, T. Fladstad and H.A. Hauge (2020) 'Trajectories of ambivalence and trust: experiences of unaccompanied refugee minors resettling in Norway', *European Journal of Social Work*, 23(4): 554–565.

Eurostat (2021) '13,600 unaccompanied minors seeking asylum in the EU in 2020'. https://ec.europa.eu/eurostat/en/web/products-eurostat-news/-/ddn-20210423-1 [Accessed 24/6/21].

FRA (2011) *Separated, Asylum-Seeking Children in European Union Member States, Comparative Report*, Luxembourg: Publication Office of the European Union.

Gimeno-Monterde, C. and J.D. Gutiérrez-Sánchez (2019) 'Fostering unaccompanied migrating minors. A cross-border comparison', *Children and Youth Services Review*, 99: 36–42.

Gower, M. (2020) *Brexit: The End of the Dublin III Regulation in the UK*, Briefing Paper 9031, House of Commons Library. https://researchbriefings.files.parliament.uk/documents/CBP-9031/CBP-9031.pdf.

Griffiths, M. and C. Morgan (2017) *Immigration Enforcement and Article 8 Rights: Mixed-Immigration Status Families*, Policy Report 19, University of Bristol. http://www.bris.ac.uk/media-library/sites/policybristol/briefings-and-reports-pdfs/2017-briefings--reports-pdfs/PolicyBristol_Report_November_2017_mixed-immigration_status_families.pdf.

The Guardian (2021) 'Kent council refuses to accept more unaccompanied child migrants', *The Guardian*, 11 June. https://www.theguardian.com/uk-news/2021/jun/11/kent-county-council-refuses-accept-unaccompanied-child-migrants.

Gupta, A. (2019) 'Caring for and about unaccompanied migrant youth', in S. Clayton, A. Gupta and K. Willis (eds) *Unaccompanied Young Migrants: Identity, Care and Justice*, Bristol: Policy Press, pp. 77–101.

Hamedullah: The Road Home (2013) film, directed by Sue Clayton, Eastwest Pictures.

Herz, M. and P. Lalander (2017) 'Being alone of becoming lonely? The complexity of portraying "unaccompanied children" as being alone in Sweden', *Journal of Youth Studies*, 20(8): 1062–1076.

HM Inspectorate of Prisons (2021) *Report on an Unannounced Inspection of the Detention of Migrants at Dover and Folkestone*. https://www.justiceinspectorates.gov.uk/hmiprisons/wp-content/uploads/sites/4/2021/12/Kent-detention-facilities-web-2021.pdf.

Home Office (2020) *Children's Asylum Claims*, Version 4.0. https://assets.publishing.service.gov.uk/government/uploads/system/uploads/attachment_data/file/947812/children_s-asylum-claims-v4.0ext.pdf.

Home Office (2021) 'Asylum applications, initial decisions and resettlement – Asy_D02'. https://www.gov.uk/government/statistics/immigration-statistics-year-ending-march-2020/how-many-people-do-we-grant-asylum-or-protection-to (accessed 24 June 2021).

Hopkins, P. and M. Hill (2010) 'The needs and strengths of unaccompanied asylum-seeking children and young people in Scotland', *Child and Family Social Work*, 15: 399–408.

Hughes, G. (2019) 'From individual vulnerability to collective resistance: responding to the emotional impact of trauma on unaccompanied children seeking asylum', in S. Clayton, A. Gupta and K. Willis (eds) *Unaccompanied Young Migrants: Identity, Care and Justice*, Bristol: Policy Press, pp. 135–158.

Humphris, R. and N. Sigona (2019) 'Outsourcing the "best interests" of unaccompanied asylum-seeking children in the era of austerity', *Journal of Ethnic and Migration Studies*, 45(2): 312–330.

Jani, J.S. (2017) 'Reunification is not enough: Assessing the needs of unaccompanied migrant youth', *Families in Society: Journal of Contemporary Social Services*, 98(2): 127–136.

Kalverboer, M., E. Zijlstra, C. van Os, D. Zevulun and M. ten Brummelar (2017) 'Unaccompanied minors in the Netherlands and the care facility in which they flourish best', *Child and Family Social Work*, 22: 587–596.

Kauko, O. and H. Forsberg (2018) 'Housing pathways, not belonging and sense of home as described by unaccompanied minors', *Nordic Social Work Research*, 8(3): 210–221.

Lidén, H. (2019) 'Unaccompanied migrant youth in the Nordic countries', in S. Clayton, A. Gupta and K. Willis (eds) *Unaccompanied Young Migrants: Identity, Care and Justice*, Bristol: Policy Press, pp. 235–278.

Lundberg, A. and L. Dahlquist (2012) 'Unaccompanied children seeking asylum in Sweden: Living conditions from a child-centred perspective', *Refugee Survey Quarterly*, 31(2): 54–75.

Middelburg, A. and A. Balta (2016) 'Female genital mutilation/ cutting as a ground for asylum in Europe', *International Journal of Refugee Law*, 28(3): 416–452.

Mishori, R., D. Ottenheimer and E. Morris (2020) 'Conducting an asylum evaluation focused on female genital mutilation/cutting status or risk', *International Journal of Gynecology and Obstetrics*, 153: 3–10.

Ní Raghallaigh, M. and A. Sirriyeh (2015) 'The negotiation of culture in foster care placements for separated refugee and asylum seeking young people in Ireland and England', *Childhood*, 22(2): 263–277.
Office of the High Commissioner for Human Rights (OHCHR) (2015) *Report of the Detailed Findings of the Commission of Enquiry on Human Rights in Eritrea*, A/HRC/29/CR.P1. https://www.ohchr.org/Documents/HRBodies/HRCouncil/CoIEritrea/A_HRC_29_CRP-1.pdf.
Office of the High Commissioner for Human Rights (OHCHR) (2021) 'Convention on the Rights of the Child'. https://www.ohchr.org/en/professionalinterest/pages/crc.aspx.
Papadogiannakis, N. (2020) 'Flashpoint: Brussels', in S. Clayton (ed.) *The New Internationalists: Activist Volunteers in the European Refugee Crisis*, London: Goldsmiths University Press, pp. 267–274.
Passarlay, G. with N. Ghouri (2015) *The Lightless Sky: My Journey to Safety as a Child Refugee*, London: Atlantic Books.
Pobjoy, J.M. (2017) *The Child in International Refugee Law*, Cambridge: Cambridge University Press.
Raithelhuber, E. (2021) '"If we want, they help us in any way": how "unaccompanied refugee minors" experience mentoring relationships', *European Journal of Social Work*, 24(2): 251–266.
Rip, J., E. Zijlstra, W. Post, M. Kalverboer and E.J. Knorth (2020) '"It can never be as perfect as home": An explorative study into the fostering experiences of unaccompanied refugee children, their foster carers and social workers', *Children and Youth Services Review*, 112: 104924. https://doi.org/10.1016/j.childyouth.2020.104924.
Sirriyeh, A. (2013) 'Hosting strangers: Hospitality and family practices in fostering unaccompanied refugee young people', *Child and Family Social Work*, 18: 5–14.
Sirriyeh, A. (2015) '"All you need is love and £18,600": Class and the new UK family migration rules', *Critical Social Policy*. doi: 10.1177/0261018314563039.
Sirriyeh, A. and M. Ní Raghallaigh (2018) 'Foster care, recognition and transitions to adulthood for unaccompanied asylum seeking young people in England and Ireland', *Children and Youth Services Review*, 92: 89–97.
Söderquist, Å., Y. Sjöblom and P. Bülow (2016) 'Home sweet home? Professionals' understanding of "home" within residential care for unaccompanied youth in Sweden', *Child and Family Social Work*, 21: 591–599.
Thommessen, S.A., P. Corcoran and P. Todd (2015) 'Experiences of arriving to Sweden as an unaccompanied asylum-seeking minor from Afghanistan: An interpretive phenomenological analysis', *Psychology of Violence*, 5(4): 374–383.
UNHCR (2013) *Too Much Pain: Female Genital Mutilation and Asylum in the European Union. A Statistical Overview*, UNHCR.
UNICEF Innocenti Research Centre (2006) *General Comments of the Committee on the Rights of the Child*, Florence: UNICEF Innocenti Research Centre.
UNICEF and Save the Children (2017) *Keeping Families Together: Retaining Children's Rights to Family Reunion Through Brexit*. https://downloads.unicef.org.uk/wp-content/uploads/2017/06/KeepingFamiliesTogether_FINAL.pdf.
Van Holen, F., L. Trogh, E. Carlier, L. Gypen and J. Vanderfaeillie (2020) 'Unaccompanied refugee minors and foster care: A narrative literature review', *Child and Family Social Work*, 25(3): 506–514.
Wade, J., A. Sirriyeh, R. Kohli and J. Simmonds (2012) *Fostering Unaccompanied Asylum-Seeking Young People: A Research Project*, London: BAAF.
Wells, K. (2011) 'The strength of weak ties: The social networks of young separated asylum seekers and refugees in London', *Children's Geographies*, 9(3–4): 319–329.
Williams, L. (2019) '"Durable solutions" when turning 18', in S. Clayton, A. Gupta and K. Willis (eds) *Unaccompanied Young Migrants: Identity, Care and Justice*, Bristol: Policy Press, pp. 187–208.
York, S. and R. Warren (2019) 'Dilemmas and conflicts in the legal system', in S. Clayton, A. Gupta and K. Willis (eds) *Unaccompanied Young Migrants: Identity, Care and Justice*, Bristol: Policy Press, pp. 39–76.

PART III

POWER, SOCIAL INEQUALITIES AND SOCIAL MOBILITY

13. Families in educational migration: strategies, investments and emotions
Johanna L. Waters and Zhe Wang

INTRODUCTION

In *The Geographies of International Student Mobility,* Beech (2019) critiques what she describes as the 'myth of the individualistic student'. The family, she writes, is instrumental in facilitating and enabling students' migration for education. It represents a form of social network that provides students with information and inspiration as well as practical support in their quest to study overseas. Sometimes, the family's influence is subtle: students referred to the influence of a family history (parents, grandparents) of educational migration on their decision to study abroad. This history forms part of students' 'habitus', rendering study abroad a possibility, or even an expectation (within the social context of the family). For many international students, however, the support they receive from their family is practical, overt and necessary. Families have been shown to pay student fees, flights and living costs, as well as providing day-to-day emotional support (Sanchez-Serra and Marconi, 2018; Mulvey and Mason, 2022). Without familial support, study abroad would be a rare occurrence. Even students able to benefit from an educational scholarship are still (at least partially) reliant on the assistance of their family (Mulvey and Mason, 2022). Redmond et al. (2022) state this relationship between family, education and the child in emphatic terms:

> Families are rendered ... responsible for the human capital development and educational outcomes of their children, and this responsibility is internalised and enacted by both parents and children. Parents are responsibilised to invest in their children's productive futures. At the same time, young people are responsibilised to actively engage [sic] with their schoolwork and enhance their educational outcomes. (pp. 84–85)

For other young people, however, the influence of the family in educational migration can be less benign and supportive, and more overtly repressive. As Walton-Roberts (2015) has shown in relation to women Indian international students in Canada, the family exerts a controlling pressure, even from afar. She writes: 'Women have a right to be mobile for employment and educational purposes, but it is part of a larger strategy. Their mobility rights are exercised *for* family and *from within* the protective shield of particular migratory channels' (pp. 78–79). Martin (2022) describes the pressures that young women from China studying abroad (in Australia) face from family at home, where they have to seek to counter the stereotype of the 'promiscuous female overseas student' (p. 169). This chimes with Ong's (1999) description of the transnational family as a regime that functions to control certain members for the overall good of the family (see also Waters, 2002; Huang and Yeoh, 2011):

> Family regimes that generally valorize mobile masculinity and localized femininity shape strategies of flexible citizenship, gender division of labor, and relocation in different sites. Transnational

publics based on ethnicized mass media, networks of Asian professionals, and circuits of capital add a geometric dimension to Asian male mobility, power and capital vis-à-vis women, not only in the domestic domain but also in transnational production, service and consumer realms. (Ong, 1999, p. 21)

Here, Ong highlights the gendered inequalities that beset many transnational families. Children's education is seen as an issue for the domestic realm and therefore a primary concern of women and mothers. For many women, transnational mobility can (ironically) confine them to the domestic sphere (they become localised through transnationalism) (Ong, 1999; Waters, 2002). Individuals' needs and desires are sacrificed for 'the greater good', demonstrating the importance of power dynamics underpinning and shaping migration for education in a wider familial social context.

The primary goal of this chapter is to discuss, through a critical review of the literature, the pivotal role that family plays in what might be called educational migration (migration principally motivated by education-related concerns). We first focus on the arguments pertaining to capital accumulation (within the family unit) as, for many years, this focus has been ascendent (see also Chapter 7, this *Handbook*). The chapter then explores the limits to this perspective by focusing on emotions. We expose the fallacy that different family members work together unproblematically in the quest for education. We also consider examples of where strategies might be seen to fail, and how various emotions complicate how educational migration is enacted 'strategically'. The chapter seeks to present a more nuanced and differentiated account of family encounters, emphasising the heterogeneity of experiences and how these may vary by class, gender and generation, and may additionally be difficult, problematic and dysfunctional (Abelmann and Kang, 2014; Walton-Roberts, 2015; Waters, 2015). We begin with an overview of debates relating to educational migration and the family, to provide some necessary context.

INTELLECTUAL CONTEXT AND OVERVIEW OF DEBATES

Over the past decade, interest amongst scholars in the important role that education plays in international and transnational migration has grown significantly (Waters and Brooks, 2021). Educational migration refers to the practice of seeking an education outside of one's 'home' country, whether at primary, secondary or tertiary level, through migration. The family is most obviously present in the migration of young children (for example, for pre-college study abroad where one family member will accompany the child) but can likewise have a strong (if more indirect) influence on older children and young adults studying at university level. Education is increasingly seen as a key driver of migration flows (Findlay et al., 2017; Li et al., 1996). Emerging scholarship demonstrates that education, broadly conceived, is frequently a critical consideration in the decision-making of migrants, and particularly transnational migrants (Waters 2008). Furthermore, education (notably higher education) is increasingly linked to states' strategies around immigration, permanent residency and citizenship (Robertson, 2011; Koh, 2017; Pottie-Sherman, 2018; Sidhu et al., 2016; Sidhu et al., 2019).

The immediate (localised) social context within which education-related migration decisions are made is invariably the family sphere, or household. The family can encompass extended members, including grandparents, aunts and uncles, and siblings, as well as parents. The household, on the other hand, includes family (and non-family) members, living either under one roof or separately through a transnational householding arrangement (but still conceived as a unit). As Yeoh et al. indicate, the family is a 'deep-rooted social institution' and yet one that 'continues to retain its significance in the face of distance, dispersal and translocality' (Yeoh et al., 2018, p. 413; see also Hardill, 2004). Thus, it makes sense to consider the role of the family in education-related migration, just as work on family and household migration is increasingly highlighting the importance of concerns around (usually children's) education.

Rarely is young people's education viewed as something acquired individually. As mentioned above, the family plays a significant role in facilitating migration for education; for example, through familial socialisation (or 'habitus') and in the practical, material support offered by family members, including financing and social connections. Additionally, the family is often in the background, influencing the decisions young people make about whether to study abroad, what to study and where to study (see, e.g., Yang, 2018; Brooks and Waters, 2010; Beech, 2015). According to this view, education is seen as a form of familial investment (Huang and Yeoh, 2005; Waters, 2006; Kajanus, 2016). Xu and Montgomery (2021), for example, discuss Chinese rural parents' roles in their children's access to elite universities (in China), where education is framed as a household concern. They propose using a 'cross-cultural application of Bourdieusian explanation in educational inequalities' to explore 'the complexity of rural (less privileged) parents' roles in their children's access to elite universities' (p. 556). This view – giving parents a central role in decision-making around higher education – is common within the literature focused around East and Southeast Asia (Seth, 2002; Murphy, 2004; Gupta, 2020). Deciding to invest in a child's educational success is habitually weighted up against other (more immediate and future) considerations, such as household employment, business or property opportunities, citizenship acquisition and lifestyle aspirations (Ley, 2011), or the desire to avoid debt (Collins and Ho, 2018). Ultimately, the household is concerned with its social reproduction and relative positioning within a class hierarchy. Investing in a child's education is perceived as a means of either securing one's class position or enabling social mobility.

Such a relationship has been perhaps articulated most forcefully by Lareau (2011) in her book *Unequal Childhoods*. Middle-class parents become intimately involved in the daily lives of their children as well as with the institutions that support schooling and other related activities. Education is part of a strategy of 'concerted cultivation': the process of acquiring a wider set of skills and talents that will pay dividends down the line. A child's activities become inseparable from those of the parents, and parents' social lives are invariably dominated by the actions and interests of the child. In this vein, we turn now to address arguments specifically pertaining to educational migration as an investment, emphasising the strategic accumulation of different forms of capital.

EDUCATIONAL MIGRATION AS CAPITAL ACCUMULATION

Education-related migration has frequently been conceptualised as something pursued strategically by households to ensure the reproduction or enhancement of status and privilege (Huang and Yeoh, 2005, 2011; Park and Bae, 2009; Waters, 2006, 2008). As noted by Yang (2018, 2022) and Lipura and Collins (2020), research on education-related migration has overwhelmingly focused on its role in the accumulation of capital. The concepts proposed by Bourdieu (1984, 1986, 1996) relating to the forms of capital have provided a dominant theoretical lens for this work. Bourdieu argues that there are three primary forms of capital circulating amongst individuals (and in turn constituting society): economic, social and cultural. Economic capital refers to finance, goods and services; social capital includes meaningful and valuable social relationships that can facilitate social reproduction; and cultural capital can be 'embodied' (within the individual), 'institutionalised' (within the prestige and value of a particular educational establishment and represented by credentials, for example) and 'objectified' (found in valuable cultural artefacts, such as paintings or books). As Bourdieu (1986) has written:

> the structure of the distribution of the different types and subtypes of capital at any given moment in time represents the immanent structure of the social world, i.e., the set of constraints, inscribed in the very reality of that world, which govern its functioning in a durable way, determining the chances of success for practices. (p. 242)

To maintain their positioning in the structure of the social world (that is, the class structure), households must engage continuously in the accumulation of different types of capital. This relates to a sense that education is becoming increasingly important in the lives of young people and their parents, globally. Academic achievement (notably graduation from a top university) is seen as crucial for a family's future, as it is directly linked to career and lifestyle success (Findlay et al., 2012). 'Credentialisation' has meant that access to a greater number of jobs depends on holding academic qualifications, and these qualifications are themselves significantly differentiated: not all signal the necessary distinction required for success (Brown et al., 2001). In the next subsections, we consider how these arguments relate specifically to the international mobility of students, differentiating between privileged and less-advantaged types of migration.

Privileged Migration and Capital Accumulation

Existing scholarship on international student mobility (ISM) often draws on Bourdieu's theories to explain how and why more privileged families use mobility as a strategy of capital accumulation, thereby reproducing their social advantage. This perspective stems from (and additionally reinforces) a 'rationalistic and calculative' interpretation of student mobility (Yang, 2018, p. 698). Indeed, migration can offer families a double advantage when it comes to education. Not only are young people able to escape a highly competitive and stressful education system at home, but they are also at the same time able to acquire more valuable credentials than those available domestically, with an international degree from a university overseas – in North America, for example – providing a preferred form of credential in their home country (within particular sectors of the job market) (Waters, 2006; Xiang and Shen, 2009). Thus, migration provides an opportunity for young people and their families to maximise the amount of cultural capital they are able to accumulate within the household, and to avoid a highly stressed and cut-throat domestic academic environment.

In terms of the forms of cultural capital that privileged young people accumulate when studying abroad, students are said to acquire various embodied skills, including language fluency and a range of what might be called cosmopolitan competencies that facilitate 'global positioning' and, consequently, household social reproduction (Ong, 1999; Gu et al., 2010). Cosmopolitan traits are habitually described in relation to an openness towards cultural difference, which includes an enjoyment of eating a range of styles of foods and other forms of multicultural consumption (films, music, art). It can involve comportment or sense of humour. In addition, it can involve a greater understanding of how different societies 'work' (signifying an ability to access resources across a range of cultural settings). Translated into the language of capital accumulation, these traits are seen to be favoured by employers, particularly international and global industries such as banking and commerce (Waters 2008; Zhang and Xu, 2020).

Less-Advantaged Families and Educational Migration

Within less-advantaged migrant groups, capital accumulation remains strategic but less obviously related to the outcomes described above. By shifting the focus away from South-to-North or East-to-West migration, it has been shown that alternative (less overtly strategic and capital-focused) interpretations of student mobility emerge. In addition, by considering the migration of non-elite or less-privileged individuals, a more nuanced account of international student mobility takes shape. As Yang (2018) has argued, those less-affluent Indian students pursuing English-language medium medical degrees (MBBS) at a provincial university in China suggest a form of 'knowledge mobility' that involves both compromise and complicity on the part of students and their families in the process of realising 'educational desires, social aspirations, and organizational objectives amidst realities of class disadvantage and resource inadequacy' (p. 694). In other words, many students were seen to 'settle for' a degree from China despite its relative lack of value, where parents 'turn[ed] a blind eye' in the hope that their aspirations for a better future could be realised. It is hard to fit such an example into theories positing a straightforward case of maximising the accumulation of capital.

Other work, too, has focused on less-privileged migrants pursuing education abroad and the complex influence on and involvement of the family in students' decision-making and experiences. This focus has complicated the view that educational migration is primarily about the strategic accumulation of capital. An example is found in Collins and Ho (2018), whose discussion of 'discrepant' knowledge mobilities within Asia highlights the conditions of uncertainty and relative deprivation that sometimes beset educational migrants (education may overlap with contract labour and involve household debt; see Fong's account of indebtedness, below), and the necessity to disentangle educational migration from its primary association with elite and privileged 'projects' of capital accumulation.

Ho (2017) has considered the motivations and experiences of African students undertaking degree programmes in China. She noted that many of the students in her research had families who ran businesses importing Chinese-origin goods to Africa (such as textiles). One aspect of students' educational goals was to learn the Chinese language, to facilitate directly the running of the family business (and not to advance their own, individual career goals per se). Their school work ran alongside facilitating familial business activities, and this often proved challenging to young people having to juggle these competing goals. Families kept a close eye on the young person, as one undergraduate from Tanzania noted:

> relatives and friends grill her about her education and business activities when she returns home during the summer vacation, while her father is watchful over how she spends her time in China because he wants her to acquire business skills for personal growth and to improve the social status of the family through her educational stint abroad (Ho, 2017, p. 22)

Thus, it can be seen that these goals do not reflect common assumptions in the literature around (largely privileged) cultural capital acquisition, education and migration. Young people in this case are engaged is some aspects of this (improving the social status of the family through attaining a prestigious overseas degree), but in addition, and often superseding these goals, are those related to enhancing the family business.

There is also a nascent literature on the role of social media in 'democratising' access to study abroad and, interestingly, expanding the notion of what constitutes 'family' within educational migration. In Jayadeva's (2020) study of Indian students in Germany, many described their online community as a 'family', and articulated with clarity the emotional support such a community ('family') provided (we discuss emotions in more detail below).

Non-Educational Capital: Other Benefits of Educational Migration

Educational migration can, in addition, be pursued with other (non-educational) objectives in mind that are envisaged to benefit the wider family, such as the acquisition of permanent residency or citizenship in the host country (Baas, 2006; Yang, 2016). Some international students have been seen to switch their visa status whilst abroad (Robertson, 2011), with a view to reuniting with family members once their permanent status is secured (a family strategy of a different kind). Here, education is seen as a relatively easy route into a desirable country. Since the late 1990s, Australia's migration policies have shifted from viewing international students as 'transient consumers' to 'potential citizens' (Robertson, 2011). As Robertson (2011, p. 2194) has written, 'student switching' policies, developed since the late 1990s, have favoured international students. These policies awarded extra migration points for Australian qualifications, allowing students to switch their status from student to migrant by applying for permanent residency. A similar story is found in Liu-Farrer's (2011) account of Chinese international students in Japan's labour market. She highlights the typical struggles found in the Chinese student-migrant experience: from low-wage worker, to entering the corporate sector, to (eventual) success in the transnational economy between Japan and China. Students' goals included seeking to reunite with family members in Japan, or indeed to start families themselves. These examples are suggestive of the significant yet diverse roles that families play within the process of educational migration.

Exemplifying this complexity through ethnography, Fong (2011) describes the quest for 'developed world citizenship' undertaken by young students from China. Her research prioritises the context of the family and household-level decision-making. She discusses the case of Gao Neng, who Fong had first met in China when she was only 13 years old. Fong describes Neng's parents' occupations (factory workers), their limited earnings and her family's living arrangements (a one-bedroom apartment). Fong visited Gao Neng again three years later, when she was 16 and attending high school in preparation for college. She talked to her parents, and no mention was made of any plans for her to study abroad. Fong's third visit came when Gao Neng was 18, and she spoke to her parents. They reported that they had spent 60 000 yuan of their life savings and had borrowed additional money to send their daughter to live in Ireland, where she was working in a shop and attending English-language classes with the hope that she would eventually be able to apply to college there. It turned out that Gao Neng's parents had begun the process of applying for a visa for her to study in Ireland without telling her. Such stories fill Fong's (2011) ethnographic account of study abroad; notable is parents' central involvement at all stages of the process. Parents view an international education as invaluable, not just as an educational experience, but for what it gives access to in terms of citizenship, and a whole life future trajectory. This example, illustrating the complexity of decision-making around study abroad, provides a useful link to the next subsection of the chapter, where accounts of capital accumulation within the household are problematised and alternative conceptions of educational migration considered.

When Educational Migration Strategies Fail

When individual family members' experiences are considered, and particularly the emotional responses of women and children (Yang, 2018), arguments privileging capital accumulation and other beneficial strategies appear inadequate at worst, and partial at best. In this subsection we consider examples of where strategies of capital accumulation variously fail (see also Chapter 9, this *Handbook*, for a discussion of household strategies).

Family strategies relating to education and migration do not always go as planned. They can fail, or result in unforeseen (and negative) consequences for the individual or multiple family members. This can be seen in our work on so-called 'satellite children' (Waters, 2000, 2003) where families from Hong Kong and Taiwan migrated to Canada primarily to give their children access to better educational opportunities and, ultimately, a Western university degree. However, the transnational family strategy was undermined when, due to an absence of adult supervision, children failed to do their school work and some failed to attend school at all. In these households, both parents had returned to East Asia to work, leaving their children unsupervised for most of the time. The children had to get themselves to school on time, and many did not comply. Consequently, the household strategy of capital accumulation articulated so clearly by the parents, who had seen migration and education as a way of securing their and their and their children's futures, was undermined by their failure to anticipate the challenges of disciplining, from a distance, wilful teenage children.

In another example of the fallibility of capital accumulation strategies, Abelmann and Kang (2014) address the charge that Korean mothers pursuing pre-college study abroad (PSA) for their children's sake are overly 'instrumental' and 'family centred', worried only about the reproduction of the household and forsaking all else. They draw on the memoirs of PSA mothers to demonstrate the complexities and contradictions found in women's experiences. PSA was frequently unsuccessful; for example, many children were doomed to fail in the United States education system, and returning to Korea as a failure was not an easy option. Some mothers found American traits distinctly unappealing. Others chose to stress the extent of their labour: how bringing up a Korean child in America was simply difficult and arduous. The arduous nature of study abroad is something we return to in more detail below (Waters and Leung, 2022). Thus, as a strategy of capital accumulation, educational migration is sometimes flawed. In what follows, we turn to discuss more directly the emotional challenges of educational migration within the context of the family, stressing further the human side of educational strategizing.

EMOTIONAL TRANSNATIONAL GEOGRAPHIES AND EDUCATIONAL MIGRATION

In this section, we consider some examples from the literature of where emotions and educational migration in the context of family life clearly intersect. We begin with a discussion of care work, before providing a more detailed empirical example from the literature on cross-border schooling (where education and family life are inextricably tangled). We finish with a discussion of familial control and how educational migration can in some instances offer an escape from oppressive circumstances.

As Boccagni and Baldassar (2015) have noted in relation to migration research more broadly, 'emotions are part and parcel of everyday life' and yet 'the emotional side of the migrant condition seems still relatively understudied' (p. 73). They go on to claim: 'mixed and contracting emotions and feelings such as hope and nostalgia, guilt and ambition, affection and disaffection – to name but a few – are an integral part of the life experiences of migrants. The everyday relevance of emotions can be easily appreciated in migrant family and group relationships' (p. 73). Thus, emotions are integral to the migrant experience, emotions are most easily apprehended amongst and within families, and the kinds of emotions we might associate with migration (hope, anxiety, fear, guilt and ambition) can also be associated with concerns related to a child's education: hope for the future, for example, or guilt related to forcing a child to relocate for their schooling, or leaving another child behind (e.g. Yeoh and Lam, 2007; Waters, 2003). Boccagni and Baldassar (2015) additionally suggest that the emotional dimensions of migration should not be framed as the opposite of strategy (what they call the 'instrumental' or 'economically driven' dimensions), but rather they should be seen as 'linked intimately' (p. 77), and part of the ambivalence inherent within much migration. Especially when it comes to families, most migration encompasses both instrumental decision-making and such feelings of love/desire/hope.

More specifically, researchers are increasingly acknowledging the emotional and affective implications of educational migration for the individuals and family members involved (Sidhu and Ishikawa, 2022; Sinanan and Gomes, 2020). Sometimes this can entail the emotional strain of maintaining transnational household relations at a distance, when some household members migrate and others do not (Waters, 2003; Jeong et al., 2014). As we have noted elsewhere, migration for education can occasionally indicate dysfunctionality and a degree of chaos (Waters, 2015). We return here, briefly, to the case of Indian medical students in China, as documented by Yang (2018), to illustrate some of this complexity. The students in Yang's sample came from less-affluent families, from either small-town or rural India. They did not fit the stereotypical view of international students as middle-class or wealthy individuals attempting to reproduce their privileged status through migration and education. Yang's (2018) analysis of students' motivations for and experiences of pursuing medical qualifications in China centres on the parents. He describes parents' moral obligation to provide (through financial support) the best education for their child that they can afford, whilst not asking too many questions about the quality of the education their children were experiencing (not to undermine the sense that they were providing children with an education that could lead to a prestigious medical career down the line). Likewise, children have a moral obligation to 'pursue social mobility with parents' investment in their education' (p. 703). Yang (2018) continues:

As a result, none of my informants could bring themselves to disclose to their parents CNU's [Chinese National University] disqualification by the Chinese MOE [Ministry of Education] [the qualifications were not seen as eligible by the Chinese state] – a 'heartbreaking' fact (as one informant put it) that would rudely shatter both sides' performance of their duties, owed to each other. To avoid such a crisis scenario, a complicitous silence and lack of detailed communication prevailed between the students and their parents. (p. 703)

This example brings to the fore the sacrifices involved in educational migration for the whole family, as well as the differential experiences and emotions attached to that process. It paints a picture very far removed from one of the strategic accumulation of capital by transnational families (Ong, 1999). Next, we continue to unpack the black box of the transnational household by illustrating the ways in which educational migration can result in highly differentiated and emotionally fraught experiences.

Emotional Fragility and the Weight of Familial Expectations

Sancho (2017) describes the complex emotional drivers of educational migration for students from India in Australia, and how these are tied in inextricable ways to a desire for familial social mobility (the emotional and the strategic are closely related in this account). These students were not wealthy, but young people who aspired *to* middle-class status. Migration to Australia offered a possibility to fulfil their aspirations, and the decision was (as in Yang's, 2018 work) very much framed by wider familial concerns. Notably, Sancho (2017) writes that most Indian international students desired to 'return to India after making enough money to attend to responsibilities as sons, husbands and respected men' (p. 526). Parents were seen to privilege 'a competitive, economic, and status-based conception of aspiration, producing growing anxieties' and the prospect of failure (p. 525). Thus, young migrant students were caught up in their parents' hopes, desires and aspirations, and their decision-making was almost entirely framed in terms of these familial social roles; these had to be reconciled with more individualistic pursuits, such as personal motivations or goals (see Martin, 2022).

Geddie (2013) drew on interviews with international science and engineering postgraduate students studying in either the United Kingdom or Canada, and demonstrated forcefully that emotive relationship considerations (such as concerns around care) were inextricably linked to (inseparable from) strategic considerations decisions that international students made about career trajectories. She noted a number of different dimensions to such relationship considerations. First was the responsibility felt for ageing parents and dependent siblings. Several students (notably from India and China) stated that there was 'no question' that they would return home sooner or later following their graduation, to take care (whether financially or in more practical terms) of ageing parents. This frequently meant that financial responsibility for the family extended to their siblings. A smaller number of students mentioned not wanting to return home because of the ongoing and undesirable influence of parents in their lives. In short, Geddie (2013) found that even amongst science and technology students with significant internationally transferable skills, parental influences were still extremely important in their lives. Tu (2016, p. 1) investigates how Chinese student-migrants from one-child transnational families 'balance ... the opportunities in the West with the filial responsibilities to aging parents back in China'. Interviewing 41 child migrants and parents, she finds that distance and borders were perceived as barriers for long-term care of ageing parents. She further illustrates how one-child migrants made 'new transnational family contracts' with their parents around emotional care, and emphasises the importance of examining the dynamics of filial behaviour within transnational families (see also Martin, 2022). Here, we see links to the growing literature on the different types of care work undertaken by international and migrant students (Deuchar, 2022; Myers-Walls et al., 2011).

Emotions and Care Work

As indicated in the work of Geddie (2013), an important aspect of the emotional side of educational migration relates to the care work that is carried out alongside or within a transnational household arrangement. Education and care are frequently closely related considerations: education is viewed as a key aspect of parenting, and parenting and care are largely inseparable. Within this literature, caring for one's children can also involve striving to give them the best educational opportunities on offer, and being willing to sacrifice one's own ambitions to achieve this (Huang and Yeoh, 2005, 2011). During the COVID-19 pandemic, families' care towards their overseas children has become apparent. For example, Hu et al. (2022, p. 1) explore the important role played by parents in Chinese students' navigation of transnational (im)mobilities during the COVID-19 pandemic. They develop the conceptualisation of 'family-mediated migration infrastructure' to explain how transnational families brokered information, mobilised essential medical resources, and coordinated 'disjointed acts of institutional players' to sustain students' transnational education (im)mobilities. They also reveal the complex ways in which transnational family members perform 'emotional engagement and detachment' as emotional work in sustaining students' transnational education (im)mobilities during the pandemic.

Another, less-discussed aspect of international students' decision-making is the influence of students' own partners and children (e.g. Brooks, 2015). This is an area where research is still rather sparse: scholarship has tended, to date, to focus on students' situations at the immediate time, despite temporality being an increasingly important aspect of discussions around international student mobility (Xu, 2021). In what follows, we highlight some specific examples from the literature of the intersection of care, parenting and emotions in relation to educational migration. This literature adds nuance to discussions that prioritise the strategic nature of capital accumulation within transnational households.

Cheung Judge (2021) has examined the care work and parenting carried out by educational institutions in private schools in Lagos. She described these as 'crucial sites of care for children with parents in the [Nigerian] diaspora' (p. 1). Cheung Judge (2021) observes a phenomenon that is regularly overlooked in the literature on migration and education; this literature tends to view migration as in one direction only: that is, children and young people going abroad for a 'better education'. Cheung Judge was interested in charting the opposite movement: the tendency for some (in this case, Nigerian) migrant families to send their children back home for schooling, in the hope of raising a 'good child'; parents are concerned with the 'whole child', and not simply with a sense that the qualifications they might be accruing in the West will be strategically more valuable. Private schools in Lagos catering to such a clientele are seen 'as "international" spaces oriented towards children's long term "global competitiveness", and spaces to inculcate "Nigerian values", including of high attainment, threatened abroad' (Cheung Judge, 2021, p. 7). Many children were seen to struggle with the rules and expectations of their homeland schools, particularly as they related to ideas around gender and social interaction. As Abotsi (2020) noted in her study of British-Ghanaian children sent by their parents to private boarding school in Ghana:

> These views of the 'good student' particularly impacted girls, who were not allowed to wear make-up or dress in 'provocative' styles (e.g., wearing short skirts), and were supposed to eschew sexual attention from boys. Staff were also under significant pressure to monitor pupils' interactions with the opposite sex, especially the girls due to fears over pregnancies. While the Ghanaian pupils did not always follow this policy, (rumours of romantic relationships among pupils were common), they did not criticise it either. Rather, it was seen as part of the accepted social norms. However, my participants from abroad found these restrictions on boy–girl interactions absurd. (p. 259)

Perhaps more work is needed on the role that schools (as institutions) play in reproducing quasi-familial relations in the context of education and migration. Certainly, in the case of 'satellite' or 'parachute' children in Canada (Ngan and Chan, 2022), schools unofficially carried out a great deal of care work in the complete absence of any parental or other adult supervision of children (Waters, 2000).

The Emotional Burden of Educational Migration: Cross-Border Schooling

'Birth tourism' represents a form of migration where educational concerns (for the unborn child) and wider family considerations are often paramount (Choi and Lai, 2022; Waters, 2008). The emotional toll on women travelling whilst pregnant to an unfamiliar environment to give birth, is significant. However, this toll is weighed against the desire for a passport for the unborn child, with all the future advantages that this passport is assumed to represent.

Cross-border schooling sometimes starts with birth tourism. In one particular example, pregnant Chinese mothers from Mainland China travelled to Hong Kong to give birth to escape the 'one-child' policy that was, at the time, in place in the Mainland. These children had no automatic right to access public schooling in Mainland China, as they possessed (unlike other family members) Hong Kong residency but lacked *hukou*.[1] Once old enough, they must attend school in Hong Kong. The emotional strain of a daily commute across the Shenzhen–Hong Kong boundary, spent in separation from the rest of the family, is palpable in extant accounts of cross-border schooling (Chan and Ngan, 2017; Leung and Waters, 2021; Waters and Leung, 2022).

In the decade between 2001 and 2011, the number of babies born in Hong Kong to Mainland parents increased from 620 to 35 000 (Chee, 2017). Chee (2017) notes the class background of mothers choosing to give birth over the border in Hong Kong. The early wave was mostly from the middle class, whilst more lately mothers have been increasingly from working-class and rural backgrounds. These children are Hong Kong residents – a status automatically granted to a person of Chinese descent born on Hong Kong soil since 2001 – and their access to education, healthcare and other social services is tied to this. In some cases, it is usual to have siblings with different residence statuses (Waters and Leung, 2019). One child will attend school in Shenzhen and another will commute daily over the boundary, creating differential experiences of educational mobilities within the household. There are currently an estimated 30 000 so-called cross-border schooling (CBS) children moving in this way daily, although estimates do vary.

The work of Chee (2017) produces a particularly impassioned account of how women, in particular, experience CBS. Chee (2017) describes how strategies that families initially enact to bypass the one-child policy, and give their child access to a better education in Hong Kong, 'turn against them'. Consequently, an initial plan becomes 'more of a trial-and-error response' (p. 203). Parents, Chee argues, had underestimated the disadvantages their child would face in being brought up on the Mainland without the benefits of having a *hukou*. 'Children without a *hukou* cannot have access to public education, medical care or other welfare, or apply for the Higher Education Entrance Examination' (p. 204). The family is therefore doomed to separation, as they cannot afford the school fees to pay for a private place in the Mainland for their child, and their child must either stay in Hong Kong to attend school during the week, or undertake the daily commute to and from Hong Kong (HK) and across the border. Chee (2017) writes:

> The border demands that Mainland families with HK-born children are doomed to be ruptured and parenthood is destined to be compromised. Underprivileged parents, like the mothers in this research, are the hardest hit by the fluctuations in policies and social ethos. They are not capable of adjusting to the changes and are not flexible enough (in Ong's term, 1999) to enjoy and manage mobilities. Instead, they are trapped by the infrastructural forms and are doomed to be circulating between platforms, whereby mobilities and immobilities, paradoxically, are out of their control. They fall into an infrastructural trap ... after the initial move, incarcerated in a non-status in a non-place, forever trapped in the current of mobilities. (p. 211)

Perhaps this view slightly overstates the extent to which families find themselves trapped. There is no doubt that, in the short term, having one child with a different residency status from the rest of the family can feel uncomfortable, anxiety-inducing, and lead to significant stress and exhaustion (Waters and Leung, 2019). However, this feeling of being trapped is unlikely to last forever. We drew slightly more nuanced and ambivalent conclusions in our own project on CBS (Waters and Leung, 2022; Leung and Waters, 2021), arguing that although children felt compelled and coerced at the time, and many regretted their time as a cross-border student, those who have now reached adulthood are able to articulate the advantages that have since accrued to them in terms of a successful school and university experience, and also employment outcomes. Thus, a longer-term perspective – away from the immediate emotional strain and physical exhaustion of CBS – may result in different conclusions being drawn about the nature of the strategy and its success (or otherwise).

Educational Migration as Escape from Control

In this subsection, we consider the claim that some individuals migrate (as students) to escape oppressive and controlling familial relations. The pressure that families place on students from a distance can also be intense and represent a form of surveillance (e.g. Yang, 2018; Ho, 2017; Martin, 2022). In fact, even when young people are allowed to travel overseas for study, they engage in a significant degree of self-regulation and self-control for fear of familial reprisals. Walton-Roberts (2015) exemplifies this, discussing the experiences of women international students from India in Canada. Parents liked to keep a watchful eye on their daughters' activities, and this included sexual behaviour (see also Martin, 2022, for a similar account of the experiences of Chinese students in Australia). Walton-Roberts (2015) writes:

> During one debriefing session in India with some of the project research assistants, we discussed the issue of sexual behaviour, and some of the researchers indicated there were penalties for such behaviour, and they spoke of families disavowing daughters ... While such extreme practices were not

mentioned during interviews, it is clear from the degree of family involvement in the whole migration process that the prospect of being disciplined or abandoned by your family would be a serious form of social enforcement, and thus likely to invoke a fairly strong degree of self-regulation. (p. 78)

For other young people, it has been found that they had to check their behaviour at the airport before boarding the plane for home. This included changing into more traditional dress to satisfy the expectations of family members waiting for their visit home (Ghosh and Wang, 2003). A reluctance to lose their freedom on returning home is also a common concern amongst (particularly women) international students from India. As Sondhi and King (2017) observed in their piece on the gendering of international student migration, using India as a case study, return home involved being subjected to the disciplinary gaze both of parents and the wider society. Hence, 'a new round of intergenerational negotiation had to take place for daughters [on their return]' (p. 1320).

CONCLUSIONS: UNPACKING THE FAMILY IN EDUCATIONAL MIGRATION

Historically, migration research has tended to treat the family or household as a black box. Over the past few decades, however, migration scholars have been increasingly attentive to the ways in which different family/household members' experiences of migration can be highly differentiated. This tendency to homogenise the familial experience in relation to educational migration was increasingly apparent in discussions of East Asian migration during the 1990s. Families were seen as invariably wealthy, privileged, and able to undertake international mobility (and pursue international education) with ease. Following on from this was a related tendency to see education as part of a household strategy. The Chinese family was viewed as particularly adept at functioning as a unit, to its overall advantage. What this argument overlooked, of course, was the emotional strain and ambivalent feelings of some family members, and the differentiated ways in which migration was experienced. For some individuals within the household, migration can offer opportunities and has been relatively liberating, for others it might have been experienced as oppressive and regressive. In reality, of course, individuals' experiences could comprise both positions, either at the same time or changeably over time (Waters 2002; Martin, 2022). In this chapter, we have sought to illustrate some of these complex experiences.

Underpinned by this understanding, this chapter has discussed the now substantial scholarship on educational migration and families. Education is increasingly seen as an important driver of migration, globally. Until relatively recently, the literature has tended to focus on the strategic or instrumental importance of educational migration, and conceptualised this in terms of the accumulation of cultural capital (e.g. Waters, 2006). Over the past few years, researchers have challenged this tendency to view migration as largely or purely strategising, instead emphasising either the ostensibly non-strategic nature of some educational migration (e.g. Yang, 2018), or significantly attenuating this view by emphasising the complex emotional dimensions of migration. These emergent perspectives have enabled us to see beyond the black box of the successful transnational household, towards understanding the differentiated experiences of different family members.

This chapter has also given us the opportunity to reflect on what we know, and where the gaps in our knowledge around educational migration and families lie. It is apparent that we still know very little about the experiences of men as adult members of households in educational migration (cf. Lee and Koo, 2006; Waters, 2010; Hoang and Yeoh, 2011). There is more work now on lone male migrants and the influence of their families on their migration (for education) (e.g. Yang, 2018). Qualitative research is beginning to suggest that family plays as large a part in influencing the migration of male students as it does for female students' (im)mobility (see Forsberg, 2017, on middle-class students from Kerala, India). The role that education plays in the migration of queer or non-binary families is, at present, unknown (see Chapter 17 of this *Handbook* for a discussion of the heterosexual family 'ideal' in migration). And we also hear very little from children in educational migration (Part II of this *Handbook* discusses age and intergenerationality; Chapters 8, 11 and 12 focusing specifically on children and young people). It is notoriously difficult, from a practical and ethical perspective, to garner children's views, but their voices would be a valuable addition to what is increasingly a rich literature. Conversely, more research has examined mothers specifically; whether in the influence of mothers over their children or in the instrumental role that mothers play in facilitating migration for education (and in post-migration transnational lives). Women bear the disproportionate burden of migration: they sacrifice their own careers, social lives and leisure pursuits for the 'good of the family' (Waters, 2015). There is little that is equalising about educational migration.

NOTE

1. The *hukou* system, also known as the household registration system, identifies each Chinese citizen as a resident of a specific area. Usually students can only access the public education resources in the area where their *hukou* is registered.

REFERENCES

Abelmann, N., and Kang, J. (2014). Memoir/manuals of South Korean pre-college study abroad: defending mothers and humanizing children. Global Networks, 14(1): 1–22.
Abotsi, E. (2020). Negotiating the 'Ghanaian'way of schooling: transnational mobility and the educational strategies of British-Ghanaian families. Globalisation, Societies and Education, 18(3): 250–263.
Baas, M. (2006). Students of migration: Indian overseas students and the question of permanent residency. People and Place, 14(1): 8–23.
Beech, S.E. (2015). International student mobility: the role of social networks. Social and Cultural Geography, 16(3): 332–350.
Beech, S.E. (2019). The Geographies of International Student Mobility: Spaces, Places and Decision-Making. Springer.
Boccagni, Paolo, and Loretta Baldassar. 2015. Emotions on the move: mapping the emergent field of emotion and migration. Emotion, Space and Society, 16(August): 73–80. https://doi.org/10.1016/j.emospa.2015.06.009.
Bourdieu, P. 1984. Distinction: A Social Critique of the Judgement of Taste. Harvard University Press.
Bourdieu, P. 1986. "The Forms of Capital." In Handbook of Theory and Research for the Sociology of Education, edited by J.G. Richardson. Greenwood Press.
Bourdieu, P. (1996). The State Nobility: Elite Schools in the Field of Power. Stanford University Press.
Brooks, R. (2015). Social and spatial disparities in emotional responses to education: feelings of 'guilt'among student-parents. British Educational Research Journal, 41(3): 505–519.

Brooks, R., and Waters, J. (2010). Social networks and educational mobility: the experiences of UK students. Globalisation, Societies and Education, 8(1), 143–157.

Brown, P., Green, A., and Lauder, H. (2001). High Skills: Globalization, Competitiveness, and Skill Formation. Oxford University Press.

Chan, A.K., and Ngan, L. L. (2017). Investigating the differential mobility experiences of Chinese cross-border students. Mobilities, 13(1): 142–156.

Chee, W.C. (2017). Trapped in the current of mobilities: China-Hong Kong cross-border families. Mobilities, 12(2): 199–212.

Cheung Judge, R. (2021). 'The best of both worlds': Lagos private schools as engaged strategists of transnational child-raising. Journal of Ethnic and Migration Studies: 1–19. DOI: 10.1080/1369183X.2020.1857233.

Choi, S.Y., and Lai, R.Y. (2022). Birth tourism and migrant children's agency: the 'double not' in post-handover Hong Kong. Journal of Ethnic and Migration Studies, 48(5): 1193–1209.

Collins, F.L., and Ho, K.C. (2018). Discrepant knowledge and interAsian mobilities: unlikely movements, uncertain futures. Discourse: Studies in the Cultural Politics of Education, 39(5): 679–693.

Deuchar, A. (2022). The social practice of international education: analysing the caring practices of Indian international students in Australian universities. Globalisation, Societies and Education. DOI: 10.1080/14767724.2022.2070130.

Findlay, A.M., King, R., Smith, F.M., Geddes, A., and Skeldon, R. (2012). World class? An investigation of globalisation, difference and international student mobility. Transactions of the Institute of British Geographers, 37(1): 118–131.

Findlay, A., Prazeres, L., McCollum, D., and Packwood, H. (2017). 'It Was Always the Plan': International Study as 'Learning to Migrate'. Area, 49(2): 192–199. https://doi.org/10.1111/area.12315.

Fong, V. (2011). Paradise Redefined. Stanford University Press.

Forsberg, S. (2017). Educated to be global: transnational horizons of middle class students in Kerala, India. Environment and Planning A, 49(9): 2099–2115.

Geddie, K. (2013). The transnational ties that bind: relationship considerations for graduating international science and engineering research students. Population, Space and Place, 19(2): 196–208.

Ghosh, S., and Wang, L. (2003). Transnationalism and identity: a tale of two faces and multiple lives. Canadian Geographer/Le Géographe canadien, 47(3): 269–282.

Gu, Q., Schweisfurth, M., and Day, C. (2010). Learning and growing in a 'foreign'context: intercultural experiences of international students. Compare, 40(1), 7–23.

Gupta, A. (2020). Heterogeneous middle-class and disparate educational advantage: parental investment in their children's schooling in Dehradun, India. British Journal of Sociology of Education, 41(1): 48–63.

Hardill, I. (2004). Transnational living and moving experiences: intensified mobility and dual-career households. Population, Space and Place, 10(5): 375–389.

Ho, E.L. (2017). The geo-social and global geographies of power: Urban aspirations of 'worlding' African students in China. Geopolitics, 22(1): 15–33.

Hoang, Lan Anh, and Yeoh, B.S.A. (2011). Breadwinning wives and 'left-behind' husbands: men and masculinities in the Vietnamese transnational family. Gender and Society, 25(6): 717–739. https://doi.org/10.1177/0891243211430636.

Hu, Y., Xu, C.L., and Tu, M. (2022). Family-mediated migration infrastructure: Chinese international students and parents navigating (im) mobilities during the COVID-19 pandemic. Chinese Sociological Review, 54(1): 62–87.

Huang, S., and Yeoh, B.S. (2005). Transnational families and their children's education: China's 'study mothers' in Singapore. Global Networks, 5(4): 379–400.

Huang, S., and Yeoh, B.S. (2011). Navigating the terrains of transnational education: Children of Chinese 'study mothers' in Singapore. Geoforum, 42(3): 394–403.

Jayadeva, S. (2020). Keep calm and apply to Germany: how online communities mediate transnational student mobility from India to Germany. Journal of Ethnic and Migration Studies, 46(11): 2240–2257.

Jeong, Y.J., You, H.K., and Kwon, Y I. (2014). One family in two countries: mothers in Korean transnational families. Ethnic and Racial Studies, 37(9): 1546–1564.

Kajanus, A. (2016). Chinese Student Migration, Gender and Family. Springer.

Koh, S.Y. (2017). Race, Education, and Citizenship: Mobile Malaysians, British Colonial Legacies, and a Culture of Migration. Springer.

Lareau, A. (2011). Unequal Childhoods. University of California Press.

Lee, Yean-Ju, and Koo, Hagen (2006). 'Wild geese fathers' and a globalised family strategy for education in Korea. International Development Planning Review, 28(December): 533–553. https://doi.org/10.3828/idpr.28.4.6.

Leung, M.W., and Waters, J.L. (2021). Making ways for 'better education': placing the Shenzhen–Hong Kong mobility industry. Urban Studies, 00420980211042716.

Ley, D. (2011). Millionaire Migrants: Trans-Pacific Life Lines (Vol. 97). John Wiley & Sons.

Li, F.L.N., Findlay, A.M., Jowett, A.J., and Skeldon, R. (1996). Migrating to learn and learning to migrate: a study of the experiences and intentions of international student migrants. International Journal of Population Geography, 2(1): 51–67.

Lipura, Sarah Jane, and Collins, Francis Leo (2020). Towards an integrative understanding of contemporary educational mobilities: a critical agenda for international student mobilities research. Globalisation, Societies and Education, 18(3): 343–359.

Liu-Farrer, G. (2011). Making careers in the occupational niche: Chinese students in corporate Japan's transnational business. Journal of Ethnic and Migration Studies, 37(5): 785–803.

Martin, F. (2022). Dreams of Flight. Duke University Press.

Mulvey, B., and Mason, M. (2022). 'It's kind of becoming a culture': how habitus influences the migration trajectories of African students in China. Journal of Ethnic and Migration Studies, 48(13): 3005–3021.

Murphy, R. (2004). Turning peasants into modern Chinese citizens: 'population quality' discourse, demographic transition and primary education. China Quarterly, 177: 1–20.

Myers-Walls, J.A., Frias, L.V., Kwon, K.A., Ko, M.J.M., and Lu, T. (2011). Living life in two worlds: acculturative stress among Asian international graduate student parents and spouses. Journal of Comparative Family Studies, 42(4): 455–478.

Ngan, L.L., and Chan, A.K. (2022). Transnational familyhood and migration strategies among parachute kids-turned-parents from Hong Kong. Asian Studies Review, 46(2): 197–214.

Ong, A. (1999). Flexible Citizenship: The Cultural Logics of Transnationality. Duke University Press.

Park, J.S.Y., and Bae, S. (2009). Language ideologies in educational migration: Korean jogi yuhak families in Singapore. Linguistics and Education, 20(4): 366–377.

Pottie-Sherman, Y. (2018). Retaining international students in northeast Ohio: opportunities and challenges in the 'age of Trump'. Geoforum, 96: 32–40.

Redmond, G., Skattebol, J., Hamilton, M., Andresen, S., and Woodman, R. (2022). Projects-of-self and projects-of-family: young people's responsibilisation for their education and responsibility for care. British Journal of Sociology of Education, 43(1): 84–103.

Robertson, S. (2011). Student switchers and the regulation of residency: the interface of the individual and Australia's immigration regime. Population, Space and Place, 17(1): 103–115.

Sanchez-Serra, D., and Marconi, G. (2018). Increasing international students' tuition fees: the two sides of the coin. International Higher Education, 92: 13–14.

Sancho, D. (2017). Escaping India's culture of education: Migration desires among aspiring middle-class young men. Ethnography, 18(4): 515–534.

Seth, M.J. (2002). Education Fever. University of Hawaii Press.

Sidhu, R.K., Chong, H.K., and Yeoh, B.S. (2019). Student Mobilities and International Education in Asia: Emotional Geographies of Knowledge Spaces. Springer Nature.

Sidhu, R., Collins, F., Lewis, N., and Yeoh, B. (2016). Governmental assemblages of internationalising universities: mediating circulation and containment in East Asia. *Environment and Planning A*, 48(8): 1493–1513.

Sidhu, R., and Ishikawa, M. (2022). Destined for Asia: hospitality and emotions in international student mobilities. Compare: A Journal of Comparative and International Education, 52(3): 399-417.

Sinanan, Jolynna, and Gomes, Catherine (2020). 'Everybody needs friends': emotions, social networks and digital media in the friendships of international students. International Journal of Cultural Studies, 23(5): 674–691. https://doi.org/10.1177/1367877920922249.

Sondhi, G., and King, R. (2017). Gendering international student migration: an Indian case-study. Journal of Ethnic and Migration Studies, 43(8): 1308–1324.

Tu, Mengwei (2016). Chinese one-child families in the age of migration: middle-class transnational mobility, ageing parents, and the changing role of filial piety. Journal of Chinese Sociology, 3(1): 1–17.
Walton-Roberts, M. (2015). Femininity, mobility and family fears: Indian international student migration and transnational parental control. Journal of Cultural Geography, 32(1): 68–82.
Waters, J.L. (2000). Flexible families? The experiences of astronaut and satellite households among recent Chinese immigrants to Vancouver, British Columbia. Masters dissertation, University of British Columbia.
Waters, Johanna L. (2002). Flexible families? 'Astronaut' households and the experiences of lone mothers in Vancouver, British Columbia. Social and Cultural Geography, 3(2): 117–134.
Waters, J.L. (2003). 'Satellite Kids' in Vancouver. In: Charney M.W., Yeoh B.S.A., and Kiong T.C. (eds) Asian Migrants and Education. Education in the Asia-Pacific Region: Issues, Concerns and Prospects, Vol 2. Springer.
Waters, J.L. (2006). Geographies of cultural capital: education, international migration and family strategies between Hong Kong and Canada. Transactions of the Institute of British Geographers, 31(2): 179–192.
Waters, J.L. (2008). Education, Migration, and Cultural Capital in the Chinese Diaspora. Cambria Press.
Waters, J.L. (2010). Becoming a father, missing a wife: Chinese transnational families and the male experience of lone parenting in Canada. Population, Space and Place, 16(1): 63–74. https://doi.org/10.1002/psp.578.
Waters, J.L. (2015). Dysfunctional mobilities: international education and the chaos of movement. In Wyn, J., and Cahill, H. (eds) Handbook of Children and Youth Studies. Springer.
Waters, J., and Brooks, R. (2021). Student migrants and contemporary educational mobilities. In Student Migrants and Contemporary Educational Mobilities. Palgrave Macmillan.
Waters, J.L., and Leung, M.W. (2019). Rhythms, flows, and structures of cross-boundary schooling: state power and educational mobilities between Shenzhen and Hong Kong. Population, Space and Place, 26(3): e2298.
Waters, J. L., and Leung, M.W. (2022). Children's bodies are not capital: arduous cross-border mobilities between Shenzhen and Hong Kong. Positions, 30(2): 353–375.
Xiang, Biao, and Wei Shen (2009). International student migration and social stratification in China. International Journal of Educational Development, 29(5): 513–522.
Xu, C.L. (2021). Time, class and privilege in career imagination: exploring study-to-work transition of Chinese international students in UK universities through a Bourdieusian lens. Time and Society, 30(1): 5–29.
Xu, Y., and Montgomery, C. (2021). Understanding the complexity of Chinese rural parents' roles in their children's access to elite universities. British Journal of Sociology of Education, 42(4): 555–570.
Yang, P. (2016). International Mobility and Educational Desire: Chinese Foreign Talent Students in Singapore. Springer.
Yang, P. (2018). Compromise and complicity in international student mobility: the ethnographic case of Indian medical students at a Chinese university. Discourse: Studies in the Cultural Politics of Education, 39(5): 694–708.
Yang, P. (2022). China in the global field of international student mobility: an analysis of economic, human and symbolic capitals. Compare: A Journal of Comparative and International Education, 52(2): 308–326.
Yeoh, B.S., and Lam, T. (2007). The costs of (im) mobility: children left behind and children who migrate with a parent. Perspectives on Gender and Migration, 38: 120–149.
Yeoh, B.S., Huang, S. and Lam, T. (2018) Transnational family dynamics in Asia. In Triandafyllidou, A. (ed.), Handbook of Migration and Globalisation. Edward Elgar Publishing.
Zhang, S., and Xu, C.L. (2020). The making of transnational distinction: an embodied cultural capital perspective on Chinese women students' mobility. British Journal of Sociology of Education, 41(8): 1251–1267.

14. Privileged migration and the family: family matters in corporate expatriation
Sophie Cranston and George Tan

INTRODUCTION

The term 'expatriate' can be contentious due to the racialised and privileged imaginaries associated with it (Fechter and Walsh, 2010; Cranston, 2017). From an organisational perspective, however, 'expatriate' refers to someone who moves overseas as part of their employment.[1] Undertaking an international assignment is a key form of temporary work-led skilled migration, to the extent that this takes on a variety of types, with people moving abroad by finding work (self-initiated), those who do a series of assignments in different locations (global careerists), as well as those who follow the home–abroad–home again model (traditional expatriates) (Lämsä et al., 2017).

While the term 'expatriate' has multiple meanings, there is a general acceptance in the literature of the assumption of temporariness: that the migrant does not plan to settle in the country, but to move on (McNulty and Brewster, 2017). Few obstacles are imagined as the individual moves through time and space. This is clearly a form of privileged mobility in multiple ways. First, privilege is often theorised as agency (Benson, 2014). While an expatriate assignment is sponsored by an organisation, individuals mostly have the choice as to whether they migrate. This is also privilege because the individual has the support and the resources to migrate, those which are not available to all. Second, corporate expatriation is usually not framed as a problematic form of mobility, hence those who inhabit this mobility are usually seen to be in place, as opposed to out of place (Cai and Su, 2020).[2] Third, because mobility is sponsored, corporate expatriation tends to be thought of as smooth. Organisations often invest in their employees, in terms of pre-departure and post-arrival support, in order to make the process of moving through a location successful (Cranston, 2016). The ease through which the corporate expatriate is seen to migrate is their privilege in migration; they have the passport, the body, the capital and/or resources to move and be welcomed by the different places in which they live.

Visions of corporate expatriate migration as a form of privileged migration contain within them an imaginary of the free-floating cosmopolitan who moves around the world with ease (Lan, 2011). It is this character, seen as the epitome and hero of neoliberal globalisation (Duplan, 2022), who is often depicted as a man crossing the globe in corporate visualisations (Cranston, 2016). However, in this chapter we follow others (e.g., Cangià and Zittoun, 2018; Coles and Fechter, 2008; Fechter, 2007; Walsh, 2018; Ryan and Mulholland, 2014) to argue that the construction of the ease of the corporate expatriate's mobility tends to imagine only one person moving. Thinking about the family of the corporate expatriate, their partner, their children, parents, siblings, and so on, starts to complicate a smooth narrative of migration. For example, framings of the corporate expatriate from a business perspective in international human resource management often frame the family as the reason for the failure of an expatriate assignment: 'Often ignored by companies sending employees abroad, the families of expatriates have a significant impact on their success. If a spouse or child is struggling to settle into the new environment, it is highly likely to impact on the employee's performance and willingness to complete the assignment' (Allianz Care, 2018).

In this framing, the family is seen to potentially impinge on the economic success of the expatriate's move (see discussion in Chapter 1, this *Handbook*). It draws upon wider discourses of gender, family and working lives (Frone et al., 1996; Yang et al., 2000; Boyar et al., 2005) that suggest the family is a problem which needs to be addressed.

In wider discussions of transnational mobility, the framing of migrants, such as the corporate expatriate, as *Homo economicus* has been questioned (Ley, 2004; Chapter 1, this *Handbook*). As Conradson and Latham (2005) argue, the everyday practices and ordinary experiences of 'elite' transnational lives revolve around eating, sleeping, attending to family obligations and responsibilities, and maintaining relationships. Through this chapter we explore the role of the family within corporate expatriation. We begin by reviewing existing literature within the social sciences on the expatriate family, demonstrating that this existing body of research establishes the family as central actors within the experiences and practices of corporate expatriation. By tracing literature on the 'expatriate' through wider theoretical developments in migration studies, the chapter then draws on cutting-edge perspectives on the corporate expatriate family through spatial–temporal life-course and mobilities perspectives. Using the example of Australian and British migrants in Singapore, the need to consider the temporal and relational within the understanding of privileged forms of mobility is highlighted.

THE FAMILY AND EXPATRIATE MIGRATION

Research that looks specifically at contemporary expatriates or groups of migrants who could be considered expatriates has followed wider trends in migration studies and the social sciences. In the 1990s and early 2000s the focus was on corporate expatriates as highly skilled migrants – often as individuals – in the context of the role that they played within economic processes of the global city (Beaverstock, 2002; Findlay et al., 1996). More generally, research on transnational professionals traditionally missed an understanding of gender and family, with an emphasis on labour as opposed to social reproduction (Coles and Fechter, 2008). Historically, female migrants were seen to be simply following men (Houstoun et al., 1984; Pedraza, 1991) as 'trailing spouses', regarded as passive and generally invisible in the migration process (Yeoh and Khoo, 1998). However, in the 2000s, two key developments influenced thinking on expatriates. The first of these was the emergence of social and cultural approaches to professional migration (e.g., Yeoh and Willis, 2005; Knowles and Harper, 2009). The second stemmed from scholarship that sought to explore transnationalism from below, or the everyday lives of migrants (e.g., Walsh, 2006; Fechter, 2007; Lundström, 2014; Walsh, 2018). These developments in the literature shifted focus from the individual to include the wider expatriate family, with a few exceptions (Leonard, 2010; Cranston, 2016). The discussion below focuses on literature that specifically includes a discussion of family within 'expatriation' (excluding studies which focus on individuals). The literature demonstrates that, rather than representing a hinderance or 'add-on' to our understanding of corporate expatriation, the family helps to determine both mobility and the experience of mobility.

Research on accompanying partners shows how the 'trailing spouse' holds an imaginary of two differing forms of relationships to the individual moving (see Chapter 1, this *Handbook*).

First, 'trailing' evokes the notion of baggage, suggesting a level of inconvenience or considered an afterthought. Second, the trailing spouse can be framed as being 'incorporated' (Callan and Ardener, 1984), facilitating the career of the moving partner through the pursuit of their work–social relations. These discussions involved examining practical and emotional support, which included handling the logistics of the move and looking after children. To an extent, this represents the institutionalisation of trailing spouses in corporate ideologies within organisations which saw the role of the spouse as to ensure the success of the expatriate in the workplace (Fechter, 2010). The vision of corporate expatriates moving around the world with ease, unencumbered by their partners, rests on the assumption that their partners' role is to support their endeavours (Kunz, 2020). However, despite partners practising mobility differently, it should not be assumed that partners do not have agency in shaping the decision to move.

The increasing focus on gendered perspectives on privileged migration (e.g., Yeoh and Khoo, 1998; Willis and Yeoh, 2000; Kofman, 2000) has engaged wider changes in gender ideologies, reflecting a shift from positioning women as 'incorporated' within their husbands' company to thinking about the challenges of dual-career couples (Coles and Fechter, 2008). This literature highlights how the practice of mobility differs between partners, contesting the smooth narrative of corporate expatriation as being masculinist (Fechter, 2007; Walsh, 2018; Duplan, 2022). For example, an emphasis is placed on the limitations that are imposed on accompanying partners' careers, in terms of the ability of partners to work, by host country governments (Büchele, 2018; Cangià, 2018). Studies also highlight how some women as accompanying partners face a reinstatement or reinforcement of gender roles that they would consider outdated, creating limits and boundaries to both their careers and their lives abroad (Büchele, 2018; Fechter, 2007; Cangià, 2018; Lundström, 2014; Walsh, 2018). The change in roles within the family also demonstrate how migration can reconfigure our understanding of gender, domesticity and the family itself (Walsh, 2018; see Chapters 2, 3, 5 and 9, this *Handbook*). For example, Lundström (2014) revisits the role of the 'mother' in contexts where domestic help is readily available. Contrary to normative expectations of how one ought to feel as a 'privileged' expat spouse, Cangià's (2017) work highlights more broadly the complex 'emotion work' of expat spouses and the myriad ways in which they manage how they feel while negotiating a new life, status and culture. Research therefore shows how gender ideologies are reflected in family dynamics. For example, Spiegel (2018) looks at the labour involved in being an accompanying spouse in ensuring the success of the move, settling in and maintaining a sense of belonging. Comparing male and female accompanying spouses, she shows how women perform the majority of this work regardless of which partner is working.

With a stronger emphasis on partners and spouses in research on corporate expatriation migration, the role of children is also elucidated (see Chapters 7 and 12, this *Handbook*). The insight of parents – as people who interact closely with them – can highlight how children feature as actors in the migration process. In wider migration studies, children have been portrayed as passive and dependant members, or constructed as 'luggage', inconvenient and a source of anxiety to otherwise mobile parents (Dobson, 2009, p. 357; Orellana, 2001, p. 588; Thorne et al., 2003, p. 248). However, Ackers and Stalford (2004) and Orellana (2001) maintain that children are at the centre of family migration decision-making. In their respective studies, they interviewed both parents and their children and, while in many cases parents had not consulted their children directly, the researchers found that children's needs were foremost in parental deliberations. It is often through a discussion of partners in expatriation that family motivations surface. Ryan and Mulholland (2014), for example, highlight women's agency in shaping the family's migration through the responsibilities they feel towards not disrupting their children's education. However, the role children play in 'expatriate' migration tends to be presented through adult voices, reflecting broader migration studies where research tends to be adult-centric. Exceptions include Sander's (2016) work on expatriate children in Shanghai, and Tanu's (2018) exploration of belonging in international schools. These texts, however, focus on young people's everyday belonging in place without necessarily situating children within the wider family unit.

When considering the family in corporate expatriate migration, heteronormativity is often presumed, along with a tendency to assume what might be considered as a 'traditional' family as opposed to other family types (single parent, split family) (McNulty 2015; see Chapter 17, this *Handbook*). More limited in scope than that of children in existing research on corporate expatriates is the role that wider family members play in shaping mobility. However, we do see glimpses. For example, Walsh (2018) argues that we should 'account for the varied mobility of any non-migrant family members' (p. 141) when exploring both the mobility decisions and experiences of British migrants. In this context, Walsh refers to two types of family members: grown-up children who may not move or live in the same location as their parents, and the parents of those who move. In discussions about whether to leave a location, the desire and need to care for elderly parents/relatives has been highlighted as a catalyst (Michielin et al., 2008). It is important to note that experiences in place and mobility decisions can still be impacted by the wider family, despite the absence and distance of them from everyday lives (Greco, 2018).

Therefore, the family are not simply an 'add-on' to our understanding expatriate mobility, as partners, children and other family members can be central to understanding the motivations and experiences of privileged migration. The literature on partners highlights the importance of a relational approach: that migration is experienced differently by different members of the family. Approaching migration as a family as opposed to individual project also hints at the importance of a temporal approach, alerting us to attending to changes in family dynamics over time.

SPATIAL–TEMPORAL APPROACHES: THE LIFE-COURSE AND MOBILITIES

Recent developments in migration studies have sought to emphasise the temporality of migration, taking two approaches (see Part IV of this *Handbook*). First, Bailey and Mulder (2017) suggest that a life-course perspective tends to be missing within the analysis of highly skilled migration, including corporate expatriation. Foregrounding the need to understand 'linked lives', they argue that that a life-course approach allows us to understand how the life events of an individual and their family helps to determine and explain mobility (Bailey and Mulder, 2017). This leads to a specific emphasis on how spatial and temporal approaches feature in migration. Second, mobilities approaches in migration studies re-orient the focus of research from the relationships between migrants and place to exploring how migrants move. This work extends understandings of mobility as relational; for example, by looking at the relationship between immobility and mobility and how this is constituted and practiced (Cresswell, 2010). Within this research is an emphasis on temporalities; for example, by using the journey as an analytical lens to trace the movement of a migrant through space and time, looking at how movement and periods of stasis are negotiated and experienced (Schapendonk et al., 2018).

As this chapter will demonstrate, there is a need to further develop temporal approaches to understanding the corporate expatriate family over the life-course, which tease out who the family is and how priorities can evolve. For example, some corporate expatriates are single, and the meeting with a desired partner, the formation of a family, or the breakdown of relationships may impact upon their experiences and mobility decisions. The role that children play in migration decisions also becomes clearer when framed within the lifecourse. In a way, 'proper family timing' is crucial in facilitating international work as pauses in gender contracts and family democracy come into play (Boström et al., 2018). The age of children is key in the decision to move, with the availability of partners to take on care-giving responsibilities or the availability of domestic help shaping mobility decisions (Kofman, 2000; Toader and Dahinden, 2018). These decisions often reinforce gender roles, which themselves change through the mobility journey. That said, by extending Cangià's (2018) use of imagination as a coping mechanism for expat spouses, the decision to move overseas is captured through the notion that parents were acting in their children's best interests (Hutchins, 2011; Korpela, 2018). Benefits for their children include the acquisition of a more international or cosmopolitan outlook (Weenink, 2008), or the unique opportunity to experience a better quality of life in an environment different to their home country (Korpela, 2018). In relation to familial and social narratives which drive return migration (Chepulis, 1981; Ní Laoire et al., 2012), parents imagine lives for themselves and their children through the connections they retain to their home country. Such imaginations can be tied to nostalgic constructions of the parents' own childhood experiences which are projected onto their own children (Ní Laoire, 2011).

However, explicit temporal approaches to the corporate expatriate family are in their infancy (Cangià and Zittoun, 2018; Suter, 2020). In Cangià and Zittoun's (2018) special issue on when expatriation becomes 'a matter of family', they argue for the significance of changing family dynamics over time and space in influencing the migration decisions of the expatriate family. As part of this special issue, Büchele (2018) examines rupture and routine as a means to understand the rhythm through which mobilities are practised by expat spouses who are unable to work. More broadly, Suter (2020) considers the 'pacing' of mobility decisions by expatriate families, showing how 'the ideal duration' of mobility is often arrived at through negotiation among different family members with different requirements.

Cangià and Zittoun (2018) argue that it is by looking at the dual concerns of space and time that the influence of the family on migration is clearly articulated. In the rest of this chapter, we further develop this argument by exploring the mobility journeys of British and Australian migrants through Singapore. Using a relational perspective, we focus specifically on the partner and children as actors in the mobility journey of corporate expatriation. In this way, we attend to how one individual relates to other members of the family, primarily their partners and children, to broaden discussion on how the decision to move to and imagined departures from Singapore revolves around the family unit. Through this, we highlight the spatial–temporal dimensions of corporate expatriate family migration by examining how the life-course and migration journey intersect.

To explore the spatial–temporal dimensions of the corporate expatriate family, we draw upon two different research projects involving interviews with Australian and British migrants who were moving through Singapore in 2012. A direct focus on the family was not the primary research aim behind either research project; however, our respondents highlighted family within their wider discussions. As the chapter draws on a small proportion of the larger interview samples, we make no claims about the representativeness of the selected interviewees; rather, the issues we discuss are illustrative of the concerns relating to family in corporate expatriate migration. The interview transcripts were analysed by looking for mentions of family, and exploring how different members of the family were discussed. The chapter includes the voices of the lead migrant, as well as working and non-working partners. All participants in the research are anonymised.

MOVING TO

As highlighted above, for the corporate expatriate, the job that they are offered acts as the catalyst for mobility. The move to Singapore is linked to the primary expatriate, with accompanying partners typically moving as dependents. Some of the accompanying partners in our study, however, were able to secure international transfers with their companies who were keen to retain them, thus becoming a corporate expatriate themselves. Others, on the other hand, moved with their partner and then secured work in Singapore after their move.

However, for some of our respondents the move to Singapore represented an opportunity not to work. For example, Edward highlighted how the differing financial climate in Singapore resulted in the ability to give up work without this impacting upon the family finances: 'It wasn't a huge step financially for us cause I had to give up my job to come here but with the tax incentives here, we're almost if just as not well off with having one person working in Singapore as having both of us working in Australia' (Edward, Australian, non-working partner, no children).

The move to Singapore was Edward's 'turn' to give up his role, as his wife had previously supported him in his mobility for work. For others, especially those with young children, the financial ability not to work in Singapore was a welcome change of pace of family life, especially if they employed live-in domestic help to assist with household chores and babysitting. This is what Lucy refers to as the chance to 'properly be a mum':

> Actually part of the reason for me being keen to come is that it will give me more time to be a mum again, umm, like properly be a mum rather than be like being a mum who works three days a week and then does all the cleaning and the washing and the ironing and the rest of it on the rest of the days. (Lucy, British, accompanying partner, 2 children)

For Lucy, the re-domestication of family life is seen as an opting-out of her busy life back home. In part, this is due to the ease of securing domestic help in places such as Singapore. Others saw domestic help as freeing up time in different ways, which Bethany alludes to in relation to leisure: 'I know a lot of people who come here and they'll have an extra child because they got help and the lifestyle is better. In terms of mums we go out a lot here because we can, you know?' (Bethany, Australian, dual career, 2 children).

Both Bethany and Lucy refer to how their domestic helper undertakes the domestic shift. For Lucy, this gives time for more focused parenting, while Bethany frames this time spent as becoming available for leisure activities, investing time in pursuit of the self. The place of Singapore, the financial attractiveness of working there, allowed for a different pace of life. Far from the move to Singapore being solely an economic decision for one family member, the decision was a negotiation between partners and the anticipated family life they could lead was a factor.

The 'right' time for global mobility was also raised in interviews when thinking about children. The age of children can facilitate the move to Singapore:

> When Kevin asked if he should put his hand up [for the job position in Singapore which was offered by his employer], I said yup! This is our chance, our kids were 6 and 7 at that time and I thought this was a good chance to move them to experience living overseas [as it was easier to do so]. (Bethany, Australian, dual career, 2 children)

Others cited how having young children was an advantage when moving to Singapore, as the move was seen to present fewer challenges. The role of time in the decision to move when it comes to children is signposted by adolescence and the commencement of high school, a natural and important juncture which demonstrates how time in the life-course can shape migration decisions. For some, changing schools was an opportune time to move to Singapore: 'for my daughter, she was moving from [last year of primary] to [first year of secondary], so she was changing school anyway, so it was no ordeal just to change schools to another school here, it worked fine' (James, British, working partner, 2 children).

The natural progression from primary to high school for James's daughter was convenient and matched the timing of the family moving to Singapore. This demonstrates that despite the lack of agency of the child, the life-course of the child is vital to the plans of their parents. In addition, it is important to note how time factored when imagining the futures of children. Discussions of cultural capital around international education acted as motivation for parents in their desire for their children to develop a cosmopolitan outlook through their mobility to Singapore:

> This is why a place like this is great for children, at the [international school] there were 73 nationalities. You went to a kid's birthday party and there were Afghanis, Indians, Japanese – people from all over the world. No one looked and said anything about the colour of their skin – paid no attention to creed, race, colour, religion. (Tom, British, working partner, 1 child)

Better cultural understanding was not only seen as a benefit for children but was also framed by some respondents in relation to their own localised childhood. They wanted something different for their children through their child's interaction with other cultures. The motivation for some parents to move to Singapore was constructed around the imagined future of their child, particularly in terms of the cultural capital that global mobility is often seen to produce. The mobility of the family was an investment in the future of the child, as well as the career of the parent.

The corporate package is fundamental to making the move in the first place which generally implies a power imbalance with the primary expat seen as the key decision maker. Although the move to Singapore might not entirely hinge on wider family members, our findings in this section suggest that spouses/partners and children are not unimportant. This largely revolves around timing, the age of the child(ren) and also circumstance, or the opportunity for the spouse/partner to opt out of work in favour of quality time with the family. How these different elements that fall in place can impact on the smoothness of the migration and life experiences of the expatriate family as a collective unit.

MOVING FROM

For migrants undertaking corporate assignments, the expectation is that their stay in Singapore is temporary and tied to their job roles. While these jobs were temporally structured by fixed-contract terms, there was some degree of flexibility, with respondents choosing to leave earlier or stay longer. As this section will demonstrate, how these decisions were framed often took into account the family.

While children's age and educational trajectories were related to arrivals to Singapore, they also shaped considerations for future departures from Singapore. These discussions were often linked to children's sense of belonging:

> I think actually that kids are a big thing [factor in return migration]. I was having a conversation with someone recently and they were saying that when they were a kid their father was in the Navy or something and they lived all over the world and as great as it was, they never had an identity ... So they were saying that when their kids reached a certain age they want to go back and settle in one country, from an educational perspective so their child would have a sense about who they are. (Mary, Australian, non-working partner, no children)

Over time, those with younger children began to frame departures around their children's identity, often with an idealisation of teenage children growing up in their home country. This further underlines how the life-stage of children punctuates the migration decision-making process:

> I remember going there every Sunday almost [to her grandparents' house] ... but what's [son] going to remember? I don't know, what is he going to remember? ... But for [son] it's completely different and sometimes you feel like ... I don't know if I'm short-changing him. Whereas at least if we were in Australia ... at least you have those roots, they've no roots yet. (Felicity, Australian, non-working partner, 1 child)

This was also reported in the case of Mary, whose children were younger when they first moved to Singapore. The right time for the family to return to Australia was linked to their children commencing high school, and a perceived notion that their teenage years in high school represented the formative years for their children in establishing lifelong friendships and their Australian identity. Children's sense of belonging was framed around putting down roots in Australia or the United Kingdom. This anchor was constructed around the everyday experiences of children whilst in these countries, visiting grandparents, playing sport, the making of life-long friends. Staying in Singapore limited children's participation in these everyday activities in the home country, presenting a potential challenge to fostering belonging, and hence this was a reason to depart Singapore.

Family considerations also framed other reasons for leaving Singapore. While the desire for children to connect to their roots was often expressed, so was the desire to be close to and care for increasingly elderly parents: 'But the pull is strong and I think it will definitely get stronger as family and friends get older ... realistically family will need us' (Abigail, British, dual career, 2 children).

As time passed, caring responsibilities extended to considering family at home, particularly parents. Abigail focused on the potential problems that caring at a distance may involve, with the move back to the United Kingdom as a means to mitigate this potential issue. For single female corporate expatriates, the desire to form a family also figured in their planning to leave.

Privileged migration and the family: family matters in corporate expatriation 225

For example, Lily, a British migrant, had moved to Singapore with a partner but their relationship ended. Having at this time been in Singapore for a year and secured her own employment, she decided to stay. However, her considerations were affected by her feeling that it was too hard for single Western women to find a suitable partner in Singapore. She therefore planned to leave Singapore within a year, before she got 'too old' to have children. Her imagined future revolved around family formation, which acted as a catalyst for mobility.

Other types of family life considerations featured in framings of departure. In families where one partner works and the other does not, the pace of life in Singapore can differ. For working partners, much of their time was invested in their work, which they might find rewarding while advancing their careers: 'so it's easy for me I come to do a job that's rewarding and I'm very busy and da da da, it's your wife and your children that are the possible pinch points in this, aren't they? If they don't settle that makes it very difficult for me' (James, British, working partner, 2 children).

As James suggested, the time invested in his job could put him at odds with his spouse and family. This was a point which Elliot also highlighted:

> If you're used to your spouse being home for tea [evening meal] every evening by six or seven then think again. The work hours plus obligatory 'networking' in the evenings, on top of frequent overseas travel, makes for little quality home life Monday to Friday ... Usually the manager loves Asia, loves the diversity, loves the regional roles, the travel, the excitement, for the families, it's often a case of Where's Daddy this week then? (British, working partner, 3 children)

From an international human resource management perspective, James's and Elliot's accounts illustrate where the family may potentially affect the corporate expatriate's work, productivity and career prospects (Frone et al., 1996; Yang et al., 2000; Boyar et al., 2005). Neither Elliot nor James suggested that the working practices were an issue; instead, the underlying suggestion was that the family posed a problem for not accepting their busy work schedules and long hours. The work commitments of the corporate expatriate can thus result in their absence from family life. This has implications for family well-being. The differential pace of life experienced by corporate expatriates, their partners and family members can in some extreme cases result in a premature departure: 'I know someone whose marriage fell apart because they had a regional role and didn't see each other at the same time. These stories are terrible. This family, they had young kids, and when divorced the wife was left on her own' (Mick, British, dual career, 2 children).

The breakdown of relationships was highlighted in relation to not only differing work practices, but also infidelity, which could speed up the departure of the other (usually female) partner and children. Although this experience of other expat families was recounted by our respondents, rather than a reflection of their own experiences, it serves to highlight some of the gendered anxieties of everyday life within liminal and transient places (Fechter, 2007; Walsh, 2018).

Other decisions to leave were centred on the careers and aspirations of the non-working partners. While some accompanying partners embraced not working, others were less positive. Some respondents actively rejected the term 'trailing spouse', which they felt had hedonistic connotations opposed to what was construed as meaningful work (Cranston, 2019). For others, they rejected the idea of the trailing spouse because they wanted to be treated on their own terms, as opposed to being regarded as dependents of their partners. It was these respondents who often highlighted their frustrations at not being able to secure a job role. For example,

Gloria 'found it quite difficult to get work' due to her status on a short-term dependent's visa (Australian, non-working partner, adult children in Australia). For Gloria, not working in Singapore was described in terms of loss, something missing from her everyday life, and a factor that would ultimately result in her departure:

> I do, I do miss it [working]. It has implications [not working in Singapore] for me when I return. If we're here longer than five years, I can't work when we move back to Melbourne. You become de-credited if you haven't worked for five years, you to do [*sic*] some sort of bridging course to show you're up to date.

Gloria's experience sits within how Cangià (2018) frames the career immobility of spouses who are linked to the global mobility of their partners: as a period of stasis. How the period of stasis resonated with each respondent was dependent on the family's situation prior to moving to Singapore, and also whether unemployment represented a welcomed continuation of, or rupture to, the individual's aspirations.

The operation of power shifts as factors that previously facilitated the move to Singapore evolve, gradually impinging on the decision to return home. Career pauses that are earlier welcomed may be replaced by the need to resume an inactive career, while the convenience of relocating young children may give way to decisions to return home to cater to the needs of children reaching adolescence. Ageing parents and the desire to be closer to them for various reasons may also begin to tug at the heartstrings, pulling them closer to home. We also see how relationship breakdown can lead to the move away. In short, over time, the family may move to the centre of the decision-making process to return home. This is not to say that the primary expat does not have agency in shaping the decision to leave. The key point, however, highlights how the needs of the family emerge more strongly over time, in contrast with how the career of the primary expat acted as the driving force in the initial move to Singapore.

DISCUSSION AND CONCLUSIONS

The findings from Australian and British corporate expatriates support the existing literature that frames the family as being central in both the motivations to move, and the experiences of mobility itself. The move to, and potential move from, Singapore was not framed in terms of an individual or career, but relationally in terms of a wider family project. By taking a life-course perspective, we emphasise the time-spaces of mobility journeys and underscore the current time and the future for each family member in terms of the individual and as a collective. In terms of partners, the findings highlight different ways in which the journey through Singapore is experienced and reported, looking at how working and non-working partners reflect upon their own and each other's experiences. For some accompanying partners, moving to Singapore presents the opportunity to pause their career; for others, this is experienced as career immobility. This enables Singapore to be experienced differently to previous experiences, where some revel in the shift to family or leisure time, and others begrudge the pause on jobs and careers. The age of children in relation to education, the desire for them to develop cultural capital, and for the family to experience a different type of family life, all feature as part of the decision to undertake a corporate expatriate assignment. Amongst our respondents, these factors expedited mobility both to and from Singapore. The key points raised in this chapter on the role of children in the mobilities of the expatriate family relates to the nexus of time with children's age, belonging and education, which together shape mobility. For our respondents, the question was not whether to move, but when was the best time to move (see also Suter 2020).

The image of the corporate expatriate crossing the globe, the masculinist hero of globalisation (Duplan, 2022), is further challenged as it hides the fact that the family acts as an 'important anchoring yet shifting entry point through which people live movement' (Cangià and Zittoun, 2018, p. 4). This once again highlights the need to contest grand narratives of mobility, by grounding the lived experiences of migration within the everyday lives and decision-making by migrants, showing how migrant lives are lived in relation to others (Conradson and Latham, 2005; Walsh, 2006). As relational, the differing experiences, aspirations, desires of the family can rub against each other, with the potential to interrupt (im)mobility. However, this does little to contest the notion of expatriate migration as being privileged. As highlighted, privilege in migration is often understood and underpinned by the ease that someone can move through space and time, framed in terms of an individual having the capital, the passport and the body to both be able to move, and be tolerated in the place where they are living. In the relational analysis of the corporate expatriate family, we extend this understanding from the individual to the family. Privilege is itself necessarily understood as relational, as the ability of someone as an individual or as part of a group to access resources that others cannot, as an effect of wider power structures (Benson, 2014). The corporate expatriate experiences a relative lack of bureaucratic friction in comparison to other migrants. For example, the discussions of when is the best age for the mobility of children reflects the ease of these migrants to access dependent visas, in stark contrast with other migrants such as domestic workers who have to leave their children behind (Parreñas, 2005). The ability of one partner to temporarily suspend their career, and to have access to domestic helpers, shows a privilege of capital. This family project is also intergenerational. The desire for children to develop cultural capital through a cosmopolitan outlook reflects wider discourses of mobility as cultural capital which will help children to get ahead in their imagined futures (Waters, 2006). As this chapter has shown, this facilitates the mobility decision of the corporate expatriate; their motivations for moving to Singapore are a way in which the privileges and opportunities of the parent's generation can reproduce themselves for their children.

A temporal approach to exploring the family in corporate expatriation therefore enables us to explore how mobility is not an individual pursuit, but an entanglement between the different family member's journeys through time and space. However, in terms of moving together, tensions do emerge, not only between family members but also at different points of the migrant journey, which in turn determines the level of tension felt and placed on the migration decision-making process. This chapter demonstrates the need to understand the operations of power within the everyday articulations and practices of the privileged family migration. By seeing the family and the life-course as relational, we elucidate the frictions that shape the migration journey for corporate expatriation. Through this, we see wider points relating to gendered privilege, which raises questions on the operation of power within and beyond the nuclear family structure. Our research shows how unequal power relationships, often pegged to masculine subjectivities under the guise of cosmopolitanism, can determine mobility and stasis (Skeggs, 2003), for example, in terms of dual-career households. It is these frictions in the family that can jar the experience of mobility. There is scope to further explore the complexities of privileged migration, and to develop how everyday approaches influence the asymmetry of power, and how it ebbs and flows between members within the family across time and space within both the nuclear and the extended family. There is also further scope to explore the voices of children and their experiences of mobility, as compared to how their parents narrate them.

NOTES

1. Discussions about the term 'expatriate' are now commonplace within migration studies. These discussions focus on how this term is often seen as reserved for white Westerners who move abroad, and the power relations imbued within this. In this chapter, we use the term 'corporate expatriate' to refer to a specific form of organisational global mobility, where an individual moves abroad to undertake a fixed-term work assignment. We use 'expatriates' in reference to other literature that uses this terminology. We refer to our respondents as migrants.
2. Discussions of belonging in place, in accounts of privileged migration, are often highly racialised. Our respondents were not all white, as is often assumed in accounts of 'Western' migration. We do not discuss race in this chapter, as discussions of race were not related to the family by our respondents.

REFERENCES

Ackers, L. and Stalford, H. (2004) *A Community for Children? Children, Citizenship, and Internal Migration in the EU*. Research in Migration and Ethnic Relations series. Ashgate.

Allianz Care (2018) Reasons for expatriate failure and how HR can help, Allianz Care. Available at: https://www.allianzcare.com/en/employers/employer-blogs/2018/09/expat-failure.html (accessed: 5 October 2020).

Bailey, A. and Mulder, C.H. (2017) 'Highly skilled migration between the Global North and South: gender, life courses and institutions', *Journal of Ethnic and Migration Studies*, 43(16), pp. 2689–2703. doi: 10.1080/1369183X.2017.1314594.

Beaverstock, J.V. (2002) 'Transnational elites in global cities: British expatriates in Singapore's financial district', *Geoforum*, 33(4), pp. 525–538. doi: 10.1016/S0016-7185(02)00036-2.

Benson, M. (2014) 'Negotiating privilege in and through lifestyle migration', in Benson, M. and Osbaldiston, N. (eds) *Understanding Lifestyle Migration*. Migration, Diasporas and Citizenship Series. Palgrave Macmillan, pp. 47–68.

Boström, K.W., Öhlander, M. and Pettersson, H. (2018) 'Temporary international mobility, family timing, dual career and family democracy. A case of Swedish medical professionals', *Migration Letters*, 15(1), pp. 99–111. doi: 10.33182/ml.v15i1.337.

Boyar, S.L., Maertz, C.P. and Pearson, A.W. (2005) 'The effects of work–family conflict and family–work conflict on nonattendance behaviors', *Journal of Business Research*, 58(7), pp. 919–925. doi: 10.1016/j.jbusres.2003.11.005.

Büchele, J. (2018) '"We live a life in periods." Perceptions of mobility and becoming an expat spouse', *Migration Letters*, 15(1), pp. 45–54.

Cai, X. and Su, X. (2020) 'Dwelling-in-travelling: Western expats and the making of temporary home in Guangzhou, China', *Journal of Ethnic and Migration Studies*, pp. 1–18. doi: 10.1080/1369183X.2020.1739392.

Callan, H. and Ardener, S. (eds) (1984) *The Incorporated Wife*. Croom Helm.

Cangià, F. (2017) '(Im)Mobility and the emotional lives of expat spouses', *Emotion, Space and Society*, 25, pp. 22–28. doi: 10.1016/j.emospa.2017.10.001.

Cangià, F. (2018) 'Precarity, imagination, and the mobile life of the "trailing spouse": precarity, imagination, and the mobile life', *Ethos*, 46(1), pp. 8–26. doi: 10.1111/etho.12195.

Cangià, F. and Zittoun, T. (2018) 'When "expatriation" is a matter of family. Opportunities, barriers and intimacies in international mobility', *Migration Letters*, 15(1), pp. 1–16. doi: 10.33182/ml.v15i1.336.

Chepulis, R. (1981) 'Return migration: an analytical framework', in Kubat, K. (ed.) *The Politics of Return: International Migration in Europe*. Centre for Migration Studies, pp. 239–245.

Coles, A. and Fechter, A.-M. (2008) 'Introduction', in Coles, A. and Fechter, A.-M. (eds) *Gender and Family among Transnational Professionals*. Routledge, pp. 1–20.

Conradson, D. and Latham, A. (2005) 'Transnational urbanism: attending to everyday practices and mobilities', *Journal of Ethnic and Migration Studies*, 31(2), pp. 227–233. doi: 10.1080/1369183042000339891.

Cranston, S. (2016) 'Imagining global work: producing understandings of difference in "easy Asia"', *Geoforum*, 70, pp. 60–68. doi: 10.1016/j.geoforum.2016.02.008.

Cranston, S. (2017) 'Expatriate as a "good" migrant: thinking through skilled international migrant categories', *Population, Space and Place*, 23(6), p. e2058. doi: 10.1002/psp.2058.

Cranston, S. (2019) 'British migrant orientations in Singapore'. in Leonard, P. and Walsh, K. (eds) *British Migration: Privilege, Diversity and Vulnerability*. Routledge, pp. 58–74.

Cresswell, T. (2010) 'Towards a politics of mobility', *Environment and Planning D: Society and Space*, 28(1), pp. 17–31. doi: 10.1068/d11407.

Dobson, M.E. (2009) 'Unpacking children in migration research', *Children's Geographies*, 7(3), pp. 355–360. doi: 10.1080/14733280903024514.

Duplan, K. (2022) 'Expatriate as hero of globalization? Critical insights on privileged migration and neoliberal ideology', in *Expats/Migrants: The Two Faces of the Same Reality?* Beck, S. (ed.) Brill Publishers, pp. 157–183.

Fechter, A.-M. (2007) *Transnational Lives: Expatriates in Indonesia*. Ashgate.

Fechter, A.-M. (2010) 'Gender, empire, global capitalism: colonial and corporate expatriate wives', *Journal of Ethnic and Migration Studies*, 36(8), pp. 1279–1297. doi: 10.1080/13691831003687717.

Fechter, A.-M. and Walsh, K. (2010) 'Examining "expatriate" continuities: postcolonial approaches to mobile professionals', *Journal of Ethnic and Migration Studies*, 36(8), pp. 1197–1210. doi: 10.1080/13691831003687667.

Findlay, A.M., Li, F.L.N., Jowett, A.J. and Skeldon R. (1996) 'Skilled international migration and the global city: a study of expatriates in Hong Kong', *Transactions of the Institute of British Geographers*, 21(1), pp. 49–61. doi: 10.2307/622923.

Frone, M.R., Russell, M. and Barnes, G.M. (1996) 'Work–family conflict, gender, and health-related outcomes: a study of employed parents in two community samples', *Journal of Occupational Health Psychology*, 1(1), pp. 57–69.

Greco, S. (2018) 'The role of family relationships in migration decisions: a reconstruction based on implicit starting points in migrants' justifications', *Migration Letters*, 15(1), pp. 33–44.

Houstoun, M., Kramer, R. and Barrett, J. (1984) 'Female predominance in immigration to the United States since 1930: a first look', *International Migration Review*, 18(4), pp. 908–963.

Hutchins, T. (2011) '"They told us in a curry shop": child–adult relations in the context of family migration decision-making', *Journal of Ethnic and Migration Studies*, 37(8), pp. 1219–1235. doi: 10.1080/1369183X.2011.590926.

Knowles, C. and Harper, D. (2009) *Hong Kong: Migrant Lives, Landscapes and Journeys*. University of Chicago Press.

Kofman, E. (2000) 'The invisibility of skilled female migrants and gender relations in studies of skilled migration in Europe', *International Journal of Population Geography*, 6: 45–59.

Korpela, M. (2018) 'Moving to paradise for the children's sake', *Migration Letters*, 15(1), pp. 55–65.

Kunz, S. (2020) 'A business empire and its migrants: Royal Dutch Shell and the management of racial capitalism', *Transactions of the Institute of British Geographers*, 45(2), pp. 377–391. doi: 10.1111/tran.12366.

Lämsä, A.-M., Heikkinen, S., Smith, M. and Tornikoski, C. (2017) 'The expatriate's family as a stakeholder of the firm: a responsibility viewpoint', *International Journal of Human Resource Management*, 28(20), pp. 2916–2935. doi: 10.1080/09585192.2016.1146785.

Lan, P.-C. (2011) 'White privilege, language capital and cultural ghettoisation: Western high-skilled migrants in Taiwan', *Journal of Ethnic and Migration Studies*, 37(10), pp. 1669–1693. doi: 10.1080/1369183X.2011.613337.

Leonard, P. (2010). *Expatriate Identities in Postcolonial Organizations: Working Whiteness*. Studies in Migration and Diaspora. Ashgate.

Ley, D. (2004) 'Transnational spaces and everyday lives', *Transactions of the Institute of British Geographers*, 29(2), pp. 151–164. doi: 10.1111/j.0020-2754.2004.00122.x.

Lundström, C. (2014) *White Migrations Gender, Whiteness and Privilege in Transnational Migration*. Palgrave Macmillan.

McNulty, Y. (2015) Acculturating non-traditional expatriates: a case study of single parent, overseas adoption, split family, and lesbian assignees. *International Journal of Intercultural Relations* 49, 278–293. https://doi.org/10.1016/j.ijintrel.2015.05.006.

McNulty, Y. and Brewster, C. (2017) 'Theorizing the meaning(s) of "expatriate": establishing boundary conditions for business expatriates', *International Journal of Human Resource Management* 28, 27–61. https://doi.org/10.1080/09585192.2016.1243567.

Michielin, F., Mulder, C.H. and Zorlu, A. (2008) 'Distance to parents and geographical mobility', *Population, Space and Place*, 14(4), pp. 327–345. doi: 10.1002/psp.509.

Ní Laoire, C. (2011) 'Narratives of "innocent Irish childhoods": return migration and intergenerational family dynamics', *Journal of Ethnic and Migration Studies*, 37(8), pp. 1253–1271. doi: 10.1080/1369183X.2011.590928.

Ní Laoire, C., Tyrrell, N. and Carpena-Méndez, F. (2012) 'Children and young people on the move: geographies of child and youth migration', *Geography*, 97(3), pp. 129–134.

Orellana, M.F. (2001) 'The work kids do: Mexican and Central American immigrant children's contributions to households and schools in California', *Harvard Educational Review*, 71(3), pp. 366–390. doi: 10.17763/haer.71.3.52320g7n21922hw4.

Parreñas, R.S. (2005) *Children of Global Migration: Transnational Families and Gendered Woes*. Stanford University Press.

Pedraza, S. (1991) 'Women and Migration: The Social Consequences of Gender', *Annual Review of Sociology*, 17, pp. 303–325.

Ryan, L. and Mulholland, J. (2014) 'Trading places: French highly skilled migrants negotiating mobility and emplacement in London', *Journal of Ethnic and Migration Studies*, 40(4), pp. 584–600. doi: 10.1080/1369183X.2013.787514.

Sander, M. (2016) *Passing Through Shanghai: Ethnographic Insights into the Mobile Lives of Expatriate Youths*. Heidelberg University Publishing.

Schapendonk, J., van Liempt, I., Schwarz, I. and Steel, G. (2018) 'Re-routing migration geographies: migrants, trajectories and mobility regimes', *Geoforum*, p. S0016718518301799. doi: 10.1016/j.geoforum.2018.06.007.

Skeggs, B. (2003) *Class, Self, Culture*. Routledge.

Spiegel, A. (2018) 'Gendered mobilities, gendered cosmopolitanism: male and female expatriate managers and their accompanying spouses', in Spiegel, A., Mense-Petermann, U. and Bredenkötter, B. (eds) *Expatriate Managers: The Paradoxes of Living and Working Abroad*. Routledge, pp. 103–133.

Suter, B. (2020) 'European corporate migrants in Chinese metropolises and the pacing of family mobility', in Amit, V. and Salazar, N.B. (eds) *Pacing Mobilities. Timing, Intensity, Tempo and Duration of Human Movements*. Berghahn, pp. 120–141.

Tanu, D. (2018) *Growing up in Transit: The Politics of Belonging at an International School*. Berghahn Books.

Thorne, B., Faulstich Orellana, M., Lam, W.S.E. and Chee, A. (2003) 'Raising children, and growing up, across national borders: comparative perspectives on age, gender, and migration.', in *Gender and U.S. Immigration: Contemporary Trends*. University of California Press, pp. 214–262.

Toader, A. and Dahinden, J. (2018) 'Family configurations and arrangements in the transnational mobility of early-career academics: does gender make twice the difference?', *Migration Letters*, 15(1), pp. 67–84. doi: 10.33182/ml.v15i1.339.

Walsh, K. (2006) "Dad says I'm tied to a shooting star!' Grounding (research on) British expatriate belonging', *Area*, 38(3), pp. 268–278. doi: 10.1111/j.1475-4762.2006.00687.x.

Walsh, K. (2018) *Transnational Geographies of The Heart: Intimate Subjectivities in a Globalising City*. Wiley.

Waters, J.L. (2006) 'Geographies of cultural capital: education, international migration and family strategies between Hong Kong and Canada', *Transactions of the Institute of British Geographers*, 31(2), pp. 179–192. doi: 10.1111/j.1475-5661.2006.00202.x.

Willis, K.D. and Yeoh, B.S.A. (2000) 'Gender and transnational household strategies: Singaporean migration to China', *Regional Studies*, 34(3), pp. 253–264. doi: 10.1080/00343400050015096.

Yang, N., Chen, C.C., Choi, J. and Zou, Y. (2000) 'Sources of work–family conflict: a Sino–U.S. comparison of the effects of work and family demands', *Academy of Management Journal*, 43(1). https://doi.org/10.5465/1556390.

Yeoh, B.S.A. and Khoo, L.-M. (1998) 'Home, work and community: skilled international migration and expatriate women in Singapore', *International Migration*, 36(2), pp. 159–186. doi: 10.1111/1468-2435.00041.

Yeoh, B.S.A. and Willis, K. (2005) 'Singaporean and British transmigrants in China and the cultural politics of "contact zones"', *Journal of Ethnic and Migration Studies*, 31(2), pp. 269–285. doi: 10.1080/1369183042000339927.

15. Not as safe as houses: experiences of domestic violence among international migrant women
Cathy McIlwaine

INTRODUCTION

It is widely acknowledged that international migration processes can profoundly shape and be shaped by intersectional gendered power relations (Herrera, 2013). Negotiations around gender norms and practices play out transnationally and locally across multiple spheres, from the state to labour markets, but are crucially centred within households. Yet the nature of such negotiations varies intersectionally, but also according to whether women move independently or with partners, as workers or for marriage, or as victims/survivors of trafficking and smuggling (Yeoh and Ramdas, 2014). In destination contexts, migrant households can act as arenas of refuge from wider societal hostilities and discrimination as well as places where some re-negotiation of gender norms might occur (Boehm, 2008). Yet, they may also become domains where hierarchies of gendered power, wider forms of structural violence linked to migration regimes, and unfree labour relationships within households, may lead to violence and abuse (Huang and Yeoh, 2007). Although migrant women are vulnerable to multiple forms of domestic violence, the incidence of abuse is not always routinely higher than for non-migrants. Indeed, there are dangers in assuming that domestic violence is higher among migrants, as this is often linked with arguments that blame such violence on the cultures of the societies from where women migrate (see Chapter 4, this *Handbook*, for an alternative discussion of violence). This neglects the gendered, racialised, structural and institutional inequalities of immigration processes that contribute to the incidence of abuse that are experienced in intersectional ways (Sokoloff and Dupont, 2005). These wider structures of power and control influence whether and how women seek support, as well as the nature of assistance made available for survivors by the state and civil society (Erez et al., 2009). Bearing these issues in mind, this chapter explores a series of key debates around delineating domestic abuse among international migrants, also exploring its prevalence, its diversity and multidimensionality, the core drivers underlying its incidence, as well as barriers to reporting. While the discussion draws on debates among international migrants in a wide range of contexts, it also draws empirically where relevant on recent research with international migrant women in London.[1]

SITUATING DOMESTIC VIOLENCE AMONG INTERNATIONAL MIGRANT WOMEN

According to the 1993 United Nations (UN) Declaration of the Elimination of Violence against Women, domestic violence is a specific form of gender-based violence against women and girls. Here, violence refers broadly to physical, sexual or psychological acts of harm, including the threat of violence, coercion and arbitrary detention in private and public spheres that include the family, community and the state. The declaration also identifies dowry-related violence, marital rape, female genital mutilation and other traditional practices harmful to women, as well as violence related to exploitation (UN Women, 2015). Most domestic violence against women and girls takes psychological, physical, sexual, financial and emotional forms within the home, perpetrated by male intimate partners. However, it can also be committed by other household members of different genders and sexualities, including parents, siblings, grandparents, extended kin as well as employers. Femicide, which refers to the intentional murder of women because they are women, is also a key dimension of domestic violence. While femicides are often associated with the public sphere, the World Health Organization (WHO, 2012) also identifies 'intimate femicide' where a woman is killed by a former or current intimate partner; 'honour'-related murders relating to murders of a girl or woman by a family member because of an assumed transgression to family reputation; and dowry femicide where newly married women are killed over conflicts linked with dowries by family members.

Domestic violence, as a specific form of gender-based violence, can also be perpetrated against men or those with gender non-conforming identities. However, most research focuses on heterosexual, cis-gender women as they disproportionately experience such violence at the hands of men. Yet it is important to be aware of heterosexism and to acknowledge that lesbian, gay, bisexual, transgender, queer and intersex (LGBTQI+) migrants also experience domestic violence, even if this is only recently being acknowledged and reported (see Chapter 17, this *Handbook* for a discussion of migration amongst LBGTQI communities). Indeed, there is a lack of research on the experiences of domestic violence among these groups in general, and especially among migrants, with most work focusing instead on the structural violence exercised by the state through immigration control that creates precarious legal status (Lee, 2019 on queer and trans migrants in Canada).

Certain types of migrant women have been identified as especially vulnerable to gender-based violence, such as refugees and migrant workers, and especially domestic workers (see Chapter 2, this *Handbook*) according to the Beijing Platform for Action, with child, early and forced marriage as well as trafficking identified as specific forms of violence against women in themselves (UN Women, 2015). Different forms of violence are also associated with specific migrant and minoritised groups as forms of 'culturally specific abuse'. For example, so-called 'honour-based violence' that is usually associated with families of South Asian origin is defined as violence perpetrated against women where the main justification 'is the protection of a value system predicated on norms and traditions concerned with "honour"' (Gill and Brah, 2014, p. 73). The term itself is widely contested as a misnomer, as it is deeply dishonourable to perpetrate violence, and because of the culturally essentialist connotations. This relates to the fact that it is all too easy to blame an amorphous idea of 'culture' as a cause of gender-based violence, when in reality it is often linked with the ways that gender inequalities intersect with structural exclusions and discrimination in cultural ways (see below).

Indeed, debates around what constitutes domestic violence vary across cultures and countries, often bolstered by prejudicial perceptions of migrants and minoritised groups (Gonçalves and Matos, 2016). It is important to acknowledge migrant women's experiences of domestic violence across a transnational continuum and across their life-course rather than focus only on their destination contexts. Experiences back home may influence how women delineate domestic violence, especially in relation to psychological violence and coercion. For example, research from my Brazilian migrant project in London has shown that women had been socialised into accepting certain types of abuse (McIlwaine and Evans, 2018). For example,

Valentina, who was in her fifties and who had settled in London in 2007, noted: 'I didn't even realise that it was violence because as I was used to hearing the stories from my grandmother, from my mother, my cousins and my sisters who went through this; for me that wasn't even abuse, it was normal, for me it was part of every marriage.' It was often only through engagements with service providers when women sought help for other issues that they began to realise that they were suffering from domestic violence (McIlwaine and Evans, 2020).

However, care must be taken in situating domestic violence as an individual behavioural issue and portraying women as helpless victims (Burman and Chantler, 2005). Indeed, an individualist approach entails a damaging tendency to naturalise and pathologise experiences of gendered violence against migrant and minoritised women as being inherent to their home and/or group cultures in religious, ethnic, racial and nationality terms (Erez et al., 2009). While there is an ongoing debate around the role of culture in explaining domestic violence, there is very limited evidence that certain ethnic or national cultures generate and facilitate intimate partner violence (Menjívar and Salcido, 2002). Of course, there are different social and cultural geographies of domestic violence rooted within variations in gendered power inequalities, and which influence experiences and help-seeking (Reina et al., 2013). In turn, understanding the cultures of migrant communities can be extremely valuable in supporting women (O'Neal and Beckman, 2016). However, blaming certain cultures for being more prone to violence ignores how migrants and ethnic groups also experience systemic material inequalities, gender, racial and ethnic discrimination, which contributes to its preponderance among certain groups. It can also further marginalise migrant women as 'victim others' while stigmatising migrant men as 'barbaric others'. Furthermore, the emphasis on certain types of violence, such as honour killings, can shift attention away from other forms of more commonly occurring types of gender-based violence, thus perpetuating their normalisation (Montoya and Rolandsen Agustín, 2013).

A culturally essentialist interpretation of domestic violence therefore underplays the complex challenges faced by migrant women through their location within a matrix of power from an intersectional viewpoint (Collins, 2009). Indeed, intersectionality has taken centre stage in many recent analyses of women migrants, such that they have been identified as potentially 'the new quintessential intersectional subject' (Bastia, 2014, p. 240). Crenshaw's (1991) classic work on intersectionality explicitly refers to immigration status as influencing experiences of domestic violence among African American women in the United States as part of their racial identity. In turn, this situates women's oppression at the intersections of racial, ethnic, class, sexual orientation, and other systems of power. Yet, while this work has been crucial in acknowledging the diversity of women's experiences of oppression and domestic violence, some have emphasised the need to separate immigration status and racial identity, and to focus on social location over individual identities (Sokoloff, 2008). This has revolved around the importance of challenging the notion that immigration is a variable within constructing a racial identity, but rather is part of a complex process of subordination that fundamentally shapes domestic violence (Erez et al., 2009). Therefore, migrant women have diverse racial, ethnic, class and sexual orientation identities that are further affected by the ways in which migration itself can be a violent process. Indeed, domestic violence is part of a wider system of violence that shapes family life for migrant women who experience abuse within their communities and from wider society (Sokoloff and Dupont, 2005). In turn, while cultural differences should be acknowledged, they do not explain domestic violence among immigrant women who are situated within wider processes of colonialism, state power and global migration dynamics (Sokoloff, 2008) (as elaborated below).

PREVALENCE OF DOMESTIC VIOLENCE AMONG MIGRANT WOMEN

Migrant women, like non-migrant women, experience domestic violence through an intersectional prism. While both groups of women may experience a range of diverse and overlapping types of domestic violence over their life-course, there remains considerable debate over whether such violence is more prevalent among migrant communities compared with their non-migrant counterparts. Indeed, it is essential not to 'hyper-fixate on gendered violence as representative of these communities' (Fluri and Piedalue, 2017, p. 541). Meaningful comparisons between migrant and non-migrant communities are difficult to carry out in light of underreporting and related data collection challenges. Also, many surveys among migrant communities focus only on intimate partner violence, are often small-scale, and do not systematically compare migrants' experiences with the population as a whole. Furthermore, there is much greater focus on migrants from various countries of the Global South who have migrated to North America and Europe, with much less attention paid to South–South and intra-regional movements. Given the challenges, it is not surprising that rates of prevalence reflect huge variations. For example, a systematic review of 24 studies between 2003 and 2013 on intimate partner violence victimisation among immigrant women in the United States and Europe reported prevalence ranging from between 17 per cent and 70.5 per cent (Gonçalves and Matos, 2016).

Within these broad patterns, there are also variations according to country and types of violence. For example, a study in Spain among 1607 migrant women from Ecuador, Morocco and Romania showed that 16 per cent of Ecuadorian, 11 per cent of Moroccan, and 9 per cent of Romanian women experienced intimate partner violence in the previous year (Torrubiano-Dominguez and Vives-Cases, 2013). In terms of types of violence, psychological intimate partner violence tends to be the most widely experienced among migrants. For instance, in a study among 495 women of Korean descent in the United States, 27 per cent reported psychological aggression by a partner over the past year, with 17 reporting sexual coercion, 2 per cent experiencing physical assault, and 1 per cent another injury (Liles et al., 2012). In my own research on the Brazilian migrant project in London with 175 women, 82 per cent had experienced gender-based violence in their lifetime, with almost half suffering emotional/psychological violence, followed by physical violence (38 per cent), and sexual violence (14 per cent) (McIlwaine and Evans, 2018). Almost a third of this was domestic violence (30 per cent), with a quarter perpetrated by an intimate partner (McIlwaine and Evans, 2020). In my London migrant project with 50 migrant women survivors with insecure immigration status in London from 22 different countries, 78 per cent experienced psychological violence within the home, 68 per cent suffered physical violence perpetrated by intimate partners, 62 per cent reported financial abuse, and 46 per cent sexual violence (McIlwaine et al., 2019).

However, the key debate is not so much about variances in prevalence among migrant women from different countries and nationalities, but about whether they are more likely to experience domestic violence compared with those born in destination contexts. It is often claimed that migrant women are more vulnerable to domestic violence than non-migrants;

for example, it has been reported in the European context that rates of gendered violence are higher among non-citizen women (European Union Agency for Fundamental Rights, 2014). However, the opposite is the case in other contexts. For example, Wright and Benson (2010) explore the notion of the 'immigrant or Latino paradox' at the neighbourhood level in Chicago, noting that those with higher concentrations of immigrants have lower incidence of intimate partner violence. In another study comparing Mexican migrants across generations in El Paso, Texas, family violence was substantially lower among first-generation Mexicans compared with 1.5, second- and third-generation Americans (Curry et al., 2018). Yet it is also important to note that although incidence is not necessarily higher, women's risks and vulnerabilities are exacerbated by inequalities inherent in the immigration system (Menjívar and Salcido, 2002). These are further compounded by a host of factors around language competencies, insecure immigration status, social isolation, institutional racism, lack of welfare support, and fear of reporting that can make migrant women more unsafe vis-à-vis their non-migrant counterparts (O'Neill and Beckman, 2016). In addition, while the degree of violence may be similar among migrant and non-migrant groups, the severity and multiplicity of violence may be more marked (Sokoloff, 2008), and the intersections with other forms of structural and symbolic violence more intense (Dominguez and Menjívar, 2014).

DIVERSITIES OF DOMESTIC VIOLENCE AMONG MIGRANT WOMEN

Turning to the diverse nature of domestic violence among migrant women, as noted above, domestic abuse extends beyond intimate partner violence to include that perpetrated by other household members, and can occur beyond the confines of the home. Certain types of migration are themselves forms of gendered violence and/or create circumstances that make women migrants particularly vulnerable to domestic violence. While the discussion focuses on the multiplicity of the types of domestic violence experienced by migrant women, their multiple identities and social locations must also be taken into account in mutually intersecting ways from an intersectional perspective.

Focusing first on domestic violence experienced by migrant women in general who have moved either independently or as part of wider family migration processes among co-nationals, a key characteristic is its multiplicity. The incidence of domestic violence is rarely a one-off occurrence (Walby and Towers, 2017), and invariably entails a series of complex overlapping events and types that take place over space, across borders and over time. Returning to my Brazilian migrant project in London, a huge range of different types of gender-based violence were identified, much of which was based in the home. In five focus groups conducted with 15 women and six men, a total of 18 different types of gendered violence were identified, most of which was intimate partner violence. These included forced detention, jealousy, defamation, stalking, moral aggression, femicide, financial abuse and gender stereotyping. Interviews with women revealed similar diversity. One woman, Cristina, 37, originally from São Paulo and who arrived in London in 2009, spoke of how she had experienced 21 different types, including being kicked, slapped, throttled, controlled, defamed, stalked, and threatened with a knife and scissors, all by her former partner (McIlwaine and Evans, 2018).

Even within one broad type of domestic violence such as psychological abuse, there are multiple forms among migrant women survivors from different contexts and backgrounds and nationalities (Erez et al., 2009; Pearce and Sokoloff, 2013). For example, in my London migrant project, a huge range of types of psychological domestic violence were identified, revolving mainly around coercive control and manipulation linked to imprisonment at home, domestic servitude and verbal abuse. For example, Mona, 41, from Libya (with a Moroccan passport) was prevented by her husband from going out with her friends, speaking with her family and leaving home without the Islamic headscarf. These types of violence were often reinforced through 'tech abuse', where technologies are exploited to harass or control women, such as inserting spyware into mobile phones (McIlwaine et al., 2019).

Psychological violence intersects with other forms of violence, especially economic and financial abuse, which was experienced by 62 per cent of women in my London migrant study. This invariably entailed partners refusing to give any money to their wives and children for food and rent, controlling or refusing access to bank accounts or welfare benefits, as well as taking out loans in women's names without their knowledge. Estela, 31, from Mexico, for example, arrived in London with a domestic service visa but was coerced into marrying her boyfriend when she fell pregnant, in order to remain in the country when her employers refused to renew her visa. Estela spoke of how he withheld welfare support earmarked for them as a family: 'He was being paid housing benefit at that time and spent all the money ... I had to pay all the rent and was frustrated with the fact that I have to pay all the expenses and have the baby' (McIlwaine et al., 2019, p. 8). Economic abuse and control of family finances as core dimensions of intimate partner violence were also reported among West African migrants in Australia (Ogunsiji et al., 2012).

Sexual violence is another important type of abuse perpetrated by intimate partners, even if it is not always treated as rape by migrants themselves. For example, West African migrant women in the United States identified sexual abuse, but most accepted it as part of marriage (Akinsulure-Smith et al., 2013). In my London migrant study, although half of the women experienced sexual violence, several service providers noted that many only accepted this as violence after they had disclosed other forms. For example, a service provider stated:

> Because almost every single rape case is that we'll ask, 'Did you experience rape at the hands of this perpetrator?' They'll say 'No!' And then we'll say, 'Were you ever forced to have sex when you didn't want to?' 'Yes!' And then we say, 'That is rape!' and they [say] 'No, no! Because he is my husband! It is part of my obligations to provide that for him! So, I don't see that something he did to me, that is just part of my job.' (McIlwaine et al., 2019, p. 10)

Non-intimate partner domestic violence among migrants takes many different forms. One important form relates to ex-partners in situations where they continue to harass their partners after separation. In a study in Canada, prevalence of former partner violence was very high among both immigrants (61 per cent) and non-immigrants (61.5 per cent of women) (Du Mont et al., 2012). Drawing on my London migrant project, Estela (see above) recalled how her ex-husband continued to harass her after 18 months of separation: 'I didn't know what to do, I was so anxious I could hardly endure it, I cried all the time of anxiety. I felt that he would come back and that again it was going to be the same!' (McIlwaine et al., 2019, p. 10).

Other types of domestic violence are very explicitly linked with the immigration process itself. Indeed, it is now widely acknowledged that immigration status can become a powerful tool of manipulation and abuse on the part of intimate partners with secure status over those without (Erez et al., 2009; O'Neal and Beckman, 2016; Voolma, 2018). This means that state practices and immigration law closely interact to 'equip perpetrators with a powerful tool to oppress minoritized women further, but it also indicates how state structures thereby come to impact directly on women's distress' (Burman and Chantler, 2005, p. 59). This instrument of domination can be used by partners from the same and different backgrounds, with the power differentials especially marked in the latter. Addressing the former, in my Brazilian migrant project in London, a service provider noted: 'if the woman is in this country "illegally", and the husband is "legal", he will do whatever he wants with her, because she is at his mercy' (McIlwaine and Evans, 2020, p. 106). In my London migrant study, this violence was sometimes referred to by service providers as 'status VAWG' (violence against women and girls) or 'bureaucratic abuse'. For example, Aisha, 33, from India, who had a spouse visa, recalled how her husband (with British citizenship) threw her out of their house, telling her to return home and that he had only married her to appease his parents because he was gay: 'After he cancelled my [spouse] visa, he booked my ticket, he called me and said "don't come to my house, I cancelled your visa, you are illegal in this country"' (McIlwaine et al., 2019, p. 7). Being on a spouse/partner visa meant that Aisha, and many others, had no recourse to public funds (NRPF), meaning that she could not access any state benefits or support (see Anitha, 2010; also Kim et al., 2017 for similar processes in the United States).

Aisha's case also constitutes a form of 'transnational marriage abandonment' identified as a key dimension of domestic violence primarily but not exclusively among those of Asian origin. This involved women being maliciously ousted from their marital household in the destination context, as in Aisha's experience, or where they are deceived into visiting relatives back home and subsequently abandoned, or when a woman marries on the basis of a promise of sponsorship for migration that never materialises (Anitha et al., 2018). In my London migrant study, this was identified by half the service providers, primarily those working with South Asian, Middle Eastern and North African women. In one case, a man from Kurdistan took his wife back to her family, returning to London without her after taking her passport and belongings, and subsequently cutting all ties and cancelling her visa on grounds that she had divorced him. These women are further stigmatised back home through rejection from their communities as they battle to seek recourse across two legal systems (McIlwaine et al., 2019).

Transnational marriage abandonment is also a specific form of so-called 'honour-based' violence linked to dowries, forced marriages, domestic servitude and other potentially harmful practices. These are especially complex as they are often perpetrated by extended family members with or without the complicity of the intimate partner (Abraham, 2002 on the United States). In my London migrant study, several service providers reported the prevalence of domestic servitude by extended family and partners, as noted by a woman from India:

> My husband and in-laws were always controlling and they treated me like a slave ... [They were] always disrespectful and my in-laws behaviour was intolerable sometimes. Physically also they hit me. They threaten me if I said about reporting them to social services; they will deport me to my country and take my daughter from me. (McIlwaine et al., 2019, pp. 10–11)

While these types of domestic violence are usually associated with South Asian migrants, they are also experienced by migrant women from a range of different backgrounds. For example, in London, a Latin American service provider spoke of forced abortions and marriages within their community, including young women being made homeless in cases where protecting the honour of the family was more important than the rights of the women (McIlwaine et al., 2019, p. 12). It is also important not to essentialise or overstate this type of violence. Montoya and Rolandsen Agustín (2013) note in relation to Europe that 'honour' killings among migrant and minoritised groups are subject to outrage and specific legislation, despite the fact that 'everyday' domestic murders among all populations are much more widespread.

Much of this discussion on 'status VAWG' has focused on different aspects of 'marriage-related migration' and 'spousal migration', which refers to 'all situations where marriage plays a substantial role in an individual's migration' (Charsley et al., 2012, p. 864). Yet, as noted above, it is when female marriage migrants depend on their sponsor for their immigration status that abuses are most marked (Erez et al., 2009). Even within this group, there are huge variations depending on nationality, citizenship status of sponsors, and immigration policies of country of origin and destination. In relation to Indian migrants in the United States, for example, Kapur et al. (2017) note that abused marriage migrants sponsored by US citizens, and permanent residents, have more rights and safeguards than their more vulnerable counterparts sponsored with more insecure visas. Furthermore, when marriage migration entails partnerships between different nationalities, power asymmetries and abuse are often intensified. This often refers to women migrating as part of what Constable (2005) calls 'marrying up' through heterosexual marriage as part of 'global spatial hypergamy', entailing movement from poorer to wealthier countries. Such marriages can result in intersectional abuses undergirded by racism. In my London migrant study, Estela from Mexico, who ended up marrying her Portuguese boyfriend to secure her status, discussed not only the physical violence but also the racist tropes that he consistently used in verbal attacks, and especially when she reported him to the authorities. She said, 'he tells me "how is it possible that a small and ugly Third Worlder [sic] has done this to me?" He thinks he's of the first world because he is Portuguese/I'm Third World because I come from Mexico.' However, it is also important to acknowledge that although marriage migrants, and especially dependents on sponsors, are vulnerable to multiple forms of domestic violence, they also have agency (Kim, 2010). Indeed, exercising agency is important in relation to all types of migration for marriage, regardless of nationality (see Abraham, 2002; Chaudhuri et al., 2014 on South Asians in the US) (see below).

Examining domestic violence among marriage migrants also highlights the debate around the blurred boundaries between domestic servitude and migrant domestic workers, where the latter are paid to carry out reproductive tasks in the home and the former are not (Kim, 2010; Piper and Roces, 2003). This leads to a consideration of domestic violence by non-family members that occurs within the space of the home. There is a huge literature on the nature of exploitative working practices among female migrant domestic workers globally that documents the myriad abuses they experience in their workplaces (Hondagneu-Sotelo, 2001; Parreñas, 2015; Yeoh et al., 1999). Much research has focused on abuse at the hands of employers and by receiving states, with the latter being conceived as structural violence, or what Parreñas et al. (2020) call 'slow violence' in relation to precarious work and unfree labour. As live-in migrant domestic workers occupy the liminal space between the workplace and their home, direct forms of violence against them perpetrated by male and female employers constitutes domestic violence. While this violence is invariably gendered, it is also deeply intersectional across racial, class and nationality grounds, reflecting insidious micro- and macro-level power relations and perpetrated under the guise of being 'one of the family' (Huang and Yeoh, 2007). Indeed, the femicide or 'feminicide' (where the state is actively involved in producing and maintaining the killing) of migrant domestic workers is gaining increasing attention around the world. With reference to Lebanon and Bahrain, Al-Hindi (2020) discusses the increasing numbers of deaths of migrant domestic workers, mainly from

Ethiopia, Sri Lanka and the Philippines, linked with the *kafala* (sponsorship) system and where the murders are often passed off as suicides.

While largely beyond the scope of this chapter, it is also important to recognise that various forms of forced labour, servitude and slavery which entail and overlap with the trafficking of women into domestic and sex work in particular, make women extremely vulnerable to domestic (and other forms of) violence. Violence among migrant domestic and sex workers is largely produced through exploitative labour relations that play out within the household sphere (Zimmerman et al., 2011). In my London migrant project, a former trans woman sex worker, Nina, from Brazil spoke of physical and sexual abuse on the part of clients and her boyfriend within her home (McIlwaine et al., 2019). In my Brazilian migrant research, Sabrina, 44 from Ceará, was brought to London by a Brazilian family to work as a nanny. Although they paid for flights, Sabrina entered on a tourist visa which subsequently expired, and her bosses confiscated her passport. In addition to working as a nanny, she was expected to clean their house, and work for their cleaning business, all for £100 per week. As well as being imprisoned in the house and only allowed out only to work, she was sexually abused by her male boss (McIlwaine and Evans, 2018). As with the governance of migrant domestic work, state migration regimes are primary drivers of violence among these workers, and among migrants more broadly.

DRIVERS OF DOMESTIC VIOLENCE AMONG MIGRANT WOMEN

While the root causes of gender-based violence are deep-seated gendered power inequalities based on patriarchal hierarchies (McIlwaine, 2013), these strongly interrelate with structural and symbolic violence (Dominguez and Menjívar, 2014). They play out in multiscalar ways at individual, local, national and transnational scales as part of unequal global systems that situate migrant women in the lowest echelons (Fluri and Piedalue, 2017; McIlwaine et al., 2020). Not only is the migration process inherently violent, but violence is a major driver of migration across a 'spatial continuum of violence' (Menjívar and Walsh, 2019). This feeds into feminist interpretations of how gendered violence must be understood across a continuum of types, where indirect forms of routinised gendered exploitation and discrimination bolster direct types of physical, sexual and psychological gendered violence (Kelly, 1988). It should also be noted that while a multiscalar and geopolitical approach has been developed in relation to understanding gendered and especially domestic violence from the scale of the body to the global power structure (Pain, 2014), there has been less work done among migrant women. It is therefore important to understand the transnational continuum of gender-based violence in relation to migrant women (McIlwaine and Evans, 2020). This must entail acknowledgement of how the migrant journey incorporates multiple forms of direct and indirect gendered violence that should be understood through an intersectional prism, foregrounding the structural and symbolic violence of immigration regimes, and wider processes of racism and discrimination, as part of a challenge to culturally essentialist arguments.

Indeed, it is now commonplace to conceptualise the consequences of immigration laws as forms of structural and symbolic violence, with the gendered nature of these being increasingly acknowledged (Dominguez and Menjívar, 2014). Following Galtung and others, structural violence encompasses historically embedded inequalities and exploitation in labour markets, education systems that result in poverty and discrimination; while symbolic violence, following Bourdieu, denotes the actions that have negative consequences based on internalised and legitimised expressions of sexism, racism and class power (Bourgois, 2001). While structural and symbolic violence are inherently gendered, they underpin and bolster direct gender-based violence against female migrants. However, most analyses from this perspective focus on women's experiences after migration, with much less research on how such violence plays out across the migration trajectory.

It is essential to acknowledge that gender-based violence can initiate women's migration in the first place (Menjívar and Walsh, 2019). This might refer to the specific reasons why women migrate, such as the symbolic violence generated due to stigma following divorce, or the gendered structural violence of exploitative labour processes (Menjívar and Walsh, 2019). Drawing on the notion of 'feminised onward precarity', which captures the spatio-temporal precarious circumstances embedded across the migrant journey, I have explored these processes in my earlier study (Towards Visibility) conducted with Latin American migrants who have ended up in London after migrating via Spain (McIlwaine and Bunge, 2016, 2019). For example, 46-year-old Miriam from Ecuador spoke of how the social and familial opprobrium she faced after divorcing twice by the age of 20 led her to migrate to Spain. Another Ecuadorian woman, Helena, discussed widespread labour discrimination in her job in a machine-knitting workshop, and that lack of social protection led her to move to Spain (McIlwaine, 2020). In what Pearce and Sokoloff (2013) refer to as 'contexts of exit', the political, economic and social circumstances that women leave fundamentally shape their departure, which are in turn influenced by the specificities of women's identity positions.

However, direct forms of gender-based and especially domestic violence are also important in driving migration. In the context of Central America, femicides have been identified as forcing women – especially from Honduras, Guatemala and El Salvador, which have the highest rates in the region – to attempt to migrate to the United States (Parish, 2017). While gang violence is often blamed for femicides, other forms of gender-based violence have also led women to flee north. The structural violence of post-conflict poverty, inequality and institutional neglect, combined with symbolic violence of patriarchal and racial subjugation, has created a toxic situation where domestic violence is endemic and perpetrated with impunity (Obinna, 2020). Tragically, these women migrants then face more gendered violence on their journeys by intimate partners and others as they traverse north (Menjívar and Walsh, 2019). Similarly, Calderón-Jaramillo et al. (2020) note that Venezuelan migrants who have fled the humanitarian crisis back home and crossed the border into Colombia cite high levels of domestic violence prompting their migration. They then experienced further gender-based violence on the journey and when they arrived in Colombia. In my Brazilian migrant study London, the vast majority (77 per cent) reported having experienced gender-based violence prior to migration, of which a third was perpetrated by intimate partners and other family members, with a further 20 per cent by friends (McIlwaine and Evans, 2018).

On arrival, in the 'context of reception' (Pearce and Sokoloff, 2013), some migrant women experience an intensification in domestic violence. Recognising that migrant women do not necessarily experience more gendered violence than non-migrants, the challenges faced by many due to their insecure immigration status, labour exploitation and widespread precarity, can lead to escalations in domestic violence. In my Brazilian migrant study in London, more than half of women who suffered gender-based violence in Brazil also experienced it again in the United Kingdom (UK). For some, this was at the hands of their existing partner with whom they had migrated; while for others, the violence was perpetrated by men who they met after settling in London. For example, Juliana, from Paraná, fled her violent and alcoholic husband in Brazil, only to meet another Brazilian man in London who subjected her to various forms of emotional, physical and sexual violence, including attempts to kill her following their marriage (McIlwaine and Evans, 2018). Gender roles often become destabilised during migration and settlement as female and male migrants change their occupational status, providing fertile ground for domestic violence to take place as hegemonic masculinities come under threat (Bui and Morash, 2008 on Vietnamese in the US; also McIlwaine, 2010). This must also be understood within the wider context of uneven global development, as Kim et al. (2017: 635) note in relation to Mexicans in the US: 'the challenges faced by female migrants are not *caused* by migration, but rather are the result of global systems of inequity'. This also relates to increasing calls for a decolonial perspective, to acknowledge how racialised, gendered and classed forms of oppression in colonial systems undergird migration processes and the resulting forms of gender-based violence that emerge (Lopes-Heimer, 2022). In relation to Maria Lugones's (2010) 'coloniality of gender', Mayblin and Turner (2021, p. 193) note how this 'shows alternative ways of considering how heteropatriarchal systems of gender and sexuality continue to be imposed and structure dispossession and violence globally'. These relations of power are also fundamental in understanding the nature of reporting among migrant women survivors of domestic violence, as discussed below.

REPORTING DOMESTIC VIOLENCE AMONG MIGRANT WOMEN

The large literature on the multiple barriers faced by migrant women in disclosing and reporting domestic violence focuses mainly on issues such as lack of information, isolation, immigration status, language competencies, and exclusion from criminal justice systems (Erez et al., 2009; O'Neal and Beckman, 2016). While there is a tendency within some of this literature to focus on individual barriers, it is also important to give weight to the role of immigration laws, welfare provision and domestic violence policies (Menjívar and Salcido, 2002; Voolma, 2018). Generally speaking, the immigration context in many countries of the Global North is inherently hostile, and based on the principle that migrants are a cheap source of labour to be used when required by capital, and neglected when they are no longer useful (Wills et al., 2010). In this context, while some provisions have been made for migrant women survivors in several countries such as Canada, Australia, New Zealand, the US and the UK, the burden of proof when seeking help is often so onerous that migrant women are actively dissuaded from reporting (Menjívar and Salcido, 2002).

Thus, informal reporting or disclosure, especially to friends and family, is more common than formal reporting (Rahmanipour et al., 2019), which is used as a last resort when women feel unable to cope with the abuse or have experienced multiple incidences of abuse (Vidales, 2010). In my Brazilian migrant study in London, more than half of women survivors did not report formally, stating that they thought nothing would be done (27 per cent); that they did not know how to report (15 per cent); because they felt community opprobrium (20 per cent); or as a result of feeling ashamed (9 per cent) (McIlwaine and Evans, 2018). Many aspects of women's reluctance are bound up in 'victim-shaming', which can be more intense among some migrant groups (Abraham, 2002; Rahmanipour et al., 2019). The notion of the 'home country as a frame of reference' (Menjívar and Salcido, 2002, p. 910) also plays an important role, particularly in the case of women who come from contexts where domestic violence is not taken seriously and where impunity for perpetrators is widespread. For example, in the Brazilian migrant research, Carolina spoke of not reporting her abusive partner because:

> the shame of it! I felt so bad, so humiliated! ... I didn't know how I was going to be treated here, because given that in my own country, in my own language, nobody had ever done anything to help me, here I thought, 'I'm nothing, I'm no one. They won't help me at all.' (McIlwaine and Evans, 2018, p. 26)

Erez et al. (2009, p. 48) refer to this as the 'abuse tolerant–intolerant continuum' in home cultures where, at one end, communities refuse to believe that domestic violence exists, and at the other end, it is treated as an unacceptable crime. They note that 65 per cent of women migrants in their sample in the United States stated that domestic violence was not treated as a crime. This continuum is further compounded by 'abuse-tolerant and privacy-affirmative perspectives' (p. 49) linked with shame and stigma, where women are expected to keep domestic violence either a secret or private and not to disclose to anyone, informally or formally.

As noted above, insecure immigration status plays a fundamental role in whether women report their experiences, as this question is linked with the fear of immigration enforcement. For example, in Los Angeles in the United States, analysis of calls to the police department and of Google searches found a 'chilling effect' resulting from the potential threat of immigration enforcement on Latino immigrant populations, who were less likely to report domestic violence (Muchow and Amuedo-Dorantes, 2020). This also emerges in qualitative research around the world from the perspective of migrant women who discuss being afraid of being deported, or because their intimate partner perpetrator has told them that they will be deported (Erez et al., 2009; Reina et al., 2013; Voolma, 2018). The same processes occur among migrant domestic workers, where survivors of abuse are unlikely to report abuse, both direct and indirect, because of their restricted immigration status and the 'extreme power of the employer' (Poinasamy, 2011, p. 97). In my London migrant study, a quarter of women cited fear of deportation as the main reason preventing reporting, followed by lack of access to information (18 per cent) and not knowing where to go (18 per cent). This was compounded by language barriers, fear of losing custody of their children, and fear of losing their home and/or income. Interactions with the police, while not uniformly negative, were characterised as favouring perpetrators, while migrant women were not believed, often as a result of language barriers which the women confronted (McIlwaine et al., 2019). In my Brazilian migrant study in London, for example, Maria spoke of ending up in a police cell overnight after reporting her husband's domestic abuse. As she did not speak English and had insecure status, he managed to persuade the police that she was the perpetrator (McIlwaine and Evans, 2020). Even when women do report, various legal barriers prevent them from securing welfare and judicial assistance, creating other forms of violence identified by Menjívar and Abrego (2012) as 'legal violence', where the state becomes complicit in the exclusion of migrants from support. Such 'legal violence' can also be conceptualised as a form of 'infrastructural violence', where much statutory support infrastructure actively and passively alienates migrants, and especially women survivors of gender-based violence (McIlwaine et al., 2021; McIlwaine and Evans, 2022). These processes are inherently racialised, classed and gendered (Erez et al., 2009).

CONCLUSION

This chapter has outlined some of the key issues that have emerged in research on the nature of domestic violence among international migrants in relation to identifying its prevalence, the diverse nature of such abuse, the main drivers that lead to its perpetration, and the challenges faced by migrant women in reporting it. Understanding of domestic violence must be situated within wider processes of the continuities and disruptions in gendered power relations, norms and practices among migrants, with abuse often constituting a key dimension of their family lives (Erez et al., 2009; McIlwaine, 2010; Sokoloff, 2008). However, domestic violence must also be positioned beyond the individual and household levels, and within multiscalar local and global structural relations (Fluri and Piedalue, 2017; Pain, 2014). In turn, explanations for the incidence of domestic violence among international migrants need to challenge culturally essentialist interpretations of 'other' migrant women and men, while laying the blame for abuse on the cultures of countries where migrants come from (Sokoloff and Dupont, 2005). Instead, the structural and symbolic violence experienced by women migrants across their migration trajectories fundamentally intersect with hierarchies of gendered power that lead to the perpetration of domestic abuse in multiple ways (Menjívar and Walsh, 2019). Domestic violence can lead women to migrate in the first place, they may experience abuse on their onward journeys, and this may intensify when they settle elsewhere. This abuse might be within the context of familial relations committed by intimate partners and other household members, as well as through exploitative and violent working relations, especially when immigration status is insecure and/or dependent on the perpetrators. Migrant women therefore often bear the brunt of geopolitical racialised gendered relations of power, as seen in the ways in which these intersect with structural and symbolic violence to intensify domestic violence, even if the incidence is not routinely higher than among non-migrants. Yet seeking and securing support as victims/survivors of domestic violence, while extremely challenging for all women, is exacerbated for migrant women by insecure immigration status, language competencies, and lack of information and social networks. This situation often allows perpetrators to act within impunity, sometimes conjoined to institutional racism on the part of the criminal justice system and welfare agencies (O'Neal and Beckman, 2016; Vidales, 2010). However, although they might not always have been recognised, migrant women do have rights, even if only in the eyes of international law rather than the legislative environments of individual destination countries. Furthermore, migrant women and migrant support organisations are fighting for the rights of these women to be upheld, such as the Step Up Migrant Women campaign[2] in the UK, of which my London migrant study discussed in this chapter was part. In the words of one of the migrants in this research who inspired the title of the report, they have 'the right to be believed' (McIlwaine et al., 2019).

ACKNOWLEDGEMENTS

I would like to thank the ESRC and Newton Fund for funding the Brazilian migrant project reported in this chapter (ES/N013247/1), and especially the People's Palace Projects, the Latin American Women's Rights Service, Yara Evans and Aline Littlejohn. I am also grateful to the Latin American Women's Rights Service and the Step Up Migrant Women campaign as partners in the London migrant women project funded by Lloyds Bank Foundation, particularly Lucila Granada and Illary Valenzuela-Oblitas. Finally, I would like to thank the Trust for London, which funded the Towards Visibility research, especially Diego Bunge.

NOTES

1. This research comprises two main projects. The first, referred to here as the Brazilian migrant project/study, entailed research exploring the nature, causes and responses to violence against women and girls among Brazilian migrant women in London and among women residing in the *favelas* of Maré in Rio de Janeiro, Brazil and conducted between 2016 and 2018 (the latter is not discussed here; see Krenzinger et al., 2018). In London, a survey with 175 Brazilian women was carried out, as well as 25 in-depth interviews, six focus groups (five with women and one with men), and interviews with 12 service providers (McIlwaine and Evans, 2018; McIlwaine et al., 2020).
    The second, referred to here as the London migrant project/study, aimed to examine the lives of migrant women who had experienced gender-based violence and insecure immigration status as part of a wider campaign, Step Up Migrant Women. It involved a survey with 50 migrant women from 22 countries, most of whom used services of specialist migrant organisations, semi-structured interviews with 11 migrant women, and a further ten with representatives from organisations supporting them, together with two focus groups (one with representatives and one with service users) (McIlwaine et al., 2019).
    I also make reference to another study, 'Towards Visibility', which explored the experiences of Latin American (female and male) migrants who had migrated to London from Latin America via other countries and mainly from Spain. This entailed a survey with 250 migrants from a range of Latin American countries, and 20 in-depth interviews (McIlwaine and Bunge, 2016, 2019; McIlwaine, 2020).
2. See https://stepupmigrantwomen.org/ (accessed 13 February 2021).

REFERENCES

Abraham, M. (2002) *Speaking the Unspeakable: Marital Violence among South Asian Immigrants in the United States*. New Brunswick, NJ: Rutgers University Press.
Akinsulure-Smith, A.M., Chu, T., Keatley, E., and Rasmussen, A. (2013) Intimate partner violence among West African immigrants, *Journal of Aggression, Maltreatment and Trauma*, 22, 109–126.
Al-Hindi, M. (2020) A comparative analysis of the femicide of migrant domestic workers in Bahrain and Lebanon, *Contemporary Challenges*, 1, 59–75.
Anitha, S. (2010) No recourse, no support: state policy and practice towards South Asian Women facing domestic violence in the UK, British Journal of Social Work, 40:2, 462–479.
Anitha, S., Yalamarty, H., and Roy, A. (2018) Changing nature and emerging patterns of domestic violence in global contexts, *Women's Studies International Forum*, 69, 67–75.
Bastia, T. (2014) Intersectionality, migration and development, *Progress in Development Studies*, 14:3, 237–248.
Boehm, D.A. (2008) "Now I am a man and a woman!": Gendered moves and migrations in a transnational Mexican community, *Latin American Perspectives*, 35:1, 16–30.
Bourgois, P. (2001) The power of violence in war and peace, *Ethnography*, 2:1, 5–34.
Bui, H., and Morash, M. (2008) immigration, masculinity, and intimate partner violence from the standpoint of domestic violence service providers and Vietnamese-origin women, *Feminist Criminology*, 3:3, 191–215.
Burman, E., and Chantler, K. (2005) Domestic violence and minoritisation, *International Journal of Law and Psychiatry*, 28:1, 59–74.
Calderón-Jaramillo, M., Diana Parra-Romero, D. Forero-Martínez, L.J., Royo, M., and Rivillas-García, J.C. (2020) Migrant women and sexual and gender-based violence at the Colombia–Venezuela border, *Journal of Migration and Health*, 1–2, 1–20.

Charsley, K., Storer-Church, B., Benson, M., and Van Hear, N. (2012) Marriage-related migration to the UK, *International Migration Review*, 46:4, 861–890.

Chaudhuri, S., Morash, M., and Yingling, J. (2014) Marriage migration, patriarchal bargains, and wife abuse: a study of South Asian women, *Violence Against Women*, 20:2, 141–161.

Collins, P.H. (2009) *Black Feminist Thought: Knowledge, Consciousness, and the Politics of Empowerment*. London: Routledge.

Constable, N. (2005) *Cross-Border Marriages: Gender and Mobility in Transnational Asia*. Philadelphia, PA: University of Pennsylvania Press.

Crenshaw, K. (1991) Mapping the margins: intersectionality, identity politics, and violence against women of color, *Stanford Law Review*, 43, 1241–1299.

Curry, T.R., Morales, M.C., Zavala, E., and Hernandez, J.L. (2018) Why is family violence lower among Mexican immigrants?, *Journal of Family Violence*, 33, 171–184.

Dominguez, S., and Menjívar, C. (2014) Beyond individual and visible acts of violence, *Women's Studies International Forum*, 44, 184–195.

Du Mont, J., Hyman, I., O'Brien, K., White, M.E, Odette, F., and Tyyskä, V. (2012) Factors associated with intimate partner violence by a former partner by immigration status and length of residence in Canada, *Annals of Epidemiology*, 22:11, 772–777.

Erez, E., Adelman, M., and Gregory, C. (2009) Intersections of immigration and domestic violence, voices of battered immigrant women, *Feminist Criminology*, 4, 32–56.

European Union Agency for Fundamental Rights (2014) *Violence against Women: An EU-Wide Survey*. Luxembourg: Publications Office of the European Union

Fluri, J.L., and Piedalue, A. (2017) Embodying violence: critical geographies of gender, race, and culture, Gender, Place *and* Culture, 24:4, 534–544.

Herrera, G. (2013) Gender and international migration: contributions and cross-fertilizations, Annual Review of Sociology, 39:1, 471–489.

Hondagneu-Sotelo, P. (2001) *Doméstica. Immigrant Workers Cleaning and Caring in the Shadows of Affluence*. Berkeley, CA: University of California Press.

Huang, S., and Yeoh, B.S.A. (2007) Emotional labour and transnational domestic work: the moving geographies of 'maid abuse' in Singapore, Mobilities, 2:2, 195–217.

Gill, A.K., and Brah, A. (2014) Interrogating cultural narratives about 'honour'-based violence, European Journal of Women's Studies, 21:1, 72–86.

Gonçalves, M., and Matos, M. (2016) Prevalence of violence against immigrant women: a systematic review of the literature, *Journal of Family Violence,* 31, 697–710.

Kapur, S., Zajicek, A., and Hunt, V. (2017) Immigration provisions in the Violence Against Women Act, *Journal of Women, Politics and Policy*, 38:4, 456–480.

Kelly, L. (1988) *Surviving Sexual Violence*. Oxford: Polity.

Kim, M. (2010) Gender and international marriage migration. *Sociology Compass*, 4:9, 718–731.

Kim, T., Draucker, C.B., Bradway, C., Grisso, J.A., and Sommers, M.S. (2017) Somos hermanas del mismo dolor (we are sisters of the same pain): intimate partner sexual violence narratives among Mexican immigrant women in the United States, *Violence Against Women*, 23(5): 623–642.

Krenzinger, M., Sousa Silva, E., McIlwaine, C., and Heritage, P. (eds) (2018) Dores que Libertam: Falas de Mulheres das Favelas sa Mare, no Rio de Janeiro sobre Violencias. Rio de Janeiro: Appris Editora.

Lee, E.O.J. (2019) Responses to structural violence: the everyday ways in which queer and trans migrants with precarious status respond to and resist the Canadian immigration regime, *International Journal of Child, Youth and Family Studies*, 10:1, 70–94.

Liles, S., Usita, P., Irvin, V., Hofstetter, C., Beeston, T., and Hovell, M. (2012) Prevalence and correlates of intimate partner violence among young, middle, and older women of Korean descent in California, *Journal of Family Violence*, 27:8, 801–811.

Lopes-Heimer, R.D.V. (2022) Travelling cuerpo-territorios: a decolonial feminist geographical methodology to conduct research with migrant women, *Third World Thematics: A TWQ Journal.* DOI: 10.1080/23802014.2022.2108130.

Lugones, M. (2010) Toward a decolonial feminism, *Hypatia*, 25:4, 742–759.

Mayblin, L., and Turner, J. (2021) *Migration Studies and Colonialism*. Polity Press: Cambridge.

McIlwaine, C. (2010) Migrant machismos: exploring gender ideologies and practices among Latin American migrants in London from a multi-scalar perspective, *Gender, Place and Culture*, 17:3, 281–300.
McIlwaine, C. (2013) Urbanization and gender-based violence: exploring the paradoxes in the global South. *Environment and Urbanization*, 25:1, 65–79.
McIlwaine, C. (2020) Feminized precarity among onward migrants in Europe, *Ethnic and Racial Studies*, 43:14, 2607–2625.
McIlwaine, C., and Bunge, D. (2016) *Towards Visibility: The Latin American Community in London*. London: Trust for London.
McIlwaine, C., and Bunge, D. (2019) Onward precarity, mobility and migration among Latin Americans in London, *Antipode*, 51:2, 601–619.
McIlwaine, C., and Evans, Y. (2018) *We Can't Fight in the Dark: Violence against Women and Girls (VAWG) among Brazilians in London*. London: King's College London.
McIlwaine, C., and Evans, Y. (2020) Urban violence against women and girls (VAWG) in transnational perspective, *International Development Planning Review* 42:1, 57–71.
McIlwaine, C., and Evans, Y. (2022) Navigating migrant infrastructure and gendered infrastructural violence: reflections from Brazilian Women in London, *Gender, Place and Culture*. https://doi.org/10.1080/0966369X.2022.2073335.
McIlwaine, C.J., Granada, L., and Valenzuela-Oblitas, I. (2019) *The Right to be Believed: Migrant Women Facing Violence Against Women and Girls (VAWG) in the 'Hostile Immigration Environment'*. London: Latin American Women's Rights Service.
McIlwaine, C., Krenzinger, M., Evans, Y., and Sousa Silva, E. (2020) Feminised urban futures, healthy cities and violence against women and girls (VAWG), in M. Keith and A. Aruska de Souza Santos (eds) *Urban Transformations and Public Health in the Emergent City*. Manchester: MUP Press, 55–78.
McIlwaine, C., Krenzinger, M., Rizzini Ansari, M., Evans, Y., and Sousa Silva, E. (2021) O direito à cidade de mulheres: uma análise sobre suas limitações a partir de violências infraestruturais de gênero contra brasileiras em Londres e na Maré, Rio de Janeiro, *Revista de Direito da Cidade*, 13:2, 954–981.
Menjívar, C., and Abrego, L.J. (2012) Legal violence: immigration law and the lives of central American immigrants, American Journal of Sociology, 117:5, 1380–1421.
Menjívar, C., and Salcido, O. (2002) Immigrant women and domestic violence: common experiences in different countries, *Gender and Society*, 16:6, 898–920.
Menjívar, C., and Walsh, S.D. (2019) Gender, violence and migration, in K. Mitchell, R. Jones and J.L. Fluri (eds) *Handbook on Critical Geographies of Migration*. Cheltenham, UK and Northampton, MA, USA: Edward Elgar Publishing, 45–57.
Montoya, C., and Rolandsen Agustín, L. (2013) The others of domestic violence: the EU and cultural framings of violence against women, *Social Politics*, 20:4, 534–557.
Muchow, A.N., and Amuedo-Dorantes, C. (2020) Immigration enforcement awareness and community engagement with police, *Journal of Urban Economics*, 117, 103253.
Obinna, D.N. (2020) Seeking sanctuary: Violence Against Women in El Salvador, Honduras, and Guatemala, *Violence Against Women*. DOI: 10.1177/1077801220913633.
Ogunsiji, O., Wilkes, L., Jackson, D., and Peters, K. (2012) Suffering and smiling: West African immigrant women's experience of intimate partner violence, *Journal of Clinical Nursing*, 21, 1659–1665.
O'Neal, E.N., and Beckman, L. (2016) Intersections of race, ethnicity, and gender: reframing knowledge surrounding barriers to social services among Latina intimate partner violence victims, *Violence Against Women*, 23, 643–665.
Pain, R. (2014) Everyday terrorism: connecting domestic violence global terrorism, *Progress in Human Geography*, 38, 531–550.
Parish, A. (2017) *Gender-Based Violence against Women: Both Cause for Migration and Risk along the Journey*. Washington, DC: Migration Policy Institute.
Parreñas, R.S. (2015) *Servants of Globalization*. Stanford, CA: Stanford University Press.
Parreñas, R.S., Kantachote, K., and Silvey, R. (2020) Soft violence: migrant domestic worker precarity and the management of unfree labour in Singapore, *Journal of Ethnic and Migration Studies*. DOI: 10.1080/1369183X.2020.1732614.

Pearce, S.C., and Sokoloff, N.J. (2013) This should not be happening in this country: private-life violence and immigration intersections in a U.S. gateway city, *Sociological Forum*, 28:4, 784–810.
Piper, Nicola, and Roces, Mina (eds) (2003) *Wife or Worker? Asian Women and Migration*. Lanham, MD: Rowman & Littlefield.
Poinasamy, K. (2011) Protecting migrant domestic workers in the UK, Gender *and* Development, 19:1, 95–104.
Rahmanipour, S., Kumar, S., and Simon-Kumar, R. (2019) Underreporting sexual violence among 'ethnic' migrant women, Culture, Health *and* Sexuality, 21:7, 837–852
Reina, A., Maldonado, M.M., and Lohman, B.J. (2013) Undocumented Latina networks and responses to domestic violence in a new immigrant gateway, *Violence Against Women*, 19:12, 1472–1497.
Sokoloff, N.J. (2008) Expanding the intersectional paradigm to better understand domestic violence in immigrant communities, *Critical Criminology*, 16, 229–255.
Sokoloff, N.J., and Dupont, I. (2005) Domestic violence at the intersections of race, class, and gender, *Violence against Women* 11:1, 38–64.
Torrubiano-Dominguez, J., and Vives-Cases, C. (2013) Application of the putting women first protocol in a study on violence against immigrant women in Spain. *Gaceta Sanitaria*, 27:6, 555–557.
UN Women (2015) *A Framework to Underpin Action to Prevent Violence against Women*. New York: UN Women.
Vidales, G.T. (2010) Arrested justice: the multifaceted plight of immigrant Latinas who faced domestic violence, *Journal of Family Violence*, 25, 533–544.
Voolma, H. (2018) 'I must be silent because of residency': barriers to escaping domestic violence in the context of insecure immigration status in England and Sweden, *Violence Against Women*, 24:15, 1830–1850.
Walby, S., and Towers, J. (2017) Measuring violence to end violence, Journal of Gender-Based Violence, 1:1, 11–31.
WHO (2012) *Understanding and Addressing Violence against Women: Femicide*. Geneva: WHO.
Wills, J., Datta, K., Evans, Y., Herbert, J., May, J., and McIlwaine, C. (2010) *Global Cities at Work*. London: Pluto.
Wright, E.M., and Benson, M.L. (2010) Immigration and intimate partner violence, Social Problems, 57:3, 480–503.
Yeoh, B.S.A., Huang, S., and Gonzalez, J. (1999) Migrant female domestic workers: debating the economic, social and political impacts in Singapore, *International Migration Review*, 33:1, 114–136.
Yeoh, B.S.A., and Ramdas, K. (2014) Gender, migration, mobility and transnationalism, Gender, Place *and* Culture, 21:10, 1197–1213.
Zimmerman, C., Hossain, M., and Watts, C. (2011) Human trafficking and health, *Social Science and Medicine*, 73:2, 327–335.

16. Academic mobility and the family
Yanbo Hao and Maggi W.H. Leung

INTRODUCTION

Academic mobility – studying, training and working in the academic field abroad – is a proliferating global phenomenon. This has stimulated a large number of education and migration/mobilities studies, which are dominated by two perspectives. The first focuses on mobile students or scholars (see Chapter 13, this *Handbook*). These individuals are presented mainly as rational individuals seeking human capital that can be translated into social distinctions, economic benefits and other forms of personal advancement. This focus has inspired a wealth of academic research on students' and scholars' motivations (e.g. Nilsson and Ripmeester, 2016; Zheng, 2014; Pawar et al., 2020) and experiences (e.g. Kronholz and Osborn, 2016; Bryła, 2015; Teichler and Janson, 2007). The second perspective emphasises the role of macro structures such as the state (e.g. Ye, 2016; Pan, 2013; Gillan et al., 2003), the broader political–economic system (e.g. Choudaha, 2017; Mok and Montgomery, 2021; Komljenovic and Robertson, 2017) and higher education or research institutions (e.g. Askehave, 2007; Kleibert, 2021; Findlay et al., 2017) in commodifying education, and promoting and regulating academic mobility flows. Less attention has been paid to the role of the key meso-level institution, namely the family, in this mobility field. This is not to say that we lack knowledge on the role of the family in academic mobility. As we show in the following literature review, research has documented, on the one hand, the importance of the family in facilitating or hindering academic mobility, and on the other hand, how the family is affected by academic mobility.[1] Yet, the family is rarely positioned at the centre of this body of work.

Our literature review is structured as follows. We begin by sketching the overall scope of the literature, which has an impact on how the family is conceptualised. We then present examples of works that predominantly consider the family as a factor contributing to or hindering academic mobility. The subsequent section looks at research that examines the impact of academic mobility on the family. We then unpack 'the family' and discuss a line of insightful research conducted from gendered or intersectional perspectives, which helps to decipher the unevenness of the academic mobility field. Finally, we pinpoint several blind spots in the literature and suggest a few directions for future studies.

MAPPING THE STUDY FIELD

A review of the publications on academic mobility shows the clear dominance of research conducted in the United States of America (USA), the United Kingdom (UK), Australia and Canada, which are the most popular host countries for international students (Gümüş et al., 2020). While this spatial focus can be justified because of the 'weight' of these study destinations, researchers including Lipura and Collins (2020) have criticised this bias in presuming such mobility to flow 'from East to West, South to North and non-English to English speaking contexts' (p. 353). They argue that most theories pertaining to student mobility have been formulated and tested in Western contexts, mostly by scholars from the UK; for example, Findlay (2010) and Findlay et al. (2012) on student mobility as transnational class reproduction, or Findlay (2010) in his theorisation on the supply and demand of international student mobility. This bias in the literature has also limited the overall conceptualisation of the relation between academic mobility and the family.

Indeed, the geography and directionalities of academic mobility are being constantly shaped or reshaped by global politics and the process of the marketisation of education. In the UK, for example, Brexit has led to a drop in the number of students from the European Union, while other countries – such as Germany and France – have become more popular due to their lower tuition fees and more favourable job markets for international graduates (Redden, 2016). Choudaha (2017) argues that the election of Donald Trump sent an anti-migration message to potential students that diverted them to more migration-welcoming countries such as Canada and Australia. These developments also signal a need to decentre our research attention from the USA and the UK.

The need is also clear considering that emerging 'peripheral' countries are becoming destinations for international students. Data show that East Asia, the Pacific, Central and Eastern Europe, and Arab states are taking over the international education market from North America and Western Europe (UNESCO, 2019). These countries attract students and their families with their lower tuition and living costs, and in some cases the availability of scholarships (Lin, 2014; Mulvey, 2021). In addition, Robertson and Kedzierski (2016) explain the rising popularity of China and India as study destinations as being a result of families' consideration of the shifting global power relations when making decisions concerning their children's study abroad. A series of more recent studies have analysed these new geographies of academic mobility. For instance, Yang (2018a) provides a case study of medical students from India in China. Lin (2014) compares the motivations and performance of lower-class and higher-class Chinese students at Thai universities, while Lee and Kuzhabekova (2018) examine the mobility of scholars from 'core' countries to Kazakhstan. Ho's (2017) research on African students in China is particularly interesting to us here, as she also refers to, among other themes, the ways academic mobility is practised as a part of broader family livelihood projects.

Finally, the COVID-19 pandemic has also made waves in the field of international student mobility. Mok et al. (2021) maintain that distance from home and a country's ability to control a public health crisis have become important factors for parents. The authors conclude that in the early phase of the pandemic, destinations in East Asia – such as Hong Kong, Japan and Taiwan – gained popularity among potential students in China, the biggest source of international students.

THE FAMILY AS AN EXPLANATORY FACTOR FOR ACADEMIC MOBILITY

Although not positioned at the centre of the scholarship, the family is found to play an important role in shaping the mobility capacity and experiences of students and scholars (see Chapter 13, this *Handbook*). In this body of work, the family is primarily considered the source of resources for academic mobility aspiration. Due to the additional costs that international education away from home entails, researchers have logically focused on the impact of the socioeconomic status of the family on the propensity for and the experiences of study abroad. Family support has been found to influence, and sometimes determine, the decision concerning overseas education and the destination. A lack of financial resources has been found to be the main cause for deviation from or termination of the ideal educational mobility (Netz, 2015; Bryła and Ciabiada, 2014; Finn and Darmody, 2017). In many cases, students also obtain other financial resources, such as scholarships, or find side jobs (Carlson, 2013). During the COVID-19 pandemic, students had trouble finding work to finance themselves, thus underlining the importance of family support (Hari et al., 2021).

Research on diverse geographical contexts has confirmed the importance of class: youngsters from more privileged socioeconomic backgrounds (usually upper and middle class) are more likely to have access to overseas education than those from lower-class families, as shown by the studies by Brooks and Waters (2009) on students from the UK, by Huang and Yeoh (2011) on Chinese students and 'study mothers' in Singapore, and by Liu-Farrer (2014) on Chinese student mobility in Japan. Most analyses of the impact of international student mobilities show that there are advantages to studying abroad. In particular, many researchers (Brooks and Waters, 2009; Findlay et al., 2012; Murphy-Lejeune, 2002; Waters, 2006, 2009; Xiang and Shen, 2009) have conceptualised these advantages with the concept of 'capital', after Pierre Bourdieu (1986). In general, these studies find that upper- and middle-class families can use academic mobility to reproduce their social, cultural and economic capitals, and hence social status and accompanying advantages vis-à-vis their less affluent counterparts. As such, international education is argued to increase both social and economic inequalities.

Studies that analyse larger datasets help to generate a broader picture of these socioeconomic inequalities. Using a nationally representative panel dataset from the German School Leavers Survey, Lörz et al. (2016) apply logistic regressions and effect decomposition methods to explain the lower likelihood of underprivileged students intending to study abroad. They conclude that a key factor in this is the low socioeconomic status of the family, which shapes previous life-course events, that in turn account for worse academic performance in previous education, higher cost sensitivity and lower expectation of benefiting from studying abroad.

Some studies have nuanced our understanding of the inhibiting factor of costs, and hence the impact of the family's class status, in student mobilities. Tran (2016) draws attention to the agency families have in escaping the class trap. In her study on international students in Australia, the cost of student migration is often not manageable, relying only on the economic resources of the students' immediate family. However, to facilitate their children's route to capital accumulation, families would come up with additional financial solutions, such as selling their houses, getting loans or borrowing money from friends and relatives, in order to send their children abroad. This calls for more diverse thinking about the notion of 'family'. In many cultural contexts, relatives are considered members of 'the family', as opposed to the classical definition in the West, which denotes a more nuclear nature. Tran further observes that these students show more eagerness to obtain economic capital and upgrade their class status. Her research hence shows that overseas education not only reproduces social advantages and disadvantages, but can also be a means fought for by disadvantaged social groups to climb the social ladder. Lin's (2014) research on Chinese undergraduate students at Thai universities also illustrates the agency of families with fewer resources in facilitating international education for their children. They tend to choose destinations that are more affordable – such as Thailand, Malaysia and South Africa – than the conventional destinations in the West.

While these examples do not challenge the fact that, in most cases, overseas education is still a privileged project dominated by wealthier families, the voices of the lower class and their strategies to escape the class trap deserve more attention. As the field of international education expands, the impact of new study destinations and the emergence of products such as transnational education that offers 'international' education in situ (Waters and Leung, 2012), especially among the expanding middle-class populations worldwide, should be highlighted.

Rather than seeing class as clear cut, dividing families into 'can pay' versus 'cannot pay' categories, researchers have offered a more elastic understanding of family socioeconomic status. For a great number of families, even though it is within their capacity to pay for tuition, it is a struggle to provide their children with a quality of life in the study destination that is comparable to that at home. As Liu-Farrer (2014, p. 194) notes in her study on Chinese students in Japan, most students are not from wealthy families who can fund the overseas education easily; rather, they are 'ordinary' people whose salaries are above average in China, but not when converted to the standard in Japan. This reminds us to situate class in a transnational frame. Arthur (1997) reports that international students often adjust their class-related expectations and practices by, for instance, lowering their living standards concerning food and clothing, in order to lighten the burden on their families. For some families, their children's education abroad can cost their entire life savings. The willingness of 'ordinary' families to make large investments in their children's overseas education can be explained by their expectations of a high return from their children's study (Brooks and Waters, 2010; Pimpa, 2005; Waters and Leung, 2021). Liu-Farrer (2014) underlines the influence of ethnoculture in family expectations. She argues that parental devotion in Chinese and, more broadly, Asian cultures raises the likelihood of such investment, which in turn makes those students' academic performance more a family issue than is the case among students from Europe or North America (Fritz et al., 2008).

The family shapes academic mobility not only by paying for it. Some research has underlined the other influences that families have on students' decision-making process (e.g. Cubillo et al., 2006; Li and Bray, 2007; Murphy-Lejeune, 2002). Studies have found that family shapes students' decisions in different phases of the mobility trajectories: from starting as an enabling or hindering factor in the pre-mobility decision-making phase, to its role in shaping the experiences of students and scholars during their stay abroad, and as an aspect that influences the return/further mobility decision after their initial study or research abroad. A few studies report that families with international backgrounds are more likely to encourage their children to study abroad. In his investigation of students from the UK who joined the Year Abroad exchange project, King (2003) reports that one-third of his participants have at least one non-UK parent. Families or relatives who are living abroad or had a pleasant experience of international education or travel (Mazzarol and Soutar, 2002; Jahr and Teichler, 2002; King et al., 2010; Souto-Otero and McCoshan, 2006; Cairns and Smyth, 2011; Murphy-Lejeune, 2002), or who are familiar with the culture of a certain foreign country (Brooks and Waters, 2010), are more likely to recommend their children to study abroad and to choose the country and/or institution of experience.

On the other hand, emotional bonds between students and their families have been found to hinder, subtly yet in an important way, overseas education decisions and experiences (e.g. Finn and Darmody, 2017; Frieze et al., 2004; Cairns, 2014; Souto-Otero et al., 2013), as well as post-graduation mobility plans. Based on their survey of youths in Ireland, Finn and Darmody (2017) report that more than a quarter of stayers do not pursue an overseas education due to their unwillingness to leave their partners and families. This is also the second most important reason for Polish university students to remain in their country (Bryła and Ciabiada, 2014). Drawing on their research on students from Austria, Belgium, Italy, Norway, Poland and the UK, van Mol and Timmerman (2014) conclude that romantic relationships and their own families (partner and children) are very strong factors that prevent students from pursuing an education abroad. Adopting a life-course approach in their study on Belgian first-year students, de Winter et al. (2021) observe similarly that the romantic relationships of students are negatively associated with studying abroad and complicate the decision-making process, even though such relationships are not, or not yet, formalised by cohabitation or marriage. These findings highlight the dynamics of the 'family' notion for students in early adulthood when the formation of their own family complicates their social role and, in turn, aspirations for and practices of academic mobility.

The role of the family does not stop after the completion of an education degree. It is commonly noted that family is a factor taken into consideration by graduating international students with respect to their career paths and job locations (e.g. Baruch et al., 2007; Cheung and Xu, 2015; Marcu, 2015). Ageing parents are presented by a few studies as a pull factor for graduating students to return home (e.g. Lee and Kim, 2010; Frieze et al., 2006). Asian students' devotion to their parents is more pronounced. For example, Cheung and Xu (2015) found that family ties are the most influential factor prompting Chinese students to return from the USA upon graduation. Comparing graduates of US universities from six countries, Alberts and Hazen (2005, p. 147) also confirm that 'the desire to be close to family members was not only a societal value, but also a moral obligation' especially among Asian students. In their study, some Japanese graduates said that being the family's eldest son obliged them to take care of their parents and thus they had to return to Japan. Yet, returning does not necessarily mean a complete return. Many studies pointed out that Singapore has become a popular post-graduation destination for Asian graduates from universities in the West (Ortiga et al., 2019; Paul and Long, 2016). Such quasi-return allows the graduates to be close enough to their parents while being able to boost their career in a regional global city. As we have illustrated, how family ties shape international students' mobility is multidimensional, depending on the cultural expectations and practices, their position in the family and the family type (Elmelech, 2005; Hwang et al., 2018; Kingminghae et al., 2019), as well as the evolving global job market.

IMPACT OF ACADEMIC MOBILITY ON THE FAMILY

We now move on to a body of work that focuses on the impact of academic mobility on the family. As we mentioned in the previous section, academic mobility is commonly found to reproduce class-based social advantages. Here, we emphasise a line of research that examines how education mobility is practised as a family strategy for capital accumulation, particularly in Asia. Ong's (1999) book *Flexible Citizenship* depicts wealthy Asian families that 'dispatch' their children, who are endowed with various forms of capital, to study overseas. The Education mobilities of these children can be considered part of a broader family investment aiming at further capital accumulation by these elite transnational families. Waters' (2005) research also examines overseas education among Hong Kong students as a family strategy to facilitate the social reproduction of their families' class status. Inspired by these pieces of seminal work, more research has documented the efforts made by middle-class families in, for example, Central Asia (Holloway et al., 2012) and lower-class families in, for instance, China (Lin, 2014) to invest in their children's international education in order to climb the social ladder through getting better jobs. Drawing on her research on international students and academic staff from vocational educational institutions in Australia, Tran's (2016) paper underlines that overseas education has reproduced social advantages in the domestic and international labour market, as well as making those with such an education successful inheritors of family businesses. For some families, an overseas degree is a way to bypass certain inequalities back home. For example, some Chinese parents have been found to advise their daughters to stay abroad after graduation, because they perceive migration as a way to escape gender discrimination that is common in the Chinese labour market (Geddie, 2013; Yang, 2018b).

A series of studies have drawn attention to the sacrifices families make in pursuing education mobility for their children. Family separation is often part of the price when younger children are involved (Waters, 2012). Scholars have termed these families as 'astronaut families' (Ho, 2002; Waters, 2002) or '*kirŏgi* families' (Finch and Kim, 2012; Kang and Abelmann, 2011), the children as 'parachute kids' (Zhou, 1998) or 'satellite kids' (Waters, 2003), and the mothers as 'study mothers' (Huang and Yeoh, 2011). These 'student migration projects' entail different family members struggling and making sacrifices in different periods. For instance, Huang and Yeoh (2005) examine education mobility among younger Chinese students who moved to Singapore with their mothers. They document the challenges 'study mothers' face, such as the lack of permission to work in Singapore in the initial stage of migration, and the difficulty of maintaining their long-distance relationships with their husbands, who stay in China, while accompanying their children to study. Departing from the usual split-family situations, Waters (2010) discusses the pains and gains of lone husbands who stay in Canada with their children for education while their wives remain in East Asia to work and provide for their families. This study portrays the difficulties of these male homeworkers in negotiating their masculine identity and self-pride. On the other hand, it highlights the improved father–child relationships in this less-common type of family migration arrangement.

Academic mobility also forms families. A survey conducted by the European Commission (2014) estimated that around 1 million babies were likely to have been born to 'Erasmus couples' between the programme's inception in 1987 and 2014. Forming a family is sometimes more than a 'natural' life-course event, as shown by the Erasmus survey. Marriage has also been found to be a method that some international students use to stay on in their place of study. Kringelbach (2015), for example, reports that some African students opt for marriage to obtain residency and formal employment in France; rights that are not accessible to foreign graduates. This underlines that the link between academic mobility and the family is fluid and highly context-specific, and should be understood as embedded in broader and linked socioeconomic and political domains.

UNPACKING THE FAMILY: GENDERED ROLES AND ACADEMIC MOBILITY

The examples of family separation given above are important in showing the efforts made by scholars who have unpacked the family from a gendered perspective. Although we have witnessed a growth of such work, prominent figures in the field (e.g. Raghuram and Sondhi, 2021; de Winter et al., 2021) recently reiterated the plea for a stronger focus on the gendered decision-making process related to academic mobility. In this section, we present important pieces of work on academic mobility that feature a distinct focus on gendered roles and positions in the family. This line of work, especially research using a life-course approach (e.g. Mosneaga and Winther, 2013), touches on how the individual or individualised academic migrant is situated, spatially and temporally, within a (changing) family constellation. Multiple familial relationships have been examined in diverse transnational contexts, including the linked lives of parent and child (e.g. Waters, 2012; Tu, 2016), partners in romantic relationships (e.g. Geddie, 2013; Mosneaga and Winther, 2013), and wives and husbands (e.g. Leung, 2017; Vohlídalová, 2014). Special attention has been paid to important life-phase junctures such as marriage, childbirth and parents' ageing (e.g. Martin, 2018; Tu and Nehring, 2020).

Based on her study on visiting researchers in Germany, Jöns (2011) underlines the importance of life-course. In her database, female students and academics at a younger age are equally mobile as, or even more mobile than, their male counterparts. However, women's mobility reduces at around the age of 35. The reason is conventional, namely the gendered division of labour at home. Academic mobility becomes difficult for many women to realise due to their family role as wives and/or mothers. More recent research among fresh university students in Belgium and Germany concludes with the rather disturbing finding that the perceived high likelihood of future conflicts between career advancement and uxorial duties reduces female students' incentive to study abroad (de Winter et al., 2021; Cordua and Netz, 2021).

Raghuram and Sondhi (2021) emphasise the need to contextualise the dynamic notions of family and gender in explaining the gendered pattern of student mobility. Gendered positions, and hence expected mobility practices, play an important role in determining academic mobility in particular cultural contexts. In the Middle East, for instance, Findlay (2010) notes there were twice as many male as female outbound students. This can partially be explained by the patriarchal family structure that restrains women from travelling and living far away from their parents or husbands. It is important to recognise the fluid nature of gender and family embedded in different social and political contexts. For example, in China, the one-child policy has increased the number of daughter-only households, which has reduced the gender gap of overseas education participation in China (Kajanus, 2015). Beyond differences in number, gendered differences in experiences of academic mobility have also been underlined. In Sondhi and King's research on Indian students (Sondhi and King, 2017; King and Sondhi, 2018), both males and females face the stress of negotiating overseas education because of their socially perceived gender roles. Men need to convince their families about the uncertain time and the high cost of staying abroad, which become obstacles to taking care of ageing parents as good sons; while women need to convince their families that they will be safe, being 'alone' in an unfamiliar country.

It is not surprising that conflicts between career and family duties present students, especially female students, with a stay-or-return dilemma after they graduate. Recent studies also show how mostly female graduates from particular sociocultural, mainly non-Western contexts extend their stay abroad in order to avoid the perceived undesirable gendered expectations in their countries of origin. Basford and van Riemsdijk (2017), for instance, observe such a tendency among Israeli female students in Norway. Drawing on her study on Chinese students in Australia, Martin (2018, p. 688) coins the term 'zone of suspension' to denote the strategy taken by female students to remain abroad and avoid the wifely and motherly duties that are expected of them at that age, which they hope to delay or avoid as time passes. In general, this line of research mainly focuses on female students from Asia studying in the West (for example, South Korean students in the USA, see Yoon and Kim, 2019; Indian students in Canada, see Sondhi and King, 2017). Our research (Hao, 2019) on the mobility of fresh Chinese graduates from Dutch universities reveals that young men are also often engaged in difficult negotiations because of their gendered expectations in Chinese society. Hao shows that the perceived social rule in China that men should own an apartment as a condition for marriage steered young male graduates to remain in their study destination and start a family.

The power of highly normative familial notions such as 'a good child', 'a good spouse' and 'a good parent' is often illustrated in staff mobility research. Age, marriage status and family composition have been found to have a strong impact on scholars' mobility trajectories. Based on their study of mobile academics working in Kazakhstan, Lee and Kuzhabekova (2018) map out how age is a factor that determines their freedom to move. The findings show that young scholars in their twenties and thirties can be highly mobile due to their lack of family obligations. Scholars who are married and have school-aged children when they are in their thirties and forties can still be mobile, because relocation causes less disruption to the education of their children, compared to that of older children. Scholars in their sixties and seventies, many of whom are 'empty nesters' relieved of familial responsibilities, are also mobile if they are in good health. Lee and Kuzhabekova's findings underline the importance of life-course, the fluidity of 'the family', and the associated expectations with regard to being a 'good' or 'responsible' member of the family when academic mobility decisions are being made.

As shown by Jöns (2011), gendered effects are also apparent in academic staff mobility. Ackers (2004) concludes that the high levels of mobility expected in the scientific profession often lead to tensions in partnerships. In the face of these tensions, women tend to sacrifice their careers, by either leaving the profession altogether or foregoing opportunities to develop their careers. Ackers and Gill (2008) further examine the gender bias of life-course dynamics, such as the impact of partnering and children on academic mobility and career development. In their investigation of scientists' mobility from Bulgaria and Poland to the UK and Germany, women in dual-career partnerships were found to be tied to a place by familial responsibilities. The challenges of maintaining a work–life balance among women scientists have also been studied in various European countries (Geddie, 2013; Leemann, 2010; Pettersson, 2011; Shinozaki, 2014; Vohlídalová, 2017) and the USA (Scheibelhofer, 2008). Cooke's (2007) research on Chinese academic couples in the UK, and our previous work (Leung, 2014) on Chinese scholars in Germany, both highlight the gendered price of mobility and the impact of the family in restraining women's mobility aspirations.

While in most cases women have been found to be the secondary movers (e.g. Ledin et al., 2007; Lee and Kim, 2010; Ackers, 2004), some exceptions have been noted. Schaer et al. (2017) use the stories of three couples from Switzerland, the USA and France who graduated from universities in the UK, Switzerland and the USA, respectively, to illustrate three types of dual-career management. In their study, women were not always followers. Apart from the male-primary mobility that is dominant, they also identified female-primary mobility when the female is the lead mover with the job and dual-career mobility. This last type was found to favour the career of both partners. However, in their study the dual-career trajectory only lasted till the birth of the couple's children. After that, the female academic shifted to part-time positions in order to coordinate work and family duties while the husband worked full-time. Clearly, the impact of gender on academic mobility is highly context-specific. While this research cannot be read as a revision of dominant findings that women, especially the mothers of younger children, are less mobile than their male and childless counterparts, Schaer et al. (2017) present the diversity of experiences that is often sidelined in the literature.

While not de-emphasising gender inequalities in academic mobility, Leung (2017) calls for an agent-centred perspective to gain insights into females' negotiations to make sense of and gain value from their 'trailing spouse' experiences. In her paper, she narrates the reflections of a highly skilled Indonesian woman in her late twenties who, as a mother of two young children, had accompanied her husband to Germany so that he could do a PhD, and then returned home as a family of six. The narrative illustrates how she created meanings to the 'downward' class mobility experiences that confronted her: putting her professional career on hold for almost five years, residing in student accommodation and living on her husband's relatively small scholarship. Her predominantly joyful recollection of their temporary migration experience was dotted with terms such as 'feeling empowered', having the opportunity 'to be a capable mother' (without domestic help) and being able to spend much 'precious time with her children'. Again, her reflections should not be used to belittle the discriminatory German labour market and broader society in which this woman found herself. Yet, the study reminds us that simplistically assessing a migrant woman's sacrifice could mean that we overlook how individuals, as active agents, negotiate their subjectivities and social positions (class, gender, family role, and so on), as well as the mobility trajectories of their family.

CONCLUSIONS AND FUTURE RESEARCH AGENDAS

As shown by our overview of the literature on academic mobility from a family perspective, 'the family' has been examined as a factor that facilitates or hinders and shapes the experiences of academic mobility. Research has also examined the positive and negative impacts of academic mobility on families. From gender and intersectional perspectives, a series of work has unpacked 'the family' and uncovered the differentiated experiences of academic mobility among women and men, married or single, and parents with older or younger children. We learn from this growing body of work the importance of situating academic mobility flows in particular socio-spatial and temporal contexts. Even though 'the family' is often part of the research questions, it is rarely the focus of discussion and systematically examined in relation to a scholar's mobility aspirations and experience.

We consider a family perspective to be productive in our conceptualisation of academic mobility in four ways. First, it helps us appreciate individuals' complex subjectivities as much more than just being a student or an academic whose only agenda is to study and conduct research. Their relationships with and positionality vis-à-vis other members of their families – in intersection with their other prescribed roles as, for instance, citizens of particular countries and members of ethnic, religious and other communities – influence and are affected by their subjectivity as mobile scholars. A recognition of the multiple identities and positionalities of these individuals helps us understand their mindsets, actions and experiences. Second, the family provides a useful analytical scale to map gendered power geometries (Mahler and Pessar, 2001; Massey, 1994) traversing the academic mobility field. The power contours are expressed at and across individual, interpersonal and broader institutional levels (Risman, 2004) that span transnational space. Third, analysing academic mobility as a familial process reveals the impact of the life-course processes of individuals and their linked family members in shaping their often individualised mobility trajectories. Fourth, a family perspective enriches the hitherto predominantly economistic view on academic mobility in the scholarship and policy discourses. It advances our understanding of the multiple values attached to academic mobility. Hence, rather than considering academic mobility as a project only for career advancement, we gain a more systemic and realistic understanding of the ways it is also embedded in other important sociocultural and political spheres.

Our literature review has revealed some blind spots in the scholarship that deserve more attention in future research. The first concerns the still rather limited and bounded definitions used in the field. Above, we presented studies that have gone beyond conventional definitions and scopes, such as those examining students from poorer, rural backgrounds, studying in 'new' study destinations, and so on. Yet, we know little about students and scholars who, for example, are forced to move because of violence and oppression, often having to leave their families behind (but see Kmak and Farzamfar, 2022). In our increasingly fragile world, it is imperative to pay more attention in migration and mobilities studies to individuals and families who need to move.

Second, 'the family' deserves further unpacking. Family structures have not been sufficiently studied. Only a few scholars have looked at how family structures influence the level and kind of family support for, or obstacles to, a student's mobility decision. For instance, the number of children can influence what and how much resource parents can assign to each child, and whether students feel more or less obliged to follow their parents' advice, or return after their studies to take care of them. Pimpa (2005) concludes that Thai students from households composed of a nuclear family are more influenced by their families than those from extended or non-traditional (for example, single-parent, homosexual parents, co-parenting after divorce) family households. Whether students or scholars from other family structures (for example, single-parent households, with non-heterosexual parents, or from extended or rainbow families) that share care and responsibilities differently arrange their mobility in different ways than those from the default nuclear family type deserves attention.

This leads to the third blind spot. The gender lens applied thus far to understand the impact of marriage and children and other key life-phase events is usually from a heterosexual perspective. Beyond the typical men versus women discourse, we recommend also looking at gender diversities and sexualities in the family domain, the academic field and broader transnational socio-political contexts.

Fourth, we observe that parents are usually silent in studies on academic mobility. It would be beneficial to also hear from them, as they play the role of consultants and investors in their children's academic mobility projects. Their perspectives would further our understanding of the ways in which academic mobility and the family are related and worked out in the quest for upward social mobility across generations. This could then generate insights into the changing meanings of mobility, education and the family across time, and often across space.

Finally, we recommend further diversifying the contexts of academic mobility that we study. Reflecting the overall tendency in migration studies, international and intra-national academic mobility are treated separately. It would be fruitful to make conceptual and empirical links across these seemingly disparate mobility contexts. We can compare and contrast the role of the family in academic mobility projects that span different spatio-temporalities. In our work on cross-border schooling across the Shenzhen–Hong Kong boundary, for example, we identified a number of intriguing links to the family, ranging from the value of education as a means of familial social mobility, the long-term planning and huge investments parents make to put their children through the daily, hours-long cross-border commute to go to school in Hong Kong, and the gendered burden of such schooling practices, especially on the mothers (Waters and Leung, 2021).

It is our hope that our review of the literature and the above observations will motivate students and scholars to further study academic mobility with more emphasis on the family. There is still much to be done concerning the ways in which the geographies of academic mobility and the notions of 'the family' continue to be transformed. Paying attention to new developments, producing critical insights into processes of inclusion and exclusion, inequalities and empowerment, as well as giving voice to those not yet heard, would enrich the debates.

NOTE

1. Our literature review covers only English-language literature. Reflecting the overall spatial focus of the literature, we offer a review of research on international academic mobility, rather than domestic or intra-national academic mobility.

REFERENCES

Ackers, L. (2004). Managing relationships in peripatetic careers: Scientific mobility in the European Union. *Women's Studies International Forum*, *27*(3), 189–201.

Ackers, L., and Gill, B. (2008). *Moving People and Knowledge: Scientific Mobility in an Enlarging European Union*. Edward Elgar Publishing.

Alberts, H.C., and Hazen, H.D. (2005). 'There are always two voices…': International students' intentions to stay in the United States or return to their home countries. *International Migration*, *43*(3), 131–154.

Arthur, N. (1997). Counselling issues with international students. *Canadian Journal of Counselling*, *31*(4), 259–274.

Askehave, I. (2007). The impact of marketization on higher education genres – The international student prospectus as a case in point. *Discourse Studies*, *9*(6), 723–742.

Baruch, Y., Budhwar, P.S., and Khatri, N. (2007). Brain drain: Inclination to stay abroad after studies. *Journal of World Business*, *42*(1), 99–112.

Basford, S., and van Riemsdijk, M. (2017). The role of institutions in the student migrant experience: Norway's quota scheme. *Population, Space and Place*, *23*(3), e2005.

Bourdieu, P. (1986). The forms of capital. In J.G. Richardson (ed.) *Handbook of Theory and Research for the Sociology of Education*. Greenwood Press, 241–258.

Brooks, R., and Waters, J. (2009). A second chance at 'success': UK students and global circuits of higher education. *Sociology*, *43*(6), 1085–1102.

Brooks, R., and Waters, J. (2010). Social networks and educational mobility: The experiences of UK students. *Globalisation, Societies and Education*, *8*(1), 143–157.

Bryła, P. (2015). The impact of international student mobility on subsequent employment and professional career: A large-scale survey among Polish former Erasmus students. *Procedia – Social and Behavioral Sciences*, *176*, 633–641.

Bryła, P., and Ciabiada, B. (2014). Obstacles to international student mobility: The case of Poland. *Trends Journal of Sciences Research*, *1*(1), 12–16.

Cairns, D. (2014). 'I wouldn't stay here': Economic crisis and youth mobility in Ireland. *International Migration*, *52*(3), 236–249.

Cairns, D., and Smyth, J. (2011). I wouldn't mind moving actually: Exploring student mobility in Northern Ireland. *International Migration*, *49*(2), 135–161.

Carlson, S. (2013) Becoming a mobile student – A processual perspective on German degree student mobility. *Population, Space and Place* 19, 168–180.

Cheung, A.C.K., and Xu, L. (2015). To return or not to return: Examining the return intentions of mainland Chinese students studying at elite universities in the United States. *Studies in Higher Education*, *40*(9), 1605–1624.

Choudaha, R. (2017). Three waves of international student mobility (1999–2020). *Studies in Higher Education*, *42*(5), 825–832.

Cooke, F.L. (2007). 'Husband's career first': Renegotiating career and family commitment among migrant Chinese academic couples in Britain. *Work, Employment and Society*, *21*(1), 47–65.

Cordua, F., and Netz, N. (2021). Why do women more often intend to study abroad than men? *Higher Education*, 83, 1079–1101.

Cubillo, J.M., Sánchez, J., and Cerviño, J. (2006). International students' decision-making process. *International Journal of Educational Management*, *20*(2), 101–115.

De Winter, T., Van Mol, C., and de Valk, H.A. (2021). International student mobility aspirations: The role of romantic relationships and academic motivation. *Journal of Studies in International Education*, *25*(5), 505–523.

Elmelech, Y. (2005). Attitudes toward familial obligation in the United States and in Japan. *Sociological Inquiry*, *75*(4), 497–526.

European Commission (2014). Erasmus Impact Study confirms EU student exchange scheme boosts employability and job mobility. Press release, Brussels, 22 September. https://ec.europa.eu/commission/presscorner/detail/en/IP_14_1025.

Finch, J., and Kim, S.K. (2012). Kirŏgi families in the US: Transnational migration and education. *Journal of Ethnic and Migration Studies*, *38*(3), 485–506.

Findlay, A.M. (2010). An assessment of supply and demand-side theorizations of international student mobility. *International Migration*, *49*(2), 162–190.

Findlay, A.M., King, R., Smith, F.M., Geddes, A., and Skeldon, R. (2012). World class? An investigation of globalisation, difference and international student mobility. *Transactions of the Institute of British Geographers*, *37*(1), 118–131.

Findlay, A.M., McCollum, D., and Packwood, H. (2017). Marketization, marketing and the production of international student migration. *International Migration*, *55*(3), 139–155.

Finn, M., and Darmody, M. (2017). Examining student immobility: A study of Irish undergraduate students. *Journal of Higher Education Policy and Management*, *39*(4), 423–434.

Frieze, I.H., Boneva, B.S., Šarlija, N., Horvat, J., Ferligoj, A., Kogovšek, T., ... and Jarošová, E. (2004). Psychological differences in stayers and leavers: Emigration desires in Central and Eastern European university students. *European Psychologist*, *9*(1), 15–23.

Frieze, I.H., Hansen, S.B., and Boneva, B. (2006). The migrant personality and college students' plans for geographic mobility. *Journal of Environmental Psychology*, *26*(2), 170–177.

Fritz, M.V., Chin, D., and DeMarinis, V. (2008). Stressors, anxiety, acculturation and adjustment among international and North American students. *International Journal of Intercultural Relations*, *32*(3), 244–259.

Geddie, K. (2013). The transnational ties that bind: relationship considerations for graduating international science and engineering research students. *Population, Space and Place*, *19*(2), 196–208.

Gillan, M., Damachis, B., and McGuire, J. (2003). Australia in India: Commodification and internationalisation of higher education. *Economic and Political Weekly*, *38*(14), 1395–1403.

Gümüş, S., Gök, E., and Esen, M. (2020). A review of research on international student mobility: Science mapping the existing knowledge base. *Journal of Studies in International Education*, *24*(5), 495–517.

Hao, Y. (2019). *Wandering at a Crossroad: An Exploration of Gendered Mobility Aspirations in the Study-to-work Transition of Chinese Graduates at Dutch Universities*. Master's thesis.

Hari, A., Nardon, L., and Zhang, H. (2021). A transnational lens into international student experiences of the COVID-19 pandemic. *Global Networks*, *2021*, 1–17.

Ho, Elaine L.E. (2017). The geo-social and global geographies of power: Urban aspirations of 'worlding' African students in China, *Geopolitics*, *22*(1), 15–33.

Ho, E.S. (2002). Multi-local residence, transnational networks: Chinese 'astronaut' families in New Zealand. *Asian and Pacific Migration Journal*, *11*(1), 145–164.

Holloway, S.L., O'Hara, S.L., and Pimlott-Wilson, H. (2012). Educational mobility and the gendered geography of cultural capital: The case of international student flows between Central Asia and the UK. *Environment and Planning A*, *44*(9), 2278–2294.

Huang, S., and Yeoh, B.S. (2005). Transnational families and their children's education: China's 'study mothers' in Singapore. *Global Networks*, 5(4), 379–400.

Huang, S., and Yeoh, B.S. (2011). Navigating the terrains of transnational education: Children of Chinese 'study mothers' in Singapore. *Geoforum*, 42(3), 394–403.

Hwang, W., Ko, K., and Kim, I. (2018). Parent–child relationship quality and filial obligation among American and Korean college students: The moderating role of children's gender. *Journal of Comparative Family Studies*, 49(3), 271–294.

Jahr, V., and Teichler, U. (2002). Employment and work of former mobile students. In Ulrich Teichler (ed.) *ERASMUS in the SOCRATES Programme: Findings of an Evaluation Study*. Lemmens Verlag.

Jöns, H. (2011). Transnational academic mobility and gender. *Globalisation, Societies and Education*, 9(2), 183–209.

Kajanus, A. (2015). *Chinese Student Migration, Gender and Family*. Springer.

Kang, J., and Abelmann, N. (2011). The domestication of South Korean pre-college study abroad in the first decade of the millennium. *Journal of Korean Studies*, 16(1), 89–118.

King, R. (2003). International student migration in Europe and the institutionalisation of identity as 'young Europeans'. *Migration and Immigrants: Between Policy and Reality*. Aksant Academic Publishers, 155–179.

King, R., Findlay, A., and Ahrens, J. (2010). *International Student Mobility Literature Review*. HEFCE.

King, R., and Sondhi, G. (2018). International student migration: A comparison of UK and Indian students' motivations for studying abroad. *Globalisation, Societies and Education*, 16(2), 176–191.

Kingminghae, W., Lin, Y., and Wu, X. (2019). Family obligations and the post-international-study migration plans of Thai students graduating from China. *Thammasat Review*, 22(2), 186–207.

Kleibert, J.M. (2021). Geographies of marketization in higher education: Branch campuses as territorial and symbolic fixes. *Economic Geography*, 97(4), 315–337.

Kmak, M., and Farzamfar, M. (2022). Personal and academic narratives of exiled and displaced scholars. In *Refugees and Knowledge Production*. Routledge, 109–127.

Komljenovic, J., and Robertson, S.L. (2017). Making global education markets and trade. *Globalisation, Societies and Education*, 15(3), 289–295.

Kringelbach, H.N. (2015). Gendered educational trajectories and transnational marriage among West African students in France. *Identities*, 22(3), 288–302

Kronholz, J.F., and Osborn, D.S. (2016). The impact of study abroad experiences on vocational identity among college students. *Frontiers: The Interdisciplinary Journal of Study Abroad*, 27, 70–84.

Ledin, A., Bornmann, L., Gannon, F., and Wallon, G. (2007). A persistent problem: Traditional gender roles hold back female scientists. *EMBO Reports*, 8(11), 982–987.

Lee, J.J., and Kim, D. (2010). Brain gain or brain circulation? US doctoral recipients returning to South Korea. *Higher Education*, 59(5), 627–643.

Lee, J.T., and Kuzhabekova, A. (2018). Reverse flow in academic mobility from core to periphery: motivations of international faculty working in Kazakhstan. *Higher Education*, 76(2), 369–386.

Leemann, R.J. (2010). Gender inequalities in transnational academic mobility and the ideal type of academic entrepreneur. *Discourse: Studies in the Cultural Politics of Education*, 31(5), 605–625.

Leung, M.W.H. (2014). Unsettling the yin–yang harmony: An analysis of gender inequalities in academic mobility among Chinese scholars. *Asian and Pacific Migration Journal*, 23(2), 155–182.

Leung, M.W.H. (2017). Social mobility via academic mobility: Reconfigurations in class and gender identities among Asian scholars in the global north. *Journal of Ethnic and Migration Studies*, 43(16), 2704–2719.

Li, M., and Bray, M. (2007). Cross-border flows of students for higher education: Push–pull factors and motivations of mainland Chinese students in Hong Kong and Macau. *Higher Education*, 53(6), 791–818.

Lin, Y. (2014). Family background and overseas education of Chinese students in Thai universities. *Thammasat Review*, 17(1), 122–149.

Lipura, S.J., and Collins, F.L. (2020). Towards an integrative understanding of contemporary educational mobilities: A critical agenda for international student mobilities research. *Globalisation, Societies and Education*, 18(3), 343–359.

Liu-Farrer, G. (2014). Tied to the family and bound to the labor market: Understanding Chinese student mobility in Japan. In *Emerging International Dimensions in East Asian Higher Education*. Springer, 185–206.

Lörz, M., Netz, N., and Quast, H. (2016). Why do students from underprivileged families less often intend to study abroad? *Higher Education, 72*(2), 153–174.

Mahler, S.J., and Pessar, P.R. (2001). Gendered geographies of power: Analyzing gender across transnational spaces. *Identities, 7*, 441–459.

Marcu, S. (2015). Uneven mobility experiences: Life-strategy expectations among Eastern European undergraduate students in the UK and Spain. *Geoforum, 58*, 68–75.

Martin, F. (2018). Overseas study as zone of suspension: Chinese students re-negotiating youth, gender, and intimacy. *Journal of Intercultural Studies, 39*(6), 688–703.

Massey, D. (1994). *Space, Place, and Gender*. University of Minnesota Press.

Mazzarol, T., and Soutar, G. N. (2002). 'Push–pull' factors influencing international student destination choice. *International Journal of Educational Management, 16*, 82–90.

Mok, K.H., and Montgomery, C. (2021). Remaking higher education for the post-COVID-19 era: Critical reflections on marketization, internationalization and graduate employment. *Higher Education Quarterly, 75*(3), 373–380.

Mok, K.H., Xiong, W., Ke, G., and Cheung, J.O.W. (2021). Impact of COVID-19 pandemic on international higher education and student mobility: Student perspectives from mainland China and Hong Kong. *International Journal of Educational Research, 105*, 101718.

Mosneaga, A., and Winther, L. (2013). Emerging talents? International students before and after their career start in Denmark. *Population, Space and Place, 19*(2), 181–195.

Mulvey, B. (2021). 'Decentring' international student mobility: The case of African student migrants in China. *Population, Space and Place, 27*(3), e2393.

Murphy-Lejeune, E. (2002). *Student Mobility and Narrative in Europe: The New Strangers*. Routledge.

Netz, N. (2015). What deters students from studying abroad? Evidence from four European countries and its implications for higher education policy. *Higher Education Policy, 28*(2), 151–174.

Nilsson, P.A., and Ripmeester, N. (2016). International student expectations: Career opportunities and employability. *Journal of International Students, 6*(2), 614–631.

Ong, A. (1999). *Flexible Citizenship: The Cultural Logics of Transnationality*. Duke University Press.

Ortiga, Y.Y., Chou, M.H., Sondhi, G., and Wang, J. (2019). Working within the aspiring center: Professional status and mobilities among migrant faculty in Singapore. *Higher Education Policy, 32*(2), 149–166.

Pan, S.Y. (2013). China's approach to the international market for higher education students: Strategies and implications. *Journal of Higher Education Policy and Management, 35*(3), 249–263.

Paul, A.M., and Long, V. (2016). Human-capital strategies to build world-class research universities in Asia. In *The Transnational Politics of Higher Education: Contesting the Global/Transforming the Local*. Taylor & Francis, 130–155. https://doi.org/10.4324/9781315625379-13.

Pawar, S.K., Dasgupta, H., and Vispute, S. (2020). Analysis of factors influencing international student destination choice: A case of Indian HE. *Journal of Further and Higher Education, 44*(10), 1388–1400.

Pettersson, H. (2011). Gender and transnational plant scientists. Negotiating academic mobility, career commitments and private life. *GENDER – Zeitschrift für Geschlecht, Kultur und Gesellschaft, 3*(1), 15–16.

Pimpa, N. (2005). A family affair: The effect of family on Thai students' choices of international education. *Higher Education, 49*(4), 431–448.

Raghuram, P., and Sondhi, G. (2021). Gender and international student migration. In C. Mora and N. Piper (eds) *The Palgrave Handbook of Gender and Migration*. Palgrave Macmillan, 221–235.

Redden, E. (2016). British universities brace likely drop in EU students. *Inside Higher Ed*.

Risman, B.J. (2004). Gender as a social structure: Theory wrestling with activism. *Gender and Society, 18*(4), 429–450.

Robertson, S.L., and Kedzierski, M. (2016). On the move: Globalising higher education in Europe and beyond. *Language Learning Journal, 44*(3), 276–291.

Schaer, M., Dahinden, J., and Toader, A. (2017). Transnational mobility among early-career academics: Gendered aspects of negotiations and arrangements within heterosexual couples. *Journal of Ethnic and Migration Studies*, *43*(8), 1292–1307.

Scheibelhofer, E. (2008). Gender still matters: Mobility aspirations among European scientists working abroad. In Tanu Priya Uteng and Tim Cresswell (eds) *Gendered Mobilities*. Routledge, 115–128.

Shinozaki, K. (2014). Career strategies and spatial mobility among skilled migrants in Germany: The role of gender in the work–family interaction. *Tijdschrift voor Economische en Sociale Geografie*, *105*(5), 526–541.

Sondhi, G., and King, R. (2017). Gendering international student migration: An Indian case-study. *Journal of Ethnic and Migration Studies*, *43*(8), 1308–1324.

Souto-Otero, M., Huisman, J., Beerkens, M., De Wit, H., and Vujić, S. (2013). Barriers to international student mobility: Evidence from the Erasmus program. *Educational Researcher*, *42*(2), 70–77.

Souto-Otero, M., and McCoshan, A. (2006). *Survey of the Socio-economic Background of ERASMUS Students DG EAC 01/05*. Brussels: European Commission.

Teichler, U., and Janson, K. (2007). The professional value of temporary study in another European country: Employment and work of former ERASMUS students. *Journal of Studies in International Education*, *11*(3–4), 486–495.

Tran, L. T. (2016). Mobility as 'becoming': A Bourdieuian analysis of the factors shaping international student mobility. *British Journal of Sociology of Education*, *37*(8), 1268–1289.

Tu, M. (2016). Chinese one-child families in the age of migration: Middle-class transnational mobility, ageing parents, and the changing role of filial piety. *Journal of Chinese Sociology*, *3*(1), 1–17.

Tu, M., and Nehring, D. (2020). Remain, return, or re-migrate? The (im)mobility trajectory of mainland Chinese students after completing their education in the UK. *International Migration*, *58*(3), 43–57.

UNESCO (2019). UNESCO Institute of Statistics data on international student mobility. http://data.uis.unesco.org/.

Van Mol, C., and Timmerman, C. (2014). Should I stay or should I go? An analysis of the determinants of intra-European student mobility. *Population, Space and Place*, *20*(5), 465–479.

Vohlídalová, M. (2014). Academic mobility in the context of linked lives. *Human Affairs*, *24*(1), 89–102.

Vohlídalová, M. (2017). Academic couples, parenthood and women's research careers. *European Educational Research Journal*, *16*(2–3), 166–182

Waters, J.L. (2002). Flexible families? 'Astronaut' households and the experiences of lone mothers in Vancouver, British Columbia. *Social and Cultural Geography*, *3*(2), 117–134.

Waters, J.L. (2003). 'Satellite kids' in Vancouver: Transnational migration, education and the experiences of lone children. In M.W. Charney, B.S.A. Yeoh and T.C. Kiong (eds) *Asian Migrants and Education*. Kluwer Academic Publishers, 165–184.

Waters, J.L. (2005). Transnational family strategies and education in the contemporary Chinese diaspora. *Global Networks*, *5*(4), 359–377.

Waters, J.L. (2006). Geographies of cultural capital: Education, international migration and family strategies between Hong Kong and Canada. *Transactions of the Institute of British Geographers*, *31*(2), 179–192.

Waters, J.L. (2009). In pursuit of scarcity: Transnational students, 'employability', and the MBA. *Environment and Planning A*, *41*(8), 1865–1883.

Waters, J.L. (2010). Becoming a father, missing a wife: Chinese transnational families and the male experience of lone parenting in Canada. *Population, Space and Place*, *16*(1), 63–74.

Waters, J.L. (2012). Geographies of international education: Mobilities and the reproduction of social (dis)advantage. *Geography Compass*, *6*(3), 123–136.

Waters, J., and Leung, M.W.H. (2012). Young people and the reproduction of disadvantage through transnational higher education in Hong Kong. *Sociological Research Online*, *17*(3), 239–246.

Waters, J., and Leung, M.W.H. (2021). Geographies of education: Cross-border schooling between Shenzhen and Hong Kong. *Geography*, *106*(2), 60–65.

Xiang, B. and Shen, W. (2009) International student migration and social stratification in China. *International Journal of Educational Development*, *29*, 513–522.

Yang, P. (2018a). Compromise and complicity in international student mobility: The ethnographic case of Indian medical students at a Chinese university. *Discourse: Studies in the Cultural Politics of Education*, *39*(5), 694–708.

Yang, P. (2018b). Understanding youth educational mobilities in Asia: A comparison of Chinese 'foreign talent' students in Singapore and Indian MBBS students in China. *Journal of Intercultural Studies*, *39*(6), 722–738.
Ye, R. (2016). Transnational higher education strategies into and out of Singapore: Commodification and consecration. *TRaNS: Trans-Regional and-National Studies of Southeast Asia*, *4*(1), 85–108.
Yoon, H., and Kim, H. (2019). Seeking a sense of belonging: The exclusion of female doctorate holders in South Korea and the US. *Gender, Place and Culture*, *26*(5), 638–658.
Zheng, P. (2014). Antecedents to international student inflows to UK higher education: A comparative analysis. *Journal of Business Research*, *67*(2), 136–143.
Zhou, M. (1998). 'Parachute kids' in southern California: The educational experience of Chinese children in transnational families. *Educational Policy*, *12*(6), 682–704.

17. The heterosexual family ideal and its limitations for bi-national same-sex family formations

Claire Fletcher

INTRODUCTION

In 1989, Denmark became the first country in the world to provide a legal framework for the recognition of same-sex unions. Since this moment, there have been rapid advancements in the socio-legal rights of lesbian, gay, bisexual, transgender, queer and intersex (LGBTQI) people. Particularly within the Global North, there is also increased awareness of the range of intimate and sexual lives of individuals and families that fall outside of the heteronormative frame (Kollman, 2018; see Chapter 12, this *Handbook*). While increased protections for same-sex families and their intimate lives is encouraging, there remain discrepancies in legal provision for LGBTQI people; for example, there is greater legal provision for same-sex unions, whilst legal protection for same-sex reproduction and parental rights has been slower and less progressive (Digoix, 2020; Rydström, 2011). Rydström (2011) has argued, however, that the legal rights that have been granted have been provided only to same-sex unions that replicate the heteronormative ideal. Relationships, family and kinship formations that fall outside of this 'ideal' formation are not recognised within legal protection. Additionally, legal advancements for same-sex family formations often prioritise citizens, and there has been slower progression towards provision of legal rights for those whose family formations are not formed within a nation-state boundary. This chapter is a contribution towards understandings of family and migration that challenge the heterosexual ideal and that are not contained within a nation-state boundary. Using the example of bi-national same-sex partnerships in the United Kingdom (UK), this chapter explores how immigration rules, which seemingly have equal provision for both heterosexual and same-sex relationships, in actuality limit which families are seen as legitimate and 'deserving' and therefore granted entry and citizenship rights.

Advances have been made in the legal recognition of same-sex partners in immigration rules, again mainly in the Global North. Changes in immigration rules are also reflective of national changes towards the legal recognition of same-sex relationships and families. Whilst the betterment of rights for LGBTQI people is to be celebrated, there remains vast policy variation between countries. Worldwide, a large number of countries fail to provide state and legal protection for those with non-normative subjectivities; for example, at the time of writing, consensual same-sex activity is still criminalised in 67 countries, with the death penalty still a possibility in 11 countries (Human Dignity Trust, 2023). Discrepancies in states' protection for LGBTQI people has led to persistent inequalities and tensions within states. In addition, inconsistencies in policy-making between states that have made efforts towards providing legal protection for sexual minority identities have left diverse communities not represented within LGBTQI politics, and therefore outside of the state protections for recognised embodiments of LGBTQI identities (Stychin, 2003; Chávez, 2010; Ayoub, 2016; Velasco, 2018). This uneven global geography in protection and rights for LGBTQI people has led to an increasing number of individuals choosing to migrate in search of safer spaces to live and love in. States in the Global North, which have made the most substantial steps towards provision of legal rights for sexual minorities, portray themselves as progressive, liberal havens for the persecuted queer body. By co-opting sexual and gender liberationist politics within their nationalist discourse, these states have increasingly positioned themselves as liberators and protectors of sexual minorities against the illiberal, traditional/religious and repressive Global South (Murray, 2014a; Jenicek et al., 2009; Murray, 2016). Despite the rhetoric and purported concern for LGBTQI migrants, this has not actually led to tangible pathways for legal migration (Shakhsari, 2014). Countries in the Global North have steadily reduced access to their territories for all but a minority type of migrants. Borders are marked by heightened surveillance, targeting the 'possibility of state-sanctioned residency rights' (White, 2013: 39). This restriction to access and securitisation of borders has caused a 'global mobility divide' and made nationality the key determining factor in the possibility of international migration (Mau et al., 2015). The divide is caused by the securitisation of borders in the Global North that disproportionately targets those in the Global South in a move to restrict access to resources. Border security has been justified and intensified since the events of 9/11 and the process constructs certain marginalised groups as a security threat, particularly along gendered, racialised and classed lines (Puar, 2007; Rygiel, 2008). White (2013) has used the term 'global apartheid' to refer to this uneven access to territory and resources, which has been created and naturalised through a matrix of citizenship, border security and immigration regimes. Immigration rules and policies are not neutral and have been developed by states to ensure a monopolisation of control over nation state borders. Immigration policies are shaped by histories of capitalism, colonialism, slavery, exploitation of minorities and controlling the movements of the poor (Luibhéid, 2014; Torpey, 1998).

Since the 1990s onwards, scholars exploring the intersection of queer subjectivities and migration have critiqued immigration policies of nation-states in the Global North. By drawing on this literature, situated mainly within migration studies, I argue that states in this region have developed immigration policies in line with a heteronormative ideal, prioritising citizens and families who are recognised within this heteronormative frame. Heteronormativity is a system that privileges cis-gender men and women, heterosexuality, and the nuclear family, of which the institutions of marriage and the family are keys for organising and upholding heteronormativity (Allen and Mendez, 2018; Ingraham, 2005, 1994). Oswald et al. state: 'Heteronormativity entails a convergence of at least three binary opposites: "real" males and "real" females versus gender "deviants," "natural" sexuality versus "unnatural" sexuality, and "genuine" families versus "pseudo" families. Each of these binaries is commonly believed to have an unambiguous and stable boundary separating the poles' (Oswald et al., 2005, p. 144).

As can be seen, heteronormativity promotes an idea of family that is constructed out of a 'real' man and woman, that is, cis-gendered and heterosexual, and considered the ideal unit for procreation. The result of this image is that 'male–female marriages have been promoted as the desired sexual norm in virtually all societies' (Luibhéid, 2014, p. 124). This societal privileging of heteronormativity is also maintained by state immigration regimes, and results in immigration processes which enforce a construction and embodiment of sexuality that 'upholds relations of power that are not only gendered and sexualized, but also materially constituted through racial, class, religious and geopolitical hierarchies' (Luibhéid, 2013,

p. 216; Luibhéid, 2014). As a result, individuals, family, or kinship configurations that cannot be established within this narrow framing, are prevented from accessing entry, recognition and legal citizenship rights abroad.

Due to the contemporary hostile geopolitical environment surrounding migration, states increasingly classify the movement of people through a legal/illegal binary. The histories of state classification of people have legacies in postcolonial imaginaries that have targeted specific migrants who have been identified by states in the Global North as in need of management (Turner, 2015). Queer migration scholarship has largely focused on the movement of LGBTQI people seeking asylum in countries offering a safer socio-legal context for sexual minorities. It has therefore been criticised for failing to consider fully the diversity *within* queer migration (Canaday, 2009; Epstein and Carrillo, 2014). However, the focus in queer migration scholarship on asylum can be attributed to the fact that seeking asylum was previously one of the few routes open to queer people fleeing persecution and violence. Historically, many countries did not recognise same-sex couples or define them as a 'family' within immigration, and therefore legal migration possibilities, outside of the asylum context, were limited.

Nonetheless, there are important insights that we can draw from this large body of scholarship. First, it has demonstrated how asylum regimes in the Global North enforce Westernised conceptions of queer bodies by extending protection only to those rendering themselves visible within these stereotypical embodiments of queer subjectivities; subjectivities that also do not challenge liberal norms in the receiving states (Akin, 2017; Dhoest, 2019; Puar, 2007; Dustin, 2018; Jordan and Morrissey, 2013; Murray, 2014a, 2014b, 2016; Raboin, 2017). There has been more limited research that has focused on same-sex couples and non-heteronormative family formations escaping persecutory conditions in asylum-seeking contexts. This research found that those who fall outside of cis-heteronormativity kinship and family frames are currently excluded from the refugee protection regime (Fobear, 2019; Ritholtz and Buxton, 2021). Additionally, queer people who do not conform to hetero/homonormative family configurations face even greater discrimination and barriers. As stated, while privilege attached to normative forms of intimacy is often invisible, those who step outside these normative frames become visible, and therefore can be targeted or excluded within policy-making. For example, Rambukkana (2015) showed how Canada's Criminal Code criminalised any formal concurrent 'conjugal unions' but, he argues, those who were targeted under this code were usually 'foreign subjects' and often only those who were simultaneously interacting with Canadian immigration policy. These policies on polygamy were designed to exclude certain others on racial, ethnic and gendered lines – namely, Muslims – from accessing the Canadian state (Rambukkana, 2015, pp. 89–90). This case illustrates how those who do not conform to heteronormative ideals – that is, non-monogamous migrants – can also affect their access to global mobility rights, as their chosen family formation is not recognised, and is indeed policed, within immigration policies. Recently, there has been a small, but burgeoning, academic enquiry into bi-national[1] same-sex couples and their interactions with immigration regimes in the Global North (Chauvin et al., 2021; Dreher, 2017; Hoffmann and Velasco, 2021; Jesus Rafi, 2017; Luibhéid, 2018; Nakamura and Kassan, 2020). As of now, the topic of bi-national, same-sex couples' migratory experiences and opportunities remains an understudied area (Hoffmann and Velasco, 2021), and further academic research is needed to explore the experience of queer individuals and family structures within regular state immigration controls. Given the limited options for queer people to seek protection through asylum, due to increasingly hostile asylum policies, critical enquiry into alternative queer migration possibilities seems an important area for further scholarship.

This chapter will argue that the heteronormative family ideal, which is pervasive within the institution of state immigration policies, limits the movement and choices of those who do not fit into this category. The example of bi-national same-sex partners, within the context of the UK, will be used to explore how immigration policies and rules for bi-national same-sex partners support heteronormative conceptualisations of family. Immigration policies also ensure legal entry and citizenship rights only to those families who can make themselves visible within heteronormative conceptualisations of family. As previous research in both queer and sexualities studies has shown, queer family-making can take a diverse range of forms (Weeks et al., 2001; Weston, 1997) that are not accounted for in current immigration policies. Using insights from queer migration and sexuality scholarship, this chapter will highlight that whilst within legal immigration frameworks same-sex couples should be on a par with their heterosexual counterparts, immigration regimes organised through heteronormative logics are discriminatory towards queer people and queer family formations. UK immigration rules are designed to exclude certain categories of people, and especially impact upon marginalised applicants who reside in stigmatised and feared geographic areas (Neumayer, 2006). As Chauvin et al. (2021), have noted, bi-national couples who are co-ethnic and socially heterogamous are considered a threat to migration controls. Treated with suspicion by states, they are required to prove the 'genuine' nature of their relationship that replicates heteronormative liberal Westernised ideals of family (Turner and Vera Espinoza, 2021). As will be shown later, immigration rules especially discriminate against and limit migration possibilities for queer people who are in country-of-origin contexts that have hostile and persecutory environments towards queer people.

Before moving on to the main discussion, a brief outline of the use of 'queer' within this chapter is provided. Browne and Nash (2010) use the term 'queer' to 'challenge the normative social ordering of identities and subjectivities along the heterosexual/homosexual binary as well as the privileging of heterosexuality as "natural" and homosexuality as its deviant and abhorrent "other"' (Browne and Nash, 2010, p. 5). LGBTQI categories have been found to be limiting as sexual identity categories, and are recognised as exclusionary and inadequate regarding the diversity of non-normative embodiment (Manalansan, 2006). Therefore, with regard to understanding the term 'queer' as it applies to individual subjectivities, Luibhéid (2008a, p. 197) has argued that identity categories are 'burdened by legacies that must be interrogated', and that identities cannot be directly applied in other temporal and geographical locations, but are transformed by local, regional and transnational movements. Therefore, whilst 'LGBTQI' will be used interchangeable with 'queer' throughout this chapter, the term 'queer' is more inclusive when trying to include the wide range of diverse range of sexualities, subjectivities and contextual influences that people might embody.

THE HETERONORMATIVE IDEAL AND SAME-SEX FAMILY FORMATIONS

Heteronormativity, a term introduced by Michael Warner (1991), is a concept that relates to the privileging of heterosexuality in the everyday, and it is also the foundational principle upon which institutions are organised, especially social institutions such as family and marriage.

Ingraham (1994) has argued that institutionalised heterosexuality is seen as the legitimate form of organising sexual lives. Heterosexuality is constructed as the natural order of family life which has its foundations in essentialist understanding of sex and gender. Heteronormativity is the process of privileging heterosexuality over other sexual identities or non-normative presentations of gender (Brown, 2009). This presumed naturalness of heteronormativity prevents any other sexuality or gender expression remaining invisible or unnoticed (Berlant and Warner, 1998; Corber and Valocchi, 2003; Warner, 1991, 1993). This subordination of non-normative sexualities and non-conforming gender identities is maintained through the binary construction of heterosexuality/homosexuality, which Sedgwick (2008) argued was constituted by a relation of asymmetry in which one term was always positioned as inferior to the other. The pervasiveness of heteronormativity means that 'it is produced in almost every aspect of the forms and arrangements of social life: nationality, the state, and the law; commerce; medicine; and education; as well as in the conventions and affects of narrativity, romance and other protected spaces of culture' (Berlant and Warner, 1998, pp. 554–555).

In Western liberal democracies, heteronormativity remains the dominant societal norm. Queer theorists have challenged the privileging of heterosexuality, the heterosexual couple and the heterosexual nuclear family as the main referent for societal organising. Yet, even within practices that are not explicitly sexual, it remains a pervading societal norm. Rubin (1984, p. 12) argues that sexuality is organised into systems of power (and oppression); those who practice 'good' sexuality are 'rewarded with certified mental health, respectability, legality, social and physical mobility, institutional support, and material benefits', and those who engage with what is considered within Western culture to be abnormal sexuality 'are subjected to a presumption of mental illness, disreputability, criminality, restricted social and physical mobility, loss of institutional support, and economic sanction'. Different sexualities are stratified, with heterosexual, procreative and monogamous sex at the top of the hierarchy, and supported by the institution of the family, as opposed to those who adopt undesirable, abnormal and condemned sexuality that includes homosexual, unmarried, promiscuous, non-procreative, casual, cross-generational or sadomasochistic sex. Rubin is critical of the heteronormative family ideal as she sees it as a site for enforcing sexual conformity to prevent deviation away from the ideal of 'good' sex.

As stated above, the family is recognised as a key institution in which heterosexuality is promoted by the state (Butler, 2002; Edelman, 2004). The heterosexual family, as an institution, is maintained by the state in the ways that it recognises and privileges it, conferring rights such as taxation benefits. Butler (2002, p. 16) argues that variations of family/kinship that 'depart from normative, dyadic heterosexually based family forms secured through the marriage vow are figured not only as dangerous for the child, but perilous to the putative natural and cultural laws said to sustain human intelligibility'. Lee (2013) illustrates how the United States (US) has used family reunification policy since the 19th century to privilege certain constructions of family, and how this is closely connected to who the US welcomes into the nation. Chávez (2017) has challenged thinking within migration scholarship and argued that there is a need to queer what is defined as family within immigration policy, to allow recognition for more diverse configurations with less emphasis on traditional notions, such as biological ties.

Historically, there has been a lack of toleration of non-normative subjectivities, which has developed since the 18th century in 'the West'. Sexuality, and different variations of sexuality, are socially constructed, and pervading negative discourses on non-normative subjectivities are a hangover from 18th century medical, psychological and legal categorisations (Weeks,

1981). Assumptions of sexual essentialism (Rubin, 1984) have meant that individuals who divert away from heterosexual norms have been labelled as sexual and gender 'deviants'. Immigration is seen as a crucial tool that states can use to construct and enforce 'normalizing dominant forms of heteronormativity' (Luibhéid, 2008b, p. 269). In addition, it is important to recognise that within immigration regimes, sexuality also intersects with processes of racialisation, gender, class and geopolitical factors. Therefore, the lens of heteronormativity is particularly useful in articulating how normalising regimes, such as immigration, (re)produce heterogenous marginalised subjects to ensure that they do not challenge the dominant racial and ethnic groups (Luibhéid, 2008a).

STATES AND THE DISCRIMINATORY EXCEPTION IN IMMIGRATION

First, an important distinction must be made between asylum (the exception) and regular immigration controls that states use to maintain their citizenry. The right of a person to seek protection is set out in international law under the Refugee Convention 1951 and its 1967 Protocol relating to the Status of Refugees. The right to asylum is also embedded in the norms of the international refugee regime, and confers legal and moral obligation on states to provide protection to those fleeing persecution (Betts, 2017; Gibney, 2018; Hathaway, 2005). However, regular immigration is under the control of states and is conceived very differently, as immigration is seen as the prerogative of a sovereign state to decide who is permitted to enter and stay. The 'regulation of movement contributes to constitute the very "state-ness" of states' (Torpey, 1998, p. 240). This distinction is important to make in the context of this chapter, as while asylum is influenced and regulated by international human rights norms, immigration control is regulated by the individual sovereign state. As a result, state immigration policy can be carried out in a discriminatory fashion, meaning that a state can give preferential treatment not only to its citizens, but also towards certain non-citizens over other non-citizens (Cantú and Luibheid, 2005, p. xii). Research examining the evolution of visa restrictions designed for immigration control shows how they reproduce racial, ethnic and class distinctions, which has led to inequality of access, and restrictions mainly targeting the mobility of people from the Global South (Mau, 2010; Mau et al., 2015; Neumayer, 2006). Visa restrictions and immigration requirements for people from certain geographical contexts are steeped in colonial legacies and reveal how anxieties over otherness and alienation within host communities and legacies effect how 'people are mapped out in relationship to ideas of civility, inferiority and "otherness"' (Turner, 2015, p. 625). Whilst the Universal Declaration of Human Rights states that all humans have 'inalienable rights to live with dignity, to the ability to form a family, and freedom from legal discrimination, among others' (United Nations, 1948), unjust immigration and border regimes frequently deny queer people the right to live within their chosen family configurations. Mau et al. (2015) have argued that restrictionist immigration policies will persist, due to global disparity of wealth, as states will continue to limit options for movement for the world's most marginalised people.

INSIGHTS FROM QUEER MIGRATION SCHOLARSHIP

As stated in the introduction to this chapter, queer migration scholarship has centred sexuality in questions and critiques of migratory processes (Cantu et al., 2009; Decena, 2008). While this scholarship has been criticised for focusing on the individual, and has largely ignored queer family and kinship migrations, important insights can still be drawn (Chauvin et al., 2021). Critical engagement on the dominance of heteronormativity within immigration regimes has illustrated how diverse queer embodiments have been rendered invisible and unrecognisable. Immigration and marriage are two main institutions where citizen rights can be conferred on foreign-born nationals, but this is a benefit only achieved by a very small minority through a selective integration of only a minority of LGBTQI persons, with the aim of supporting neoliberal and military agendas. This selective integration results in the abandonment of the most vulnerable within the queer community (Chávez and Luibhéid, 2020; Luibhéid, 2008b, 2014). Yue's (2008) research focuses on Australian immigration policies and how they are 'historically coded family'. This has implications for how same-sex migration organises sexuality, using heteronormative configurations of intimacy and the institute of the family to impose a self-cultivation on the queer migrant to emulate a particular ideal citizen. This imposition has a disciplinary element, ensuring entry of only a "good citizen" who is compliant with heteronormative expectations (Yue, 2008, p. 240). Rendering relationships readable to a state's immigration process is crucial for recognition and entry. Queer families or couples that do not conform with heteronormative formations are not recognised for privileges attached to citizenship. White (2013), discusses what she terms 'intelligible intimacy', which results in a 'kind of currency exchanged for nationalized residency privileges' (p. 39). However, she argues that this always comes at the expense of others whose queer subjectivities have been framed as undeserving and undesirable, and who are therefore ineligible for entry or legal status.

Luibhéid's (2008b) work on US immigration policies has shown a long history of privileging certain people that is implicated in the nationalist agendas of states to produce and maintain an ideal citizenry. In the US until 1965, immigration policies were designed around racial and ethnic preference, and were intended to exclude Asian, Latin American and Caribbean migrant populations. After 1965, US policy changed to offering immigration possibilities mainly through family ties, therefore assuring heteronormative dominance. Within this change, immigration policy specifically denied entry to lesbian and gay migrants, labelling them 'sexual deviates', a label not removed until 1990 (Reimers, 1985). In other research, Luibhéid (2008b) uses the debate over the recognition of same-sex marriages in US immigration law (which was not legal at the time of her research) to interrogate the construction of il/legality of people by states. She showed how the construction of US citizenry and immigration technologies left thousands of people living in the US as 'illegals'. The inability to have their same-sex partners formally acknowledged within US immigration laws led couples to employ wide-ranging strategies to retain their family unit. The difficulties of continuously ensuring legal recognition for the foreign-born partner meant that couples had to labour consciously to secure legality through other means. However, the only strategies available were predominantly short-term and precarious, and held the threat of the foreign-born partner falling into undocumented or illegal status if other visa strategies failed (Luibhéid, 2008b). States often identify certain groups of migrants as illegal (therefore justifying their exclusion), but as Luibhéid's example shows, people can move in and out of illegality due to restrictionist immigration policies. Illegality, therefore, cannot be attributed to certain bodies, but instead it is a process which one can move between (Ngai, 2014). One of the most interesting aspects of Luibhéid's argument focuses on whether the recognition of same-sex relationships in the immigration regime would lead to full recognition within the US citizenry. She refers us back to the how sexuality cannot be considered alone, but intersects with gender, race, class and geopolitics; which, in turn, influence how states structure their immigration regimes in terms of who is permitted entry (Luibhéid, 2002, 2008b).

Furthering this enquiry, Duggan's (2003) coined the concept of homonormativity to refers to a sexual minority identity that does not contest dominant heteronormative identity or institutions, but instead sustains them. Homonational embodiments are linked to white, male gay culture and political agendas, which Duggan argues are situated in domesticity and consumption. Applying this to immigration regimes, queer subjectivities that are compliant (read: those that are recognised within predominantly white, male, gay culture) can make their queerness recognisable within heteronormative frames (that is, homonormativity) and are permitted entry. Academics have shown how people with non-normative or queer relationship formations face difficulties in having their relationships recognised and legitimated within immigration regimes of the Global North (Luibhéid and Cantú, 2005; Luibhéid, 2008b). Puar (2007) demonstrates in her arguments how the racialisation of certain people in relation to national norms, in addition to homonormative ideals of queer bodies, has also restricted access to territory in the global North. She developed the concept of 'homonationalism':

> This brand of homosexuality operates as a regulatory script not only of normative gayness, queerness, or homosexuality, but also of the racial and national norms that reinforce these sexual subjects. There is a commitment to the global dominant ascendancy of whiteness that is implicated in the propagation of the United States as empire as well as the alliance between this propagation and this brand of homosexuality. (p. 2)

The 'ascendancy of whiteness' that Puar incorporates into her arguments is important for understanding immigration regimes within the Global North. In the context of the post 9/11 'War on Terror', Puar argues that the US used the protection of LGBTQI US citizens within the US's domestic politics to demonstrate a US exceptionalism. The pitting of the Muslim terrorist body against the American queer body was used to frame the former as barbaric, traditional and backward, and as 'other', that queer US citizens needed protecting from. This conceptualisation of sexuality justifies the exclusion of this 'other' (namely Muslims) – religious, cultural and nationalist – from accessing the Global North, and is also used to defend restrictionist immigration policies. The development of an acceptable queer identity helps to sustain and promote the neoliberal status quo of the Global North, but it requires an 'other' or the production of an 'external enemy' for the state to position as a threat to a liberal society of white, upwardly mobile queers (Agathangelou et al., 2008).

Another point to be drawn from Puar is that states within the Global North use liberation rhetoric, such as the protection of LGBTQI rights, to justify geopolitical hierarchies and geopolitical interests. Murray's (2014a) critique of the migration to liberation trope supports this argument. By troubling the homonationalist, queer migration to liberation narrative, he shows how Canada's asylum regime was used to validate the Canadian state as a liberal safe haven that would provide protection to those fleeing homophobic persecution 'over there', meaning those states situated in the global South (Murray, 2014a, 2016). Shakhsari (2014, p. 1011) points out that in order to be recognised as in need of protection due to a non-normative identity, one has to be recognised as 'the right refugee', and this recognition is tied into the

The heterosexual family ideal and its limitations 273

'geopolitical clock and the interests of the international human rights regimes'. Fassin (2010, p. 522) critiques the commitment of states in the Global North to international human rights by highlighting the hypocrisy of such states. He argues that the use of liberal rhetoric about sexual equality by states is a political tool to bolster global political dominance of Western states, and the rhetoric on sexual democracy is incorporated into 'an instrumentalization in the logic of anti-immigration politics'. States draw on equality rights rhetoric to place refugees within the binary of deserving/underserving, and this categorisation of people fits the geopolitical interests of states and validates the discrimination against certain populations to deny them entry.

IMMIGRATION POSSIBILITIES FOR SAME-SEX COUPLES IN THE UK

Little scholarly attention has been given to same-sex bi-national relationships in relation to immigration. Previously, marriage migration scholarship has had a straight bias, and queer migration scholarship has assumed queer migration to be an individual as opposed to a family project (Chauvin et al., 2021). Bringing these two bodies of scholarship into dialogue with one another allows for a more rounded critique of immigration policies and rules, exposing the difficulties created by this heteronormative bias for people within queer family formations. While heterosexual couples are more likely to benefit from marriage as an avenue to migration and legal citizenship, the rise in legal recognition of same-sex marriage and civil partnerships in many liberal democracies has led to an increase in same-sex binational relationship migration (Chauvin et al., 2021). This is when either or both members of the couple choose to migrate, or when a foreign partner joins a partner who is a citizen or has full or partial leave to remain[2] within a state. This is a very narrow definition and does not take into consideration families who cannot make themselves visible for legal migration. Here I show how the UK's immigration rules and evidentiary requirements restrict entry to those who challenge the norms of the state. Visa waiver policies are used by states to foster desired forms of mobility and citizenry by controlling and prohibiting the entry of less-desired others (Steinbugler, 2005). As outlined earlier, states have historically used immigration regimes to preserve heteronormativity and the nuclear family, and this ideal of family is reflected in the construction of immigration policy. Using the UK as a case study, it is apparent that those with queer subjectivities are discriminated against by immigration rules and the evidentiary requirements needed for entry.

The UK first recognised same-sex partner applications for immigration and visa purposes in 1997 after a lobbying group, organised through Stonewall, petitioned the Home Office to allow their foreign partners to be granted leave to remain in the UK. In October 1997, the Unmarried Partners Concession was announced, which recognised same-sex relationships, and it was the first time that lesbian and gay couples were recognised in British law. This concession was limited, as it only allowed foreign partners to remain in the UK if they had already been living with their partner for four years. This restriction meant that only a limited number of bi-national same-sex relationships qualified. The concession was amended in June 1999 to bring the time required down to two years, and in October 2000 the concession was implemented into the UK's immigration rules. In November 2004 the Civil Partnership Bill was passed, and once this legislation came into use in December 2005, it ensured equal immigration rights for same-sex couples. These immigration rules supposedly recognised same-sex relationships on a par with heterosexual couples, based on three types of partnership: marriage or civil partnership (treated as the same in UK immigration law), two years of cohabitation (commonly known as unmarried or same-sex partnered) and fiancé/proposed civil partnership. Therefore, UK immigration rules are, on paper, the same for heterosexual couples and same-sex couples.

To apply for a visa as a married or civil partnered same-sex couple, documentation proving their marriage or civil partnership is required, and it must be considered legal in the country where it (the union) took place. Couples are required to prove that their relationship is a genuine one, and evidence of this is expected as part of the application. There is also a financial component to the application, and the applicant's spouse or partner must earn at least £18,600 per year or, if they are not earning, the level of savings required is at least £62,500. The applicant must prove there is also adequate housing for them to live in, which must be owned or occupied by the family, and documentation is required to show that the couple will legally occupy the property. Applicants must also prove a certain level of English language proficiency, and the competence required varies depending on the stage of the application process. An exemption from the English language requirement part of the visa application is only available for certain English language-speaking countries, or those with certain educational attainments, such as an English-taught academic degree, Master's, or PhD from a university in the UK. An academic degree undertaken from outside of the UK is acceptable, but only if it is taught in English. The requirements for those applying for the two years of cohabitation and fiancé/proposed civil partnership spouse visa have similar requirements to that of the marriage visa. The main difference in the fiancé/proposed application is that couples who are not married must demonstrate that they have lived together for a least two years, either in the UK or abroad. Crucially, they must provide evidence to prove their cohabitation. If neither of these options are possibilities, couples can apply to come to the UK as a proposed civil partner or fiancé, and once granted entry they have six months to marry or enter a civil partnership in the UK, but this route obviously relies on the grant of this visa to enter the UK. Again, as part of this application the Home Office expects extensive evidence of the couple's relationship and the plans for the couple's intention to wed.

DISCRIMINATION WITHIN UK VISA REGIMES FOR BI-NATIONAL SAME-SEX COUPLES

The application and evidentiary requirement to apply for leave to remain for a same-sex partner in the UK is meant to be on a par with heterosexual bi-national couples, but is in fact discriminatory. The requirement to provide documentation to prove a marriage is a good example, as the uneven distribution of equality rights for LGBTQI people globally makes it impossible for people in certain countries to marry or provide legal partnership recognition for their same-sex relationships. Likewise, in many countries, LGBTQI couples are unable to cohabit with their partner without serious fear for their safety. Given that 67 countries still have laws criminalising same-sex consensual sex, it can be seen why some of the requisite evidence is prohibitive for individuals in certain geographical locations. The requirements for the visa are also framed within the dominant societal norm of heteronormativity and the privilege attributed to the heterosexual frame of relationships and family, which are seen as the superior moral and cultural forms of domesticity and kinship structures (Berlant and Warner, 1998). Stipulations to provide evidence of a legally recognised marriage, or 'proof' of cohabitation over a two-year period, has two main consequences. First, it ensures entry only to queer bodies that comply with, and do not challenge, the heteronormative ideal of the intimate couple. Second, it makes it virtually impossible for those from certain geographic locations, which are mainly situated in the Global South, to access territories in the Global North because they cannot meet the cohabitation requirements as it is simply unsafe to do so. In research focusing on queer asylum, it is common for LGBTQI people to engage in clandestine relationships with their same-sex partners to avoid persecution and harassment (Jansen and Spijkerboer, 2011; Jordan and Morrissey, 2013; Millbank, 2009). Therefore, it can be reasonably assumed that this would be the case for others in hostile geographical locations who choose a migratory route other than asylum. However, as in asylum, past history of a heterosexual relationship can be used to discredit an application and question the genuineness of a same-sex relationship.

HETERONORMATIVE IDEALS AND THE GENUINE RELATIONSHIP

For bi-national same-sex couples, the need to prove that their relationship is 'genuine' is a necessary part of the UK immigration process. If the couple's relationship is not legally recognised, they must include proof that they have been cohabitating for a two-year period. Unlike heterosexual couples, the focus of this 'genuineness' of same-sex relationships is on each member's sexual orientation (Fassin and Salcedo, 2015). If both, or one of the couple, is from a country where LGBTQI people are not accepted, it is unlikely that they would be able to obtain the requisite evidence of their relationship as a couple, such as holidays together, living together in a home, and socialising with friends and family. Evidentiary requirements are very much designed around the heteronormative ideal of heterosexual intimate lives, and also assume a level of relative privilege, that is, the ability to have holidays. The need to prove a 'genuine' relationship is driven by suspicions of migrants' motivations for entry in increasingly protectionist regimes in the Global North: suspicion has grown now that many migratory routes are closed to lower-skilled migrants. This climate of suspicion and disbelief around the authenticity of cross-border marriages is especially present in cases of couples who are co-ethnic or socially heterogamous (Chauvin et al., 2021).

Insights from forced migration scholarship on the construction of categories of deserving and undeserving migrants can be useful when considering how 'genuine' relationships are established. This large body of scholarship, focusing mainly on queer asylum, has concentrated on Westernised conceptualisations of non-normative subjectivities and how queers are forced to embody or emulate a small number of Western-centric categories of sexuality and gender expression. However, these conceptualisations have been at the cost of erasing the presence of others who do not fit into these narrow categorisations (El-Tayeb, 2012; Luibhéid, 2008b; Dahl and Gabb, 2020; Giametta, 2017). Within the European legal framework, academics have also demonstrated how Western conceptualisations of non-normative subjectivities are riddled with Eurocentric stereotypes of LGBTQI individuals (Jansen and Spijkerboer, 2011). Decision-makers rely on subjective knowledge to assess a person's right to refugee status, 'often based on culturally constrained understandings of sexualities and genders', or 'ignorance or (potentially subconscious) heterosexual biases' (Jordan and Morrissey, 2013, p. 14). While the idea of a trans-historical, universal and essentialist gay identity has been challenged by queer theorists (Akin, 2017), as has the notion that explicit displays of sexuality or gender identity are a sign of a fully liberated queer (Decena, 2008), there remains an expectation in legal decision-making on how those with queer subjectivities should present. Fassin and Salcedo (2015) demonstrate the need to Westernise non-normative sexualities by using the example of identity checks on couples to prove the veracity of their relationship. They showed that checks imposed Westernised 'gay' and 'lesbian' identities on migrant partners that they did not connect with. One man had to assume a purely 'gay' identity to ensure that his identification as a 'gay man in a same-sex relationship' was recognised by French immigration authorities as legitimate. The conceptualisation of a 'gay man' in the French context excluded the option of participating in sex with women, regardless of the motivation of this sexual conduct. However, he recognised that within the French state his own self-definition of his sexuality would have led to a refusal in terms of his immigration claim. Fassin and Salcedo's (2015, p. 1121) research shows that their participants had an awareness of what was required to be considered for inclusion and citizenship rights in states of the Global North, explaining that 'subjects do feel obligated to betray what they sometimes call their "real nature" to play the (Western) part of the homosexual'.

Murray (2014a, p. 27) explored the impact of asylum regimes in the Global North on those who had non-heteronormative subjectivities. His research demonstrated that if a person's self-understanding and identification was incompatible with 'specific formations of socio-sexual identity reflecting on Euro-American white, middleclass, cisgender subjectivities', then their asylum claim had a higher chance of failure. If their embodiment did not match Euro/American understandings of queer subjectivities, their actual subjectivities would be misinterpreted within the refugee determination process, and lead to accusations that their identity was a 'false identity'. When thinking about the need for bi-national same-sex couples to evidence a 'genuine' relationships, for their relationship to be considered authentic it has to be constructed in such a way as to ensure that it can be rendered intelligible, and they are able to 'translate their sexuality' (Akin, 2017). Therefore, queer migrants need to be able to perform their subjectivities in ways that are legible to decision-makers (Fiddian-Qasmiyeh, 2016). As with queer asylum seekers, bi-national, same-sex couples need to ensure that their personal narratives make 'what is hidden visible' (Jordan and Morrissey, 2013, p. 14), but to do so requires an understanding of the local context, which is often dependent on other intersectional identities, such as class and gender (Jansen, 2013; Lewis, 2013). This finding would also suggest that immigration policies privilege those who are in couples where one member is a citizen of the country in which the visa is sought.

ONLY THE PRIVILEGED CAN MOVE

The 'global mobility divide' makes nationality a key determinant in people's ability to effectuate international moves (Mau et al., 2015); access to economic, cultural and social capital, and individual and family class positions, can significantly alter international mobility (Carling, 2002; Van Hear, 2014; see Chapter 14, this *Handbook*). The ability to move to the UK to be with a same-sex partner also has financial implications. The amount of financial capital needed to migrate often means that it is only attainable for those with greater privilege (Turner and Vera Espinoza, 2021). Chauvin et al. (2021) found that couples could circumvent uneven geography of same-sex marriage legislation if they had enough economic and social resources to do so, and as a result were often from the more privileged classes in society. Couples with low resources were disadvantaged in migratory contexts, as the lack of economic capital made it practically impossible to obtain a visa. Lesbian couples find it harder to obtain visas, as female-only households are more likely to experience economic precarity (Kofman, 2018). The financial requirements to be considered as eligible are grounded in the 'liberal character of the visa which is concerned with securing the citizen-migrant household as an economic unit which sustains the "genuine" family free of state benefits' (Turner and Vera Espinoza, 2021, p. 360). The financial component, in terms of income and savings, is restrictive; and in the UK also enforces a dependency on the partner who already has established citizenship rights, as those coming from other countries cannot apply for resident permits independently. This finding is supported by Pravattiyagul (2021) who carried out research with *kathoeys* (transgender women in Thailand) and found that they were dependent on their European partners for the first few years after migration, in terms of their finances and citizenship. The result of this dependency meant that *kathoey* felt the need to emulate a European male ideal of a good traditional woman to ensure that they did not lose favour with their husbands, which would also have resulted in a loss of residency rights in Europe. Financial dependency can lead to an unequal power imbalance in relationships, even ones that were seemingly equal in privilege before the migration process. Ahlstedt (2016) highlighted how the migration process caused negative emotions within the migrating partner, especially in relation to loss of independence and the necessary dependence on the other partner. In addition, financial requirements within the immigration process are also found to directly affect the emotional and mental well-being of couples (Ahlstedt, 2016; Turner and Vera Espinoza, 2021). Aline Jesus Rafi's (2017) research is illustrative these issues and barriers for bi-national couples and focused on the US during the Defence of Marriage Act (DOMA) era and beyond. DOMA was a federal law, passed in 1996, that recognised marriage as the union of one man and one woman, and because of DOMA, US states had the right to refuse to recognise same-sex marriages granted under the laws of other states. DOMA was subjected to numerous legal challenges, and was finally repealed in 2013. This was due to *United States V. Windsor* (2013), which required federal government to recognise same-sex marriages. Aline Jesus Rafi's research exposed the financial strain on couples trying to regularise the immigration of a foreign-born partner. One couple stated: 'it probably took about a year for me to truly understand just how unforgiving the immigration system was; how unfair it was … They are going to empty your pockets, and if you are lucky you get to stay, and if not they kick you out' (Jesus Rafi, 2017: 43).

Financial requirements within immigration regimes put an additional strain on couples already in precarious situations. It also ensures that those who migrate are not entitled to support of the state, and are therefore financially dependent on their partner for at least two years in the majority of cases. This has implications especially for the partner who has a subordinate legal position, and can leave them vulnerable as they are reliant on their partner for not only their financial security but also their legal right to be in their host state.

PUSH FACTORS IN SAME-SEX FAMILY MIGRATION

As can be seen in the preceding discussion, there are numerous barriers for bi-national couples in same-sex partnerships; however, people continue to move despite the hardships. Therefore, this section will consider the motivations for migration for same-sex partners. The ability to live in national contexts which are considered welcoming to LGBTQI people is an oft-noted reason why queer migrant and queer migrant families choose to migrate (Chauvin et al., 2021). LGBTQI people who live in countries that are hostile to queer people can encourage migration to states with greater equality. The concept of same-sex 'love exiles' was first developed to capture the case of professional expatriate same-sex couples who migrated to the Netherlands, as its national laws recognised same-sex relationships. However, migration was only possible due to the fact that one member of the couple was regarded as highly skilled and their employability made migration to a European country a possibility (McDevitt-Pugh, 2011). Pravattiyagul's (2021) participants deliberately used the strategy of bi-national partnership as a means of achieving their migration to Europe. Desire to migrate was motivated by better equality for trans women, better employment opportunities and, through bi-national marriage, an ability to achieve increased social status in Thailand. In addition, other participants felt that their long-term relationships were not recognised in Thailand, as there are no same-sex marriage or civil partnership rights, and they worried about the consequences of this, such as their partner becoming ill. Traditional migration is not only expensive but also restrictive, and therefore *kathoeys* viewed finding a *farang* (white) partner as the most convenient means to facilitate migration. Conversely, Fassin and Salcedo (2015, p. 1122) found that one of their participants from Benin was forced to migrate when his relationship with a white partner made him visible as a 'gay man', as 'whiteness is associated with gayness because it makes gayness visible'. His visibility as a gay man alienated him from his friends and family, and he was therefore forced to migrate to remain with his partner and also to escape harassment and abuse.

Another common theme in research focusing on bi-national same-sex relationships is that couples who are unable to regularise their status through immigration regimes are forced constantly to search for strategies to remain together, including migration to another national context to ensure the relationship's survival (Luibhéid, 2008b). There is a large body of queer migration research that focuses on the US and Canada, including a proliferation of research in the lead-up to, and as a result of, the *United States V. Windsor* (2013) decision that led to the repeal of DOMA. Nakamura and Kassan (2020) examined resilience amongst same-sex, bi-national couples in Canada, and found that migration was an attempt to continue relationships in contexts outside of anti-LGBGT immigration policies, predominantly in the US. Migrating had a profound impact on the couple's mental well-being, which was attributed to leaving behind existing support structures, extreme financial strain, career regression due to migration, and not being able to access typical heterosexual support structures in host countries. In classic migration literature, focusing on heterosexual couples, support structures are identified as co-ethnic immigrant communities, but in terms of same-sex couples these communities can be hostile toward sexual minority members (Nakamura et al., 2013). Research has found that if only one person in the relationship is foreign-born, the stressful events stemming from the immigration process and attempts to regularise their status creates a ripple effect on the entire family and can negatively impact upon relationships (Domínguez et al., 2012). Despite these numerous strains, couples did report feelings of relief attributed to no longer needing to plan their every step with strict adherence to wider constraints of legal and social barriers, due to their same-sex family configuration.

Ahlstedt's (2016) exploration of narratives of queer intimacies in partner migration has considered the intersection of queer migration, intimate migration and privileged migration, with a focus on the emotions of the migrating and non-migrating partners. It is telling that, as her research concentrated on the privileged end of migration, the process of immigration itself was reported as unproblematic by most participants. Despite this, couples reported that they found the immigration process itself put pressure on them and their relationship. Factors for this pressure and anxiety were not solely related to the application process and grants of stay, but also associated to the waiting times for permanent residence, and the stress and fear that permanent status would not be granted (Ahlstedt, 2016; Turner and Vera Espinoza, 2021). One of the main limitations of the research discussed above is that it has only considered the experiences of families whose configurations are visible within heteronormative frames. The next section will consider those whose relationships and family are not recognised, and who therefore struggle to make themselves visible as legitimate.

QUEER EXCLUSION IN IMMIGRATION REGIMES

The example of the UK immigration visa requirement for same-sex couples has shown how, on one level, entry is gained through visibility within a heteronormative framing which does not threaten the heteronormative ideal of the state. The umbrella encompassing LGBTQI people is broad, and whilst there has been progress for some who identify as LGBTQI it is argued that many others remain invisible, particularly migrants and people of colour (Ayoub, 2016). It has been argued that the rights of queer people have narrowly focused on gaining the legal right to same-sex marriage. Kollman (2018) argues that the result of a large amount of energy and focus of LGBTQI activists in Western liberal democracies having centred on the rights of people in same-sex relationships to marry, has come at the expense of those who are rendered invisible within homonationalist frames. Whilst bi-national same-sex migration offers opportunities to a privileged few, still more people with queer subjectivities cannot make themselves visible and are therefore prevented from migratory possibilities. Chávez (2010) argues against immigration that requires people to render themselves visible within the framework of the white, middle-class, heteronormative family. Queer and trans people are frequently unable to rely on traditional support structures, such as the wider family. Subsequently, trans people rely on each other and build close familial ties within the trans and queer community vernacular, such as 'chosen family' (Ritholtz and Buxton, 2021). However, chosen family structures such as these are not seen as legitimate within immigration regimes, and therefore those who chose these familial arrangements are prohibited from migrating and accessing citizenship rights.

CONCLUSION

Bi-national same-sex migration is an option for those who can engage in privileged migration, but as we have seen, it is limited to those whose queer subjectivities can be realised and do not challenge the norm of heteronormativity within the Global North. Immigration regimes in the Global North use the granting of citizenship to only certain queers to justify their global standing within the global geopolitical hierarchy. Queer migration scholarship has provided a much-needed critique of this, drawing attention to those whose queer subjectivities are refused recognition and therefore legitimate entry by immigration regimes. This chapter has shown that there is a need for immigration regimes in the Global North to assess their immigration laws and rules to ensure that they accommodate the wide range of diverse family formations (see also Chapters 2 and 12, this *Handbook*). Further enquiry is needed into how narrow, heteronormative conceptions of family impact upon people in diverse family formations, and from different geographic contexts. Immigration rules in the UK for same-sex couples interact with issues explicitly tied to processes of racialisation, class and gender, and geopolitical hierarchies. Requirements not only serve nationalist agenda of states within the Global North in terms of granting access to those they deem deserving of citizenry, but also immigration regimes are complicit in creating categories of underserving/deserving, legal/illegal and normal/deviant. Furthermore, having only certain non-normative sexualities and subjectivities recognised within immigration regimes has a policing effect against undesirable 'others' from accessing the Global North. Only allowing those who can make themselves visible within dominant norms – in this case, the heteronormative ideal of the family – is exclusionary and impacts upon bi-national same-sex family configurations that stand outside this ideal, whilst also disproportionality impacting upon the world's most marginalised migrant families. Further research into how 'alternative' families are rendered invisible by different immigration regimes is still badly needed.

NOTES

1. With regard to the term 'bi-national', it should be noted that this is based on a legal categorisation (individuals' nationality) imposed on individuals by the state. Within this chapter, it is only used to acknowledge the difference of nationality between partners. It does not presuppose the existence of other differences in terms of culture or language (Bénédicte, 2013).
2. Leave to remain (partial leave) means that you have been granted permission to remain in the UK for a specified period; there can be restrictions and limitations to your activities such as the right to work. Indefinite leave to remain refers to a person who has been granted permanent lawful status in the UK and is no longer subject to immigration status.

REFERENCES

Agathangelou, A., Bassichis, M. and Spira, T. (2008) Intimate Investments: Homonormativity, Global Lockdown, and the Seductions of Empire. *Radical History Review* 100: 120.
Ahlstedt, S. (2016) *The Feeling of Migration: Narratives of Queer Intimacies and Partner Migration.* Linköping University Electronic Press. DOI: 10.3384/diss.diva-129930.
Akin, D. (2017) Queer Asylum Seekers: Translating Sexuality in Norway. *Journal of Ethnic and Migration Studies* 43(3): 458–474.
Allen, S.H. and Mendez, S.N. (2018) Hegemonic Heteronormativity: Toward a New Era of Queer Family Theory: Hegemonic Heteronormativity. *Journal of Family Theory and Review* 10(1): 70–86.
Ayoub, P. (2016) *When States Come Out: Europe's Sexual Minorities and the Politics of Visibility.* Cambridge: Cambridge University Press.
Bénédicte, B. (2013) The Politics of Bi-nationality in Couple Relationships: A Case Study of European Bi-national Couples in Manchester. *Journal of Comparative Family Studies* 44(6): 699–714.
Berlant, L. and Warner, M. (1998) Sex in Public. *Critical Inquiry* 24(2): 547–566.
Betts, A (2017) *Protection by Persuasion : International Cooperation in the Refugee Regime.* Ithaca, NY: Cornell University Press.
Brown, G. (2009) Thinking beyond Homonormativity: Performative Explorations of Diverse Gay Economies. *Environment and Planning A* 41(6): 1496–1510.
Browne, K. and Nash, C.J. (2010) *Queer Methods and Methodologies.* London: Taylor & Francis.
Butler, J. (2002) Is Kinship Always Already Heterosexual? *Differences (Bloomington, Ind.)* 13(1): 14–44.
Canaday, M. (2009) *The Straight State: Sexuality and Citizenship in Twentieth-Century America.* Princeton, NJ: Princeton University Press.

Cantú, L. and Luibheid, E. (2005) *Queer Migrations: Sexuality, U.S. Citizenship, and Border Crossings*. Minneapolis, MN: University of Minnesota Press.

Cantu, L., Naples, N.A. and Vidal-Ortiz, S. (2009) *The Sexuality of Migration: Border Crossings and Mexican Immigrant Men*. New York: New York University Press.

Carling, J. (2002) Migration in the age of involuntary immobility: Theoretical reflections and Cape Verdean experiences. *Journal of Ethnic and Migration Studies* 28(1): 5–42.

Chauvin, S., Salcedo Robledo, M., Koren, T., et al. (2021) Class, Mobility and Inequality in the Lives of Same-Sex Couples with Mixed Legal Statuses. *Journal of Ethnic and Migration Studies* 47(2): 430–446.

Chávez, K.R. (2010) Border (In) Securities: Normative and Differential Belonging in LGBTQ and Immigrant Rights Discourse. *Communication and Critical/Cultural Studies* 7(2): 136–155.

Chávez, A.E. (2017) Intimacy at Stake: Transnational Migration and the Separation of Family. *Latino Studies* 15(1): 50–72.

Chávez, K.R. and Luibhéid, E. (2020) Introduction. In: Luibhéid, E. and Chávez, K.R. (eds), *Queer and Trans Migrations: Dynamics of Illegalization, Detention, and Deportation*. Chicago and Springfield, IL: University of Illinois Press.

Corber, R.J. and Valocchi, S.M. (2003) *Queer Studies: An Interdisciplinary Reader*. Malden, MA: Blackwell.

Dahl, U. and Gabb, J. (2020) Trends in Contemporary Queer Kinship and Family Research. *Lambda Nordica* 24(2–3): 209–237.

Decena, C. (2008) Tacit Subjects. *GLQ* 14(2-3): 339–359.

Dhoest, A. (2019) Learning to be Gay: LGBTQ forced Migrant Identities and Narratives in Belgium. *Journal of Ethnic and Migration Studies* 45(7): 1075–1089.

Digoix, M. (ed.) (2020) *Same-Sex Families and Legal Recognition in Europe*. Cham: Springer International Publishing.

Domínguez, D.G., Solórzano, B.H. and Peña, E. (2012) Nonheterosexual Binational Families: Resilient Victims of Sexual Prejudice and Discriminatory Immigration Policies. *Journal of GLBT Family Studies* 8(5): 496–508.

Dreher, T. (2017) The 'Uncanny Doubles' of Queer Politics: Sexual Citizenship in the Era of Same-Sex Marriage Victories. *Sexualities* 20(1–2): 176–195.

Dustin, M. (2018) Many Rivers to Cross: The Recognition of LGBTQI Asylum in the UK. *International Journal of Refugee Law* 30(1): 104–127.

Edelman, L. (2004) *No Future: Queer Theory and the Death Drive*. Durham, NC, USA and London, UK: Duke University Press.

El-Tayeb, F. (2012) 'Gays Who Cannot Properly Be Gay': Queer Muslims in the Neoliberal European City. *European Journal of Women's Studies* 19(1): 79–95.

Epstein, S. and Carrillo, H. (2014) Immigrant Sexual Citizenship: Intersectional Templates among Mexican Gay Immigrants to the USA. *Citizenship Studies* 18(3–4): 259–276.

Fassin, É. (2010) National Identities and Transnational Intimacies: Sexual Democracy and the Politics of Immigration in Europe. *Public Culture* 22(3): 507–529.

Fassin, E. and Salcedo, M. (2015) Becoming Gay? Immigration Policies and the Truth of Sexual Identity. *Arch Sex Behav* 44(5): 1117–1125.

Fiddian-Qasmiyeh, E. (2016) The Faith–Gender–Asylum Nexus: An Intersectionalist Analysis of Representations of the 'Refugee Crisis'. In: Mavelli, L. and Wilson, E.K. (eds), *The Refugee Crisis and Religion: Secularism, Security and Hospitality in Question*. London: Rowman & Littlefield International.

Fobear, K. (2019) 'Wherever We Would Go, We Would Be Together': The Challenges for Queer Refugee Couples Claiming Joint Asylum in Canada. In: Güler, A.S.M. and Venturi, D. (eds), *LGBTI Asylum Seekers and Refugees from a Legal and Political Perspective*. Cham: Springer.

Giametta, C. (2017) *The Sexual Politics of Asylum: Sexual Orientation and Gender Identity in the UK Asylum System*. Abingdon, UK and New York, USA: Routledge.

Gibney, M.J. (2018) The Ethics of Refugees. *Philosophy Compass* 13(10): e12521.

Hathaway, J.C. (2005) *The Rights of Refugees under International Law*. Cambridge: Cambridge University Press.

Hoffmann, N.I. and Velasco, K. (2021) Making Migration Sexy: Immigrants in Same-Sex Couples in the United States. *SocArXiv*, 15 February. doi:10.31235/osf.io/hxjkt.

Human Dignity Trust (2021) *Map of Countries that Criminalise LGBT People*. https://www.humandignitytrust.org/lgbt-the-law/map-of-criminalisation/ (accessed 23 March).

Ingraham, C. (1994) The Heterosexual Imaginary: Feminist Sociology and Theories of Gender. *Sociological Theory* 12(2): 203–219.

Ingraham, C. (2005) *Thinking Straight: The Power, Promise and Paradox of Heterosexuality*. New York, USA and London, UK: Routledge.

Jansen, S. (2013) Introduction: Fleeing Homophobia, Aslyum Claims Related to Sexual Orientation amd Gender Identity in Europe. In: Spijkerboer T. (ed.), *Fleeing Homophobia: Sexual Orientation, Gender Identity and Asylum*. London: Routledge.

Jansen, S. and Spijkerboer, T. (2011) Fleeing Homophobia, Asylum Claims Related to Sexual Orientation and Gender Identity in Europe. https://www.refworld.org/docid/4ebba7852.html (accessed 17 February 2019).

Jenicek, A., Wong, A. and Ou Jin Lee, E. (2009) Dangerous Shortcuts: Representations of Sexual Minority Refugees in the Post-9/11 Canadian Press. *Canadian Journal of Communication* 34(4): 635–658.

Jesus, Rafi A. (2017) One Step at a Time: The Dilemmas, Strategies, and Outcomes of Bi-National Same-Sex Relationships During DOMA and Beyond. Dissertation, Georgia State University. doi: https://doi.org/10.57709/9996865.

Jordan, S. and Morrissey, C. (2013) 'On What Grounds?' LGBT Asylum Claims in Canada. *Forced Migration Review* 42: 13–15.

Kofman, E. (2018) Family Migration as a Class Matter. *International Migration* 56(4): 33–46.

Kollman, K. (2018) *The Same-Sex Unions Revolution in Western Democracies: International norms and domestic Policy Change / Kelly Kollman*. Baltimore, MD: Project Muse.

Lee, C. (2013) *Fictive Kinship: Family Reunification and the Meaning of Race and Nation in American Immigration*. New York: Russell Sage Foundation.

Lewis, R. (2013) Deportable Subjects: Lesbians and Political Asylum. *Feminist Formations* 25(2): 174–194.

Luibhéid, E. (2002) *Entry Denied: Controlling Sexuality at the Border*. Minneapolis, MN: University of Minnesota Press.

Luibhéid, E. (2008a) Queer/Migration: An Unruly Body of Scholarship. *GLQ* 14(2–3): 169–190.

Luibhéid, E. (2008b) Sexuality, Migration, and the Shifting Line between Legal and Illegal Status. *GLQ* 14(2–3): 289–315.

Luibhéid, E. (2013) Sexualities and International Migration. In: Gold, S.J. and Nawyn, S.J. (eds), *Routledge International Handbook of Migration Studies*. New York: Routledge.

Luibhéid, E. (2014) Sexuality and International Migration. In: Buffington, R.M., Luibhéid, E. and Guy, D.J. (eds), *A Global History of Sexuality: The Modern Era*. Chichester: Wiley Blackwell.

Luibhéid, E. (2018) Same-Sex Marriage and the Pinkwashing of State Migration Controls. *International Feminist Journal of Politics* 20(3): 405–424.

Luibhéid, E. and Cantú Jr, L. (2005) *Queer Migrations: Sexuality, U.S. Citizenship, and Border Crossings*. Minneapolis, MN: University of Minnesota Press.

Manalansan, M.F. (2006) Queer Intersections: Sexuality and Gender in Migration Studies. *International Migration Review* 40(1): 224–249.

Mau, S. (2010) Mobility Citizenship, Inequality, and the Liberal State: The Case of Visa Policies. *International Political Sociology* 4(4): 339–361.

Mau, S., Gülzau, F., Laube, L., et al. (2015) The Global Mobility Divide: How Visa Policies Have Evolved over Time. *Journal of Ethnic and Migration Studies* 41(8): 1192–1213.

McDevitt-Pugh, L. (2011) The Mobility of Corporate Lesbians. *Signs: Journal of Women in Culture and Society* 36(4): 798–806.

Millbank, J. (2009) 'The Ring of Truth': A Case Study of Credibility Assessment in Particular Social Group Refugee Determinations. *International Journal of Refugee Law* 21(1): 1–33.

Murray, D. (2014a) Real Queer: 'Authentic' LGBT Refugee Claimants and Homonationalism in the Canadian Refugee System. *Anthropologica* 56(1): 21–32.

Murray, D.A. (2014b) The (Not So) Straight Story: Queering Migration Narratives of Sexual Orientation and Gendered Identity Refugee Claimants. *Sexualities* 17(4): 451–471.

Murray, D.A.B. (2016) *Real Queer? Sexual Orientation and Gender Identity Refugees in the Canadian Refugee Apparatus.* London: Rowman & Littlefield International.

Nakamura, N., Chan, E. and Fischer, B. (2013) 'Hard to Crack': Experiences of Community Integration among First- and Second-Generation Asian MSM in Canada. *Cultural Diversity and Ethnic Minority Psychology* 19(3): 248.

Nakamura, N. and Kassan, A. (2020) Living in Exile: The Experiences of Individuals in Same-Sex Binational Relationships in Latin America. *Journal of Homosexuality* 67(14): 2014–2033.

Neumayer, E. (2006) Unequal Access to Foreign Spaces: How States Use Visa Restrictions to Regulate Mobility in a Globalized World. *Transactions – Institute of British Geographers (1965)* 31(1): 72–84.

Ngai, M.M. (2014) *Impossible Subjects: Illegal Aliens and the Making of Modern America.* Princeton, NJ: Princeton University Press.

Oswald, R., Blume, L. and Marks, S. (2005) Decentering Heteronormativity: A Proposal for family studies. In: Bengtson, V., Acock, A., Allen, K., et al. (eds), *Sourcebook of Family Theories and Methods: An Interactive Approach.* Thousand Oaks, CA: SAGE.

Pravattiyagul, J. (2021) Thai Transgender Women in Europe: Migration, Gender and Binational Relationships. *Asian and Pacific Migration Journal – APMJ* 30(1): 79–101.

Puar, J.K. (2007) *Terrorist Assemblages: Homonationalism in Queer Times.* Durham, NC: Duke University Press.

Raboin, T. (2017) *Discourses on LGBT Asylum in the UK: Constructing a Queer Haven.* Manchester: Manchester University Press.

Rambukkana, N. (2015) *Fraught Intimacies: Non/monogamy in the Public Sphere.* Vancouver and Toronto: UBC Press.

Reimers, D.M. (1985) *Still the Golden Door: The Third World Comes to America.* New York: Columbia University Press.

Ritholtz, S. and Buxton, R. (2021) Queer Kinship and the Rights of Refugee Families. *Migration Studies.* DOI: 10.1093/migration/mnab007.

Rubin, G. (1984) Thinking Sex: Notes for a Radical Theory of the Politics of Sexuality. *Social Perspectives in Lesbian and Gay Studies: A Reader* 1: 100–133.

Rydström, J. (2011) *Odd Couples: A History of Gay Marriage in Scandinavia.* Amsterdam: Uitgeverij Aksant.

Rygiel, K. (2008) The Securitized Citizen. In: Isin, E.F. (ed.), *Recasting the Social in Citizenship.* Toronto: University of Toronto Press.

Sedgwick, E.K. (2008) *Epistemology of the Closet.* Berkeley, CA: University of California Press.

Shakhsari, S. (2014) The Queer Time of Death: Temporality, Geopolitics, and Refugee Rights. *Sexualities* 17(8): 998–1015.

Steinbugler, A.C. (2005) Visibility as Privilege and Danger: Heterosexual and Same-Sex Interracial Intimacy in the 21st Century. *Sexualities* 8(4): 425–443.

Stychin, C. (2003) *Governing Sexuality: The Changing Politics of Citizenship and Law Reform.* Oxford: Hart Publishing.

Torpey, J. (1998) Coming and Going: On the State Monopolization of the Legitimate 'Means of Movement'. *Sociological Theory* 16(3): 239–259.

Turner, J. (2015) The Family Migration Visa in the History of Marriage Restrictions: Postcolonial Relations and the UK Border. *British Journal of Politics and International Relations* 17(4): 623–643.

Turner, J. and Vera Espinoza, M. (2021) The Affective and Intimate Life of the Family Migration Visa: Knowing, Feeling and Encountering the Heteronormative State. *Geopolitics* 26(2): 357–377.

United Nations (1948) UN General Assembly, Universal Declaration of Human Rights. 10 December, 217 A (III). https://www.refworld.org/docid/3ae6b3712c.html (accessed 5 December 2022).

Van Hear, N. (2014) Reconsidering Migration and Class. *International Migration Review* 48(s1): S100–S121.

Velasco, K. (2018) Human Rights INGOs, LGBT INGOs, and LGBT Policy Diffusion, 1991–2015. *Social Forces* 97(1): 377–404.

Warner, M. (1991) Introduction: Fear of a Queer Planet. *Social Text* 29: 3–17.

Warner, M. (1993) *Fear of a Queer Planet: Queer Politics and Social Theory.* Minneapolis, MN, USA and London, UK: University of Minnesota Press.
Weeks, J. (1981) *Sex, Politics and Society: The Regulation of Sexuality since 1800.* London: Longman.
Weeks, J., Heaphy, B. and Donovan, C. (2001) *Same Sex Intimacies: Families of Choice and other Life Experiments.* London: Routledge.
Weston, K. (1997) *Families We Choose: Lesbians, Gays, Kinship.* New York: Columbia University Press.
White, M.A. (2013) Ambivalent Homonationalisms: Transnational Queer Intimacies and Territorialized Belongings. *Interventions (London, England)* 15(1): 37–54.
Yue, A. (2008) Same-Sex Migration in Australia: From Interdependency to Intimacy. *GLQ: A Journal of Lesbian and Gay Studies* 14(2–3): 239–262.

PART IV

SPATIALITIES AND TEMPORALITIES

18. Migrant family separation, reunification and recalibration
Denise L. Spitzer and Sara Torres

INTRODUCTION

Movement and migration have been features of world human history. In recent decades, however, transformations in transportation modalities and communication technologies, fleeing the exigencies of conflict, poverty and environmental disasters in search of new economic opportunities and social mobility, and the longing for new adventures, have propelled both travel and permanent resettlement in other locales. Over the past 50 years, shifts in the world economy evidenced by global production chains have entrenched a transnational division of labour, which is grounded in seeking out (and retaining) low labour costs (Castles, 2011; Delgado Wise et al., 2013). Poor salaries and the concomitant neoliberal prescriptions for economic growth touted by multinational corporations, some governments, and multilateral institutions such as the World Bank and the International Monetary Fund (IMF), which advocate the withdrawal of state support for social programmes, have impelled transnational labour migration (Delgado Wise et al., 2013). Neoliberal globalization has thus propelled the out-migration of an estimated 100 million persons (Delgado Wise et al., 2013). This burgeoning number of transnational migrant workers has resulted in social transformations, as families often experience prolonged separation across political and social borders, followed by reunifications under changed circumstances, whether within homelands or in lands of resettlement. Focusing primarily on Europe and North America as regions of family reunification and resettlement, in this chapter we examine the impact of familial separation on transnational families, and the processes and consequences of familial reunification.

Although the United Nations Convention on the Rights of the Child and the International Convention on the Protection of the Rights of All Migrant Workers and Members of their Families enshrine the right to family reunification (IOM, 2015), national immigration policies, informed by both neoliberal constructs of productivity and burgeoning racism and xenophobia, further structure migrant inclusions and exclusions (Strasser et al., 2009; Watson, 2018; Wray, 2009). Moreover, implementation of these Conventions is weak (Delgado Wise et al., 2013). While research demonstrates that family members are important sources of social support and facilitate migrant integration (Bragg and Wong, 2016; IOM, 2015; Oliver, 2013; Spitzer and Torres, 2014a; Strasser et al., 2009; Wray, 2009), rising moral panic about expanding numbers of migrants from the Global South, in particular, through family reunification or chain migration has contributed to increased concerns about, and greater limitations of, family migration (Block, 2015). In particular, some countries fear that the presence of family members may disrupt integration, as migrants are regarded as bearers of traditional beliefs and practices that may conflict with their nationalist progressive self-images (Oliver, 2013). This discourse (in conjunction with concerns about sham marriages) is used to shore up stricter migration controls and surveillance (Wray, 2009).

Moves towards greater border controls and managed migration imbued with neoliberal notions of human capital, and hence a migrant's market worth, has resulted in a proliferation of migrant categories, each of which turns on definitions of skill, desirability and age, *inter alia*. This complex (and often shifting) taxonomy of migrants structures options for either permanent or temporary resettlement and therefore has significant implications for the possibilities of family reunification (Beine et al., 2015; Social Planning Council of Ottawa, 2010). Migrant designation as temporary foreign worker, permanent resident, naturalized citizen, undocumented worker or foreign student, as well as economic status, education and national origin, are all implicated in the possibilities for family reunification (Block, 2015; Hooper and Sallant, 2018; see Chapters 2, 3 and 20, this *Handbook*).

Increasingly, migrants and their families from wealthy countries confront fewer barriers to their mobility, and professionally credentialed migrants and their families are granted opportunities for permanent resettlement, while workers classified as semi- or low-skilled are permitted temporary resettlement as sojourners (Block, 2015; Castles, 2011; Craig, 2015; Wray, 2009; see Chapter 12, this *Handbook*). Moreover, family members of migrants constructed as low-skilled often face stricter admission criteria than relatives of high-skilled migrants moving to the same country (Beine et al., 2015). Some countries, such as the United States of America (USA), issue limits on family visas by country. For example, in 2018, US citizens hoping to sponsor siblings from the Philippines or Mexico would be expected to wait over 20 years (Hooper and Salant, 2018).

Furthermore, migrants hoping to reunite with their families are often expected to demonstrate that they have the financial resources and adequate housing to sustain and accommodate them. At times, they are compelled to sign an undertaking of financial responsibility for incoming family members, who will be prohibited from partaking in social welfare programmes for a specified period of time (Block, 2015). In the United Kingdom (UK), for instance, in 2012, spousal sponsors were required to earn £23,000 a year, an income threshold that approximately half of Britons could not meet (Block, 2015). Given that women and racialized workers are more apt to be situated at the lower echelons of the labour market, they face even greater obstacles sponsoring family (Block, 2015). Moreover, these policies reinforce dependency on the sponsor, which has gendered consequences (DeLaet, 1999). Despite these myriad challenges, approximately 40 per cent of migrants to Organisation for Economic Co-operation and Development (OECD) countries are categorized as family class; however, as family members may migrate under disparate categories or circumstances, kin-based migration may comprise from 57 per cent (UK) to over 80 per cent (in the USA) (Hooper and Salant, 2018).

This chapter explores the contours of our knowledge about migrant family separation and reunification to uncover what we understand about the impacts on transnational families in the Global North and South. Given the stratification of migrants within the context of managed migration, and the disparate opportunities for family reunification that are subsequently on offer, we deploy an intersectional lens that attends to the dynamic interactions amongst social indicators such as gender, ethnicity/nationality, age and place, and other factors, to help nuance our understanding of this phenomenon, and to aid in the identification of gaps in our current research. Notably, the parameters of our review are structured by a number of issues. Firstly, we acknowledge that we focus here on experiences of families in Europe and North America. Some regions of the world – for example, broadly speaking, Asia – have limited opportunities for permanent familial resettlement. Moreover, our findings reflect the geographical foci of the research published in English, French and Spanish that we were able to locate. The final issue, which we will discuss later in the chapter, is the discursive cultural and socio-political construction of family structures policy, which will in turn circumscribe the type of family that will become the topic of research. Resultantly, the experiences of queer, polygynous, unmarried, chosen, and other families may be underrepresented in the literature.

TRANSNATIONAL PARENTING AND THE IMPACT OF FAMILIAL SEPARATION

The impact of familial separation on household members who have migrated or are left behind is multi-fold, and contingent on myriad socio-political, gendered, economic and personal contexts. This variation further underscores the need for intersectional analysis to discern more carefully the interactions of social location, oppression and privilege as individuals and families navigate this transnational space. Family separation is commonly characterized by temporal elasticity. Migrants, often setting off as sojourners, may anticipate being separated from their families for a set period of time, only to have that absence prolonged, and to have their return or reunification in their host country indefinitely postponed as restrictive immigration policies and/or insufficient capital to enable reunification serve as obstacles to their plans (Carling et al., 2012; Social Planning Council of Ottawa, 2010).

Familial separation engenders shifts in household arrangements and relations, which are attenuated across geographic and temporal borders. The upheavals associated with the transition to transnational household include a redistribution of economic and social power within the family, which may contribute to intra-familial tensions (Carling et al., 2012). In some instances, migration may subvert gender norms as breadwinning roles are reversed, even though labour migration is both normalized and encouraged by the state and in popular discourse (Spitzer and Piper, 2014). In addition, family members left at home may enjoy the benefits of financial remittances and gifts (IOM, 2015), which may elevate their economic, educational and social status, yet also render them feeling indebted to their migrant family member (Pratt, 2006). Moreover, prolonged familial disjuncture is often associated with a host of psycho-social as well as economic impacts. Conjugal and parental relationships may be challenged by the physical, temporal and socio-cultural distance that each family fragment and individual household member experience (IOM, 2015; Pratt, 2006; Social Planning Council of Ottawa, 2010). Importantly, while some unwanted outcomes such as deteriorating interest in education, uptake of illegal substance use, and early marriage, have been reported (IOM, 2015), not all children in migrant households are negatively affected (Zentgraf and Chinchilla, 2012).

Out-migration of household members often requires the rearrangement of familial roles and responsibilities. Given the gendered nature of household labour and care work, these responsibilities often fall to female kin involving multiple distant households (Parreñas, 2005). Migrant domestic workers whose care labour is purchased predominantly by women in more affluent countries and contexts, and whose own immediate caregiving work is taken on by female relations (for example, daughters, mothers, sisters, cousins), comprise a global care chain (Parreñas, 2005; Yeates, 2004), the nodes of which are characterized by disparities in power within and across locations, which Sarvasy and Longo (2004) characterize as feminized neocolonialism.

Familial separation alters, but does not eliminate, parenting roles. Labour migration is often rationalized as a means of supporting and improving the wherewithal of families, particularly children; however, parenting responsibilities persist transnationally (Zentgraf and Chinchilla, 2012). Migrant women in particular continue to assume the primary role of parenting children (Carling et al., 2012). Gendered constructions of parenthood task mothers with maintaining the 'ritualized practices of everyday life' (Falicov, 2007, p. 159, in Carling et al., 2012, p. 196). Whilst both migrant mothers and fathers are expected to send financial remittances and gifts, mothers regardless of their geographic location are deemed responsible for the provision of ongoing support for their children (Carling et al., 2012; Parreñas, 2005). The entrenchment of gender ideologies that equate parenting with womanhood further complicate transnational parenting. Migrant mothers often bear the opprobrium of others, including their own family members, who accuse them of abandoning their children – a sentiment they may internalize themselves – even though, as mentioned, they generally migrate with the purpose of enhancing their children's material well-being (Carling et al., 2012; Parreñas, 2005; Zentgraf and Chinchilla, 2012). Notably, migrant fathers are not generally subject to the same expectations (Carling et al., 2012). In fact, Yeoh et al. (2020) revealed that Indonesian and Filipino women regarded men as incapable of providing the emotional care labour associated with the maternal role, and of meeting the demands of being the left-behind parent, which would require them to engage in both paid and unpaid labour, and therefore favoured male migration. In their study, some Filipino and Indonesian fathers in migrant households sought to reconfigure their constructs of masculinity to include care labour (Yeoh et al., 2020); however, Parreñas (2005) found that many Filipino fathers failed to assume household responsibilities – with the exception of men engaged in hyper-masculinized occupations such as policing.

Shaw (2020) argues that gender roles and masculinity push children to play a central role in the relationship among family members left behind. If and when fathers are unavailable or unwilling to participate in household chores, are not up to take responsibility for caregiving, or choose to focus on romantic attentions elsewhere, girls feel compelled to take up the mothering role of keeping the family together by buffering relations within the family, carrying on household responsibilities, and taking care of siblings (Shaw, 2020). Therefore, girls' responses and fathers' actions or inactions produce and reproduce gender and intergenerational inequalities in the pre-reunification period (Yuval-Davis, 2015). The migration of Senegalese men to Italy and Spain results in another pattern of familial relations and parenting. Families accept their 'perpetual separation' or families being 'together but apart'. Entrenched gender roles, however, still dictate that women left behind are put under the tutelage and surveillance of the husband's family (Mazzucato et al., 2015). This context, which seeks to guarantee in-laws' support for women, may curtail women's independence and enhance control of women by their husband's family.

Communication technologies have greatly altered transnational parenting. Mobile phones, text messaging and video meeting applications have enabled greater immediacy in connections at little to no cost (Carling et al., 2012). Ongoing contact may help to sustain family relationships, but these are also complicated by shifting intra-familial power dynamics that may result in the changing lines of authority that may be confusing particularly for children (Zentgraf and Chinchilla, 2012). Moreover, migrant mothers must adapt to the temporal rhythms of their family members at home, which can be challenging when time zones and working hours are particularly disparate (Yeoh et al., 2020). Retrospective interviews with youth, however, suggests that communication with migrant parents was less meaningful for them than it was for the adults and that they would have preferred their parent's presence rather than the gifts they sent in their absence (Suárez-Orozco et al., 2011). Return visits further help to sustain parent–child relationships; however, even the possibility to do so depends on their contract and provisions for leave, employer consent (even when leave is mandated by the contract, employers may exert control over its timing and length) and financial resources. Furthermore, visits are particularly challenging for undocumented migrants, as crossing borders may threaten their ongoing employment (Fresnoza-Flot, 2015). Undocumented Filipino migrant mothers in France reportedly compensated for their prolonged absences by communicating more often with their children, and by remitting more money and gifts than their documented counterparts (Fresnoza-Flot, 2015).

The impact of familial separation on children appears to depend on the children's age at parental migration, the length of time apart, and the gender of the migrant parent. Adjusting to a parent's absence can be particularly trying for children; however, the effects can be mitigated if children are given adequate preparation for their parent's departure, especially if explanations are provided by their mothers who emphasize the temporary nature of their separation (Suárez-Orozco et al., 2011; Zentgraf and Chinchilla, 2012). In the initial year of separation from their mothers, children report elevated rates of depression and anxiety; however, little or only transient impact on mental health was noted amongst children with migrant fathers, and over time these psychological impacts dissipated (Suárez-Orozco et al., 2011). Separation from migrant mothers also appears to be less critical in early childhood; however, compared to migrant fathers their absence has a more profound effect on children once they have started school (Tarroja and Fernando, 2013; Yeoh et al., 2020). Although responses to parental absence may differ – some children becoming resentful, others accepting of the new circumstances – younger children appear to withdraw more emotionally, whilst adolescents may respond by becoming either more independent or more aggressive (Suárez-Orozco et al., 2011; Tarroja and Fernando, 2013).

Students with migrant mothers have poorer attendance records and grades than their counterparts with resident mothers, report higher rates of behavioural and emotional difficulties, higher drop-out rates and substance abuse issues (Fresnoza-Flot, 2015; IOM, 2015; Suárez-Orozco et al., 2011; Tarroja and Fernando, 2013). These problems may be rooted in local conditions. Some youth with migrant mothers experience bullying and intimidation by peers at school, and some assume caregiving and other household responsibilities in the family, which reduces the time and energy required for schoolwork (Tarroja and Fernando, 2013). Pratt (2017), argues that children's experiences during separation and reunification represent a form of violence, which is expressed in 'the mundane, chronic, and everyday violence of poverty, social and economic marginalization, and feelings of abandonment' (Pratt, 2017, p. 388).

FAMILY REUNIFICATION: PROCESS AND EXPERIENCE

Family reunification and the right to sponsor family (as constructed by the host country) is generally proffered to citizens and to some migrants legally residing in another country (Strasser et al., 2009). Despite commitments to international Conventions and human rights, and research which suggests that the presence of family facilitates integration, some governments hesitate to embrace family reunification as they fear that immigrant families will become dependent on state-sponsored programmes and resources, or fail to embrace 'modern' and 'progressive' values (Oliver, 2013; Social Planning Council of Ottawa, 2010; Strasser et al., 2009). Prolonged family separation not only engenders social and financial costs that are often unrecognized in the policy environment, but may also preoccupy migrants to such a degree as to distract them from making contributions to their country of resettlement (IOM, 2015; Zentgraf and Chinchilla, 2012). For example, the perceived obligation to continue sending remittances to family in their home countries may reduce migrant workers' abilities to retain financial resources for immigration and resettlement expenses for their families, to contribute to their local communities as volunteers, or to invest in their own education and retraining in their host country.

According to the Migration Integration Policy Index (2015), which includes data from 52 nations, from the OECD and European Union (EU) member states to BRIC (Brazil, Russia, India, and China) countries, the five countries most open to family reunification are Spain, Portugal, Slovenia, Canada and Sweden; the USA and the UK were ranked 14th and 38th, respectively. In all cases, social and cultural constructions of family, and their respective economic value, inform policies which further reinforce which type of families are admitted for resettlement. In Europe, most countries employ a definition that restricts access to nuclear families (Bonjour and Kraler, 2015); in Canada, single migrants with adequate financial resources are eligible to sponsor a sibling, parent or more distant relation (Spitzer and Torres, 2014a). The immigration status of the principal migrant/sponsor often determines their eligibility to be accompanied or to be later joined by family members. Family sponsorship requirements are often reduced for refugees; however, Germany and Sweden have recently imposed restrictions on family reunification rights of newly arrived asylum seekers (Hooper and Salant, 2018). In Japan, some children of asylum seekers who were born in or brought to Japan at a young age have reportedly been offered permanent status as they reach the age of majority, if their parents are willing to return to their home country (Funakoshi et al., 2016). Most countries permit citizens and permanent residents to bring or be reunited with family members, particularly children and spouses (Hooper and Salant, 2018); however, the definitions of spouse and child are not uniform. For example, Canada permits the sponsorship of same- and opposite-sex married, common-law and conjugal partners; whereas the USA accepts only legally married couples (Halpert and Baldwin, 2013). In many EU countries, civil partnerships are acceptable, although in some nations, including the UK, couples are on probation for two years (Oliver, 2013; Wray, 2009). Many countries require couples regardless of marital status to reside together for a specific period of time (Strasser et al., 2009; Wray, 2009). Concern about forced and arranged marriage have led to the implementation of age thresholds for spousal migrants that range from 24 years in Denmark; to 21 in Austria, Belgium and the Netherlands; and 18 in most other European countries (Block, 2015; Oliver, 2013). Denmark further demands that migrant couples affirm their commitment to gender equality and mutual respect (Strasser et al., 2009). Generally, only one spouse in a polygynous family is eligible for sponsorship (Wray, 2009).

Age informs the construction of the category of child for the purposes of migration, the limit of which for most EU countries is 18 (15 in Denmark), while the USA accepts unmarried children under 21, Canada under 22, and Australia under 23 years of age (Hooper and Salant, 2018). There is general consensus that migrant parents and grandparents must be over 65 years of age to be eligible for sponsorship, although the UK allows relations under 65 who are wholly dependent on British family members to join them in exceptional circumstances (Wray, 2009).

Importantly, dependency is often embedded in the sponsorship process. Some countries demand evidence that sponsored relations are unable to care for themselves – whether children or elders – and have no one in proximity to be of material assistance (Strasser et al., 2009; Wray, 2009). While all countries ask that migrant sponsors accept financial responsibility for incoming family members in most circumstances, the specific demands of migrant sponsors and the processing of sponsorship applications can differ according to migrant status, nationality and country of resettlement (Strasser et al., 2009; Wray, 2009).

Whereas permanent residents and naturalized citizens in Canada had the right to sponsor parents and grandparents, but had to wait many years for their application to be processed because of the backlog in the system, new policies established between 2014 and 2017 by two successive federal governments (representing two different political governing parties) introduced more onerous policies for family reunification. In 2014, new measures for adult children wanting to sponsor their parents or grandparents were passed which included a 30 per cent increase in the income threshold required from sponsors, and a significant increase in the length of time sponsors are required to support parents or grandparents, from a prior ten years to the current standard of 20 (Bélanger and Candiz, 2020). Only after this extended period are parents or grandparents eligible for government assistance. In addition, the first government regime created an annual quota system, whilst the second established a lottery system. Under the quota system, there were 5000 available places for parents or grandparents, whose applications were accepted on a first come, first served basis. Under the lottery system, still in operation at the time of writing in 2021, 10,000 random applicants win the right to have their applications processed, making family reunification a matter of luck and no longer a right (Bélanger and Candiz, 2020). In other words, what was once the right of those with legal status to family reunification has been curtailed (Bonjour and Kraler, 2015).

In Europe, potential family sponsors in Belgium, Germany, France and Sweden must meet housing provisions, while the income thresholds required to meet expectations of long-term financial support has increased dramatically in many cases (Block, 2015). Australia requires an individual sponsoring parents to earn a minimum of AU$86 606, while couples must have an income of AU$115,475 (Knaus, 2018). Sponsors may opt for a contributory visa whereby they pay between AU$50,000 and AU$115,000 to facilitate processing of their applications, reducing the wait time from approximately 30 years to two (Askola, 2016; Hooper and Salant, 2018). In France, migrants who wish to sponsor family members may do so after living in the country for at least one year, and must demonstrate that they earn at least €1445 per month and pay for a highly priced application processing fee, which is sometimes unattainable for migrant domestic workers (Fresnoza-Flot, 2015). For many migrants, the financial demands of sponsorship present a major challenge that prolongs the reunification process (Social Planning Council of Ottawa, 2010), which can engender further stress if they fear that children will age out of the category of dependent for the purposes of migration.

Like Canada, other countries set quotas on visa allocations for some family members (Hooper and Salant, 2018). While sponsors must address specific requirements to be reunited with relations, family members too must often meet additional criteria either pre-migration or prior to becoming permanent residents, as many countries initially grant family migrants temporary status (Block, 2015; Oliver, 2013; Strasser et al., 2009). Depending on the country, family migrants may undergo language testing in the application phase, while others assess language skills and knowledge of local contexts and values after partaking in local courses; all of these evaluations are meant to determine family migrants' ability to integrate into local society (Block, 2015; Oliver, 2013). Despite the availability of instructional assistance and settlement services in many regions, family migrants and their sponsors remain the primary agents of integration (Chen and Thorpe, 2015; Oliver, 2013). Overall, these policies reinforce dependency on the migrant sponsor, which may create resentment amongst family members who may feel permanently indebted, but it also enhances their vulnerability should the sponsor lose their job or pass away (Pratt, 2006; Social Planning Council of Ottawa, 2010; Strasser et al., 2009).

Reunification can bring family members face-to-face with realities they had not anticipated. The struggles faced by migrants and migrant households are generally concealed – and remain opaque due to the silences maintained after reunification (Spitzer et al., 2012; cf. Suárez-Orozco et al., 2011) – allowing for an imagined and idealized existence upon reunification (Zentgraf and Chinchilla, 2012). Often, after a honeymoon period, tensions may emerge (Spitzer et al., 2012; Suárez-Orozco et al., 2011; Zentgraf and Chinchilla, 2012). Most notably, reunification is also often accompanied by upheavals in socio-economic status and downward mobility as many migrant workers undergo a process of deskilling, which has compelled the settled migrant to work multiple jobs, leaving little time for aiding the family with material and emotional adjustments to their new environment and to each other, which appears to facilitate adaptation for youth to a lower standard of living (Carling et al., 2012; Lam et al., 2005; Ogaya, 2015; Pratt, 2006; Spitzer et al., 2012). As Ogaya (2015) noted of Filipino live-in caregivers in Canada: 'While transmigrant mothers long deeply for family reunification to enable them to be "ideal mothers", this dream goal sometimes clashes with the reality of their lives as migrant workers' (p. 214). In addition, reunified families may have difficulties in locating affordable and suitable accommodation, while children face challenges in transitioning to a new education system, resulting in high drop-out rates (Pratt, 2006; Social Planning Council of Ottawa, 2010). Despite these challenges, the presence of family appears to be salutary overall, as household members contribute to the group's material and emotional well-being (Social Planning Council of Ottawa, 2010).

Family reunification in a new land is often met with ambivalence, as it also signals separation from family and friends at home, particularly for children who have been parted from caregivers who were often grandparents (Bernhard et al., 2005; Pratt, 2006; Suárez-Orozco et al., 2011). Consequently, children may display emotional distance from their migrant parent in proportion to the amount of time they have been apart and their age at separation; they are also more likely to report low self-esteem and depression in this novel setting (Carling et al., 2012; Fresnoza-Flot, 2015; Pratt, 2006; Suárez-Orozco et al., 2011). They may struggle with the adaptation to disparate parenting styles and the changes to familial roles (Fresnoza-Flot, 2015; Spitzer et al., 2012). In addition, couples contend with stressors as they learn how to live together and renegotiate their relationships (Pratt, 2006; Spitzer et al., 2012).

In particular, recently arrived family members often depend on the sponsor for help in navigating both unfamiliar systems including health, education and employment, and the norms, values and attitudes of their new host society. Strasser et al. (2009) found that when women are the sponsors, serious renegotiation of traditional gender roles is required. Research with Filipino families reuniting in Canada found that further problems ensued when men were able to work, as they expected their wives to return to reproductive roles and relinquish their breadwinning responsibilities in Canada (Spitzer et al., 2012). Yeoh et al. (2020) observed similar efforts to 're-domesticate' women migrant workers who had returned to their home country. In other cases, women felt pressure to continue being active in the labour force whilst still performing household responsibilities without spousal or children's support (Oishi, 2008). One former live-in caregiver in Canada, disillusioned by the lack of support from her husband and children whose arrival she had worked for and greeted with great joy, shared that she 'felt like a slave' (Spitzer and Torres, 2014b). In addition, some husbands reported feeling emasculated when they did not secure immediate access to the labour market, or when they could not find work commensurate with their previous experience and education, and were consequently financially dependent upon their wives. According to Strasser et al. (2009), women who are sponsored by their partners often felt that it affected their self-esteem and reduced their opportunities for regaining the sense of autonomy developed after their partners left the home country.

An additional impact of separation is linked to unintended reconfiguration of the family. Some Filipino women migrant workers who entered Canada as live-in caregivers, and endured a prolonged period of separation while working to reunite with and resettle their families, had spouses who declined to join their migrating children. Resultantly, they became lone parents, which engendered additional stress. In some of these cases, children blamed their mothers for the rupture of the family, and remained unforgiving of them post-arrival in Canada (Spitzer et al., 2012).

Another phenomenon that leads to families being separated is that of twice-migrant families. Twice-migrant families are those who migrate to one destination country via a third country. Agrawal (2016) found that a number of male skilled migrants from South Asia, China and the Philippines, who migrated to Canada with their families from the Middle East, were unable to find comparable job opportunities in Canada, and subsequently decided to return to the region. Families were then separated once again across multiple borders, as mothers and children stayed in Canada. Twice-migrant families who returned to their lucrative jobs in the Middle East did so because they were disillusioned with the lack of job opportunities stemming from failure to recognize their credentials and skills. This split familial context is particularly challenging for women, who have to bear the responsibility of raising children as a single mother often whilst working to upgrade skills or to support their families (Agrawal, 2016).

RECALIBRATION

In the same way that family separation and reunification reflect the interplay amongst socio-economic and political contexts that shape labour migration, gender relations and restrictive immigration policies, recalibration of family relationships also reflects the intersection of such factors occurring in the post-reunification period. Despite these challenges, therefore, families tend to adjust over time (Fresnoza-Flot, 2015). For example, Suárez-Orozco et al.'s (2011) longitudinal study of migrant children in the USA discovered that psychological symptoms dissipated by the fifth year of reunification. Studies in Canada and France revealed that Filipino migrant youth often embraced a greater sense of independence than they exhibited at home (Fresnoza-Flot, 2015; Ogaya, 2015; Seki, 2015). Notably, their greater autonomy, which often included finding employment, was often connected with the desire to contribute to their families, kin and friends at home (Ogaya, 2015; Seki, 2015). In France, young Filipino migrant women adopted French social values and habits such as drinking alcohol and smoking, while young men became more serious about their education, which they regarded as critical to upward mobility (Fresnoza-Flot, 2015). In Canada, Spitzer et al. (2012) also found that within the first five years of reunification families coalesced around enhancing the financial well-being of the household, as children and spouses contributed to collective coffers. Nearly 43 per cent of participants (12 out 28 migrant women) interviewed were actively working towards purchasing a home. Of those who owned a home in this study, the majority had purchased by the five-year mark owing to their own thrift and collective efforts.

As families renegotiate their relationships, socio-economic factors and the reproduction of gender roles are paramount to family dynamics. For example, Kazemipur and Nakhaie's (2014) analysis of data from the Longitudinal Survey of Immigrants to Canada found a link between a sense of attachment or a sense of connection to a country, and positive economic experiences in the country. For these authors a sense of attachment is shaped by a 'dynamic process of interaction between immigrants and the host society's population and institutions' (Kazemipur and Nakhaie, 2014, p. 629). Attachment to the new country in the recalibration period might also be determined by participation in the labour market of children, and retirement plans of parents. A study in France, where Filipino parents brought their children to the country to have a better life, found that parents themselves planned to retire and return to live permanently in the Philippines (Fresnoza-Flot, 2015).

Finding employment is particularly important for family recalibration (Spitzer and Torres, 2014a). The inability to secure meaningful employment for family members in this period perpetuates structures of inequalities when children and youth are unable to receive the financial support necessary to access training that leads to competitive jobs. Pratt (2017) argues that these obstacles frequently relegate migrant children and youth to the next generation of the low-skilled and marginalized workforce. With regard to spouses, lack of employment among reunited husbands, combined with patriarchal norms, often enhances the risk of violence against women in the recalibration period. For example, Oishi (2008) reports that in the USA, Asian and Central American migrant women experienced domestic violence from their reunited husbands who faced hurdles adapting to the new country and did not receive kin and community support.

Parents and children dreamed that upon reunification in their new country, families would live happily ever after, but most of the literature finds that such dreams are often shattered. Fresnoza-Flot (2015) indicated that, despite generational differences and clashes associated with family separation and reunification, parents and children developed 'tolerance towards each other, allowing the social reproduction of the family in its new land' (Fresnoza-Flot, 2015, p. 1165). Other authors also found that in the initial months and years following reunification, parents and youth acknowledged having acute discomfort, but most 'demonstrated remarkable strength, determination, resourcefulness, and resilience in dealing with the imposed challenges' (Suárez-Orozco et al., 2011, p. 249). Recalibration is about being able to live as a family and all the effort – perfect and imperfect – that it requires to make the best of the circumstances to re-establish the family in the new country with the support of the host society.

In Canada, Spitzer et al. (2012) found that over time reunited Filipino families recalibrated their relationships and managed to attain a new equilibrium, often accompanied by markers of migrant resettlement such as working towards (or attaining) home ownership, and children establishing their own families on Canadian soil. Relationships with children improved as children came to appreciate the sacrifices their mothers had made for them. One woman's daughter apologised for her poor treatment of her mother. The mother, a former live-in caregiver from the Philippines, explained: 'she told me one time. She says "Mom at first I don't understand you, but now I realize the more I grew up the more I realize what you're going through. So, I'm sorry it was such, I'm sorry I was such a bad girl to you."'

For some daughters, the recalibration of the relationship with the mother came when they became mothers themselves and realized the benefits of being in Canada. One daughter shared:

> I feel like – at that time, when I was a child, when I came here I kind of felt mad, like '[sigh] I don't wanna be here, I don't wanna be with these friends.' … I felt like I hated my mom back then, but now, I'm like, I felt grateful now, I'm like 'OK now I can give my kids like, a better health system. They don't have this back home …' They have a better future in here than back home, now that I'm a mom myself.

Recalibration is also about straddling between two (or more) cultures in the context of changing social and economic status, and migrant parents' attempt to keep their culture and language of origin, while children adapt to the culture and language of the new country. Filipino parents in France and Canada insisted on exposing their children to Filipino culture, such as food traditions and languages (Fresnoza-Flot, 2015; Spitzer et al., 2012). This often conflicts with children's desire to blend into the host community, including fitting in at school. For example, parents may insist on their children taking their home-country food for school lunches, and this may cause children to be shamed by their peers (Spitzer et al., 2012). Notably, school is often the site of racism and discrimination for newcomer youth, and parents may be ill-prepared to cope with these issues as they are novel to their experience. Moreover, some youth prefer not to share negative experiences and encounters, to avoid burdening their parents; resultantly, these issues remain unaddressed and unresolved. Differences in parents' and children's views toward cultural norms of the new society in migrant families also contribute to intergenerational conflicts. These are considered normal in the development processes of all families, but are particularly exacerbated by social, political and economic elements of the acculturation processes (Rania et al., 2018). Taken together, all of these processes and contexts are implicated in the recalibration of reunited migrant family life (Spitzer et al., 2012).

CONCLUSION

Neoliberal globalization has engendered an unprecedented movement of peoples across the globe in the pursuit of employment opportunities and economic survival. Although United Nations Conventions guarantee the right of immigrants to family reunification, nation-states have established a host of policies that stratify and delimit opportunities for families to resettle as a unit. Intersectionality – which highlights how the multiplicity of social identifiers including gender, ethnicity, socio-economic class, sexuality and migration status, amongst others, are co-constituted and situate individuals and groups of individuals within social hierarchies where they are subject to various oppressions and access various privileges – offers a lens that is salient to this issue (Spitzer et al., 2019). Specifically, intersectionality illuminates the socio-political inequalities experienced by migrants under neoliberalism that obscures racism, sexism, hetero-sexism, and other forms of xenophobia under the banner of migration policies that often purport to treat everyone on a level playing field (Hill-Collins and Bilge, 2016).

Nation-states, through their implementation of migration policy regimes, cross state borders and penetrate private households to extract, confine and situate individual family members and reconfigure intra-familial relationships. Policies that bestow certain nationalities, skills and genders with greater prestige based on their perceived economic value, mean that these people are granted admission and opportunities for migration and permanent resettlement – with families in tow – to countries in the Global North, whilst those deemed low-skilled, often but not solely racialized women, are more often admitted on a temporary basis. Importantly, the designation of low-skill does not always cohere with educational background, nor with the complexity of the work. For example, 63 per cent of participants in Canada's Live-In Caregiver Program, who may have been called upon to perform tasks that were once the domain of nurses or teachers, possessed undergraduate degrees; a proportion that far exceeded the one of university-educated economic immigrants (Kelly et al., 2011).

Whilst countries in the Global North extract the labour of migrant workers, policies and discourses erect barriers to familial reunification by delimiting and defining the construct of family. Most Northern countries privilege heteronormative nuclear families, who are perceived as a more mobile and economically effective family form that is more readily capable of integration. In comparison, multigenerational families are regarded both as a potential threat to progressive values and as a possible burden on government support programmes. In addition to policies that constrain the potential reunification with select family members, including adult children, grandparents and siblings, particular obstacles may be established based on nationality, as is seen in the USA.

Prolonged family separation of uncertain duration, and delayed family reunification, has become normalized and is thus not often the subject of public protest and outrage. The impacts on family members have been well documented, including worsening educational outcomes for left-behind children, the burdens of care work that are generally assumed by women and girls – including the reconfiguring of parenting roles – and intra-familial and spousal tensions. Remittances may help to alleviate some financial burdens, but in our study left-behind youth opined that they would have preferred the presence of their mother rather than her presents (Spitzer et al., 2012).

Throughout the familial separation, reunification and recalibration process, the Northern nation-state asserts control over the household and household relations. Notably, many countries through their sponsorship agreements entrench dependence on sponsors, and invariably create impediments to integration and a sense of belonging. Reunited family members are tasked with recalibrating their relationships. Although these entanglements are often regarded as the purview of the private household, the context of the state's multiple interventions in migrants' lives, societal attitudes and their intersectional status, further complicate their renegotiations. Notably, most reunited families are able to achieve some form of equilibrium over the long term, as their goals are tempered by the realities they face.

Despite its ubiquity, more research on family separation and reunification is urgently needed. To date, much of the work on the impact of separation on family members has focused on the effects on mental health and the educational outcomes of left-behind and migrant youth. Although more research on these topics is needed, further examination of the impact on gender roles and gender ideologies, including potential shifts and renegotiations, also requires investigation, particularly with respect to breadwinning and parenting roles, care work responsibilities, and prolonged dependence compelled through migrant family sponsorship agreements. Comparative case studies could help to tease out the effects of place, including policies, programmes and the presence or absence of co-ethnic communities, on reunited families. The dearth of literature on the recalibration process indicates the need for more research on the intergenerational effects of downward social mobility and the trauma induced by prolonged and indeterminate separation. This gap also calls for rethinking recalibration of reunited families' experiences in light of similar processes of adaptation and integration by migrants who benefit from policies favouring their arrival together with families.

Recalibration of family life is therefore about looking at the relationship between migrant family members, but also about the relationship that all members of society have with migrant families. In other words, recalibration of migrant families' lives cannot be seen in isolation from the dynamics of the host society, but needs to be understood within the societal structures that foster or undermine families' efforts for autonomy and to live permanently – and in dignity – in their new country (Nedelsky, 2011).

REFERENCES

Agrawal, S.K. (2016). 'Twice Migrants in Canada: Who are They and How Do They Perform Economically?' *Journal of International Migration and Integration* 17: 669–686. doi: 10.1007/s12134-015-0428-y.

Askola, H. (2016). 'Who Will Care for Grandma? Older Women, Parent Visas, and Australia's Migration Program.' *Australian Feminist Law Journal* 42(2): 297–319.

Beine, M., A. Boucher, B. Burgoon, M. Crock, J. Gest, M. Hiscox, P. McGovern, H. Rapoport, J. Schaper and E. Thielemann. (2015). 'Comparing Immigration Policies: An Overview from the IMPALA Database.' *International Migration Review* 50(4): 827-863.

Bélanger, D. and G. Candiz. (2020). 'The Politics of "Waiting" for Care: Immigration Policy and Family Reunification in Canada.' *Journal of Ethnic and Migration Studies* 46(16): 3472–3490. doi: 10.1080/1369183x.2019.1592399.

Bernhard, J., L. Landolt and L. Goldring. (2005). *Transnational, Multi-Local Motherhood: Experiences of Separation and Reunification Among Latin American Families in Canada.* CERIS Working Paper No. 40. Toronto: Joint Centre of Excellence for Research in Immigration and Settlement.

Block, L. (2015). 'Regulating Membership: Explaining Restriction and Stratification of Family Migration in Europe.' *Journal of Family Issues* 36(11): 1433–1452.

Bonjour, S. and A. Kraler. (2015). 'Introduction: Family Migration as an Integration Issue? Policy Perspectives and Academic Insights.' *Journal of Family Issues* 36(11): 1407–1432.

Bragg, B. and L. Wong. (2016). '"Cancelled Dreams": Family Reunification and Shifting Canadian Immigration Policy.' *Journal of Immigrant and Refugee Studies* 14(1): 46–85.

Carling, J., C. Menjívar and L. Schmalzbauer. (2012). 'Central Themes in the Study of Transnational Parenthood.' *Journal of Ethnic and Migration Studies* 38(2): 191–217.

Castles, S. (2011). 'Migration, Crisis, and the Global Labour Market.' *Globalizations* 8(3): 311–324.

Chen, X. and S.X. Thorpe. (2015). 'Temporary Families? The Parent and Grandparent Sponsorship Program and the Neoliberal Regime of Immigration Governance in Canada.' *Migration, Mobility, and Displacement* 1(1): 81–98.

Craig, G. (2015). *Migration and Integration: A Local and Experiential Perspective.* IRIS Working Paper Series, No. 7/2014. Birmingham: Institute for Research Into Superdiversity.

DeLaet, D. (1999). 'Introduction: The Invisibility of Women in Scholarship on International Migration.' In G. Kelson and D. DeLaet (eds), *Gender and Immigration.* New York: New York University Press, pp. 1–17.

Delgado Wise, R., H. Covarrubias and R. Puentes. (2013). 'Reframing the Debate on Migration, Development and Human Rights.' *Population, Space and Place* 19: 430–443.

Fresnoza-Flot, A. (2015). 'The Bumpy Landscape of Family Reunification: Experiences of First- and 1.5-Generation Filipinos in France.' *Journal of Ethnic and Migration Studies* 41(7): 1152–1171.

Funakoshi M., A. Miyazaki and T. Wilson. (2016). 'Japan Forces a Harsh Choice on Children of Migrant Families.' https://www.reuters.com/investigates/special-report/japan-detention-children/ (accessed 24 April 2018).
Halpert, D. and A. Baldwin. (2013). 'Who is Family? A Look at Canadian and U.S. Immigration Law on the Definition of Qualifying Relatives.' *Law Now*. https://www.lawnow.org/who-is-family/ (accessed 24 April 2018).
Hill-Collins, P. and S. Bilge. (2016). *Intersectionality: Key Concepts.* Cambridge: Polity Press.
Hooper, K. and B. Salant (2018). *It's Relative: A Cross-Country Comparison of Family-Migration Policies and Flows.* Washington, DC: Migration Policy Institute.
International Organization for Migration (IOM) (2015). *Migration and Families: International Dialogue on Migration.* Geneva: International Organization for Migration.
Kazemipur, A. and M.R. Nakhaie. (2014). 'The Economics of Attachment: Making a Case for a Relational Approach to Immigrants' Integration in Canada.' *International Migration and Integration* 15: 609–632. doi: 10.1007/s12134=013-0284-6.
Kelly, P., S. Park, C. de Leon and J. Priest. (2011). *Profile of Live-In Caregiver Immigrants to Canada, 1993–2009.* Toronto: TIEDI.
Knaus, C. (2018). 'Australia Doubles Financial Requirement for Families of New Migrants.' *The Guardian.* https://www.theguardian.com/austrailia-news/2019/apr/13/australia-doubles-financial-requirement-for-families-of-new-migrants (accessed 24 April 2018).
Lam, A.M.C., T.S. Chan and K.W. Tsoi. (2005). 'Meaning of Family Reunification as Interpreted by Young Chinese Immigrants.' *International Journal of Adolescent Medicine and Health* 17(2): 105–122.
Mazzucato, V., D. Schans, K. Caarls and C. Beauchemin. (2015). 'Transnational Families Between Africa and Europe.' *International Migration Review* 49(1): 142–172. doi:10.1111/imre.12153.
Migration Integration Policy Index (MIPEX). (2015). 'Family Reunion.' Retrieved 1 May 2018, from http://www.mipex.eu/family-reunion.
Nedelsky, J. (2011). *A Relational Theory of Self, Autonomy, and Law.* Oxford: Oxford University Press.
Ogaya, C. (2015). 'When Mobile Motherhoods and Mobile Childhoods Converge: The Case of Filipino Youth and Their Transmigrant Mothers in Toronto, Canada.' In I. Nagaska and A. Fresnoza-Flot (eds), *Mobile Childhoods in Filipino Transnational Families: Migrant Children with Similar Roots in Different Routes.* Houndmills: Palgrave Macmillan, pp. 205–221.
Oishi, N. (2008). 'Family without Borders? Asian Women in Migration and the Transformation of Family Life.' *Asian Journal of Women's Studies* 14(4): 54–79.
Oliver, C. (2013). *The Impact of Restrictions and Entitlements on the Integration of Family Migrants: A Comparative Report.* Oxford: COMPAS, University of Oxford.
Parreñas, R.S. (2005). *Children of Global Migration: Transnational Families and Gendered Woes.* Stanford, CA: Stanford University Press.
Pratt, G. (2006). 'Separation and Reunification Among Filipino Families in Vancouver.' *Canadian Issues* (Spring): 46–49.
Pratt, G. (2017). 'Children and the Intimate Violence of Transnational Labor Migration.' In C. Harker and K. Hörschelmann (eds), *Conflict, Violence and Peace* (Vol. 11). Singapore: Springer Singapore, pp. 387–408.
Rania, N., L. Migliorini and L. Rebora. (2018). 'Family Acculturation in Host and Immigrant Couples: Dyadic Research in an Italian Context.' *Europe's Journal of Psychology* 14(4): 914–931.
Sarvasy, W. and P. Longo. (2004). 'Kant's World Citizenship and Filipina Migrant Domestic Workers.' *International Feminist Journal of Politics* 6(3): 392–415.
Seki, K. (2015). 'Identity Construction of Migrant Children and Representation of the Family: The 1.5 Generation Filipino Youth in California, USA.' In I. Nagaska and A. Fresnoza-Flot (eds), *Mobile Childhoods in Filipino Transnational Families: Migrant Children with Similar Roots in Different Routes.* Houndsmills: Palgrave Macmillan, pp. 151–178.
Shaw, J.E. (2020). 'Tender Labor: Transnational Young People and Continuums of Familial Care.' *Anthropology of Work Review* 41(1): 14–23. doi: 10.1111.awr.12186.
Social Planning Council of Ottawa. (2010). *Immigrant Children, Youth and Families: A Qualitative Analysis of the Challenges of Integration.* Ottawa, ON: Social Planning Council of Ottawa.

Spitzer, D.L. and N. Piper. (2014). 'Retrenched and Returned: Filipino Migrant Workers During Times of Crisis.' *Sociology* 48: 1007–1023.

Spitzer, D.L. and S. Torres. (2014a). *Familiar Strangers: Migrant Family Reunification in Canada*. Paper Prepared for United Nations' North American Experts' Group, Mexico City, Mexico.

Spitzer, D.L. and S. Torres. (2014b). '"At Home, Men were Kings": Transnational Filipino Families in Canada Re-Negotiating Gender Roles.' Paper presented to the 16th National Metropolis Conference, Gatineau, Quebec, 14 March.

Spitzer, D.L., S. Torres, A. Beboso, C. Bernardino, N. Berkes, A. Calzado and J. Pallard. (2012). *Transnational Families in Transition: Filipino Families, Canadian Issues*. Unpublished report. Ottawa.

Spitzer, D.L., S. Torres, A. Zwi, E.N. Khalema and E. Castro-Palaganas. (2019). 'Towards Inclusive Health Care.' *BMJ* 366: 14256. doi: 10.1136/bmj.14256.

Strasser, E., A. Kraler, S. Bonjour and V. Bilger. (2009). 'Doing Family: Responses to the Constructions of the "Migrant Family" Across Europe.' *History of the Family* 14: 165–176.

Suárez-Orozco, C., H.J. Bang and H.Y. Kim. (2011). 'I Felt Like My Heart Was Staying Behind: Psychological Implications of Family Separations and Reunifications for Immigrant Youth.' *Journal of Adolescent Research* 26(2): 222–257.

Tarroja, M.C. and K. Fernando. (2013). 'Providing Psychological Services for Children of Overseas Filipino Workers (OFWs): A Challenge for School Psychologists in the Philippines.' *School Psychology International* 34(2): 202–212.

Watson, J. (2018). 'Family Ideation, Immigration, and the Racial State: Explaining Divergent Family Reunification in Britain and the US.' *Ethnic and Racial Studies* 41(2): 324–342.

Wray, H. (2009). 'Moulding the Migrant Family.' *Legal Studies* 29(4): 592–618.

Yeates, N. (2004). 'Global Care Chains: Critical Reflections and Lines of Enquiry.' *International Feminist Journal of Politics* 6(3): 369–391.

Yeoh, B.S.A., B.C. Somaiah, T. Lam and K. Acedera. (2020). 'Doing Family in "Times of Migration": Care Temporalities and Gender Politics in Southeast Asia.' *Annals of the American Association of Geographers* 110(6): 1709–1725. DOI: 10.1080/24694452.2020.1723397.

Yuval-Davis, N. (2015). 'Situated Intersectionality and Social Inequality.' *Raisons politiques* 58(2): 91–100.

Zentgraf, C.M. and N.S. Chinchilla. (2012). 'Transnational Family Separation: A Framework for Analysis.' *Journal of Ethnic and Migration Studies* 38(2): 345–366.

19. 'Maybe in the future I'll have two homes': temporalities of migration and family life among Vietnamese people in London
Annabelle Wilkins

INTRODUCTION

The impact of complex and multidirectional migration trajectories on intimate relationships has been of increasing interest within the field of migration studies, as scholars investigate the challenges of '"doing family" across distance' (Acedera and Yeoh 2019: 250). The growing importance of migration as a livelihood strategy, combined with the feminization of labour migration and the (im)mobility facilitated and constrained by immigration regimes, has resulted in increased attention to relationships and care practices within transnational family lives (Baldassar and Merla 2014; Hoang et al. 2015; Lam and Yeoh 2019; Merla et al. 2020; Parreñas 2014; Yeoh et al. 2005). Recent contributions reflect a growing focus on the temporal dimensions of family life in contexts of migration (Acedera and Yeoh 2019; Baas and Yeoh 2019; Merla et al. 2020; Yeoh et al. 2020). As argued by Acedera and Yeoh (2019), 'not only are the spatial aspects of the family altered when members are dispersed across different nations, the temporal dynamics of the family are also reconstituted, as members rework and reimagine their familial relationships across different temporalities, negotiating the rhythms and tempo of everyday family life from afar' (p. 252). Studies focusing on the temporalities of transnational family life are situated within a broader body of scholarship that examines migration through the lens of time and temporality, challenging the long-standing emphasis on space in migration research (Amrith 2020; Baas and Yeoh 2019; Cwerner 2001; Griffiths et al. 2013; Mavroudi et al. 2017; Ortiga and Macabasag 2020; Robertson 2014, 2019; Stevens 2019; Waters 2011; Yeoh et al. 2020). This literature has examined the multiple temporalities that shape and are shaped by migration, and has demonstrated how the everyday rhythms of migrant mobilities are embedded within the power-laden timescales of immigration policies (Acedera and Yeoh 2019; Robertson 2014, 2019).

Alongside the emergence of pioneering scholarship on time-related aspects of migration and transnational family life (see other chapters in Part IV of this *Handbook* for a wider discussion of this), parallel developments have taken place in scholarship on the temporalities of home. In addition to understanding home as a material and symbolic location that can be experienced at different spatial scales, research has recognized home as a site of multiple temporalities (Boccagni 2017; Blunt et al. 2021; Liu 2020; Pink et al. 2017). Home has been understood as a site in which the past, present and future are connected, and as an emotional experience that is re-made throughout the life-course (Blunt and Dowling 2006). Time and temporality are of particular importance in studies connecting home, migration and diaspora (Blunt and Bonnerjee 2013; Blunt et al. 2021; Walsh and Näre 2016). Boccagni proposes that, for migrants, 'Home can ... be appreciated as a starting point for individual biographies, as a source of meaningful memories and biographical continuity, even as an aim for the future' (Boccagni 2017: 65). Recent research has called for a relational perspective on the temporalities of home, highlighting how domestic temporalities are encompassed within multiple 'timescapes' encompassing the routines of everyday time and large-scale time, such as individual and collective senses of the past and the future (Liu 2020: 10). Another recent intervention explores how the temporalities of home are bound up with the timescales of urban change (Blunt et al. 2021).

While the themes of these studies overlap with scholarship on the temporalities of transnational familyhood, most research on time and migration within 'home studies' has focused on material or symbolic temporalities of home, or how migrant imaginaries of home change over the life-course, rather than how the everyday rhythms of domestic life are negotiated in contexts of migration. In this chapter, I aim to demonstrate how bringing these areas into closer dialogue can contribute to understanding family life in situations of mobility, in terms of both the micro-temporalities of family practices and the larger-scale temporal structures of migration policies. The chapter begins with an overview of how time has been explored in research on migration and the family, followed by a discussion of recent literature that examines temporality in relation to home. The chapter then draws upon interviews and ethnographic research with Vietnamese migrant and refugee participants in London (Wilkins 2019). I demonstrate how the micro-temporalities of migrant home-making are shaped by timescales of migration and urban change, as well as exploring how migrants' imaginaries of home and mobility change over the life-course.

TIME AND TEMPORALITY IN MIGRATION STUDIES

While Cwerner (2001) advocated for a dedicated framework to study the 'times of migration', the migration literature, until recently, has remained dominated by questions of space (Griffiths et al. 2013; Yeoh et al. 2020). Over the last decade, however, there has been a growing recognition of the significance of time in migration and mobility (Baas and Yeoh 2019; Robertson 2019; Stevens 2019; Yeoh et al. 2020). A substantial and developing body of scholarship has focused on the roles of time and temporality in immigration policy and their impacts on migrant (im)mobilities (Allen and Axelsson 2019; Andersson 2014; Mezzadra and Neilson 2013; Tazzioli 2018). This includes attention to liminal experiences of waiting among asylum seekers, refugees and immigration detainees (Conlon 2011; Griffiths 2014); the temporalities of border controls and appropriation of migrants' time by state authorities (Andersson 2014; Tazzioli 2018); and how labour migrants are impacted upon by the intersections between temporality, precarity and legal status (Axelsson et al. 2017; Clayton and Vickers 2019). This scholarship has facilitated understandings of how immigration regimes establish what Mezzadra and Neilson (2013) conceptualize as 'temporal borders', how these operate to structure migrant mobilities and their effects on the everyday lives of marginalized migrant populations.

A related but distinctive body of research examines the significance of time in the migration experiences of 'middling' and highly skilled migrants (Axelsson 2017; Robertson 2020; Marcu 2017) and international students (Baas 2015; Collins and Shubin 2017; Maury 2017, 2022; Robertson 2013). This scholarship has contested the assumption that skilled migrants experience frictionless mobility, drawing attention to the multiple insecurities that are connected with the temporal structures of immigration regimes (Axelsson 2017: 974). Robertson (2019) explores migrants' experiences of temporality within 'staggered' or multi-stage migration, drawing upon Meeus's (2012) concept of the timescale to theorize relations between everyday, institutional and biographical time. Robertson argues that attention to multiple timescales enables an understanding of:

> how time can function contemporaneously and in mutually constitutively ways: as a mode of governance that disciplines when and under what conditions migrant bodies move; as a component of migrants' own understandings of their biographies in mobility ... and as the rhythms of daily social life that constitute particular spaces and places (Robertson 2019: 182)

Robertson (2019) identifies how migrants negotiate the institutional timescales of migration alongside significant biographic events including marriage and the birth of children. Maury (2022) develops the concept of 'punctuated time' to theorize the experiences of student-migrants in Finland. The author discusses how waiting for the renewal of residence permits impacted on students' family life, as they were unable to travel to visit family for prolonged periods (Maury 2022). These examples highlight the effects of temporal migration controls on the negotiations of care and intimate relationships within transnational families.

TEMPORALITIES OF MIGRATION AND TRANSNATIONAL FAMILY LIFE

An emerging and rapidly developing body of literature examines the temporal dimensions of the transnational family, building upon research on time and migration, and bringing this into dialogue with scholarship on caregiving, gender relations and transnational family practices in both sending and receiving contexts (Acedera and Yeoh 2019; Baas and Yeoh 2019; Yeoh et al. 2020). Much of this recent research is empirically situated in Asia, where regimes of temporary labour migration are dominant (Acedera and Yeoh 2019; Yeoh et al. 2020). Other studies have investigated the temporalities of transnational family care among Chinese immigrant families in Canada (Zhou 2015), and temporary labour migrants in Israel (Harper and Zubida 2020). These contributions reveal how transnational caregiving practices and intimate relationships are shaped by multiple temporalities in both 'home' and host contexts, also examining how these timescales intersect with gender relations and political contexts. In a study of the relationships between the 'micro-temporalities' of transnational family life and the 'meso-temporalities' of immigration policies, Acedera and Yeoh (2019) draw upon interviews with migrant wives in Singapore and their husbands in the Philippines to explore how couples negotiate transnational relationships (Acedera and Yeoh 2019: 255). The authors combine the concepts of rhythms and ruptures as developed in the timescale framework (Robertson 2014; cf. Meeus 2012) with those of liminality and simultaneity (Cwerner 2001). The findings demonstrate how couples used both synchronous and asynchronous communication technology to 'resynchronize' their intimate lives (Acedera and Yeoh 2019: 258). The authors emphasize the importance of considering the intersections between structure and agency in migration temporalities, arguing that 'the micro-temporalities of transnational families' everyday lives cannot be understood without considering the meso-temporalities of immigration policies that instill temporariness and precarity in the lives of the transnational family, deterring the imagination of stable family futures' (Acedera and Yeoh 2019: 268).

Drawing on life-story interviews with families in rural areas of Indonesia and the Philippines, Yeoh et al. (2020) examine the diverse 'care temporalities' that shape the gendered dynamics of caregiving for left-behind children in sending communities. The authors build upon the temporal concepts of rhythm, rupture and reversal to theorize 'how care relations are molded, negotiated, or transformed across modalities of temporal experience linked to the vicissitudes of temporary migration' (Yeoh et al. 2020: 2). The research identifies that while women are becoming increasingly active as migrant breadwinners, the gendered cultural expectations of women as caregivers continue to shape the everyday rhythms of transnational family life (Yeoh et al. 2020: 11). The study's findings demonstrate that while the 'rupture' of women's migration opens up the potential for 'polyrhythmic' care temporalities (Yeoh et al. 2020: 15), these must be considered alongside existing gender dynamics within families and cultural contexts, as well as the temporal constraints of institutional migration regimes.

Recent research on the temporalities of transnational family relationships articulates how concepts of home are reconfigured in and through migration. For example, in Acedera and Yeoh's (2019) study, the proximity of Singapore to the Philippines was considered a major advantage in facilitating visits home, enabling migrant women to maintain a sense of their identities as caregivers. In reality, visits home were often restricted by the temporal requirements of visa categories and the demands of work (Acedera and Yeoh 2019). The authors argue that migrants' perspectives on (potential) return visits are intertwined with gendered associations between women, home and domesticity:

> When wives migrated not only out of the homeland but out of the home, which was associated with their primary identity as homemakers, they often experienced a sense of guilt and ambivalence. The importance of the potential to come home, then, needs to be understood in the context of migrant wives' attempts to find a middle ground between their new identities as primary breadwinners, while tempering the guilt of not being able to be present in the homespace. (Acedera and Yeoh 2019: 260)

Later sections of this chapter will expand upon connections between home, family and migration to explore how the micro-temporalities of home intersect with the dynamics of family life as well as being shaped by the timescales of immigration policy.

MIGRATION, FAMILY AND THE LIFE-COURSE

An understanding of the impact of biographic transitions and family events such as relationship formation, reproduction, childrearing and ageing processes is vital to understanding how family life is reconfigured in migration. Recent research has brought the literature on time and migration into dialogue with life-course perspectives in order to examine how migration journeys, aspirations and imaginaries are interpreted by migrants at different stages of their lives (Amrith 2020; Findlay et al. 2015; Kilkey and Palenga-Möllenbeck 2016; Kilkey and Ryan 2020). A life-course perspective is central to the approach of an edited book on migration and family life by Kilkey and Palenga-Möllenbeck (2016). As the editors argue, 'an understanding of migration and mobility as *dynamic* processes includes an acknowledgement that such dynamism is present *within* each stage of the family life-course as well as across different stages' (Kilkey and Palenga-Möllenbeck 2016: 5). The above book combines an analysis of the subjective, relational and emotional elements of time with the macro-level timeframes of legal and policy frameworks. The chapters map onto different stages of the life-course in diverse global contexts, including chapters on the impact of marriage migration policies on migrant relationships in South Korea (Kim and Kilkey 2016), and how the family lives of Ghanaian women migrants in the Netherlands are constrained by restrictive migration and welfare policies (Poeze and Mazzucato 2016). Other chapters focus on ageing and intergenerational care strategies, including the case of older Albanian migrants wishing to avoid becoming 'elderly orphans' by following their children to Italy and Greece, where they provide care for their grandchildren (King et al. 2016). The book as a whole demonstrates the value of considering the analytical lenses of migration, mobility and the life-course alongside each other to enable an understanding of the uneven impacts of migration policies, and how these are intertwined with experiences and outcomes of migration at different life-stages.

Drawing upon ethnographic research with migrant care workers from the Philippines, and building on Cwerner's (2001) notion of 'temporal horizons', Amrith (2020) explores how migrants' imaginaries of their journeys shift over time as a result of personal experiences, family transitions and political-economic factors. Adopting a life-course perspective challenges perceptions of migration trajectories as linear pathways, revealing how journeys become disrupted, uncertain or 'stuck' at different stages of the migration experience, including as a result of immigration policies, but also due to life-events such as ageing and family formation (Amrith 2020: 16). Examining migration in relation to the life-course also foregrounds the intertwined relationships between time and emotions in migrant journeys. As Amrith argues, 'The temporal dimensions that shape migrant trajectories engender affective responses that are both mobilizing and immobilizing at different points in migrants' lives' (ibid.: 5). Along with reflections on migrants' shifting imaginaries of mobility and settlement, life-course perspectives have also been drawn upon by research that explores how migrants' complex relationships with home are reconfigured over time, and particularly in relation to return migration (Amrith 2020; Walsh 2018; Walsh and Näre 2016). These studies highlight the complex connections between migration, home and family life, and how these change at different points of the migrant journey, as well as in relation to biographical transitions.

TEMPORALITIES OF HOME AND MIGRATION

Research on time in relation to home has explored how domestic practices and relations both shape and are shaped by multiple temporalities, including the rhythms and routines of domestic work, care and family life (Nansen et al. 2009; Pink et al. 2017). Other perspectives have focused on domestic objects and interiors as sites of connection to other times and places, including across transnational and diasporic space (Miller 2001; Tolia-Kelly 2004a, 2004b; Walsh 2006). Time and temporality are of particular relevance when considering experiences of home within contexts of mobility and displacement (Boccagni 2017; Brun and Fábos 2015; Blunt and Dowling 2006; Walsh and Näre 2016). For refugees and people living in conditions of protracted displacement, the temporalities of home are profoundly disrupted by what Brun and Fábos conceptualize as 'immobilized temporariness'; yet the authors demonstrate that even in liminal and precarious circumstances, 'homemaking nevertheless takes place as people try to recreate familiarity, improve their material conditions, and imagine a better future' (Brun and Fábos 2015: 11).

A new agenda on the temporalities of home is advanced in recent research by Blunt et al. (2021), who explore 'the living of time' through the 'multi-layered and entangled temporalities of home and the city' in the context of urban change in East London (Blunt et al. 2021: 149). In establishing their perspective, Blunt et al. (2021: 149) point out that while the themes of time and temporality are prominent in literature on both home and the city, there has been relatively little research that draws these perspectives together. The authors build upon insights from literature on time in relation to the city, including how time is implicated in processes of urban change, including regeneration and gentrification (Amin 2008, cited in Blunt et al. 2021: 151). This approach also extends the authors' previous work on 'home-city geographies' (Blunt and Sheringham 2019), and on the city as a site of home in diaspora, in which the city is understood as a 'site of dwelling and mobility, shaped by connections within and across different cities and communities in both the past and the present' (Blunt and Bonnerjee 2013: 225). Blunt et al. (2021) draw upon home-city biographies with residents of an East London estate, demonstrating how their experiences of home are intertwined with personal migration trajectories, family and housing histories, and feelings of belonging or exclusion. This perspective enables studies of home to attend to relations between mobility and immobility at different scales, from the domestic to the urban, across transnational space and over time.

Recent scholarship by Liu (2020) offers a relational perspective on time and space that opens up new pathways for theorizing temporality in the geographies of home. Liu develops the concept of 'timescape', which recognizes the intertwining of time and space, and draws attention to how practices are shaped by multiple dimensions of time, including rhythms, tempos and timeframes, and individual and collective senses of past, present and future (Adam 1998, cited in Liu 2020: 3). These connections are reflected in migrant home-making, including how diasporic homes are linked to other spaces and times through material possessions (Tolia-Kelly 2004a, 2004b; Walsh 2006). While a growing body of research has explored how migrant home-making is bound up with multiple temporalities, Liu contends that 'mobile and politicized geographies of dwelling need to pay more attention to regular and occasional practices in relation to home-making/-unmaking practices across places, in order to sketch out the changing ways of life in a precarious contemporary world' (Liu 2020: 14). Building on connections between migrant home-making and temporalities of migration and family life, the next section of this chapter explores how the intersecting temporalities of home, migration and family relationships are experienced among Vietnamese migrant participants in London.

TEMPORALITIES OF MIGRANT HOME-MAKING AND FAMILY LIFE

Domestic Objects and Home-Making Practices

Vietnamese refugees first arrived in the United Kingdom (UK) following the British government's acceptance of a quota of 10 000 refugees from camps in Hong Kong in 1979 (Chan 2011). Alongside those who came as refugees (and the second and third generations of their families), the UK Vietnamese population also includes migrants on temporary visas and international students, as well as unknown numbers of irregular and undocumented migrants (Sims 2007). The 2011 census estimated around 30 000 people living in England and Wales who were born in Vietnam, of whom around half live in London, though this is substantially lower than the 55 000 estimated by community organizations (Sims 2007). The Vietnamese diaspora in the UK is diverse in terms of language, ethnicity and religious practice, and includes followers of Buddhism, Catholicism and ancestor veneration.

This section illustrates the key arguments of the chapter through reference to research involving in-depth interviews, ethnographic research and visual methods that explored relationships between home, work and migration among Vietnamese communities in London (Wilkins 2019). Participants were all first-generation migrants with diverse migration backgrounds and trajectories, including individuals who had arrived as refugees, and migrants who had come to the UK for work or education in recent years. The research took place in East London, where local Vietnamese communities have become established, particularly within the borough of Hackney. The study examined connections between home and work for migrants, as well as exploring their experiences of home in relation to the wider city, and how their imaginaries of home and migration had changed over time. Participants were positioned within various categories with regard to immigration status, including individuals on temporary work visas and postgraduate student visas, and those who had arrived as refugees and had since received indefinite leave to remain or citizenship through naturalization. Participants' different migration circumstances and their temporal boundaries influenced the types of work, housing and familial relationships in which they were embedded, and also shaped their practices and imaginaries of home.

Domestic possessions and everyday practices in participants' homes demonstrated the multiple temporalities involved in home-making in contexts of migration. In addition to connections between domestic objects and senses of 'large-scale' time (Liu 2020: 10), participants' home-making practices were also structured through the meso-scale temporalities of immigration policies that impacted upon the everyday rhythms of home-making. These overlapping timescales are illustrated by the practices, possessions and imaginaries of home in the narrative of one participant named Son, who was born in rural Central Vietnam in 1968, and arrived in the UK in 1979 aged 11 after leaving Vietnam by boat with his mother and two siblings. After being rescued at sea, the family spent several months in a refugee camp in Hong Kong before being resettled in the UK. Son's family were initially dispersed to a small town in Scotland, where Son lived until moving to Hackney at the age of 16. Son's home contained an extensive and diverse collection of objects, including artwork depicting rural Vietnamese landscapes that had been bought on return visits to Vietnam, as well as devotional objects and altars to the Buddha and to his ancestors (Wilkins 2019: 98). Son's possessions connected with Vietnamese concepts of the 'original homeland' (quê hương): the ancestral home that is associated with birth and childhood. These objects embedded memories of Son's past home and family in Vietnam in domestic practices in the present (cf. Liu 2020; Tolia-Kelly 2004a, 2004b), and also stretched the temporalities of home to include relationships with the ancestors. Son's home was not only a site of connection to remembered homes, but also linked to his imagined future home and family relationships (Walsh 2006). His living room contained photographs of his wife and daughter, who were based in Vietnam and were hoping to reunite once Son was earning enough to apply for their visas to come to the UK. This echoes Brickell's (2011: 31) theorization of migrant home spaces as translocal sites of 'emplaced mobility', in which domestic objects and practices not only relate to creating a sense of continuity with the past, but also become part of an imagined and desired future.

Participants' home-making practices and imaginaries were variously shaped and constrained by the temporal dimensions of their immigration statuses. Those who were on temporary visas commonly lived in shared rental accommodation, moved house relatively frequently, and described themselves as being less concerned with home-making through material objects than participants with longer-term immigration statuses and more secure accommodation. However, for Ngoc, a student who lived with her sister and fellow students whom she had known since school in Vietnam, domestic objects and practices were important in creating a sense of a 'family household' (quoted in Wilkins 2019: 100). These included practices of communal cooking as a social activity and maintaining a cleaning rota so that the house felt more 'homely'. In addition to these everyday domestic rhythms, Ngoc asked her mother for guidance on installing a Buddhist altar in her student house, which she described as enabling a sense of closeness to her home and family in Vietnam.

Participants emphasized that communication technologies were among the most crucial aspects of home-making, as these technologies enabled them to maintain transnational family relationships. These were of particular importance for migrants on temporary visas, but also for participants with permanent residence who maintained contact with family members in Vietnam. Participants used synchronous and asynchronous communication technologies for differing purposes (cf. Acedera and Yeoh 2020: 262). This included leaving synchronous applications such as Skype connected for long periods while they relaxed or studied, as well as using asynchronous communication platforms such as Facebook Messenger to send brief communications during work or study periods. This combination of technologies enabled an ongoing sense of connection to their family and everyday life in Vietnam. These findings echo research by Madianou (2016) on how the use of multiple communication media creates a sense of 'ambient co-presence', as well as supporting Acedera and Yeoh's (2020: 262) analysis of how transnational couples used varied communication technologies to 'resynchronise their intimate lives'. Participants also described how the feelings of familiarity and continuity engendered through these practices contributed to a new sense of home that bridged the gap between their family lives in London and in Vietnam.

Temporal Connections between Home, Migration and the City

Building upon recent perspectives by Blunt et al. (2021), I argue in this section that understandings of the temporalities of migration and home can be usefully extended to encompass the temporal dimensions of urban dwelling and mobility. Participants who had lived in London for several decades generally expressed a sense of home in relation to the particular areas of London in which they had grown up or been resident in for longer periods. This sense of home was often intertwined with where their family was located, but also reflected frequently ambivalent relationships with processes of urban change. Uyen, who arrived as a refugee in the 1980s, described the now-fashionable Shoreditch district as having been a 'run-down' area and a 'dead industrial wasteland' when she was first resettled there in temporary accommodation with her family (quoted in Wilkins 2019: 55). Uyen expressed a sense of home in relation to her neighbourhood in Hackney, which was intertwined with having seen it 'evolve over time' (quoted in Wilkins 2019: 66). Son's memories of Hackney were dominated by his mother's experience of being mugged there during the 1990s, which had left him with a long-term sense of insecurity about the area as a whole. Despite these associations, Son described a sense of feeling at home in Hackney because of its proximity to family, friends and Vietnamese community spaces, and expressed a sense of appreciation to the local authority for offering housing to Vietnamese refugee families.

Participants who had arrived in more recent years generally had a more transient sense of attachment in relation to particular areas of the city. Hien, a postgraduate student, described feeling 'attached to London in a very general sense ... someone who is living here for a short time ... trying to experience as much as I can and bring it with me on the next journey' (Hien, quoted in Wilkins 2019: 70). Other participants who had arrived more recently drew upon their memories of cities in Vietnam as points of comparison with London. Brick Lane market in Shoreditch was described by some participants as being reminiscent of the atmosphere of street food markets in Hanoi's Old Quarter, and generated a feeling of home through memories of spending time with their families and friends in Vietnam. For some participants in particularly insecure housing, public spaces in the city were regarded as more significant sites of attachment than the residential dwelling. Taken together, participants' diverse temporal relationships with home and the city echo the findings of Blunt et al. (2021), who argue that '[U]rban dwelling is shaped by multiple and multi-layered temporalities, intertwining the past, present and future, generations and life-courses, and housing, family and migration histories' (Blunt et al. 2021: 159). In the next section, I explore how participants' and imaginaries of future homes and family arrangements were shaped by the temporalities of their immigration status.

Future Imaginaries of Home, Migration and Family Life

Considering the temporalities of home, migration and family life opens up what Liu (2020: 11) conceptualizes as the 'futurescape of home', which includes 'the futures of both the material and immaterial (social/emotional) aspects of home', and is continuously affected by present practices as well as by wider power relations. Participants' imaginaries of future homes and migration journeys were inseparable from their different stages of the life-course. Son described how his idea of home encompassed his ancestral home in Vietnam, but had shifted over time towards his house in Hackney and the UK as a whole. As his plans moved towards the longer-term future, Son described an aspiration to move between homes in London and Vietnam:

> When I retire, probably, if I can afford it I'll probably buy a home there [in Vietnam] and spend maybe six months there, to avoid the winter, start going back in September when it starts getting into autumn or something, until like, I don't know, spring or summer. If I can afford it, I'd have two homes and just go back and forth, that would be nice, yeah. (quoted in Wilkins 2019: 124)

For younger participants and those who had migrated more recently, plans for the future were generally fluid and uncertain. While in some cases this reflected a sense of mobility and freedom, other people's imaginaries of future homes were more precarious and constrained by the temporal borders of the immigration regime (Maury 2022; Mezzadra and Neilson 2013; Stevens 2019). Ty, who arrived in London as an undergraduate student, wanted to stay in the UK in the longer term but had been affected by the UK government's decision to suspend the post-study work visa in 2012. During his first year in London, he was also affected by the tightening of other immigration policies on international students, when his college lost its sponsorship status and he was forced to enrol on another course or lose his student status. Ty experienced this as a temporal rupture (Cwerner 2001; Yeoh et al. 2020) that had disrupted his everyday life in London and engendered a sense of anxiety about his future. This uncertainty directly impacted on his intimate relationship, as Ty hoped to live with his partner in London but did not know whether this would be possible in the longer term. In this sense, Ty's experience articulates Robertson's (2019) concept of 'contingent temporality', within which 'life transitions within the biographic timescale, such as graduating, buying homes, getting married, having children, or building careers, were frequently described as disrupted and restructured by the institutional timescale of migration governance' (Robertson 2019: 174). Like the migrants in Robertson's study, Ty had decided to retrain in a career subject that would give him greater opportunities within the immigration system (in this case, accountancy), but still felt that his future had been interrupted, and expressed a sense of anxiety as a consequence of constantly shifting institutional requirements (cf. Robertson 2019: 175). Ty's experience demonstrates how the temporalities of home, family and migration are structured through the complex timescales of immigration governance.

CONCLUSION

This chapter has examined the growing body of scholarship that approaches migration and transnational family life through the lens of time and temporality, and has argued that this literature can be brought into dialogue with research on the temporalities of home to enable a holistic perspective on the multiple timescales of family life in contexts of mobility. Recent research on the temporalities of 'doing family' across distance provides crucial insights into how the rhythms of family relationships are intertwined with temporal boundaries of immigration governance (see, for example, Chapters 10 and 17, this *Handbook*), and literature on the temporalities of home considers how domestic practices and imaginaries change over time and space. These bodies of research have tended to approach these overlapping topics from different disciplinary standpoints, and to consider either the relations and practices of transnational familyhood, or material and symbolic temporalities of home in contexts of migration and diaspora. Recently, however, scholars have begun to consider these themes alongside one another, notably the aforementioned study by Acedera and Yeoh (2019), who examine the relationships between the temporalities of the transnational family and gendered concepts of home.

Drawing on recent studies and the empirical example of Vietnamese migrant participants in London, I have demonstrated how bringing the temporalities of transnational family practices together with time-related frameworks of home opens up new possibilities for an expansive and integrated view of the relationships between the micro-temporalities of family life, the meso-scale impacts of institutional timescales, and personal life-course transitions. Attention to the temporal dimensions of home and migration emphasizes the emotional and embodied dynamics of family life, and foregrounds the non-linear nature of migrant journeys (cf. Amrith 2020), while attention to the interactions between different timescales shows how migrants' home-making practices and imaginaries are embedded within and often constrained by temporal boundaries (cf. Robertson 2019). Drawing on theoretical approaches from within studies of home enables insights into the roles of domestic objects, practices and spaces in transnational family life, and how migrants' imaginaries of home change over the life-course in relation to family events and biographic transitions (Tolia-Kelly 2004a, 2004b; Walsh 2006, 2018). Furthermore, recent scholarship on the temporalities of urban dwelling facilitates understanding of the city as a site of home that stretches beyond the domestic space and is intertwined with migration and family histories (Blunt et al. 2021). Approaching from the alternative perspective, studies of home can benefit from a close examination of the care temporalities and everyday rhythms of transnational family life, and how these intersect with the temporal structures of immigration policies in different geographical and political contexts (Acedera and Yeoh 2019; Yeoh et al. 2020).

The study of temporalities of migration, home and the family offers multiple directions for future research, in which a number of topics and contexts remain underexplored. The research covered in this chapter has predominantly focused on the temporalities of migration and home among nuclear families and heterosexual couples. Further research is required to shed light on the temporalities of home, migration and care practices among diverse family formations and relationships. A growing number of studies are exploring the temporalities of migration for migrants in lesbian, gay, bisexual and/or transgender relationships. Oswin (2014) examines how heteronormative expectations of the family act to 'other' migrant workers in Singapore. Building upon and developing the concept of 'queer temporalities' (see Oswin 2014), Baas (2019) explores how sexuality intersects with the temporalities of migration for gay Indian migrants in Singapore. Other research by Luo (2020) investigates the temporal aspects of migration among Chinese intra-national migrant young gay men, demonstrating how the concept of *jia* (family/home) motivates their migration experience in relation to the past, present and imagined future homes. Future research on the temporalities of home, family and migration requires a multidimensional approach to analysing how migrant mobilities, family lives and relationships are intertwined with institutional and cultural temporalities.

The empirical focus of much recent research on time in transnational family life has been in Southeast and East Asia, where feminized labour migration and temporary contract labour regimes are of particular importance (Acedera and Yeoh 2019; Yeoh et al. 2020). Other research on the temporalities of migration has focused on migration flows from the Global South to the North, including to Australia (Baas 2015; Robertson 2019, 2014; Stevens 2019), the United States (Coe 2015; Zhou 2015) and Europe (Axelsson 2017; Maury 2022; Merla et al. 2020). Further research is needed to understand the temporalities of migration and family life in diverse global contexts, particularly in relation to internal migration and South–South trajectories. The research discussed in this chapter reveals the uneven impacts of migration policies on the family lives and home-making practices of those with diverse immigration trajectories and circumstances, including those who might be categorized as 'middling' or skilled migrants, as well as those in particularly marginalized groups (Robertson 2019). As the timescales of state immigration and welfare policies circumscribe not only the right to move, but also the right to make a home, it becomes ever more important to understand how migrants negotiate the temporalities of family life in contexts of mobility.

REFERENCES

Acedera, K.A. and Yeoh, B.S.A. (2019) 'Making time': Long-distance marriages and the temporalities of the transnational family. *Current Sociology Monograph* 67(2): 250–272.

Acedera, K.A.F. and Yeoh, B.S.A. (2020) 'Until death do us part'? Migrant wives, left-behind husbands, and the negotiation of intimacy in transnational marriages. *Journal of Ethnic and Migration Studies* 4 6(16): 3508–3525. DOI: 10.1080/1369183X.2019.1592414.

Allen, J. and Axelsson, L. (2019) Border topologies: The time-spaces of labour migrant regulation. *Political Geography* 72: 116–123.

Amrith, M. (2020) The linear imagination, stalled: changing temporal horizons in migrant journeys. *Global Networks*. DOI:10.1111/glob.12280.

Andersson, R. (2014) Time and the migrant other: European border controls and the temporal economics of illegality. *American Anthropologist* 116(4): 795–809.

Axelsson, L. (2017) Living within temporally thick borders: IT professionals' experiences of Swedish immigration policy and practice. *Journal of Ethnic and Migration Studies* 43(6): 974–990.

Axelsson, L., Malmberg, B. and Zhang, Q. (2017) On waiting, work-time and imagined futures: Theorising temporal precariousness among Chinese chefs in Sweden's restaurant industry. *Geoforum* 78: 169–178.

Baas, M. (2015) The fluidity of return: Indian student migrants' transnational ambitions and the meaning of Australian permanent residency. In M. Baas (ed.) *Transnational Migration and Asia: The Question of Return*. Amsterdam: Amsterdam University Press, pp. 39–54.

Baas, M. (2019) Queer temporalities: The past, present and future of 'gay' migrants from India in Singapore. *Current Sociology Monograph* 67(2): 206–224.

Baas, M. and Yeoh, B.S.A. (2019) Introduction: Migration studies and critical temporalities. *Current Sociology Monograph* 67(2): 161–168.

Baldassar, L. and Merla, L. (2014) Introduction: Transnational family caregiving through the lens of circulation. In L. Baldassar and L. Merla (eds) *Transnational Families, Migration and the Circulation of Care. Understanding Mobility and Absence in Family Life*. New York: Routledge, pp. 3–24.

Boccagni, P. (2017) *Migration and the Search for Home: Mapping Domestic Space in Migrants' Everyday Lives*. New York: Palgrave Macmillan.

Blunt, A. and Bonnerjee, J. (2013) Home, city and diaspora: Anglo-Indian and Chinese attachments to Calcutta. *Global Networks* 13(2): 220–240.

Blunt, A. and Dowling, R. (2006) *Home*. London: Routledge.

Blunt, A., Ebbensgaard, C.L. and Sheringham, O. (2021) The 'living of time': Entangled temporalities of home and the city. *Transactions of the Institute of British Geographers* 46: 149–162. https://doi.org/10.1111/tran.12405.

Blunt, A. and Sheringham, O. (2019). Home-city geographies: Urban dwelling and mobility. *Progress in Human Geography* 43(5): 1–20.

Brickell, K. (2011) Translocal Geographies of 'Home' in Siem Riep, Cambodia. In K. Brickell and A. Datta (eds) *Translocal Geographies: Spaces, Places, Connections*. Aldershot: Ashgate, pp. 23–38.

Brun, C. and Fábos, A. (2015) Making homes in limbo? A conceptual framework. *Refuge* 31(1): 5–18.

Chan, Y.W. (2011) Revisiting the Vietnamese refugee era: An Asian perspective from Hong Kong. In Y.W. Chan (ed.) *The Chinese/Vietnamese Diaspora: Revisiting the Boat People*. Abingdon: Routledge, pp. 3–19.

Clayton, J. and Vickers, T. (2019) Temporal tensions: European Union citizen migrants, asylum seekers and refugees navigating dominant temporalities of work in England. *Time and Society* 28(4): 1464–1488.

Coe, C. (2015). The temporality of care: Gender, migration, and the entrainment of life courses. In A. Erdmute and H. Drotbohm (eds) *Anthropological Perspectives on Care*. New York: Palgrave Macmillan, pp. 181–205.

Collins, F. and Shubin, S. (2017) The temporal complexity of international student mobilities. In E. Mavroudi, B. Page and E. Christou (eds) *Time, Space and International Migration*. Cheltenham, UK and Northampton, MA, USA: Edward Elgar Publishing, pp. 17–32.

Conlon, D. (2011) Waiting: Feminist perspectives on the spacings/timings of migrant (im)mobility. *Gender, Place and Culture* 18(3): 353–360.

Cwerner, S.B. (2001) The times of migration. *Journal of Ethnic and Migration Studies* 27(1): 7–36.

Findlay, A., McCollum, D., Coulter, R. and Gayle, V. (2015) New mobilities across the life course: A framework for analysing demographically linked drivers of migration. *Population, Space and Place* 21: 390–402. doi: 10.1002/psp.1956.

Griffiths, M. (2014) Out of time: The temporal uncertainties of refused asylum seekers and immigration detainees. *Journal of Ethnic and Migration Studies* 40(12): 1991–2009.

Griffiths, M., Rogers, A. and Anderson, B. (2013) Migration, time and temporalities: Review and prospect. COMPAS Research Resources Paper. Oxford: COMPAS.

Harper, R.A. and Zubida, H. (2020) Thinking about the meaning of time among temporary labor migrants in Israel. *Time and Society* 29(2): 536–562.

Hoang, L.A., Lam, T., Yeoh, B.S.A. and Graham, E. (2015) Transnational migration, changing care arrangements and left-behind children's responses in Southeast Asia. *Children's Geographies* 13(3): 263–277.

Kilkey, M. and Palenga-Möllenbeck, E. (2016) Introduction: Family life in an age of migration and mobility: Introducing a global and family life-course perspective. In M. Kilkey and E. Palenga-Möllenbeck (eds) *Family Life in an Age of Migration and Mobility: Global Perspectives through the Life Course*. London: Palgrave Macmillan, pp. 1–18.

Kilkey, M. and Ryan, L. (2020). Unsettling events: Understanding migrants' responses to geopolitical transformative episodes through a life-course lens. *International Migration Review*. DOI: 10.1177/0197918320905507.

Kim, G. and Kilkey, M. (2016) Marriage migration policy as a social reproduction system: The South Korean experience. In M. Kilkey and E. Palenga-Möllenbeck (eds) *Family Life in an Age of Migration and Mobility: Global Perspectives through the Life Course*. London: Palgrave Macmillan, pp. 137–162.

King, R., Vullnetari, J., Lulle, A. and Cela, E. (2016) Contrasts in ageing and agency in family migratory contexts: A comparison of Albanian and Latvian older migrants. In M. Kilkey and E. Palenga-Möllenbeck (eds) *Family Life in an Age of Migration and Mobility: Global Perspectives through the Life Course*. London: Palgrave Macmillan, pp. 261–286.

Lam, T. and Yeoh, B.S.A. (2019) Parental migration and disruptions in everyday life: Reactions of left-behind children in Southeast Asia. *Journal of Ethnic and Migration Studies* 45(16): 3085–3104.

Liu, C. (2020) Rethinking the timescape of home: Domestic practices in time and space. *Progress in Human Geography*. DOI: 10.1177/0309132520923138.

Luo, M. (2020) Sexuality, migration and family: Understanding *Jia* and its impact on Chinese young gay men's migration motives from a temporal perspective. *Journal of Ethnic and Migration Studies*. DOI : 10.1080/1369183X.2020.1821615.

Madianou, M. (2016) Ambient co-presence: transnational family practices in polymedia environments. *Global Networks* 16(2): 183–201. https://doi.org/10.1111/glob.12105.

Marcu, S. (2017) Tears of time: A Lefebvrian rhythmanalysis approach to explore the mobility experiences of young Eastern Europeans in Spain. *Transactions of the Institute of British Geographers* 42(3): 405–416.

Maury, O. (2017) Student-migrant-workers: Temporal aspects of precarious work and life in Finland. *Nordic Journal of Migration Research* 7(4): 224–232.

Maury, O. (2022) Punctuated temporalities: Temporal borders in student migrants' everyday lives. *Current Sociology* 70(1): 100–117. https://doi.org/10.1177/0011392120936315.

Mavroudi, E., Page, B. and Christou, A. (eds) (2017) *Timespace and International Migration*. Cheltenham, UK and Northampton, MA, USA: Edward Elgar Publishing.

Meeus, B. (2012) How to 'catch' floating populations? Research and the fixing of migration in space and time. *Ethnic and Racial Studies* 35(10): 1775–1793. doi: 10.1080/01419870.2012.659272.

Merla, L., Kilkey, M. and Baldassar, L. (2020) Introduction to the special issue 'Transnational Care: Families Confronting Borders'. *Journal of Family Research*. DOI: 10.20377/jfr-420.

Mezzadra, S. and Neilson, B. (2013) *Border as Method, or, the Multiplication of Labor*. Durham, NC, USA and London, UK: Duke University Press.

Miller, D. (ed.) (2001) *Home Possessions: Material Culture behind Closed Doors*. Oxford: Berg.

Nansen, B., Arnold, M., Gibbs, M.R. and Davis, H. (2009) Domestic orchestration: Rhythms in the mediated home. *Time and Society* 18(2–3): 181–207. https://doi.org/10.1177/0961463X09338082.

Ortiga, Y.Y. and Macabasag, R.L.A. (2020) Temporality and acquiescent immobility among aspiring nurse migrants in the Philippines. *Journal of Ethnic and Migration Studies*. DOI: 10.1080/1369183X .2020.1788380.

Oswin, N. (2014) Queer time in global city Singapore: Neoliberal futures and the 'freedom to love'. *Sexualities* 17(4): 412–433.

Parreñas, R. (2014) The intimate labour of transnational communication. *Families, Relationships and Societies* 3(3): 425–442.

Pink, S., Mackley, K.L., Moroşanu, R., Mitchell, V. and Bhamra, T. (2017) *Making Homes: Ethnography and Design*. London: Bloomsbury.

Poeze, M. and Mazzucato, V. (2016) Transnational mothers and the law: Ghanaian women's pathways to family reunion and consequences for family life. In M. Kilkey and E. Palenga-Möllenbeck (eds) *Family Life in an Age of Migration and Mobility: Global Perspectives through the Life Course*. London: Palgrave Macmillan, pp. 187–212.

Robertson, S. (2013) *Transnational Student-Migrants and the State: The Education Migration Nexus*. London: Palgrave Macmillan.

Robertson, S. (2014) The temporalities of international migration: Implications for ethnographic research, in S. Castles, D. Ozkul and M. Cubas (eds) *Social Transformation and Migration: National and Local Experiences in South Korea, Turkey, Mexico and Australia*. Basingstoke: Palgrave Macmillan, pp. 45–60.

Robertson, S. (2019) Migrant, interrupted: The temporalities of 'staggered' migration from Asia to Australia. *Current Sociology* 67(2): 169–185.

Robertson, S. (2020) Suspending, settling, sponsoring: the intimate chronomobilities of young Asian migrants in Australia. *Global Networks*, 20 (4), 677–696. doi: https://doi.org/10.1111/glob.12291.

Stevens, C. (2019) Temporary work, permanent visas and circular dreams: Temporal disjunctures and precarity among Chinese migrants to Australia. *Current Sociology Monograph* 67(2): 294–314.

Sims, J.M. (2007) *The Vietnamese Community in Great Britain: Thirty Years On*. London: Runnymede Trust.

Tazzioli, M. (2018) The temporal borders of asylum: Temporality of control in the EU border regime. *Political Geography* 64: 13–22.

Tolia-Kelly, D. (2004a) Locating processes of identification: Studying the precipitates of re-memory through artefacts in the British Asian Home. *Transactions of the Institute of British Geographers* 29(3): 314–329.

Tolia-Kelly, D. (2004b) Materializing post-colonial geographies: Examining the textural landscapes of migration in the South Asian home. *Geoforum* 35(6): 675–688.

Walsh, K. (2006) British expatriate belongings: Mobile homes and transnational homing. *Home Cultures* 3(2): 123–144.

Walsh, K. (2018) Materialities and imaginaries of home: Geographies of British returnees in later life. *Area* 50: 476–482.

Walsh, K. and Näre, L. (2016) *Transnational Migration and Home in Older Age*. Abingdon, UK and New York, USA: Routledge.

Waters, J.L. (2011) Time and transnationalism: A longitudinal study of immigration, endurance and settlement in Canada. *Journal of Ethnic and Migration Studies* 37(7): 1119–1135.

Wilkins, A. (2019) *Migration, Work and Home-Making in the City: Dwelling and Belonging among Vietnamese Communities in London*. London: Routledge.

Yeoh, B., Huang, S. and Lam, T. (2005) Transnationalizing the 'Asian' family: Imaginaries, intimacies and strategic intents. *Global Networks* 5(4): 307–315.

Yeoh, B., Somaiah, B.C., Lam, T. and Acedera, K.F. (2020) Doing family in 'times of migration': Care temporalities and gender politics in Southeast Asia. *Annals of the American Association of Geographers*. DOI: 10.1080/24694452.2020.1723397.

Zhou, Y.R. (2015) Time, space and care: Rethinking transnational care from a temporal perspective. *Time and Society* 24(2): 163–182.

20. Offshoring social reproduction: low-wage labour circulation and the separation of work and family life

Thomas Saetre Jakobsen, Sam Scott and Johan Fredrik Rye

INTRODUCTION

International Organization for Migration (IOM) data show how important labour migration now is, especially that occurring over a low-income to high-income economic gradient (IOM 2020). The increasing presence of low-wage labour migration as part of the total labour force in high-income regions needs to be understood against the backdrop of an uneven and unequal global capitalist geography, with core economies (high-income regions) continually probing ways to exploit labour and other resources in more peripheral areas (lower-income regions) (Smith et al. 1984; Wallerstein 1976, 1982).

The importance of transnational family dynamics in relation to low-wage labour migration has been extensively explored by feminist scholars (see Chapters 2, 3 and 4, this *Handbook*). They have, in particular, focused on migration to provide care services in core economies. This form of (usually temporary) migration underpins what have been termed 'global care-chains' (Hochschild 2000) whereby migrants provide paid care in host countries whilst also balancing family care responsibilities back home. A range of issues are raised by this literature, which we review below, that include: the importance of maintaining 'transnational intimacy' (Parreñas, 2005) with family back home; the sacrifices and costs of physical family separation as a result of labour migration; the role and importance of migrants' remittances to support family left behind; and the importance of economic contexts, and specifically 'jumping scale' (Katz 2001a) across a periphery–core gradient, to make global care chains work from the perspective of the employer, the migrant and the migrants' wider family.

The literature on labour migration and transnational families has tended to focus on a particular sector (care work) and region (Asia) and this chapter, having reviewed the extant literature, is designed to show how ideas and concepts from it can also be applied to other sectors and other regions. In our case, we look specifically at European horticulture and the impact of temporary/circulatory harvest migration on (transnational) family structures and dynamics. The core question that we pose is: how is our understanding of low-wage labour migration from peripheral to core economies advanced by examining the physical separation of migrants and their families? To answer this, we combine existing literature with new empirical material.

The physical separation of migrants and their families, as occurs in both care and horticultural sectors, seems to underpin a strong work ethic whilst also allowing wages to remain low. Employers are able to access '*Homo economicus*' when migrants are separated from normal family and communal life, as they are when they live at the workplace (on the farm or with the host family). Migrants provide their labour power at one place and their family's maintenance is realized at another. Moreover, workers retreat to home communities when work dries up and, in the process, relieve employers, host communities and host states of reproduction costs (Hart 2002; Jakobsen 2018). They also often send vital remittances back home whilst working abroad (Lund et al. 2013; Wells et al. 2014; Willis and Yeoh 2000). We conceptualize these transnational family arrangements as the 'offshoring of social reproduction', whereby farm owners and farmworkers 'jump scale' (Katz 2001a) within a highly uneven geography of development, which allows greater surplus value to be realized within horticulture than would otherwise be possible. This chapter therefore adds to, and complements, the feminist literature on transnational householding, by placing the question of labour's social reproduction at the heart of our analysis.

In the sections that follow we first use the existing literature to examine transnational household practices amongst low-wage labour migrants and explore the tensions generated by the separation between working life (in the host country) and family life (in the home country). We then use this literature to help understand the case of low-wage labour migration to the horticultural sectors of two high-income countries – Norway and the United Kingdom (UK) – and flesh out how labour migrants and employers manage the tensions associated with the separation of work and family life.

LOW-WAGE LABOUR MIGRATION AND TRANSNATIONAL HOUSEHOLDING

Core economies across the globe import low-wage workers; however, families are often left behind. For workers in some industries, contracts are typically seasonal or relatively short-term and often tied to a single job/employer for a defined period, either by lack of alternatives or by formal requirements in visa programmes. Thus, labour circulation rather than permanent settlement can predominate for many low-wage migrants (Yeoh et al. 2020). Under such circumstances it is no wonder that transnational families emerge, where workplace production and household social reproduction are physically distanced (Burawoy 1976; Douglass 2015; Lam et al. 2006; Safri and Graham 2010). Yet how this separation works – how it shapes employers' and workers' experiences, practices and strategies, and adds to the accumulation of surplus value – is addressed in the literature for some sectors and some regions more than others.

For example, since the 1990s, feminist scholars have identified the relationship between care needs in the Global North, international labour migration and the family 'left behind' (Chant 1998; Kofman 2012; Pearson and Kusakabe 2012). Through innovative concepts such as 'global care-chains' (Hochschild 2000), transnational or global householding (Bryceson and Vuorela 2002; Douglass 2006; Willis and Yeoh 2000; Yeoh et al. 2020), and the 'migration left-behind nexus' (Toyota et al. 2007), this literature highlights the importance of the physical separation of migrants and their families in the migration process. It also opens up the 'black box' of households in terms of decision-making, distribution of resources and gendered divisions of labour (Folbre 1986; Kofman and Raghuram 2006; Wolf 1990).

Scholars have discussed how the dual-breadwinner model in core economies has created a shortage of 'hands and hearts' to provide care within the household, generating a demand for migrant labour to supplement family labour (Douglass 2006; Fraser 2016; Kofman 2012). Migrant labour's simultaneous presence (in host-country households) and absence (from the family left behind) constitutes what Hochschild (2000) has labelled 'global care-chains'. The constitution of these care-chains points to how care provisioning is increasingly solved on a private basis by moving labour across a core–periphery gradient (Douglass 2015; Hoang et al. 2015; Lan 2008). Feminist scholars, for instance, have argued that the privatization of care produces a more generalized crisis of social reproduction under neoliberal capitalism (Bakker 2007; Bakker and Gill 2019, 2003; Fraser 2016). This is because care needs in core economies are solved privately by hiring low-wage international labour migrants. This then generates a care deficit in the migrant's household back home (Isaksen et al. 2008).

Transnational householding thus emerges, involving care arrangements that are organized and carried out across borders (Douglass 2006, 2012; Parreñas 2000). Migrants, who are often also care providers, take on breadwinner responsibilities in foreign labour markets while other household members stay back home. While it is not unusual that high-skilled labour migrants bring their spouse and/or their children with them when working abroad, for low-wage labour migrants this is often not possible due to the family's lack of economic capital and/or the visa regulations of the host country (Nakache 2018; Scott and Jakobsen forthcoming).

The feminist literature specifically emphasises how the absence of the migrant breadwinner, often women but also men, affects the (gendered) divisions of labour within the household and the family practices of raising children and/or caring for the infirm (Kilkey et al. 2014; Parreñas 2000). It also points towards the maintenance of intimacy across borders to maintain (transnational) family units. Parreñas (2005), for instance, has emphasized the importance of communication technologies for Filipino migrant mothers and their children left behind. This underscores how transport and communication technologies facilitate the possibility of providing for material and emotional needs even under conditions of 'global householding' (Douglass 2006).

Labour migrants contribute materially to the needs of their family back home through remittances: money wired from the country of wage-work to the country of household reproduction. Wells et al. (2014), for instance, detail how migrant workers employed within Canada's agricultural sector regularly send money home to Mexico to help their families pay for basic needs such as food, accommodation and healthcare. As such, they realize 'arbitrage' by exploiting economic gradients (different wage rates, exchange rates, cost of living, and so on) between home (more peripheral) and host (core) countries.

From the perspective of transnational householding, both the remittances sent back home by migrant workers and the care provisioning by those left behind contributes to the everyday and intergenerational social reproduction of split households (Jakobsen 2017; Kofman 2012; Nguyen and Locke 2014). However, while remittances are often hailed as a redistributive solution to the inequalities of an uneven global economy (Bock et al. 2016; Faist 2008), and communication technologies go some way to making transnational intimacy among family members possible, the physical separation and often long-term absence of a household member comes at a price (Nguyen et al. 2006; Toyota et al. 2007).

Investigations of the social costs paid by those left behind (children, partners and elderly relatives) at the 'labour-sending end' of the global care-chains is a central theme in the literature: what has been termed the 'migration left-behind nexus' (Toyota et al. 2007). The global domestic work industry probably represents the clearest manifestation of how the cost and rewards of labour migration are distributed across global care-chains between labour-receiving and labour-sending households. The literature highlights how absentee mothers and their left-behind children manage the physical separation of the migration process, but also how the left-behind fathers need to adjust their caregiving work to changing divisions of labour within the household. Yeoh et al. (2020), for example, illustrate some of these dynamics as they explore how 'doing family' for households that are split across national borders for prolonged periods of time involves reconfiguring the gender politics of care among 'left-behind families'. In their study, the left-behind Filipino daughter resents her mother's absence, as she feels that their relationship is 'just about the money', and while she is closer to her father, he is left vulnerable to insinuations from his in-laws that he is an undeserving beneficiary of his wife's remittances (Yeoh et al. 2020: 1719).

The costs of migration to transnational households are also evident in other contexts. For instance, McLaughlin et al. (2017) identify the adverse effects of male farm labour migration to Canada on left-behind households in Mexico. For children, the absence of a father appears to have negative impacts on school performance, and children also react to separation 'by becoming sick, depressed, or both' (McLaughlin et al. 2017: 691). For the women staying behind, the absence of their spouse involves an intensification of household work and a wider responsibility both for their children's well-being and for the family farm (see also Rosales-Mendoza and Campos-Flores, 2019). Thus, while migrants and wider household members rely on each other during an often protracted spell of migrant work, through care arrangements, emotional ties and pooling of common resources (for example, remittances, unpaid household labour), their physical separation comes at a price. While the price of family separation can be discerned within migrant households, such as for left-behind children or relatives, the dynamics separating labour power from household social reproduction also form part of an extended geography of uneven development, as we highlight in the next section.

OFFSHORING SOCIAL REPRODUCTION

Much like labour mobility within and across national borders, and the associated family separation that follows in its wake, offshoring – the relocation of activities across national borders – is one of the defining features of globalization (Peck 2017). While much of the literature on offshoring has centred on the theme of outsourcing production, and jobs, to lower-wage countries, at its core, 'the primary function of offshore space of all kinds is to provide opportunities for *arbitrage*: the exploitation of difference for profit' (Potts 2019: 199).

Price differentials between onshore and offshore locations work to allow the realization of surplus value within an uneven geography of global production. Looking beyond the relocation and outsourcing of production facilities, importing workers (but not their families) is another means through which arbitrage can be realized. This is particularly the case in industries where offshoring production is not as feasible, such as care work and horticulture (Scott 2013a). In the case of arbitrage for wages, labour contractors play a key role in linking onshore and offshore locations, by putting these 'markets' in touch with each other (Peck 1996). These transnational 'labour chains' allow an employer, a human resources manager or a labour market intermediary to recruit low-wage workers in economically peripheral areas, and pass some of the risk of a competitive commodity market onto the workers who are called upon in part for their flexibility (Barrientos 2013). Low-wage labour is then relocated into an 'onshore' production facility where considerable value is added: as, for various reasons, low-wage migrant workers are not only attractive due to lower wage demands, but are also known to be compliant to employers' demands and to work especially hard (Scott 2013b; Scott and Rye

2021). Thus, a central background condition to the activities of offshoring and onshoring are the uneven and unequal geographies of 'actually existing' capitalism (Peck 2017).

Crucially for the discussion here, the costs of socially reproducing the workforce are often offloaded to households when capital withdraws from the social wage, partly through offshoring its commitment to particular places (Katz 2001b, 2008). Social reproduction represents the work and social arrangements that allow people and nature to come to life, be sustained and replenished on a daily and long-term basis (Bakker 2007). It is, in short, the biological and social maintenance of labour power on a daily and intergenerational basis. Under capitalism it is important to note that in order to secure life, every person needs to engage with the market to obtain basic necessities (Wood 2002). This makes wage-work important to any notion of social reproduction. However, no one can live on wages alone: households under capitalism combine wage-work with unpaid work and relationships. While this makes capitalism less all-encompassing as a part of our daily lives (Gibson-Graham 2006), scholars have pointed to how keeping activities 'unaccounted for' in market terms allows capital to free-ride (Fraser 2016). That is, as unpaid care work, socialization and maintaining relationships are carried out without capital or states taking them into account, their costs mostly remain hidden (Waring 1999). Yet, they are essential to the reproduction of capitalism (Smith et al. 1984). Thus, the work of social reproduction is a background condition for capitalism, providing for and maintaining a workforce, yet it remains hidden in most accounts of the economy.

Marxist scholars working in the South African and Chinese contexts have extended the argument above around the 'subsidy' that the social reproduction of labour provides capitalism (Hart 2002; Arrighi 2009; Zhan 2019a; Zhan and Scully 2018). They argue that by keeping the added value and cost to workforce provisioning (for example, giving birth, socialization) and maintenance (for example, care-work) outside the official accounts, the price of labour power is cheapened, as both states and employers receive the added 'surplus' from household and community work for 'free'. At the same time, the costs of this work (for example, handling work injuries, infirm care-needs or 'worn out' workers) are 'offloaded' to workers' households and communities (Arrighi et al. 2010; Hart 2006; Zhan 2019b).

In the case of international labour migration, as discussed above, these tensions manifest themselves quite differently. On the one hand, there are dual-breadwinner families in core economies who solve their household needs by hiring (largely migrant) domestic workers. On the other hand, there are the transnational households made up of low-wage migrants working in core economies and families left behind in more peripheral areas. Crucially, the presence of low-wage labour migrants without family members joining them appears to be becoming more commonplace in core economies, with the 21st century revival of guestworker-type migration schemes.

To summarize, employers now require highly productive workers; and an absence of *in situ* family ties and responsibilities, allied with a core–periphery mobility gradient, seem to be key in giving low-wage labour migrants a particularly strong work ethic. Whilst the literature on low-wage labour migration and transnational families has tended to focus on care-work, in the next section we intend to show how ideas from this literature are also relevant in other migrant-dense sectors such as horticulture. In fact, central to the system of migrant labour in horticulture, we argue below, is family separation and the offshoring of costs associated with the reproduction of workers.

LOW-WAGE MIGRANT LABOUR IN EUROPEAN HORTICULTURE

European food production over the last three decades has become reliant on low-wage migrant labour, following a number of structural transformations (Rye and Scott 2018). Amongst other things, we have seen: the consolidation of farms; vertical integration in the production network, with wholesalers and supermarket chains commanding a stronger influence on quality and quantity; just-in-time delivery requirements in the production network; and a growing appetite within the population for fresh fruit and vegetables (Geddes and Scott 2010; Richards et al. 2013). Whereas horticulture before this period of restructuring generally solved its seasonal labour needs through mobilizing residual populations locally, including family labour and the underemployed (Newby 1979; Strauss 2013; Verdon 2017), low-wage international labour migrants have become the norm, especially after European Union enlargement in 2004 and 2007. Moreover, the preferences of employers in the horticulture sector for deferent, flexible and hard-working labour plays an important role in making migrant labour the dominant workforce in the fields (Hellio 2014, 2017; Rogaly 2008; Scott and Rye 2021; Waldinger and Lichter 2003).

As with migrant domestic workers going from the Philippines to the United States (US), or Indonesia to Singapore (Parreñas 2000; Yeoh et al. 2020), migrant labour in Europe's horticultural sector has largely been drawn in from more peripheral economies. We have had, for example, Ukrainian workers moving to Polish farms (Górny and Kaczmarczyk 2018), and Polish workers moving to German farms (Fialkowska and Piechowska 2016) and beyond, in a kind of east-to-west, periphery-to-core migration 'conveyor belt'. Similarly, the Mediterranean agricultural industries recruit large numbers of migrant workers from Africa and Central and Eastern Europe (Gertel and Sippel 2014; Corrado et al. 2017), and there are numerous other examples of migrants from more distant locations, such as the Thai wild berry harvesters in the Nordic forests, and Bangladeshi strawberry pickers in Greece (Rye and O'Reilly 2021). Beyond Europe, there is also a North American literature documenting a long history of international labour migration from south (Mexico, Central America and the Caribbean) to north (the US and Canada) to solve harvest labour needs (Daniel 1981; Mitchell 2012; Reid-Musson 2017).

Though the conditions of work and life in the horticulture industry are harsh compared to most other occupations in the host country, low-wage labour migrants in the food industry do have agency. This is especially evident when migrants' lives are viewed within a transnational *milieu*. In fact, one of the primary ways in which individual workers and their families can assert their influence on the resource distribution within the uneven geography of capitalism is by moving across space to earn wages in more affluent core regions, as foreign currency can be used for household consumption (Alberti 2014; Mitchell 1996). In the literature on migrant farm workers, it is often pointed out that seasonal migrants accept low wages and harsh working conditions, as the wages go further back home (Holmes 2013; Rogaly 2009). The concept of a 'dual frame of reference' (Suárez-Orozco and Suárez-Orozco 1995; Waldinger and Lichter 2003) articulates the observation that the deference of migrants to the low wages of the industry are partly attributed to the way migrants compare price differentials between the country of work and the wages accrued there, and the country of family reproduction (Scott 2013b; Waldinger and Lichter 2003). This is not to gloss over the fact that labour migration comes at a price for the individual migrants who toil within precarious employment, and for the family members staying behind (as noted above).

CASE STUDY: NORWEGIAN AND UK HORTICULTURE

As the literature reviewed above illustrates, though seldom argues explicitly, in the horticultural sector of core economies the tensions between capital accumulation and social reproduction are 'solved' through temporary and seasonal low-wage labour circulation and an accompanying arbitrage. The underpinning conditions for these arrangements are an uneven economic geography (differential wages, employment/unemployment, exchange rates, costs of living, and so on), transnational migration across this unevenness, and family separation.

We will now illustrate our core arguments through case study material (qualitative in-depth interviews) from western England (18 interviews) and south-eastern Norway (18 interviews). In both locations, horticulture has traditionally formed the backbone of the economy and still plays a dominant role, despite its declining relative importance. Food production in each area is dominated by labour-intensive crops, particularly fruit and vegetables, that today rely on large numbers of low-wage and temporary/seasonal labour migrants. The workforces in both countries at the time of the research were mainly recruited from Central and Eastern Europe, though in the Norwegian study locality there were also migrants travelling longer distances, for instance from Vietnam.

Across the two locations, we interviewed a total of 36 individuals: sampling migrant farmworkers (N = 14), employers (N = 10) and local community representatives (N = 12). Interviews lasted for about 45 minutes to 90 minutes, and followed largely similar semi-structured interview guides, covering some common topics related to the migrant worker phenomenon in the locality but also tailored to capture specific aspects for the different interviewee categories.

The migrant farmworkers were from Central and Eastern Europe working on a temporary or seasonal basis, though some for longer periods of the year, often in a circular mode (moving annually between home and host countries) spanning many years. Most of the migrant workers lived onsite in tied accommodation, with employers deducting rent from the wage. Given their long working hours, isolated location and limited integration with the local community, we faced considerable difficulties in recruiting migrant farm workers. Thus, employers acted as gatekeepers, and whilst we acknowledge the potential pitfalls of such a recruitment strategy – such as selection of workers who are particularly loyal, or the potential effect it had on how our loyalties were perceived by the interviewees (Scott 2013c) – other strategies were less optimal (see also Holmes 2013). Migrant interviews were conducted in English, which required recruitment of interviewees who had mastered the language and, therefore, were among those with longer histories of circulatory migration. While this represents a selection bias – the migrant interviewees were most likely not among the worst-off farm workers in the localities, as they had stayed year after year – it also provided accounts that reflected back on many years of experience. The fact that most of the migrant farmworkers are male in our sample reflects the demography of the workers on the particular food production worksites visited.

The employers were selected in order to enhance sample variance. All had long-standing experiences within the horticultural industry, and appeared forthcoming in the interviews. Similarly, the community representatives were selected based on their accumulated knowledge of the local farming sector and/or migrant farmworker communities. Employer and community interviewees all represented the majority population in the locality: ethnic white, born in the country (except for one Irish interviewee in the UK), and higher socio-economic status (vis-à-vis migrants). They were also older. Among community representatives there is a more even gender balance of interviewees. The employer and community interviews were conducted in the mother-tongue language in their respective countries.

OFFSHORING SOCIAL REPRODUCTION AND TRANSNATIONAL ARBITRAGE

In the remainder of the chapter, we draw the extant literature and our new empirical material together. We examine why temporary and seasonal low-wage migrant workers are so attractive to employers in the UK and Norwegian contexts, and argue that a large part of their appeal is connected to the fact that they leave social (family and communal) ties back home. With these transnational family regimes, social reproduction is 'offshored' for the benefit of the employers. However, we also show how low-wage migrants manage this offshoring and gain benefits from it, engaging in what we call two-way transnational arbitrage. Our focus on low-wage labour migration and family separation can be contrasted with higher wage international business migration: where the (usually) male breadwinner is normally able to move with his 'trailing wife' who performs invisible care and emotional work in the host country (Kunz 2020).

Labour Circulation and the Separation of Work and Family Life

In horticulture, labour needs vary by season. In Norway, the main growing and harvesting season is three to four months long, from around June to September. In the UK the peak season is a little longer, from around April to October. In both contexts, and related to this seasonality (which is also crop-dependent), there were relatively few examples of permanent migrant farm workers. The vast majority of workers, instead, lived in temporary onsite farm accommodation. Most returned home during the off-season, where they may take short-term jobs or go unemployed and rely on savings from their seasonal work. The work patterns of migrant farm workers are, thus, often circular and multi-nodal, dividing their work and personal lives between host and home localities.

For seasonal workers, who are mostly housed on the farm, it was often difficult (and in practice prohibited by many employers) to have young family members join them. Spouses may join usually only if they are part of the workforce. Housing on the farm, in the form of caravans, cabins or refurbished barns, was typical, with two to six people often sharing. The cost of lodging was usually deducted from the wage, and was certainly cheaper (and much easier) than living offsite.

It is not only the housing arrangements that deter workers from moving as a family, but also the short-term nature of their stay and the low and uncertain income when compared to the living costs in the host country. Moreover, except for a wish to stay and spend time together, other family members had few reasons to travel to Norway or the UK, which to them primarily represent the migrating family member's workplace. Illustratively, some of the employer interviewees referred to seasonal farm work as 'North Sea shifts', alluding to the cyclical work arrangements on the oil installations off the coast of Norway, which combines the distinctive temporal and spatial separation between work and home, and at the same time lacks separation between work and place of rest while at work. Others have argued that these 'disruptive' rhythms to the mobility process of circular migrants are important in explaining their sought-after work ethic (Yeoh et al. 2020; Collins and Bayliss 2020).

Migrant Work Ethic

The uncertainty of the temporary/seasonal work and the need to secure new employment each year, not to mention the months when work is not available, can be difficult to bear for workers. It is also problematic for employers. At all farms visited, in both the west of England and south-eastern Norway, recruitment was an ongoing concern for farmers, who typically start the process in January and see the first workers arrive in March. Much of the recruitment in Norway was peer-to-peer, though in the UK agencies and direct recruitment were also evident. Peer recruitment is usually carried out by more permanent staff, often some of the few migrant workers who are employed for the whole year.

The recruitment process is thus characterised by uncertainty and affected by factors beyond the employers' direct control. Yet farmers appeared generally content with the mode of recruitment, relying on migrants instead of local workers. Part of the explanation for this is the fact that while migrant farmworkers earn a relatively low wage in Norway and the UK, the wage differential between the host (core) country and the home (more peripheral) country is large enough to make seasonal agricultural work attractive. This reflects the 'dual frame of reference' of migrant workers noted above and helps to explain the motivation for moving abroad to take up low-wage work (Waldinger and Lichter 2003). On the other hand, local workers without this dual frame of reference do not realistically consider the wages and working conditions on offer in seasonal horticulture.

Alongside the dual frame of reference, migrants are considered a very productive labour force because they are housed onsite and there is therefore little separation between home and work. This makes workers very flexible and reliable, to be deployed as and when needed. As one of the farm workers reflected: 'Ya. We all [in] our company, which are working here, are living on farm and we save a lot of time too for this. Because ... our job is in our yard [chuckles]. Just enough to go out through the door, and it is ... in you are on the job' (Gabriel, migrant farmworker for 17 years, south-eastern Norway).

Commensurate with this, employers tended to boast about the good work ethic of their seasonal migrants. They explicitly related this to the workers' lack of family obligations. Beth (a UK employer) explained:

> It's not a nine to five job. So it's very difficult to work around families ... This is growing. It hasn't got time for somebody to, pick the children up from school. The focus needs [to be on] picking there and then, and it's so time precious. We don't know from one day to the next what days the shifts are going to be. So with the guys working here, living here, they are a lot more flexible. They kind of give the hundred percent of their time and their life to the farm once they're here ... Cause they haven't got their children ... We don't overwork them by any means. I mean there are rules and they can't work too [long]. [But] you know, they haven't got that all 'I've got to go tomorrow to go watch my daughter's play or whatever'. So they are one hundred per cent committed to the job.

Essentially, low-wage circulatory migrants from more peripheral economies are seen by agricultural employers in core countries as the optimal source of labour. This relates very clearly to the lack of *in situ* family/communal ties and obligations, and to a dual frame of reference (Scott 2013b; Scott and Rye, 2021).

Limited Integration

Linked to their strong work ethic, migrants were seen to pose little or no cost to the local community. They were seen to be focused on working hard, with thoughts of rural integration often sidelined (Scott and Visser 2022). The combination of seasonality, onsite housing, and a '*Homo economicus*' outlook amongst migrants, means that the workforce on farms is often invisible:

> No, they're [people in the local community] probably not aware of the scale. Also, I think, you know, most of the people who come into, or traditionally most of the people who have been coming in to do this migrant work are often single or if they're not single, they've left, they often left their families back in their native countries. They're not elderly, so they don't have a great impact on schools or hospitals or care. And so if they are happy to have a few beers with their friends in, you know, somewhere isolated where they're not visible, by their community, they don't even have that impact on society, you know, because they're not filling up hospitals or schools or things like that. (Connor, police officer who grew up in the study area, western England)
>
> There are many who are seasonal workers, quite a few, who come here for a short period. This is my impression, right. And then I do not think that they are interested in getting that integrated, they are here to work and ... they have some weeks, a month or one and a half. I am not sure if they have much time to integrate. (Ida, agricultural officer who grew up in the study area, south-eastern Norway)

Thus, alongside a strong work ethic, it seems that temporary/circulatory migrants, even if they return year after year to the farm, tend to remain quite distanced from the rural host communities (for more on low-wage migrant invisibility in rural spaces, see Lever and Milbourne 2017; Licona and Maldonado 2014). Low-wage migrants are principally in the host country to work, they tend to live where they work; the work they do is often all-consuming and, on top of this, many have families and commitments back in the home country to focus on during the off season.

Family Sacrifice and Transnational Arbitrage

The separation between family and employment, allied with the strong work ethic, comes at a price. The migrants we interviewed told of how they and their family members left behind can suffer:

> I think it is more bad things. Because of ... because of family. Because, I have a young family. Young children so ... everyday without them is ... you know ... its ... it won't return, you know what I mean. And children get older and it won't return so ... I do not know. Maybe the people who have older children or have adult children have other problems, I think so, but for me the most problematic is the separation with the family. And the good thing is ... hmm ... [silence] ... good things ... only the money. Nothing else. Yeah, I think so. Maybe I see other country, and that is also, but alone, yeah. Its ... (Gorski, migrant farmworker for five years, south-eastern Norway)

Family separation, and most notably not being around while children are growing up, is managed through the narrative of sacrifice, a theme much discussed in the literature on migrant mothers and left-behind children (Asis 2002; Asis et al. 2004; Bloch 2017; Hewett 2009). The migrant interviewees sacrificed part of the household's present emotional well-being for improved material consumption back home, and for future joint household endeavours. Thus, migrant farm workers must bridge the physically distanced spheres of work and home life.

Despite the problems and sacrifices associated with this, many migrants also emphasized how the wages earned in the host country actually helped them to achieve some of their aspirations back home via transnational investment and consumption practices:

> If you want to work, if you're not lazy, you can come here, you can, you can make money, you can send money to your family, your parents and stuff. You can help Bulgarian economics, because most of the money in Bulgaria is from immigrants. We are sending to many money to Bulgaria. Like that we are helping the country. (Anthony, migrant farmworker for seven years, western England)

There is clearly a longer-term objective associated with seasonal employment and migrants' hard work, and onsite living is accepted with this longer-term objective in mind. Indeed, this is likely one of the key factors that explains why migrants work as hard as they do at the bottom of the labour market, as demonstrated across a wide variety of political and national contexts (Dawson et al. 2017; Rigg 2013; Shen 2016; Tacoli and Mabala 2010).

Work in the host country was most commonly explained with reference to house building and/or remittances to one's family back home:

> Yes. I make a house, a brand-new house. Yeah. I move the money from UK to Romania, and do that. As long as you've got the house, if tomorrow it's finished. You have to work. You need to live, but I got somewhere to go. Anybody is like that. They think: 'All right. If I make some money, I'll make money and make something.' (Arthur, migrant farmworker for seven years, western England)
>
> Yeah. So far I would like to keep going this way because, yeah ... I build a house. I collect the money for that for some years and I will not finish with that and ... maybe I have a bit ... backup and maybe in some years I shall start in Poland to do something, just to be close to the family. But as long as I can, and as long as it is valuable, I try to work like that. (Gaspar, migrant farmworker for 17 years, south-eastern Norway)

While there is a literature highlighting the costs of transnational household arrangements (Biao 2007; Hoang et al. 2015; Nguyen et al. 2006; Ye et al. 2016) for family members involved, there is nonetheless scope for analysing further how the costs and benefits of these arrangements are distributed by actors beyond the household unit, and how they are experienced and rationalized by different actors.

Undoubtedly labour (migrant workers) and capital (low-wage employers) benefit from 'the exploitation of difference for profit' (Potts 2019: 199), in what could be described as a two-way, though uneven, process of transnational 'arbitrage'. However, the maintenance of transnational family arrangements and the ways in which these underpin the reproduction of labour power (migrants' work ethic) and also offshore many of the costs of labour reproduction (that is, importing workers but not families) seems ultimately to serve the economic interests of core economies first and foremost.

CONCLUSIONS

The chapter has reviewed the literature on low-wage labour migration and transnational families and applied insights from this to a horticultural case study. We have argued that the offshoring of social reproduction accompanies certain forms of contemporary low-wage labour migration. In particular: migration related to temporary/seasonal employment (and thus labour circulation); migration related to the need to live at work (in horticulture and in domestic work); and migration related to a move across a periphery-to-core economic divide, are all associated with the separation of the work from the family and communal spheres. To capture these structural underpinnings, we have advanced the related concepts of the 'offshoring of social reproduction' and two-way transnational 'arbitrage'.

The transnational strategy of offshoring social reproduction, and the resultant physical separation between the spaces of production (work) and social reproduction (family and community), appears to provide capital in core economies with an additional degree of labour power. At the same time, migrants also appear able to negotiate this separation, navigating their constrained choices by adding value to their low-wage work. Even if this comes at a considerable cost to themselves, their family and their community, for many migrants the offshoring of social reproduction is still preferable to staying put. This is why we speak of two-way transnational 'arbitrage' with respect to low-wage labour migration, whereby movement from peripheral to core economies, and the associated 'jump in scale' (Katz 2001a), increases the labour power available to core capital and, at the same time, migrants are also able to exploit scalar inequalities, albeit with major sacrifices. It may well be a two-way arbitrage, but it is still a highly uneven one in terms of the distribution of both benefits and costs.

To date, migration has been viewed primarily through an economic lens centred upon productive wage labour. Yet as a broad feminist literature now attests to, behind every worker is a wider familial and communal milieu. Capital and states know that this wider milieu sustains labour, but also know that in certain contexts it can pay to keep it at a distance. Given this, it is time for much more attention to be directed towards the hinterlands underpinning, enabling and sustaining migration and migrant work. Specifically, more research is now needed methodologically to shift attention away from a workplace, host-country lens towards a social reproduction, transnational lens. This shift would help us to understand better the 'solution' of particular forms of low-wage labour migration within the context of a spatially and socially unequal capitalist system. This shift towards placing social reproduction at the centre of research would help us to explain better the 'matching' interests of labour migrants and capital; though with highly uneven points of departure and outcomes. Moreover, by methodologically shifting to more comparative research on low-wage labour migration, we can better consider the costs and benefits, as conceptualized by the actors themselves, in labour regimes that involve transnationally embedded labour market participation.

Summing up, migration can challenge conventional understandings of the family and bring into relief the often competing economic and social dimensions of contemporary life. For many low-wage workers, inequalities in the global economy mean that transnational household arrangements must prevail. They prevail because migrants seek out better work opportunities than are available domestically, and because capital and the state often prefer to import low-wage workers more than parents, carers, friends and human beings. Low-wage labour migration from peripheral to core economies, then, is associated with both an economic dividend (for employers and the migrant) but also a social (familial and communal) cost. The balance between economic rewards and household sacrifice is a delicate one, but an increasingly prominent one as far as low-wage migrants (especially temporary guestworkers) are concerned.

ACKNOWLEDGEMENTS

The chapter has been made possible through the 2017–2022 Global Labour in Rural Societies (GLARUS) research project financed by the Norwegian Research Council (grant no. 261864/F10). We are very grateful to the funder for the support received. We would also like to thank the editors of this *Handbook* (Professor Johanna Waters and Professor Brenda Yeoh) for extremely helpful and constructive comments on earlier drafts of this chapter.

REFERENCES

Alberti, Gabriella. 2014. Mobility Strategies, 'Mobility Differentials' and 'Transnational Exit': The Experiences of Precarious Migrants in London's Hospitality Jobs. *Work, Employment and Society* 28 (6): 865–881. https://doi.org/10.1177/0950017014528403.

Arrighi, Giovanni. 2009. *Adam Smith in Beijing: Lineages of the 21st Century*. London: Verso.

Arrighi, Giovanni, Nicole Aschoff and Ben Scully. 2010. Accumulation by Dispossession and Its Limits: The Southern Africa Paradigm Revisited. *Studies in Comparative International Development* 45 (4): 410–438. https://doi.org/10.1007/s12116-010-9075-7.

Asis, Maruja Milagros B. 2002. From the Life Stories of Filipino Women: Personal and Family Agendas in Migration. *Asian and Pacific Migration Journal* 11 (1): 67–93. https://doi.org/10.1177/011719680201100104.

Asis, Maruja Milagros B., Shirlena Huang and Brenda S.A. Yeoh. 2004. When the Light of the Home is Abroad: Unskilled Female Migration and the Filipino Family. *Singapore Journal of Tropical Geography* 25 (2): 198–215. https://doi.org/10.1111/j.0129-7619.2004.00182.x.

Bakker, Isabella. 2007. Social Reproduction and the Constitution of a Gendered Political Economy. *New Political Economy* 12 (4): 541–556. https://doi.org/10.1080/13563460701661561.

Bakker, Isabella and Stephen Gill. 2003. Global Political Economy and Social Reproduction. in Gill, Stephen and Isabella Bakker (eds), *Power, Production and Social Reproduction*. Basingstoke, UK and New York, USA: Palgrave Macmillan, pp. 3–16. http://www.palgraveconnect.com/doifinder/10.1057/9780230522404.

Bakker, Isabella and Stephen Gill. 2019. Rethinking Power, Production, and Social Reproduction: Toward Variegated Social Reproduction. *Capital and Class* 43 (4): 503–523. https://doi.org/10.1177/0309816819880783.

Barrientos, Stephanie Ware. 2013. 'Labour Chains': Analysing the Role of Labour Contractors in Global Production Networks. *Journal of Development Studies* 49 (8): 1058–1071. https://doi.org/10.1080/00220388.2013.780040.

Biao, Xiang. 2007. How Far Are the Left-behind Left behind? A Preliminary Study in Rural China. *Population, Space and Place* 13 (3): 179–191. https://doi.org/10.1002/psp.437.

Bloch, Alexia. 2017. 'Other Mothers,' Migration, and a Transnational Nurturing Nexus. *Signs: Journal of Women in Culture and Society* 43 (1): 53–75. https://doi.org/10.1086/692441.

Bock, Bettina., Giorgio Osti and Flaminia Ventura. 2016. Rural Migration and New Patterns of Exclusion and Integration. In Shucksmith, Mark and David L. Brown (eds), *Routledge International Handbook of Rural Studies*. London, UK and New York, USA: Routledge, pp. 71–84.

Bryceson, Deborah and Ulla Vuorela. 2002. *The Transnational Family: New European Frontiers and Global Networks*. Oxford, UK and New York, USA: Berg Publishers.

Burawoy, Michael. 1976. The Functions and Reproduction of Migrant Labor: Comparative Material from Southern Africa and the United States. *American Journal of Sociology* 81 (5): 1050–1087.

Chant, Sylvia. 1998. Households, Gender and Rural–Urban Migration: Reflections on Linkages and Considerations for Policy. *Environment and Urbanization* 10 (1): 5–22. https://doi.org/10.1177/095624789801000117.

Collins, Francis L. and Thomas Bayliss. 2020. The Good Migrant: Everyday Nationalism and Temporary Migration Management on New Zealand Dairy Farms. *Political Geography* 80 (June): 102193. https://doi.org/10.1016/j.polgeo.2020.102193.

Corrado, Alessandra, Carlos de Castro and Domenico Perrotta. 2017. Cheap Food, Cheap Labour, High Profits: Agriculture and Mobility in the Mediterranean. In Corrado, Alessandra, Carlos de Castro and Domenico Perrotta (eds), *Migration and Agriculture: Mobility and Change in the Mediterranean Area*. London, UK and New York, USA: Routledge, pp. 1–24.

Daniel, Cletus E. 1981. *Bitter Harvest: A History of California Farmworkers, 1870–1941*. Berkeley, CA: University of California Press.

Dawson, Chris, Michail Veliziotis and Benjamin Hopkins. 2017. Understanding the Perception of the 'Migrant Work Ethic'. *Work, Employment and Society* 32 (5): 811–830. https://doi.org/10.1177/0950017017706306.

Douglass, Mike. 2006. Global Householding in Pacific Asia. *International Development Planning Review* 28 (4): 421–446. https://doi.org/10.3828/idpr.28.4.1.

Douglass, Mike. 2012. Global Householding and Social Reproduction: Migration Research, Dynamics and Public Policy in East and Southeast Asia. Asia Research Institute Working Paper Series, no. 188: 29.

Douglass, Mike. 2015. Global Householding and Social Reproduction in Migration Research. SSRN Scholarly Paper ID 2583197. Rochester, NY: Social Science Research Network. http://papers.ssrn.com/abstract=2583197.

Faist, Thomas. 2008. Migrants as Transnational Development Agents: An Inquiry Into the Newest Round of the Migration–Development Nexus. *Population, Space and Place* 14 (1): 21–42. https://doi.org/10.1002/psp.471.

Fialkowska, Kamila and Maria Piechowska. 2016. New Way, Old Pattern: Seasonal Migration From Poland to Germany. *Arbor* 192 (777): a285. http://dx.doi.org/10.3989/arbor.2016.777n1001.

Folbre, Nancy. 1986. Hearts and Spades: Paradigms of Household Economics. *World Development* 14 (2): 245–255. https://doi.org/10.1016/0305-750X(86)90056-2.

Fraser, Nancy. 2016. Contradictions of Capital and Care. *New Left Review*. 100: 99–117.

Geddes, Andrew and Sam Scott. 2010. UK Food Businesses' reliance on low-wage migrant labour: a case of choice or constraint. In Ruhs, Martin and Bridget Anderson (eds), *Who Needs Migrant Workers?* Oxford: Oxford University Press, pp. 193–218.

Gertel, Jörg and and Sarah Ruth Sippel (eds). 2014. *Seasonal Workers in Mediterranean Agriculture: The Social Costs of Eating Fresh*. Abingdon, UK and New York, USA: Routledge.

Gibson-Graham, J.K. 2006. *The End of Capitalism (as We Knew It): A Feminist Critique of Political Economy*. Minneapolis, MN: University of Minnesota Press.

Górny, Agata and Paweł Kaczmarczyk. 2018. A Known but Uncertain Path: The Role of Foreign Labour in Polish Agriculture. *Journal of Rural Studies* 64, 177–188.

Hart, Gillian Patricia. 2002. *Disabling Globalization: Places of Power in Post-Apartheid South Africa*. Berkeley and Los Angeles, CA: University of California Press.

Hart, Gillian Patricia. 2006. Denaturalizing Dispossession: Critical Ethnography in the Age of Resurgent Imperialism. *Antipode* 38 (5): 977–1004. https://doi.org/10.1111/j.1467-8330.2006.00489.x.

Hellio, Emmanuelle. 2014. 'We Don't Have Women in Boxes'. In Gertel, Jörg and Sarah Ruth Sippel (eds), *Seasonal Workers in Mediterranean Agriculture: The Social Costs of Eating Fresh*. Abingdon, UK and New York, USA: Routledge, pp. 141–157.

Hellio, Emmanuelle. 2017. 'They Know That You'll Leave, like a Dog Moving on to the next Bin': Undocumented Male and Seasonal Contracted Female Farmworkers in the Agricultural Labour Market of Huelva, Spain. In Corrado, Alessandra, Carlos de Castro and Domenico Perrotta (eds), *Migration and Agriculture: Mobility and Change in the Mediterranean Area*. London, UK and New York, USA: Routledge, pp. 198–216.

Hewett, Heather. 2009. Mothering across Borders: Narratives of Immigrant Mothers in the United States. *Women's Studies Quarterly* 37 (3–4): 121–139.

Hoang, Lan Anh, Theodora Lam, Brenda S.A. Yeoh and Graham Elspeth. 2015. Transnational Migration, Changing Care Arrangements and Left-Behind Children's Responses in South-East Asia. *Children's Geographies* 13 (3): 263–277. https://doi.org/10.1080/14733285.2015.972653.

Hochschild, Arlie Russell. 2000. Global Care Chains and Emotional Surplus Value. In Giddens, Anthony and Will Hutton (eds), *On the Edge: Living with Global Capitalism*. London: Jonathan Cape, pp. 130–46.

Holmes, Seth. 2013. *Fresh Fruit, Broken Bodies: Migrant Farmworkers in the United States*. Berkeley and Los Angeles, CA, USA; and London, UK: University of California Press.
International Organization for Migration (IOM). 2020. *World Migration Report 2020*. Geneva: International Organization for Migration.
Isaksen, Lise Widding, Sambasivan Uma Devi and Arlie Russell Hochschild. 2008. Global Care Crisis: A Problem of Capital, Care Chain, or Commons? *American Behavioral Scientist* 52 (3): 405–425. https://doi.org/10.1177/0002764208323513.
Jakobsen, Thomas Sætre. 2017. *Living in Transition: Peasant-Workers Working Between Farmland and the Workplaces of the Urban in Post-Deng China*. Doctoral thesis at NTNU, 2017:178. https://brage.bibsys.no/xmlui/handle/11250/2448913.
Jakobsen, Thomas Sætre. 2018. From the Workplace to the Household: Migrant Labor and Accumulation without Dispossession. *Critical Asian Studies* 50 (2): 176–195. https://doi.org/10.1080/14672715.2018.1443018.
Katz, Cindi. 2001a. On the Grounds of Globalization: A Topography for Feminist Political Engagement. *Signs* 26 (4): 1213–1234. https://doi.org/10.1086/495653.
Katz, Cindi. 2001b. Vagabond Capitalism and the Necessity of Social Reproduction. *Antipode* 33 (4): 709–728. https://doi.org/10.1111/1467-8330.00207.
Katz, Cindi. 2008. Bad Elements: Katrina and the Scoured Landscape of Social Reproduction. *Gender, Place and Culture* 15 (1): 15–29. https://doi.org/10.1080/09663690701817485.
Kilkey, Majella, Ania Plomien and Diane Perrons. 2014. Migrant Men's Fathering Narratives, Practices and Projects in National and Transnational Spaces: Recent Polish Male Migrants to London. *International Migration* 52 (1): 178–191. https://doi.org/10.1111/imig.12046.
Kofman, Eleonore. 2012. Rethinking Care Through Social Reproduction: Articulating Circuits of Migration. *Social Politics: International Studies in Gender, State and Society* 19 (1): 142–162. https://doi.org/10.1093/sp/jxr030.
Kofman, Eleonore and Parvati Raghuram. 2006. Gender and Global Labour Migrations: Incorporating Skilled Workers. *Antipode* 38 (2): 282–303. https://doi.org/10.1111/j.1467-8330.2006.00580.x.
Kunz, Sarah. 2020. A Business Empire and Its Migrants: Royal Dutch Shell and the Management of Racial Capitalism. *Transactions of the Institute of British Geographers* 45 (2): 377–391. https://doi.org/10.1111/tran.12366.
Lam, Theodora, Brenda S.A. Yeoh and Shirlena Huang. 2006. Global Householding in a City-State: Emerging Trends in Singapore. *International Development Planning Review* 28 (4): 475–498.
Lan, Pei-Chia. 2008. New Global Politics of Reproductive Labor: Gendered Labor and Marriage Migration. *Sociology Compass* 2 (6): 1801–1815. https://doi.org/10.1111/j.1751-9020.2008.00176.x.
Lever, John and Paul Milbourne. 2017. The Structural Invisibility of Outsiders: The Role of Migrant Labour in the Meat-Processing Industry. *Sociology* 51 (2): 306–322. https://doi.org/10.1177/0038038515616354.
Licona, Adela C. and Marta Maria Maldonado. 2014. The Social Production of Latin@ Visibilities and Invisibilities: Geographies of Power in Small Town America. *Antipode* 46 (2): 517–536. https://doi.org/10.1111/anti.12049.
Lund, Ragnhild, Kyoko Kusakabe, Smita Mishra Pand and Wang Yunxian (eds). 2013. *Gender, Mobilities, and Livelihood Transformations: Comparing Indigenous People in China, India, and Laos*. London, UK and New York, USA: Routledge.
McLaughlin, Janet., Don Wells, Aaraón Mendiburo, André Lyn and Biljana Vasilevska. 2017. 'Temporary Workers', Temporary Fathers: Transnational Family Impacts of Canada's Seasonal Agricultural Worker Program. *Relations Industrielles / Industrial Relations* 72 (4): 682–709. https://doi.org/10.7202/1043172ar.
Mitchell, Don. 1996. *The Lie of the Land*. Minneapolis, MN: University of Minnesota Press.
Mitchell, Don. 2012. *They Saved the Crops: Labor, Landscape, and the Struggle over Industrial Farming in Bracero-Era California*. Athens, GA: University of Georgia Press.
Nakache, Delphine. 2018. Migrant Workers and the Right to Family Accompaniment: A Case for Family Rights in International Law and in Canada. *International Migration* 56 (6): 221–235. https://doi.org/10.1111/imig.12444.
Newby, Howard. 1979. *The Deferential Worker: A Study of Farm Workers in East Anglia*. Madison, WI: University of Wisconsin Press.

Nguyen, Liem, Brenda S.A. Yeoh and Mika Toyota. 2006. Migration and the Well-Being of the 'Left Behind' in Asia. *Asian Population Studies* 2 (1): 37–44. https://doi.org/10.1080/17441730600700507.
Nguyen, Minh T.N. and Catherine Locke. 2014. Rural–Urban Migration in Vietnam and China: Gendered Householding, Production of Space and the State. *Journal of Peasant Studies* 41 (5): 855–876. https://doi.org/10.1080/03066150.2014.925884.
Parreñas, Rhacel. 2000. Migrant Filipina Domestic Workers and the International Division of Reproductive Labor. *Gender and Society* 14 (4): 560–580. https://doi.org/10.1177/089124300014004005.
Parreñas, Rhacel. 2005. Long Distance Intimacy: Class, Gender and Intergenerational Relations between Mothers and Children in Filipino Transnational Families. *Global Networks* 5 (4): 317–336. https://doi.org/10.1111/j.1471-0374.2005.00122.x.
Pearson, Ruth and Kyoko Kusakabe. 2012. Who Cares? Gender, Reproduction, and Care Chains of Burmese Migrant Workers in Thailand. *Feminist Economics* 18 (2): 149–175. https://doi.org/10.1080/13545701.2012.691206.
Peck, Jamie. 1996. *Work-Place: The Social Regulation of Labor Markets*. New York, USA and London, UK: Guilford Press.
Peck, Jamie. 2017. *Offshore: Exploring the Worlds of Global Outsourcing*. Oxford, UK and New York, USA: Oxford University Press.
Potts, Shaina. 2019. 'Offshore'. In Antipode Editorial Collective, *Keywords in Radical Geography: Antipode at 50*. Hoboken, NJ, USA and Oxford, UK: John Wiley & Sons, pp. 198–201. https://doi.org/10.1002/9781119558071.ch36.
Reid-Musson, Emily. 2017. Grown Close to Home™: Migrant Farmworker (Im)Mobilities and Unfreedom on Canadian Family Farms. *Annals of the American Association of Geographers* 107 (3): 716–730. https://doi.org/10.1080/24694452.2016.1261683.
Richards, Carol, Hilde Bjørkhaug, Geoffrey Lawrence and Emmy Hickman. 2013. Retailer-Driven Agricultural Restructuring – Australia, the UK and Norway in Comparison. *Agriculture and Human Values* 30 (2): 235–245. https://doi.org/10.1007/s10460-012-9408-4.
Rigg, Jonathan. 2013. From Rural to Urban: A Geography of Boundary Crossing in Southeast Asia. *TRaNS: Trans-Regional and -National Studies of Southeast Asia* 1 (1): 5–26. https://doi.org/10.1017/trn.2012.6.
Rogaly, Ben. 2008. Intensification of Workplace Regimes in British Horticulture: The Role of Migrant Workers. *Population, Space and Place* 14 (6): 497–510. https://doi.org/10.1002/psp.502.
Rogaly, Ben. 2009. Spaces of Work and Everyday Life: Labour Geographies and the Agency of Unorganised Temporary Migrant Workers. *Geography Compass* 3 (6): 1975–1987. https://doi.org/10.1111/j.1749-8198.2009.00290.x.
Rosales-Mendoza, Adriana Leona and Linamar Campos-Flores. 2019. Family Separation and Emotional Bonds: Women of Chiapas and Yucatan, Mexico, Facing Male Migration to Quebec, Canada. *International Journal of Care and Caring* 3 (2): 279–294. https://doi.org/10.1332/239788219X15567157927222.
Rye, Johan Fredrik and Karen O'Reilly (eds). 2021. *International Labour Migration to Europe's Rural Regions*. London: Routledge.
Rye, Johan Fredrik and Sam Scott. 2018. International Labour Migration To/In Rural Europe: a Review of the Evidence. *Sociologia Ruralis* 58 (4): 928–952.
Safri, Maliha and Julie Graham. 2010. The Global Household: Toward a Feminist Postcapitalist International Political Economy. *Signs: Journal of Women in Culture and Society* 36 (1): 99–125. https://doi.org/10.1086/652913.
Scott, Sam. 2013a. Labour, migration and the spatial fix. *Antipode* 45 (5), 1090–1109.
Scott, Sam. 2013b. Migrant-Local Hiring Queues in the UK Food Industry. *Population, Space and Place*, 19 (5), 459–471.
Scott, Sam. 2013c. Migration and the Employer Perspective: Pitfalls and Potentials for a Future Research Agenda. *Population, Space and Place* 19 (6): 703–713. https://doi.org/10.1002/psp.1790.
Scott, Sam and Thomas Sætre Jakobsen. Forthcoming. 'Migration and the Spatial Fix: Geographies of Low-Wage Labour Migration to Core Economies'. In Herod, A. (ed.), *Handbook of Labour Geography*. Cheltenham, UK and Northampton, MA, USA: Edward Elgar Publishing.

Scott, Sam and Johan Fredrik Rye. 2021. Praised, Prized, yet Penalised: A Critical Examination of Low-wage Hiring Queues in the Global Strawberry Industry. *Journal of Rural Studies*. https://doi.org/10.1016/j.jrurstud.2021.04.014.

Scott, S. and M.A. Visser. 2022. Constraining Labour: The Integration Dynamics of Working-Class Horticultural Migrants in Rural Areas of Norway, the UK and the US. *Sociologia Ruralis* 62 (1): 112–130. https://doi.org/10.1111/soru.12363.

Shen, Yang. 2016. Filial Daughters? Agency and Subjectivity of Rural Migrant Women in Shanghai. *China Quarterly* 226 (June): 519–537. https://doi.org/10.1017/S0305741016000357.

Smith, Joan, Immanuel Wallerstein and Hans-Dieter Evers (Eds). 1984. *Households and the World Economy*. London, UK and New Delhi, India: SAGE Publications.

Strauss, Kendra. 2013. Unfree Again: Social Reproduction, Flexible Labour Markets and the Resurgence of Gang Labour in the UK. *Antipode* 45 (1): 180–97. https://doi.org/10.1111/j.1467-8330.2012.00997.x.

Suárez-Orozco, M. and C.E. Suárez-Orozco. 1995. The Cultural Patterning of Achievement Motivation: A Comparison of Mexican, Mexican Immigrant, Mexican American, and Non-Latino White American Students. In Rumbaut, Ruben and Wayne A Cornelius (eds), *California's Immigrant Children: Theory, Research, and Implications for Educational Policy*. San Diego, CA: University of California, pp. 161–190.

Tacoli, Cecilia and Richard Mabala. 2010. Exploring Mobility and Migration in the Context of Rural–Urban Linkages: Why Gender and Generation Matter. *Environment and Urbanization* 22 (2): 389–395. https://doi.org/10.1177/0956247810379935.

Toyota, Mika, Brenda S.A. Yeoh and Nguyen Liem. 2007. Bringing the 'Left behind' Back into View in Asia: A Framework for Understanding the 'Migration–Left Behind Nexus'. *Population, Space and Place* 13 (3): 157–161. https://doi.org/10.1002/psp.433.

Verdon, Nicola. 2017. *Working the Land: A History of the Farmworker in England from 1850 to the Present Day*. London: Palgrave Macmillan.

Waldinger, Roger and Michael I. Lichter. 2003. *How the Other Half Works: Immigration and the Social Organization of Labor*, 1st edition. Berkeley, CA: University of California Press.

Wallerstein, Immanuel. 1976. *The Modern World-System: Capitalist Agriculture and the Origins of the European World-Economy in the Sixteenth Century*. New York: Academic Press.

Wallerstein, Immanuel. 1982. 'The Rise and Future Demise of the World Capitalist System: Concepts for Comparative Analysis'. In Alavi, Hamza and Teodor Shanin (eds), *Introduction to the Sociology of 'Developing Societies'*. London: Macmillan Education UK, pp. 29–53.

Waring, Marilyn. 1999. *Counting for Nothing: What Men Value and What Women Are Worth*. 2nd edition. Toronto and Buffalo: University of Toronto Press.

Wells, Don, Janet McLaughlin, André Lyn and Aaraón Diaz Mendiburo. 2014. Sustaining Precarious Transnational Families: The Significance of Remittances From Canada's Seasonal Agricultural Workers Program. *Just Labour* 44: 144–167. https://doi.org/10.25071/1705-1436.9.

Willis, Katie D. and Brenda S.A. Yeoh. 2000. Gender and Transnational Household Strategies: Singaporean Migration to China. *Regional Studies* 34 (3): 253–264. https://doi.org/10.1080/00343400050015096.

Wolf, Diane L. 1990. Daughters, Decisions and Domination: An Empirical and Conceptual Critique of Household Strategies. *Development and Change* 21 (1): 43–74. https://doi.org/10.1111/j.1467-7660.1990.tb00367.x.

Wood, Ellen Meiksins. 2002. *The Origin of Capitalism: A Longer View*. London, UK and New York, USA: Verso.

Ye, Jingzhong, Congzhi He, Juan Liu, Weijing Wang and Shidong Chen. 2016. Left-behind Elderly: Shouldering a Disproportionate Share of Production and Reproduction in Supporting China's Industrial Development. *Journal of Peasant Studies* 44 (5): 971–999. https://doi.org/10.1080/03066150.2016.1186651.

Yeoh, Brenda S.A., Bittiandra Chand Somaiah, Theodora Lam and Kristel F. Acedera. 2020. Doing Family in 'Times of Migration': Care Temporalities and Gender Politics in Southeast Asia. *Annals of the American Association of Geographers* 110 (6): 1709–1725. https://doi.org/10.1080/24694452.2020.1723397.

Zhan, Shaohua. 2019a. Accumulation by and without Dispossession: Rural Land Use, Land Expropriation, and Livelihood Implications in China. *Journal of Agrarian Change* 19 (3): 447–464. https://doi.org/10.1111/joac.12304.

Zhan, Shaohua. 2019b. *The Land Question in China: Agrarian Capitalism, Industrious Revolution, and East Asian Development*. New York: Routledge.

Zhan, Shaohua and Ben Scully. 2018. From South Africa to China: Land, Migrant Labor and the Semi-Proletarian Thesis Revisited. *Journal of Peasant Studies* 45 (5–6): 1018–1038. https://doi.org/10.1080/03066150.2018.1474458.

21. Growing over time: left-behind children in the past three decades

Theodora Lam

INTRODUCTION

At the turn of the second millennium, 'left-behind children' or 'children left behind' were terms that were more commonly associated with the 'No Child Left Behind' Act on standardising education programmes for all children in the United States.[1] Fast-forward 20 years, 'left-behind children', in their various permutations and/or hyphenations, have become a focus within migration studies, describing an increasingly prevalent family formation where children remain in their homes while one or both parents migrate for work elsewhere (UNICEF 2020). These children are often knitted into a web of caregivers comprising the remaining parent (if available), other relatives such as grandparents and/or paid help in the parents' absence (Lam and Yeoh 2019a). The increasing – albeit still relatively limited – interest in children left behind by migrant parents within the migration scholarship can be attributed to two significant shifts in the field. First, there is heightened research interest in the tenets of new economics of labour migration (NELM) highlighting that migration decisions are often made conjointly with other members of the household, and that the ensuing costs and benefits of migration are also shared by these same members regardless of age and gender (Stark and Bloom 1985). As a result, there is greater understanding that migration does not simply affect the mobile individual alone, but also involves those who do not move (Van Hook and Glick 2020). While the predominantly adult-centric studies have traditionally focused mainly on the migrants themselves, scholars have since contributed to the second shift in the field by gradually turning their attention toward the immobile others including minors who have stayed behind, either voluntarily or involuntarily (see Chapters 5 and 6, this *Handbook*).

It is timely, at the start of a new decade, to reflect on and examine the evolving scholarship on children left behind in origin countries by migrant parents, whilst identifying gaps and exploring possible avenues for future research. The chapter begins by broadly reviewing the developments in the scholarship on left-behind children by focusing on the challenges in researching them, the different methodological approaches used and the resultant findings. In particular, the chapter refers mainly to studies from Southeast Asia. Though children are left behind in many corners of the world, the majority are purportedly situated in Asia, with high numbers from China and other Southeast Asian countries such as the Philippines and Indonesia (Buchanan 2015). This is also reflected in the higher number of studies published on left-behind children from these regions. Migrants from Southeast Asia are also often caught in a temporary labour migration regime with relatively limited opportunities of bringing their families or reuniting with them in the destinations (Yeoh 2020). Apart from identifying existing research issues and lacunae, the chapter also proposes future research directions. In so doing, the chapter seeks to provide a holistic view of the different ways of researching and understanding the experiences of left-behind children, and to propose ways of conducting future research in order to produce meaningful and useful findings.

RESEARCHING LEFT-BEHIND CHILDREN: CHALLENGES AND DEVELOPMENTS

Challenges in Research

Before delving into existing research on left-behind children, the chapter first addresses key debates concerning definitions as well as the challenges of researching them. Recognising the issues associated with researching left-behind children from the onset helps to raise awareness of the constraints and limitations of existing findings. The seemingly straightforward description of left-behind children given earlier belies the complexity of the research and the subject itself. Each part of the term, be it 'left-behind' or 'children', is inherently contentious and must be carefully explained to prevent any confusion. A frequent debate is over some scholars' preference for the term 'stay behind' versus 'left behind' to describe children with labour migrant parents (recent examples include Cebotari et al. 2016; Galvan and Beltran 2016), as the latter often carries with it negative connotations akin to passiveness, abandonment and neglect (Graham and Yeoh 2013). However, existing studies on such split households from around the world tend to use 'left behind' to highlight the lack of choice and agency faced by the parents – mostly low-waged migrants from rural and/or developing countries on fixed-term contracts – as well as their children over their respective (im)mobilities. As noted earlier, the primarily temporary labour migration regime in many parts of Asia and elsewhere does not allow labour migrants to bring their families, including children, with them (Hoang and Yeoh 2015a; UNICEF 2020; ILO n.d.). Similarly, internal labour migrants in China also encounter restrictive structural constraints in migrating with their families, as the country's household registration or *hukou* system would prevent accompanying children from accessing many social amenities outside of their home towns (Ge et al. 2019). Finally, the precarious conditions of labour migration, lack of safe migration pathways, as well as higher costs in destinations, are just some of the numerous factors that make it difficult for many migrants seeking to maximise economic returns to bring their families with them (Dreby 2010; Ivlevs et al. 2019; Fong and Shibuya 2020; UNICEF 2020). For these reasons, and as is evident from the greater number of published research using this term, it appears that 'left behind' has become more dominant in the literature.[2]

'Children' is yet another much deliberated term, as to date there is no universal definition of what constitutes a child. While the Convention on the Rights of the Child defines a child as 'every human being below the age of 18 years unless under the law applicable to the child, majority is attained earlier', the age limit may vary from 14 to 21 according to countries and policies (OHCHR 1989; Yeoh and Lam 2007). There may even be variations within countries, with different jurisdictions setting their respective limits. The wide age range – from infants to toddlers to teenagers, adolescents and youth – makes studying left-behind children challenging on many methodological fronts. Aside from the difficulties and sensitivities involved in researching young respondents, it is not possible to conduct comprehensive or representative studies (whether quantitative or qualitative) on each age cohort. Subsequent research decisions made over numerous parameters, such as sample size, age range and age-appropriate research instruments, thus have significant implications on the data gathered, and inevitably delineate the knowledge gleaned on these children.

To complicate matters further, some studies use educational levels/grades or simply vague categories such as adolescents or youth to identify their respondents, masking the true ages of those being studied (Parreñas 2005; Wang et al. 2015). Such ambiguities not only impede efforts to calculate the magnitude of children left within countries, but may also result in difficulties in comparing findings across studies, misinterpretations of study outcomes, and a lack of precise understanding on the impacts of migration and policies on specific age groups. While there are currently no comprehensive solutions to these issues, recognising the limitations of the research upfront serves as a critical reminder when reviewing the scholarship. In order to provide a more wide-ranging review, this chapter thus uses 'left-behind children' – broadly defined – to refer collectively to all children, teens and/or adolescents under 21 living separately, whether by choice or otherwise, from at least one internal or international migrant parent who is working in another city/country for a sustained time-period.[3] Nonetheless, this chapter also acknowledges that there may be other terms that are more appropriate in describing children left by migrant parents within specific cultures or circumstances, and is not proposing that 'left-behind children' is or becomes the universally accepted term.

Another ongoing challenge confronting researchers studying left-behind children since the early years has been determining the number of children affected, as rough estimates could only be pulled together from calculated guesses of different data sources which are in themselves often inaccurate or incomplete (Whitehead and Hashim 2005; Rossi 2009). To date, minimal progress has been made in attempts to acquire a more accurate or representative picture of the numbers of left-behind children around the world, and some estimates have not been updated for over a decade. Aside from the difficulty in defining children, variability in the calculation methods and the lack of consensus over the types of migrants to be included in the count are some of the factors hindering the construction of a comprehensive database (Cortés 2007). It also appears that left-behind children continue to remain an afterthought and/or are overlooked by many governments, possibly being relegated as a family concern rather than national concern. Thus far, only a few countries have endeavoured to collect relevant information on left-behind children from surveys, census or immigration forms. In contrast, data on child migrants appear more readily accessible (Roy et al. 2015). Available figures, however, seem to hint at an ever-expanding number of left-behind children around the globe as data from more countries as well as migration types are added to the mix. The largest estimate thus far appears to be from China, where according to surveys conducted by the All China Women's Federation and National Health and Family Planning Commission (NHFPC), between 60 and 70 million children are possibly left behind in rural areas by parents migrating to cities for work (Li 2015; Tong et al. 2019). Estimates from other parts of Asia over the past two decades suggest that there are between 3 and 9 million left-behind children in the Philippines (Reyes 2008; Tobin 2008); 1 million in Indonesia estimated to be left by international migrants in 2005, and possibly millions more when considering children of internal as well as irregular migrants (Bryant 2005; UNDESA 2019); 1 million in Sri Lanka left by mother migrants alone (Perera and Rathnayaka 2013); 0.5 million in Thailand (Bryant 2005); and around 259 000 in Kyrgyzstan (UNICEF 2020). Where numerical estimates are not readily available, others have put forward that over a third of all children in Ecuador (36 per cent), Georgia (39 per cent), Ghana (37 per cent) and Moldova (36 per cent), and more than 40 per cent in rural South Africa, are being left behind (Fellmeth et al. 2018; Antia et al. 2020). Compared to popular perceptions, especially those proposed by non-governmental organisations (NGOs) and media, that there are hundreds of millions of left-behind children globally,[4] the number of studies on them – particularly in Southeast Asia – is still disproportionately small. The absence of detailed data continues to obscure the demographic profile of the left-behind children population (and the magnitude of the problem), thus hindering efforts to conduct nationally representative studies as well as to implement relevant policies and interventions.

The following sections will now turn to discussing some of the findings and research issues that different methodological approaches used in studying left-behind children have revealed.

Existing Research on Left-Behind Children

Though migrants leaving families behind in origin countries is not a new phenomenon, studies focusing solely on left-behind children only emerged sporadically in the 1990s (see Battistella and Conaco 1996, 1998, for studies from the Philippines). The limited studies (leaning towards unfavourable outcomes), coupled with negative media attention and reports over the seemingly large numbers of neglected and delinquent left-behind children, underscore to scholars, policy-makers and representatives from NGOs the urgent need to conduct more rigorous studies on the impacts of migration on these children. Thereafter, research on left-behind children from several geographic regions including Africa, Asia, Latin America and Eastern Europe started gathering speed after mid-2000, with most of the English-language publications appearing in the last ten years (Yeoh and Lam 2007; Antia et al. 2020). While the scholarship was initially driven by research on left-behind children with international migrant parents from Southeast Asian countries such as the Philippines, as well as Latin American countries such as Mexico (see e.g. Parreñas 2005; Dreby 2007), a significant proportion of the published studies are now on left-behind children of internal migrant parents in China. The research on left-behind children has thus mainly focused on studying the impacts of either international or internal migration, and has constantly been criticised for omitting the other migration type.[5] The recent overwhelming predominance of research findings from China may also possibly begin to skew the general understanding of left-behind children from other parts of the world, given the unique rural–urban migration contexts and country-specific policies in which these children are embedded.

Over the years, left-behind children in a number of Asian cities in Cambodia, China, Indonesia, the Philippines, Thailand and Vietnam, as well as other countries including Ghana, Moldova, Mexico and Romania (recent examples include Cojocaru et al. 2015; Mazzucato et al. 2015; Jampaklay et al. 2018; Zimmer and Van Natta 2018; Arlini et al. 2019; Botezat and Pfeiffer 2020), have attracted the scholarly attention of researchers from different disciplines working within their respective subject silos. Research on left-behind children has grown progressively varied over the years, with expanding sample sizes (from tens to thousands), and diverse use of quantitative, qualitative and mixed research methodologies as well as research instruments/tools, whilst incorporating more interdisciplinary, multi-sited and comparative approaches in recent years (Van Hook and Glick 2020). The perspectives used in existing studies on left-behind children are generally observed to follow the three paradigms outlined by Ge et al. (2019: 125), namely, diagnostic approaches listing the simple cause of parents leaving and the presumably negative effects on the children; advanced diagnostic approaches incorporating theories and techniques developed from other countries into the local research; and sociologically oriented approaches that integrate more complex and novel theoretical frameworks, research designs and domains to examine 'the broader social dimensions of LBC [left-behind children]'. While the scholarship on left-behind children has been evolving over the years, the bulk of the scholarship is still being criticised by some as being predominantly descriptive, making it difficult to test theoretical relationships, establish detailed causal relationships or develop new theories (Fong and Shibuya 2020; Van Hook and Glick 2020).

The above research paradigms are generally or partially observed within three broad strands of current research investigating the impacts of migration on multiple aspects of children's well-being: primary research (quantitative, qualitative or mixed-methods); largely quantitative secondary studies drawing on existing national datasets or systematic reviews and meta-analyses of data from existing studies; and a third, emerging, strand emphasising children's personal viewpoints and experiences of the effects of parental absence (see Chapters 7 and 12, this *Handbook*). The following sections explore these strands in detail.

Quantitative Research

Numerous schools of scholars ranging from epidemiologists and psychologists to other social scientists have been investigating the various impacts of parental absence, due to either internal or international migration, on the different aspects of children's physical, emotional, mental, economic, educational and social well-being (Lam et al. 2018). These studies may involve primary research on specific groups of children, often using standardised quantitative outcome measures (examples of publications from 2015 include Zhou et al. 2015; Jampaklay et al. 2018; Arlini et al. 2019; Mordeno et al. 2019; Nazridod et al. 2019), or secondary statistical analyses conducted on publicly available national datasets to derive understandings of children of migrant parents (selected publications from 2015 include Cortes 2015; Nguyen and Nguyen 2015; Sarma and Parinduri 2016; Ng 2019; Treleaven 2019). Multiple variables usually related to the characteristics of left-behind children and their migrant parents, carers and environment – such as age, gender, length of separation, education levels, household size/structure, types/amount/frequency of remittances, place of origin, destinations and social support – are tested against a developing list of hypotheses typically postulating the negative impacts of parental absence. To increase validity and further understanding, control groups such as children with non-migrant parents, or other appropriate controls, are included in some of the larger studies (see e.g. Graham and Jordan 2011; Mazzucato et al. 2015; Gassmann et al. 2018).

Given the diverse possibilities and plausible variables in the thousands of published studies on left-behind children, it is unsurprising to find that the scholarship has generated very heterogeneous, sometimes even conflicting, findings thus far (Fellmeth et al. 2018; Lam et al. 2018; Antia et al. 2020). Certain studies revealed findings that were more positive than expected, while many others painted a rather dire scenario with depressing outcomes for left-behind children (see, for example, overviews in Arguillas and Williams 2010; Valtolina and Colombo 2012; Antman 2013; Mazzucato 2015; Wickramage et al. 2015; Gassmann et al. 2018). These findings are evidently not generalisable, or even comparable across studies, and each outcome being studied is highly intertwined with fairly specific yet complex combinations of 'socio-cultural contexts and a host of factors encompassing the age of left-behind children, gender of migrants/carers/children, length of parental migration, migrant destination as well as the situations in the home communities' (Mazzucato and Schans 2011; Lam et al. 2018: 257). This observation has resonance with Antia et al.'s (2020: 1) conclusion from their systematic analysis that left-behind children's mental health and well-being outcomes are dependent on the 'gender of the migrant parent, culture and other transnational family characteristics'. At times, it is also difficult to place the impacts of migration on left-behind children's well-being in clear dichotomous good/bad, positive/negative categories, given that perceptions of the benefits or detriments of migration are also dependent on one's priorities: economic gains vis-à-vis family togetherness (Gassmann et al. 2018). Overall, many studies would agree that the financial situation of most left-behind children would normally improve as a result of their parents' migration (in turn leading to better education and health outcomes), and that the negative impacts of parental physical absence can be mitigated through regular communication (Antman 2013; Lam et al. 2018; Lam 2019). There is also evidence that such split family formations may become increasingly normalised over time, and a growing 'culture of migration' may have possible impacts on changing mindsets and developing better adjustment strategies (Hoang and Yeoh 2015b; Fong and Shibuya 2020).

Analysing Secondary Data

To form a better understanding of these disparate findings, scholars in the past few years have begun conducting systematic reviews and/or meta-analyses on the growing pool of research on left-behind children in search of a more definite sense of impacts of parental migration/ absence on specific well-being outcomes for children. Researchers conducting such analyses have spent much time and laborious effort utilising different research databases, using all possible combinations of related search terms, sometimes in different languages, to sieve out relevant literature for their purpose. Each step of the process needs to be well documented, and specific inclusion and exclusion criteria (such as children's age, type of study and use of control groups) according to the parameters of the analysis must be clearly outlined to account for the final conclusion. Unsurprisingly, given that the bulk of the scholarship is based on left-behind children in China, the large proportion of the over 20 published (and found) English-language systematic reviews and/or meta-analyses to date are conducted on or comprise mainly of research from China. A number of these systematic reviews and/or meta-analyses are particularly concerned with children's socio-emotional well-being, covering topics such as depression and loneliness, and mental well-being of left-behind children (see Cheng and Sun 2015; Zhao and Yu 2016; Liang et al. 2017; Chai et al. 2019; Ding et al. 2019; Y.Y. Wang et al. 2019; Wu et al. 2019; Antia et al. 2020; Wang et al. 2020; Xu et al. 2020). Others, to highlight a few examples, are interested in investigating resilience (Dong et al. 2019), personality traits (L.L. Wang et al. 2019), social adaptation (Zhang et al. 2018) and child development (Wang and Mesman 2015). Only a handful of the published systematic reviews and/or meta-analyses are not based on studies from China per se, but are focused on analysing findings on the impacts of parental migration on left-behind children's health (Fellmeth et al., 2018; Račaitė et al. 2019; Račaitė et al. 2021), mental well-being (Antia et al. 2020), healthcare seeking behaviours and nutritional status (Kunwar et al. 2020), and the influence of grandparental care on child health and development (Sadruddin et al. 2019). These will be discussed in this chapter.

In a systematic review of a final count of 30 studies focused on the impacts of parents' international migration on the mental health and well-being of left-behind children, Antia et al. (2020: 1) stressed that 'mental health and well-being outcomes of left-behind children differed across and sometimes even within regions', and that only findings from the Americas and South Asia are completely negative. They concluded that, as compared to children in non-migrant households, left-behind children show abnormal Strengths and Difficulties Questionnaire (SDQ) scores, and report higher levels of loneliness and depression. Fellmeth et al. (2018), in their meta-analysis on 111 studies of left-behind children from both internal and international migrant households, also found increased risk of depression, suicidal ideation and anxiety among those left behind. Overall, the systematic reviews and meta-analysis conducted by Račaitė et al. (2019), Račaitė et al. (2021) and Fellmeth et al. (2018) indicated that parental migration, whether internal or international, has negative health implications for left-behind children, such as stunting, unhealthy habits and partaking in vice behaviours, as compared to non-left-behind children. Such outcomes led Fellmeth et al. (2018: 2567) to strongly conclude that, '[p]arental migration is detrimental to the health of left-behind children and adolescents, with no evidence of any benefit'. On the other hand, Kunwar et al. (2020) were unable to find any conclusive impacts of international parental migration on healthcare seeking behaviours for common child ailments and the nutritional status of left-behind children under five due to insufficient research. Finally, though not a systematic review focusing solely on left-behind children, Sadruddin et al.'s (2019) finding of the substantial heterogeneous influences of grandparental care on child health and development invoke some thoughts for consideration and future research, especially since some of the reviewed studies are on left-behind children placed under their grandparents' care.

Primary Qualitative and Mixed-Methods Research

Although results from the earlier two strands of studies tend to stress the negative outcomes for children, many would still argue that they do not provide a comprehensive understanding of left-behind childhoods versus those from non-migrant households. The systematic reviews reinforce the argument that there may be no, positive or negative impacts of parental migration on left-behind children, as any outcomes are largely contingent on context and country. More importantly, children's voices and agency are still often missing from these studies, which portray children as relatively passive dependents of adults. Given the nature of their examination, qualitative studies facilitating more intimate understandings of children's experiences are also often left out of systematic reviews and meta-analyses, thus possibly skewing their outcomes. To counter this, we turn to studies from Southeast Asia for some alternative perspectives. Parreñas (2005) is among the first scholars to proffer a closer, retrospective insight into the gendered experiences of a group of Filipino left-behind young adults who have grown up in the absence of migrant parents. Her study highlighted the children's expressions of emotions (mostly sadness, confusion and a sense of abandonment) as well as estrangement from both left-behind and migrant fathers. On the other hand, another study by Scalabrini Migration Centre (SMC) found that the left-behind school-going Filipino children studied were fairly similar to those from non-migrant households, being socially well adjusted, receiving strong support and getting along with other family members (ECMI/AOS-Manila et al. 2004). Parental migration did not affect the socialisation and development of critical values and spirituality for the left-behind children in this study. Instead, they were still schooled in responsibilities by being assigned chores (though, on average, they had more chores than children from non-migrant households) from surrogate carers in place of their absent parent. Drawing from the same study, Asis (2006) concluded that children demonstrated agency in determining migration outcomes, playing an active role in minding their own well-being, coping with parental absence and also keeping the family together. Left-behind children can grow independently in the absence of restrictive parental control and may acquire many important life skills in the process. Generally, this scholarship reveals that the childhoods of left-behind children need not necessarily be very different from those from non-migrant households, although this may also be largely dependent on the quality of care provided by surrogate carers (Battistella and Conaco 1998; Asis and Baggio 2003; Asis 2006).

To counter critics who question the rigour and scale of qualitative research, the chapter now turns to a large-scale mixed-methods study on the impacts of transnational migration on children in four Southeast Asian countries: Indonesia, the Philippines, Thailand and Vietnam. The CHAMPSEA[6] project not only investigated the effects of parental migration, but also drew attention to the gendered migration experiences of left-behind children aged 9 to 11 vis-à-vis the non-migrants. Through household surveys as well as structured interviews conducted with selected left-behind children from different types of migrant families and care-giving arrangements, scholars from the team shed further light on Indonesian, Filipino and Vietnamese children's views, sentiments and agency in negotiating the migration decision-making process, arrangements of care, managing relationships with migrants and left-behind carers and their personal well-being (see Graham et al. 2012; Hoang and Yeoh 2012; Hoang et al. 2015; Hoang and Yeoh 2015b). Having grown up in the absence of one or both parents, left-behind children are able to express their mixed feelings on migration which are often not clearly black or white. They – left-behind children from CHAMPSEA as well as other studies – appreciate the financial benefits of migration, but would at times prefer their parents to remain at home, and may personally decide against migrating themselves in order to avoid splitting up their families in the future (Lam and Yeoh 2019a; de los Reyes 2020). Overall, these studies affirm that children are not simply passive subjects of migration, establishing how they are both simultaneously powerful and powerless within the family's livelihood strategy that is intertwined with mobility.

Using CHAMPSEA as an illustration, it is also one of the few large-scale studies in this field offering a longitudinal perspective on the impacts of migration on left-behind families. Its researchers returned to the field sites in Indonesia, the Philippines and Thailand some eight years later to conduct follow-up studies with the same households, whose two groups of children have since grown to middle childhood (ages around 11 to 13) and young adulthood (ages around 17 to 19). From their interviews, Somaiah et al. (2020) found that successful parental migration has afforded left-behind female Indonesian adolescents greater educational opportunities and life choices. In pursuing higher qualifications in their desired course of study, the girls are mindful of the wider career and life options available to them. Though the study found that left-behind female Indonesian adolescents were more likely to emulate their migrant parents by developing migration aspirations, it also revealed those who are now choosing to counter the ingrained migration culture by staying (Somaiah et al. 2020). Such studies are important in tracing and revealing the 'immobile' children's growth over their life-course, agency and strategies in coping with parental migration and familial adjustments through the changing times of parental migration, whilst exploring how children express their resilience and demonstrate their creativity in the face of parental absence (see Lam and Yeoh 2019a, 2019b). These are findings that cannot be easily captured and revealed via standardised measurement tools and quantitative means.

Besides acknowledging left-behind children's agency, which is often missing from quantitative studies, the various studies from the CHAMPSEA project are among the few in the scholarship that also recognised left-behind children's inability and incapacity due to the larger structures of power and inequality. Oftentimes, left-behind children are rendered relatively 'passive' within the larger migration and communication decisions that are usually controlled by the adults or the structural setting at large. Nonetheless, left-behind children do not remain in stasis, but learn and acquire the necessary skills and knowledge over time to navigate the perils of transnational living. Changes in children's everyday lives, educational choices, parental migration or return, as well as caregiving decisions, may be effected through seemingly small actions made by left-behind children. Generally, the interactions between left-behind children and the adults can make 'a difference – to a relationship, a decision, to the workings of a set of social assumptions or constraints' (Mayall 2002: 21).

Overview and Ways Forward

The growing scholarship on left-behind children regardless of methodological approaches and paradigms highlights the importance of understanding the complex roles that children play within migrant households, both as young agents of influence as well as recipients of the effects of migration (Orellana et al. 2001; Dobson 2009; Ní Laoire et al. 2010; Hoang and Yeoh 2015b) (as also seen in various chapters within Part II in this *Handbook*). In tracing the developments in researching left-behind children, and informed by the challenges and findings, it is evident from the overview of the scholarship that many gaps remain despite its advancements. As mentioned earlier, the relative dearth of research on the impacts of international migration on left-behind children, as compared to those on internal migration, skews research findings and prevents comparisons across studies (Antia et al. 2020). It is also telling that many of the studies on left-behind children are still largely confined within individual countries/languages, independent subject silos, and keeping to their respective fixed research techniques/methodologies. For instance, a psychologist or sociologist may not only prefer to collaborate with fellow colleagues, but perhaps also will only largely refer to the work of those in the same discipline, country or language, and persist in using the same quantitative or qualitative research practice, and so on. Informed by studies such as the CHAMPSEA project and those by Mazzucato et al. (2015), more collaborative, multidisciplinary, mixed-methods, intergenerational, bi-national and cross-contextual/country studies are definitely needed to provide a more comparative and holistic interpretation of the experiences of left-behind children (Mazzucato and Schans 2011; Schapiro et al. 2013; Van Hook and Glick 2020).

Existing studies on left-behind children are still fairly one-dimensional in that only typical profiles of left-behind children, such as those left by international or internal labour migrant parents, or from heteronormative nuclear households, are included in the studies. Besides acknowledging the presence of different types of migrants within a country, McKay (2018) reminds us that there are other types of 'left-behind' children, such as those who may have been sent home by their migrant parents. In addition, Constable (2018) stresses the importance of giving equal attention to children from other non-heterosexual forms of household formations. At the same time, Dumitru (2014) prompts scholars undertaking research on left-behind children to break out of sexist stereotypes by incorporating other perspectives of care for them into their research and, in the process, to develop new theories of care that may actually be gained through migration. In short, moving away from conventional understandings of family formations, and existing negative biases in hypotheses of a care drain or deprivation, may actually generate new findings and understandings in scholarship on left-behind children.

To date, many of the studies focus on school-going children in middle childhood below the age of 16. It is thus more difficult to find the voices of older left-behind youth – who are themselves on the cusps of adulthood and beginning to encounter migration decisions – reflecting on how their worldviews and aspirations may have been shaped by their parents' migration or by the prevalent 'culture of migration' in which they dwell (see overview in Mazzucato and van Geel 2022). There are also limited studies offering gender-differentiated outcomes of migration for left-behind boys versus girls (Lam 2019). More importantly, aside from CHAMPSEA, studies offering a longitudinal investigation into the longer-term impacts of migration on left-behind children over their personal life-course are still very scarce. In this respect, this chapter seeks to initiate the process of gaining an in-depth understanding of left-behind children's lives through the years they have spent apart from their parents. The studies by Lam and Yeoh (2019a), Somaiah et al. (2020) and Somaiah and Yeoh (2021) have already given us a glimpse of viewing the experiences of (non-)migration through the independent eyes of left-behind children over time, and how migration and parental absence may have shaped their growth and development thus far. Following the example of CHAMPSEA, there is much research potential for in-depth longitudinal mixed-method research on left-behind children by combining the use of different measurement tools to first interrogate the impacts of parental migration, and subsequently follow up with in-depth interviews at different junctures of their lives.

CONCLUSION

Research scholarship on left-behind children simultaneously reveals encouraging advancements in the field through rising interest in the topic, alongside the expansion of research design, methodologies and instruments (selected examples include Graham et al. 2012; Graham and Yeoh 2013; Mazzucato et al. 2015; Cebotari and Dito 2021), whilst exposing existing gaps in knowledge. As new understandings are gained on the topic, there are also increasing realisations that new variables need to be added into future studies on left-behind children. Rapid societal and/or environmental changes, such as the COVID-19 pandemic and climate change, are also introducing new complications into children's lives, thus requiring further exploration. An inclusion of children's own voices would further enhance the research potential of conducting dedicated mixed-method longitudinal research over the children's own life-course as well as a household's migration life-course of leaving and returning. Combining the 'well-established [quantitative] methods to approximate casual effects' with the 'deeper understanding of processes, mechanisms, and motivations underlying the relationships seen in quantitative work' afforded through qualitative investigations in a multi-site longitudinal study will contribute greatly to revealing the long-term impacts of migration on children's well-being (Van Hook and Glick 2020: 236). A greater understanding of left-behind children within their household context can help to broaden existing rhetoric and provide further clarity over the phenomenon, assist future generations of migrant families in reconfiguring their households cum relationships, as well as facilitate government and relevant bodies in developing appropriate policies and mitigating strategies. More importantly, these quality insights can contribute to much-needed new theorisations of migration and the transnational family project, whilst helping to build a sustainable migration project for all households (Schapiro et al. 2013).

ACKNOWLEDGEMENTS

Parts of this chapter are adapted from Lam et al. (2018). Copyright ©2018 from *Growing up in Transnational Families: Children's Experience and Perspectives* by T. Lam, S. Huang, B.S.A. Yeoh, and J.O. Celero. Reproduced by permission of Taylor & Francis Group, LLC, a division of Informa plc.

NOTES

1. See Hunter and Bartee (2003) for more information on this Act, which has since been replaced.
2. The chapter also recognises that children may be left behind for other reasons, including death/sickness, parental divorce, incarceration, war and climate change. However, it is only able to review the research on left-behind children within the context of temporary labour migration.
3. Most studies reviewed set the time criteria as a minimum of six months apart (examples include Valtolina and Colombo 2012; Fellmeth et al. 2018; Antia et al. 2020), though studies by Mazzucato et al. (2015) have set it at three months.
4. Citing available United Nations Children's Fund statistics, Kunwar et al. (2020: 352) stated that up to one-quarter of children under five 'in developing countries have at least one parent living abroad'.
5. This is finally changing, with a study by Cebotari and Dito (2021) that includes both migration types in their investigations.
6. CHAMPSEA, or Child Health and Migrant Parents in Southeast Asia, employs both quantitative and qualitative methodologies to investigate the impacts of parental migration on the well-being and health of children aged 3 to 5 and 9 to 11, from migrant and non-migrant households. For a detailed explanation of the study, refer to Graham and Yeoh (2013).

REFERENCES

Antia, K., J. Boucsein, A. Deckert, P. Dambach, J. Racaite, G. Surkiene, et al. 2020. 'Effects of International Labour Migration on the Mental Health and Well-Being of Left-Behind Children: A Systematic Literature Review.' *International Journal of Environmental Research and Public Health* 17 (12). doi: 10.3390/ijerph17124335.

Antman, F.M. 2013. 'The Impact of Migration on Family Left Behind.' In *International Handbook of the Economics of Migration*, edited by A.F. Constant and K.F. Zimmermann, 293–308. Cheltenham, UK and Northampton, MA, USA: Edward Elgar Publishing.

Arguillas, M.B., and L. Williams. 2010. 'The Impact of Parents' Overseas Employment on Educational Outcomes of Filipino Children.' *International Migration Review* 44 (2): 300–319. doi: 10.1111/j.1747-7379.2010.00807.x.

Arlini, S.M., B.S.A. Yeoh, C.Y. Khoo and E. Graham. 2019. 'Parental Migration and the Educational Enrolment of Left-Behind Children: Evidence from Rural Ponorogo, Indonesia.' *Asian Population Studies* 15 (2): 190–208. doi: 10.1080/17441730.2019.1609294.

Asis, M.M.B. 2006. 'Living with Migration: Experiences of Left-Behind Children in the Philippines.' *Asian Population Studies* 2 (1): 45–67. doi: 10.1080/17441730600700556.

Asis, M.M.B., and F. Baggio. 2003. 'The Other Face of Migration: Children and Families Left Behind.' In the Workshop on 'Taking the lead: successful partnership initiatives for the delivery of settlement services' at the 8th International Metropolis Conference, Vienna, Austria.

Battistella, G., and M.C. Conaco. 1996. 'Impact of Migration on the Children Left Behind.' *Asian Migrant* 9 (3): 86–91.

Battistella, G., and M.C. Conaco. 1998. 'The Impact of Labour Migration on the Children Left Behind: A Study of Elementary School Children in the Philippines.' *Sojourn: Journal of Social Issues in Southeast Asia* 13 (2): 220–241.

Botezat, A., and F. Pfeiffer. 2020. 'The Impact of Parental Labour Migration on Left-Behind Children's Educational and Psychosocial Outcomes: Evidence from Romania.' *Population, Space and Place* 26 (2). doi: 10.1002/psp.2277.

Bryant, J. 2005. 'Children of International Migrants in Indonesia, Thailand, and the Philippines: A Review of Evidence and Policies.' Innocenti Working Paper No. 2005-5.

Buchanan, E. 2015. 'Who Are the "Left Behind Children" around the World?' *BBC News: Asia*. https://www.bbc.com/news/av/world-33996631.

Cebotari, Victor, and Bilisuma B. Dito. 2021. 'Internal and International Parental Migration and the Living Conditions of Children in Ghana.' *Children and Youth Services Review* 121: 105821. doi: https://doi.org/10.1016/j.childyouth.2020.105821.

Cebotari, V., M. Siegel and V. Mazzucato. 2016. 'Migration and the Education of Children Who Stay Behind in Moldova and Georgia.' *International Journal of Educational Development* 51: 96–107. doi: 10.1016/j.ijedudev.2016.09.002.

Chai, X.Y., H.F. Du, X.Y. Li, S.B. Su and D.H. Lin. 2019. 'What Really Matters for Loneliness among Left-Behind Children in Rural China: A Meta-Analytic Review.' *Frontiers in Psychology* 10. doi: 10.3389/fpsyg.2019.00774.

Cheng, J., and Y.H. Sun. 2015. 'Depression and Anxiety among Left-Behind Children in China: A Systematic Review.' *Child Care Health and Development* 41 (4): 515–523. doi: 10.1111/cch.12221.

Cojocaru, S., M.R. Islam and D. Timofte. 2015. 'The Effects of Parent Migration on the Children Left at Home: The Use of Ad-Hoc Research for Raising Moral Panic in Romania and the Republic of Moldova.' *Anthropologist* 22 (3): 568–575.

Constable, N. 2018. 'Assemblages and Affect: Migrant Mothers and the Varieties of Absent Children.' *Global Networks* 18 (1): 168–185. doi: 10.1111/glob.12176.

Cortes, P. 2015. 'The Feminization of International Migration and Its Effects on the Children Left Behind: Evidence from the Philippines.' *World Development* 65: 62–78. doi: 10.1016/j.worlddev.2013.10.021.

Cortés, R. 2007. *Children and Women Left Behind in Labor Sending Countries: An Appraisal of Social Risks*. New York: United Nations' Children Fund.

de los Reyes, E.J.Y. 2020. '"Left-Behind" to "Get-Ahead"? Youth Futures in Localities.' *Globalisation Societies and Education* 18 (2): 167–180. doi: 10.1080/14767724.2019.1700351.

Ding, L.Y., L.W. Yuen, E.S. Buhs and I.M. Newman. 2019. 'Depression among Chinese Left-Behind Children: A Systematic Review and Meta-Analysis.' *Child Care Health and Development* 45 (2): 189–97. doi: 10.1111/cch.12642.

Dobson, M. 2009. 'Unpacking Children in Migration Research.' *Children's Geographies* 7 (3): 355–360. doi: 10.1080/14733280903024514.

Dong, B., D.D. Yu, Q.Q. Ren, D.D. Zhao, J. Li and Y.H. Sun. 2019. 'The Resilience Status of Chinese Left-Behind Children in Rural Areas: A Meta-Analysis.' *Psychology Health and Medicine* 24 (1): 1–13. doi: 10.1080/13548506.2018.1487986.

Dreby, J. 2007. 'Children and Power in Mexican Transnational Families.' *Journal of Marriage and Family* 69 (4): 1050–1064. doi: 10.1111/j.1741-3737.2007.00430.x.

Dreby, J. 2010. *Divided by Borders: Mexican Migrants and Their Children*. Berkeley, CA: University of California Press.

Dumitru, S. 2014. 'From "Brain Drain" to "Care Drain": Women's Labor Migration and Methodological Sexism.' *Womens Studies International Forum* 47: 203–212. doi: 10.1016/j.wsif.2014.06.006.

ECMI/AOS-Manila (Episcopal Commission for the Pastoral Care of Migrants and Itinerant People/Apostleship of the Sea-Manila), SMC (Scalabrini Migration Center) and OWWA (Overseas Workers Welfare Administration). 2004. *Hearts Apart: Migration in the Eyes of Filipino Children*. Quezon City: Scalabrini Migration Center.

Fellmeth, G., K. Rose-Clarke, C. Zhao, L.K. Busert, Y. Zheng, A. Massazza, et al. 2018. 'Health Impacts of Parental Migration on Left-Behind Children and Adolescents: A Systematic Review and Meta-Analysis.' *The Lancet* 392 (10164): 2567–2582. doi: 10.1016/S0140-6736(18)32558-3.

Fong, E., and K. Shibuya. 2020. 'Migration Patterns in East and Southeast Asia: Causes and Consequences.' In *Annual Review of Sociology, Vol 46*, edited by K.S. Cook and D. S. Massey, 511–531. Palo Alto, CA: Annual Reviews.

Galvan, R.T., and M.T.G. Beltran. 2016. 'Discourses of Legitimation and Loss of Sons Who Stay Behind.' *Discourse and Society* 27 (4): 423–440. doi: 10.1177/0957926516634542.

Gassmann, F., M. Siegel, M. Vanore and J. Waidler. 2018. 'Unpacking the Relationship between Parental Migration and Child Well-Being: Evidence from Moldova and Georgia.' *Child Indicators Research* 11 (2): 423–440. doi: 10.1007/s12187-017-9461-z.

Ge, Y., L. Song, R.F. Clancy and Y. Qin. 2019. 'Studies on Left-Behind Children in China: Reviewing Paradigm Shifts.' *New Directions for Child and Adolescent Development* 2019 (163): 115–135. doi: 10.1002/cad.20267.

Graham, E., and L.P. Jordan. 2011. 'Migrant Parents and the Psychological Well-Being of Left-Behind Children in Southeast Asia.' *Journal of Marriage and Family* 73 (4): 763–787. doi: 10.1111/j.1741-3737.2011.00844.x.

Graham, E., L.P. Jordan, B.S.A. Yeoh, T. Lam, M. Asis and S. Kamdi. 2012. 'Transnational Families and the Family Nexus: Perspectives of Indonesian and Filipino Children Left Behind by Migrant Parent(S).' *Environment and Planning A* 44 (4): 793–815. doi: 10.1068/a4445.

Graham, E., and B.S.A. Yeoh. 2013. 'Child Health and Migrant Parents in South-East Asia: Risk and Resilience among Primary School-Aged Children.' *Asian and Pacific Migration Journal* 22 (3): 297–314. doi: 10.1177/011719681302200301.

Hoang, L.A., T. Lam, B.S.A. Yeoh and E. Graham. 2015. 'Transnational Migration, Changing Care Arrangements and Left-Behind Children's Responses in Southeast Asia.' *Children's Geographies* 13 (3): 263–277. doi: 10.1080/14733285.2015.972653.

Hoang, L.A., and B.S.A. Yeoh. 2012. 'Sustaining Families across Transnational Spaces: Vietnamese Migrant Parents and Their Left-Behind Children.' *Asian Studies Review* 36 (3): 307–325.

Hoang, L.A., and B.S.A. Yeoh. 2015a. 'Introduction: Migration, Remittances and the Family.' In *Transnational Labour Migration, Remittances and the Changing Family in Asia*, edited by L.A. Hoang and B.S.A. Yeoh, 1–23. Basingstoke: Palgrave Macmillan.

Hoang, L.A., and B.S.A. Yeoh. 2015b. 'Children's Agency and Its Contradictions in the Context of Transnational Labour Migration from Vietnam.' *Global Networks* 15 (2): 180–197. doi: 10.1111/glob.12057.

Hunter, R.C., and R. Bartee. 2003. 'The Achievement Gap – Issues of Competition, Class, and Race.' *Education and Urban Society* 35 (2): 151–160.

ILO. n.d. 'Labour Migration in Asia and the Pacific.' ILO, Accessed 28 December 2020, https://www.ilo.org/asia/areas/labour-migration/WCMS_634559/lang--en/index.htm.

Ivlevs, A., M. Nikolova and C. Graham. 2019. 'Emigration, Remittances, and the Subjective Well-Being of Those Staying Behind.' *Journal of Population Economics* 32 (1): 113–151. doi: http://dx.doi.org/10.1007/s00148-018-0718-8.

Jampaklay, A., K. Richter, K. Tangchonlatip and S. Nanthamongkolchai. 2018. 'The Impact of Parental Absence on Early Childhood Development in the Context of Thailand.' *Asian and Pacific Migration Journal* 27 (2): 209–230. doi: 10.1177/0117196818767439.

Kunwar, R., C.M. Vajdic and D.J. Muscatello. 2020. 'Parental International Migration Is Not Associated with Improved Health Care Seeking for Common Childhood Illnesses and Nutritional Status of Young Children Left-Behind in Nepal.' *Public Health* 186: 137–143. doi: 10.1016/j.puhe.2020.06.049.

Lam, T. 2019. 'Young Women and Girls Left Behind: Causes and Consequences.' In *Supporting Brighter Futures: Young Women and Girls and Labour Migration in South-East Asia and the Pacific*, edited by IOM, 11–28. Geneva: IOM.

Lam, T., S. Huang, B.S.A. Yeoh and J.O. Celero. 2018. 'Growing up in Transnational Families: Children's Experience and Perspectives.' In *Routledge Handbook of Asian Migrations*, edited by G. Liu-Farrer and B.S.A. Yeoh, 250–263. Abingdon: Routledge.

Lam, T., and B.S.A. Yeoh. 2019a. 'Parental Migration and Disruptions in Everyday Life: Reactions of Left-Behind Children in Southeast Asia.' *Journal of Ethnic and Migration Studies* 45 (16): 3085–3104. doi: 10.1080/1369183X.2018.1547022.

Lam, T., and B.S.A. Yeoh. 2019b. 'Under One Roof? Left-Behind Children's Perspectives in Negotiating Relationships with Absent and Return-Migrant Parents.' *Population, Space and Place* 25 (3): 1–10. doi: 10.1002/psp.2151.

Li, Y. 2015. 'Left Behind Child Psychological Condition White Paper.' China: Beijing Normal University Scientific Communication and Education Research Center.

Liang, Y., L. Wang and G.Q. Rui. 2017. 'Depression among Left-Behind Children in China.' *Journal of Health Psychology* 22 (14): 1897–1905. doi: 10.1177/1359105316676333.

Mayall, B. 2002. *Towards a Sociology for Childhood : Thinking from Children's Lives*. Buckingham: Open University Press.
Mazzucato, V. 2015. 'Transnational Families and the Well-Being of Children and Caregivers Who Stay in Origin Countries Introduction.' *Social Science and Medicine* 132: 208–214. doi: 10.1016/j.socscimed.2014.11.030.
Mazzucato, V., V. Cebotari, A. Veale, A. White, M. Grassi and J. Vivet. 2015. 'International Parental Migration and the Psychological Well-Being of Children in Ghana, Nigeria, and Angola.' *Social Science and Medicine* 132: 215–224. doi: 10.1016/j.socscimed.2014.10.058.
Mazzucato, V., and D. Schans. 2011. 'Transnational Families and the Well-Being of Children: Conceptual and Methodological Challenges.' *Journal of Marriage and Family* 73 (4): 704–712. doi: 10.1111/j.1741-3737.2011.00840.x.
Mazzucato, V., and J. van Geel. 2022. 'Transnational Young People: Growing up and Being Active in a Transnational Social Field.' In *Handbook on Transnationalism*, edited by B.S.A. Yeoh and F. Collins, 198–210. Cheltenham, UK and Northampton, MA, USA: Edward Elgar Publishing.
McKay, D. 2018. 'Sent Home: Mapping the Absent Child into Migration through Polymedia.' *Global Networks* 18 (1): 133–150. doi: 10.1111/glob.12174.
Mordeno, I.G., I.M.J.S. Gallemit, S.S.B. Lantud and B.J. Hall. 2019. 'Personal Psychological Resources Mediate Parent–Child Relationship and Mental Health among Left-Behind Children.' *PsyCh Journal* 8 (3): 318–329. doi: 10.1002/pchj.288.
Nazridod, S., C.P.D.C. Pereira and M.D.D.H. Guerreiro. 2019. 'Adolescents Who Stay, Parents Who Migrate: Gender Inequalities, Resilience and Coping Strategies in Tajikistan.' *Journal of Ethnic and Migration Studies*. doi: 10.1080/1369183X.2019.1662716.
Ng, J. 2019. 'Labor Migration in Indonesia and the Health of Children Left Behind.' *IZA Journal of Development and Migration* 10 (2). doi: 10.2478/izajodm-2019-0006.
Nguyen, C.V., and H.Q. Nguyen. 2015. 'Do Internal and International Remittances Matter to Health, Education and Labor of Children and Adolescents? The Case of Vietnam.' *Children and Youth Services Review* 58: 28–34. doi: 10.1016/j.childyouth.2015.09.002.
Ní Laoire, C., F. Carpena-Méndez, N. Tyrrell and A. White. 2010. 'Introduction: Childhood and Migration – Mobilities, Homes and Belongings.' *Childhood* 17 (2): 155–162. doi: 10.1177/0907568210365463.
OHCHR. 1989. 'Convention on the Rights of the Child.' Accessed 28 December 2020, https://www.ohchr.org/en/professionalinterest/pages/crc.aspx.
Orellana, M.F., B. Thorne, A. Chee and W.S.E. Lam. 2001. 'Transnational Childhoods: The Participation of Children in Processes of Family Migration.' *Social Problems* 48 (4): 572–591. doi: 10.1525/sp.2001.48.4.572.
Parreñas, R.S. 2005. *Children of Global Migration: Transnational Families and Gendered Woes*. Stanford, CA: Stanford University Press.
Perera, N., and M.R. Rathnayaka. 2013. *Sri Lanka's Missing Mothers: A Working Paper on the Effects of Mother Migration on Children*. Sri Lanka: Save the Children.
Račaitė, J., J. Lindert, K. Antia, V. Winkler, R. Sketerskienė, M. Jakubauskienė, et al. 2021. 'Parent Emigration, Physical Health and Related Risk and Preventive Factors of Children Left Behind: A Systematic Review of Literature.' *International Journal of Environmental Research and Public Health* 18 (3): 1167–1180.
Račaitė, J., G. Surkiene, M. Jakubauskiene, R. Sketerskiene and L. Wulkau. 2019. 'Parent Emigration and Physical Health of Children Left Behind: Systematic Review of the Literature.' *European Journal of Public Health* 29: 392.
Reyes, M. 2008. 'Migration and Filipino Children Left-Behind: A Literature Review.' Paper prepared for the United Nations Children's Fund (UNICEF).
Rossi, A. 2009. 'The Impact of Migration on Children Left Behind in Developing Countries: Outcomes Analysis and Data Requirements.' MHR Measurement and Human Rights Working Paper. doi: 10.2139/ssrn.2490380.
Roy, A.K., P. Singh and U.N. Roy. 2015. 'Impact of Rural–Urban Labour Migration on Education of Children: A Case Study of Left Behind and Accompanied Migrant Children in India.' *Space and Culture, India* 2 (4): 17–34. doi: 10.20896/saci.v2i4.74.

Sadruddin, A.F.A., L.A. Ponguta, A.L. Zonderman, K.S. Wiley, A. Grimshaw and C. Panter-Brick. 2019. 'How Do Grandparents Influence Child Health and Development? A Systematic Review.' *Social Science and Medicine* 239. doi: 10.1016/j.socscimed.2019.112476.

Sarma, V.J., and R.A. Parinduri. 2016. 'What Happens to Children's Education When Their Parents Emigrate? Evidence from Sri Lanka.' *International Journal of Educational Development* 46: 94–102. doi: 10.1016/j.ijedudev.2015.11.007.

Schapiro, N.A., S.M. Kools, S.J. Weiss and C.D. Brindis. 2013. 'Separation and Reunification: The Experiences of Adolescents Living in Transnational Families.' *Current Problems in Pediatric and Adolescent Health Care* 43 (3): 48–68. doi: 10.1016/j.cppeds.2012.12.001.

Somaiah, B.C., and B.S.A. Yeoh. 2021. 'Temporal Emotion Work, Gender and Aspirations of Left-Behind Youth in Indonesian Migrant-Sending Villages.' *Journal of Youth Studies*. Online First. doi: 10.1080/13676261.2021.1952170.

Somaiah, B.C., B.S.A. Yeoh and S.M. Arlini. 2020. '"Cukup for Me to Be Successful in This Country": "Staying" among Left-Behind Young Women in Indonesia's Migrant-Sending Villages.' *Global Networks* 20 (2): 237–255.

Stark, O., and D.E. Bloom. 1985. 'The New Economics of Labor Migration.' *American Economic Review* 75 (2): 173–178.

Tobin, V. 2008. 'Gender, Migration and Children's Rights.' In *The International Conference on Gender, Migration and Development: Seizing Opportunities, Upholding Rights*. Hotel Sofitel Philippine Plaza Manila, Philippines.

Tong, L., Q. Yan and I. Kawachi. 2019. 'The Factors Associated with Being Left-Behind Children in China: Multilevel Analysis with Nationally Representative Data.' *PLoS ONE* 14 (11): e0224205. doi: 10.1371/journal.pone.0224205.

Treleaven, E. 2019. 'Migration and Investments in the Health of Children Left Behind: The Role of Remittances in Children's Healthcare Utilization in Cambodia.' *Health Policy and Planning* 34 (9): 684–693. doi: 10.1093/heapol/czz076.

UNDESA. 2019. 'International Migrant Stock 2019: Country Profiles.' Accessed 9 April 2020, https://www.un.org/en/development/desa/population/migration/data/estimates2/countryprofiles.asp.

UNICEF. 2020. 'Children "Left Behind".' Accessed 14 December, https://www.unicef.org/documents/children-left-behind.

Valtolina, G.G., and C. Colombo. 2012. 'Psychological Well-Being, Family Relations, and Developmental Issues of Children Left Behind.' *Psychological Reports* 111 (3): 905–928. doi: 10.2466/21.10.17.pr0.111.6.905-928.

Van Hook, J., and J.E. Glick. 2020. 'Spanning Borders, Cultures, and Generations: A Decade of Research on Immigrant Families.' *Journal of Marriage and Family* 82 (1): 224–243. doi: 10.1111/jomf.12621.

Wang, L.L., W. Wu, G.B. Qu, X. Tang and Y.H. Sun. 2019. 'The Personality Traits of Left-Behind Children in China: A Systematic Review and Meta-Analysis.' *Psychology Health and Medicine* 24 (3): 253–268. doi: 10.1080/13548506.2018.1540787.

Wang, L.M., and J. Mesman. 2015. 'Child Development in the Face of Rural-to-Urban Migration in China: A Meta-Analytic Review.' *Perspectives on Psychological Science* 10 (6): 813–831. doi: 10.1177/1745691615600145.

Wang, M., R. Sokol, H. Luan, B.E. Perron, B.G. Victor and S.Y. Wu. 2020. 'Mental Health Service Interventions for Left-Behind Children in Mainland China: A Systematic Review of Randomized Controlled Trials.' *Children and Youth Services Review* 117. doi: 10.1016/j.childyouth.2020.105304.

Wang, X., L. Ling, H. Su, J. Cheng, L. Jin and Y.H. Sun. 2015. 'Self-Concept of Left-Behind Children in China: A Systematic Review of the Literature.' *Child: Care, Health and Development* 41 (3): 346–355. doi: 10.1111/cch.12172.

Wang, Y.Y., L. Xiao, W.W. Rao, J.X. Chai, S.F. Zhang, C.H. Ng, G.S. Ungvari, H.P. Zhu and Y.T. Xiang. 2019. 'The Prevalence of Depressive Symptoms in "Left-Behind Children" in China: A Meta-Analysis of Comparative Studies and Epidemiological Surveys.' *Journal of Affective Disorders* 244: 209–216. doi: 10.1016/j.jad.2018.09.066.

Whitehead, A., and I. Hashim. 2005. 'Children and Migration: Background Paper for Dfid Migration Team.' Brighton: DRC on Migration, Globalisation and Poverty, University of Sussex.

Wickramage, K., C. Siriwardhana and S. Peiris. 2015. 'Promoting the Health of Left-Behind Children of Asian Labour Migrants: Evidence for Policy and Action.' *Issue in Brief* September (14): 1–12.

Wu, W., G.B. Qu, L.L. Wang, X. Tang and Y.H. Sun. 2019. 'Meta-Analysis of the Mental Health Status of Left-Behind Children in China.' *Journal of Paediatrics and Child Health* 55 (3): 260–270. doi: 10.1111/jpc.14349.

Xu, D.D., W.W. Rao, X.L. Cao, S.Y. Wen, F.R. An, W.I. Che, et al. 2020. 'Prevalence of Depressive Symptoms in Primary School Students in China: A Systematic Review and Meta-Analysis.' *Journal of Affective Disorders* 268: 20–27. doi: 10.1016/j.jad.2020.02.034.

Yeoh, B.S.A. 2020. 'Temporary Migration Regimes and Their Sustainability in Times of Covid-19.' Geneva: International Organization of Migration (IOM).

Yeoh, B.S.A., and T. Lam. 2007. 'The Costs of (Im)Mobility: Children Left Behind and Children Who Migrate with a Parent.' In *Perspectives on Gender and Migration*, edited by United Nations ESCAP, 120–149. Bangkok: United Nations Economic and Social Commission for Asia and the Pacific.

Zhang, J.H., L.X. Yan, H.Y. Qiu and B.R. Dai. 2018. 'Social Adaptation of Chinese Left-Behind Children: Systematic Review and Meta-Analysis.' *Children and Youth Services Review* 95: 308–315. doi: 10.1016/j.childyouth.2018.11.012.

Zhao, F.Q., and G.L. Yu. 2016. 'Parental Migration and Rural Left-Behind Children's Mental Health in China: A Meta-Analysis Based on Mental Health Test.' *Journal of Child and Family Studies* 25 (12): 3462–3472. doi: 10.1007/s10826-016-0517-3.

Zhou, C.C., S. Sylvia, L.X. Zhang, R.F. Luo, H.M. Yi, C.F. Liu, et al. 2015. 'China's Left-Behind Children: Impact of Parental Migration on Health, Nutrition, and Educational Outcomes.' *Health Affairs* 34 (11): 1964–1971. doi: 10.1377/hlthaff.2015.0150.

Zimmer, Z., and M. Van Natta. 2018. 'Migration and Left-Behind Parents and Children of Migrants in Cambodia: A Look at Household Composition and the Economic Situation.' *Asian Population Studies* 14 (3): 271–289. doi: 10.1080/17441730.2018.1513111.

22. Transnational families and mobility regimes
Franchesca Morais and Brenda S.A. Yeoh

INTRODUCTION

The modern world is in continual flux, with people, objects, capital, information and ideas constantly circulating globally. With the immense increase in the scale of travel across the world, as more people are able to travel more often, 'all the world seems to be on the move' (Sheller and Urry, 2006, p. 207). The ability and freedom to move internationally has become a normality, with horizontal mobility across geographical borders frequently associated with vertical economic, social and cultural progress (Salazar and Smart, 2011). With the advent of transnationalism approaches since the 1990s, scholarship on the border-spanning activities and practices of migrants in developing and maintaining multiple economic, social, organisational, religious and political linkages has burgeoned (Glick-Schiller et al., 1992; Basch et al., 1994; Yeoh and Collins, 2022). In the same vein, research on migration and the family has turned attention to exploring geographically dispersed families across borders as an increasingly common living arrangement (Bryceson and Vuorela, 2002; Yeoh et al., 2005).

Foregrounding the prominence and primacy of the family, transnational family scholarship acknowledges that the family, in whatever configuration, remains the primary arrangement that meets 'certain social, emotional, and economic needs ... [and is where] decisions about work, care, movement, and identity are negotiated, contested, and resolved' (Trask, 2010, p. 185). This has spawned a rich corpus of literature on the role of information and communication technologies (ICTs) in allowing families to remain connected digitally and maintain bonds of familyhood despite living apart (Sinanan and Horst, 2022; see Chapter 6, this *Handbook*). At the same time, scholars have also reiterated the importance of visits, repatriations or migrations, as it nevertheless remains an eventual goal and implicit preference for families to be physically co-present (Skrbiš, 2008; Baldassar et al., 2007; Merla et al., 2020a). Inasmuch as migration often signifies a form of rupture to family rhythms and relations, return is usually thought of as family reunion, the restoration of the desired state or the 'normal' order of things in the family (Yeoh et al., 2020).

Mobility across international borders, or the aspiration and possibility for such mobility, is hence an integral feature of maintaining a sense of transnational familyhood. Yet, particularly in comparison to the abounding work on ICTs, how 'doing family' across national territory is affected by border controls, increasing securitisation and the rise of what Turner (2007) calls 'immobility regimes' has not been given sufficient attention. Scholars argue that mobility has to be framed in relation to the global political system of nation-states which, in order to assert nation-state sovereignty, set and control the parameters of transnational movements, often through policies reflecting the rhetoric of 'closure, entrapment and containment' (Shamir, 2005, p. 199; see also Glick-Schiller and Salazar, 2013; Martin and Dragojlovic, 2019). This has important implications for migrants and their family members, who face complex bureaucracies to manage their compliance with an ever-shifting array of rules and obligations governing entry and residence. While national borders are increasingly becoming closed off for some individuals, others are conditionally and exclusively selected for entry (Hawthorne, 2005). This has led scholars to think in terms of 'regimes of mobility', where the rules and conditions for border-crossing facilitate the mobility of some, while impeding or disrupting the mobility of others, leading to situations in which certain kinds of mobility or certain types of mobile individuals 'become the subjects of praise or condemnation, desire, suppression or fear' (Glick-Schiller and Salazar, 2013, p. 196). Increasingly stringent 'mobility regimes' significantly impact upon not only migrants or prospective migrants, but also their transnational family members living across nation-state boundaries (Merla et al., 2020a). Conversely, families absorb, resist, process and act on opportunities or constraints produced by changing regime rules and regulatory practices, thus acting as the crucial link between the micro-level processes (for example, migrant decision-making) and macro-level regimes (for example, visa requirements) that implicate and influence transnational migration.

This chapter thus approaches transnational family dynamics in relation to mobility regimes in order to encapsulate the complex modes of differentiation within governing structures of mobility and their implications for family life. The current political climate of restrictive mobility has dramatically affected the contexts in which some transnational families are able to maintain kinship ties across distance and territorial borders (Merla et al., 2020a). In addition, the spatial dispersion of transnational families across borders is often driven by mobility regimes, where immigration policies around visit visas, family reunification, residency, naturalisation and citizenship can affect the ability or possibility for families to stay together.

In interrogating the scholarship on mobility regimes and the implications for transnational family formation and practices, we structure our argument as follows. First, we draw on a rich body of scholarship centred on immigration policies and border practices to highlight the value of researching mobility regimes in migration studies. Traditional migration research has long been criticised for being state-centric, and as a response, has more recently become more subject-oriented or migrant-centric (Anderson, 2019). As a reflection of this general trend in migration studies, much research on mobility regimes has similarly focused on the aforementioned two ends of the spectrum: either the nation-state or the individual migrant.

This leads us to the second strand of our argument, which centres on the need to foreground the family in understanding the differentiating power of mobility regimes on primary social relations. By drawing on a small but growing body of work that explores the intersections between individual migrant decision-making, family relations and configurations, and nation-state border practices, we explore the mutually constitutive effects of family formations and practices on the one hand, and prevailing migration regimes on the other. We emphasise the importance of time and temporality for understanding the interconnections between transnational families and mobility regimes. At the scale of the family, migrants' life-stage progressions are entrained alongside the lives of their family members (Coe, 2016), which can often be disrupted by mobility regimes. For example, restricted mobility can result in delayed childbirth, the inability to provide eldercare, or forgoing a migration opportunity in order to care for a family member (Merla et al., 2020a). We argue that transnational families are not only predicated on spatiality-based dynamics, as is often the focus, but also that mobility regimes have important implications for the temporal rhythms of transnational family life.

The chapter concludes with a discussion of how mobility regimes have affected transnational families in the context of the COVID-19 pandemic. At the time of writing – from 2021 to 2022 – the widespread closure of international borders and the disruptions to air travel have had significant implications for the mobility rights and capacities of transnational families. We consider the possible impact of the pandemic on transnational family life in the longer term, and also whether the global crisis is likely to lead to a re-imagination of how family life may be done differently across borders.

MOBILITY REGIMES AND REGIME RESEARCH IN MIGRATION STUDIES

Generally understood as 'networks of rules, norms, and procedures that regularize behaviour and control its effects' (Krasner, 1982, p. 2), the concept of 'regime' has long been used in migration studies. Ghosh (2000) was among the first scholars to call for the development of an 'international migration regime' for the orderly movement of people, where destination countries permit legal migration of labour, and source countries facilitate the repatriation of their nationals and suppress illegal migration (see also Koslowski, 2008; Jandl and Stacher, 2004). Focusing instead on the national rather than the international scale, Boucher and Gest (2015) look at regimes as models or types of immigration control adopted by different nation-states. In the same vein, some migration scholars who have used regime terminology in their analyses of migration management and nation-state border control practices (e.g. Hess, 2012; Tsianos, 2010) have tended to treat regimes as 'governing arrangements constructed by states to coordinate their expectations and organize aspects of international behaviour in various issue areas' (Wilson, 2000, p. 256). Migration regime research highlighting state policies and border regulations from a macro-level approach (Merla et al., 2020a, p. 530) has been particularly prominent in two geopolitical settings: the European Union's border zones and the border between Mexico and the United States (e.g. Hess et al., 2016; Heimeshoff et al., 2014; Heyman, 2009; Nail, 2016 as cited in Schwarz, 2018).

Drawing from mobilities research and the 'new mobilities paradigm' that highlights the multiple, complex and fluid movements of migrants across the globe (Urry, 2000; Sheller and Urry, 2006; Sheller, 2011), other accounts in migration research have adopted the term 'mobility regimes' instead as an all-encompassing bridge between migration studies, mobility studies and border studies. In doing so, mobility regimes are not merely synonymous with nation-state migration apparatuses, but bind together state actors, commercial parties, international organisations, and local practices and regulations that aim at regulating movement (Schwarz, 2018). Although the different regime terminologies might often be conflated, this turn of phrase – along with the companion term 'immobility regimes' – gives emphasis to the complexities of global mobility, power and inequality (Horvath et al., 2017). Some mobility regimes have long-standing global traditions, including the instalment of visas and passport systems by the League of Nations after World War I and international provisions for refugees based on the United Nations Refugee Convention in 1951 (Koslowski, 2011; Torpey, 1999). Other mobility regimes such as border controls (e.g. Andersson, 2014) and deportation systems (e.g. Kalir and Wissink, 2016) are constantly emerging and shifting through interactions with 'a universal paradigm of suspicion' directed toward 'the agents of mobility ... [who are] suspected of representing the threads of crime, undesired immigration, and terrorism' (Shamir, 2005, p. 201).

Indeed, despite increased levels of global mobility, Shamir (2005, p. 199) proposes reconceptualising globalisation 'not as a system of liquid mobility', but as one that also produces 'closure, entrapment and containment'. Noting that mobility is still a scarce resource for the overwhelming majority of the world's population who are not a part of the hypermobile global elite (see also Bauman, 2002; Doyle and Nathan, 2001; Cunningham and Heyman, 2004; Turner, 2007), he argues that anxieties over terrorism and urban violence have created a 'fear of diversity', triggering 'new forms of enclosure' (Yeoh and Lam, 2012, p. 70, citing Shamir). Paradoxically, the rise of mobility has been accompanied by the proliferation of physical gates and fences at borders, sophisticated border surveillance systems that rely on electronic fences and infrared cameras, complex bureaucratic barriers, exclusionary visa classification schemes, and the use of biosocial profiling technology to screen people based on race, ethnicity and nationality (Shamir, 2005). In his paper, Shamir also signals very briefly in a footnote how conditional and exclusionary limits on travel opportunities might also impact upon transnational families, citing the example of Asian families in the United Kingdom whose family members 'encounter growing difficulties in obtaining permission to visit them' (p. 206).

Building on Shamir's idea of a single global mobility regime, Glick-Schiller and Salazar (2013) postulate that there are in fact 'several different intersecting regimes of mobility that normalise the movements of some travellers while criminalising and entrapping the ventures of others' (p. 189). The authors deploy a 'regimes-of-mobility approach' that calls attention to the role of a wide range of actors, from individual states to changing international regulatory and surveillance systems, in order to explore the contradictory relationship between the privileged movements of some, on the one hand, and the stigmatised and forbidden movement of the poor and the powerless, on the other (ibid.). While acknowledging the important role of the nation-state as a key actor in the formation and legitimisation of mobility regimes, Glick-Schiller and Salazar also argue that 'scholars must examine the role of nation-states and the influence of national identities in shaping the experience of migrants without confining their study and analysis within the parameters of the nation-state' (p. 192). The authors thus call for an approach to understanding mobility regimes that does not automatically use the nation-state as a unit of analysis. Rather, studying the movement of people across space needs to take into account a variety of forces that shape mobility, which often include, but are not confined to, states and their policies. Similar to Shamir's work, Glick-Schiller and Salazar only very briefly allude to the importance of the family and the household as a scale of analysis. Quoting King and Skeldon (2010, p. 1640), they point to the (then) recent mobility turn in migration studies (see also Faist, 2013) that acknowledges the importance of a range of scales from the 'family/household, community, national, and the constellation of countries linked by migration flows' (p. 184).

Positioned within a wider critique of methodological nationalism in migration studies, this emerging body of work also moves beyond understanding the inner workings of mobility regimes in themselves to consider the consequences of mobility regimes for the lived experiences of migrants more explicitly. This scholarship gives weight to how people move through, interact with and negotiate the opportunities and constraints inhering in prevailing mobility regimes. Through a combination of in-depth interviews, telephone calls and online conversations, as well as follow-up visits to the migrants in different places and at different times in their migration journeys, Schapendonk and Steel's (2014) research provides insight into the border-crossing experiences of Sudanese and Nigerian migrants heading for Europe. The research showed that the experiences of migrants varied drastically between the individuals, even though they were from or living in the same country, and were contending with similar rules and regulations within the same mobility regime. As argued by scholars such as Schapendonk et al. (2018) and Schwarz (2018), visualising mobility regimes through boundaries and territories framed by a geopolitical map can be problematic, as borders are seen as homogeneous and thus do not represent the differential and unequal ways in which mobility regimes impact upon and are experienced by migrant subjects. Instead, a border 'only materializes through border practices that are geographically scattered and in many cases invisible' (Schwarz, 2018, p. 3). In order to maintain a subject-oriented approach that takes the migrants' perspectives and their embodied experiences and feelings of movement as the starting points of analysis, Schapendonk et al. (2018), utilise a migration trajectory approach as a methodological tool that follows the 'twists and turns' of migration processes (p. 3). In doing so, the authors take on the task of 're-routing migration geographies' (p. 1), in two ways. First, the approach allows them to re-route attention in mobility regime research away from the dominant discussion on state-led regulations and agendas. Second, by analysing in detail where, when and how often the migrants encounter mobility regimes, and attending to the continuous process of navigation and readjustment, the approach also re-routes the implications for the migrants in question. Schwarz (2018) similarly highlights the importance of both individual action and the regime structure of mobility in arguing for the value in studying the intersection between the two. In doing so, migrants' active navigation through mobility regimes becomes a basis for self-positioning of migrants (ibid.). Thus, mobility regimes in themselves are not seen as structurally determined, but the approach also gives focus to the migrant as subject in highlighting the migrant's agency and ability to circumvent these structures.

The interplay between migrants and mobility regimes is well illustrated by emerging literature focusing on the space of encounter between migrants and border agents on a day-to-day basis (Singer and Massey, 1998). As part of what Heyman (1995) calls a 'ritualized border game', migrants draw on a range of tactics and bureaucratic coping strategies to navigate both the formal and the implicit 'rules' of border crossing (Papadopoulos and Tsianos, 2013; Winters, 2020; Wilson Janssens, 2020; Massa, 2020; Wissink et al., 2020). Massa's (2020) work, for example, considers how Eritrean refugees and Ethiopian returnees 'play' with legal categories in order to shape and direct their own migration pathways. She argues that mobility regimes not only restrict mobility pathways, but also give migrants an opportunity to find solutions. As McDowell (2008) notes, border restrictions can be questioned by migrants through processes of social negotiation, such as through the adaptation of their physical appearances (for example, choice of clothing, haircut and facial hair), conforming to stereotypes with a higher acceptance of moving freely (for example, businessmen or international students) in order to avoid negative reactions (ibid.). In Khosravi's (2011) auto-ethnography of his migratory journey from Iran to Sweden, he illustrates the experience of illegalisation not only in relation to the crossing of a geopolitical border, but also as a continuing process that accompanies the traveller long after the migration journey is complete. In Khosravi's case, he navigated a multiplicity of border-crossings by pursuing a longer-term strategy to eke out a pathway towards citizenship where, over time, he managed to change his legal status from illegalised traveller to asylum seeker, then to recognised refugee, and finally to Swedish citizen. However, the change in his legal status had not changed the constant racial discrimination he faced in public, demonstrating the persistence of 'bordered identities' (De Genova, 2014) for those who are indelibly marked out as 'stateless, un-documented, failed asylum seekers ... constantly caught in the position of being the border' (Khosravi, 2011, p. 99). Mobility regimes hence operate beyond the physical border-crossing to shape the opportunity structure for identity-making among migrants. In a similar vein, Yeoh et al. (2017) argue that temporary migration as a mobility regime binds low-waged construction workers to a cycle of indebtedness and transience governed by short-term contracts, with few opportunities for upward mobility and many barriers against integration into the host society. As a consequence, these migrant workers inhabit the city as transient subjects, expected to labour but not stay. Under the temporary regime, precarity – mediated by state agencies, the migration industry and labour markets – is produced across a continuum, from the migrant's accumulation of debt before migration, and the endurance of risks faced during recruitment and training, to compliance under difficult workplace conditions in the destination country. In this sense, the migrant's body at borders, in workplaces and public spaces can become key sites of racial and gender marginalisation, and of struggles against exclusion and prejudice (Winters, 2020).

The emerging body of scholarship on mobility regimes in migration research, however, has tended to unpack the causes and consequences of (im)mobility by focusing on the state apparatus (and to a lesser extent on non-state assemblages such as the migration industry and humanitarian agencies) on the one hand (see, for example, Chapters 12 and 17, this *Handbook*), and the individual migrant subject negotiating the regime of power on the other. Much less attention has been given to the relational effects of migration regimes where 'the mobilities of some people could have the effect of immobilizing other people' (Schapendonk and Steel, 2014, p. 264). To plug this gap, we move the discussion forward in the next section to consider the intermediate scale of the family in reconstituting relationalities and (im)mobilities. In our analysis of transnational families, we set out to operationalise the term 'mobility regimes' specifically (rather than just 'border regimes' or 'migration regimes'), as a useful conceptual framework that emphasises the 'various structures of power' that 'accord rights to move, settle, and stay in place to individuals of certain classes and racialized categories and deny both mobility and stasis to others' (Glick-Schiller, 2018, p. 208). By engaging with literature that explores the intersections between mobility regimes and family relations, we argue for the importance of a regimes-of-mobility perspective (Glick-Schiller and Salazar, 2013) that gives weight not just to the situated agency of the individual migrant, but also to 'the whole affective register of familial connections and practices' (Valentine, 2008, p. 2101). Such an approach usefully helps us to avoid the trap of assuming that the migrant is 'a subject freed from the obligations of social ties and traditions to make choices in a global economy' (Valentine, 2008, p. 2106, paraphrasing Cole and Durham, 2007). It also reminds us that the impacts of mobility regimes are not just trained on migrant lives, but also on families left behind (Yeoh et al., 2020).

TRANSNATIONAL FAMILIES AND MOBILITY REGIMES FROM A TEMPORAL PERSPECTIVE

Bryceson and Vuorela (2002), in their pivotal book, define transnational families as 'families that live some or most of the time separated from each other, yet hold together and create something that can be seen as a feeling of collective welfare and unity, i.e. "familyhood", even across national borders' (p. 3). Migration literature identifies spatial dispersion and relational interdependency as two primary dimensions of transnational families, where 'dispersion' refers to having members of the family spread across several nation-states, while 'interdependency' denotes maintaining a bond despite the long distance (Wall and Bolzman, 2014). Both of these interrelated dimensions of the transnational family are largely implicated by mobility regimes, where border policing and immigration laws can affect patterns of family migration and settlement (Massey et al., 2015, 2016; Sandberg, 2018) and also determine the ways in which transnational families are able to stay connected over long distances (Bonizzoni, 2018; Merla et al., 2020a, 2020b).

Importantly, these mobility regimes are not only rooted in space (for example, at international borders), but also in time. One of the first scholars to engage with the question of time and temporality in relation to mobility regimes was Saulo Cwerner (2001), who drew attention to the ways in which immigration policies and visa regimes operate as a tool of discipline. According to Cwerner, migrants have limited control over their own time, but temporal control is instead shaped by visa regimes that can require migrants to wait, put their lives on hold, and place migrants in unclear and precarious situations. Since then, a substantial body of work has followed, focusing on the crucial role of time and temporality in the enforcement of border regulations and immigration policies and their impacts on the mobility of migrants. 'Temporal borders' was a term later conceptualised by Mezzadra and Neilson (2013) in order to encapsulate the various ways in which border techniques for regulating migration are enacted by exerting control over and through time (see also Andersson, 2014; Tazzioli, 2018). Little (2015) also highlights the complex temporality of borders by distinguishing between 'tempo', 'pace' and 'temporality', and the different speeds that different processes and changes take place across different aspects of bordering, and how this is experienced by the migrant.

The different time-elements within migration structures and policies are important for understanding the implications of mobility regimes on transnational families. As Acedera and Yeoh (2019) argue, 'not only are the spatial aspects of the family altered when members are dispersed across different nations, the temporal dynamics of the family are also reconstituted, as members rework and reimagine their familial relationships across different temporalities, negotiating the rhythms and tempo of everyday family life from afar' (p. 252). In this section, we highlight three different lines of transnational family research where a combined conceptual focus on mobility regimes and temporality yields important insights: life-course stages, remittances and transnational family strategies.

Mobility Regimes vis-à-vis Transnational Family Life-Course Stages

Migration has primarily and almost instinctively been viewed as a spatial process, where migrants move from one spatial territory to another. This idea is reflected in the classical representation of migration in geographical maps, with a cartographic arrow pointing from point A to point B (Griffiths et al., 2013). The long-standing preoccupation with space in migration scholarship has meant that it is often overlooked, or taken for granted, that the process of migration happens over time as well. Adopting a temporal lens thus allows for a better understanding of the migration process; that is, the migration journey across a migrant's life-course (ibid.). Especially in today's world, migration journeys rarely conform to expected sequential trajectories of one-off movements from point A to permanent residency in point B. Instead, they often involve diversion, repetition and simultaneity, and can take hours, years and even generations (ibid.).

Scholars have increasingly adopted a life-course perspective (Elder, 1998) in order to advance research on migration and temporality so as to examine how migration journeys and aspirations are implicated by different stages of a migrant's life (e.g. Amrith, 2020; Kilkey and Palenga-Möllenbeck, 2016; Kilkey and Ryan, 2020). As Kilkey and Ryan (2020) argue, the life-course framework highlights the 'situatedness of migrant experiences as lived in particular times (both personal and historical), places, and relationships' (p. 229) where lives are socially organised into both biographical and historical time. A life-course framework thus enables researchers to understand how important historical events impact migrants' personal life narratives (Carling, 2017). The life-course framework set out by Elder (1998) also highlights the principle of 'linked lives' or how 'lives are lived interdependently', which is particularly relevant in emphasizing that migration decision-making is often made in relation to networks of relationships that are situated in specific life-stages (Kilkey and Ryan, 2020). Key life-course stages such as relationship formation, reproduction, childrearing and ageing are vital to understanding how family life is reconfigured in migration (Kilkey and Palenga-Möllenbeck, 2016).

We argue that a migrant's life-stages linked to the lives of their extended family support networks can often be 'disrupted in time' by mobility regimes. For instance, Cati Coe (2016) shows how the temporal barriers of immigration laws and policies, through their 'rigid categories of persons ... narrow definitions of family, and the slow pace of ... bureaucratic processes' (p. 44) are significant as they prolong family separation and create uncertainty around the possibility for future family reunification. Her research considers how Ghanian migrants have to synchronise and coordinate their lives with their family members, where younger women who move overseas for employment have to pay attention to the 'life courses of those in other generations, to relatives' deaths, physical frailty, births, and need to earn a livelihood' (p. 42), and use these life-events as cues for when they would need to return to live in their home towns. These decisions are often further complicated by the lags and delays of the temporally inflexible mobility regimes, which can be incompatible with the biological temporal processes of migrants and their family members; for example, when adults or elderly people decline in health suddenly.

The temporalities of a transnational family's life-course in relation to the temporalities of mobility regimes highlight the importance of different 'scales' of time – everyday, institutional and biographical time[1] – where migrants have to negotiate the institutional time scales of migration alongside significant biographic events such as marriage and the birth of children (Robertson, 2019). For instance, the extension of waiting periods for family reunification, access to welfare provisions and gaining citizenship status, highlight the ways in which the temporalities of mobility regimes have implications for the life-course of a family, as migrants would have to slow down or put on hold their family plans, causing 'specific forms of suspension or delay in migrants' desired or intended trajectories' (ibid., p. 179).

Mobility Regimes vis-à-vis Precarity, Debt and Remittances

'Permanent temporariness' (Carciotto, 2018), conjoined to a sense of precarity, has become a pervasive feature of mobility regimes, especially in the case of temporary labour migration. The temporal delays and insecurity associated with a temporary migration regime can produce social and financial pressures on migrant family networks (Boyce, 2020), which in turn affects the lived experiences of time for transnational migrants and their families. Acedera and Yeoh (2019) consider the temporary labour migration regime in Singapore, where the mobility of low-skilled migrant workers are governed by policies that produce transience and temporariness through short-term permits and quotas that make permanent residency and family reunification in the host country virtually impossible. They argue that the meso-temporalities of immigration policies instil temporariness and precarity for transnational families, and ultimately deter their aspirations and imaginations for stable family futures (ibid.)

Temporary labour migration regimes are often interlaced with different degrees and forms of indebtedness, which have important implications for migrants' salaries and remitting capabilities as they undertake precarious labour in order to fulfil their migration goals and aspirations (Platt et al., 2017). Harrison and Lloyd (2012) point out how migrants accept long hours of labour under abusive and exploitative conditions so as to be able to send remittances home as quickly as possible, in order to avoid the risk of deportation before paying off their debts. Paul's (2017) work also reflects the never-ending need for labour migrants to send remittances back home, where migrants internalise a sense of obligation to send money back home as well as a sense of self-pride in becoming their family's benefactor. The low wages and indebtedness of temporary labour migrants, coupled with persisting remittance obligations (see also Silvey and Parreñas, 2019), have implications for the temporalities of transnational families, where migration timelines can be indefinitely extended and family separation constantly prolonged.

Mobility Regimes vis-à-vis Transnational Family Strategies and Care Arrangements

Care circulation is defined as 'the reciprocal, multidirectional and asymmetrical exchange of care that fluctuates over the life course within transnational family networks subject to the political, economic, cultural and social contexts of both sending and receiving areas' (Baldassar and Merla, 2014, p. 22). Care exchanges between migrants and their families can be in the form of emotional love, practical care and financial support (ibid.). In transnational families where caregiving occurs across national borders, care strategies and arrangements are often complicated by divergent prevailing mobility regimes across countries with different migration and family-related laws, regulations and policies. A special issue on 'Transnational care: Families confronting borders' in the *Journal of Family Research* in particular highlights a range of these strategies, which include gathering and circulating information to plan and organise individual and family mobility, trying to secure access to refugee status or family reunification, mobilising ICTs to provide and receive care across distance, and focusing on long-distance forms of care (see Merla et al., 2020b for the Introduction). Baldassar and Wilding (2022) also emphasise the impact of immigration policies on the division of caregiving in transnational families, especially in cases of undocumented or temporary labour migrants who are denied citizenship and do not have the same access to social services as wealthier, high-skilled migrants (see also Boccagni, 2014; Bryceson, 2019).

Migrants and their transnational families often have to develop coping strategies in order to deal with and adapt to the temporalities of mobility regimes (for example, see Chapter 13, this *Handbook*). For instance, they might delay migration plans and aspirations, in anticipation of mobility restrictions, in order to stay home and fulfil familial care obligations. As Merla et al. (2020a) argue, the circulation of care across borders is particularly sensitive to the temporal controls of migration regimes, as it often involves the physical crossing of borders, especially for proximate care needs and obligations, which may require migrants to make frequent visits home or permanently return to their country of origin. These different caregiving arrangements are in turn reliant on different temporal configurations, through short-term visits, or long-term expatriations or constant circulation within the family network (see also Kilkey and Merla, 2014). The authors argue that increasingly selective migration policies such as limits on dependent passes, the unattainability of parent visas, restrictions on reunifications with children, and restricted access to citizenship, dramatically affect the contexts in which transnational families maintain their kinship and caregiving relationships across territorial borders, and in turn have significant implications on the temporal configurations of care arrangements (ibid.). This seems to be especially so for intergenerational care relationships, as the elderly are often not able to secure more permanent visas because they are typically viewed as economically inactive and hence a 'burden' on public funds (Bonizzoni, 2018). Migrant children who are not able to provide proximate care for their elderly parents work often resort to working around these visa restrictions by planning frequent short visits and regular trips (De Silva, 2018). In some cases, as a result of increasingly strict mobility regimes that are constantly changing, families have to rely on the exchange of care across national borders using ICTs and new technologies as a way of maintaining a sense of familyhood transnationally instead of proximate care (Benítez, 2012; Nedelcu and Wyss, 2016). However, this is not always an option in the cases where older migrants might not be as familiar with using new technologies (Kryżowski and Mucha, 2014). As such, the multiple temporalities of mobility regimes, also attuned to the biographical times of family members, have important implications on the care strategies and arrangements of transnational families.

CONCLUDING THOUGHTS AND THE COVID-19 PANDEMIC

In this chapter, we contribute to research on families and migration by situating two crucial concepts – mobility regimes and temporality – more prominently within the transnational research agenda. In order to make sense of the complex and fluid transnational flows of people across borders that do not always conform to the nation-state's boundary-making work (see Hui, 2016), migration research is increasingly enriched and influenced by mobilities studies. The concept of mobility regimes serves to emphasise how 'intensifying mobilities in the contemporary period is not a claim about increasing freedoms or a celebration of supposedly unrestricted "flows" in globalization', but they are 'always attended by forces of immobilization' (Martin and Dragojlovic, 2019, p. 279). While mobility regimes research has thus far attended to immigration regimes operating at the nation scale on one hand, and the complex and varied experiences of individual migrants as they encounter these regimes on the other, the concept remains underutilised in relation to the scale of the family.

In addition to foregrounding mobilities, another important paradigmatic shift in migration research that this chapter pays heed to is a recent focus on time and temporality that elucidates how migration is 'not necessarily always about trans/national mobility but often about not moving at all' (Baas and Yeoh, 2019, p. 162). However, despite the importance of time and temporal dimensions, apart from a few exceptions, work focusing on critical temporalities in transnational family research remains relatively limited (Waters, 2011; Yeoh et al., 2020). As such, we set out to emphasise the ever-shifting and temporal nature of mobility regimes and how this has important implications for the temporalities of transnational family life.

The chapter proposes three strands of transnational family scholarship that would benefit from a critical understanding of the intersections between mobility regimes, transnational families and temporalities: transnational family life-course stages; debt and remittances; and care strategies and arrangements. We note, however, that these three research areas do not serve as an exhaustive or all-encompassing list of the ways in which the concepts of mobility regimes and temporality can be applied to transnational family research. Instead, we signal the growing literature on temporalities and mobility regimes as a way to develop a more critical understanding of the intersections between transnationalism and family relations. For instance, a temporal understanding of mobility regimes in light of rapidly altering conditions of migration also allows for an understanding of the ways in which the fundamental alterations of mobility regimes across time and space are implicated by key historical moments and processes (Glick-Schiller, 2018). Historical moments, or key 'unsettling events' that create drastic political, social and economic transformations, have the potential to disrupt migration decisions and projects (Kilkey and Ryan, 2020). Glick-Schiller (2018) writes about the current world situation of rising nationalism and right-wing political movements that target migrants, where the possibilities for migrants to live transnational lives are becoming increasingly difficult. Moments in history importantly produce new politics, cultures and forms of governmentality (ibid.). In the rest of this concluding section, we explore the ways in which an analysis of mobility regimes and temporality might be particularly useful in the context of the COVID-19 pandemic, as an important moment in time that has seen the convergence of different (im) mobility regimes. A macro-level understanding of the longer-term and broader historical contexts of mobility regimes thus allows us to consider how the COVID-19 pandemic – as a specific moment of stalled mobilities – impacts transnational family lives.

Some scholars have argued that the COVID-19 pandemic and its associated resurgence of borders is indicative of a 'new global border regime' which will likely outlive the pandemic (Radil et al., 2020). The COVID-19 crisis has seen the rapid creation of new national and subnational borders in order to limit the movement of people and curb the spread of disease. The increasingly stringent mobility regimes, with the closure of national borders, curfews and worldwide international travel restrictions, could place transnational families in highly uncertain and precarious situations. The nature of a crisis means that pandemic-related policies need to be 'fast-acting', yet each country also operates on different timescales in reacting and adapting to the pandemic. The pandemic has seen fast-shifting benchmarks and notions of best practices around the world for pandemic response, which in turn have continually informed and shaped local border control policies. The multiple and complex temporalities in which mobility regimes have been assembled in light of the COVID-19 pandemic have important consequences on the still-ongoing biographical times of transnational migrants and their family members, who would then have to adapt their care strategies and migration plans to the precarious conditions of the COVID-19 pandemic.

Importantly, the COVID-19 pandemic reinforces the uneven power relations that govern access to mobility, which impact not only individual migrants but also their family members abroad. As pointed out by Schling et al. (2020, p. 1):

> the global lockdown associated with the fight against Covid-19 has transformed the privileges, power, violence and hierarchies of im/mobility. The capacity to be immobile, by 'staying at home' is both premised upon, and has radically different embodied consequences depending on articulations of age, class, gender, racialization, migration/residency status and dis/ability.

Merla et al. (2020b) also write that the COVID-19 pandemic is likely to affect transnational family solidarities, but especially in the cases where migrants are disproportionately excluded from the social protection measures introduced by many governments to compensate for lost income, jeopardising their own livelihoods as well as those of their transnational family members. Interestingly, the COVID-19 pandemic has also led to new 'paradoxes in mobility control' (Lin and Yeoh, 2021, p. 97), where mobility regimes that might have previously existed along specific categories of class, gender and race have become upturned by a virus that does not discriminate along the same differentiated categories. As Lin and Yeoh (2021) point out, at the start of the pandemic, the highest risk of transmission was associated with the classes of people who would be normally deemed desirable (for example, businessmen and tourists), where the 'very groups once presumed to be "non-risky" turned out to be the root pathological source' (p. 101). The increasing unpredictability of borders over time could have important implications for future social formations, and the COVID-19 pandemic raises important questions about how transnational families in particular might regroup and strategise in times of crisis and uncertainty.

NOTE

1. Institutional time relates to 'policy and governance', biographic time relates to 'life events and imaginaries of pasts, presents and futures' and everyday time relates to the 'lived time' of migrants experiencing staggered migration trajectories (Robertson, 2019, p. 174, drawing from Meeus, 2012).

REFERENCES

Acedera, K.A. and Yeoh, B.S.A. (2019). 'Making time': Long-distance marriages and the temporalities of the transnational family. *Current Sociology Monograph*, 67(2), 250–272.

Amrith, M. (2020). The linear imagination, stalled: Changing temporal horizons in migrant journeys. *Global Networks*. DOI:10.1111/glob.12280.

Anderson, B. (2019). New directions in migration studies: Towards methodological de-nationalism. *Comparative Migration Studies*, 7(1), 1–13. https://doi.org/10.1186/s40878-019-0140-8.

Andersson, R. (2014). Time and the migrant other: European border controls and the temporal economics of illegality. *American Anthropologist*, 116, 795–809. https://doi-org.libproxy1.nus.edu.sg/10.1111/aman.12148.

Baas, M. and Yeoh, B.S.A. (2019). Introduction: Migration studies and critical temporalities. *Current Sociology Monograph*, 67(2): 161–168.

Baldassar, L., Baldock, C.V. and Wilding, R. (2007). *Families Caring across Borders: Migration, Ageing and Transnational Caregiving*. London: Palgrave Macmillan UK.

Baldassar, L. and Merla, L. (eds) (2014). *Transnational Families, Migration and the Circulation of Care: Understanding Mobility and Absence in Family Life*. New York: Routledge.

Baldassar, L. and Wilding, R. (2022). Transnationalism and care circulation: mobility, caregiving and the technologies that shape them. In Brenda S.A. Yeoh and Francis L. Collins (eds), *Handbook on Transnationalism*. Cheltenham, UK and Northampton, MA, USA: Edward Elgar Publishing, pp. 388–403.

Basch, L.G., Schiller, N.G. and Szanton Blanc, C. (1994). *Nations Unbound: Transnational Projects, Postcolonial Predicaments, and Deterritorialized Nation-States*. London, UK and New York, USA: Gordon & Breach.

Bauman, Z. (2002). *Society Under Siege*. Cambridge: Polity Press.

Benítez, J.L. (2012). Salvadoran transnational families: ICT and communication practices in the network society. *Journal of Ethnic and Migration Studies*, 38(9), 1439–1449. doi:10.1080/1369183X.2012.698214.

Boccagni, P. (2014). Caring about migrant care workers: From private obligations to transnational social welfare? *Critical Social Policy*, 34(2), 221–240. doi:10.1177/0261018313500867.

Bonizzoni, P. (2018). Policing the intimate borders of the nation: A review of recent trends in family-related forms of immigration control. In J. Mulholland, N. Montagna and E. Sanders-McDonagh (eds), *Gendering Nationalism: Intersections of Nation, Gender and Sexuality*. Cham: Springer International Publishing, pp. 223–237.

Boucher, A. and Gest, J. (2015). Migration studies at a crossroads: A critique of immigration regime typologies. *Migration Studies*, *3–2*, 182–198.
Boyce, G.A. (2020). Immigration, policing, and the politics of time. *Geography Compass*, 14, e12496. https://doi-org.libproxy1.nus.edu.sg/10.1111/gec3.12496.
Bryceson, D.F. (2019). Transnational families negotiating migration and care life cycles across nation-state borders. *Journal of Ethnic and Migration Studies*, *45*(16), 3042–3064. doi:10.1080/1369183X.2018.1547017.
Bryceson, D.F. and Vuorela, U. (2002). *The Transnational Family: New European Frontiers and Global Networks*. Abingdon, UK and New York, USA: Routledge.
Carciotto, S. (2018). The regularization of Zimbabwean migrants: A case of permanent temporariness. *African Human Mobility Review*, *4*(1), 1101–1116.
Carling, J. (2017). On conjunctures in transnational lives: Linear time, relative mobility and individual experience. In E. Mavroudi, B. Page and A. Christou (eds), *Timespace and International Migration*. Cheltenham, UK and Northampton, MA, USA: Edward Elgar Publishing, pp. 33–47.
Coe, C. (2016). Orchestrating care in time: Ghanaian migrant women, family, and reciprocity. *American Anthropologist*, *118*, 37–48. https://doi.org/10.1111/aman.12446.
Cole, J. and Durham, D.L. (2007). *Generations and Globalization: Youth, Age, and Family in the New World Economy*. Bloomington, IN: Indiana University Press.
Cunningham, H. and Heyman, J. (2004). Introduction: Mobilities and enclosures at borders. *Identities*, *11*(3), 289–302. DOI: 10.1080/10702890490493509.
Cwerner, S.B. (2001) The times of migration. *Journal of Ethnic and Migration Studies*, *27*(1), 7–36.
De Genova, N. (2014), Ethnography *in* Europe, or an anthropology *of* Europe? *Social Anthropology/Anthropologie Sociale*, *22*, 293–295. https://doi-org.libproxy1.nus.edu.sg/10.1111/1469-8676.12077.
De Silva, M. (2018). Making the emotional connection: Transnational eldercare circulation within Sri Lankan–Australian transnational families. *Gender, Place and Culture: A Journal of Feminist Geography*, *25*(1), 88–103. doi:10.1080/0966369X.2017.1339018.
Doyle, J. and Nathan, M. (2001). *Wherever Next: Work in a Mobile World*. London: Industrial Society.
Elder, G.H. (1998). The life course as developmental theory. *Child Development*, *69*(1), 1–12.
Faist, T. (2013). The mobility turn: A new paradigm for the social sciences? *Ethnic and Racial Studies*, *36*(11), 1637–1646. doi:10.1080/01419870.2013.812229.
Ghosh, B. (2000). *Managing Migration: Time for a New International Regime?* Oxford: Oxford University Press.
Glick-Schiller, N. (2018). Theorising transnational migration in our times: A multiscalar temporal perspective. *Nordic Journal of Migration Research*. doi:10.2478/njmr-2018-0032.
Glick-Schiller, N., Basch, L. and Blanc-Szanton, C. (1992). Transnationalism: A new analytic framework for understanding migration. *Annals of the New York Academy of Sciences*, *645*(1), 1–24. doi:10.1111/j.1749-6632.1992.tb33484.x.
Glick-Schiller, N. and Salazar, N.B. (2013). Regimes of mobility across the globe. *Journal of Ethnic and Migration Studies*, *39*(2), 183–200. https://doi.org/10.1080/1369183X.2013.723253.
Griffiths, M., Rogers, A. and Anderson, B. (2013). *Migration, Time and Temporalities: Review and Prospect*. COMPAS Research Resources Paper. Oxford: COMPAS.
Harrison, J.L. and Lloyd, S.E. (2012). Illegality at work: Deportability and the productive new era of immigration enforcement. *Antipode*, *44*(2), 365–385. doi:10.1111/j.1467-8330.2010.00841.x.
Hawthorne, L. (2005). 'Picking winners': The recent transformation of Australia's skilled migration policy. *International Migration Review*, *39*(3), 663–696. https://doi.org/10.1111/j.1747-7379.2005.tb00284.x.
Heimeshoff, L.-M., Hess, S., Kron, S., Schwenken, H. and Trzeciak, M. (eds) (2014). *Grenzregime II: Migration – Kontrolle – Wissen. Transnationale Perspektiven*. Berlin: Assoziation A.
Hess, S. (2012). De-naturalising transit migration. Theory and methods of an ethnographic regime analysis. *Population, Space, and Place*, *18*(4), 428–40.
Hess, S., Kasparek, B., Kron, S., Rodatz, M., Schwertl, M. and Sontowski, S. (eds) (2016). *Der lange Sommer der Migration: Grenzregime III*. Berlin: Assoziation A.
Heyman, J. (1995). Putting power in the anthropology of bureaucracy: The immigration and naturalization service at the Mexico–United States border. *Current Anthropology*, *36*(2), 261–287.

Heyman, J. (2009). Ports of entry in the 'homeland security' era: Inequality of mobility and the securitization of transnational flows. In S. Martinez (ed.), *International Migration and Human Rights: The Global Repercussions of U.S. Policy*. Berkeley, CA: University of California Press, pp. 44–59.

Horvath, K., Amelinaz, A. and Peters, K. (2017). Re-thinking the politics of migration. On the uses and challenges of regime perspectives for migration research. *Migration Studies*, 5(3), 301–314. https://doi.org/10.1093/migration/mnx055.

Hui, A. (2016). The boundaries of interdisciplinary fields: Temporalities shaping the past and future of dialogue between migration and mobilities research. *Mobilities*, 11(1), 66–82. DOI: 10.1080/17450101.2015.1097033.

Jandl, M. and Stacher, I. (eds) (2004). *Towards A Multilateral Migration Regime*. Special Anniversary Edition dedicated to Jonas Widgren. Vienna: International Centre for Migration Policy Development.

Kalir, B. and Wissink, L. (2016). The deportation continuum: Convergences between state agents and NGO workers in the dutch deportation field. *Citizenship Studies*, 20(1), 34–49. https://doi.org/10.1080/13621025.2015.1107025.

Khosravi, S. (2011). *'Illegal' Traveller: An Auto-Ethnography of Borders*. Basingstoke, UK and New York, USA: Palgrave Macmillan.

Kilkey, M. and Merla, L. (2014). Situating transnational families' care-giving arrangements: The role of institutional contexts. *Global Networks (Oxford)*, 14(2), 210–229.

Kilkey, M. and Palenga-Möllenbeck, E. (2016). Introduction: Family life in an age of migration and mobility: Introducing a global and family life-course perspective. In M. Kilkey and E. Palenga-Möllenbeck (eds), *Family Life in an Age of Migration and Mobility: Global Perspectives through the Life Course*. London: Palgrave Macmillan, pp. 1–18.

Kilkey, M. and Ryan, L. (2020). Unsettling events: Understanding migrants. responses to geopolitical transformative episodes through a life-course lens. *International Migration Review*. DOI: 10.1177/0197918320905507.

King, R. and Skeldon, R. (2010). Mind the gap! Integrating approaches to internal and international migration. *Journal of Ethnic and Migration Studies*, 36(10), 1619–1646.

Koslowski, R. (2008). Global mobility and the quest for an international migration regime. *Center for Migration Studies Special Issues*, 21, 103–143. https://doi.org/10.1111/j.2050-411X.2008.tb00395.x.

Koslowski, R. (2011). *Global Mobility Regimes*. Basingstoke: Palgrave Macmillan.

Krasner, S.D. (1982). Structural causes and regime consequences: Regimes as intervening variables. *International Organization*, 36, 85–205.

Krzyżowski, Ł. and Mucha, J. (2014). Transnational caregiving in turbulent times: Polish migrants in Iceland and their elderly parents in Poland. *International Sociology*, 29(1), 22–37. doi:10.1177/0268580913515287.

Lin, W. and Yeoh, B.S.A. (2021). Pathological (im)mobilities: Managing risk in a time of pandemics. *Mobilities*, 16(1), 96–112. doi:10.1080/17450101.2020.1862454.

Little, A. (2015). The complex temporality of borders: Contingency and normativity. *European Journal of Political Theory*, 14(4), 429–447. https://doi.org/10.1177/1474885115584831.

Martin, F. and Dragojlovic, A. (2019). Gender, mobility regimes, and social transformation in Asia. *Journal of Intercultural Studies*, 40(3), 275–286. doi:10.1080/07256868.2019.1599166.

Massa, A. (2020). Borders and boundaries as resources for mobility: Multiple regimes of mobility and incoherent trajectories on the Ethiopian–Eritrean border. *Geoforum*, 116, 262–271. doi:10.1016/j.geoforum.2018.01.007.

Massey, D.S., Durand, J. and Pren, K.A. (2015). Border enforcement and return migration by documented and undocumented Mexicans. *Journal of Ethnic and Migration Studies*, 41(7), 1015–1040.

Massey, D.S., Pren, K.A. and Durand, J. (2016). Why border enforcement backfired. *American Journal of Sociology*, 121(5), 1557–1600.

McDowell, L. (2008). Thinking through work: Complex inequalities, constructions of difference and trans-national migrants. *Progress in Human Geography*, 32(4), 491–507. https://doi.org/10.1177/0309132507088116.

Meeus, B. (2012) How to 'catch' floating populations? Research and the fixing of migration in space and time. *Ethnic and Racial Studies*, 35(10), 1775–1793.

Merla, L., Kilkey, M. and Baldassar, L. (2020a). Examining transnational care circulation trajectories within immobilizing regimes of migration: Implications for proximate care. *Journal of Family Research*, *32*(3), 514–536. https://doi.org/10.20377/jfr-351.

Merla, L., Kilkey, M. and Baldassar, L. (2020b). Introduction to the special issue 'Transnational care: Families confronting borders'. *Journal of Family Research*, *32*(3), 393–414. https://doi.org/10.20377/jfr-420.

Mezzadra, S. and Neilson, B. (2013). *Border as Method, or, the Multiplication of Labor*. Durham, NC: Duke University Press.

Nail, T. (2016). *Theory of the Border*. Oxford: Oxford University Press.

Nedelcu, M. and Wyss, M. (2016). 'Doing family' through ICT-mediated ordinary co-presence: Transnational communication practices of Romanian migrants in Switzerland. *Global Networks (Oxford)*, 16(2), 202–218. doi:10.1111/glob.12110.

Papadopoulos, D. and Tsianos, V. (2013). After citizenship: Autonomy of migration, organisational ontology and mobile commons. *Citizenship Studies*, *17*(2), 178–196.

Paul, A.M. (2017). *Multinational Maids: Stepwise Migration in a Global Labor Market*. Cambridge: Cambridge University Press. http://doi.org/10.1017/9781108120357.003.

Platt, M., Baey, G., Yeoh, B.S.A., Khoo, C.Y. and Lam, T. (2017). Debt, precarity and gender: Male and female temporary labour migrants in Singapore. *Journal of Ethnic and Migration Studies*, *43*(1), 119–136. doi:10.1080/1369183X.2016.1218756.

Radil, S.M., Pinos, J.C. and Ptak, T. (2020). Borders resurgent: Towards a post-Covid-19 global border regime? *Space and Polity*, *25*(1), 132–140. DOI: 10.1080/13562576.2020.1773254.

Robertson, S. (2019). Migrant, interrupted: The temporalities of 'staggered' migration from Asia to Australia. *Current Sociology*, *67*(2), 169–185.

Salazar, N.B. and Smart, A. (2011). Anthropological takes on (im)mobility. *Identities (Yverdon, Switzerland)*, *18*(6), i–ix. https://doi.org/10.1080/1070289X.2012.683674.

Sandberg, M. (2018). 'Dearest little wife': The gender work of Polish transnational families in past and present. Versita. doi:10.2478/njmr-2018-0029.

Schapendonk, J. and Steel, G. (2014). Following migrant trajectories: The im/mobility of sub-Saharan Africans en route to the European Union. *Annals of the Association of American Geographers*, *104*(2), 262–270. https://doi.org/10.1080/00045608.2013.862135.

Schapendonk, J., van Liempt, I., Schwarz, I. and Steel, G. (2018). Re-routing migration geographies: Migrants, trajectories and mobility regimes. *Geoforum*, *116*, 211–216. https://doi.org/10.1016/j.geoforum.2018.06.007.

Schling, H., Espinoza, M.V. and Datta, K. (2020, 22 April). Transformed privileges of im/mobility and COVID-19. *Im/mobility in Coronatimes Blog*. https://www.qmul.ac.uk/geog/research/immobility-in-coronatimes-blog/.

Schwarz, I. (2018). Migrants moving through mobility regimes: The trajectory approach as a tool to reveal migratory processes. *Geoforum*, *116*, 217–225. https://doi.org/10.1016/j.geoforum.2018.03.007.

Shamir, R. (2005). Without borders? Notes on globalization as a mobility regime. *Sociological Theory*, *23*(2), 197–217. https://doi.org/10.1111/j.0735-2751.2005.00250.x.

Sheller, M. (2011), Cosmopolitanism and mobilities. In M. Nowicka and M. Rovisco (eds), *The Ashgate Research Companion to Cosmopolitanism*. Aldershot: Ashgate, pp. 344–361.

Sheller, M. and Urry, J. (2006). The new mobilities paradigm. *Environment and Planning. A*, *38*(2), 207–226. https://doi.org/10.1068/a37268.

Silvey, R. and Parreñas, R. (2019). Precarity chains: Cycles of domestic worker migration from Southeast Asia to the Middle East. *Journal of Ethnic and Migration Studies*, 1–15. doi:10.1080/1369183x.2019.1592398.

Sinanan, J. and Horst, H.A. (2022). Communications technologies and transnational networks. In Brenda S.A. Yeoh and Francis L. Collins (eds), *Handbook on Transnationalism*. Cheltenham, UK and Northampton, MA, USA: Edward Elgar Publishing, pp. 371–387.

Singer, A. and Massey, D.S. (1998). The social process of undocumented border crossing among Mexican migrants. *International Migration Review*, *32*(3), 561–592.

Skrbiš, Z. (2008). Transnational families: Theorising migration, emotions and belonging. *Journal of Intercultural Studies*, *29*(3), 231–246. https://doi.org/10.1080/07256860802169188.

Tazzioli, M. (2018). The temporal borders of asylum. Temporality of control in the EU border regime. *Political Geography*, *64*, 13–22.
Torpey, J. (1999). *The Invention of the Passport: Surveillance, Citizenship, and the State*. Cambridge: Cambridge University Press. doi:10.1017/CBO9780511520990.
Trask, B. (2010). *Globalization and Families: Accelerated Systemic Social Change*. New York: Springer. doi:10.1007/978-0-387-88285-7.
Tsianos, V. (2010). Transnational migration and the emergence of the European border: An ethnographic analysis. *European Journal of Social Theory*, *13*, 373–387.
Turner, B.S. (2007). The enclave society: Towards a sociology of immobility. *European Journal of Social Theory*, *10*(2), 287–304. https://doi.org/10.1177/1368431007077807.
Urry, J. (2000). *Sociology Beyond Societies: Mobilities for the Twenty-first Century*. London: Routledge.
Valentine, G. (2008). The ties that bind: Towards geographies of intimacy. *Geography Compass*, *2*(6), 2097–2110. doi:10.1111/j.1749-8198.2008.00158.x.
Wall, K. and Bolzman, C. (2014). Mapping the new plurality of transnational families: A life course perspective. In L. Baldassar and L. Merla (eds). *Transnational Families, Migration and the Circulation of Care: Understanding Mobility and Absence in Family Life*. New York: Routledge, pp. 61–77.
Waters, J.L. (2011). Time and transnationalism: A longitudinal study of immigration, endurance and settlement in Canada. *Journal of Ethnic and Migration Studies*, *37*(7), 1119–1135.
Wilson, C. (2000). Policy regimes and policy change. *Journal of Public Policy*, *20*(3), 247–274. Retrieved 14 July 2021 from http://www.jstor.org/stable/4007691.
Wilson Janssens, M.C. (2020). Spatial mobility and social becoming: The journeys of four Central African students in Congo-Kinshasa. *Geoforum*, 116. doi:10.1016/j.geoforum.2018.05.018.
Winters, N. (2020). Beyond the bird in the cage? Translocal embodiment and trajectories of Nicaraguan female migrants in Seville, Spain. *Geoforum*. https://doi.org/10.1016/j.geoforum.2018.05.019.
Wissink, M., Düvell, F. and Mazzucato, V. (2020). The evolution of migration trajectories of sub-Saharan African migrants in Turkey and Greece: The role of changing social networks and critical events. *Geoforum*, *116*, 282–291.
Yeoh, B.S.A., Baey, G., Platt, M. and Wee, K. (2017). Bangladeshi construction workers and the politics of (im)mobility in Singapore. *City (London, England)*, *21*(5), 641–649. doi:10.1080/13604813.2017.1374786.
Yeoh, B.S.A. and Collins, F.L. (eds) (2022). Introduction to the *Handbook on Transnationalism*. In Brenda S.A. Yeoh and Francis L. Collins (eds), *Handbook on Transnationalism*. Cheltenham, UK and Northampton, MA, USA: Edward Elgar Publishing, pp. 1–29.
Yeoh, B.S.A., Huang, S. and Lam, T. (2005). Transnationalizing the 'Asian' family: Imaginaries, intimacies and strategic intents. *Global Networks (Oxford)*, *5*(4), 307–315. doi:10.1111/j.1471-0374.2005.00121.x.
Yeoh, B.S.A. and Lam, T. (2012). Migration and DiverseCity: Singapore's changing demography, identity and landscape. In D.W. Haines, K. Yamanaka and S. Yamashita (eds), *Wind over Water: Rethinking Migration in an East Asian Context*. New York: Berghahn, pp. 60–77.
Yeoh, B.S.A., Somaiah, B.C., Lam, T. and Acedera, K.F. (2020). Doing family in 'times of migration': Care temporalities and gender politics in Southeast Asia. *Annals of the American Association of Geographers*, *110*(6), 1709–1725. doi:10.1080/24694452.2020.1723397.

Index

Đổi mới 72, 73, 74

Abelmann, N. 206
Abotsi, E. 210
Abrego, L.J. 243
'abuse-tolerant and privacy-affirmative perspectives' 243
'abuse tolerant-intolerant continuum' 243
academic achievement 203
academic conceptualisation 155
academic mobility 9
academic mobility and the family 9, 249, 257, 258
    explanatory factor for 250, 251, 252, 253
    gendered roles and 254, 255, 256, 257
    impact of 253, 254
    mapping the study field 249, 250
accommodation arrangements 190
Acedera, K.A. 301, 303, 304, 308, 310, 355, 356
Ackers, L. 104, 105, 219, 256
'actually existing' capitalism 319
Adams, M. 112, 114
affordable public daycare 20
afooshaas 62
African-Caribbean diasporic families 122
Agbenyega, J. 112
age and intergenerational relationships 7, 8
ageing parents 253
age-old patriarchal ideology 141
Aggleton, P. 110
Agrawal, S.K. 294
agricultural community 139
Ahlstedt, S. 277, 278
Al-Ali, N. 54
Alberts, H.C. 253
Al-Hindi, M. 239
All China Women's Federation 335
Allsopp, J. 186, 190
Al-Sharmani, M. 55, 59
Amarasingam, A. 57
Amber, Neil 6
'ambient co-presence' 4
'ambient intimacy' 89
Amnesty International 58
Amrith, M. 305
Anh, Nguyen Tuan 140
Anthias 109

Antia, K. 337, 338
anti-immigration politics 273
anti-LGBGT immigration policies 278
anti-Tamil pogroms 56
anti-Tamil violence 58
Anving, Terese 6
arranged marriages 41
Arthur, N. 252
Article 8 of the European Convention on Human Rights 187
'ascendancy of whiteness' 272
Asian labour migration 88
Asian masculinities 68
Asian transnational labor migration 144
Asis, M.M.B. 339
Assam tea plantations 170, 172, 174, 178, 180
    political economy of 173, 174, 175, 176, 177
astronaut families 106, 254
asylum claims 185
asylum process 185
asylum regimes 195, 276
asylum seekers 291
asylum system 184, 188, 193
au pair market 25
au pair schemes 16, 17, 19, 20, 28
    and 'family-like' care in the UK 21, 22, 23, 24, 25
    and nannies 'doing family' in Sweden 25, 26, 27, 28
Australian immigration policies 271
auto-ethnography 353
Avila, E. 54, 55

Baas, M. 311
Bailey, A. 220
Baldassar, L. 159, 160, 207, 357
Bankston III, Carl L. 146
Basch, L. 3
Basford, S. 255
Bauman, Z. 84, 85, 95
Beck-Gernsheim, E. 36, 84, 85, 86, 95
Beck, U. 84, 85, 86, 95
Beech, S.E.
    The Geographies of International Student Mobility 200
Behrendt, M. 188, 190, 194
Beijing Platform for Action 233

"being family" 137
Bélanger, D. 34, 35, 46
Belloni, M. 187, 189
Benson, M.L. 236
Bernstein, H. 174
Bex, C. 193, 194
Bhuyan, R. 42
bilateral kinship system 71
bi-national couples 268
bi-national marriage 278
bi-national same-sex couples, UK visa regimes for 274, 275
bi-national same-sex family formations
   heteronormative ideal and same-sex family formations 268, 269, 270
   heteronormative ideals and the 'genuine' relationship 275, 276
   immigration possibilities for same-sex couples in the UK 273, 274
   insights from queer migration scholarship 271, 272, 273
   push factors in same-sex family migration 277, 278, 279
   queer exclusion in immigration regimes 279
   states and the discriminatory exception in immigration 270
   UK visa regimes for bi-national same-sex couples 274, 275
bi-national same-sex migration 279
bi-national same-sex partners 268
bi-national same-sex partnerships 10, 265
bi-national same-sex relationships 278
biographic transitions and family events 304
biopolitical governance 39
biosocial profiling technology 352
'birth tourism' 210
Black-American women 19
Block, L. 37
Blunt, A. 305, 306, 308, 309
Boccagni, Paolo 207, 301
Bojarczuk, S. 157
"bordered identities" 353
border enforcement 34
border surveillance systems 352
Börjesson, U. 189, 193
Botswana 136
Boucher, A. 351
Bourdieu, P. 105, 106, 120, 202, 203, 251
Boyd, M. 157
Brazilian migrant project 233, 236, 238
Brazilian migrant research 243
Brazilian migrant study 243
Brexit transition period 186
Brickell, K. 307
British Au Pairs Agencies Association

(BAPAA) 17
British colonial rule 174
British labour market 155
British migration regime 87
broader political–economic system 249
Brooks, R. 251
Browne, K. 268
Bryant, John 146
Bryceson, D.F. 354
Büchele, J. 221
'bureaucratic abuse' 238
business immigration programs 2
Butler, J, 269

Cabalquinto, Earvin Charles 7
'the cage' 56
Cairns, D. 127
Calderón-Jaramillo, M. 241
Call, Maia A. 138
Canada's Immigration and Refugee Protection Act 39
Canadian family migration 42
Canadian immigration policies 40, 42, 44, 45, 267
Cangià, F. 219, 221, 226
capital accumulation 201, 204, 206, 209, 251, 253
   educational migration as 202, 203, 204, 205, 206
   privileged migration and 203, 204
   strategies 206
   through global mobility 105, 106, 107, 108
capital acquisition, conversion, and transfers 108, 109
capital and transnational (im)mobility 110
care arrangement 160
care circulation 357
Care for children in an era of private market services: A study of nannies, children and parents 17
care labour 289
care regimes 19, 21
'care temporalities' 304
care workers, international movement of 16
   career immobility 226
caregiving arrangement 148
'cash-for-care' system 21
cash remuneration 181
cash-strapped rural households 71
CBS 211
Cebotari, Victor 343
Celtic Tiger economic boom period 125, 126
central public responsibility 25
chain migration 122, 286
Chamberlain, M. 122

Index 367

Chan, Kam Wing 145
channel transnational migration 88
Chant, Sylvia 141
Charsley, K. 35
Chase, E. 186, 188, 190
Chauvin, S. 268, 276
Chávez, K.R. 269, 279
Chee, W.C. 210, 211
Chen, Chen 140, 141, 143, 145
Chen, Chuanbo 140
Cherlin, A.J. 84, 85, 95
Cheung, A.C.K. 253
Child Health and Migrant Parents in Southeast Asia (CHAMPSEA) 340, 341, 342, 343
child welfare services 192
child welfare systems 185
childcare arrangements 76
'childcare crisis' 22
childcare regimes 18, 20, 28
child-centred creative arts 113
childhood/family migration 124
childhood left-behind experience 145
childhood mobility experiences 102
childhood socialisation 78
children, impacts on 145, 146
'chilling effect' 243
China migration 146
Chinese circular migrants 139
Chinese immigrant families in Canada 303
Chinese labour market 254
Chinese-related cultural capital 110
Chinese student mobility 251
Chinese-Western intermarriage 93
Choi, S.Y. 69, 78, 143
"chosen family" 279
Choudaha, R. 250
circular migrants 139
circular migration 137, 138, 139, 140
circumvent immigration rules 43
cisheteronormativity kinship 267
civic awareness and engagement 61
Civil Partnership Bill 273
civil partnership rights 278
Clayton, Sue 8
Coe, Cati 356
co-ethnic communities 298
co-ethnic immigrant communities 278
Cole, J. 354
collective childcare 23
collective forms of care 22
'collective obligation to family' 188
collective welfare and unity 354
Collins, F.L. 202, 204, 249
'coloniality of gender' 242
commodification 35

'commodification of intimacy' 35
communication technologies 92
communicative asymmetries 94
'commuter migration' 155
conditional permanent residence (CPR) 37, 42
    governance 39, 40, 43
Confucian ideologies of social order 71
Confucian worldview of social harmony 71
conjugal and parental relationships 288
'conjugal unions' 267
Connell, R.W. 69
Conradson, D. 218
Constable, N. 35, 239, 341
contemporary mobility 11
contemporary transnational family practices 154
contemporary transnational households 1
'contingent temporality' 310
Convention on the Rights of the Child 334
conventional familial arrangements 70, 143
Cooke, F.L. 256
Cooke, Thomas J. 141
corporate expatriates 217, 225, 226, 227
    experiences 227
    family 218, 221, 227
    family migration 221
    migration 217, 220, 222
corporate expatriation 217, 218, 219, 221, 227
'cosmopolitan capital' 106
'cosmopolitan' competencies 203
cosmopolitan traits 203
cosmopolitanism 109, 227
Cox, Rosie 6
Cranston, Sophie 9
credentialisation 203
Crenshaw, K. 234
'crisis of masculinity' 68
cross-border intimate communication 90
cross-border marriages 43, 275
    migration 38
cross-border mobility 106
cross-border schooling 210
'cross-cultural kids' (CCK) 103
crucial economic contributions 72
cultural and religious community 36
cultural and social practices 35
cultural attitudes 21
cultural capital 105, 106, 107, 110, 123, 129, 203, 212, 223, 226, 227
cultural care norms 163
'cultural chameleons' 107
cultural conflict 121
cultural exchange scheme 20
cultural marriage traditions 46
'culturally specific abuse' 233
"culture of migration" 338, 342

cutting-edge scholarship 5
Cwerner, S.B. 302, 305, 355

'daddy quotas' 20, 29
Dahinden, J. 158
Dahlquist, L. 188
D'Aoust, A.M. 36, 37, 39, 40
Darmody, M. 252
daycare institutions 26
decision-making process 43, 45, 104, 226
'deep-rooted social institution' 1, 202
de facto households 77
Defence of Marriage Act (DOMA) 277, 278
De Graeve, K. 193, 194
degree of violence 236
denationalisation policies 88
'dependent applicant' 44
dependent immigrants 3
'dependents' 1
De Tona, C. 123
de Winter, T. 253
diaspora families 57
diaspora-generated transnational families 56
"diaspora geopolitics" 51
diasporic communities 60, 123
diasporic family narratives 123
Dick, Eva 139
differential digital literacy 94
differential technological accesses and competencies 90
digital colonisation 96
digital communications media 7
digital communication technologies 89, 90
digital connectivity 95
digital devices 91
digital media 4, 89, 91, 94
digital platforms 92
digital ruptures 90, 91, 92
digital technologies 92
digitalisation and mediation of transnational intimacy 89, 90
digitally mediated familial intimacy 92
digitally mediated transnational familial intimacy 92
direct gender-based violence 241
direct gendered violence 240
'distributed geography' 56
Dito, Bilisuma B. 343
diversity 109
divorce 41
Dixon, P. 107
'doing family' 17, 19, 148, 191, 310, 349
doings of care 27
domestic labour market 254
domestic objects and home-making practices 306, 307, 308
domestic 'private' sphere 56
domestic services 21, 25
    in Sweden 25
domestic temporalities 302
domestic violence 40
domestic violence among international migrant women 232, 233, 234, 235, 244
    diversities of 236, 237, 238, 239, 240
    drivers of 240, 241, 242
    prevalence of 235, 236
    reporting 242, 243
domestic workers 16, 19, 21, 28
    in Nordic countries, re-emergence of 20, 21
    international movement of 16
dominant neoliberal policy 42
Doná, G. 122
Dorrit, Posel 139, 146
double income middle-class families 21
Douglass' concept of 'householding' 136, 172
Douglass, Michael 136, 144
'downward' class mobility experiences 257
Drammeh, L. 191
dual-career households 227
dual-career management 256
dual-career mobility 256
dual-career trajectory 256
'dual carer' ideal 27
dual-earner families 141
'dual-frame of reference' 320, 323
Dublin III regulation 186
Duchêne-Lacroix, Cédric 139
Duggan (2003) 272
Dumitru, S. 341
Durham, D.L. 354
Dutch culture 191

East Asian migration 212
economic accumulation 46
economic capital 55, 203
'economic migrants' 2
economic mobility 88
'economic' towards migration 3
economic transactions 35
economic transnationalism 63
Education mobilities of children 253
education system 171
educational migration, families in 9, 200, 212, 213
    as capital accumulation 202, 203, 204, 205, 206
    capital accumulation 205
    emotional transnational geographies and educational migration 207, 208, 209, 210, 211, 212

intellectual context and overview of debates 201, 202
educational scholarship 200
egalitarian gendered division of labour 76
Eide, K. 184, 190
Eldén, Sara 6
Elder, G.H. 356
'elite migrants' 9
Elliott, A. 90
emigrant women 35
emotional and physical labour 55
emotional attachment and obligation 190
emotional burden of educational migration 210, 211
emotional care labour 289
emotional estrangement 111
emotional fragility and weight of familial expectations 208, 209
emotional lives of transnational kinship 59, 60, 61
emotional/psychological violence 235
emotional transnational geographies 207, 208, 209, 210, 211, 212
emotional wellbeing 195
emotions and care work 209, 210
employment or career mobility 2
employment regimes 18
'enfolded mobilities' 119
equal immigration rights for same sex couples 273
Erez, E. 243
Eritrean migrants in Ethiopia 187
Esping-Andersen, G. 18, 20, 28
Ethiopian regime 58
ethnic identities 121
ethnomorality framework 161
ethnomorality of care 159, 160
    framework 160, 165
ethnonational group 58
ethnonational identity 60
ethnonational kinship 54, 56, 57, 58, 59, 60, 61, 62, 63, 64
EU enlargement 155
EU Reception Directive 187
EU referendum 162
European Agreement on Au Pair placement 29
European agreement on free movement of labour 25
European Dublin III regulation (Regulation (EU) No. 604/2013) 186
European food production 320
European horticulture, low-wage migrant labour in 320
expatriate and globally mobile children 103, 104, 105

expatriate family 223
expatriate migration 227
    family and 218, 219, 220
expatriate mobility 220
expensive transnational marriages 54
exploitative labour processes 241
Ezaki, M. 73

faaltu labour 174
Faier, L. 35
familial adjustments 340
familial business activities 204
familial capital accumulation 105, 107, 110
familial capital/mobility projects 103
familial cultural capital 122
familial global mobility project 105, 108, 112
    capital acquisition, conversion, and transfers 108, 109
    capital and transnational (im)mobility 110
    unintended consequences and human cost 111
familial intimacy 84, 85, 87, 88, 91
    transformation of 86, 95, 96
    transnationalisation of 7
familial investment 202
familial migration 127
    decision-making process 105, 112
familial migratory decision-making 105
familial mobility
    project 113
familial mobility capital 105, 106
familial mobility project 111, 112, 113
familial mobility projects 109, 113
familial responsibilities 93
familial reunification 286, 297
familial separation 288
    on children 290
familial social mobility 208, 258
familial social roles 208
familial socialisation 202
families and households in migration research 136, 137
family and care issues, emergence of 155, 156
family class immigrants 43
family decision-making 71
family displacement 188
family expatriation 105
family finances 23
family formation 45, 46
    and reunification 34, 45
    migration 36
'family household' 308
family imaginary 90
family immigration 42
    policy 43

rules, change in 43
family in law, role of 185, 186, 187
family, intergenerational dynamics and social reproduction 120, 121
family-led transnational mobility 102
'family-like' relationship 17, 191, 195
'family-mediated migration infrastructure' 209
family memories, role of 121
family migrants 34
  households 10
family migration 2, 33, 34, 36, 42, 46, 105, 286
  arrangement 254
  benefits of 37
  decision-making 219
  pattern 156
  policies 33
  processes 236
  projects 8
  rules 37
  strategies 41, 159
family migration in Europe 33
family regimes 200
family relationships
  unaccompanied child migrants and 184
family reputation 233
family reunification 10, 33, 41, 42, 46, 154, 164, 187, 190, 195, 286, 287, 290, 291, 292, 293, 294, 295, 296, 297, 356
  policies 195
family reunification policy 269
family-reunion strategies 155
family sacrifice and transnational arbitrage 324, 325
family separation 288
family socioeconomic status 252
family sponsorship requirements 291
family strategies 206
family structures policy 288
family violence 236
'family wage' 19
family's capital accumulation 107
Fan, C. Cindy 8, 139, 140, 141, 142, 143, 145
Fassin, E. 273, 276, 278
father–child relationships 254
"fear of diversity" 352
Fellmeth, Gracia 339
female contract workers, rate of 70
female genital mutilation (FGM) 189
female internal migration 69
female labour force participation 72, 76
female labour migrants 79
  independent 73
  Vietnamese 71
female labour migration 69, 71, 73, 74, 75, 76, 77, 78, 79, 143

female migration 70
  for families 159
female-primary mobility 256
female rural-urban migrants 143
femicides 233, 239, 241
feminine attributes 72
femininity 69, 79
feminisation of labour migration in post-reform Vietnam 69, 70, 71
feminised migration 70
'feminised onward precarity' 241
feminist approaches 3, 4, 5
feminist framework 136
feminist scholarship 3
feminization of labor migration 142, 148
feminized labour migration 311
feminized neo-colonialism 288
Filipino culture 296
Filipino migrant youth 294
financial capital 276
financial dependency 277
financial remittances and gifts 288
financial wellbeing of the household 295
Finch (2007) 191
Finch typology 159
Findlay, A.M. 250, 255
Finnis, Elizabeth 139
Finn, M. 252
first-generation immigrants 146
first-generation migrants 146
Flemish foster families 192
Fletcher, Claire 9
Flexible Citizenship (Ong) 253
flexible masculinities 73, 74, 75, 76
Flynn, A. 34, 35, 46
Fong, V. 204, 205
forced labour 240
forced migration 51
forced migration scholarship 275
'foreign brides' 1
'Foreign Direct Investment sector' 69
formal care systems 194
'forms of capital' 202
Forsberg, H. 194
foster families 190, 191, 192
fraudulent marriages 43
'freedom of choice' 17, 21, 26
freedom of movements 154, 155, 163, 164
Fresnoza-Flot, A. 295

Gaetano, Arianne M. 142
gang violence 241
Gavanas, Anna 18
Ge, Yan 336
Geddie, K. 208, 209

gender
  and intergenerational inequalities 289
  based inequalities 35
  differences in Punjab 45
  division of labor 143, 144
  equal family 17
  equality 21, 25, 26, 28
  gap 45
  ideologies, entrenchment of 136, 143
  ideology 136, 143
  inequalities in academic mobility 257
  politics 3
  relations 18, 54, 55, 170
  relations and subjectivities 6, 7
  roles 170
    in immigration decision making 46
    within the household 74
  segregated labour market 69
  selectivity of migration 141, 142
  split households and 141, 142, 143, 144
  subjectivities 54, 55
gender-based violence 72, 233, 234, 236, 240, 241, 242, 243
'gender-blind' discussions of migration 1
'gender doings' of stay-behind men 78
'gender equality' 28
gender (in)equality
  au pair schemes
  and 'family-like' care in the UK 21, 22, 23, 24, 25
  and nannies 'doing family' in Sweden 25, 26, 27, 28
  conceptualising regimes of care and family 17, 18, 19, 20, 21
gendered care duties 55
gendered caring practices 158
gendered decision-making process 255
gendered division of labour 73, 74, 75, 76
gendered dynamics of transnational family relations 54, 55, 56
'gendered geographies of power' 34
gendered governmentality 34
gendered power inequalities 234
gendered productions of pain and suffering 63
gendered roles
  academic mobility and 254, 255, 256, 257
'gendered translocal householding' practice 75
gendered transnational cultural practices 7
gendered violence 234, 236
generationed political economy 8, 174, 180
generationed political economy of plantation 176
The Geographies of International Student Mobility (Beech, S. E.) 200
geopolitical episodes 162
German labour market 257

German School Leavers Survey 251
Gest, J. 351
Ghosh, B. 351
Gibson, Mhairi 140
Giddens, A. 84, 85, 86, 94, 95
Gill, B. 256
Glick-Schiller, N. 87, 352, 359
'global apartheid' 266
global capitalism 88
global capitalist economy 35
'global care chain' 93
global economic competitiveness 42
'global householding' 136
global job market 107
global labour and education mobilities 88
global mobilities 107, 108
  and digitalisation 84
  and transnationalism 95
  capital accumulation through 105, 106, 107, 108
  of family members 85
  parent-led project of 110
'global mobility divide' 266, 276
Global North multilocality 139
global seafarer labor market 142
'global spatial hypergamy' 239
'good manhood' 71
'good parenting' 27, 28
Grabska, K. 54
Grace, B.L. 53, 54
'graduate mobility habitus' 127
Graham, E. 144, 343
guardianship schemes 193
Gulf Cooperation Countries (GCC) 142
Gupta, Anna 8
Gurmu, Eshetu 140

Hall, Katharine 139, 146
Hao, Y. 9, 256
'happy family' discourse 74
Harrison, J.L. 357
Hart, J. 173
Hayden, M. 107
Hazen, H.D. 253
hegemonic breadwinner ideal 71
hegemonic cultural ideals 123
hegemonic heteronormativity 94
hegemonic masculinities 69, 78, 242
  values 79
Herz, M. 194
heterogeneity 109
heteronormative conceptions of family 279
heteronormative conceptualisations of family 268
heteronormative family ideal 268, 269
heteronormative framing 93, 279

heteronormative ideals 266, 267
    and same-sex family formations 268, 269, 270
    and the 'genuine' relationship 275, 276
heteronormativity 266, 268, 269
    within immigration regimes 271
heterosexism 233
heterosexual couples 275
heterosexual family 269
heterosexual ideal 265
heterosexuality/homosexuality 269
heterosexual marriage 239
heterosexual nuclear family 269
Heyman, J. 353
Hill, M. 188
Ho, E.L. 204
Ho, E.S. 250
Ho, K.C. 204
hộ khẩu 138
Hoang, Kimberly Kay 68
Hoang, Lan Anh 7, 144
home-based care 24
homecare workers 16
homo economicus 2, 218, 324
homonational embodiments 272
homonationalism 272
Hondagneu-Sotelo, P. 54, 55
'honour-based violence' 233, 238
'honour' killings 238
Hopkins, P. 188
horticulture industry 320
Horton, P. 69
hostile asylum policies 268
household arrangements 135, 139, 141, 147, 148
household consumption 320
household decision-making processes 72, 76
household divisions of labor 136
household incomes 75
household labour 288
household livelihood strategies 140
household registration instruments 138
household registration system 138
household responsibilities 289, 294
household scale 55, 56
'household strategy' 212
household's sustenance 72
householding 136, 148
Hu, Yang 7, 93
Huang, S. 107, 251, 254
Hugo, Graeme 138
Huijsmans, R. 8, 171
hukou system 145, 147, 213
'human capital' approaches 2, 5
human capital development 200
human capital perspectives 2

human rights abuses 58
human rights atrocities 58
human trafficking 174
    discourse 176
Humphris, R. 194
Hutchins, T. 105, 112
Hyndman, Jennifer 6, 7, 56, 57
hypermasculine behaviours 78
hypermasculinity 76, 77, 78
hyper-masculinized occupations 289
hypermobility 110

ideal educational mobility 251
idealized national community 46
imaginaries of home, migration and family life 309, 310
immigrant families 42
immigrant groups 36
immigrant labour 41
immigrant service providers 44
immigrant status 44
immigrant women 44
immigrant youth 124
immigration 277
    and regulations 38
    and rules 273
        meso-scale temporalities of 307
        meso-temporalities of 303
    and welfare policies 187
    decision making, gender roles in 46
    enforcement 243
    governance of marriage migration 46
    governance processes 46
    in Canada 42
    in the Global North 279
    laws 190, 240, 242
    laws and policies 6, 356
    of countries 45
    policies 6, 7, 34, 36, 38, 41, 44, 46, 266, 268, 271, 276, 355, 356, 357
    possibilities for same-sex couples in the UK 273, 274, 280
    process, financial requirements within 277
    queer exclusion in 279
    regimes 10, 280, 301, 303, 309
    rules 265
        and policies 266
        same-sex partners in 265
    states and discriminatory exception in 270
    system 39, 236
    systems 125
Immigration and Nationality Act 1965 146
immigration regimes 358
immobility 110
    mobility and 120

im/mobility dispositions and narratives 127, 128, 129, 130
'immobility regimes' 349, 351
'incomplete migration' 155
independent female labour migrants 73
Indian popular culture 178
indirect gendered violence 240
individual host families 23
individual migrations 119
individualisation thesis 85
influential theory 136
informal reporting or disclosure 242
information and communication technologies (ICTs) 349, 357, 358
'infrastructural violence' 243
Innes, A. J. 39
insecure immigration status 243
Institute for Public Policy Research (IPPR) 155
Institute for Social Development Studies 77
institutional migration regimes 304
institutional racism 244
institutionalised heterosexuality 269
intellectual context and overview of debates 201, 202
'intelligible intimacy' 271
intense emotional mobilisation 94
intentional transnational formation of household 54
'intentional unpredictability' 155
intergenerational capital accumulation 113
intergenerational care relationships 358
inter-generational care strategies 305
intergenerational family 122
intergenerational migration dynamics 130
intergenerational mobility aspirations 108
intergenerational negotiation 212
intergenerational negotiations 121
intergenerational social reproduction 8, 102
  and mobility 103, 105, 108, 109
intergenerational tensions 121
intergenerationality 7
  in migrant families 123
internal labour migrants 334
internal migrants 146
internal migration, research on 146
international community 58
International Convention on the Protection of the Rights of All Migrant Workers 10, 286
International Dialogue on Migration 170
international education 251, 252
  market 250
international family formation 37
international female labour migration 74
international human resource management 217, 225

international human rights 273
  organizations 58
international labour market 254
International Labour Organisation (ILO) 16
international law 244
international marriage 35
  migration 40, 41, 42, 43, 44, 45
international migrant women, domestic violence among 232, 233, 234, 235
  diversities of 236, 237, 238, 239, 240
  drivers of 240, 241, 242
  prevalence of 235, 236
  reporting 242, 243
international migration 6, 34, 35, 36, 46, 146, 184, 266
  and developments 33
  and globalization 45
  on left-behind children 341
'international migration regime' 351
'international mindedness' 106
international mobility 212
International Organisation for Migration (IOM) 170
international parental migration 339
international schooling 110, 113
international schools and boarding schools 106
international student migration 212
international student mobility (ISM) 203, 204, 209, 250, 251
International Telecommunication Union 91
interpenetration of mobility regimes 95
interrupted transnational intimacy 90, 91, 92
intersectional violence 45
interurban and intraurban population movements 136
intimate family relationships 84, 86
'intimate femicide' 233
intimate gendered governmentality, new forms of 39, 40
intimate partner violence 236, 237
intra-familial tensions 288
intra-family relationships 144
intra-household dynamics 135, 143, 148
'involuntary immobility' 173
Irish child return migrants 108, 110
Irish diasporic cultural activities 128
Irish diasporic networks 126
Irish migration 127
Irish return-migrant parents 125
Irish transnational families 125, 127

Jacka, Tamara 141
James, A. 120, 121
James-Hawkins, L. 72
Jamieson, L. 85

Jayadeva, S. 205
Jesus Rafi, A. 277
'jigsaw puzzle' 27
    of family life 27
    of life 27, 29
joint decision making 77
Jöns, H. 255, 256
Jónsson, G. 173
Jordan, L.P. 343
Judge, Cheung 209
Junge, Vera 140

Kandel, W. 127
Kang, J. 206
Kapur, S. 239
Kauko, O. 194
Kazemipur, A. 295
Kedzierski, M. 250
Kelly, M. 128
Kenney, Jason 39
Kent Intake Unit (KIU) 191
Kenyan refugee camps 54
Khanh, Ha Thi Van 143
Khosravi, S. 353
Kikon, Rhondeni 8
Kilkey, M. 159, 162, 304, 355
Kim, J. 107
Kim, M. 242
King, R. 212, 252, 255, 352
kinship-based social networks 71
kinship care, transnational practices of 64
kirogi kajok 106
Kloc-Nowak, Weronika 8, 165
'knowledge mobility' 204
Kofman, Eleonore 142
Koh, Sin Yee 8
Kollman, K. 279
Korean language competency 37
Korean Nationality Act 37
Kõu, Anu 140, 144, 145
Kringelbach 254
Kuzhabekova, A. 250, 256
Kwon, J. 108
Kyle, D. 93

labour circulation and the separation of work and family life 322, 323
labour discrimination 241
labour export policies 16
labour force 20, 76, 294
labour market 2, 25, 38, 44, 68, 125, 141, 171, 172, 205, 232, 240, 295, 354
    marginalisation 125
labour migrant parents 334
labour migrants 54
labour migration 33, 52, 69, 70, 76, 88, 93, 137, 289, 320, 334
    feminization of 142, 148, 301
    theory 136, 148
labour migration in Europe 33
labour migration laws 26
labour regime 174, 180
labour relations 68
Lahaie, Claudia 146
laissez-faire approach to employment 18
Lalander, P. 194
Lam, Theodora 11, 143, 342
Lareau, A.
    Unequal childhoods 202
'late modernity' 95
Latham, A. 218
Latin American migrant families 125
Latin American migrants 241
Lauko and Forsberg (2018) 190
"laws of migration" 136
Lawson, Victoria A. 136
Lee (2013) 269
Lee, Everett 136, 137
Lee, J.T. 250, 256
left-behind children 144, 145, 146, 148, 333, 341, 342
    analysing secondary data 338, 339
    challenges in research 334, 335, 336
    existing research on 336, 337
    primary qualitative and mixed-methods research 339, 340, 341
    quantitative research 337, 338
    research scholarship on 342
left-behind families 340
left-behind husbands 143
left-behind wives 148
legal migration 266
'legal violence' 243
lesbian, gay, bisexual, transgender, and queer (LGBTQ) 94
    families 94
    people 94
    transnational families 93
lesbian, gay, bisexual, transgender, queer and intersex (LGBTQI) 268, 271, 279
    categories 268
    couples 274
    families 12
    identities 266
    individuals 275
    migrants 10
    people 265, 266, 267, 274, 275, 277, 278, 279
    politics 265
    rights 272
less-advantaged families and educational migra-

tion 204, 205
Leung, M.W.H. 9, 257
Levitt, P. 53, 122
Ley, D. 2
Li, Tianjiao 139
liberal national community 37
Liberation Tigers of Tamils Eelam (LTTE) 56, 57, 58
Lievens, J. 36
lifecourse and mobilities 220, 221, 222, 223, 224, 225, 226
life-course approach 253
Lim, S.L. 54
Lin, Liyue 147
Lin, W. 359
Lin, Y. 250, 251
Lindquist, J. 87
Lipura, Sarah Jane 202, 249
Little, A. 355
Liu, C. 306, 309
Liu, Jianbo 145
Liu-Farrer, G. 205, 251, 252
Live-In Caregiver Program 20, 297
Lloyd, S. E. 357
local childcare cultures 24
Locke, Catherine 74, 140, 143
London migrant project 237, 240
London migrant study 238
long distance caring relations
    Brexit and the COVID-19 pandemic 162, 163
    conceptualisation of care in Polish migrants' families 159, 160, 161
    emergence of family and care issues 155, 156
    social networks and their role for families 156, 157, 158
'long-distance intimacy' 89
longitudinal migration research 119
longitudinal qualitative research 120
Longitudinal Survey of Immigrants to Canada 295
Longo, P. 288
Lörz, M. 251
lottery system 292
low- and middle-income countries 91
low-skilled labor 142
low-wage circulatory migrants 323
low-wage labour migrants 320
low-wage labour migration 316, 317, 318, 322, 325, 326
low-wage labour mobility 11
low-wage migrant labour in European horticulture 320
Lucas, Robert E.B. 136

Lugones, Maria 242
Luibhéid, E. 268, 271, 272
Lundberg, A. 188
Lundström, C. 219
Luo, M. 311

Mabala, Richard 142
Mablin, L. 242
"macro-level" approach 351
Madianou, M. 4, 89, 308
Mahler, S.J. 3
mainstream platform, state censorship of 92
'male breadwinner' model 19
male-female marriages 266
male-primary mobility 256
Mannheim, Karl 173
Mannheimian analytics 173
Mannheimian approach 173
Mannheimian interpretation of generation 173
marital transactions 35
market-based solutions 21
market-focused mechanism 19
market transactions 35
marriage migrants 46
    in South Korea 37
    positioning 34, 35, 36
marriage migration 1, 6, 33, 34, 35, 36, 38, 39, 40, 45, 46, 93
    control and management of 37
    governmentality of 37
    immigration governance of 46
    in Germany 37
    policies 305
    policy 39, 40
    practices 46
    processes 38
    rules 38
    scholarship 273
    strategies 46
marriage or civil partnership 274
marriage practices 38
'marriage-related migration' 239
'marriages of convenience' 39
marriage union 41
Marston, S.A. 55
Martin, F. 200, 255
masculine behaviour 78
masculine identity 76
masculinities 69, 76, 79
Massa, A. 353
Massey, D. 127
matrimonial advertisements 45
Mau, S. 270
Maury, O. 303
Maxwell, C. 110

Mazzucato, V. 341
McDowell, L. 353
McIlwaine, Cathy 9
McKay, D. 341
Mclachlan, D.A. 106, 111
Meeus, B. 303
men and masculinities in post-reform Vietnam 71, 72, 73
Menjívar, C. 75, 243
mental health problems 72
Merla, L. 159, 357, 359
Mesman, Judi 145
meso-scale temporalities of immigration policies 307
'meso-temporalities' of immigration policies 303
methodological nationalism 7
Mezzadra, S. 302, 355
micro-temporalities of migrant home-making 302
'micro-temporalities' of transnational family life 303
middle-class families 106
middle class parents 202
migrant background and mobility capital 124, 125, 126, 127
migrant-background identity 129
migrant care workers 20, 28
migrant categories 287
migrant children 104
migrant communities 36, 38
    cultures of 234
migrant contract workers, deployment of 70
migrant designation 287
migrant domestic work 240
migrant domestic workers 18, 19, 288
migrant families 121, 122, 123, 130, 342
    care in 159
    intergenerationality in 123
    'sandwich generation' of 8
    sponsorship agreements 297
migrant labor market 142
migrant mobilities 87, 93
migrant remittances 140, 144
migrant resettlement 295
migrant work ethic 323
migrant work labor force 142
migration 1
    and care 144, 145
    as relational, enfolded and linking lives over time 119, 120
    decision-making 136, 148, 172, 178, 356
    decision-making process 224, 227, 340
    family and the life course 304, 305
    financial benefits of 340
    gender 46
    industry 70
    infrastructure 88
    legislation and policies 90
    management 38, 45, 351
    policies 87, 91, 205, 305, 311
    policy 10
    policy regimes 297
    regimes 18, 19, 20, 21
    research, families and households in 136, 137
    scholarship 142
    studies, time and temporality in 302
    temporalities 303
    temporalities of home and 305, 306
    theory 171
    trajectory approach 353
    transgenerational reproduction of 8
migration-decision making 172, 177
    reconfiguration 178
'migration-left behind nexus' 140
migration policies 21
Migration Policy Index 291
Miller, D. 89
Mincer, J. 2
mixed-methods research 339, 340, 341
mobile children
    expatriate and globally 103, 104, 105
mobility 217
    and immobility 120
    lifecourse and 220, 221, 222, 223, 224, 225, 226
    narratives of young people in multigenerational transnational Irish families 128
mobility and intergenerational transfers of capital
    capital accumulation through global mobility 105, 106, 107, 108
    expatriate and globally mobile children 103, 104, 105
    familial global mobility project 108, 109, 110, 111
    parent-child decision-making 112, 113
'mobility bias' 69
mobility capital 118, 123, 124, 125, 126, 127, 130
    and young people in transnational multigenerational Irish families 125, 126, 127
mobility regimes 11, 87, 88, 90, 92, 350
    and infrastructures 86, 87, 88, 89, 95
    and 'regime' research in migration studies 351, 352, 353, 354
    multiple temporalities of 358
    transnational families and 349
modern communication technologies 90
Mok, K.H. 250
Money Advice Service 22
Montgomery, C. 202

Montoya, C. 238
Morais, Francesca 11
Morgan (1996) 191
Moriarty, E. 127
mosaic masculinity 78
mosaic transnational family change 95
mother migrant families 75
mother-migrant households 75
Mühlau, P. 157
Mulder, C.H. 220
Mulholland, J. 219
multi-generational families 297
multi-generational migrant families 130
multigenerational transnational families 130
multigenerational transnational Irish families, young people in 128
multilocality 137, 138, 139, 140
multi-locational households 137, 139
multi-sited ethnography 53
Murray, D. 272, 276

Naganathan, G. 57
Nakamura, N. 278
Nakhaie, M.R. 295
Nash, C.J. 268
national au pair schemes 21
national childcare regimes 18
National Health and Family Planning Commission (NHFPC) 335
national imaginary 6, 46
national immigration policies 286
National Internal Migration Survey 69
National Minimum Wage (NMW) 22
Neilson, B. 302, 355
Neng, Gao 205
neoliberal austerity policies 37
neoliberal globalisation 68, 78, 217, 296
neoliberal structuring of policies 42
neoliberalism 37
network-based arrangement 161
new economics of labour migration (NELM) 171, 333
new-generation migrants 146, 147, 148
new-generation migrations 146
'new global border regime' 359
'new immigration paradigm' 2
'new mobilities paradigm' 351
Newland, Kathleen 139
Nguyen, Liem 144
Nguyen, Minh T.N. 140, 143
Nguyen, T.D. 73
Ní Laoire, C. 8, 108, 110, 112, 171
Ní Raghallaigh, M. 192
'No Child Left Behind' 333
No Recourse to Public Funds (NRPF) 238

non-conforming gender identities 269
non-educational capital 205, 206
non-familial forms of intimacy 85
non-family households 137
non-family related networks 177
non-governmental organisations (NGOs) 336
non-heteronormative family formations 267
non-heteronormative subjectivities 276
non-heterosexual relationships 94
non-intimate partner domestic violence 237
non-migrant children 145
non-migrant counterparts 236
non-migrant groups 236
non-migrant households 146, 339, 340
non-monogamous migrants 267
non-normative embodiment 268
non-normative identity 272
non-normative sexualities 269, 280
non-parental party 27
nonpermanent mobility 138
Nordic countries
    re-emergence of domestic workers in 20, 21
'Nordic exceptionalism' 19
normative familial notions 256
normative nuclear family model 87
North India-Canada migration 40, 41, 42, 43, 44, 45
Norwegian and UK horticulture 321, 322
nuclear family 87
    obligations 160
NVivo 57, 59

Oakes, Tim 140
'offshoring of social reproduction' 325
offshoring social reproduction 318, 319, 326
    and transnational arbitrage 322
    family sacrifice and transnational arbitrage 324, 325
    labour circulation and the separation of work and family life 322, 323
    limited integration 324
    low-wage labour migration and transnational householding 316, 317, 318
    low-wage migrant labour in European horticulture 320
    migrant work ethic 323
    Norwegian and UK horticulture 321, 322
Ogaya, C. 293
Oishi, N. 295
Okazaki, S. 107
Okólski, M. 165
old-generation migrants 146, 147, 149
'one and a half breadwinner' pattern 19
one-child policy 210, 211, 255
Ong, A. 3, 200, 201

Flexible Citizenship 253
'open-mindedness' 106
Orellana, M.F. 102, 219
'Oriental' youth identities 128
Oromo diaspora 59, 61
Oromo refugees 58
Oswin, N. 311

paid labour 25
    force 20
pain and suffering, gendered productions of 63
Palenga-Möllenbeck, E. 304
pandemic-related policies 359
parental decision-making of Polish migrants 156
parental leave schemes 20
parental migration 146, 338, 339, 340, 341
parent-centric approach 102, 105
parent–child decision-making 105, 112, 113
parent–child relations 111, 145
parent-child relationships 290
parent-led familial migration project 111
parent-led transnational mobility strategies 111
Parreñas, R.S. 1, 93, 239, 289, 339
partner violence 237
Passarlay, Gulwali 189
patriarchal and gender subordination 35
patriarchal family 143
patriarchal hierarchies of power 70
Paul, Anju Mary 141, 357
Pearce, S.C. 241
Peng, Y. 69
Peng, Yuk-Ping Yinni 143
permanent migration 140
'permanent temporariness' 356
'perpetual separation' 289
personal relationships, individualisation of 85
personalised communication technologies 89
Pessar, P.R. 3
physical immobility 90
physical mobilities 111
physical violence 239
Pimpa, N. 258
place-based capital 130
plantation labour force 176
plantation labour regime 8, 175, 180
plantation youth 175, 181
Polish familialistic care culture 160
Polish migrants
    families 154, 156, 159
    families, conceptualisation of care in 159, 160, 161
    in Dublin 157
    population 155
    to the UK 155, 156
Polish post-accession migrants 154, 159, 160

Polish post-accession migration 155
political transnationalism 51, 52, 53
politico-cultural formations 46
polymedia 89
'polyrhythmic' care temporalities 304
post-colonial cultural imaginaries 88
post-communist transformation 155, 156
post-EU enlargement 159
post-graduation mobility plans 252
post-industrial societies 85
post-materialism 85
post-materialist families 86
post-reform Vietnam
    feminisation of labour migration in 69, 70, 71
    men and masculinities in 71, 72, 73
potential family sponsors 292
power, social inequalities and social mobility 9, 10
Pratt, G. 290, 295
Pravattiyagul, J. 277, 278
pre-college study abroad (PSA) 206
pre-migration gendered division of labour 75
pre-mobility decision-making phase 252
primary qualitative and mixed-methods research 339, 340, 341
private childcare 28
private domestic services 26
private household 297
private housing 19
privatised childcare in the Anglophone 'North' 19, 20
privileged migration 203, 204
privileged migration and family 217, 218
    family and expatriate migration 218, 219, 220
    spatial-temporal approaches 220, 221, 222, 223, 224, 225, 226
prolonged familial disjuncture 288
prolonged family separation 291, 297
prolonged immigration processes 38
'pro-mobility' habitus 127
Provincial Nominee Programs 42
psychological abuse 236
psychological domestic violence 237
psychological intimate partner violence 235
psychological violence 235, 237
Puar, J.K. 272
public and affordable daycare 25
public daycare 20, 21, 26
    affordable 20
    system 25
public health crisis 250
Punjab transnational marriage unions 41
Punjabi-Canadian community 41, 44

formation 40
Punjabi diaspora 44
push factors in same-sex family migration 277, 278, 279
"push-pull" framework 136

qualified nannies 22
queer asylum 275
queer community 271
queer exclusion in immigration regimes 279
queer families or couples 271
queer family formations 273
queer intimacies 278
queer migration 278
   research 278
   scholarship 267, 271, 272, 273, 279
queer people 267
queer subjectivities
   and migration 266
   stereotypical embodiments of 267
'queer temporalities' 311

Račaitė, Justina 339
racial identity 234
racism 296
Radziwinowiczówna, A. 160, 162, 165
Raghuram, Parvati 142, 255
Rambukkana, N. 267
Ramos, C. 125
'range of return spatialities and temporalities' 119
rapid social stratification 68
rapid societal and/or environmental changes 342
rational cost-benefit analysis 74
rational decision-making 136
Ravenstein, E.G. 136, 137
recalibration 294, 295, 296
   of family life 298
Red River Delta 69, 73, 74, 75, 77
Redmond, G. 200
re-emergence of domestic workers in the Nordic countries 20, 21
Refugee Convention 1951 185, 190, 270
'refugee diasporas' 57
refugee protection regime 267
refugee transnationalism 52, 53, 54, 55
"regimes of mobility" 350
'regimes-of-mobility approach' 352
regional cultural capital 110
religious organisations 194
Ren, Yuan 145
'renationalisation of policies' 88
reproductive labour, transnational division of 93
"re-routing migration geographies" 353
restrictionist immigration policies 270, 272
restrictive contract labour migration regimes 74
restrictive immigration policies 37
restrictive immigration regimes 120
restrictive migration regimes 91
restrictive policies 36
Resurreccion, Bernadette P. 143
return migrants 140
return migration 140
return mobilities 119, 122
reunification migration 45
reunified families 293
Reynolds, T. 122, 123
right-wing political movements 359
rigid patriarchal system 70
Rip, J. 192
'ritualized border game' 353
'ritualized practices of everyday life' 289
Roberts, Kenneth D. 139
Robertson, S. 205, 303, 310
Robertson, S. L. 250
Rolandsen Agustín, L. 238
Rosińska, Anna 165
Rubin, G. 269
rural female migrants in Hanoi 74
rural marriage in Japan 35
rural out-migration 69
rural-to-urban migration in Africa 136
rural-urban disparities 69
rural-urban labor migration 139
rural-urban migrants 138, 140, 143, 148
   in China 139, 140, 143, 148
rural-urban migration 74, 140, 142, 336
rural-urban multilocality 139
RUT 25
   tax deduction 25
Ryan, L. 8, 156, 157, 158, 162, 219, 355
Rydstrom, H. 69
Rydström, J. 265
Rye, Johan 11

Sadruddin, A.F.A. 339
safe migration pathways, lack of 334
Salazar, N. 87
Salazar, N. B. 352
Salcedo, M. 276, 278
same-sex binational relationship migration 273
same-sex couples 6, 267, 278
   immigration rules in the UK for 280
   in the UK 273, 274
   UK immigration visa requirement for 279
same-sex families 265
   configuration 278
   formations 265, 268, 269, 270
   migration, push factors in 277, 278, 279
same-sex marriages 273, 277, 278, 279
same-sex migration 271

same-sex partners in immigration rules 265
same-sex relationships 279
same-sex unions 265
Sancho, D. 208
Sander, M. 110, 220
Sarvasy, W. 288
'satellite children' 206
Save the Children 75
Scalabrini Migration Centre (SMC) 339
Scandinavian countries 20
Schaer, M. 256, 257
Schapendonk, J. 352, 353
Schein, Louisa 140
Schiller, Glick 154
Schmidt-Kallert, Einhard 139
schooling system 105
Schwarz, I. 352, 353
Scott, Sam 11
second-generation immigrants 146
second-generation migrants 146, 147, 148
'servant culture' 18
sexual democracy 273
sexual essentialism 270
sexual identity categories 268
sexual infidelity 77
sexual violence 237
Shakhsari, S. 272
Shamir, R. 87, 351, 352
Shaw, J.E. 289
Sigona, N. 194
Silvey, Rachel M. 136, 142
single female corporate expatriates 224
Sin, I Lin 8
Sirriyeh, Ala 37, 191, 192
Skeldon, R. 352
'slow violence' 239
social care system 159
'social democratic welfare regime' 20
social inequalities 9, 10, 28
social mobility 9, 10, 76
social network analysis (SNA) 157
social networks and their role for families 156, 157, 158
'social remittances' 53
social reproduction 120
social security system 20
socialisation 73, 121
socially-sanctioned obligations 188
socio-economic inequality 18
socio-economic mobility 36, 46
socio-emotional relationships 113
socio-political inequalities 296
Söderquist Forkby, Å. 189, 193
Sokoloff, N.J. 241
Somaiah, B.C. 173, 342

Somali Zigula refugee community 53
Sondhi, G. 212, 255
Southern Sudanese refugees 54
'spatial continuum of violence' 240
spatialities 10, 11
spatial-temporal approaches 220, 221, 222, 223, 224, 225, 226
Spiegel, A. 219
Spitzer, D.L. 10, 295
split households and migration in the Global South 135
    and gender 141, 142, 143, 144
    and intergenerational perspectives 144
    circular migration and multilocality 137, 138, 139, 140
    families and households in migration research 136, 137
    impacts on children 145, 146
    migration and care 144, 145
    next generation 145
    second-generation and new-generation migrants 146, 147, 148
sponsored immigrants 37
sponsorship regimes 39
spousal law 39
'spousal migration' 239
spousal sponsorship policy 42
spousal sponsorship rules 39, 46
Stalford, H. 104, 105, 219
Stark, Oded 136
state bordering practices 39
state censorship of mainstream platform 92
state immigration policy 268, 270
state immigration regimes 266
state socialism 18
states and discriminatory exception in immigration 270
Statham, J. 188
'status VAWG' 238, 239
stay-behind husbands 76, 77, 78
stay-behind men 74, 75, 77, 78
Steel, G. 352
Steele, B.J. 39
Step Up Migrant Women campaign 244
Strasser, E. 293, 294
Strengths and Difficulties Questionnaire (SDQ) scores 339
structural inequalities 90, 91, 92
structural violence 233, 240, 241, 244
    of post-conflict poverty 241
student migration
    cost of 251
student mobility 250
'student switching' policies 205
subaltern peasant men 78

'sunny day technologies' 91
Suter, B 221
Swedish immigration laws 190
Swedish system 193
symbolic capital 123
symbolic capital of mobility 111
symbolic violence 240, 241, 244

Tacoli, Cecilia 142
'Taiwan villages' 74
Tamil diaspora 51, 56, 57, 58
Tamil nationalism 64
Tan, George 9
Tanu, D. 220
tax deduction 25, 26
Taylor, R. 120, 127
teessoos 62
temporal connections between home, migration and the city 308, 309
'temporal horizons' 305
temporalities 10, 11, 12
    in migration studies, time and 302, 303
    of home and migration 305, 306
    of migrant home-making and family life 306, 307, 308, 309, 310
    of migration 303, 304
    of transnational familyhood 302
    of transnational family life 301
temporary contract labour regimes 311
temporary labour migrants 357
temporary labour migration 303, 343
    regime 333
    regimes 356, 357
temporary migration 138, 353
temporary migration experience 257
Thai, Hung Cam 68
Thiranagama, S. 57
'Third Culture Kids' (TCK) 103, 104, 111
Thommessen, S.A. 188, 193
Thomson, R. 120, 127
time-related underemployment 73
Timmerman, C. 253
Todaro, Michael P. 136
Torres, Sara 10
Toyota, Mika 140
traditional beliefs and practices 286
traditional destination countries 107
traditional family relations 92
traditional femininity ideals 70
traditional gender norms 141
traditional gender-role expectations 41
traditional gender roles 293
traditional geographical mappings 190
traditional migration 278
    research 350

traditional notion of the family 138
traditional research methods 114
'trailing spouse' 44
Tran, L.T. 251, 254
transformation of intimacy 95
transgenerational family dynamics 123
transgenerational migration dynamics 121
transgenerational mobilities 127
transgenerational reverberations in migrant 121, 122, 123, 124
transgenerational temporal connection 122
transitional societies 136
translocal householding 70
translocal households 74, 75, 77, 137, 140, 143
translocality 140
translocational positionality 109
transnational affective capital 89
transnational arbitrage 322, 324, 325
'Transnational care: Families confronting borders' 357
transnational caregiving practices 303
transnational caring practices 154
transnational communication 89, 91
transnational contract labour migration 70, 74
transnational contract workers 76
transnational cross-border mobilities 86
transnational cultural practices 64
transnational dimensions of well-being 61
transnational education migration 106
transnational emotional labour 55
transnational familial belonging 190
transnational familial intimacy 86, 88, 90, 91, 92, 93, 94, 95
transnational families 4, 5, 10, 11, 51, 52, 53, 54, 55, 63, 64, 86, 87, 88, 89, 91, 93, 94, 95, 119, 126, 127, 200, 208, 209, 303, 325
    and mobility regimes
    and 'regime' research in migration studies 351, 352, 353, 354
    arrangements 87, 316, 325
    care, temporalities of 303
    COVID-19 pandemic 358, 359, 360
    from temporal perspective 354, 355, 356, 357, 358
    formation in Canada 52
    habitus 122
    in Vietnam 75
    life 10, 84, 89, 162, 301, 303, 304, 310, 311
    life course stages 355, 356
    links 187, 188, 189, 190
    lives 301
    members 86, 89, 90, 91, 94
    networks 159, 164, 190
    practices 11, 162, 164, 195
    project 342

regimes 322
relations 6, 54, 55, 56, 88, 89, 91, 93, 94, 95
relationships 86, 87, 89, 90, 94, 158
relationships, temporalities of 304
scholarship 349, 358
solidarities 359
strategy 206
tale of two diasporas 56, 57, 58, 59, 60, 61, 62, 63
temporalities of 310
transgenerational reverberations in migrant and 121, 122, 123, 124
transnational kinships 53, 54
transnational familyhood 310
temporalities of 302
'transnational fathering' practice 92
transnational grandparenting 4
transnational household 208, 288
arrangement 209
arrangements 325, 326
relations 207
transnational householding 316, 317, 318
transnational households 74, 75
transnational (im)mobility 110, 113, 114
transnational intimacy 7, 89, 95
transnational Irish families 118
transnational kinships 53, 54, 55, 64
emotional lives of 59, 60, 61
gendered practices of well-being among 61, 62
networks 54
transnational labour migration 286
transnational linkages 89
transnational lives 10
transnational marriage abandonment 238
transnational marriage migration 6, 34, 35, 46
international marriage migration 40, 41, 42, 43, 44, 45
marriage migration policy 39, 40
policy and state control 36, 37, 38, 39
positioning marriage migrant 34, 35, 36
transnational marriages 54
transnational migrant families 69, 118
transnational migrant workers 74, 286
transnational migration 3, 36, 38, 39, 87, 93, 102, 139, 340
networks 45
processes 46
transnational migrations and im/mobilities
family, intergenerational dynamics and social reproduction 120, 121
migration as relational, enfolded and linking lives over time 119, 120
transgenerational reverberations in migrant and transnational families 121, 122, 123, 124
young people from migrant backgrounds and their transgenerational connections 124, 125, 126, 127, 128, 129, 130
transnational mobilities 87, 95, 122, 128
and cosmopolitanism 129
political economy of 88
regime 87
transnational mobility 68, 102, 105, 110, 111, 113, 155, 157, 201, 218
research 102
transnational motherhood 54
'transnational mothering practice' 92
transnational mothers 54, 55
transnational multigenerational Irish families
mobility capital and young people in 125, 126, 127
transnational networks 158
transnational notions of family 51
transnational opportunities 45
transnational or migrant families 123
transnational parenting and impact of familial separation 288, 289, 290
transnational politics 51
transnational processes and practices 54
transnational publics 201
transnational scholarship 51
transnational social capital 123
transnational social fields 122
transnational social space 87
'transnational social spaces' 4
transnational surrogacy 94
transnationalisation of familial intimacy 7, 89, 92, 93, 95
transnationalisation of family life 88
transnationalisation of intimacy 7, 84, 89, 92, 95, 96
digitalisation and mediation of 89, 90
mobility regimes and infrastructures 86, 87, 88, 89
mosaic of continuity and change 92, 93, 94, 95
role of transnationalism 85, 86
structural inequalities, digital ruptures, and interrupted 90, 91, 92
transnationalism 10, 52, 53, 158, 160, 162, 218
and family 3, 4, 5
gendered nature of 55
role of 85, 86
Trudeau Liberal government 42
Trump, Donald 92, 250
Tse, J.K.H. 111
Tu, Mengwei 111, 208
Turner, B.S. 349

Turner, J. 242
twice-migrant families 294
'twists and turns' of migration processes 353
Tyldum, G. 38
Tyrrell, N. 124, 125

ubiquitous digital communication technologies 89
UK immigration
   process 275
   rules 268, 273, 274
   visa requirement for same-sex couples 279
UK study 'Au Pairing After the Au Pair Scheme 17
UK visa regimes for bi-national same-sex couples 274, 275
UN Declaration of the Elimination of Violence against Women 1993 232
UN Refugee Convention in 1951 351
'unaccompanied child migrants' 8
unaccompanied child migrants and family relationships
   foster families 190, 191, 192
   role of family in law 185, 186, 187
   support and significant relationships 192, 193, 194, 195
   transnational family links 187, 188, 189, 190
unaccompanied minor (UAM) 184, 185, 187, 188, 190, 191, 192
uncontracted labour 73
underemployment 73
'undesirable' immigration 39
'undoing gender' 148
unequal childhoods 202
unintended consequences and human cost 111
United Nations Convention on the Rights of the Child (CRC) 10, 185, 186, 286
United States education system 206
United States V. Windsor 277, 278
'universal breadwinner model' 21
'universal caregiver model' 20
Universal Declaration of Human Rights 270
'universal worker' model 19
Unmarried Partners Concession 273
urban labor market 147
urban small trade 70
Urry, J. 90
US immigration policies 271
US-Sino trade war 92

valuable mobility related capital 113
value of capital 109
Van Hear, N. 57
Van Mol, C. 253
van Riemsdijk, M. 255
Veale, A. 122

Vietnam emphasises continuity 74
Vietnamese construction of masculinity 72
Vietnamese female labour migrants 71
Vietnamese labour exports 70
Vietnamese labour migrants 70
Vietnamese masculinities in transition
   feminisation of labour migration in post-reform Vietnam 69, 70, 71
   flexible masculinities 73, 74, 75, 76
   hypermasculinity 76, 77, 78
   men and masculinities in post-reform Vietnam 71, 72, 73
Vietnamese masculinity centre 71
Vietnamese migrant households 78
Vietnamese moral womanhood 77
Vietnamese refugee families 308
Vietnamese scholarship 70
Vietnamese stay-behind men 69
Vietnam Household Living Standards Survey 2012 73
violence
   against women 233
   among migrant domestic and sex workers 240
   and displacement, dynamics of 53, 54
   domestic 232
'virtual intimacy' 89
visa applications, evaluation of 40
visa regimes 355
Visa waiver policies 273
vocational educational institutions 254
Vuorela, U. 354

Waddling, J. 109
Wade, J. 191
'wait and see' approach 162
Wallace, Claire 136
Walsh, K. 220
Walter, B. 127
Walton-Roberts, M. 6, 200, 211
Wang, Lamei 145
Wang, Xiaobing 145
Wang, Zhe 9
Warner, Michael 268
Waters, Johanna L. 9, 10, 53, 111, 144, 251, 253, 254
Waters, M. 122
Weenink, D. 106
'welfare regimes' 17
Wellman, B. 156
Western liberal democracies 269
Western-related cultural capital 110
Westernise non-normative sexualities 276
whilst reunification 10
White, A. 156

White, M.A. 266, 271
'wider generational order' 171
Wilding, R. 357
Wilkins, Annabelle 10, 11
Wilkins, S. 110, 113
Williams, A. 119
Williams, Fiona 18
Willis, Katie 8
wives' labour migration 78
woman-carer model 75
women
    economic participation 44
    migrants in Indonesia 136
    vulnerability in Canada 44
'women and migration' research 170
work-family conflict 28
World Bank 76
Wright, E.M. 236

Xiang, B. 87
Xie, Yu 145
Xu, Hongwei 145
Xu, L. 253
Xu, Y. 202

Yang, P. 202, 204, 207, 250
Ye, Jingzhong 143
'Year Abroad' exchange project 252
Yeh, D. 124, 128
Yeoh, B. S. 11, 107, 143, 144, 202, 251, 254, 289, 293, 301, 303, 304, 308, 310, 342, 353, 355, 356, 359
young people
    from migrant backgrounds and their transgenerational connections 124
    im/mobility dispositions and narratives 127, 128, 129, 130
    migrant background and mobility capital 124, 125, 126, 127
Yousuf, B. 6, 7, 58, 59, 61
youth migrations 8, 170, 171, 174, 180
    and diverse interpretations of generation 171, 172, 173
    badli 178, 179, 180
    generationed political economy of Assam's tea plantations 176
    generationed political economy of Assam tea plantations 173, 174, 175, 176, 177
    migration-decision making reconfiguration 177, 178
Yue, A. 271

Zelinsky, Wilbur 136, 138
Zhou, Chengchao 145, 146
Zhou, Min 146
Zhu, Yu 139, 147
Zittoun, T. 221
'zone of suspension' 255
Zontini, E. 122, 123